Venezuela

Titles in ABC-CLIO's *Latin America in Focus Series*

Venezuela   Elizabeth Gackstetter Nichols and Kimberly J. Morse

Titles in ABC-CLIO's *Africa in Focus Series*

Eritrea   Mussie Tesfagiorgis G.
Ethiopia   Paulos Milkias

Titles in ABC-CLIO's *Asia in Focus Series*

China   Robert André LaFleur, Editor
Japan   Lucien Ellington, Editor
The Koreas   Mary E. Connor, Editor

VENEZUELA

*Elizabeth Gackstetter Nichols
and Kimberly J. Morse*

 ABC-CLIO

Santa Barbara, California • Denver, Colorado • Oxford, England

Library of Congress Cataloging-in-Publication Data

Nichols, Elizabeth Gackstetter.
  Venezuela / Elizabeth Gackstetter Nichols and Kimberly J. Morse.
    p. cm. — (Latin America in focus)
  Includes bibliographical references and index.
  ISBN 978-1-59884-569-3 (alk. paper) — ISBN 978-1-59884-570-9 (ebook)
1. Venezuela. 2. Venezuela—Social life and customs. 3. Venezuela—Politics and government. 4. Venezuela—Economic conditions. I. Morse, Kimberly J. II. Title.
  F2308.N49   2010
  987—dc22   2010031885

ISBN: 978-1-59884-569-3
EISBN: 978-1-59884-570-9

14 13 12 11 10   1 2 3 4 5

This book is also available on the World Wide Web as an eBook.
Visit www.abc-clio.com for details.

ABC-CLIO, LLC
130 Cremona Drive, P.O. Box 1911
Santa Barbara, California 93116-1911

This book is printed on acid-free paper ∞

Manufactured in the United States of America

Contents

About the Authors

Elizabeth Gackstetter Nichols is a professor of Spanish and chair of the Department of Languages at Drury University. She has published articles on Venezuelan literature and culture and appears in the edited volume *Bottom Up or Top Down: Participation and Clientelism in Venezuela's Bolivarian Democracy*.

Kimberly J. Morse is an associate professor of history at Washburn University. She has published articles on 19th-century Venezuelan history in academic journals in the United States and in Venezuela.

Preface

Venezuela is not just oil any more than Angola is just diamonds. Hugo Chávez no more represents the ideas and aspirations of every individual Venezuelan anymore than Barack Obama shares identical ideologies with every person in the United States. Economics and politicians, however, for good or ill, come to represent nations in ways that oversimplify complex histories and realities. When we know little of a nation's history or reality it is all too easy to form an opinion about that country based on nothing more than a story in a newspaper or a 30-second segment on cable news. Reporters call what they write stories. The word "story" in English also implies fiction. Reporters clearly do not intend to write fiction when they write their stories. The word is apt, nevertheless, because the stories only reflect one person's interpretation of a select body of evidence that can never be, because of the story's brevity, representational of an entire nation's reality. When we, as teachers, scholars, students, or businesspeople, draw general conclusions from those brief stories, we, in a sense, create the lens through which we understand an entire country, and that understanding is more unintentionally fictional than factual.

We intend to help you move past an understanding of Venezuela as a story and toward nuanced insight into Venezuela as a nation. Trying to understand Venezuelan reality within the context of interrelated struggles over modernization, Westernization and Western power, race, class, gender, politics, economics, culture, and oil is what this book is about. In the following chapters, we will do our best to pull all of those threads apart and examine them carefully to help readers understand why Venezuela is truly unique and why it is important in the world we live in today—why it is so much more than oil and headlines.

The first chapter, "Geography" will introduce readers to issues associated with Venezuelan geography and demography. This chapter pays special attention to issues of land use and the environment. The second chapter, "History," provides the essential background necessary in Venezuelan history to help readers understand the Venezuelan present. Chapter 3, "Government and Politics," explains the Venezuelan system of government and the significant changes to the political structure in the years from 1989 to 2010. The chapter introduces issues surrounding the election of President Hugo Chávez and explores issues pertinent to those who support and oppose his rule today. Chapter 4, "Economy," analyzes the importance of the petroleum industry in the 20th and 21st century. The chapter also assesses the role of labor in politics and society. It concludes with an evaluation of multiple economic issues pertinent to understanding the presidency of Hugo Chávez. Chapter 5, "Society," explores the intersections of race, ethnicity, and class as well as the significance of religions of all sorts in Venezuela, past and present. Chapter 5 also assesses issues of gender and sexuality, outlining the historical development of the women's movement and representation in Venezuela and the role women play in Venezuela today. The chapter concludes with an evaluation of the education system, a topic that brings race, class, ethnicity, religion, and gender together in one schoolhouse. Chapter 6, "Culture," covering the past to the present, evaluates the state of the arts in Venezuela—literature, visual arts, architecture, and music. Art in Venezuela was frequently not art for art's sake; artists' work reflected evolving complexities in Venezuelan society. Chapter 6 also incorporates an analysis of elements of popular culture such as food, sports, and leisure activities. Sections in Chapter 6 on language and etiquette assess not only what languages people speak, but how they use language and codes of conduct to convey expectations of proper, formal, respectful behavior even in a culture that seems informal. Chapter 7, "Contemporary Issues," covers those topics that are in the news and on the minds of those who live in and work with Venezuela. Issues of instability, corruption, foreign policy, and energy conclude our examination of Venezuelan reality. This interdisciplinary examination of Venezuelan reality, from colonization to the first decade of the 21st century, also contains a glossary of important Spanish-language terms and acronyms, a timeline of events both historical and cultural, tables of relevant facts and figures, a list of major Venezuelan holidays, and an annotated bibliography to assist readers with further research.

Certainly we do not know what exactly will happen in Venezuela as it moves through the 21st century, but as we move through this text, we will look at Venezuela's past and present to consider how Venezuela will face the challenges ahead.

¡*Manos a la orden*!

Scholars incur many debts when they write. We are no different. We are quite fortunate to be two of a small and extremely dedicated corps of Venezuelan scholars in Venezuela, the United States, and Japan. Many of those scholars are cited in this text. Many of them are our friends. We cannot wait for the time when we can be friends and scholars again without having to avoid talking about painful, divisive topics. We owe special thanks to Daniel Hellinger, Haydeé Vílchez Cróquer, Jun Ishibashi, Miguel Tinker Salas, Peter Linder, David Smilde, Tomás Straka, Fernando Coronil, and Jesús "Chucho" García for their counsel at different points in this work. At Drury University, Robert Weddle provided expertise on architecture, and Daniel Ponder provided clarity on electoral processes. Kathy Jester and Mallory Newcomb worked extraordinarily hard in the editing process. All were of invaluable assistance. Marj Murray, the interlibrary loan librarian at Washburn University, is a goddess to whom all Washburn scholars bow in humble praise. We are grateful to our colleagues in small departments in teaching universities who patiently let us become obsessed with scholarship at the wrong time of the year. Those colleagues occasionally helped us find just the right words to write. Kimberly Morse is forever indebted to her Venezuelan families for teaching her what it means to be *venezolana por matrimonio*. Kimberly Morse and Elizabeth Gacksetter Nichols are equally indebted to their parents for reasons beyond words. To our spouses, Nelson Córdova and Dale Nichols, thank you for putting up with us through this process, for picking up the slack when we were going crazy. Your patience is (nearly) infinite and we are in your debt. We are most indebted to each other. The book is better because of what we learned together.

To our children, Ben and John Córdova and Kira Nichols, Mommy does not have to work tonight. This book is for you.

Geography

DEATH IN EL DORADO

One of the most pervasive myths in the colonization of Latin America is El Dorado, the land where gold is so common that the ruler covers himself in its dust. Many Spanish explorers suffered and died in South American forests seeking the mythical place. In Venezuela, the 16th-century explorer Sir Walter Raleigh lost his fortune and his son in his search for the fabled land.

The city was a mirage, but the gold deposits in the south of Venezuela were not. Deep in Bolívar State in the southeast, miners, Indians, and the state fight bloody battles over huge deposits of gold and diamonds to this day. Over the past several decades, however, successive Venezuelan governments have failed to organize large-scale mining operations except in the mining town of El Callao. This has led to a general modern-day gold rush of small-scale, informal miners. These miners (Venezuelan and Brazilian) invade the traditional lands of the indigenous tribes in the area, like the Yanomami, who find their territory, human rights, and very survival threatened. These informal wildcat miners cause great environmental damage, destroying the once-pristine rainforest. The miners use high-pressure hoses to churn up the riverbed, leaving mud holes that become breeding grounds for malaria-carrying mosquitoes. In addition, wildcatters use mercury to process the gold, contaminating water and wildlife. The modern-day battle for El Dorado gives one example of how geographic issues of modernization and development, land use, and environment come together to create challenges for contemporary Venezuelan society.

GEOGRAPHIC OVERVIEW

Venezuela sits on the northern hump of South America and is bounded on the north by the Caribbean Sea and the Atlantic Ocean, on the east by the nation of Guyana, on the south by Brazil, and on the west by Colombia. Venezuela is roughly twice the size of California in land area and shaped like an inverted triangle. This configuration places Venezuela at the crossroads of six different geographical regions: the Maracaibo lowlands in the west, the mountains of the northwest, the beach resort area and islands of the north, the Guiana highlands of the southeast, and the Orinoco plains of the south and center. Amazonia is in the far south.

As Venezuela lies just north of the equator, it lies wholly in the tropics. Venezuela's climate is, generally, tropical, with a rainy season (November through May) usually referred to as "winter" and a dry "summer" season that falls in the months of June to October. Many of Venezuela's major cities (including the capital, Caracas) have a temperature range of 45° to 91°F (7° to 33°C), with an annual average temperature of 70°F (21°C), though temperatures around the nation can vary because of elevation (*Venezuela* 1993).

THE MARACAIBO LOWLANDS: FOUNTAIN OF BLACK GOLD

In the west, the area is dominated by Lake Maracaibo, where Alfonso de Ojeda and Amerigo Vespucci first set foot on South American soil. The country around the lake is ringed by a mountain range (the northernmost extension of the Andes), creating an oval that opens out to the Caribbean Sea and dividing the area from the rest of the nation. The land between the lake and the foothills of the mountains is swampy and

---

SIR WALTER RALEIGH'S SEARCH FOR EL DORADO

Early explorers of northern South America heard tales of a king who covered himself in gold dust. Based on these stories, the explorers launched expeditions into what is now Brazil and Venezuela, hoping to find a wealth of gold. The Englishman Sir Walter Raleigh was one who undertook this search.

Raleigh, believing that El Dorado was located in what is now Venezuela, sailed in 1595 and began his search at the mouth of the Orinoco River, dubbing the area "Guiana." Raleigh never found the fabulous golden city (or even much gold), but that did not stop him from publishing *The Discovery of Guiana*, which exaggerated his discoveries on the Orinoco and fed the myth of El Dorado. In 1612 Raleigh, spending time in the Tower of London for his attacks on Spaniards, promised King James a fortune if he were released and allowed to return to Guiana. In 1616 Raleigh mounted this second expedition to the Orinoco, but found trouble with the Spanish instead of gold and was forced to return home in disgrace to his own execution.

flat. At only six meters of elevation (16.96 feet), Maracaibo is one area of Venezuela whose annual average temperature is hotter than the norm, with an annual average temperature of 82°F (28°C). The population in the area is concentrated in the booming city of Maracaibo, the second largest in Venezuela after Caracas.

Maracaibo, home to more than 2 million people, is a major rival to Caracas politically, economically, and culturally. In 1917, the oil rush began in the Maracaibo lowlands, as British and American multinational oil companies rushed to develop what was under Lake Maracaibo. It is estimated that at least 7 percent of the world's proven oil reserves lie under the lake (*Venezuela* 1993). Massive oil derricks and processing plants dominate the lake, which was once characterized by the indigenous huts on stilts that greeted Ojeda and Vespucci. This industrial activity has meant frequent oil spills, both in the lake and in the rivers that feed the lake. For this reason, the lake now suffers from significant environmental degradation.

In addition to the introduction of chemical agents from the petroleum industry, pollution from agricultural industries in the area and raw sewage from the capital city pollute the waters. The lake is fed by both salt water from the Caribbean and fresh water from several inland rivers. The lighter fresh water floats on top of the lake and traps pollutants with the heavier salt water below. Additional chemicals, like pollutants from oil spills, products used to clean up spilled oil, and nutrients from the sea also become trapped under the fresh water at the bottom of the lake. Scientists from the University of Zulia have determined that levels of nitrogen and phosphorus, for example, have jumped nearly 1,000 percent in the last three decades (Marzuola 2004).

Oil rigs sit in Lake Maracaibo in Western Venezuela, South America's richest oil producing area, on November 17, 1970. While oil revenues are the backbone of Venezuela's economy, supplying 70 percent of government income, the black gold has created a host of problems. Thousands of acres of the nation's land lie fallow while Venezuela has to import foodstuffs it could produce. (AP/Wide World Photos)

The mix of chemicals and the balance between the lower and upper levels of water may be upset, as in the spring of 2004, when heavy rains allowed the nutrients in the lower levels of the lake to rise to the top. The result was a potentially disastrous bloom of invasive duckweed that grew at an alarming rate, fed by the unnaturally high levels of nutrients. The plant eventually covered 20 percent of the lake's surface, cutting off oxygen to existing plants and animals in the lake. The problem became so severe that the Venezuelan government was forced to spend nearly 2 million dollars a month in clean-up efforts to stop duckweed growth (Leng, Preston, and Rodriguez 2004).

Despite environmental concerns, the city itself is seen by many *maracuchos*, or citizens of Maracaibo, as significantly better than Caracas. People who live in Maracaibo sing the praises of its lower crime rate and laud its excellent university, the University of Zulia. The *maracuchos* are extremely proud of their city and the unique cultural traditions of the area that formed because of the traditional geographic separation from the rest of the nation. Some of these artistic traditions, like the musical style *gaita zuliana*, have gained popularity throughout Venezuela.

THE MOUNTAINS OF THE WEST AND NORTH: FROM ANDES TOWNS TO CAPITAL CITY

Two mountain ranges, continuations of the Andes range that extends the length of South America, define the western and northern borders of the nation. The first range runs along the eastern edge of Venezuela, surrounding Lake Maracaibo, separating it from the rest of the nation, and stretching southwest, toward the border with Colombia. The mountains of the west contain some peaks that reach above

---

THE *GAITA ZULIANA*

The *gaita zuliana* is a unique musical form invented in Zulia State that dates back to the early years of the 19th century. It is performed in 2/4 time with lyrics written in octosyllabic meter. The form usually contains three verses, each separated by a chorus.

First sung as part of Catholic masses, the *gaita* is a musical form that combines Afrovenezuelan, Spanish, and Venezuelan heritage. The percussion used in the *gaita*—drums known as *furros* and maracas—are the contribution of Africa, while the use of the guitar is of Spanish heritage. The inclusion of the *cuatro*, a four-stringed guitar native to Venezuela, rounds out the combination of cultural influences.

While the origins of the *gaita* are religious, modern-day *gaitas* may also be protest songs, celebratory love songs, or historical ballads that tell unique stories of Zulia. The most well known, however, continues to be the *gaita de furro*, which is performed in honor of the Virgen de Chiquinquirá at the celebration of Candelaria, a religious festival.

4,500 meters, (14,763.78 feet) the highest of which is El Pico Bolívar, at 5,007 meters (16,427.17 feet).

The city of Mérida, found in this western range, is a university town with a deep colonial heritage and is home to 260,000 people. Located in a valley between two high peaks, Mérida sits at an elevation of 1,603 meters above sea level, a mile-high city. Mérida offers education in the form of the Universidad de los Andes, the second-oldest university in Venezuela, serving 40,000 students, with campuses in Tachira and Trujillo as well. In addition, in Mérida, a visitor can take a trip in the world's longest and highest cable car to near the top of the Pico Espejo, elevation 4,765 meters (*Venezuela* 1993). At the top, travelers are treated to an amazing view of Mérida and the mountains and, if they are lucky, contact with some of the only snow in Venezuela. In winter, citizens of Mérida run for the cable-car station when they see clouds on the peak, hoping to find snow at the top.

Separated by a gap from the western range, the northern coast of the nation is bordered by a pair of ranges that divide the interior of the nation from the sea. The valleys between these two mountain ranges, known as the Cordillera Central, are home to a great number of the Venezuelan population. The capital, Caracas, is located at the foot of Mount Avila, and can only be reached from the coastal airport either through a series of tunnels that bore through the mountains that separate it from the sea or by the colonial mountain highway that winds over the Avila itself. In 2007, the United Nations estimated that the Caracas urban area was home to

The majestic top of Pico Bolívar in Merida, Venezuela. (Kristina Mahlau/Dreamstime.com)

Teleferico—a cable car from Merida to Pico Bolívar. (Venezuela, Sierra Nevada de Merida) (Ryszard Laskowski/Dreamstime.com)

THE CARACAS-LA GUAIRA HIGHWAY

Until the middle of the 20th century, travel from the northern Venezuelan coast into Caracas was a lengthy process, up and over the Avila and other mountains of the Cordillera Central.

In order to facilitate the flow of traffic from the nation's principal port in La Guaira and airport in Maquetia, Marcos Pérez Jiménez reinvested some of Venezuela's new petroleum wealth in a new highway, the Autopista Caracas-La Guaira, a road that would reduce travel time between La Guaira and Caracas to less than an hour.

Engineers designed a series of tunnels through the mountains and viaducts over valleys. The resulting highway, completed in 1953, included two tunnels, one of nearly 2,000 meters in length, and three viaducts. In the 21st century, however, engineers became increasingly concerned about Viaduct #1, and in March of 2006, after years of heavy rain and earth movement, the viaduct collapsed. Even though a small emergency side route had been constructed the previous year, until the new Viaduct #1 was completed in June of 2007, travel between Caracas and the coast was severely delayed.

2.9 million citizens, which at the time represented 11.6 percent of Venezuela's population (United Nations 2007). Its situation is unique, spread out in valleys in between the hills and mountains of the Cordillera Central. One of the things a first-time visitor usually notices is the looming Mount Avila, which dominates the northern skyline like a storm cloud on the horizon. The mountainsides that surround the city are home to many citizens as well. Barrios (neighborhoods) of *ranchitos* (cement block homes, one to three stories tall) climb the mountainsides and are home to most of Caracas's poor. As you approach the center of the city, however, monuments to business, industry, and art rise up, cars whiz by, and pollution grows.

Caraqueños love their cars, and despite the heavy traffic, most citizens of Caracas who can afford a car prefer to drive. The result is a morass of traffic that rivals any large city congestion in the United States, with casual regard for traffic laws or speed limits. The love of modern engineering embodied by the automobile is mirrored in the construction visible in skyscrapers and high-rise apartment buildings as well. The majority of Caracas residents live in apartments, and the city is dominated by large concrete buildings that tower over the city like the Avila and the neon signs that line the highways. The truly elite live in luxurious single-family homes in the eastern valleys of the city, and yes, they drive as many *caraqueños* prefer, despite a reliable public transportation system that includes buses and a growing subway system. This dominance of cars in the capital does have an effect on air quality. While favorable winds do help disperse some of the smog, the gas burned by the thousands of cars produces levels of sulfur dioxide and nitrogen dioxide that both exceed World Health Organization standards for acceptable air quality in the city (Air Pollution 2006).

Highway traffic in Caracas, Venezuela. (Juan Manuel Silva/StockPhotoPro)

This is not to say that the nation's capital is without artistic charm or respite from traffic and pollution. The city is also the *distrito federal*, or federal district, and the *capitolio* area of the government contains a collection of pleasant neoclassical architecture and gleaming golden domes. In this area, one can also find the childhood home of the South American liberator Simón Bolívar, restored hacienda homes

THE CARACAS SUBWAY SYSTEM

As millions of *caraqueños* know, one of the most efficient ways to move around Caracas is to avoid the choking automobile traffic and ride the subway, known as the Metro. The metro is clean, well run, and very popular. High traffic times can be very crowded, but the Metro is very economical (in 2009, a one-way fare was .50 *bolívares* /$.23 U.S.) and fast.

The Caracas Metro opened its first line in 1983 with service between the neighborhoods of Propatria in the west and La Hoyada in the east, encompassing the government district. In 1987, a second line was completed that stretched south from the *capitolio* government district to Las Adjuntas. In 1994, the Metro extended its length with the addition of another north-south line further to the east, from Sábana Grande to La Riconada, and an additional east-west line that linked Sabana Grande with Guaraira Repano. Finally, in 2006, a fourth line was added in the center of the city in order to alleviate the very high usage of the #1 line. New suburban lines are planned.

Caracas, Venezuela subway train. (Art Directors.co.uk/Ark Religion.com/Stock-PhotoPro)

converted to museums, and lovely public art. Caracas is also home to the country's main public and private universities, the Universidad Central de Venezuela (UCV) and the Universidad Católica Andrés Bello, respectively. The UCV, whose campus was designed by the renowned architect Carlos Raúl Villanueva, is a marvel of urban planning and has been named a World Heritage Site by the United Nations Educational, Scientific and Cultural Organization (UNESCO). It is the only university campus designed in the 20th century to have been given this recognition. Caracas also has two main parks, the Parque del Este, a huge oasis of greenspace in the midst of the urban jungle, and the Parque Central, adjacent to the monuments to Venezuelan art that are represented by the main museums and theaters in the downtown area.

BEACHES, OIL, AND COFFEE!

Just over (or through) Mount Avila, a 40-minute ride from the crowded urban center of Caracas, begins the 1,700 miles of Venezuela's Caribbean coastline. Much of this coast is lined with the kind of sandy white beaches and lush tropical plant life that attract tourists, and, as such, the area is a major draw both for Venezuelans on holiday and for vacationers from around the world. On the first weekend of holy week, the highways between Caracas and the beaches of the coast are jammed full of families making their way to the beaches of the coast, from Coro in the west to Cumaná in the east, for a vacation on the sand.

The mainland beaches are popular, but Venezuela's properties in the sea are perhaps even more enticing. Just north of Caracas and the port of La Guaira is an archipelago of 50 small islands, or coral cays, known as Los Roques. These peaceful islands, many of them very small, may be reached only by boat. The islands are filled with wildlife such as birds and sea turtles and were declared a national park in 1972. Further east is the larger, and more heavily developed, Isla Margarita. Margarita is filled with large hotels and restaurants and offers a wide array of beach and water sports, including surfing, windsurfing, and parasailing. In recent years, modernization and development of Margarita has reached a level where the demand for water has placed a strain on supply, causing frequent shortages as the island's population exceeds its ability to provide water and treat waste.

Barcelona is the coastal capital of the state of Anzoategui in eastern Venezuela, but Puerto La Cruz, immediately to the east of Barcelona, became an industrial and tourism hub in the late 20th century. Tourists traveling to Margarita travel daily to the island via ferry from Puerto La Cruz. The city has its own beaches and resort hotels and is the point of embarkation for beaches farther east in Mochima National Park. More important for Venezuela, however, are the oil platforms and refineries both in the city and immediately west of Puerto La Cruz and Barcelona. Pipelines bring oil from petroleum fields in the interior, from El Tigre and Anaco or from farther east in the state of Monagas, to the refineries in Puerto La Cruz. Sitting on Playa Colorada in Mochima at sunset, one can watch local fisherman fish with drag nets and see luxury yachts and oil tankers on the ocean horizon.

Venezuela, Archipelago de Los Roques, aerial view. (Antonello Lanzellotto/StockPhotoPro)

Between the coastal beaches of the far east and the Orinoco Delta (discussed later in this chapter) is another small mountain range. The mountains around Caripe and Teresén in the state of Monagas are notable for two reasons. Venezuela's deepest cave (more than 10 kilometers deep), la Cueva del Guácharo, found by German explorer Alexander Von Humboldt in 1799, is in a national park just outside Caripe. *Guácharos* are birds who live like bats in the cave by day and hunt as far south as Brazil by night. The cool mountain environment is also perfect for shade-grown coffee. The Venezuelan elites built the national economy on coffee exports in the 19th century. Now coffee grown on small plantations in places like Caripe and Teresén serve niche markets in the United States.

FOLLOWING THE ORINOCO RIVER TO THE GUIANA HIGHLANDS: THE LOST WORLD

If one follows the coastline east from Margarita Island, white beaches give way to the marshy area of the Orinoco river delta, one of the world's largest deltas. The delta, a 10,000-square-mile wetland, is about the size of Maryland and is dominated by mangrove swamp and rich wildlife that roam the area in cycles. In addition to abundant bird species, when the waters are lower, rodents such as agoutis and pacas can be found searching the dry areas of forest floor for seeds. During times of flood, however, visitors are more likely to finds crocodiles and otters swimming in the flood-waters. In the area of the delta, the land is crisscrossed with small channels that are best navigated by small boats or canoes.

Because the Orinoco Delta is considered one of the largest intact wetland areas left on earth, it has become an increasing draw in the area of ecotourism for Venezuela. The beauty of the swamp forest, and the wide variety of animal species, draws visitors from across the globe. In the forest, jaguars pace the forest floor, while capuchin and Guianan *saki* monkeys make their homes in the trees. The swamp also provides one of the last homes for endangered Orinoco crocodiles. Companies offering Orinoco "river cruises" that promise the opportunity for "nature and adventure travel" give wildlife conservation organizations hope that the area will remain wild, as revenue from tourism outweighs any possible development interest. For this reason, wildlife conservationists have rated the area "relatively stable/intact" ("Orinoco Delta" n.d.).

Following the Orinoco south, swamps give way to more development, and therefore increased environmental impact. Where the delta comes together to form the Orinoco proper sits Ciudad Guyana, an industrial city of 800,000 people, noted for its iron industry (*Venezuela* 1993). Ciudad Guyana is a young city, founded in 1961 as part of a project to produce a modern example of city planning and organization. Geographically, Ciudad Guyana provides a center between Ciudad Bolívar, further south, and the passage through the delta to the ocean.

This part of the country, Bolívar State, is important for the potential for mining (mentioned earlier) and metal refinery including gold and aluminum. El Callao, in Bolívar, is one of the only areas in which legal, government-sanctioned gold mining takes place. This mining is carried out by skilled workers in the employ of companies renting small concessions from the Venezuelan government. Mining has traditionally

Aerial view of Orinoco river in Venezuela, May 31, 2009. (Vladimir Melnik/Dreamstime. com)

been one of the only sources of employment in El Callao. The legal and lucrative nature of the mining, however, does not necessarily equate with worker safety or sound environmental practice.

In a joint study conducted by the Venezuelan government, the Brazilian government, and the United Nations Industrial Development Organization, scientists found that the mining and processing techniques used in gold mining created serious mercury pollution for both those involved in the mining and milling process as well as innocent people living near the processing centers. The gold ore in Bolívar State comes in very fine grains; therefore, miners in El Callao still use mercury amalgamation, a process abandoned in other parts of the world because of its environmental dangers. In the course of mercury amalgamation, copper plates are coated with mercury. When the gold ore is washed over the plates, the very fine grains of gold cling to and mix with the mercury, separating from the other minerals. Contamination takes place when the abrasion of the ore causes droplets of mercury to be released with the leftover ore into the groundwater. In addition, the gold itself is contaminated with mercury. Unfortunately, the miners, millers, and citizens of El Callao do not believe in mercury poisoning and take no steps to prevent it, even allowing children to work and play in the processing centers (Veiga et al. 2005).

Mercury is a toxin that causes neurological damage: alteration of visual and spatial perception, problems with memory, and disruption of motor coordination and manual dexterity. In the previously mentioned study, the scientists discovered that 90 percent of the miners and millers tested had levels of mercury in their system that put them above the "alert" level designated by the World Health Organization. They also found signs of "serious intoxication and neurological damages in a large majority of those directly involved in the amalgamation process as well as in innocent people living near the processing centers" (Veiga et al. 2007). While the international team demonstrated cleaner mining techniques to the miners, and recommended awareness programs, it noted the significant work yet to be done.

ILLEGAL GOLD MINING IN AMAZONAS

In December of 2009, the Venezuelan government deployed its military to expel 400 illegal wildcat gold miners from Yapacana National Park in Venezuela's Amazonas State. Another 1,500 miners are believed to have escaped expulsion by hiding in the forest. The expelled miners, of Colombian and Brazilian nationality, were sent to Colombia, which reacted with anger. The government of Colombia declared that the forced expulsion was a violation of the miner's human rights. The Venezuelan government, in contrast, pointed out that gold mining in the area was illegal, as well as environmentally damaging, leaving devastated landscapes and mercury-tainted water. The expulsion heightened tensions between Colombia and Venezuela, who were embroiled in a feud over the movements of guerrilla groups along the Venezuela-Colombia border.

Energy also plays an important role in the economy of the area. Bracketing the nation with the reserves under Lake Maracaibo is the so-called Orinoco Tar Belt, a mass of sticky brown heavy and extra-heavy crude oil that is more difficult to refine than the light crude in the west but that is valuable nonetheless as a petroleum product. Current extraction and refining of the petroleum in the tar belt takes place on a smaller scale because the process is unwieldy and expensive, but future world needs for oil have produced an increase in demand. In 2009, Venezuela and Vietnam began talks aimed at agreeing on a plan to produce oil together in the Orinoco region by early 2011. Future production of oil in the Orinoco region will undoubtedly have increased environmental and economic impact on the region.

Hydroelectric energy is also produced in this part of the country through several dams on the Caroní River south of the Orinoco. Indeed, to the problems created by the wildcat mining for gold on the Caroní River we can add the issue of sediment buildup. When miners employ the high-pressure hoses on the river banks to expose the gold deposits, the soil that is removed causes sedimentary buildup in the turbines of the dams that provide hydroelectric power.

The territory south of Ciudad Bolívar is dominated by the Guiana highlands, an area of tropical forest dotted with distinctive, flat-topped mountains known as *tepuis*. *Tepuis* are only found in the Guiana highlands. These tablelike mountains are free-standing, rising abruptly above the thick forest. With their nearly vertical sides and smooth crowns, they provide individually unique ecosystems for the plant and animal life that live on their surfaces above the clouds. The life on top of the mountain is so far removed from that on the forest floor (the tallest mountain stands at more than 3,000 feet) that *tepui* wildlife exists in a different climate from that on the forest floor.

In his novel *The Lost World*, Sir Arthur Conan Doyle had his explorers find dinosaur and other fantastic creatures on the top of a *tepui*. While this is fantasy, a

THE PEMÓN AND THE *TEPUIS*

The area surrounding the most famous of Venezuela's *tepuis*, Roraima, Auyantepui, and Matawi, has been inhabited by an indigenous tribe known as the Pemón for thousands of years. There are Pemón settlements throughout the Gran Sábana area, living in many cases in mud and straw houses similar to those of their ancestors. The Pemón, however, have not been unaffected by their contact with the many tourists who come to see the *tepuis* and Angel Falls.

For the Pemón, the *tepuis* are sacred places, locations where the souls of the departed, known as *mawari* linger. Many of the Pemón's creation myths also revolve around the mountains. In traditional Pemón culture, the *tepuis* look out for and guard the savanna, and no one is allowed to ascend a *tepui*. In the 21st century, however, the economic opportunity afforded to the Pemón from guiding tours of the sacred mountains has meant a relaxing of the traditional rules, and many Pemón settlements earn a living guiding such tours.

Lost World. Unique panoramic view of the Auyantepuy table-top mountain seen from Kamarata valley in Gran Sabana south of Venezuela. (Vladimir Melnik/Dreamstime.com)

true wonder of nature does make its home on the top of one of the mountains: Angel Falls, the world's tallest waterfall, begins its descent from the top of the Auyan-tepui. The falls, named for Jimmy Angel, an American pilot who landed his plane on top of the mountain, reach 3,212 feet to the ground below and feed into the Caroní River.

THE NATIONAL FLOWER AND THE NATIONAL TREE

In 1951, the Venezuelan government proclaimed the *Cattleya* orchid to be the national flower of the nation. The *Cattleya* is indigenous to Venezuela, growing as far north as the Cordillera Central, and as far south as the Sábana Grande region. The *Cattleya* comes in a wide variety of colors, including white, red, pink, and lavender, and it is commonly known as the Easter Orchid, or Flower of May. This flower is commonly used to decorate the holy cross during the Cruz de mayo religious festivals and is also used as decoration in processions for holy week.

The *Cattleya* is hardly the only Venezuelan orchid, however. Many other orchids grow in the forests of Amazonas and Bolívar states. It is estimated that there are between 1,000 and 1,200 species of orchids native to Venezuela, with many species yet to be discovered in unexplored forest areas.

The government decreed the *araguaney* the national tree in 1948. It is unique to Venezuela, known for its huge, vibrant yellow blooms that last from February to April.

The distinctive *tepuis*, Angel Falls, and the national park created around them, Canaima National Park, are major attractions for scientific exploration and ecotourism. The government runs a resort at the shores of a lagoon of spectacular pink sand with a view of smaller, but still picturesque, waterfalls. To see Angel Falls, travelers choose either to make a flight over the forest floor to pass by the falls or to take a more extensive trip up the Caroní River from the resort to the foot of the falls. Because of its status as a national park and the lack of development, like the Orinoco Delta, the Canaima area is also popular for excursions to other areas for hiking, boating, and other adventure sports.

Most popular is an excursion to stay at a lodge at the Canaima lagoon. The lagoon is famous not only for its setting, surrounded by multiple smaller waterfalls, but also for its tea-colored water and pink sand. The water, clear but reddish-brown from the tannins released by minerals and plant life, complements the sand, which gains its color from the pink quartz of the area. Visitors generally take side trips from the resort and lagoon to fly past Angel Falls or other nearby waterfalls.

Scientists also come to the area to study the enclosed ecosystems of the *tepui* mountains. The opportunity to discover new species of plant and animal life is an amazing opportunity for wildlife biologists. However, the two groups, scientist and adventure-tourists, at times find themselves at odds on this issue of access to the *tepuis*. The highland ecosystems of the tabletop mountains are extremely fragile and have, until recently, survived because of their largely inaccessible nature in an isolated region of the nation. The growing popularity of adventure tourism, which brings more and more people to the mountaintops, brings with it the risk of human disturbance. The greatest risk is that of fire. The ecosystems are particularly vulnerable to the effects

Angel Falls. (Corel)

of fire and are particularly unable to recover from uncontrolled burning. In order to try to help preserve the delicate ecosystems of the *tepuis*, in 1993, the government declared all lands south of the Orinoco over 800 meters in height national monuments, thereby putting all the *tepuis* in a protected area system that gave officials some extra power in enforcement.

THE ORINOCO PLAINS

If one returns west, the Orinoco plains stretch out to the north and west of the Orinoco River, reaching back to the foothills of the Andes that stretch along the western boarder of the nation with Colombia. This is the home of Doña Bárbara, the wild and uncontrolled agent of Rómulo Gallegos's famous novel of the same name, a land of open plains and cattle ranches that have historically encompassed up to 1 million acres. Cattle ranching is, by far, the most important part of the economy of this area and has been since the colonial era. When early settlers arrived in the southern part of the country, they found the soil poor, with little farming potential. Ranching was the only economically feasible use of the land. The Spanish introduced cattle in 1550, and ranching took hold in the Orinoco lowlands with great success. The Orinoco plains are also known as the llanos, and the cowboys who run the cattle here are known as *llaneros.* By the middle 1800s one *llanero* could run up to 4,000 head of cattle (Otto and Anderson 1986).

The plains are mainly vast grasslands, cut through by rivers that flood seasonally. Some small forests grow along the banks of these rivers. The ecological make-up of the area not only supports ranching but also a wealth of biodiversity in animal life.

Llaneros Cattle Drive. (Bob Gaspari/StockPhotoPro)

PIRANHAS OF THE PLAINS

One of the most famous Amazonian fish is the carnivorous piranha. The rivers and ponds of Venezuela's western llanos are home to eight species of the fish, which are very common, in many locations making up the majority of fish in the water. Venezuelan piranhas grow to a length of three and a half inches, and have rows of very sharp, very small teeth placed in powerful jaws. While popular culture has portrayed piranhas as vicious man-eaters, in reality, the fish are piscavores—eaters of other fish.

Studies have shown that the majority of piranhas of western Venezuela eat a diet of fish scales and chunks of other fish's flesh. Another variety of piranha specializes in biting the fins off of other fish. The piranha's jaws are strong enough to bite off a human finger, but are normally employed in ripping off pieces of other fish.

While it is extremely uncommon for piranha to eat human flesh, humans find piranha flesh very enjoyable, mild and sweet. Fried piranha is a popular dish in the llanos.

A mounted and preserved piranha from Venezuela. (iStockPhoto)

The Orinoco plains and rivers are home to more than 1,000 species of fish, more than 300 species of birds, and more than 100 species of mammals, including capybaras, the world's largest rodent. This extensive array of wildlife makes the llanos another area of interest for ecotourists. Bird watchers flock to the area for the opportunity to see so many types of rare avian species, and adventure tour groups sell safari packages similar to those advertised for African nations.

AMAZONAS AND THE FAR SOUTH

The far southern tip of Venezuela, south of the Guiana Highlands is Amazonas State, sometimes known as Amazonia. This area of Venezuela, while named for the Amazon, is actually bisected and drained by the Orinoco River. The area is heavily forested, rich in wildlife diversity, and home of the largest concentration of indigenous peoples in the nation.

Perhaps because of the area's distance from the capital, Amazonas is the least explored and developed region in Venezuela. Puerto Ayacucho, the capital of Amazonas, is by far the most populous city in Amazonas State, and in 2009, the population estimate for Puerto Ayacucho was 83,000 people out of a total population for the state of 149,000 (City Population 2009). Given the size of the state, that leaves a lot of space for a relatively small number of people. Puerto Ayacucho is located in the very northern part of Amazonas State. Yet beginning about 40 miles south of the city, the roads end. All travel after that point is conducted by air or by boat on the Orinoco and its tributaries.

The lack of roads is not a concern to the traditional inhabitants of the region. More than a dozen different indigenous groups make the state their home. Indeed, 24 of Venezuela's 28 recognized indigenous groups can be found in Amazonas State including the Yanomami, discussed at length elsewhere in this book. While many outside the indigenous communities might find the Indian way of life poverty stricken, research has shown that by living in the Amazonian forest and consuming forest resources, the indigenous peoples of the area receive more economic and nutritional benefit than they would as low-paid and low-skilled laborers in Puerto Ayacucho (World Resources Institute n.d.). In this way, the lack of intrusion into traditional living has been a benefit to the residents of Amazonas.

The region does not, however, remain completely free of outside influences. Many of the same problems of illegal gold mining discussed in regard to Bolívar State hold true as well in Amazonas. Wildcat gold mining, while illegal, is even harder to police and control in the remote reaches of Amazonas.

REFERENCES

"Air Pollution in Selected World Cities." 2006. *The World Almanac.* www.theworldalmanac. com.

Briceño de Bermúdez, Tarcila. 1993. *Comercio por los Ríos Orinoco y Apure: Segunda mitad del siglo XIX.* Caracas: Fondo Editorial Tropykos.

"Capybara." n.d. http://www.economicexpert.com/a/Capybara.html.

City Population. 2009. "Venezuela." http://www.citypopulation.de/Venezuela.html.

Leng, R. A., T. R Preston, and Lyliana Rodriguez. 2004. "The Duckweed Invasion of Lake Maracaibo: An Evaluation of the Causes and Proposals for Future Action." http://www.penambulbooks.com/Downloads/reporteng072204.pdf.

Marzuola, Carlos. 2004. "Scientists Puzzled by Plant Invasion on Venezuelan Lake." http://www.scidev.net/en/latin-america-and-caribbean/features/scientists-puzzled-by-plant-invasion-on-venezuelan.html.

"Orinoco Delta Swamp Forests." n.d. http://www.nationalgeographic.com/wildworld/profiles/terrestrial/nt/nt0147.html.

Otto, J. S., and N. E. Anderson. 1986. "Cattle Ranching in Venezuela and Florida." *Comparative Studies in Society and History* 28: 672–683.

United Nations Department of Economic and Social Affairs. 2007. "Urban and Rural Areas 2007." http://www.un.org/esa/population/publications/wup2007/2007_urban_rural_chart.pdf.

Veiga, Marcello M., J.J. Berzas Nevado, R.C. Rodríguez Martín-Doimeadios, F.J. Guzmán Bernardo, M. Jiménez Moreno, A.M. Herculano, do J.L.M. Nascimento, M.E. Crespo-López. 2005. "Mercury Pollution from Artisanal Gold Mining." In B. Block, ed. *Dynamics of Mercury Pollution on Global and Regional Scales: Atmospheric Processes, Human Exposure around the World.* Norwell, MA: Springer.

Venezuela: A Country Study. 1993. Washington, DC: Library of Congress.

World Resources Institute. n.d. "Indigenous Communities and Forest Activities." http://www.wri.org/publication/content/8302.

History

TIMELINE

1499—Alfonso de Ojeda and Amerigo Vespucci arrive at the South American continent at what is now Venezuela.

1567—Diego de Losada establishes Caracas.

1711—Juan del Rosario Blanco, a free person of color, establishes Curiepe.

1721—Founding of the Universidad Central de Venezuela (UCV).

1723—José de Oviedo y Baños publishes the first history of Venezuela.

1728—The Guipuzcoana Company and its monopoly on cacao production are established.

1734—The Viceroyalty of New Granada (modern-day Venezuela, Colombia, and Ecuador) is established.

1776—The *audiencia* in Caracas is established. All Venezuelan territories are placed under the jurisdiction of the Caracas *audiencia.*

1783—Simón Bolívar is born.

1791—The Haitian slave revolt takes place.

1795—A revolt in Coro of slaves, ex-slaves, Indians, and peons in land dispute takes place.

1808—Napoleon Bonaparte invades Spain.

July 5, 1811—Venezuela declares independence from Spain.

1812—A massive earthquake destroys Caracas.

Francisco de Miranda is exiled to northern Africa.

February 15, 1819—The Angostura Congress begins, during which Bolívar gives his famous speech outlining ideologies and priorities for an independent Venezuela.

June 24, 1821—Bolívar's forces win the Battle of Carabobo, which leads to Venezuelan independence.

1821—Gran Colombia, incorporating Venezuela, Colombia, and Ecuador, is created.

1823—Slavery is theoretically abolished by Simón Bolívar but is continued in Venezuela until 1854.

1828—President José Antonio Paez expels Bolívar from Venezuela.

December 17, 1830—Bolívar dies in Santa Marta, Colombia.

1831—Gran Colombia is officially dissolved, and Colombia, Venezuela, and Ecuador are created as independent nations.

1838—First Bank (British Colonial Bank) opens in colonial Venezuela.

1847—*Gramática de la lengua castellana* (*Grammar of the Spanish Language*) is published by Andrés Bello.

1853—*Manual de urbanidad y buenas maneras* (*Manual of Urbanity and Good Manners*) is published by Manuel Carreño.

1854—Slavery is abolished in Venezuela.

1858–1863—The Federal War takes place.

1860—Liberal reformer and *caudillo* Ezequiel Zamora is assassinated.

1870—Guzmán Blanco decrees free and compulsory public education.

1875—Guzmán Blanco expels Caracas Archbishop Silvestre Guevara y Lira.

1878—Oil is first extracted by Antonio Manuel Pulido and his Compania Petrolia de Táchira. The well produces 60 barrels a day and supplies Cucuta (Tinker Salas 2009: 40).

1880s—New York and Bermudez Company begins to work the asphalt lake in the state of Sucre, producing asphalt, oil, and tar (Tinker Salas 2009: 41).

1895—Baseball is introduced to Venezuela.

1908—Juan Vicente Gómez orchestrates the removal of Cipriano Castro as president of Venezuela. Gómez remains president until his death in 1935.

1914—Zumaque 1 well begins to produce in Mene Grande, beginning the modern era of oil production in Venezuela. The well eventually produces 641 million barrels (Tinker Salas 2009: 46).

1922—U.S. oil companies write Venezuela's first Petroleum Law.

1924—*Ifigenia: Diario de una señorita que escribía porque se fastiaba* (*Iphigenia: The Diary of a Young Lady Who Wrote Because She Was Bored*) is published by Teresa de la Parra.

1928—Multiple movements challenge the Gómez dictatorship, including one led by university students Raúl Leoni, Rómulo Betancourt, and other future political leaders.

1929—*Doña Bárbara* is published by Rómulo Gallegos.

1930—The Venezuelan Association of Baseball is founded.

1934—The highway linking Caracas and the Andes is completed.

1935—Gómez dies.

1938—The New Petroleum Law is written to increase Venezuela's share of petroleum profits.

1939—Alex Carrasquel becomes the first Venezuelan to play Major League Baseball.

1945–1948—*Trienio democrático* under the presidency of Rómulo Gallegos.

1949—*Ana Isabel, Una niña decente* (*Ana Isabel: A Decent Girl*) is published by Antonia Palacios.

1951—Chico Carrasquel becomes the first Latino selected to play in the Major League Baseball All-Star Game.

1952–1958—Dictatorship of Marcos Pérez Jiménez.

1958—Pact of Punto Fijo is made between the political parties AD, COPEI, and Unión Repúblicana Democrática, laying the groundwork for Venezuelan democracy until 1998.

1960—Venezuela establishes the Organization of Petroleum Exporting Countries (OPEC) with Iran, Iraq, Saudi Arabia, and Kuwait.

1973—The value of Venezuelan currency against the U.S. dollar peaks.

1974—Law against Unjustified Layoffs establishes minimum wage.

1975—El Sistema music education system is founded.

Oil is nationalized and the PDVSA (Petróleos de Venezuela, S.A.) is created.

1976—The Venezuelan Gallery of National Art has its grand opening.

1977—Carlos Raúl Villanueva's design for the UCV University City is completed.

1980—Ley Orgánica de la Educación (Organic Law of Education) is implemented.

1983—*Correo del corazón* (*Letters from the Heart*) is published by Yolanda Pantin.

"Black Friday": The Bolivar is devalued from 4.3VEB to the dollar to 7VEB for imports of essential consumer goods.

1984—Luis Aparicio becomes the first Venezuelan inducted into the Major League Baseball Hall of Fame.

Telenovela *Topacio* premiers in Venezuela.

1989—*El caracazo* and other riots nationwide challenge the presidency of President Carlos Andres Pérez (CAP).

May 18, 1989—The first general strike in Venezuelan history takes place.

1990—Labor Law is signed that provides for collective bargaining rights, fringe benefits, retirement, and disability pensions.

1992—Coup attempts in February and November lead to the resignation of Carlos Andrés Pérez. Hugo Chávez leads the February coup. The November coup originated in units of the Air Force.

The *telenovela Por estas calles* dominates Venezuelan airwaves and conversations.

1993—President Pérez is forced out of office in a corruption scandal.

1994—Ley de Cinematografía Nacional, a national film law designed to protect and promote Venezuelan film, is passed. It creates the CNAC—Centro Nacional Autónomo de Cinematografía.

1998—Hugo Chávez Frías is elected as president.

1999—New version of the Venezuelan National Constitution is approved: the Bolivarian Constitution.

Severe mudslides in northern Venezuela kill 30,000.

2000—Venezuela wins the Little League World Series.

Megaelections take place. Every elected official—local, state, and federal—is required to stand for reelection.

Hugo Chávez is reelected to the presidency under the new six-year term allowed for in the 1999 Bolivarian Constitution.

Hydrocarbons Law is passed. It provides that all oil production and distribution activities will be the domain of the Venezuelan state, with the exception of the joint ventures targeting extra-heavy crude oil production. Under this law, private investors cannot own 50 percent or more of the capital stock in joint ventures involved in upstream activities.

Land Law is passed. It allows the federal government to seize private lands deemed idle or not appropriately used.

April 12, 2002—A coup attempt is made against Chávez. All Organization of American States (OAS) nations condemn the coup except the United States. Chávez returns on April 14.

December 2002–January 2003—PDVSA declares a general strike that paralyzes the country and eventually leads to greater direct government control of the company.

2003—The Social Responsibility Law is implemented.

2005—A recall election is held on the office of the president. Hugo Chávez is confirmed in office.

New Tribes Mission is expelled from Venezuela.

Ozzie Guillén leads the Chicago White Sox to victory in the World Series.

2006—Hugo Chávez is reelected to a second term as president with 63 percent of the vote.

Law of Communal Councils, authorizing and encouraging the creation of communal councils, is passed.

2007—The Simón Bolívar Youth Orchestra plays at Carnegie Hall, New York City.

2008—President Chávez severs ties with the World Bank and the International Monetary Fund (IMF).

The *bolívar fuerte*, a new currency that simplified the currency system by eliminating zeroes from the exchange rate with the dollar, is instituted. This move is a reaction to runaway inflation.

A cross-border raid by Colombia into Ecuador begins an international incident, resulting in severing of diplomatic ties between Venezuela and Colombia.

2009—Constitutional Referendum passes that lifts term limits on the presidency.

Gustavo Dudamel, graduate of El Sistema, becomes the music director of the Los Angeles Philharmonic Orchestra.

New Organic Law of Education is passed.

New Law of Law of Electoral Processes is passed.

Several banking magnates are arrested. The moves are seen as either a crackdown on corruption in the banking industry or as a purge of selected economically prominent loyalists in a bid to further consolidate President Chávez's power.

2010—The VEB is devalued for most transactions. The Venezuelan government continues to subsidize the value of the bolivar for imports of food, medicine, and other items deemed essential.

February 8, 2010—President Chávez declares an energy emergency in response to electricity and water shortages provoked by a drought and falling water levels at the Guri Dam, the nation's principle sources of hydroelectric power.

The Chicago White Sox unretire number 11, worn by Venezuelan and White Sox Hall of Famer Luis Aparicio. Omar Vizquel, 11-time gold glove Venezuelan short stop, wears 11 for the White Sox in 2010.

Don José de Oviedo y Baños published the first history of Venezuela in 1723. By that year, the central valleys were well settled, stable, and on the verge of prosperity that attracted so much royal attention that the crown reorganized the colonial administration system in order to better take advantage of the wealth the flowed out in the form of brown gold, chocolate. The central and western parts of what became Venezuela also produced cacao in significant quantities. Missionaries in the east had finally dedicated themselves to the business of "civilizing" indigenous tribes in the east. More Spaniards arrived and converted vast expanses of llanos south and north of the Orinoco River into cattle ranches. Part of Don José's mission with his tome was to attract those Spaniards. So of course he wrote of "fertile plains" and "delightful valleys," waters "clear and salubrious" (Oviedo y Baños 1987: 7). The colony he described was perfect for breeding the finest horses or grazing cattle. Farmers harvested fields of wheat, maize, rice, cotton, tobacco, sugar, cacao, vanilla, and all sorts of other fruits and vegetables. Sarsaparilla and indigo grew so prodigiously they might well have been weeds. There were tin mines, copper mines, and gold (Oviedo y Baños 1987). He did not mention the pearls. By the time Don José wrote, the pearls were gone. Indeed, Venezuela was a colonizer's dream. Natural resources enabled the colonists to support themselves while producing raw materials, cacao, tobacco, and sugar for European markets.

So why did Don José feel compelled to rescue Venezuelan history from the "oblivion of memory" so early in that same history? (Oviedo y Baños 1987: 7) The stability and prosperity that marked the era in which Don José wrote were recent. The early colonial experience had been anything but easy for anyone involved in the colonial process—Spaniards, indigenous Venezuelans, or Africans. Further, what we now know as Venezuela was divided into at least three distinct regions, regions that had more communication with other colonies or with Spain but not with the other Venezuelan colonies. Don José's drive to promote Venezuela to Europeans in order to further the process of progress challenged by regionalism and ethnic differences (or different versions of modernity) is a theme that runs through Venezuelan history.

COLONIAL BEGINNINGS

Columbus found Venezuela on his third voyage to the Americas in 1498 and wrote back to Queen Isabella about pearls. By 1499, Vespucci and Ojeda explored the western coastline, enchanted by huts on stilts in Lake Maracaibo. None of the explorers found gold or silver in the quantities found later in Mexico or Peru. Explorers did not find organized, centralized indigenous civilizations like the Aztec in Mexico or Inca in Peru, though in 1499 Spaniards had no idea those groups existed. There were dozens of indigenous groups occupying Venezuela when the Spaniards arrived in 1499. Some groups were seminomadic hunter-gatherer peoples. Other groups used agriculture to subsist. At best, groups in the center and center-west formed a loose confederation of communities that shared common culture but that did not share loyalty to one leader. The northern coast of what became Venezuela immediately interested Spaniards for two principle reasons: those pearls and indigenous slaves to be shipped to plantations in Hispaniola (Santo Domingo) and Cuba. Spaniards used outposts in Coro in the west and the Cumaná-Cubagua-Margarita Island nexus in the east as staging grounds for pearl fishing or slaving endeavors. From those points also throughout the 1500s other Spaniards and a few Germans Welsers (given a private grant by the Spanish crown in 1528) continued to explore deeper into Venezuela, always in search of El Dorado and the Venezuelan version of the Incan empire, but instead finding indigenous Venezuelans living in chiefdoms, sedentary agriculturalists or hunter-gatherers, and mosquitoes. Lots and lots of mosquitoes. The reality was, as Don José noted, that the Spaniards and the Germans in early decades were not interested in settling or developing the province but instead simply wanted to exploit Venezuela for personal gain (Oviedo y Baños 1987). That meant that not only did Spaniards and German Welsers enact violence against indigenous Venezuelans for the purpose of conquest and slave raiding, but Europeans also came into violent conflict with each other over the spoils of conquest.

Aerial view of three ships offshore; Christopher Columbus with indigenous Margarita islanders; islanders diving in foreground. (Library of Congress)

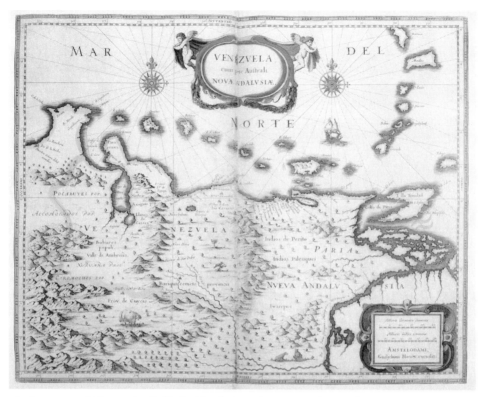

Antique map of Venezuela. Published by the Dutch cartographer Willem Blaeu in Atlas Novus *(Amsterdam 1635). (iStockPhoto)*

About the same time the German exploration contract expired in 1548, Spaniards left in Venezuela realized that they had to settle down and begin the colonization process, to develop a colony based on agricultural production. Exploitation wasn't enough. The larger colonial context had changed significantly since 1500. The conquest of indigenous empires in Mexico and Peru made those areas the focal points of the Spanish empire in the Americas. The crown's interest in Venezuela dissipated nearly immediately. Pearl fisheries did not yield much by the 1540s. Moreover, the New Laws promulgated by Spanish King Carlos V in 1542 outlawed indigenous slavery, making slave raiding into declining Venezuelan indigenous populations in the east and west illegal. With a healthy climate and a sedentary population to use for labor, Spaniards chose the valley of El Tocuyo to establish the first inland community in 1545. The problem was, however, that El Tocuyo did not have a port. So Spaniards continued to push east, establishing the city of Valencia in 1555 (Lombardi 1982). They knew that the valleys and plains farther east in the area called Aragua had the best agricultural potential and necessary ocean access, but Indians in the area put up a stiff resistance. There were probably approximately 30,000 indigenous Venezuelans in the valleys that became Caracas when the Spaniards began their conquest and settlement efforts (Lombardi 1982). Only by force did Diego de Losada finally establish Caracas in 1567, and the city's existence remained tenuous for decades after.

EL CACIQUE GUAICAIPURO (CA. 1530–1568)

El Cacique Guaicaipuro was an indigenous leader in Venezuela who formed a confederation of indigenous groups in the central valleys near what is now Caracas to resist Spanish settlement. The Spanish discovered gold in Los Teques, just north of Caracas, and commenced mining operations and settlement in the late 1550s. Guaicaipuro then organized his confederation to expel the Spaniards. His confederation removed the Spaniards in Los Teques in 1560 and repelled another invasion in 1562 before losing to Diego de Losada in 1568. Honored in the 20th and 21st century as a symbol of indigenous resistance and identity, he is also one of the three powers (along with María Lionza and Negro Felipe) at the top of the pantheon of gods in the cult of María Lionza.

Plague finished the conquest process in Caracas in 1580, reducing the indigenous population to some 10,000 to 12,000 (Lombardi 1982). As in much of the rest of Latin America, European diseases did more to conquer indigenous Americans than European swords did.

THE ESTABLISHED COLONY AND
COLONIAL INSTITUTIONS

There are two key questions to think about when we think about Venezuela as a true colony and not just a colonial outpost. The first question is what did Spain want from Venezuela? The second question is what did Venezuela want for itself? Those questions do overlap somewhat, but let us first consider them separately. To help us accomplish both tasks, we need to think about where Venezuela fit in the overall Spanish colonial structure in the Americas. About the time of the conquests of Mexico and Peru, the Spanish crown divided all of its American territories into two large administrative units, the Viceroyalty of New Spain and the Viceroyalty of Peru. New Spain included Mexico (including what became the U.S. Southwest), Central America, Florida, the Caribbean Islands, and Venezuela. The Viceroyalty of Peru included the rest of South America, except the Portuguese colony of Brazil. The Spaniards further divided their territories into subregions called *audiencias.* Through much of its colonial history, Venezuela was part of the *audiencia* that had its seat in Santo Domingo. Those divisions make sense historically, as Spaniards incorporated Venezuela into the colonial system when the system only involved the Caribbean (Santo Domingo), and then Mexico. Spaniards developed the Viceroyalty of Peru with the conquest of Peru, which began a bit later, in 1532. Venezuela's inclusion in the Viceroyalty of New Spain, *audiencia* of Santo Domingo, made a bit less sense geographically. The western regions of the colony including El Tocuyo and what became Maracaibo developed extensive overland communication and trade with

Santa Fé de Bogota (Colombia) in the *audiencia* of Santa Fé in the Viceroyalty of Peru. The eastern regions of the country—Barcelona, Cumana, and later Angostura on the Orinoco River—maintained communication and trade with the eastern parts of the Caribbean including Santo Domingo. The central coastal areas and Caracas maintained trade relationships with Mexico and the Dutch island colonies in the western Caribbean. Those relationships meant that the regions had little to do with each other despite the fact that the crown considered the colony one, not three, with Caracas the most important city in the colony. Eventually, the crown divided Venezuela into five provinces that corresponded roughly with the geographic divisions. Those provinces were, east to west, Trinidad-Guyana, Margarita Island, Nueva Andalucía (Cumaná), Venezuela (Caracas), and La Grita-Mérida-Maracaibo (Tronconis de Veracoechea 1981). Because the crown did not locate an *audiencia* in Caracas until the late 1700s local political and administrative institutions, the Caracas *cabildo* (town council) in particular, developed significant local authority and claimed authority beyond the local level (Lombardi 1982).

The crown expected Venezuela to serve particular purposes. Yes, it was supposed to be a bulwark of Spanish control in northern South America, to defend South America against any other European colonial predators. Texas served that purpose north of the Caribbean. Even though the European power plays involving American territories were real, Spain relied more on colonies in the Americas for income, Venezuela included. Venezuela never produced vast quantities of precious metals, but over the course of the 17th century, colonists learned how to excel in the production of high quality tobacco, cattle byproducts (hides and salted meat), and cacao. By the 18th century, as part of the Bourbon Reforms, the crown redrew colonial boundaries in part to take better advantage of the profit that came from Venezuelan goods, particularly cacao.

International trade benefited Spaniards and creoles (individuals born in the Americas of Spanish descent), but through most of the colonial period, Venezuelans had to work around the crown's trade rules instead of obeying those rules. Because the colonies existed to serve the needs of the mother country, Spain prohibited legal trade with anyone other than Spain. Furthermore, Spain limited the definition of legal trade to only that trade that went through Havana, Cuba to Spain. So if a tobacco plantation owner in Barinas in the southern llanos wanted to ship tobacco legally to Spain, he had to send it overland to the port of La Guaira (the port that served Caracas). The tobacco then went to Havana, then to Spain. He could not encumber a merchant in La Guaira to ship directly to Spain, nor could he legally ship down the Orinoco River to points beyond. Though Venezuelans engaged in enough legal trade to barely satisfy the crown's needs, Venezuelans profited most from illegal trade, contraband, with other Spanish colonies in the Americas or other European colonial possessions in the Caribbean. As cacao plantations prospered and began to rely even more heavily on imported African slaves, the contraband trade in slaves with the Dutch island of Curaçao became particularly important. Venezuelans also used local trade in the foodstuffs on Don José's list to support themselves more than adequately. Once Spaniards settled down to the business of settling in Venezuela, they did quite well.

There is one other colonial institution associated with settlement and the development of the economy, and that was the *encomienda*. *Encomienda* was a system through which the crown allowed Spanish colonizers to use indigenous labor to work land for the colonizers' purposes. The crown did not grant colonizing Spaniards land directly through *encomienda* but instead indirectly through the number of Indians granted to Spaniards. More important Spaniards received the right to use the labor of more Indians and thus the ability to use more land. In exchange for the right to use indigenous labor, Spaniards were supposed to Christianize and civilize their Indians and support them in times of difficulty. In practice, *encomienda* meant indigenous slavery for economic purposes with scant attention to any efforts to Christianize. And so it was that one of the first things that Diego de Losada did was to assign indigenous Venezuelans to Spaniards in *encomienda* when he arrived in the valley that became Caracas in 1567. Robert Ferry notes that even through the early decades of the 1600s, Spaniards argued that their ability to profit agriculturally from wheat depended on their ability to increase the numbers of Indians they held in *encomienda* (difficult given the declining indigenous population) augmented by African slaves (Ferry 1989). The New Laws promulgated by Carlos V in 1542 placed limits on how *encomenderos* could use Indians held in *encomienda*. *Encomenderos* were supposed to use indigenous labor only three days a week, a rule violated regularly throughout the Venezuelan provinces (Tronconis de Veracoechea 1981; Bastidas Valecillos 1997; Morales M. 1994). The time of service was not supposed to exceed one or two generations. However, *encomenderos* in Nueva Andalucía developed a different form of *encomienda* called *apuntamiento*, in which they held Indians in *encomienda* indefinitely in a system that really did have much in common with slavery (Prato Perelli 1990). Historians suggest that *encomienda* served the purpose of conquest more than almost anything else (except disease). Though undeniably exploitative, the system served the Spaniards' agenda. Through it, Spaniards and creoles obtained the labor they had to have in order to prosper, for the crown's purposes and for their own.

Gold, God, and glory. We can certainly make the argument that Spaniards perceived their colonial efforts through those three windows. Certainly, Spaniards pursued glory (not so successfully) in the early decades of the colonial experience in Venezuela. Gold became economic profit, something Spaniards and creoles mastered once they moved past the glory days. That leaves God. For some conquerors in other parts of the Americas, conquerors like Hernán Cortés in Mexico, the devotion to God and the mission to Christianize and civilize indigenous Americans was perhaps as important as any other motivation. That means that Cortés receives some of the credit for fostering a strong missionary and institutional Catholic Church presence in Mexico from the earliest years of colonial endeavors. Cortés did not have a contemporary in Venezuela. As early as 1514, Franciscans tried to establish missions in far eastern Venezuela, but all attempts failed until 1656, when missions founded in and around the community of Píritu south of Barcelona finally survived (Tronconis de Veracoechea 1981). Franciscans had much more success in the central valleys, as their attempts to convert the indigenous populations coincided somewhat with Spanish settlement agendas. The Convent of San Francisco in Caracas, founded in 1576, was first of many convents in the central valleys. As the indigenous population quickly declined, Franciscans turned their efforts to serving the growing urban populations: Spanish, creole, indigenous, African, and mixed race. Franciscans built convents, churches, libraries, and schools. They educated generations of colonial elite Venezuelans and fostered the development of a Venezuelan-born clergy, something that never happened in the east. Indeed, through the 19th century, the east remained largely dependent on Spanish clergy (Lombardi 1982; Morse 2003).

Within the first 100 years after Columbus found Venezuelan Tierra Firme, colonists established the most important institutions and patterns of domination that continued through the next 200 years. With the establishment of the missions in Píritu in 1656, Spaniards began to settle the interior in the east, using the *encomienda* and *apuntamiento* labor to develop cattle and livestock ranches that supplied colonies in the Caribbean through the port of Barcelona. German traveler Alexander Von Humboldt commented on the quantity of salted meat that shipped from Barcelona to Caribbean ports. He estimated the value of each boatload, approximately 500 to 600 pounds, at 45,000 pesos. The merchants and cattlemen made more money from the export of livestock. In 1799 and 1800, Barcelona also exported 8,000 mules to the Caribbean islands, compared to 6,000 mules shipped from Puerto Cabello, and 3,000 from Carupano (Humboldt 1941). In the central valleys and points west, the most important development in the 1600s was the shift from wheat production to cacao, a process that began in the 1630s and encompassed territory that extended from the Tuy Valley east of Caracas to Coro in the far west. The process also meant increased dependence on a growing African slave population, replacing completely indigenous labor. The cacao boom truly began in the late 1600s, continued until the 1720s, and reinforced central and western commercial and geographic patterns. The Caracas *cabildo* frequently acted as if it had de facto administrative control over much more territory than it actually, legally, could claim. Through the whole process, the *caraqueño* elite developed a coherent sense of elite identity and control unusual even in Latin America. By the time of independence, those who were the Caracas elite had been so for six or seven generations. It was not an elite that easily admitted new blood, even from other Venezuelan provinces (Ferry 1989). A common phrase today is *Caracas no es Venezuela y Venezuela no es Caracas* (Caracas isn't Venezuela and Venezuela isn't Caracas). The phrase applies to the colonial era, too.

What changed the political, economic, military, and administrative situations in the Venezuelan provinces was the introduction of the Guipuzcoana Company in 1728. The Basque-owned (the Basques were from northern Spain) Real Compañia Guipuzcoana de Caracas was the first crown-chartered commercial monopoly company. The crown granted the company the right to trade directly with Venezuela for cacao. Company ships left San Sebastian loaded with consumer goods, duty free, then after a quick stop to pay taxes in Cádiz, traveled to La Guaira, load with cacao, then returned to Cádiz (Ferry 1989). The company was also supposed to provide Venezuelan planters with a supply of African slaves adequate to meet the needs of expanding cacao cultivation. Venezuelan planters could only legally sell their cacao to the company, which generally paid at a price lower than the market rate paid in Veracruz, Venezuela's most important trading partner in cacao. In return for the perks and profit implied in the monopoly, the crown expected the company to pro-

Cocoa beans in Chuao, Venezuela. (iStockPhoto)

vide additional military protection to the northern South American coast, centered on Caracas, and to invest in administrative infrastructure that would serve to unify the divided Venezuelan provinces. In Caracas and in Venezuelan port cities, Basque company officials frequently acted with extralegal authority in noncompany affairs. Until the Juan Francisco de León Revolt, a Venezuelan revolt against multiple company practices, the crown favored appointment of Basques to provincial governor posts throughout Venezuela. Both policies made sense to the company and the crown, interested in administrative cohesion and profit, but alienated Venezuelans.

Despite the legitimate complaints Venezuelans levied at the company, they had to admit that because of the company, Venezuela in the 1760s was much more territorially and administratively cohesive than it had been before the company (Lombardi 1982), Robert Ferry argues that the all-important Bourbon Reforms actually began in the 1750s after the León Revolt in 1749 and not, as commonly thought, after the English occupation of Havana in 1762 (Ferry 1989). Royal Governor Felipe Ricardos implemented reforms intended to punish Caracas and its *caraqueño* elite for any real or imagined role in the León Revolt, a rebellion that, at its height, involved an occupation of 5,000 small cacao planters and their supporters in Caracas, then a city of only 18,000 (Ferry 1989). Governor Ricardos also wanted to create not just a modern colony but, more importantly, a loyal colony, subverting Venezuelan or company interests to those of the crown. He increased the number of royal troops stationed in Caracas from 1,200 to 1,800 and raised taxes to support them. He replaced all Venezuelans and Basques in administrative posts with non-Basque Spaniards. He enacted strict work rules to force men between the ages of 12 and 60 to work, sent poor women who did not work to "virtuous houses" where they could learn "good customs," and he assigned orphans to masters to learn trades. He hired a public defender to "serve the incarcerated poor, a director of public works, and inspector of city streets, and assessor of real property, an auditor of estates of the deceased, a recorder of mortgages, an officer who evaluated the worth of slaves, and a supervisor of food stores" (Ferry 1989: 244–246). Most important, he forced the Caracas *cabildo* to pay for a new public market emporium, which forced the heretofore independent *cabildo* into debt to the crown, therefore rendering the council dependent (Ferry 1989).

Added to these economic and moral reforms (later implemented throughout the colonies) was a significant administrative and military reorganization. In 1734, the crown created the Viceroyalty of New Granada, which included what is now Venezuela, Colombia, and Ecuador with its capital in Santa Fé de Bogotá. The crown finally placed an *audiencia*, or royal office, in Caracas in 1776 and placed all Venezuelan provinces under that *audiencia*'s jurisdiction. Also in 1776, the crown placed the provinces under the fiscal administration of an intendant, also stationed in Caracas. In 1777 the crown empowered a captain general with the military defense of all Venezuelan provinces, again from Caracas (Lombardi 1982). Venezuela finally became one colony firmly integrated into the Spanish colonial system, though not without costs or consequences. Elites in the regions, east, south, or west, paid lip service to Caracas's primacy but still favored regional identity and economic ties (*orientales*, *andinos*, etc.) over colonial Venezuelan identity and economic unity. The Caracas elite weathered fairly well Ricardos's reforms, but life for the middling and lower classes became more complicated. Increasing slave populations after 1759 led to slave revolts (Coro in 1795) that had their own ramifications. Just when the crown finally thought it knew what it wanted from Venezuela and knew how to get it, Venezuelans of all sorts began to think about rewriting the terms of the relationship.

INDEPENDENCE

Independence for any nation is not an easy process. Independence implies that a core group of people has to come up with a cohesive ideology, reasons to justify independence to those who may not quite be so enthusiastic about the idea. Independence leaders use that ideology, or at least they hope to, to create unity among populations divided regionally, economically, ethnically, and along class lines. The core group eventually may convince enough people to start the independence process, but even so, those who join may do so with a mentality of self-interest. And as independence almost always means war, a few of those independence leaders need to have the military skills necessary to lead troops into battle and the diplomatic skills necessary to convince other nations to financially and materially support the independence efforts. No guns, no independence.

So it was in Venezuela in the late decades of the 1700s. Venezuelan elite certainly resented the heavy-handed economic control exercised by the company, though the super elite had their own ships and could ship their own cacao to Veracruz without dealing with the company. It was the smaller farmers, many of them relatively recent immigrants from the Canary Islands, who fell victim to the company's exploitative pricing practices and market control. The Caracas *cabildo* lamented the loss of its independence, but the elite did not have to worry about getting shipped off to Spain to serve on some public works project because royal officials made an accusation of vagabondage. The middling and poorer classes suffered just such a threat. Yes, some of the elite, Simón Bolívar and Francisco de Miranda in particular, were highly educated and did become partisans of Enlightenment ideas that included liberty, equality, and fraternity. Bolívar, with his tutor, Simón Rodriguez, and Francisco de Miranda even embarked on European grand tours in which they soaked in those ideas firsthand. Miranda even went on a grand tour of the United States and met George Washington (Racine 2003). So while some elite may have seen the need to reform the relationship between the crown and Venezuela, and few talked idealistically about independence, most elite hesitated.

Indeed, Humboldt noted that most Venezuelan elite wanted absolutely nothing to do with independence and certainly nothing to do with any of those radical governing systems, republics or democracies, that demanded power sharing. As he said:

> They [the elite] would prefer to be deprived of certain rights than share those rights with others; they would even prefer foreign dominance to the rule of Americans of inferior castes. They abhor any constitution based on the equality of rights. (Humboldt 1941: 308)

There are two points to keep in mind. The elite all over Latin America considered themselves to be Spaniards and Americans simultaneously. Bolívar traced his lineage in Venezuela back six generations, a common situation among Venezuelan elite, but he still took a great deal of pride in his Spanish blood. For most of the elite, no matter the complaints they had with the crown, independence meant turning their backs on Spanish blood and identity, something they were not willing to do. The bigger problem, however, was racial. There were 87,000 slaves in Venezuela in 1800, many first-generation slaves, most concentrated on cacao plantations in the coastal areas. There were several thousand more runaways in the colony, plus an even larger population of *pardos*, mixed-race Africans, most free. When you add the indigenous population to that mix, the population of those of color outnumbered the white population by at least 2–1, substantially more in some places (Graham 1994). As much as the Venezuelan elite resented the Spanish military presence after 1749 and hated paying higher taxes to support it, they also depended on the Spanish military to defend them against slave revolts. The fear was well placed. In May 1795 in Coro, a well-organized force of 200 slaves, ex-slaves, Indians, and peons from 12 haciendas and one *cumbe* (community of ex-slaves and runaways) attacked and occupied four haciendas and killed an unknown number of white creoles before the creoles regained control of the region. Elites at the time feared Enlightenment ideas about liberty and the Haitian slave revolt in 1791 that eventually led to Haitian independence had sparked the Coro revolt. More recent studies argue that the revolt was not about Haiti or Enlightenment ideas but instead about land disputes between the large slave, ex-slave, Indian, and mixed-race populations who produced foodstuffs for Coro on crown-granted land and the creole elite who wanted the land for other purposes (Gil Rivas, Dovale

Simón Bolívar. (Library of Congress)

Prado, and Lismila Bello 1996). No matter the cause, the fact that the revolt happened was enough for most elites to resist any ideas about independence.

So it was that Napoleon Bonaparte's invasion of Spain in 1808 did more to provoke independence movements in the Spanish Americas than any other internal circumstance. The Caracas *cabildo* moved to simultaneously regain its independent status while proclaiming that it legitimately represented the interests of the Spanish King Ferdinand VII (deposed by Napoleon and replaced by Napoleon's brother, Joseph) in the colony. When the last captain general of Venezuela, Vicente Emparan, resigned at the *cabildo* meeting on April 19, 1810, he, in effect, granted the *cabildo*'s wish. Now a junta, the *caraqueños* acted as if they represented the interests of all Venezuelans (as usual), when in reality the provinces of Guayana, Maracaibo, and Coro openly rejected Caracas's primacy and instead declared varying degrees of loyalty to Spain. Nevertheless, the Caracas junta called a congress during the summer of 1811 and on July 5, 1811 declared Venezuelan independence with all of the eloquent language of republicanism and liberty that one could imagine.

And truly enough there were in Caracas a few elites and university students who appeared drunk on the ideologies. An Englishman, Major George Flinter, who was in Caracas at the time, noted that free people of color thought the declaration of independence meant racial equality, even though the new Venezuelan constitution clearly limited voting rights to those who owned substantial property, disenfranchising most Venezuelans of all colors (Lynch 2006). Slaves thought emancipation was around the corner (Flinter 2000). Those men who made independence happen, Francisco de Miranda (not so successfully) and Simón Bolívar, believed in the republican ideas, but these men were much more practical about implementing such ideas in Venezuela over the long course of independence. The Venezuelan First Republic, called La Patria Boba (The Foolish Republic), lasted just barely a year before Spanish forces retook Caracas and punished without mercy Venezuelan patriots. During La Patria Boba, the Venezuelan Congress gave Miranda the powers of a dictator after a massive earthquake destroyed Caracas on March 26, 1812. Once Caracas returned to royalist control in August, 1812, Spaniards shipped Miranda to exile in northern Africa in chains (Racine 2003). They granted Bolívar a passport that he used extensively in the next four years to garner the international support necessary to make Venezuela independent, while the violent excesses of Spanish forces and Venezuelan loyalists (like the *llanero* José Tomás Boves) slowly convinced more Venezuelans that independence was necessary.

The war that eventually resulted in independence was long, bloody, and often more like a civil war than an independence war. Caudillos (strongmen) in the provinces used the situation to advocate for their own interests. They developed and led armies of their own peons, who caudillos used to support the Spaniards or Venezuelan patriots, depending on who offered the best deal. Both Spaniards and Bolívar advocated using slaves and free people of color more effectively in their armies. Slaves and free people of color fought for both sides, always with the implied promise of freedom and equality in exchange for service. The limits that the elite placed on the franchise in the first Venezuelan constitution indicates clearly that they thought that whatever the Venezuelan republic was going to be, it was going to serve elite interests, despite any language about equality. The social rule breaking that George Flinter observed during the Patria Boba period—free people of color publicly engaging in discussions about equality or massive rebellions of slaves and free people of color in the Tuy valley—indicated that people of color demanded more of an independent Venezuela than white elite were willing to give (Flinter 2000; Lynch 2006). To a certain degree, the Venezuelan war for independence was also race war.

NEGRO PRIMERO OR MANUEL PIAR?

Negro Primero (Pedro Camejo) and Manuel Piar were people of color who fought for Venezuelan independence and were recognized for their bravery and military skill. Camejo entered into service during the wars as a slave but soon received attention from José Antonio Paéz and Bolívar because of his loyalty, skill, and patriotism. Mortally wounded in the decisive Battle of Carabobo, before he died he found Paéz to report, "My general, I have come to say goodbye because I am dead." Piar's fame in Venezuela is more ambiguous. A *pardo* from Curaçao whose forces were also primarily people of color, Piar was crucial in Bolívar's efforts to control the east and then the Orinoco and Angostura in 1817. He did not easily submit, however, to Bolívar's authority. Bolívar accused Piar of inciting a race war and had him executed on October 16, 1817. The legacies of both men raise troubling questions about the meaning of race and the "appropriate" role of people of color in society (Lynch 2006).

So given such complicated obstacles, how was Bolívar able to succeed? After another failed republic attempt in 1813–1814, Bolívar learned that he had to subjugate all potential patriots (those *caudillos*) before he could tackle the Spanish. Using powers of personal persuasion backed by violence, beginning in 1815 with letters and continuing with his invasion through Barcelona in 1816, Bolívar began a campaign to persuade the eastern and southern caudillos (José Antonio Paéz, most importantly) to accept his command. Finally in 1819, Bolívar had a true army, supplemented with British forces, stationed in Angostura on the Orinoco. He did something truly audacious at that point. With Spaniards still firmly in control of most of the colony, including Caracas, he called a congress in Angostura to write another constitution. He needed an ideological tool that struck the appropriate balance between idealism and pragmatism while acknowledging issues of race and class that allowed Venezuelans to support independence, which he hoped to accomplish with the his army. In his address to the congress (as important in many ways as the constitution itself), Bolívar argued that while the Spaniards' actions demanded Latin American independence, independence did not mean United States–styled republicanism or federalism. Bolívar argued that Latin Americans had a unique identity, combining, European, indigenous, and African heritage (Bolívar 1951: 176). All groups, he argued, should enjoy political sovereignty and liberty. But because Spaniards subjected Latin America to "the threefold yoke of ignorance, tyranny, and vice," Latin Americans could not "acquire knowledge, power, or [civic] virtue," which meant that they were not prepared for self-governance. Thus Bolívar argued that Venezuela could best be governed by a

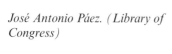

José Antonio Páez. (Library of Congress)

strong executive authority supported by a hereditary senate until that time in which the population was more capable of participating in governance. All would be equal, eventually. The Angostura Congress rejected the idea of the hereditary senate but otherwise adopted Bolívar's pragmatism laced with idealism.

In 1819, however, the constitution was a constitution without a country. Between 1819 and 1821, Bolívar and his troops (Venezuelans and British) crossed the llanos and Andes to liberate Bogotá and establish an independent New Grenada, then crossed back to liberate Venezuela as part of New Grenada. Caracas opened its doors to a victorious Bolívar on June 29, 1821 (Lynch 2006). Bolívar then turned his attention south to further consolidate control of New Grenada, then conquer Ecuador, Bolivia, and Peru. Some of his Venezuelan generals went with him. José Antonio de Sucre eventually became the first president of an independent Bolivia. José Antonio Paéz, the *llanero* caudillo, remained in Venezuela and became as adept at manipulating *caraqueño* politicians as he was at mastering guerrilla strategies. But as Venezuelans got about the business of creating a nation in the 1820s, they discovered that as horrible as the independence process had been, actually being independent was much more complicated than they had imagined.

THE LONG 19TH CENTURY

One of the issues that permeates all Venezuelan history is the struggle for modernity tied to economic prosperity. The shift from wheat to cacao in the colonial era marked one way the elite thought they could achieve economic modernity by competing more successfully in the international marketplace while not forsaking active trade in domestic foodstuffs and other goods. So for the colonial elite, modernity meant balance between international interests and domestic ones. The story of the 19th century is not any different. Venezuelan elite from day one struggled to create a functional modern nation in an era in which figuring out what modern was, and what functional was, were complicated endeavors.

Bolívar knew all too well before the war for independence ended that the country needed international investment in order to survive. The war destroyed nearly all of the cacao-producing infrastructure, trees and all. Cattle losses numbered in the millions of head. How *hacendado*s were going to obtain labor, slave or free, to work any crop after the war was an open question. In 1810, the Venezuelan population was 935,000, but it was only 600,000 in 1821. All classes and racial groups suffered (Cunill Grau 1987). Money could not help demographic recovery, but it was essential for economic recovery. Through negotiations begun by Bolívar, the British sent the Venezuelans a 2-million-pound loan in 1822 (Graham 1968). Fairly quickly, *hacendados* switched from cacao to coffee. Coffee bushes cost less than cacao trees. Coffee bushes produced a marketable harvest in three years; it took six years for a cacao tree to yield marketable beans. Increased coffee consumption in Europe and the United States meant a steady international demand, and the new Venezuelan government allowed creditors to accept repayment for loans in coffee instead of cash (Yarrington 1997).

Man harvesting coffee at El Carmen,
Venezuela. (Bildagentur/StockPhotoPro)

And so it was that independent Venezuela carried on economic practices encouraged by the Guipuzcoana Company, which meant national economic dependence on one export crop, with limited regional variety. The east and the south continued trade in cattle and hides; they also produced foodstuffs for the domestic market. Most national political and economic decisions for the next several decades were all related to furthering the coffee trade, but with an eye on an ever-increasing national debt. No matter how much coffee Venezuelans produced, it could not pay loans associated with international (primarily British) investment in infrastructure or the trade imbalance associated with importation of cheap manufactured goods. Sir Robert Kerr Porter, British Consul to Venezuela, reported that as early as 1826

> The poverty of the [Venezuelan] State is extreme, and the monthly expenses exceed the receipts of the revenue by many thousand dollars, the deficit for last year was $9,000,000. In fact, the government have been expending the British loan, and when that is all exhausted—then is to be seen the effects of an empty treasury. (Porter 1966: 69)

By 1839, the debt consumed 40 percent of public expenditures (Hellinger 1991). Given those economic and social situations, establishing a stable government would be difficult at best.

Remember that in 1821 (or 1823 when royalists finally surrendered in Puerto Cabello) Venezuela was part of a new nation called Gran Colombia, what used to be the Viceroyalty of Nueva Grenada that included Venezuela, Colombia, and Ecuador, the cornerstone of what Bolívar hoped would be a united American nation. The three regions were supposed to remain autonomous, only coming together for major congresses, but from the beginning, the Venezuelans, Paéz with his presidential aspirations in particular, resented what they saw as Colombian meddling. They certainly resisted paying taxes to the national government in Bogotá. So most were not surprised when Paéz led Venezuela out of Gran Colombia and to complete independence in 1830, though Bolívar felt betrayed. He said "The tyrants of my country have taken it from me and I am banished; now I have no homeland for which to sacrifice myself" (Lynch 2006: 269). Bolívar died in Santa Marta, Colombia on December 17, 1830 on his way to exile, not wanted in his home country or in Colombia. His remains were reburied in the cathedral in Caracas in 1842 and again in the National Pantheon in 1876 (Lynch 2006).

But the real problem was establishing a national government given the economic necessities and social complexities, not to mention regional divisions. Regional caudillos with their own mounted forces, José Tadeo Monagas among them, resisted curbing their local or regional control in favor of strong, national, central authority, to Paéz. A constitutional congress wrote a new constitution after the dissolution of Gran Colombia, and those who met the land ownership requirements elected Paéz president. Despite Congress's efforts to impose a coherent legal code throughout the country, local authorities enforced those laws local elites liked—for example, laws that declared individuals to be vagabonds in order to force their labor—but used extralegal traditions in other circumstances. Regional elites certainly resented Caracas bureaucrats who presumed to act on behalf of the nation even when those in the nation really were not sure what that nation was. Those Caracas bureaucrats became increasingly important as they were the ones who managed Venezuela's economic relationships with the North Atlantic. Despite this, Paéz, though not well educated, proved an able diplomat as he established authority within the Caracas elite and as

VICENTA OCHOA, DEAD MANY TIMES

In 1834, Vicenta Ochoa rather brutally killed María de la Cruz, a *samba* (mixed indigenous and African) slave in Caracas. Ochoa apparently owed de la Cruz, a peddler, money. De la Cruz went to Ochoa's home to collect the debt. Ochoa called de la Cruz an insolent slave and beat her to death. With the help of a corporal, Ochoa bound up the body and threw it into the sewer. She paid the soldier with earrings she took from de la Cruz's wares. The penalty at that time for murder was capital punishment. Ochoa was also a wife and a mother. While no one disputed her guilt, the death sentence provoked outrage and gendered responses. Women couched their arguments in defense of maternity. Men's arguments varied from defense of private property (de la Cruz had invaded Ochoa's home) to assertions about the role of civilized, paternal nations (they do not kill women). Courts eventually commuted Ochoa's sentence to exile. The debate continued about the death penalty, finally abolished in 1849 (Diaz 2007).

head of state in trade relations with North Atlantic nations. His military experience as a caudillo came in handy when he had to put down a rebellion led by caudillos from the east, Santiago Mariño (also an independence war leader) and Monagas. Even though the mushrooming national debt was like a ticking time bomb, high coffee prices, good harvests, and easy credit meant stable years for elites in most of the country through the 1830s.

But when coffee prices began to fall in the late 1830s and through the 1840s, the house of cards began to fall apart. One of the principle problems was the Ley del 10 de Abril de 1834. The law removed all protections debtors had against usury. According to this law, a creditor could write a contract that enforced any interest rate under any conditions, and the courts had to uphold the contract. The loan grantor could force the auction of the debtor's property and repossess that property at bargain rates (Lombardi 1971; Pino Iturrieta 1993). That created a political problem once prices fell and courts supported creditors' rights according to the law. Monthly interest rates on many debts rose to 15 percent (Hellinger 1991). Labor was the second problem. The conversion of old cacao lands into coffee plantations and expansion of coffee cultivation required a great deal of labor. Slavery as an institution designed to provide labor, though moribund after independence, existed, but because no new slaves entered the country, slavery could not supply labor needs. Falling coffee prices also meant falling free-labor wages, so peasants began to rely less on coffee plantations for economic survival and began to rely more on their own subsistence crops grown on small *conucos*, or backyard plots.

Hacienda del Carmen Coffee beans drying in the sun. (Travel Ink/StockPhotoPro)

The elite began to divide into two political groups, Conservatives and Liberals. Conservative and Liberal parties were common in Latin American in the 19th century, but the Venezuelan versions did not have much in common with their other Latin American counterparts. Venezuelan Conservatives, led by Paéz, shared with other Latin American Liberals the desire to promote foreign commerce. Venezuelan Conservatives favored creditors and counted numerous merchants in their numbers. Venezuelan Liberals, led by Antonio Leocadio Guzmán (and kin by marriage to Bolívar's family), claimed to represent agricultural interests, or indebted planters. Eventually the Liberal Party gained support among the poor and people of color, but when it began it did not pretend to be anything other than the party of the planter elite (Pino Iturrieta 1993). To make things even murkier, both parties included individuals who seemed to cross party lines—merchants who were also planters. More important in both parties were family and regional caudillo ties (Lombardi 1982). Liberals failed in rebellion attempts in 1842 and 1846, though the 1846 rebellion could have easily become more a social uprising with racial overtones than a mere political rebellion. After the 1846 rebellion, President Carlos Soublette ordered the arrest of Guzmán, and the courts sentenced him to death on the eve of the 1847 election.

Paéz raised eyebrows when he tapped José Tadeo Monagas, the eastern caudillo with some Liberal sympathies, as Soublette's successor. Monagas's electoral victory was not a surprise, but his political independence was. He commuted Guzmán's sentence to exile, filled ministry positions with Liberals, and appointed more Liberals to bureaucratic posts. Over time, he replaced many of those individuals with those who were loyal to him personally, including his kin and fellow *orientales* (easterners) from the Province of Barcelona. Concerned that Monagas pretended to undo all the Conservative Paéz had accomplished, the old caudillo led a furtive rebellion against the man he thought would be another protégé. Both because Monagas was no slouch in the caudillo category and because the elite did not see the reason to support the rebellion, Paéz found himself quickly exiled to the United States. Monagas pushed his reforms further. He abolished the Ley del 10 de Abril, fixed interest rates at no more than 9 percent per year and placed strict conditions on when creditors could begin foreclosure procedures against debtors. He enacted laws that protected debtor rights. He abolished the death penalty (Moreno Molina 2004). He promoted land reform, though his family, friends, and the elite benefited much more than did the masses (Mathews 1970).

In 1851 José Tadeo passed along the presidency to his brother, José Gregorio Monagas, and also passed along a tremendous national debt, which low coffee prices did not do much to help pay off. Worse, throughout the 1840s it had become apparent that it was time to abolish the institution of slavery completely. Some Liberals were truly committed to abolition as a moral cause. Elite slave owners would not allow that to happen without recompense for the value of the slaves they still held. Many slave owners had mortgaged their slaves as property in order to cover other debts. Compensating owners cost the Venezuelan state millions that it did not have in the 1840s or in 1854, when José Gregorio made another attempt to abolish slavery, even though 15,000 individuals remained slaves on the eve of emancipation

(Lombardi 1971). José Gregorio Monagas's state appeared magnanimous and morally upright when it abolished slavery, but in so doing the state sowed the seeds for further discontent among the elite. And no Venezuelan president had ever seriously addressed the poverty in which most Venezuelans lived, regardless of race. The Monagas brothers, as all Venezuelan presidents thus far, allowed local and regional elites to manage their relationships with the laboring classes as those elites saw fit. Practices such as debt peonage became common (Morse 2000). Debt peonage was a practice in which *hacendados*, or *amos*, used small amounts of debt owed by peons to *amos* to secure cheap labor. Debt peonage relationships often lasted generations. In some parts of the country, elites continued to find creative ways to use indigenous Venezuelans as slaves (Armellada 1954). Though the state professed to be modern and devoted to the law, exploitative local traditions often held more sway in local issues than any nationally promulgated legal code. Such social and economic issues plagued the second presidency of José Tadeo, though he seemed more interested in building his family's fortunes than avoiding the massive civil war that was on the Venezuelan horizon.

The Federal War (1858–1863) is perhaps the most important and least understood war in Venezuelan history. While elites used the war to sort out which of them would control the nation, all other Venezuelans may well have fought for more fundamental issues. Ezequiel Zamora was a true ideological Liberal who believed in land reform for the benefit of the masses and protection for the laboring classes. He was also a military man who had participated in the Liberal rebellion of 1846 and had also been condemned to death by President Soublette; José Tadeo Monagas also commuted his sentence. When Zamora again led Venezuelans into battle in 1859, he fought for "a true revolution, with the elimination of large land holdings and all forms of social and economic oppression. The fight was not only for equality, but the liquidation of all social classes" (Frankel 1976: 151). Under his leadership, empowered masses fought for a distinct Venezuelan future, one defined more by the interests of common Venezuelans than by elite priorities. Their battle cry spoke volumes: "*¡Vamos a Caracas a matar a todos los blancos, a todos los ricos y a todos que sepan escribir!*" ("Let's go to Caracas to kill all of the whites, all of the rich, and all who are literate!") (Frankel 1976: 152). This fighting force understood that the elite manipulated race, wealth, and knowledge to keep common Venezuelans oppressed. Zamora capably channeled that hatred into an effective fighting force until he died in battle on January 10, 1860.

Benjamin Frankel suggests that after Zamora's death, no leader of any faction appeared to fill the void, though after 1860 race did not drive the war. The conflict descended into a free-for-all in which local caudillos took vengeance on enemies without restraint. This war was not characterized by large opposing forces driven by common causes and common dedication to some form of ideology. The war became hundreds of smaller, bloodier, uglier, and more personal conflicts between local forces (Morse 2000). Frankel equally condemns the national leaders as "usurpers of political power and wealth, that played with the emotions of the masses, pushing their vulnerable points in order to achieve violent and destructive reflex reactions" (Frankel 1976: 146–147). Juan Falcón, who eventually became president, did not win

*Antonio Guzmán Blanco, president
of Venezuela during three separate
terms between 1870 and 1887.
(Library of Congress)*

the war to build a political vision but to enjoy the fruits of victory—to the victor go the spoils. Zamora wanted a social, political, and economic revolution (Morse 2000). That did not happen. Instead 60,000 to 100,000 Venezuelans died (Hellinger 1991).

Violence simmered throughout the 1860s, even after Juan Falcón assumed the presidency in 1863. The Monagas family led another failed revolt against the state that lasted from 1868 to 1870. By far the most important figure to emerge from the mess was Antonio Guzmán Blanco, son of the Liberal Leocadio Guzmán. He called himself the "Illustrious American," which tells us something about both his ego and his ambition. Guzmán Blanco was a Liberal Order and Progress president, bent on creating a modern nation, like many of his contemporaries in other Latin American nations in the later third of the 19th century. Their definition of Liberal was a bit different from the versions to which their Liberal predecessors adhered. They all believed in reorganizing social, political, and economic structures to encourage as much foreign investment as possible (incurring mountains of debt). Guzmán Blanco, unlike Liberal contemporaries in Mexico and Brazil, did not believe industrialization marked Venezuela's future. He continued to put all of the nation's economic eggs in the agricultural basket. None of the Liberal presidents believed in representative forms of government, as they believed masses were not capable of acting in ways civilized enough to curry North American or European favors. Indeed, the Liberal Order and Progress decades ramped up modern civilization-versus-barbarism hyperbole to a degree remarkable even in Latin American history.

Though Venezuelan historians continue to dispute the degree to which Guzmán Blanco's host of modernizing and centralizing reforms succeeded, they do not doubt that Venezuela was more modern, its government stronger and more centralized in 1888, when Guzmán Blanco left for self-imposed exile in France, than it was in 1870 when he assumed the presidency. He fostered foreign investment in railroads, roads, and telegraph systems designed to strengthen the national state and further economic integration domestically and internationally. He expanded and modernized the public administration system without significantly increasing expenditures (Ewell 1984). He modernized the national army through purchase of modern weapons. He subordinated regional elites by allowing them some autonomy but also providing benefits to them through the modernized administrative and public works infrastructure (Lombardi 1971). And even if they wanted to send caudillo armies to challenge Guzmán Blanco, how could men with old rifles and machetes defeat a modern army with modern arms?

Guzmán Blanco's legal reforms were perhaps even more important. He issued new penal and civil codes in 1873, and a new constitution in 1881. Public behavior, morality, and work habits were crucial if the world were to perceive Venezuela as a modern nation. The penal code outlawed gambling and ordered strict fines for those who owned or managed establishments where gambling occurred; it further ordered that those who won through fraudulent means would be considered thieves in the eyes of the law and prosecuted as such (*Código* 1973). The 1873 penal code also prohibited any abuses of freedom of religion, imposed penalties for grave robbing, included a section dedicated to crimes against public health, one prohibiting the sale of poor-quality food, and also included a section regulating the quality of water for public consumption (*Código* 1973). The role of the law, then, was to foster the creation of a modern state through the regulation of issues related to the public good as well as regulation of private behavior. No detail fell outside the purview of the law in the modern state, at least on paper, from the sale of a rotten *guayaba* at a public market to cheating at a game of cards in a bar. It appears that local authorities throughout the country began to adopt Guzmán Blanco's attention to modern legal

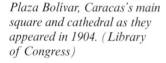

Plaza Bolívar, Caracas's main square and cathedral as they appeared in 1904. (Library of Congress)

details. Authorities began to pay more attention to witness testimony, forensics, and procedural issues at local and district court levels. Authorities argued in court that the law's obligation in a modern state was to protect the weak, not persecute them. The personal judgments of the local justice of the peace meant less (RPB 1873). When local authorities began to supplant their legal authority with the authority of the Venezuelan state, the state became stronger despite the regional autonomy Guzmán Blanco allowed local caudillos.

Guzmán Blanco understood that his ability to rule depended on his ability to balance Venezuelan and international demands simultaneously in order to create the modern, orderly, and progressive state. One way to understand that challenge is to look at how he used construction and public space. In order to attract North Atlantic money, to make the foreign investors want to invest in Venezuela, Caracas had to look good. Already a Francophile, Guzmán Blanco gave Caracas a facelift using Parisian architectural styles. He ordered the construction of wide boulevards, grand archways, plazas, and great buildings, often dedicated to his own glory but certainly good for the modern, progressive, civilized cause. Better yet, he began the construction of public water systems, sewer lines, and electrical services (Lombardi 1971). Regional elites certainly appreciated the power implied in the new buildings when they visited Caracas, but they valued other construction projects more. Guzmán Blanco was the first Venezuelan president to use Bolívar's image to cultivate Venezuelan national identity. The most important plaza built in Caracas during the Guzmán Blanco era was the Plaza Bolívar, with its grand sculpture of the Liberator riding a rearing horse. Soon a sculpture in honor of Bolívar became a prerequisite feature in all Venezuelan central plazas—some of these sculptures were good, and some were not so good. The point, however, was that although Guzmán Blanco used his European tastes to remake Caracas into a European-style city, he also used public space to reinforce his commitment to Venezuela. Nevertheless, he did not allow Venezuelans to use public spaces in Caracas in ways that Venezuelans always had. He outlawed raucous Carnival celebrations in the days before Lent that involved hurling water, eggs, and other substances and instead favored more stately costume parades (Díaz 2004). Elites in the west in Maracaibo enacted similar prohibitions in an effort to control behavior of lower classes perceived as barbarous (Linder 2006). In so doing, regional elites adopted the modern, orderly, and progressive sensibilities favored by the state.

Guzmán Blanco accomplished two things before leaving in 1888. He skimmed off enough cash through commissions on all of the international loan money coming into the country to live happily ever after at least three times over. He had also created a state strong enough to survive even more serious economic mismanagement in the decade that followed. But he had not created a state strong enough to survive falling international coffee prices or major boundary disputes with European nations. In the 1890s, the Venezuelan economy was tied to the export of three major goods: coffee, cattle, and sugar (particularly in the west). And though coffee grown on smaller farms less dependent on nonfamily labor had become more important in the decades after the Federal War, international prices still had the ability to shatter the economy (Yarrington 1997). In 1899, coffee prices plummeted,

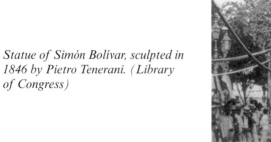

Statue of Simón Bolívar, sculpted in 1846 by Pietro Tenerani. (Library of Congress)

and Venezuela lost 90 percent of land claimed in a border dispute in the far east to the British (British Guayana). Cipriano Castro had national ambitions before the dual crises hit. He used the unrest that the coffee collapse caused in his home state of Tachira in the far west to initiate his fight for Caracas. President Ignacio Andrade left on October 19, 1899. The era of the western *tachirense* presidents began. It lasted until 1935.

International problems defined most of the decade Castro governed in Caracas. Venezuela lost the land dispute to the British three weeks before Andrade left. By 1902, the British, Germans, and the Italians began to press for repayment of loans, impossible given low coffee prices. They blockaded Venezuelan ports even after Castro agreed to settle the claims. That brought in the United States, as the direct military interference of European governments in the affairs of an American nation violated the Monroe Doctrine. The United States then brokered Venezuelan payments of European claims and negotiated the departure of the European navies. The Roosevelt Corollary to the Monroe Doctrine was born. If American nations engaged in "chronic wrongdoing," the United States reserved the right to intervene to prevent European intervention (Ewell 1984: 40) The United States used the Roosevelt Corollary to intervene in Caribbean and Caribbean basin nations numerous times before the Great Depression forced a change in U.S. foreign policy.

Consistently low coffee prices hampered Castro's ability to accomplish much domestically or economically, if he really tried to accomplish anything. Uprisings against him cost 12,000 lives between 1901 and 1903. He placated his friends by granting them monopolies on goods such as firearms and dynamite, sugar, textiles, flour, guano, tobacco, liquor, matches, and meat, all to the detriment of local pro-

CIPRIANO CASTRO: GONE, BUT HE DID NOT FORGET

Cipriano Castro went into exile in 1908, but until the day he died in 1924 he traveled Europe and the United States attempting to raise money and manpower to retake the country by force. His argument was that Gómez was turning Venezuela into a semiprotectorate of the United States. He accused the United States of pursuing "insatiable" interests in Venezuela. Worse were conditions in Venezuela. Writing from Spain in 1910 Castro said that the political situation was so bad that "gangrene has already invaded all the social body! It would not be an exaggeration to say that Venezuela is a penitentiary let loose in a lunatic asylum" (McBeth 2008: 55).

Cipriano Castro, on New York City street. (Library of Congress)

ducers and their laborers. He slowly loaded the bureaucracy and army with fellow *tachirenses*. Privately he drank and debauched so much that by 1906 he suffered from multiple serious ailments. Then he made a singularly bad decision. He appointed his chief rival, Juan Vicente Gómez as acting president while Castro attempted to recover from his ailments. Though the Castro regime did not officially end until he left the country in 1908, Gómez ruled (Ewell 1984).

Juan Vincente Gómez. (Library of Congress)

MI BENEMÉRITO JUAN VICENTE GÓMEZ

Chilean born and Venezuelan reared novelist Isabel Allende told the story of events immediately after Gómez's death this way.

> the Ministers of State, terrified at the possibility of a popular uprising, held a hasty meeting in which someone proposed they call for the Professor [the embalmer], thinking that if the cadaver of El Cid lashed to his steed could lead the charge against the Moors, there was no reason why the embalmed President for Life could not continue to govern from his tyrant's seat. (Allende 1988: 14)

Even when the state decided to acknowledge El Benefactor was dead

> The people refused to believe that the President for Life was actually dead; they thought that the old man displayed on the bier fit for a pharaoh was a hoax, another of that sorcerer's tricks to trap his critics. People locked themselves in their houses, afraid to stick a foot out the door, until the *guardia* broke down the doors, turned out the occupants by brute force, and lined them up to pay their last respects to the Supreme Leader, who was already beginning to stink. (Allende 1988: 15)

Though Allende embellished the story a bit as is a novelist's privilege, there are kernels of truth in the telling. Gómez did govern with an iron fist; he used violence and the cultivation of a personal myth (that involved witchcraft) to perpetuate his power and diminish the authority of any of his ministers and without any concessions to regional caudillos. Gómez wanted to rule Venezuela as if it was his own personal cattle ranch. From his hacienda in Maracay, Gómez micromanaged Venezuela using the telegraph and a modern military during a crucial era in the nation's history. It was during Gómez's regime that oil began to flow like black gold from Venezuelan oil fields.

Though both Castro and Gómez were *andinos* from Táchira, historians note that in many ways they were complete opposites. Castro was a libertine in private who loved to tweak foreign powers in public. Gómez fostered better foreign relations and was a taciturn teetotaler who never married, though he fathered dozens and dozens of illegitimate children who he placed in government positions throughout the country. Once he assumed the presidency in 1908, he immediately set about mending relationships with the United States. He initiated the visit of a special U.S. commissioner to repair that particular relationship and asked that the United States also send three battleships with marines to remain in port in La Guaira for the three-month talks. Then and after, the United States acted to protect Gómez's interests from anyone inside or outside of Venezuela interested in conspiring in favor of Castro until the old man died in 1924 (Hellinger 1991; Ewell 1984). Marines accomplished something else during their three-month stay, at least according to popular myth. When they left the battleships, they played baseball. Venezuelans have been playing the game ever since.

Gómez used the fortunate coincidence of rising coffee prices to mend fences with the domestic and international economically powerful and revised tax policies to curry their favor, though he ended the personal monopolies on consumer goods favored by Castro and thus brought a new revenue stream into the Venezuelan treasury. Gómez chose economic ministers wisely and listened to their advice. As a result, even before oil profits began to reach the treasury, the economic system functioned more rationally and efficiently than it ever had in Venezuelan history.

North Atlantic companies began to extract tar out of Venezuelan fields during the Castro era. By the 1910s, companies began to extract oil in addition to tar. Throughout the 1910s, Gómez and his economic ministers debated how to best manage the activities of the international companies and the extraction of subsoil resources. Though a few ministers argued for closer national control of subsoil resources similar to the clauses built into the 1917 Mexican constitution, with his penchant to favor international interests, Gomez allowed U.S. oil company lawyers to write most of what became the Petroleum Law of 1922. Of course the companies heralded the law as the best in the Americas, one that expected of them low taxes and royalties, no Venezuelan congressional oversight, and no restrictions on the amount of land international companies could own (Ewell 1984).

It would be easy to argue that Gómez sold out Venezuela by accepting the terms of the 1922 Petroleum Law. Not to pardon the old (dead) man, but the post–World

War I years had been complicated. Coffee prices began to fall. Twenty-two thousand Venezuelans died in the global influenza pandemic, including Gómez's favorite son, Ali. Gómez survived a military coup, but putting it down required more effort (and more brutality) than he expected (Ewell 1984). The years between 1922 and Gómez's death in 1935 marked the beginning of Venezuela's transition into the 20th century. Gómez governed more autocratically than ever, but the burgeoning oil industry also meant new discussions about labor rights and unions, students began to discuss a democratic future, and political parties, illegal though they were, began to organize for that eventual change.

It all goes back to that question of modernity. Venezuela did not have the skilled workers necessary to support the oil companies—Gulf, Shell, and Standard—so the companies brought those employees with them. Company skilled labor lived in company enclaves in North American–style houses with imported North American amenities. Their kids went to company schools and after school all went to play golf, baseball, tennis, or swim at the company country club. When they needed lawyers, they used company ones. When they needed hospitals, they went to modern company hospitals. Unskilled Venezuelan labor and growing numbers of unskilled West Indian labor working in oil fields began to develop class consciousness that Venezuelan laboring classes had not had before. In part because of the more easily available information through newspapers and radio, more Venezuelans understood the disparities that existed between the modernity that petroleum enclaves represented and the conditions in which most Venezuelans lived. Venezuelans resented just a bit the contempt with which foreigners regarded them. Venezuelan intellectuals respected Mexico's moves to control its own oil industry and to industrialize but lamented that Venezuela was not ready for such moves yet. The unrest that simmered beneath the surface in the later Gómez years came from all of those concerns (Ewell 1984; Díaz Sánchez 1981). Gómez used oil as a cash cow, but his Venezuela did not benefit nearly as much as other countries did. Yes, oil enabled Gómez to pay off the national debt in 1930. Oil earnings climbed to 676,769,078 bolivars in 1936 (coffee brought in 32 million bolivars) (Hellinger 1991). Venezuela quickly became the world's most important oil exporter and second to the United States in production. But the three companies that controlled 98 percent of all Venezuelan oil sent nearly all of the oil overseas for refining. Venezuelans consumed less than 3 percent of the oil that came from Venezuelan subsoil. Maracaibo's population mushroomed, and the process of polluting the lake with "the Devil's excrement" began in earnest (Ewell 1984: 65).

By 1928, Venezuelans began to voice concerns about all such issues, political, social, and economic. Young communists began organizing oil workers in the west, but many found themselves sent into exile where they continued their activities with other communists in Central American nations. A celebration of student week turned into a critical march. When Gómez predictably jailed the working-class protesters, demonstrations all over the country unpredictably demanded the students' release. Young officers launched a failed conspiracy shortly thereafter (Ewell 1984). Many of the participants in all movements joined the communists in exile, forming the core of what came to be known as the Generation of 1928. Chief among them was Rómulo

Betancourt, one of the most important figures in the development of Venezuelan democracy. But before any of the fervor for change could result in real action, Gómez had to die. He finally did, on December 17, 1935.

OIL

We absolutely cannot ignore the fact that oil influenced the politics and economics of the 20th century, and perhaps 21st century, more than anything else. Some parts of the story are similar to others in Venezuela's past. Venezuelans, past and present, see oil as the tool they can use to make their nation modern. So it was with cacao in the colonial period and coffee in the 19th century. As with those two products in centuries past, Venezuelans in the 20th century built the national economy almost exclusively around the international export of one product, forsaking, by and large, agricultural or industrial economic diversity and despite Venezuela's abundant natural wealth. As with cacao and coffee, national economic dependence on oil means national economic dependence on international pricing. When oil prices are high, huge sums flow into Venezuelan coffers, enabling Venezuelan presidents to invest more heavily in social spending and, in some cases, enrich themselves. There is absolutely no doubt that oil brought more money into the Venezuelan system than any previous export product ever did. Throughout most of the 20th century, the concessions, taxation, and royalty structure favored the private companies that extracted the oil, so they also profited to the tune of billions from the black gunk extracted from Venezuelan subsoil. When oil prices fell, the national economy suffered much more than the companies did. There is, however, a qualitative difference between international demand for oil and international demand for coffee or cacao. Coffee is a luxury good. Though perhaps we should consider oil a luxury, the reality is that the world is so hooked on oil for transportation, for industry, and for the composition of other consumer goods made from plastic (including plastic grocery bags) that oil has become a necessity. That basic fact gives oil-producing nations leverage in the global marketplace that they would not have otherwise.

Venezuelan intellectual Arturo Uslar Pietri stated the situation this way:

Petroleum is the fundamental and basic fact of the Venezuelan destiny. It presents to Venezuela today the most serious national problems that the nation has known in its history . . . Everything else loses significance. Whether the Republic is centralist or federalist. Whether the voters vote white [for Acción Democratica] or any other color. Whether they build aqueducts or not. Whether the University is open or closed. Whether immigrants come or don't come. Whether schools are built or not built. Whether the workers earn five bolívares or fifteen bolívares. All those issues lack meaning. Because they are all conditioned, determined, created by petroleum. They are all dependent and transitory. Dependent and transitory. Petroleum and nothing else is the theme of Venezuela's contemporary history. (Uslar Pietri 1972: 18)

We shall see to what extent Uslar Pietri's musings retain validity throughout the 20th century and into the 21st.

GÓMEZ IS DEAD: NOW WHAT?

Once the Venezuelan population realized that Gómez really was dead, a wave of violence exploded in urban areas. Violence continued against those most loyal to the dead president's system, as the new president Eleazar López Contreras realized the nation would not tolerate the continuation of the Gómez administration in any fashion. López Contreras and his successor, Isaías Medina Angarita, are most recognized for guiding the nation through a transitional period that eventually led to the first democratically elected government. Though neither man hesitated to resort to autocratic behavior when necessary (in the president's opinion), both began to use more modern techniques in governance, both in style and substance. López Contreras was the first Venezuelan president to use the radio to directly address the population in 1936. Uslar Pietri, a young intellectual in 1936, urged the president to "*sembrar el petróleo*" (sow the oil), which is exactly what López Contreras did. He pushed through a new petroleum law in 1938, bringing more income to Venezuela that he used to fund education and social welfare programs. Early in his presidency, López Contreras actually supported Venezuelan labor in disputes with the companies but clamped down hard during a 1936–1937 general strike. Finally, López Contreras actually shortened the presidential term to five years and handed over power to Medina Angarita without any conflict.

Though some of the 1928 exiles began to return to Venezuela during López Contreras's presidency, he drew the line at communists, particularly after the general strike. More than once he limited freedom of the press. Not so with Medina Angarita. With freedom of the press returned, political life flourished. He allowed communists, those belonging to the Partido Comunista Venezolana (PCV), to come back. University students regained their public political voice. The growing bureaucracy meant also a growing middle class who supported politically active professional organizations and new political parties, an early version of FEDECAMARAS (chambers of commerce) chief among the professional organizations; Acción Democrática (AD) quickly became the most important opposition party (Ewell 1984).

Betancourt began advocating for democratic change from the minute he returned to Venezuela in 1936. His approach was different from the beginning. In the years prior to his establishment of AD in 1941 with author Rómulo Gallegos, Betancourt began to build a multiclass alliance that included both real and urban grass roots leadership. He firmly believed in using oil wealth to create a stronger Venezuelan state that governed democratically over a more diverse economy and empowered populace. Betancourt pushed for agrarian reform, modern education and health care, and expanded labor rights (Hellinger 1991). It was a populist platform increasingly common throughout Latin America in the middle 20th century. What brought AD to power in 1945 was a schism between López Contreras and Medina Angarita that led to a military coup. The young conspirators arranged the first national elections in the 20th century using universal, direct suffrage. Betancourt became the first democratically elected president in Venezuela in 1945.

THE *TRIENIO* (1945–1948)

Betancourt ruled by decree until 1947 and had the opportunity to put into place some of what he had advocated in years prior. The oil ministry negotiated more favorable terms from the companies, which resulted in 50/50 profit sharing between the same three companies—Gulf, Shell, and Standard—and the Venezuelan state. The state began its own exploration efforts and began to invest in its own tanker fleet. The state forced the companies to pay for the construction of three refineries in Venezuela, enhancing Venezuela's ability to refine its own heavy crude and providing more skilled and unskilled employment to Venezuelan laborers. With the increased oil income, the state engaged in a limited land reform program, redistributing first lands that had belonged to Gómez. The state built hospitals, sewer systems, and invested in housing. Increased spending on public education meant that the number of children in primary schools increased from 131,000 to 500,000 (Hellinger 1991). The government formed the Venezuelan Investment Corporation to foment industrial development. In addition to pursing populist programs, AD (the ruling party at the time) used populist style. Betancourt used the media, especially radio, and colloquial language to make common Venezuelans feel a connection with their government that they never had before. AD's extensive organizational apparatus also gave peasants, urban barrio residents, and labor the ability to participate in civil society in new ways (Ellner 1999).

Continued political activity defined the *trienio* as much as it did the years before. Competition between parties was often fierce, but during the *trienio* none matched AD's influence. The most important of the new parties was COPEI (Independent Electoral Political Organizing Committee) led by a former *adeco*, Rafael Caldera. The communist party focused its activities on the all-important petroleum labor sector. Though Betancourt was a key figure in the Costa Rican communist party during his exile there in the Gómez years, once back in Venezuela he and AD did everything they possibly could to marginalize Venezuela's communist party, the PCV. Part of

Rómulo Betancourt. (Library of Congress)

the plan to create social peace for AD meant establishing a collective bargaining agreement with the petroleum workers' unions that pushed aside communists. Doing so strengthened the state and played favorably with the companies, who benefited from a pacified work force.

All in all, Betancourt's *adeco* government worked to modernize through the creation of social peace with oil wealth and favorable relationships with the companies. *Adeco* union activists associated with the Confederación de Trabajadores Venezolanos (CTV) became part of the *adeco* organizing machine. Peasant organizations, neighborhood associations, unions, and professional organizations all became part of the *adeco* process. Of all the other parties that emerged in the Venezuelan political spectrum, only COPEI developed an organizing structure as strong as that of AD. Eventually, the state sponsored a presidential election in 1947. Rómulo Gallegos won in a landslide. He was ousted in a coup a year later by Colonel Marcos Pérez Jiménez. Though the *trienio* was a brief period, many of the men who dominated Venezuelan politics between 1958 and 1998 began their political careers during that time. Later politicians used policies and patterns begun in those three short years.

MARCOS PÉREZ JIMÉNEZ

The opposition parties who welcomed the coup were quickly disillusioned when they realized that Carlos Delgado Chalbaud and Pérez Jiménez (the minister of defense) had no intentions of governing democratically. All of the parties, including AD and the PCV, were forced underground. Free press, cooperatives, and unions were all banned. One of AD's most important leaders was assassinated in 1952. Delgado Chalbaud was the first Venezuelan president assassinated while in office, in 1950. Pérez Jiménez controlled the country from his defense ministry post until a rigged election made him officially president in 1952. It was a brutal dictatorship. Pérez Jiménez jailed thousands as political prisoners and sent hundreds to a labor camp in Amazonia. Pérez Jiménez in addition used torture and assassination to control dissent.

Economically, Pérez Jiménez granted additional oil exploration concessions to the companies. That, plus his political of repression of political dissidents—including communists—did much to endear Pérez Jiménez to the companies and to North Atlantic governments enmeshed in the cold war. He slashed social service and labor spending and invested heavily in massive construction projects, about a third of all government expenditures. He and those close to him made fortunes off of the subcontracting process for the roads, bridges, hotels, refineries, and port improvement projects (Ewell 1984). The system of tunnels and bridges that connect La Guaira to Caracas was first completed during the Pérez Jiménez regime. To this day, Venezuelans appreciate the efficiency associated with the system but openly wonder how many people died in order to build it. The population of cities boomed because most public construction projects (and employment) were urban, not rural. European immigrants finally moved to Venezuela in significant numbers, particularly Spaniards, Italians, and Portuguese. Life expectancy rose and mortality rates fell in the population in general, all contributing to urban population growth and exacerbating a hous-

Marcos Pérez Jiménez. (Library of Congress)

ing crisis. The urban middle class bought radios and went to movies as they never had before. The Sabana Grande district in Caracas offered bars, nightclubs, restaurants, and fine shopping for anyone with disposable income, Venezuelan or tourist. But the gap that divided the rich and the poor grew during Pérez Jiménez's dictatorship. The poor began to build *ranchitos* on the Caracas valley slopes. The burden of poverty fell hardest on women, who often raised their children alone (Ewell 1984). The Pérez Jiménez era was like many Venezuelan phenomena. The stability and prosperity on the surface masked political oppression, corruption, and growing social inequality.

The first signs of trouble for Pérez Jiménez appeared in 1956 when the Archbishop of Caracas delivered a pastoral letter critical of social conditions. Soon all of the prominent political parties, those officially banned and those still legal, formed the Junta Patriótica in united opposition to the regime. A growing economic crisis exacerbated by unchecked corruption further complicated the situation that began to spiral out of the dictator's control. On January 21, 1958, a small media strike escalated into a general strike that involved serious street fighting. When the United States signaled that it would not support Pérez Jiménez, he left on January 23 (Hellinger 1991).

PUNTO FIJO

Scholars continue to debate exactly what sort of democracy Venezuela had between 1959 and 1989. No matter what sort of democracy and no matter how flawed, Venezuela enjoyed the longest period of stability and relative prosperity (for some more than others) than ever before in its history as an independent nation. The Pact of Punto Fijo laid the groundwork for the period. The name, Pact of Punto Fijo, comes from a meeting in October, 1959 held at the home of *copeyano* leader Rafael Caldera at Punto Fijo. The pact was more of a process that began in the waning days of the Pérez Jiménez regime. The parties, including the communist PCV, business groups represented by FEDECAMARAS, the Catholic Church, the military, and student groups realized that the disunity during the *trienio* contributed to Pérez Jiménez's ability to take over and rule between 1948 and 1958. Avoiding similar catastrophe meant securing the unity between groups who had previously spit nails at each other. Once Pérez Jiménez left, Admiral Wolfgang Larrazabal guided a junta government composed of military and civilians committed to securing democratic elections by the end of 1959. Though the year was not without conflict and complete unity did not survive (the PCV was not invited to the pact meetings in October), Larrazabal and the centrist political and civic leaders avoided disaster.

At Punto Fijo, AD, COPEI, and URD (Democratic Republican Union) agreed to share governance, no matter who won the election. In addition, FEDECAMARAS gained protection from imports, the Church gained a financial subsidy and legal autonomy, and the military received the promise that officers would not be

Rafael Caldera Rodríguez. (AP/Wide World Photos)

TABLE **2.1** Venezuelan Presidents, 1959–1989

President	Party	Years
Rómulo Betancourt	AD	1959–1964
Raúl Leoni	AD	1964–1969
Rafael Caldera	COPEI	1969–1974
Carlos Andrés Pérez	AD	1974–1979
Luis Herrera Campíns	COPEI	1979–1984
Jaime Lusinchi	AD	1984–1989

prosecuted for past actions, except Pérez Jiménez. The United States secured his return to Venezuela so that the nation could officially exile him to Spain. Labor and student groups also participated in the pact; the CTV became the officially recognized voice for labor (Hellinger 1991; Ewell 1984). Betancourt easily won the elections in December, though he showed poorly in Caracas, much to AD's great dismay. As promised in the pact, Betancourt built a government that included representatives from COPEI and URD. When URD left the pact with the party's shift left, COPEI and AD became staunch allies in pacted governments. They appointed members of both parties to government positions, avoiding serious political name calling, and transitioned easily from one president to the next. In all honesty, there was almost no difference ideologically or in practice between the two parties, although *adecos rancios* and *copeyanos rancios* (rabid *adecos* and *copeyanos*) always found something to disagree on. It was an era of government controlled by parties, or *partidocracia*, more than it was democracy.

THE GOOD, THE BAD, AND THE UGLY OF *PARTIDOCRACIA*

We would be remiss if we did not note significant positive changes during the era of *partidocracia* that came from economic development and oil wealth. Betancourt's first challenge as president was to come up with ways to increase income in an era of lower international oil prices. He needed the money, as he inherited from Larrazabal and other presidential predecessors the largest budget deficit in national history (Ewell 1984). Betancourt raised tariffs on imports to try to protect nonpetroleum industries (steel and aluminum), but oil remained the cornerstone of the national economy. Neither Betancourt nor his oil minister, Juan Pablo Pérez Alfonzo, believed that Venezuela was yet ready to nationalize oil. The nation did not have the skilled engineers and other professionals to support the industry just yet. They did move to shift more profits to Venezuela away from the companies and more closely monitored company activities. More boldly, Pérez Alfonzo led Venezuela as one of the founding members of OPEC (Organization of Petroleum Exporting Companies) in 1959. OPEC was, and is, an international oil producers association that has the ability to influence international oil prices and to set production quotas. Not all international producers are members of OPEC; the United States is not a member. Not all OPEC nations adhere to the quotas set for them. Venezuela has frequently violated that provision. That said, OPEC gives Middle Eastern and other participating nations the ability to control their economic futures in ways they would not otherwise have. As the world's dependency on oil grew during the latter half of the 20th century, so too did the organization's influence and profits to Venezuela's national treasury.

The power of OPEC internationally combined with tensions in the Middle East in the late 1960s and the early 1970s gave Venezuela leverage with petroleum and companies that it did not have before. Given the nation's increased technological proficiency, President Carlos Andrés Pérez nationalized oil in 1976. Venezuela had income to sow. Pérez appointed a transition commission in 1974 that included all involved sectors, from FEDECAMARAS to labor. The companies did not resist nationalization, as it did not mean that they would have to leave. Nationalization simply meant restructuring so that even greater profits went to the Venezuelan state. Given the money involved in oil and the reserves still untapped in Venezuela, staying and negotiating was in the companies' best interests. Nationalization created PDVSA (Petroleos de Venezuela, Sociedad Anónima), a state holding company charged with coordinating the activities of national subsidiaries and the international companies. Over time, PDVSA began its own exploration and extraction activities using a cadre of highly skilled, Venezuelan-trained engineers. The company, though state owned, paid only a portion of its profits back to the state and retained significant reserves for its own use. So long as profits remained high throughout the 1970s (the international oil crisis was a good thing for Venezuela), PDVSA's autonomy was not an issue. It would be later. But through the 1960s and 1970s, Venezuela had oil money to put to use.

We will discuss in Chapter 6 how Venezuela used oil income to subsidize artistic production, music, and architecture. In addition, during the 1960s and the 1970s, Venezuela pursued populist policies and invested oil profits heavily in the nation's social infrastructure. The nation invested in improved rural housing, health care, nutrition, and water supplies, drastically reducing deaths from malaria and other insect-borne diseases. Infant mortality rates decreased and life expectancy rose throughout the nation (Ewell 1984). The population grew, augmented by an influx of immigrants (many illegal) from Colombia, who worked often as domestic servants or street vendors in urban areas. Successive presidents invested in some urban housing to meet the housing needs of burgeoning cities, especially Caracas and Maracaibo. Puerto La Cruz in the state of Anzoategui in the east grew from a fishing village to a significant urban center with the construction of a refinery, a cement factory, a port, and oil platforms immediately west in Jose.

For populist and technical reasons, Venezuelan governments through the 1970s invested heavily in public education. Betancourt's administration sponsored the construction of over 3,000 primary schools and almost 200 secondary, normal, and technical schools (Ewell 1984). Literacy rates climbed. The World Bank recorded adult literacy rates at 89.8 percent in 1990 (World Bank n.d.). They had been 60.8 percent in 1958 (Ewell 1984). Organizations like INCE (Instituto Nacional de Cooperación

Educativa, or National Institute of Cooperative Education) provided free technical education and certification in fields such as drafting, plumbing, and electrical wiring. The state also invested in higher education, and enrollment rates climbed as primary and secondary education improved. By the 1980s, working-class Venezuelans reasonably expected to enroll in, if not graduate from, college. In 1991, 36 percent of all university students came from working-class backgrounds (Reimers 1991). Despite investment in education in rural areas, education above the primary level was most available in cities. Parents could, and did, plan life trajectories based on maximizing educational opportunities for their children. Parents who were illiterate or semiliterate cleaning ladies or longshoremen worked to ensure their children's graduation as medical professionals, engineers, and other highly skilled technicians. Lucky students received scholarships from the Gran Mariscal Ayacucho Foundation to study abroad in the United States and Europe. With increased education, a stable national bureaucracy, a prosperous national oil industry and related urban-based service industry, the Venezuelan middle class grew, though the extremes between those who had much and those who had little grew, too.

Partidocracia controlled the voices of those left out of the system for one reason or another. Parties on the political left developed in the 1960s out of the communist party when it became apparent that AD and COPEI would not move from the political center under any circumstance. Parties such as MAS (Movimiento al Socialismo), founded by Teodoro Petkoff, MIR (Movimiento de Izquierda Revolucionaria), MEP (Movimiento Electoral del Pueblo), and later Causa R advocated for real land reform (AD implemented a limited, unsuccessful program) and independent labor. The parties existed through the 1980s, some more important than others, as unelected (and unelectable) opposition voices. The disaster for the left was the guerrilla movement in the 1960s. Younger-generation communists in the far left believed that the only way to change Venezuela to the benefit of lower classes, urban and rural, was through violence. Throughout the 1960s, guerrillas staged attacks, some quite spectacular (burning a Sears department store in Caracas) in urban and rural areas (Hellinger 1991). The military responded, and civilians often found themselves caught in the middle. Fidel Castro's revolution in Cuba inspired the young Venezuelan leftists, but the situation in Venezuela in the 1960s was not comparable to Cuba in the decades prior to 1959. Yes, the Venezuelan lower classes suffered during the economic reorganizing that took place in the 1960s, but the *adeco* government was a popularly elected government that had the political will and ability to use its resources for popular good. The *adeco* and *copeyano* machines became adept at incorporating barrio leaders who could have become guerrillas into the party systems. So the violence accomplished nothing but death.

Historians and political scientists in Venezuela and elsewhere lauded Venezuelan exceptionalism, a theory that argued that economic, political, and social stability created a healthy democracy unusual in cold war–era Latin America. Oil wealth, political leaders' ability to learn from previous errors, and the development of a significant middle class placed Venezuela far along the road to political modernity, much farther than any Latin American counterparts. Indeed, exceptionalism is a theory predicated on celebrating the triumph of 20th-century modernity over 19th-century caudillo barbarism (Ellner and Tinker Salas 2007). There are several problems with the theory. It denies the 19th-century struggle for modernity while minimizing complicated and contested political, social, economic, and racial processes. But the theory became the prism through which Venezuelans (and others) understood their past and their present, leading to flawed understandings of the past that limited their abilities to see weaknesses built into the system as it existed through the 1980s.

Daniel Hellinger argues that by the end of the 1960s Venezuelan democracy devolved into crass competition between COPEI and AD for votes through control of unions, professional organizations, and universities because electoral victory meant jobs, money, and prestige for parties, which they used to build more success in the next electoral cycle. Neither party challenged the validity of the political system in which they functioned, nor did they compete over political ideas. Both parties were centrists bent on placating foreign interests and domestic elite while using oil profits to prop up the social spending that generated party support. Both parties abhorred political extremes, right or guerrilla left. Venezuelan politics had become "the politics of patronage and clientelism. The goal was not to mobilize or to represent citizens, but to incorporate them under the umbrella of a party as pawns of the larger populist game" (Ellner and Tinker Salas 2007: 116). The game worked so long as the money continued to flow. When the money stopped flowing . . .

THE VERY UGLY 1980s

The 1970s and early 1980s were the era of "Esta barato. Dame dos" ("It's cheap. Give me two") for the Venezuelan upper middle class and truly elite. They went to Miami for weekend shopping trips and Europe for vacations. But all that glitters is not a gold Rolex, more like a cheap knockoff sold by a street vendor. Global recession at that same time began to limit global demand for oil, steel, and aluminum. Even with the income Venezuela earned from oil, it had borrowed heavily from the IMF, World Bank, and private lenders like Citibank throughout the 1970s. Those loans came due just when money to pay them with began to become scarce. Worse, Venezuelan heavy industries (oil, steel, and aluminum) are extremely capital intensive and require constant investment in order to produce profits. That meant that the Venezuelan state had to find a way to obtain more loans while paying off old loans at higher interest rates with less money. Though Presidents Herrera Campíns and Lusinchi promised to increase social spending to alleviate growing poverty (74% by 1983), they actually reduced agricultural subsidies, which produced increased food prices. Real wages, the true value of salaries, fell below 1974 levels (Ellner and Tinker Salas 2007). By the early 1980s, Herrera Campíns and then Lusinchi began to devalue the bolivar. With unemployment climbing and wages stagnant or falling, that monetary policy hit the already suffering lower classes hard. Successive governments cut public spending in health care and education. While those who still had money could go to private hospitals when ill or send their children to private schools, most Venezuelans had to rely on a derelict health care system and send kids to schools that were literally decaying around them.

And so it was in 1988 when Carlos Andrés Pérez campaigned for reelection that he promised to bring back the good times associated with him in the 1970s. By 1988, most Venezuelans were willing to believe anything, and there is no doubt that Carlos Andrés (as he was popularly called) was charismatic in a slimy sort of way. Once elected and inaugurated, President Pérez announced a package (*el paquete*) of economic reforms consistent with the demands of international lenders but inconsistent with the populist expectations of the Venezuelan public, and more extreme than any of the reforms implemented by his predecessors.

The riots that came to be known as the *caracazo* began in Caracas and eventually engulfed cities throughout the country as Venezuelans rejected *el paquete.* We will assess in Chapter 4 the economic policies that led to the *caracazo* and evaluate in Chapter 3 the social and political consequences of the riots. However, it is significant to note that Venezuelan reaction to *el paquete* ended *partidocracia* (Punto Fijo period) and began the current era in Venezuelan political, economic, and social history. The democratic election of Hugo Chávez Frias in 1998 has its roots, in part, in the dissolution of the legitimacy of the political system that began in 1959. Chávez had

Accion Democratica candidate and former president, Carlos Andres Pérez, waves to journalists as he arrives to vote in the presidential election in Caracas, Venezuela on December 4, 1988. (AP/Wide World Photos)

Officer Hugo Chávez Frías talks to reporters at the Defense Ministry after surrendering to troops loyal to the government of Carlos Andres Perez, in Caracas, Venezuela in 1992 after his forces attempted a coup d'etat. Chávez was later elected to Venezuela's presidency in 1998. (AP/Wide World Photos)

the political acumen to speak directly to people's frustrations with economic instability, class, and racial inequality (topics we will analyze in Chapters 3, 4, and 5).

While his presidency (1998–) has been fraught with controversy, by 2010 opposition politicians began to acknowledge that Chávez forever changed the political landscape because he made patently public the relationships between economics, race, and class. Working-class Venezuelans could no longer be bought, as it were, with promises and favors during election season—the norm during the period of *partidocracia.* Politicians would have to address the substantial structural problems that engendered social inequality and present the electorate with real solutions. By 2010 a crashing economy, insecurity, and electricity and water shortages also began to remind Chávez that he also had to answer to the populace with reasoned solutions and not the 21st-century version of tired Venezuelan political rhetoric. Political pundits began to suspect that the ferocity of Venezuelan discontent that Chávez had harnessed in his election process and during the early years of his presidency could just as easily be unleashed. It is to the Venezuelan political system in the Chávez period to which we now turn our attention.

REFERENCES

Allende, Isabel. 1988. *Eva Luna.* New York: Alfred A. Knopf.

Armellada, Friar Cesaro de, ed. 1954. *Fuero Indígena Venezolano.* Caracas: República de Venezuela, Ministerio de Justicia, Comisión Indigenista.

Bastidas Valecillos, Luis. 1997. "Una mirada etnohistórica a las tierras indígenas de Mérida (I:Epoca colonial)." *Boletín Antropológico* 41 (Septiembre-Diciembre): 65.

Bolívar, Simón. 1951. "Address Delivered at the Inauguration of the Second National Congress of Venezuela in Angostura." In Vicente Lecuna and Harold Bierck, eds., *Selected Writings of Bolívar, Volume One.* Caracas: Banco de Venezuela.

Código penal sancionado por el General Guzman Blanco, Presidente Provisional de la República y General en Jefe de sus Ejercitos, Edición Oficial, 1873. 1973. Caracas: Imprenta del Congreso de la República de Venezuela.

Cunill Grau, Pedro. 1987. *Geografía del poblamiento venezolano en el siglo XIX, Tomo I.* Caracas: Ediciones de la Presidencia de la República.

Díaz, Arlene J. 2004. *Female Citizens, Patriarchs, and the Law in Venezuela, 1786–1904.* Lincoln: University of Nebraska Press.

———. 2007. "Vicenta Ochoa, Dead Many Times: Gender, Politics, and Death Sentence in Early Republican Caracas." In William E. French and Katherine Elaine Bliss, eds., *Gender, Sexuality, and Power in Latin America Since Independence.* Lanham, MD: Rowman and Littlefield.

Díaz Sanchez, Ramón. 1981. *Mene.* Madrid: Editorial Mediterráneo.

Dupouy, Walter, ed. 1966. *Sir Robert Kerr Porter's Caracas Diary, 1825–1842: A British Diplomat in a Newborn Nation.* Caracas: Editorial Arte.

Ellner, Steve. 1999. "The Heyday of Radical Populism in Venezuela and its Aftermath." In Michael Conniff, ed., *Populism in Latin America.* Tuscaloosa: University of Alabama Press.

Ellner, Steve, and Miguel Tinker Salas. 2007. "The Venezuelan Exceptionalism Thesis: Separating Myth from Reality." In Steve Ellner and Miguel Tinker Salas, eds., *Venezuela: Hugo Chávez and the Decline of an "Exceptional Democracy."* Plymouth, UK: Rowman and Littlefield.

Ewell, Judith. 1984. *Venezuela: A Century of Change.* Stanford, CA: Stanford University Press.

Ferry, Robert J. 1989. *Colonial Elite of Early Caracas, 1567–1767.* Berkeley: University of California Press.

Flinter, George. 2000. "The Commencement of the Revolution in Venezuela." In Christon I. Archer, ed., *The Wars of Independence in Spanish America.* Wilmington, DE: Scholarly Resources.

Frankel, Benjamin A. 1976. "La Guerra Federal y sus Secuelas." In Miguel Izard, ed., *Política y Economia en Venezuela, 1810–1976.* Caracas: Fundación John Boulton.

Gil Rivas, Pedro A., Luís Dovale Prado, and Lidia Lismila Bello. 1996. *La insurrección de los negros de la sierra coriana: 10 de mayo de 1795, notas para la discusión.* Caracas: Universidad Central de Venezuela.

Graham, Richard. 1968. *Britain and the Onset of Modernization in Brazil, 1850–1914.* Cambridge: Cambridge University Press.

———. 1994. *Independence in Latin America: A Comparative Approach, Second Edition.* New York: McGraw-Hill.

Hellinger, Daniel C. 1991. *Venezuela: Tarnished Democracy.* Boulder, CO: Westview Press.

Humboldt, Alejandro de. 1941. *Viaje a las regiones equinocciales el nuevo continente hecho en 1799, 1800, 1801, 1802,1803, y 1804 por A. de Humboldt y A. Bonpland. Tomo dos.* Lisandro Alvarado, trans. Caracas: Biblioteca Venezolana de Cultura.

Linder, Peter. 2006. "Civilizing Carnival: Popular Culture, Social Class, and Political Power in Maracaibo, 1870–1935." Paper Delivered at the XXVI International Congress of the Latin American Studies Association, March 15, 2006.

Lombardi, John V. 1971. *The Decline and Abolition of Negro Slavery in Venezuela, 1820–1854.* Westport, CT: Greenwood.

———. 1982. *Venezuela: The Search for Order, the Dream of Progress.* New York: Oxford University Press.

Lynch, John. 2006. *Simón Bolívar: A Life.* New Haven, CT: Yale University Press.

Mathews, Robert Paul. 1970. *Violencia rural en Venezuela, 1840–1858: Antecedentes socio-económicos de la Guerra Federal.* Caracas: Monte Avila Editores, 1970.

McBeth, Brian S. 2008. *Dictatorship and Politics: Intrigue, Betrayal, and Survival in Venezuela, 1908–1935.* Notre Dame, IN: University of Notre Dame Press.

Morales M., Filadelfo. 1994. *Sangre en los conucos: Reconstucción etnohistórica de los indígenas de Turmero.* Caracas: Fondo Editorial Tropykos.

Moreno Molina, Agustín. 2004. *Entre la pobreza y el desorden: El funcionameinto del gobierno en la presidencia de José Gregorio Monagas.* Caracas: Universidad Católica Andres Bello, 2004.

Morse, Kimberly J. 2000. *Aun en la muerte separados: Class, Clergy, and Society in Aragua de Barcelona, Venezuela, 1820–1875.* PhD diss., The University of Texas at Austin.

———. 2003. "When the Priest Does Not Sympathize with *el Pueblo*: Clergy and Society in *El Oriente venezolano*, 1843–1873." *The Americas: A Quarterly Review of Inter-American Cultural History* 59, no. 4: 511–535.

Oviedo y Baños, Jose de. 1987. *The Conquest and Settlement of Venezuela*, trans. Jeannette Johnson Varner. Berkeley: University of California Press.

Pino Iturrieta, Elias. 1993. *Las ideas de los primeros venezolanos.* Caracas: Monte Avila Editores.

Porter, Sir Robert Kerr. 1966. *Sir Robert Kerr Porter's Caracas Diary, 1825–1842: A British Diplomat in a Newborn Nation.* Walter Dupouy, ed. Caracas: Editorial Arte.

Prato Perelli, Antoinette. 1990. *Las encomiendas de Nueva Andalucia en el siglo XVII: Visita hecha por don Fernando de la Riva Agüero, Oidor de la Audiencia de Santo Domingo, 1688.* Caracas: Biblioteca de la Academia Nacional de la Historia.

Racine, Karen. 2003. *Francisco de Miranda: A Transatlantic Life in the Age of Revolution.* Wilmington, DE: Scholarly Resources, Inc.

Registro Principal de Barcelona, Criminales, 28, 1873, Libro 60. 1873. "Criminales, Averiguando la muerte hecha a Francisco Fuentes, 26 Diciembre de 1873, No. 59, Contra Pedro Pascacio Becerro por homicidio;" Registro Principal de Barcelona, Criminales, 1874, No. 29, Libro 18, "Criminales, Contra Hilario Arguindique por maltrato inferido a Demetria Rendon, 1874," April 6.

Reimers, Fernando. 1991. "The Impact of Economic Stabilization and Adjustment on Education in Latin America." *Comparative Education Review* 35, no. 2: 319–353.

Tinker Salas, Miguel. 2009. *The Enduring Legacy: Oil, Culture, and Society in Venezuela.* Durham, NC: Duke University Press.

Tronconis de Veracoechea, Ermilia. 1981. "Venezuela: Indígenas Siglo XVII." *Boletín de la Academia Nacional de la Historia* 64: 251, 609.

World Bank. n.d. "Edstats." http://devdata.worldbank.org/edstats/SummaryEducationPro files/CountryData/GetShowData.asp?sCtry=VEN,Venezuela,%20RB.

Yarrington, Doug. 1997. *A Coffee Frontier: Land, Society, and Politics in Duaca, Venezuela, 1830–1936.* Pittsburgh, PA: University of Pittsburgh Press.

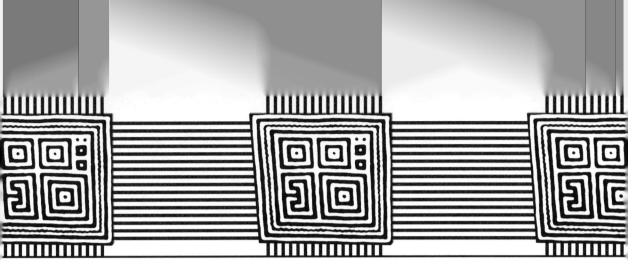

Government and Politics

The years between 1989 and the *caracazo* and 2010 have been particularly active and volatile in Venezuela, especially in the area of politics. New political parties have been formed, coup d'état have been planned and carried out, and new constitutions have been written, then amended. This chapter will begin with a basic overview of the Venezuelan system of government as it is configured in 2010, and then will provide more detailed information about the events that led to substantial changes in the system in the years between 1989 and 2010. Additional changes and challenges will be addressed in Chapter 7.

BRANCHES OF GOVERNMENT AND GOVERNMENTAL STRUCTURE

The Venezuelan government, since 1999 known as La República Boliviariana de Venezuela (The Bolivarian Republic of Venezuela) has five branches: the executive branch headed by a president, a legislative branch that consists of a unicameral legislative congress, a judiciary branch headed by a supreme tribunal, a citizens' branch, and an electoral council. Before the 1999 constitution, only the executive and legislative branches existed. The addition of the three additional branches of government is one of many changes brought about in the constitution at the end of the century. It should also be noted that the change in the name of the republic (formerly the Republic of Venezuela) is another major alteration in the period between 1989 and 2010. In those 20 years, much of the structure of the Venezuelan government has been altered. What has not changed, however, is the continuing role of a strong executive.

National Capitol, Caracas Centre, Venezuela, South America. (Jan Csernoch/ Dreamstime.com)

The Executive Branch and the Office of the President

Following Venezuela's long and well-established tradition of *caudillismo* and powerful central figures in politics and government, the Venezuelan presidency is a very strong office. The president must be Venezuelan by birth and at least 30 years old. While the 1999 constitution reflects the growing possibility of a female president, as of 2010 all presidents have been men.

The president is elected by a plurality of the vote of the people, who enjoy universal suffrage at the age of 18. As provided for in the 1999 constitution, the president serves six-year terms; until 2009, the president was limited to one term at a time and could not be reelected until two intervening presidential terms had passed. This provision of the constitution, however, was repealed in February of 2009 with a national vote in which 54 percent of Venezuelans voted to repeal the term limits (Forero 2009a). This change will likely increase the power of the presidency, as leaders such as Hugo Chávez will be allowed to stand for reelection indefinitely.

The power of the presidency is also found in the powers given to the president. The president is both chief of state and head of government. The president serves as commander in chief of the military and additionally controls foreign policy and the ability to call special sessions of the congress. In addition, the president may control the national budget, including the negotiation of loans. Finally, the president can suspend the constitution or declare a state of siege.

THE NONSEXIST MAGNA CARTA

The drafting of a new constitution in 1999 was an opportunity to make the nation's foundational document more inclusive. Women's groups were especially active in the drive to draft demands in the interests of women for the constitution and to promote the candidacy of women to the constitutional assembly.

The result of the efforts of these groups is a constitutional document commonly referred to as the "Nonsexist Magna Carta." The 1999 constitution states that women are entitled to full citizenship, and it addresses discrimination, sexual harassment, and domestic violence. In addition, the constitution makes a special effort to be gender inclusive in its language. As the Spanish language has masculine and feminine versions of job titles, in every instance in which the constitution refers to a job title within government, the possibility of both a male and a female are mentioned. The constitution, for example, always refers to the president as *presidente o presidenta* and ministers as *ministro o ministra*.

To assist him in his duties, the president is to appoint a cabinet, but as the cabinet ministers serve at the will of the president, they have little control over the president's decisions if he chooses not to listen to them. The legislative branch is not involved in the selection of cabinet ministers. Indeed, given the structure of the government, the president can adopt whatever regulations he desires, using cabinet ministers to implement the laws. These regulations, if implemented through the ministries, are not subject to approval of the congress, and the judicial branch does not have the right to review them. In this way, the concept of checks and balances is not as strong in Venezuelan governmental structure as in other systems.

There is no set number of cabinet ministers, as it is the province of each president to decide the size and composition of his cabinet. President Rómulo Betancourt in the 1940s, for example, appointed 13 cabinet ministers. In 2010, President Hugo Chávez had 25 cabinet ministers (CIA 2010a). The growth in the number of ministers may be linked to the growing legislative power of the president and the growing list of national goals. Goals such as the preservation of democracy, the maintenance of public order, or the modernization of the armed forces, along with the provision of increased social services and directing the economy, have all fallen under the purview of the presidency. Some have noted that by the 1990s, Venezuelans were referring to "the government" when in fact they meant "the president." In the popular consciousness, the man in charge, the president, was the government (Haggerty 1990).

The Legislative Congress

The legislative branch of government in Venezuela is composed of a one-house (unicameral) congress called the Asamblea Nacional (National Assembly.) This congress is composed of 167 delegates from different states and territories who are popularly elected to serve five-year terms. In addition, the 1999 constitution provided for three designated seats in congress to be reserved for the representatives of the indigenous peoples of Venezuela (CIA 2010a).

As previously mentioned, new laws are not only initiated by the National Assembly. Legislation may be initiated by the assembly but also by the president or by the judicial branch. In addition, the citizen branch (ombudsman, public prosecutor, and comptroller general) or a public petition signed by no fewer than 0.1 percent of registered voters may be used to initiate legislation in the assembly (U.S. Department of State 2009). In the case of disagreements between the legislature and the executive, the president may ask the National Assembly to reconsider portions of laws if he objects to their provisions. In this case, a simple majority of the assembly can override these objections.

The National Judiciary

The judicial branch of government is responsible for holding trials and providing due process to those people and organizations charged with crimes and those under civil court indictments. The lower courts hear a wide variety of cases in nine categories: civil, commercial, criminal, labor, tax, custom, administrative, juvenile, military, and agrarian. The judicial branch supervises and directs the activities of district courts, municipal courts, and trial and appeal courts. (Ramirez 2006). The judicial branch is headed by the Tribunal Supremo de Justicia (Supreme Justice Tribunal) or TSJ. The TSJ directs, administrates, and organizes all juridical activity in Venezuela (TSJ n.d.).

INDIGENOUS AND AFROVENEZUELAN REPRESENTATION IN CONGRESS

While indigenous peoples in Venezuela have received significantly increased recognition in the 1999 Bolivarian Constitution and through specific representation in the National Assembly, similar acknowledgement of the Afrovenezuelan population has been slow to materialize.

No reliable numbers exist of the African-descended population in Venezuela, and the 1999 constitution does not guarantee the rights of Afrovenezuelans in the same way that it does those of women and indigenous peoples. Since 2007, a movement for the official recognition of the African-descended population has grown considerably, as activists such as Jesús "Chucho" García have organized marches and letter-writing campaigns designed to bring about a rewriting of the constitution. Groups such as the Network of Afro-Venezuelan Organizations request the inclusion of a chapter that would recognize African-descended communities, protect ancestral lands, respect spiritual values, and include Afrovenezuelan history and culture in the educational curriculum. In addition, the network requested that the 2010 census consider race as a category.

While the TSJ has existed in some form in Venezuela since 1811, the judiciary has only been a branch of government since the 1999 Bolivarian Constitution. The 1999 constitution provided for 20 members of the TSJ. Constitutional reforms in 2004 added to the total number of justices. The TSJ is, in 2010, composed of 32 justices. These justices are selected by the National Assembly and serve a single 12-year term (TSJ n.d.).

The justices of the TSJ may meet in plenary session with all justices appearing or in the individual *salas* (chambers) that take care of different areas of law. Each *sala* may make decisions in their particular area of expertise, and each has its own secretary and support staff. These six *salas* are the Political-Administrative, the Social, the Civil, the Constitutional, the Electoral, and the Criminal. Additional, special *salas* may be added if 100 or more cases in a specific area are accumulated (TSJ n.d.).

The Citizens' Branch of Government

The citizens' branch of government is one of the three branches added in the 1999 constitution. The Venezuelan system consists of three components: a prosecutor general, an ombudsman, and a comptroller general. The *fiscal general* (attorney general), fills the task of protecting the citizens through investigations and public prosecutions of a wide range of crimes. Anticorruption investigations and illegal drug prosecutions are typical of this type of action. The office of *defensoria del pueblo* (ombudsman) handles investigations and prosecutions of violations of human rights and health issues. All services of the ombudsman are offered free of charge to the public, and the ombudsman maintains offices across the nation to record and handle citizen complaints and concerns. Finally, the *contraloría general* (comptroller/auditor general) is responsible for the investigation and prosecution of irregularities related to the management of public funds or properties. Holders of the directorships of these offices are elected by the National Assembly and hold seven-year terms.

Collectively, these three offices may also challenge actions of the TSJ that they believe are illegal. As a group, these offices are the Republican Moral Council, charged with general education about and defense of civil virtues and democratic principles.

The National Electoral Council

The fifth branch of government in Venezuela is the electoral branch, known as the Consejo Nacional Electoral (National Electoral Council) or CNE. This council is responsible for organizing, administering, and supervising elections and referendums at all levels: local, state and federal. This is also the organization responsible for certifying signatures in support of legislation or other petitions, and it is the body that certifies election winners. The powers of the electoral branch are exercised through the CNE, as head of the branch, but also through the subordinate organizations of the National Board of Elections: the Civil Status and Voter Registration Commission and the Commission on Political Participation and Financing (Ramirez 2006).

The members of the CNE are, like those of the citizens' branch, elected to seven-year terms by the National Assembly. In the event of a tie vote in the assembly, the TSJ may be called upon to appoint council members (U.S. Department of State 2009).

FEDERAL AND STATE STRUCTURE

The Constitution of 1961 mandated for Venezuela a structure of 20 states, two federal territories, and a federal district. In addition, Venezuela has 72 island dependencies in the Caribbean. Governmental power is divided between a national government based in the federal district in Caracas and state governments in the 23 states in 2010. Delta Amacuro, Amazonas, and Vargas achieved statehood in 1991, 1994, and 1998, respectively. Amazonas and Delta Amacuro were the two federal territories. Until 1989, state governors were appointed directly by the President of the Republic. This fact, combined with the fact that state governments were dependent on the national government for their budgets, has limited the autonomy of state governments to make their own decisions. The autonomous decision making that has taken place has generally happened through the actions of state-level unicameral legislatures selected through direct elections. In addition, each state has its own constitution, which gives it the power to administrate its own political, financial, and administrative systems. This power, combined with the change in 1989 that allowed the direct election of state governors, has allowed some decision making to be made at the state level, though in 2010, states still depended on the federal governments for their budgets.

POLITICAL PARTIES

The Punto Fijo agreement of 1959 solidified the position of COPEI and AD as the two main political parties in Venezuela. As we discussed in Chapter 2, the two parties, much like the Republicans and Democrats in the United States, took turns in Miraflores (the Venezuelan equivalent of the White House) and in controlling the National Assembly for 40 years.

That situation, however, like much else in Venezuelan politics, changed after the *caracazo*. After 1989, the stranglehold that COPEI and AD had on elected positions at all levels in Venezuela was broken, and the way was clear for other parties to be formed and for candidates from those parties to be elected. By 2009, not a single member of the National Assembly was *adeco* or *copeyano*.

In 2009, the vast majority of seats (141) in the National Assembly were held by the Partido Socialista Unido Venezolano (United Socialist Party of Venezuela, PSUV). In addition, the Patria Para Todos (Fatherland for All, PPT) party held 5 seats, the Venezuelan Communist Party (PCV) held 4 seats, the party Por la Democracia Social (For Social Democracy, PODEMOS) held 6 seats, and the party Frente Popular Humanista (Popular Humanist Front, FPH) held 5 seats. Six assembly seats were held by independents (CIA 2010a). The period from 1989 to 2009 was very active in the creation, dissolution, and consolidation of political parties. We will profile the preceding parties with the understanding that only time will tell whether they will still exist 20 years from now. The situation remains fluid. As Sujatha Fernandes observes, the time of traditional political party structure in Venezuela is likely over (Fernandes 2007a).

PSUV

The PSUV was created in 2007 by mandate of Hugo Chávez, who proposed dissolving the 24 different progovernment parties and combining them into one large party. Chavez's idea was to unite all of his supporters under one banner, eliminating interparty rivalries, the necessity for redundant party bureaucracies, and corruption. Chávez remains the president of this party in 2010. With his order, 13 of the 24 designated parties heeded the call and joined the PSUV. Among the parties that joined the PSUV were Chávez's own party, the politically powerful MVR (Fifth Republic Movement). Other progovernment parties, such as the PCV and the PPT, did not refuse outright to join but rather asked for more time to consider the idea and debate it within their membership (Fernandes 2007a).

The idea for forming the PSUV has come under criticism from a variety of sources. Community organizers see the formation of the PSUV as yet another example of top-down political organizing in the tradition of the AD and COPEI in the years before the *caracazo*. Those members of community councils and Bolivarian circles who worked hard to support the president at the local and barrio level see the declaration from the top of the government as a way for elites to consolidate their power and take decision making away from those on the ground (Fernandes 2007a). Further concerns include the stifling of dissent and the opportunity for debate caused by the consolidation of all politicians into one large party.

PODEMOS and FPH

Two major political parties that frequently stand in opposition to the administration of Hugo Chávez are PODEMOS and FPH. Between them, in 2009, the two parties only held 11 seats in the National Assembly, in part because most opposition lawmakers boycotted the 2005 legislative elections. PODEMOS, as a political party, was founded in 2002 and once formed part of the Chávez camp, supporting the president and his policies, but broke with the Chávez administration in 2007 over the push to fold all pro-Chávez parties into the PSUV. PODEMOS considers itself a center-left political party and part of the revolution committed to progressive causes and at times supports the work of the Chávez government. Members of the party objected to the move to squash debate and criticism of all executive decisions, and so they refused to join PSUV. This move to separate themselves from Chávez by not joining PSUV has actually gained PODEMOS support in the form of five lawmakers who left their previous party affiliations and have joined PODEMOS (Forero 2009b).

The FPH, similar to PODEMOS, considers itself a moderate, center-left party, though it is willing to speak against the policies of the Chávez administration. FPH is a newer political party, having been founded in 2009 as part of the debates surrounding the constitutional amendments that would eliminate term limits on the presidency.

AD, COPEI, and UNT

The traditional political parties, AD and COPEI, that date back to 1941 and 1946, respectively, have functionally sat out of politics in the period between 1999 and 2009. After losing credibility in the *caracazo*, the two establishment parties chose to boycott the 2005 legislative elections in protest of the policies of Hugo Chávez. This has later been understood as a serious strategic error for the opposition, as it allowed progovernment parties to take over the National Assembly. A new party, Un Nuevo Tiempo (A New Time, UNT), emerged at the national level in 2006 in strong opposition to the Chávez administration. For the legislative elections planned for September of 2010, the three parties planned to work together in putting together a slate of opposition candidates.

ELECTORAL SYSTEM

The CNE runs the nation's electoral system. Presidential elections are held every six years. In 2005 legislative elections, 65 members of the National Assembly were elected through a party-list proportional representation system. In this type of system, each political party constructs a list of candidates and voters cast votes for the party (not the individual candidate). After the votes are tallied, parties are allocated seats in the assembly in rough proportion to their share of the total vote. Once a party knows how many seats it has won, it then chooses that number of names from the list, and those people represent the party in the assembly for five years, after which there is another election, and the process starts all over. An additional 99 members of the assembly are elected through a straight plurality system, where each candidate runs for his or her own seat (rather than as part of a list), and the candidate who receives the *most* votes wins the seat, as opposed to some systems in which the winning candidate is required to win a majority of the votes. This is particularly pronounced in races where there are more than two viable candidates, and the winning candidate may win the seat with far less than an absolute majority of votes, sometimes as little as 25 or 30 percent. Of these 99 seats, 68 are chosen in single-member districts (as in the United States) and 31 in multimember constituencies, where more than one person represents the same geographic area. Three seats are reserved for the indigenous peoples of Venezuela. All members serve five-year terms (IFES 2005).

In 2009, the National Assembly passed a new electoral law allowing the CNE to redraw voting districts at any time and in any way the organization saw fit. In addition, the law reduced the number of seats in the assembly that would be elected through proportional representation from nearly 40 percent to just at 30 percent

(IFES 2009). The new law provides for a simple plurality voting system in elections for governor or president but institutes a "parallel" voting system for legislative and municipal councils. This system means that voters can either choose candidates individually by name, or can select party-line or grouped names of candidates. The new law also provided increased voting access in rural areas and increased fines for electoral fraud (Pearson 2009). While government supporters assured members of the opposition that the power to redraw districts would not be used in a political fashion, critics of the law worry that the Chávez administration will use the new law to redraw electoral districts to favor progovernment candidates. Additionally, members of the opposition point out that the "parallel" voting system will allow major party candidates to list their candidates twice, once as a single name and once in the party section, thus doubling the chance that someone will vote for them. This fact, opponents argue, gives preference to the large parties such as the PSUV and puts smaller parties at a disadvantage (Pearson 2009).

CONSTITUTION

In 2010 the Constitution of the Bolivarian Republic of Venezuela remained the 1999 Bolivarian Constitution, which had replaced the constitution of 1961. It is the 26th constitution in the history of the nation. As we discuss in this chapter, and throughout this book, major changes found in the constitution include: the concentration of more power in the executive branch, the dissolution of the legislative senate, the addition of the electoral and citizens' branches of government, the guarantee of a state pension for all citizens, and calls for the public examination of judicial candidates.

The drive to redraft the constitution is understandable in light of the chaotic and violent events of the preceding 10 years. The exceptional years of *partidocracia* and pacted democracy were over. New economic and political realities had emerged. To understand how these events came about, and how the new political landscape was drawn, we need to turn our attention back to 1989.

AN OVERVIEW OF FORMATIVE EVENTS IN RECENT VENEZUELAN POLITICS

The Caracazo *and Endemic Problems of Race and Class*

Many scholars and politicians acknowledged by 2010 that racism was an endemic problem in Venezuela and had been long before the election of Chávez in 1998. Academics began to research the problem in the 1980s. Sociologist Ligia Montañez documented examples of racist behavior in daily events. In one example, a lighter skinned person purposely distanced himself from a dark skinned Venezuelan at a bus stop after looking up and realizing with whom he shared space. In a second example, a company denied employment to a qualified applicant upon realizing the applicant was black (Montañez 1993: 149). The growing economic crisis in the 1980s served to exacerbate race and class problems. In 1989, the poorest 5 percent of the national population controlled 4.9 percent of national wealth, while the wealthiest five percent controlled 49.2 percent. The next wealthiest group controlled another 22.1 percent, meaning that only 10 percent of the population controlled 71.3 percent of Venezuela's national wealth (Kelly 1995: 298). The working classes complained that the public schools they sent their children to crumbled around their ears and teachers often did not come, while the elite sent their children to private schools. The working classes had to go to poorly staffed public hospitals to receive marginal care, while the elite went to private hospitals in secluded Caracas neighborhoods or, better yet, to the United States to receive medical care. There was never enough housing in urban areas for the working classes, who were forced to build more creatively on mountainsides and "appropriate" electricity when local electric services did not reach their homes. Appropriating sewage and water systems, however, was more complicated. The working classes knew that their chances of ever seeing a lawyer if they found themselves in prison were slim, as public defenders rarely visited clients. Prisoners easily spent more time in prison before their trial date than they were eventually sentenced to (Kelly 1995: 295), unless, of course, the accused was an elite. Justice in those cases could be purchased.

The tensions that had defined Venezuela from almost the beginning became more public in 1989 after the election of Carlos Andres Pérez within the context of worsening economic crisis in the global age of neoliberal economics. Twenty-five percent of Venezuelans lived below the poverty line in 1981. By 1989, depending on estimates, 40 to over 70 percent of Venezuelans lived in poverty (Kelly 1995; Hellinger 1991). Venezuela created what appeared to be a democratic miracle in the 1970s by using oil revenues to prop up social spending in education, health care, and social security but also to subsidize food and fuel. As a result, Venezuelans paid low prices for essentials like flour, coffee, milk, and sugar. Though most people still did not own cars, fuel subsidies kept the fares low for the microbuses that most Venezuelans used to go nearly anywhere in all major cities. Fuel subsidies also kept cooking gas prices low. Even though the state began to cut education, health, and social security spending in the 1980s upon the insistence of international lenders in order to pay the nation's enormous debt, Venezuelan presidents resisted touching the subsidies. Real per capita income fell 19 percent between 1977 and 1991 (Kelly 1995: 298). Had the state cut subsidies in the 1980s, the consequences for those Venezuelans falling below the poverty line and those hovering near it could have been devastating.

An event along the Colombian border that the state hoped to use to prop up its shaky legitimacy during the economic crisis in 1988 turned into a nightmare. Sixteen men went fishing in a canoe on the Arauca River on October 29. Suddenly, they were attacked by machinegun fire followed by more fire from military helicopters. Fourteen of the 16 died. Forensic doctors later found evidence to suggest that the men were shot, execution style, from behind. Some had been tortured and mutilated, their tattoos and faces burned. Within hours, the national counterinsurgency brigade, CEJAP, flew reporters in to announce a successful encounter with 50 heavily armed Colombian guerrillas who planned to "sabotage oil pipes and kidnap ranchers" on the Venezuelan side of the border (Coronil and Skurski 2006: 95). Pictures of bodies in guerrilla uniforms next to guns appeared in the media. The state, military, and the media turned injustice and tragedy into a national victory.

Or so they thought. Two of the fishermen survived and returned home, to the town of Amparo (literally "help" or "refuge") to report what actually happened. Local Congressman Walter Márquez intervened to protect the survivors from national police who threatened to take the survivors into custody. Then Márquez, the survivors, and slowly the media reported a version of events that completely contradicted the state's official story. President Lusinchi insisted that the military acted appropriately to defend democracy against a significant external threat, while others (within the context of a presidential campaign) suggested that democracy needed to be defended from internal threats through an open investigation. An investigation did happen, and the judge ordered the arrest of the survivors but not any of the soldiers responsible for the deaths. Márquez had to arrange for the survivors to take refuge, *amparo*, in Mexico until after the election in December. The survivors could not seek refuge in their own home town, Amparo, for fear of persecution from national authorities and fled to Mexico as official political refugees in December of 1988.

How the fourteen men died eventually became public. The CEJAP soldiers directly responsible for the massacre were charged with homicide, though their superiors were not. The courts cleared the survivors of any wrongdoing, and they came home in 1989. In the process, however, the state and the military used inflamed rhetoric, exacerbating the perceive differences between rich and poor. Officials implied that all rural border residents were subversives because they were poor and uneducated. General Camejo Arias actually asserted that in border areas "there is practically nobody who is not involved with some kind of crime however small it might be, out there everyone is involved" (Coronil and Skurski 2006: 96). All poor, according to Camejo Arias, were criminals. He may as well have said that all poor were barbarians.

It was in that charged context that Carlos Andres Pérez campaigned for and was elected president in 1988. A corruption scandal marked the end of his first presidency in 1979, but Venezuelans searching for a superman were willing to forgive Pérez's earlier wrongdoings. They called him the "man with energy" who would bring back the good times and save the nation from corrupt politicians. In addition to leaving office under the black cloud associated with the Amparo massacre, a nasty influence peddling scandal associated with his mistress, Blanca Ibañez, also dogged President Lusinchi in the last months of his presidency. Pérez called the International Monetary Fund the "bomb that only kills people" in reference to consequences of conditions the IMF placed on debtor nations. It was no wonder that Pérez won the election in a landslide (Coronil 1997: 375).

Privately, however, Pérez sent word to the IMF that he was willing to accept an IMF austerity program in exchange for more loans to support the government that owed 33 billion dollars to international lenders (Coronil and Skurski 2006: 130). "*El paquete*" (the package) that Pérez introduced included reductions in the number of state employees, reduced or eliminated subsidies and price controls, lowered tariffs, and ended wage regulations that benefited Venezuelan workers. Businesses began to hoard basic goods in preparation for the elimination of price controls. The hoarding resulted in shortages in nearly everything, including coins. Then in early February 1989, Pérez raised the price of domestic gasoline 30 percent. Though most Venezuelans did not own cars, they saw cheap transportation as their birthright. Raising fuel prices violated this birthright and broke the fragile thread that tied state to society. Owners of microbuses doubled their fares on February 27 to compensate for the higher gas prices. And so began five days of riots that wracked the nation (Coronil 1997: 375–376; Lopez Maya 2002).

Several hundred thousand people participated in looting and rioting in Caracas and other major cities. Residents of the poor Caracas barrios organized, took control of their own neighborhoods, then marched en masse to burn and loot over 1,000 stores in the barrios and in Caracas's commercial districts (Coronil 1997: 376). More distressing was the ferocious violence with which the government suppressed the riots. The government airlifted 10,000 troops into Caracas who, with police, fired at will on looters in the barrios and commercial districts. A suspension of constitutional guarantees protected the military and police from recriminations. Soldiers carefully protected major shopping malls and the entrances to elite neighborhoods, though rioters had not targeted those areas. The message, however, was clear. The state, through the military, meant to protect the most privileged classes, domestic and international, against any incursions from the barbaric behavior of the "primitive tribe," as Congressman Gonzalo Barrios called the protesters who lived in *ranchitos* in the *cerros*, the hillsides. Congressmen Barrios, one of the original *adecos*, referred to congressmen as "civilizing generals" (Coronil and Skurski 2006: 114).

From behind the military armed barricades and supported by elite youth armed Rambo-style, the elite universally described Venezuelans who lived in the barrios as *malandros* (thugs), drug dealers, dark-skinned foreigners, and urban guerillas. Barrio residents were all subversive, criminals, and primitive, just like all rural Venezuelans. The state adopted a similar perspective and reacted accordingly. They strafed the *ranchitos* with machine guns. Masked gunmen (suspected to be police) in civilian clothes shot people at random from motorcycles, escalating the general state of terror. Police used the opportunity of suspended legality to settle scores and follow up on personal vendettas. Security forces detained and tortured barrio community organizers, participants of student and political groups, and Jesuit priests. Only the detention of the priests and the students raised eyebrows (Coronil and Skurski 2006: 117).

The coordination and violence from both sides shocked authorities, the national elite, and the international community. In the end, between 277 and 1,000 Venezuelans died during five days of violence. The official count remains at 277, despite the discovery of mass graves and other evidence to suggest that the higher number might be more accurate (Coronil and Skurski 2006: 85). In many ways, the situation in 1989 was not all that different from the situation in the late 1700s. In both eras, the elite did not think that the masses were capable of coordinated action because, according to the elite, the masses were too primitive and too passive to organize. *Malandro*, as generalized derogatory slang, became the 20th-century version of comparable references to barbarism in the colonial era. Some lawmakers, as noted, preferred the term "barbarian" to *malandro*. Elites in both eras selectively interpreted events to fit stereotypes and minimize the importance of complex reality. Colonial elites did not think that slaves and people of color had rights, though slaves and people of color often used concepts of implied rights to structure their lives. Because the elites did not think slaves and people of color had rights, they could not comprehend how slavery and the violation of implied rights caused multi-ethnic rebellions (see Chapter 5).

Thugs, drug dealers, dark-skinned Colombian immigrants, and old leftist guerillas started the 1989 riots, according to the elite, but the protesters in 1989 were certainly not all *malandros.* On the walls the protestors wrote the phrases "*el pueblo tiene hambre*" (the people are hungry), "*basta el engaño*" (no more deception), and "*el pueblo habló*" (the people have spoken). The protesters clearly identified socioeconomic and political problems and demanded solutions. As they marched waving the Venezuelan flag, unarmed, and confronted armed military and police, the protesters sang the national anthem, "*Gloria al bravo pueblo que el yugo lanzó*" (Glory to the brave/angry people who threw off oppression). The anthem is an homage to independence-era political liberty, but the protesters used it as pointed political criticism and a call to social justice (Coronil and Skurski 2006: 110–111). The word *bravo* is important, too. It can mean either brave or angry. Protesters were definitely and defiantly both.

There were two significant differences between the late 1700s and 1989. Elite control was such in the colonial era that the elite had the ability to withstand the rebellions (with Spanish military support) and create the system of elite hegemony that lasted through much of the 20th century. The 1989 riots, the *caracazo*, marked the beginning of the end of that system. Most immediately, the riots also proved definitively that the system of *partidocracia*, pacted democracy, that the elite had created after 1959 was bankrupt. Sowing the oil did not work within the context of an economic crisis. International economic authorities controlling Venezuelan international debt had the ability to control not only economic policy but social policy as well. In that context, *partidocracia* had become no more than a paper-thin veneer covering the profound race and class divisions that had defined Venezuela from the beginning. Finally, human rights observers and the stunned international community who saw the violence in living color on their television screens asked, who was more barbaric? Were the looters more barbaric, or were agents of the state who killed anywhere between 277 and 1,000 Venezuelans during the riots more barbaric? Unless Venezuelans had cable in 1989, they did not see most of what was going on either. The major Venezuelan television networks played days of Disney movies.

Nevertheless, the Venezuelan state, supported by the elite, was not at all interested in thinking through the issues in 1989. Despite pressure from international human rights groups, the government never investigated what happened during those five days in 1989, never pursued legal action against those responsible for violent excess, and never assumed a posture of responsibility in relationships with the families of the dead or wounded (Coronil 1997). Even so, professionals, students, workers, and middle- and lower-rank members of the military began to argue that the elite used the state to the elite's advantage, sacrificing everyone else.

THE END OF *PUNTOFIJISMO* AND THE ECONOMIC CRISIS

It was not just endemic issues associated with race and poverty that undid *puntofijismo* and created the climate that led to the *caracazo*. The economic crisis also devastated the middle class that had developed in the 1960s and 1970s. *Puntofijismo* involved power sharing between the parties, AD and COPEI, and the distribution of the significant oil wealth of the nation, investing in health care and education. It was true that corruption existed, but the average Venezuelan, and even Venezuelans who lived on the margins, believed that there was the possibility for advancement through the programs provided by the state. Patricia Márquez, born in 1965, remembers that time as "the Venezuela where everything was possible," when young Venezuelans of any class could easily see going anywhere in the world to get a university degree, and people from the lower middle to upper middle class "went crazy in Miami's malls repeating 'It's so cheap, give me two'" (Márquez 2003: 199).

After the devaluation of the bolivar and steep drop in oil prices in 1986 (see Chapter 4), the middle class as well as the increasing number of poor were ready to see change in their leadership. Pérez represented hope for the middle classes who wanted the glory days to return. Márquez remembered that "One of my grandmothers simply hoped that she could travel as often as she did in the past, while the other prayed that her life savings would be secure" (Márquez 2003: 200).

Residents of Petare, a low income neighborhood in eastern Caracas, bring down the bodies of two men killed in riots on February 28, 1989. 277 people were reported killed, according to official sources. (AP/Wide World Photos)

It was not the same world, however, as we have already discussed. Politically, over the course of the 1980s and 1990s, the effects of the crisis were compounded by the fact that the crunch was not felt evenly among Venezuelans. The economic crisis actually deepened after 1989. Even as the poor grew poorer and the middle class disappeared, the rich grew richer. Between 1981 and 1997, the income share of the poorest 40 percent of the nation fell from 19.1 percent to 14.7 percent, while the income share of the wealthiest 10 percent of the nation increased from 21.8 percent to 32.8 percent (Roberts 2003). This reality of rapidly increasing poverty and stark divisions between the elite and popular classes created political unrest unseen in Venezuela for 50 years. After 50 years of being well-off, being told that their nation was wealthy and modern, what other conclusion could the average Venezuelan draw but that the rich (now getting even richer) and the politicians had stolen and mismanaged their national birthright?

All of that changed, however, in the early 1980s with the collapse of world petroleum prices. The oil boom lasted from 1973 to 1983, when it ended on what is now known in Venezuela as "Black Friday." On February 28, 1983, President Luis Herrera Campíns devalued the bolivar, signaling the beginning of the crisis. The culprit was an unprecedented series of fluctuations in international oil prices. Petroleum had a historical pattern of price consistency, with the dollar-per-barrel price remaining at a nearly constant level or edging upward. After the boom of the 1970s, however, oil began a series of sharp fluctuations that played havoc with the Venezuelan economy through the 1980s and 1990s. The effects of this rise and fall on the Venezuelan economy provided a painful reminder that Venezuela had never overcome the "permanent dilemma," their singular dependency on petroleum as a source of national income, and their failure to diversify the economy (Lombardi 2003).

After the devaluation of the bolivar and steep drop in oil prices in 1986, Venezuelans were ready to see change in their leadership. When citizens went to the polls in the presidential elections in 1988, they pinned practical wishes and impractical dreams on the candidate. Pérez was elected, and Venezuelans hoped and expected that the former president (who had presided over some of the glory days of the 1970s) would take them back to the same wealth and opportunity they had enjoyed during his first term.

It was not the same world, however, and in a surprise move, in February, only a few days after he came to power, Pérez announced that he would implement a plan called "*el paquete*" (the package), a program of economic adjustment recommended by the International Monetary Fund. Part of this program included a 30 percent increase in the cost of fuel. In response to the hike, bus drivers attempted to illegally double their fares and refuse student discounts. Students and workers, facing the increase as they tried to get to work and school that morning, were the first to begin rioting on the day of the *caracazo*.

Many see the events of the 1980s, and the *caracazo* in particular, as the first real incidence of social polarization along class lines in a generation in Venezuela, though such problems had been part of the Venezuelan story since the beginning of the colonial era. What was different about the oil years was that during those times, economic optimism had kept tension between classes at bay. Kenneth Roberts notes that during the 1970s, public opinion surveys found that the membership of both the AD and the COPEI were not divided on class lines, and that both parties were multiclass organizations that cut across class distinctions (Roberts 2003). The crisis, however, brought inequality in Venezuela into stark relief. Journalists took to calling the *caracazo* "the day the shantytowns came down from the hills" (Márquez 2003: 201), as poor Venezuelans vented their frustration.

Those who lived in the hills had much to be frustrated about. Poverty had increased dramatically in the years since the end of the oil boom. Between 1984 and 1989, the poverty rate increased from 46 to 62 percent of the population. In the same time period, the number of citizens living in extreme poverty more than doubled: from 14 to 30 percent of the population. Poverty did affect a minority of the population during the oil boom, but after the onset of the economic crisis, the majority of Venezuelans were living in economically difficult circumstances (Roberts 2003).

THE FIRST MILITARY COUP ATTEMPTS

The first significant blow to the *puntofijismo* style of rule was delivered by the economic crisis and widespread unrest generated by Black Friday and the *caracazo*. A second blow came with an attempted military coup led by Lieutenant Colonels Hugo Chávez

The chaotic architecture of the barrios, or slums, of Caracas. (iStockPhoto)

Frías and Francisco Arias Cárdenas. On February 4, 1992, Chávez and Arias led a group of military officers in an effort to take over the Venezuelan government. The group, calling itself the Movimiento Revolucionario Boliviariano (Bolivarian Revolutionary Movement) or MBR, billed itself as an anticorruption movement that would call a constitutional assembly after taking power in order to reconstruct Venezuelan government in a way that would make it more responsive to the people's needs. The military effort achieved almost all of its objectives, but failed to take President Pérez captive, and so ultimately failed in its bid to take power. The coup plotters defeat, however, was not without political gain. When it became clear that the takeover was to fail, Chávez went on national television and made an appeal for the revolutionary troops to surrender. He accepted sole responsibility for the defeat, impressing Venezuelans who were used to politicians who would do anything but accept responsibility.

Chávez and the coup failed, and he and many of the plotters were jailed, but the movement gained considerable recognition and support among people in the nation. Many citizens, feeling that government had become unresponsive to the dire situation of the people, were glad to see someone take bold action. As one university professor noted to Patricia Márquez, "People liked the coup attempt. Let's be clear about that. The fact that somebody wanted to overthrow a government through a coup was a new thing for most Venezuelans. The truth is that the largest percentage of our population is very young . . . For an eighteen-year-old it is sort

Two soldiers of the Venezuelan national guard, a unit loyal to President Carlos Andrés Pérez, open fire February 4, 1992 against military rebels hidden in the building near the air force base of La Carlota, which was captured by rebels in a coup attempt. (AP/Wide World Photos)

of cool that a man takes up arms and tries to change the government" (Márquez 2003: 201). We should also note that someone who was 18 in 1992 grew up in an era of increasing instability conditioned by parental memories of better times. The continuing popularity of the idea of a coup can be seen in the second, also unsuccessful, attempt that followed in November of the same year. People were definitely ready for change.

1998 PRESIDENTIAL ELECTIONS

The national elite were not ready. They decided that national stability depended on removing Pérez from office. Congress impeached him on corruption charges laced with adultery accusations in May, 1993. The parties, COPEI and AD, carefully selected historian Rafael Velasquez as interim president before the election of Rafael Caldera. Caldera was one of the few living politicians who combined roots in the early days of democracy in the 1940s with a squeaky clean personal reputation. He was old, people noted, but at least he was honest and had never cheated on his wife. Caldera also appeared to understand the realities of the Venezuelan people. In an interview to a Venezuelan newspaper, when talking about the coup attempts, Caldera noted "It is difficult to ask the people to burn for freedom and democracy while they think freedom and democracy are not able to feed them and impede the exorbitant increase in the cost of subsistence; when it has not been able to deal effectively with the blight of corruption" (Hellinger 2003: 32). It is perhaps for this reason that Caldera released the attempted coup plotters, as a signal that he understood the desire for change, though he did not agree with the methods they used.

Caldera did not, however, have an answer to the growing economic crisis. As mentioned before, the number of citizens living in poverty continued to grow in advance of the 1998 elections, and Hugo Chávez Frías, the charismatic leader of the attempted overthrow, was now free to run for president. For his campaign, Daniel Hellinger remembers that Chávez, and the MBR, drew upon the great history of Venezuelan caudillos, or strongmen; the liberator Simón Bolívar, Bolívar's teacher and philosopher Simón Rodríguez, and the lesser-known caudillo Ezequiel Zamora, a Liberal reformer and military leader assassinated in 1860, allegedly by his own people. The singer Alí Primera had built a mythic reputation around Zamora and his life on the Barinas plains. Chávez appropriated this myth and the music, using the anti-elite, anti-oligarchic rhetoric of both Zamora and Primera in his speeches and rallies.

Chávez was also aided in the fact that unlike the previous President Caldera, or his opponents-to-be in the coming presidential race, he was not highly educated, and he was not of the racial elite. Nor was he of the national elite. From the state of Barinas in the llanos, Chávez's parents were both school teachers. He enlisted in the military and enrolled in the Venezuelan Academy of Military Sciences after high school, a common path for young men from the lower middle class who wanted higher education but who could not afford one otherwise. He played baseball and softball on local teams, reaching the Venezuelan National Baseball Championship with the Criollitos de Venezuela. He portrayed himself truly as a "man of the people" in 1998 because he *was* a "man of the people." He shared the lower middle class background that a few Venezuelans still had and many more aspired to. He was a baseball nut like most Venezuelans. He looked like most Venezuelans. He used common Venezuelan slang, and avoided the flowery political rhetoric most politicians used. Chávez spoke to Venezuelans in language they understood about topics near and dear to their hearts. It was no wonder people seemed more willing to believe Chávez's promises that he would clean up corruption in government and the judiciary and completely change the way government worked. Indeed one of Chávez's main campaign promises was to revive his call for a constituent assembly and write a new constitution.

Many who were in Venezuela during the second coup attempt in November 1992, during the election campaigns, and in 1999 during the campaigns for the constituent assembly remember that what was most remarkable about those years was a sense of hope and optimism that permeated society. Venezuelans finally felt that there would be real change that would benefit the masses. No more unfulfilled promises. No more *adeco* or *copeyano* pet projects designed to buy votes in the next election. Venezuelans expected real change from Chávez, systematic and profound. People referred to Chávez with affection as if they knew him personally. Little old ladies called him *hijo* (son), and placed pictures of him on home altars, asking the appropriate local virgins and the popular, yet uncannonized, José Gregorio Hernández to protect him (see Chapter 5).

By presenting himself as the candidate for the masses, the outsider who was ready to shake up the oligarchy and fight for the people, Chávez stood in contrast to the other eventual candidates in the presidential race: former Miss Universe Irene Saez and businessman Henrique Salas Römer. Both Saez and Salas Römer were seen to represent the establishment, the neoliberal policies that Chávez railed against, and the elite who kept gaining ground even as the poor lost it. Saez was the Mayor of Chacao, one of the wealthiest municipalities in the Caracas metropolitan area. Salas Römer was the governor of Carabobo State. In addition, in the final days before the election, in a move that probably did more harm than good for the Carabobo governor, the two *puntofijista* parties (COPEI and AD) endorsed Salas Römer. In the end, voters chose the outsider by a significant majority of 56 percent (Hellinger 2003).

NEW PRESIDENT, NEW CONSTITUTION, MEGAELECTIONS

Chávez won the presidency in 1998, but most of what he hoped to accomplish in his first term would be blocked by the existing congress who were mostly still COPEI and AD and unlikely to go along with his plans for massive change. Chávez, therefore, moved quickly to call a popular vote for an elected assembly that would write the new document. Though Chávez favored a slate of candidates for election to the assembly, he did not limit who could participate in the elections. All sorts of people of all sorts of political stripes ran for constituent assembly: all colors, all socioeconomic classes. And though AD and COPEI ran candidates, the construction of the ballot itself harmed their chances. For the first time in many elections, the ballot was in black and white, no colors associated with old parties, only candidate names and numbers. Chávez's movement handed out cards with the ballot numbers of candidates associated with the movement to help voters. By the time the balloting was over, Chávez's movement controlled 121 of the 131 seats in the constitutional assembly.

After winning another vote for approval of the new "Bolivarian" constitution, Chávez then called for "megaelections" in July of 2001. Elections were needed to fill the seats in the new unicameral legislature provided for in the constitution. These elections were to be megaelections, however. All elected officials at the state and national level were required to stand for reelection. This was an opportunity to totally clean house of the Venezuelan political establishment, and this is in fact what happened. In July of 2001, Chávez's party won large majorities in the new legislature, and Chávez himself won the presidency again by a margin of 21 percentage points (Hellinger 2003). After the megaelections, the opposition found itself in complete disarray.

After the elections for the Constitutional Assembly in 1999, the old parties, AD and COPEI, fell apart. They no longer had the ability or the legitimacy in the eyes of the broader public to act as political parties. Part of the opposition consisted of the old political elite associated with the old parties. Also, part of the opposition was the leadership of the large labor union, the CTV, because of its association with the old parties, and FEDECAMARAS, the national chamber of commerce organization. Before the general strike in 2002–2003, the upper management and engineers of PDVSA also formed part of the opposition.

Over time, other groups became associated with the opposition for reasons that are a bit harder to divine. The leader of MAS (Movimiento al Socialismo), Teodoro Petkoff, one of the most dedicated leftists in Venezuela, gravitated toward the opposition in 1998, and his party followed. Indeed, despite some of the conservative elite's charges against Chávez that he was creating a Cuban-style communist state, many traditional leftist leaders and organizers found Chávez and his policies too centrist and joined the opposition. Former Vice President Luis Miquilena split with Chávez in 2001 only after appointing judges to the TSJ (Supreme Court) loyal to Miquilena but not necessarily loyal to the constitution (Grandin 2007). Numerous academics and intellectuals became associated with the opposition over time because of concern over the potential for human rights abuses they saw in new laws and because of Chávez's growing friendship with Fidel Castro, not always a friend to intellectuals. Many also saw corruption and cronyism in the Chávez administration that was not much different from administrations that had come before. No matter what, the opposition, as it is loosely referred to, was not and is not a homogenous and organized movement, because its participants come to it with such different perspectives and agendas. The diverse nature of the opposition has made it difficult to successfully challenge Chávez when it counts most, on election day.

We also must note that the opposition's rhetoric was frequently overtly racist. The response to the election of Hugo Chávez as president in 1998 began to show Venezuelans of all shades the profound racial and class divisions that marked the country, more so even than the *caracazo* had in 1989. Candidates who opposed Chávez and their supporters openly used racist language, calling Chávez a monkey, portraying him in cartoons with monkeylike lips and nose, a Neanderthal heavy brow. One could google "Mico Mandante" (Commander Monkey) and a host of Web sites appeared with derogatory images and speech deriding not only Chávez in racial terms but also those who followed him. Even the national newspapers, *El Universal* or *El Nacional*, from 1998 to the present, do not refrain from using racialized language and imagery in their discussion of Chávez. *Tal Cual*, begun by MAS founder, Teodoro Petkoff, began to use racial language and imagery for Chávez when Petkoff distanced himself from Chávez and became part of the opposition. *Tal Cual* cartoonists drew Chávez with whiteface and thick lips. The real problem, however, was that when Chávez's political opposition and elite-owned media outlets derided Chávez in those terms, they also derided Chávez supporters who shared Chávez's racial and class background. Further polarization was the consequence of racial and class-based attacks.

There is one other group that we must try to define, the "*ni-nis*," or "*ni uno ni el otro*" (not one or the other). *Ni-nis* are individuals who recognized that Venezuela had to change and who appreciate the structural changes Chávez has attempted. *Ni-nis* often do not like the way Chávez attempts to force change, however. Nor do they care for his strident rhetoric that may add fuel to the opposition's fire. In later years, they have become concerned about laws that might impinge on freedom of expression, a crucial topic, as many of the *ni-nis* are academics. *Ni-nis* were often critical of the opposition because they do not see that the other side understands the realities that brought Chávez to power and feel that they use language and imagery that widens racial and class breaches. *Ni-nis* condemn the opposition for its support of the failed coup in April 2002 and the general strike of 2002–2003. It may well be that the number of people who consider themselves *ni-nis* has grown over time, but exactly how many there are is hard to say. In Venezuela's charged political context, most definitely in Caracas, those who are not 100 percent Chavista or 100 percent opposition often do not feel comfortable expressing opinions publicly.

NEW POLICIES, NEW PROJECTS

With a new constitution and new representatives in place, it was time for the new government to begin work on some of its campaign promises. One of the first efforts of the Chávez administration was Plan Bolívar 200, a project that used the military to attack social problems like sanitation, health care, public transportation, and housing. The program used the organizational power and manpower of the Venezuelan military to coordinate building and clean-up projects across the nation and man health care clinics. Under the plan, Venezuelan soldiers built roads and schools. They vaccinated thousands of Venezuelans against preventable diseases. In this way, the project delivered immediate, short-term relief to many and demonstrated how the military could help the people. There was criticism of the program, however, as the military itself questioned its new role in the nation, and as problems arose in who would direct the projects.

In 2000, Chávez also garnered both praise and criticism for his foreign policy. Chávez began to build a critique of Western political and economic policies that favored developed nations at the expense, he argued, of developing nations. Immediately, that meant Chávez significantly changed the tenor of Venezuela's relationship with the United States, one of the world's most important developed nations. The era of *puntofijismo* had been significantly pro-Washington, and ties between the two nations had been cordial and cooperative. The Chávez administration would be less so. In his first years in office, Chávez refused to cooperate with the U.S. drug war in Colombia, maintaining what many saw as dangerously close ties with left-wing guerillas in that nation. Chávez also refused to endorse the resolution that would have tied participation in a hemispheric free-trade zone to electoral democracy, and even went so far as to place conditions on aid from the United States after devastating floods and mudslides hit the northern coastal region in 2000. Chávez said that Venezuela would be grateful to receive the material aid, but that Venezuelans would administer the aid, not U.S. officials. That was a position that won praise even among some opposition in Venezuela and sympathetic observers throughout Latin America. The United States had dominated relationships in Latin America since the Spanish-American-Cuban War in 1898, and certainly since the Roosevelt Corollary discussed in Chapter 2. Neoliberal economic policies in the late 20th century had further undercut Latin American nations' sovereignty. What Chávez tried to do was create a Venezuelan-led Latin American independence in foreign policy and economic matters. In the next few years, several Latin American presidents endorsed his approach, to greater or lesser degrees.

Chávez's stance on cooperation with the United States is related to his following of historical Latin American patriots. Like Simón Bolívar, or the 19th-century Cuban leader José Martí, Chávez admired the democratic tradition in the United States, the one that embraces social mobility and social equality, but he opposed Venezuela's use as a tool in Washington's desire to build a hemispheric defense. He also resisted the economic model in which nations like Venezuela provide raw materials to developed nations, often at the expense of more thorough economic development. Chávez and other leaders of developing nations also questioned the value of global economic treaties like NAFTA (North American Free Trade Agreement) in which Latin American nations become junior partners, not full partners, in the arrangements that benefit North American businesses more than Latin American nations. Rather, like Bolívar, Chávez's vision was of a united Latin America that could compete economically with the developed world.

Chávez did not only want to build coalitions with Latin American nations. He wanted to construct an economic coalition of developing nations from around the world. Evidence of Chávez's desire to build just such a coalition came in September of 2000 when Venezuela hosted the Second Summit of Heads of States and Governments of the Member Countries of OPEC in Caracas. In the declaration that was written at that summit, the heads of state agreed that among their key commitments were to (1) lead the entire underdeveloped world and (2) seek substantial reduction of the developing countries' debt and to demand "just and equitable treatment of oil in the world energy market" (Hellinger 2003: 46). These declarations give an indication of the stance that Chávez, with the other leaders, took—an us-against-them vision in opposition to the developed nations, particularly the United States. The leader began to assert a more active role in shaping global economic policy as opposed to passively accepting neoliberal reforms. The leaders of developing nations demanded a more equitable distribution of global income and recognition that the wealth of developed nations depends on the resources, material and human, of developing nations. It was a position that even some members of the opposition appreciated in the early years. That said, Chávez's rhetoric became more strident in later years. He publicly culti- vated relationships with leaders who developed nations found dangerous (Fidel Cas- tro in Cuba, Mahmoud Ahmadinejad in Iran) and the tone of public debate shifted away from recasting international relationships between developed and developing nations to an us-against-them approach. Bush Administration policies toward Latin America generally, and Venezuela specifically, contributed to the us-against-them foreign policy, according to Latin American scholars (Clement 2007).

Another example of Chávez's independent path and explicit anti-imperialist rhet- oric can be seen in his 2005 decision to expel New Tribes Mission missionaries from the southern regions of the country. As we will discuss in Chapter 5, scholars have long worried about cultural imperialism and late 20th-century missionary efforts in Latin America. Those concerns also applied to New Tribes activities in Venezuela.

Venezuela's President Hugo Chávez, right, and Iranian President Mahmoud Ahmadinejad, hug each other after Chávez was awarded the 1st grade order of the Islamic Republic of Iran during a ceremony at Tehran university in Tehran, Iran, in this 2006 photo. (AP/Wide World Photos)

Be that as it may, scholar Nicolas Kozloff places the conflict between Chávez and New Tribes in the context of the larger war of words between Chávez and U.S. televangelist Pat Robertson (Kozloff 2005a). In 2005, Robertson called Venezuela a "launching pad for Muslim extremism" and suggested on his show, *The 700 Club*, "We have the ability to take him out, and I think the time has come that we exercise that ability" (Buncombe 2005). Venezuelan officials suggested there were close ties between New Tribes and the Robertson ministry and that missions engaged in imperialist espionage. The expulsion speech also connected New Tribes Mission to imperialism. Chávez charged that New Tribes represented a "true imperialist invasion" (Kozloff 2005b).

This independent foreign policy, so different from the *puntofijismo* years has been extremely controversial in Venezuela. For the traditional Venezuelan elite, rejecting the United States and the developed world is a rejection of the modern, cosmopolitan vision of Venezuela that influential individuals in the nation have pursued for centuries in an effort to move the country forward. This independent foreign policy stand, therefore, strengthens Chávez's opponents' characterization of him as uneducated and vulgar. For Chávez's supporters in the lower classes, however, standing up to the United States and organizations such as the IMF strengthens his credentials as the strong caudillo, independent and a man of the people.

The most potentially dangerous aspect of Chávez's foreign policy has to do with relationships with its neighbor, Colombia. Relations with Colombia have rarely been pleasant. The two countries sparred numerous times in the 19th and the 20th century over the location of the boundary that divides the nations. In the 20th century, drugs and guerrillas further complicated relationships. Colombia regularly accuses Venezuela of supporting the FARC (Fuerzas Armadas Revolucionarias de Colombia), a left-leaning Colombian guerrilla organization associated with both drug running and kidnapping. Some in the United States, including Senator Richard Lugar of Indiana, suggest that Chávez is turning Venezuela into a narcostate. In 2008, Colombia raided into Ecuadoran territory and killed a FARC guerilla leader. Nations throughout Latin America condemned the raid as a violation of Ecuadoran sovereignty. As the war of words between Colombia, Ecuador, and Venezuela escalated, both Colombia and Venezuela moved troops and weapons toward their common border. Periodic troop buildups have been common since then, increasing fear among some of a war with an extremely well-armed Colombia (Forero 2009c).

THE 48-HOUR COUP OR THE CHAMBER OF COMMERCE COUP

The divide that had grown within the nation between pro-Chávez and anti-Chávez factions came to a head in April 2002. The opposition was still deeply divided and weakly represented in the National Assembly but had significant control of the major news media. As a result, most of the significant debate and argument leading up to the April 2002 coup took place on the Venezuelan airwaves. In December of 2001, the opposition, with the help of the media, set the stage by promoting and encouraging, first, a strike of the state's oil workers (in protest of Chávez's oil policies) and then, second, a general strike, both of which effectively brought the nation and the economy to a standstill. Tensions escalated in the early months of 2002. The opposition called another general strike for April 9, 2002 leading up to the coup on April 11.

Members of the opposition owned all the major newspaper and television outlets, with the exception of the state-owned radio and television stations. RCTV, Venevisión, and Globovisión, on television, were all significantly anti-Chávez, with RCTV being described, in particular as "the behind-the-scenes power broker for the opposition" ("An Opposition" 2007). During the first months of 2002, the opposition used the media, especially RCTV, to organize rallies and protest marches in the affluent eastern sections of the capital. The stations suspended regular programming in the days before the coup and broadcast statements that were openly anti-Chávez. Commentators and roundtables condemned all things Chávez, including Chávez supporters. So-called public service announcements urged Chávez to leave office, and exhorted the opposition to take to the streets to encourage him to do so.

Some private media broadcasters later admitted that their activities and inflammatory language, much of it racial, was unprofessional (Kozloff 2005a). The broadcasters, however, could neither take back the words nor undo the programming choices they had made during the coup. Cable viewers could see the color of the class divide as they watched upper-middle-class and elite (primarily light-skinned) members of the opposition protest in the Altamira Plaza in the eastern part of Caracas, while lower-middle-class and poor Chavista supporters (primarily people of color) protested in the western parts of the city. Venevisión, RCTV, Globovisión, and Televen did not show images of those protests. They ran *telenovela* reruns.

Chávez also used (and continues to use) media to deliver political, social, and economic messages. Through the state-owned VTV and a weekly radio program called ¡*Aló Presidente*! (Hello President!) Chávez marshaled his significant skills in communication and charisma to talk to his supporters. Chávez chatted with the people about government and literature, and callers phoned in with specific health or work problems that many times they blamed on the old regime. As members of the opposition rallied in the richer districts of Caracas in the months before the coup, Chávez talked to his supporters. They, in turn, held their own demonstrations in the poorer neighborhoods on the west side of the city.

In early April, Chávez attempted to fire the executive directors of the state oil company PDVSA as part of the administration's struggle to control oil policy. The oil executives, as members of the economic elite, were Chávez opponents, and were backed by the main business confederation, FEDECAMARAS, roughly equivalent to the national Chamber of Commerce. In light of these developments, PDVSA and FEDECAMARAS called for a mass demonstration in front of PDVSA headquarters, located closer to the more affluent neighborhoods in the eastern part of the city. The private Venezuelan media joined the organizational effort by advertising the plan every 10 minutes in their programming. The crowd of mostly middle-class opposition met at the PDVSA headquarters and then moved toward the presidential palace in the city center when protest organizers urged them to kick Chávez out.

In the meantime, a large crowd of Chávez supporters had come together in support of the president around the presidential palace in opposition to the PDVSA protest. Community media played a role in gathering them, as had cell phone text messaging. When the two groups met, violence broke out. Accounts vary and there is controversy yet as to who was ultimately responsible, but what is known is that gunfire was exchanged and demonstrators died on both sides.

During the chaos, on April 11, military commanders entered the presidential palace and detained Chávez. Word was prematurely released that he had resigned and he was taken out of the country. The state-owned television station VTV was taken off the air, leaving only the opposition-controlled media outlets to filter information about the coup. Despite the tightly controlled media spin, however, information about the coup made its way into the poor barrios on the western side of the city, primarily via low bandwidth community radio and television stations and cell phones. Demonstrators began to make their way to the presidential palace to protest the illegal takeover. Within hours, thousands of citizens surrounded the palace, demanding the return of the president, though the opposition media outlets refused to show the protests or any information regarding popular support for Chávez.

In the early morning hours of April 12, 2002, the coup plotters, a group of business elites, took control of the presidential palace and placed FEDECAMARAS leader Pedro Carmona in the presidency and immediately suspended the constitution, the National Assembly, and the TSJ. The United States immediately recognized Carmona. No Latin American nation recognized the new government, and the coup drew condemnation from the Organization of American States.

Counterpressures from multiple sources doomed the new, unconstitutional government. International political pressure was intense, with all of Venezuela's neighbors calling the coup a coup. In addition, some of the original supporters of the overthrow within Venezuela withdrew support when the new government announced that it would suspend the constitution. In particular, it became clear that while some of the military had been behind the coup, there was still a pro-Chávez contingent in the military, and a third segment of the armed forces that was not necessarily pro-Chávez but was certainly pro-constitution and was unwilling to support an illegal presidency. Finally, while the opposition media refused to acknowledge the massive protests demanding the return of the democratically elected president, the protests continued to grow. Indeed, the mass uprising was as much a defense of the constitution and democracy as it was in support of Chávez, but the effect was the same. By April 16, Carmona was forced to resign and Chávez returned.

The opposition remained determined to oust Chávez. Its next move proved even more devastating to the nation, and, ironically, to the opposition. On December 2, 2002, 40 groups associated with the opposition and led primarily by the CTV and PDVSA executives called for another general strike. The strike lasted for two months. The total shut down of PDVSA, other oil companies, oil-associated industries, and sympathetic businesses forced oil production to plummet from 3.2 million barrels a day to 40,000 barrels a day ("Chávez's Battle" 2003). Striking workers damaged or destroyed heavy production equipment and sabotaged computers before they left their jobs, making it difficult for new oil workers to restart the industry. The aluminum and steel industries shut down because of gas shortages. In the worst of the strike, some parts of the country began to suffer food shortages, because there was not enough gas for transportation purposes. Whereas Caracas was the only part of the nation that felt directly the April 11, 2002 coup attempt, everyone in the nation suffered the consequences of the general strike in one way or another.

Unemployment and further polarization were two direct consequences of the strike. Some 18,000 to 30,000 (figures vary) PDVSA employees lost their jobs as a result of the strike. Many more Venezuelans who worked for non-PDVSA oil companies lost their jobs when their companies either joined the strike or closed because the strike forced them out of business. Some lost their jobs when they participated in mass resignation rallies with hundreds resigning their positions at a time, chanting anti-Chávez slogans, shouting that they would not submit to Chávez the tyrant as he made Venezuela into another Cuba. Others lost their jobs when Chávez fired them for being sympathetic with the strike or for signing opposition-circulated anti-Chávez petitions. The opposition claimed that 3.7 million Venezuelans signed the petitions before the end of the strike (Bustamante 2003). Some of those signatures were not voluntary. PDVSA supervisors or supervisors in oil associated industries called meetings during the strike to inform workers about events. Workers at those meetings signed roll sheets and added their *cedula* (social security) numbers. Some of those roll sheets ended up on the opposition's petitions. An unknown number of Venezuelans, some who resigned from PDVSA, some who voluntarily signed petitions, some who involuntarily signed petitions, ended up on a blacklist called the Maisanta List ("Venezuela's Oil Blacklist" 2007). Some on the Maisanta List could not find work in any oil-related industry for years after the general strike. Others find it difficult to keep any employment in the formal economy (and certainly not oil related), as their employers feel obligated to let them go when they find out employees are on the list. As a result, some of Venezuela's most skilled engineers have either left the country or have resorted to work in the informal economy, like taxi driving.

More than the elections or the coup, the general strike polarized the nation and divided friends and families. Those who supported the strike insisted that they did so to defend the nation, while their mothers argued that politics did not feed families. Worse was the damage to PDVSA's image in the eyes of the general public. The opposition insisted that PDVSA knew best how to manage the nation's oil, even if that meant shutting off supplies of the national patrimony. Throughout the strike, Chávez insisted that the oil belonged to the nation, not PDVSA, echoing the sentiments of the general public. So even though the nation suffered during the strike, Chávez came out of the crisis stronger, with the ability to shape oil policy according to his will and hire new PDVSA employees that would be loyal to him. The opposition, in contrast, lost credibility. Many perceived that the opposition, through PDVSA, had used the nation's patrimony as a weapon against the Venezuelan population. Finally, because of Chávez's increased (but not total) control over the company, the state was able to redirect more oil income into national social projects. Indeed, much of the spending on major social projects dates to the period after the strike, not before.

THE RECALL

Having failed in an attempt to remove Chávez by extralegal means, the opposition turned to a provision in the Bolivarian Constitution that provided for a recall referendum of any elected official halfway through his or her term. This provision is considered one of the key elements of the constitution; the possibility of recalling elected officials gives citizens the ability to exercise power over their representatives in a way that they did not have in the days before the new constitution. The provision was included with the idea that it would encourage elected officials to communicate more with their constituents and respond to citizens' needs more effectively.

Opponents to Chávez grabbed onto the idea of a recall vote after the failure of the general strike, the coup, and other forms of civil disobedience. The process of coming to terms for the process of the referendum, however, was difficult. In May of 2003, the opposition succeeded in getting the government to agree to the idea of a referendum. Under the constitution, however, in order for the recall referendum to proceed, the opposition needed to collect petitions with signatures from more than 20 percent of registered voters, a number which in this case equaled 2,451,821 (Hellinger 2007). The opposition gathered over 2.5 million signatures in November of 2003 and submitted them to the National Electoral Council.

The CNE only accepted 1,900,000 of the signatures as valid. More than 800,000 of the signatures seemed to have been filled out on pages where one person had filled out the entire page except for the signature. (Each petition needed to include name, last

Opposition members display Venezuela currency (bolivar) to employees of PDVSA during a rally to demand a referendum on ending the presidency of Hugo Chávez in Caracas. (AP/Wide World Photos)

name, ID number, date of birth, voter ID number, original signature by hand, and digital fingerprint.) It was not technically illegal to fill out other parts of the form for a voter, but the electoral board's ruling to disallow the forms that had been prefilled out (all but the signature) found that it was intimidating to be presented with a form with all your vital information already on it, just awaiting a signature.

The opposition, who had organized the recall drive, accused the CNE of being a pawn of the Chávez government, and interpreting the rules too broadly. As a result, they took their case to the courts, where it eventually landed in the highly controversial TSJ. The two chambers of the court issued conflicting rulings, sending the matter to the full court. Eventually, a compromise was reached, once again referring to the constitution, which allowed for voters to verify or withdraw signatures. On May 28–30, voters were allowed to either withdraw or confirm their contested signatures. In the end, only 74,112 people withdrew their signatures, and the opposition was able to submit a full petition.

The next step, of course, was for the opposition to win a recall vote against the president. In accordance with the constitution, opponents needed to win more "yes" ("yes we want to recall him") votes than Chávez had won in his presidential election in July of 2000. In order to do this, they needed 3,757,773 signatures, a number significantly greater than the 2.5 million signatures they had collected for the recall petition (Hellinger 2007) In addition, the voters needed to cast more "yes" votes than "no" votes in order for the recall to be successful.

The opposition was mobilized, but so was Chávez. Drawing heavily on the barrios where his support was greatest, Chávez organized the Comando Maisanta, named for his great-grandfather, a nationalist guerilla fighter. The idea was that the neighborhoods would form small guerilla-style organizations (10 members each) to mobilize people for the "no" vote. The members would go door-to-door, speaking with people, encouraging citizens who had never registered to vote to sign up and mobilizing the poorer neighborhoods.

The effort was hugely successful. Hundreds of thousands of Venezuelans, mostly from lower-class neighborhoods or from immigrant families, were persuaded to register for identity cards and to vote. Researcher Sujatha Fernandes, observing the effort from the barrios during that time states, "Rather than Chávez's charisma, his subsidized social programs or the ineptitude of the opposition, the decisive factor in Chávez's ultimate victory was the mobilizing role played by local barrio organizations" (Fernandes 2007b: 44). In the end, on August 15, 2004, almost 10 million Venezuelans voted, 3 million more than in the July 2000 election, and 70 percent of the eligible population (Hellinger 2007). Venezuelans living abroad drove and flew to embassies and consulates to vote. In Venezuela, some waited up to eight hours. The opposition received more the required 3.7 million votes, but "no" votes still outnumbered "yes" votes. Chávez won 59 percent of the vote with 5.8 million votes (Carter Center 2005).

In the wake of the failed recall referendum, the opposition had little choice but to retreat and try to regroup in advance of the presidential elections set for December of 2006. Clear organization and cohesion still failed to materialize within the group of those opposed to Chávez, but what his adversaries seemed to have learned was the electoral power of the poorer economic classes. A coalition of anti-Chavistas put up Manuel Rosales as their candidate. One of his key campaign promises was "*mi negra*" (my little black one) a debit card tied directly to the state's oil wealth, which would have provided cash transfers to the poor. This proposal, which many believe would have been impossible in the pre-Chávez years, recognized that the pro-Chávez subaltern class expected direct action and involvement from their government. The ploy was unsuccessful, however, and Chávez won reelection again with a significant majority of 62 percent.

"*Mi negra*" was troubling for reasons other than the apparent pandering. *Mi negra* or *mi negro* are common terms of endearment with roots deep in Venezuela's racial past. *La negra* was the elite man's lover, the woman of color or slave whom he could never marry but kept on the side, sometimes with true affection. Women who were *la negra* must have felt combinations of shame, exploitation, privilege, and affection. Nothing was simple when you were *la negra*. Surely when Rosales named the debit card "*mi negra*" he implied the term of affection. In this case, Rosales was conjuring an affectionate state that cared for its most vulnerable population. There is no doubt, however, that *las negras* of old were society's most vulnerable members, poor women of color, just as poverty has color today. The suggestion that every citizen would be allowed to have their own chance to exploit the less fortunate must have been at best troubling, at worst highly offensive to many.

La negra occupies an ambivalent place in Venezuela's historical consciousness, simultaneously misused, adored, despised, but somehow empowered. That may well be the position people of color occupy in contemporary Venezuela. Manuel Rosales blurred the line between class and race in ways he did not intend.

DECISIONS OF THE TSJ

Those who opposed the changes to the Supreme Tribunal made in 2004 point to a series of decisions by the court in subsequent years as proof that the court has been packed with Chávez supporters. One example frequently cited is the court's 2008 decision to uphold a ban on 270 opposition candidates in the state and municipal elections of that year. The banned list had been submitted by Venezuela's comptroller general, an appointee of the pro-Chávez National Assembly. The comptroller contended that the candidates were ineligible to run for office because of accusations of corruption. He contended that his office had the right to disqualify candidates on suspicion of those charges, even if the candidates were never convicted.

Many of the accused candidates argued the disqualification under the 1999 constitution, which protects the political rights of all citizens unless they have been convicted of a crime. The TSJ, however, upheld the comptroller's ruling. The court's decision held that the disqualification did not remove all the political rights of the citizens, but only the right of running for office.

THE LESSON OF SOCIAL POLARIZATION

In the middle years of the first decade of the century, it appeared that Venezuela might once again be "exceptional" for the amount of influence that social class played in its democratic politics (Roberts 2003). In other Latin American nations, political parties have managed to draw their members from a cross section of economic classes. Rarely, if ever, had the distance between social classes evidenced in the riots of the *caracazo* been so influential in Latin American electoral politics. In Venezuela, after the collapse of *puntofijismo* and the economic crisis, Chávez moved to exploit the breach between social classes.

Whether the Venezuelan case was truly "exceptional" or not, the distance between the elite economic and political classes and the poor and underprivileged in Venezuela had never had a higher profile. Chávez won the presidency, in large part by appealing directly to the marginalized people who felt they had been left out of, or cheated out of, the benefits of Venezuela's oil wealth and prosperity. Indeed, one of Chávez's great talents is his ability to talk to the poor majority, who he calls "*el soberano*" (the sovereign) in a voice that includes them and makes them feel part of government. A large part of Chávez's appeal is that he is a great communicator. It was Chávez's ability to connect with the people that led the economic and political elite to try to limit his media access during the early years of his presidency, relegating him to the state-owned (and poorly rated) television and radio stations.

It is not just his ability with words that makes Chávez effective, however; it is also his message. When Chávez speaks, he constantly emphasizes the interests of the lower classes over those of other classes and sectors, such as business. Chávez projects what seems to be a true and genuine desire to put the people first. As his chief of staff for his 1998 campaign put it, Chávez's message is not artificially created by public relations experts but "self-constructed" (Hellinger 2006: 10). This message, designed for the marginalized, is wholeheartedly embraced by those left out of the benefits of Venezuela's oil wealth and struggling in the new economy. As Alejandro Moreno, a priest who works in the poor Caracas neighborhoods, sees it, "What is important is not what he speaks but what speaks inside him. In him speaks the convivial relations of popular Venezuela, of a convivial man . . . one elderly woman expressed it very well: 'For me, it's like my own son is president'" (Moreno 1998: 5).

The people in the hillside barrios may have loved the president for speaking to them directly. The upper classes, however, hated it. The elite were confused and offended by being left out of the country's main avenue of political discourse. Used to being the central concern of government and its programs, business and other sectors chafe at the idea of being left out of the conversation and the political process. The charges against Chávez that he exacerbated the social divisions in the nation by playing to the poor and demonizing the rich came from these feelings of marginalization in sectors that are more used to a place at the table, or perhaps even owning the table, the plates, the silverware, and the food served.

It is true that Chávez used his considerable charisma and communication skills to tap into the resentment of the people toward the elite. By constantly referring back to the strongmen of independence—Bolívar, Rodríguez, and Zamora—Chávez

CHOLERA IN THE DELTA

The fact that indigenous Venezuelans needed a strong advocate became pain-fully apparent when a cholera outbreak killed 500 people, mostly Warao Indians, in Delta Amacuro State, the Orinoco Delta, and in the far east of Venezuela in the early 1990s. Even after the epidemic, the health conditions were worse in Delta Amacuro than in nearly any other state in the nation. Medical anthropologist Charles Briggs noted in 2001 that half of all children in the region died before puberty, and 60 percent of the total population had tuberculosis, proof of a public health and infrastructure crisis more profound than any transitory epidemic (Briggs 2001).

A vicious cycle of victim blaming made the cholera crisis worse. Public health officials blamed the epidemic on Warao cultural practices. They talked about where the Warao ate, what the Warao ate, where the Warao defecated, and flies. Officials concluded that the Warao's ignorance, backwardness, and unsanitary living conditions caused the outbreak. Some critics interpreted the modern state's chronic lack of investment in public health and education in the delta and other areas with large indigenous populations as a form of institu-tionalized racism that, at best, contradicted state and elite claims that racism was not a problem in Venezuela (Briggs 2001).

reminded the people of what Daniel Hellinger calls the "historical myth associating Venezuelan national identity with a popular, egalitarian struggle for freedom against a perfidious oligarchy" (Hellinger 2006: 11). By doing this, Chávez continues to build his credentials as the "people's president," one in a great line of defenders of the citizens, but risks continuing to alienate sectors of the elite business and political classes.

Two groups in particular, Afrovenezuelans and indigenous peoples, saw in the Chávez era an avenue to social and political participation that they had not yet seen in Venezuelan history. Early in his campaign in 1998, Chávez publicly acknowledged the national debt to the indigenous population and promised to defend indigenous rights (Chávez Frías 1998). The Constitutional Assembly began to pay that debt in the 1999 Bolivarian Constitution. The constitution recognized the existence and rights of the indigenous peoples of Venezuela. Specifically, the constitution recog-nized indigenous languages as respected official languages. In addition, the constitu-tion recognized indigenous land rights as collective, inalienable, and nontransferable. Three seats in the congress now must be held by indigenous Venezuelans. But there are differences between rights in theory and rights in reality. Pressure to exploit subsoil resources in delicate ecosystems where many of the remaining indigenous Venezuelans live threatens culture, livelihood, and survival. Indigenous Venezuelans suffer from malnutrition, live in poor housing conditions, and do not have adequate access to public health facilities or education. Economic marginalization only serves to reinforce the negative stereotypes that many Venezuelans continue to hold about indigenous Venezuelans. There is no such thing as a cosmic eraser that can make those deep-seated prejudices go away.

What is different now is that official support of the indigenous movement and constitutional recognition of indigenous rights has brought the discussion to the forefront through marches, demonstrations, and conferences. One such conference, the International Conference of Resistance and Solidarity of Indians and Peasants, held in Caracas in 2003, linked discussions of issues facing indigenous populations and the rural peasantry. In a way, the conference reversed the intent of the 1960 Venezuelan Agrarian Reform Law. Peasants and indigenous populations, though different, experienced similar problems and as such, benefited from combined advocacy. Chávez instituted a controversial land reform program in 2001 with the intent of making Venezuela self-sufficient in terms of foodstuffs. The law also calls for formal protection of land indigenous communities identify as theirs, reversing the 1882 law that dissolved the *resguardos*. As of July 2007, those portions of the law had not yet been implemented.

The challenges faced by Afrovenezuelans are a bit more complicated than the ones faced by advocates for indigenous Venezuelans. Unless Venezuelans see a CONIVE-sponsored march on television or hear about protests against coal strip mining in indigenous territories in the far west or illegal gold mining in Yanomami territory in the Amazon, Venezuelans see the real problems that face indigenous Venezuelans as marginal. Confronting racism within the rest of the population means confronting what scholars and activists call endoracism as well as the open racism of the white elite. Endoracism is the consequence of the positivist project begun in the 19th century that denied the value of Venezuela's African and indigenous heritage, constructing instead the "raceless" Venezuelan identity. Endoracism is a sense of that shame Venezuelans feel toward their own African or indigenous heritage, the one many see in the mirror every day, expressed through cultural understandings of beauty, light skinned over dark skinned, for example. The media reinforces those ideas. A study by Jun Ishibashi in the late 1990s and early 2000s found that black Venezuelans participated in extremely low numbers in *telenovelas* (5% of all actors), as candidates for Miss Venezuela (3%), as actors

CONIVE

After the *caracazo*, internal human rights groups formed to address centuries-old class- and race-based human rights issues that the riots exposed. One of these groups was the National Indigenous Council of Venezuela (CONIVE), formed in 1989 by indigenous Venezuelans to argue for national recognition of indigenous Venezuelans and indigenous Venezuelans' rights. The council includes 60 different organizations representing 32 different indigenous groups, or approximately 800,000 indigenous Venezuelans, most from the far west and south of the Orinoco (Fox 2006).

in Venezuelan-produced movies (8%), or as actors on television commercials (12%) (Ishibashi 2004). Most of the actors of color in commercials were dancing to tropical rhythms on beaches and not portrayed as parents or professionals. Anthropologists like Angelina Pollack-Eltz did much to document Afrovenezuelan culture in the later part of the 20th century, true enough, but the focus on culture combined with television images of bikini-clad women dancing to drums did little to address endoracism and racism. Indeed, by the early 2000s, Afrovenezuelan activist and scholar Jesús "Chucho" García (himself a fine drummer) began to use drums and drumming as symbols of what Afrovenezuelans and all Venezuelan people of color should not talk about.

Afrovenezuelans began to form advocacy groups in the late 1980s and early 1990s. The first was the Unión de Mujeres Negras (Union of Black Women) lead by Reina Arratia. Chucho García began the Fundación Afroamérica in 1993 and the Afrovenezuelan Network in 2000. He has become a champion of sustainable development in coastal areas historically associated with populations of African descent through small business development, cooperatives, and the Instituto Universitario Barlovento. He was also a national advocate for curriculum reform that would address race and class issues faced by all people of color, African descent, mixed race, or indigenous.

While indigenous and Afrovenezuelan groups are grateful for the space in civil society to speak about complicated issues publicly, often for the first time, gratitude has not made them complicit Chavistas. As noted previously, indigenous groups must continue to fight economic plans that threaten their economic and cultural sovereignty. Chucho García protects his credibility by refusing financial support from the government or any group associated with *Chavismo* or from any opposition parties (Chucho García, personal communication with Kimberly J. Morse 2008).

THE "PEOPLE'S PRESIDENT" AND CIVIL SOCIETY

Indeed, much of the debate about the state of democracy in Venezuela focuses on civil society. The nature of the polarizing presidency and the Bolivarian emphasis on participatory democracy stimulated active participation in civil society by Chavistas and opposition, most visually apparent in the massive marches of hundreds of thousands of Chavistas or opposition supporters that shut down large portions of Caracas during election seasons. Venezuelans use marches to make their voices heard to support or oppose government action. Sectors of the opposition organized numerous marches in 2001 to oppose proposed education reforms (González de Pacheco 2003). Indigenous Venezuelans, human rights groups, environmental groups, and other participants in leftist causes, many of whom normally support Chávez, used marches to encourage Chávez to reconsider coal mining and the construction of coal-related ports in the far west in 2005 (Márquez 2005). There is another layer associated with marches and protests as forms of participation in civil society.

MISIÓN ARBOL

Not all of the Chávez government's social missions are directed squarely at the economic issues of the poorer classes in Venezuela. A range of missions, from Misión Cultura, which is designed to both provide cultural opportunities and protect cultural patrimony, to Misión Arbol, are designed to raise the standard of living for a wide range of Venezuelan citizens and to protect the nation as a whole.

Misión Arbol, one of the younger social missions, was launched in 2006 with the task of combating the deforestation of Venezuela. The mission creates community conservation committees who engage in educational work, raising consciousness about environmental issues, especially Venezuela's high rate of deforestation, one of the highest in the world. The problem is particularly severe in the areas south of Lake Maracaibo and in southern Venezuela, where forests have been destroyed by mining and logging. The mission's goal is to, by the year 2011, collect 30 tons of seeds and plant 100 million plants, reforesting 150 hectares of land. By late 2006, 15 million seedlings had been planted.

Not only is *why* people march or *who* marches important, but *where* they march is important, too. We have noted more than once the symbolic importance of the constructions and uses of space. Particularly in Caracas, marches have given public spaces political meanings they did not have before. Altamira plaza in the eastern part of the city has become the most important space associated with opposition politics. The barrios in the west, with their additional associations with poverty and crime, are Chavista territory. How civil society uses public spaces has created a new political map of the city, with commonly understood borders between Chavista areas and opposition areas (García-Gaudilla 2007).

The 1999 constitution's emphasis on participatory democracy encourages small-scale participation, too. Chávez regularly reinforces that message. As we have mentioned, there is no doubt that he has used unique communication skills, peppering speeches with baseball analogies and evangelical language to appeal to the popular classes, then uses that popularity to create grassroots organizations to further support. At different points in time, those "Bolivarian Circles" have played crucial roles in organizing mass support for Chávez during election cycles. Workers' cooperatives took their place after 2006. There is no doubt that more people participate in civil society than before the Chávez era, but such high levels of participation combined with Chávez's charisma and ability to distribute favors make many wonder if participation in civil society at the grassroots level is independent or dependent. A 2006 study by Kirk Hawkins and David Hansen found that the circles were financially independent of the state and more autonomous at the local level than perhaps the government intended. However, they were so dependent on Chávez and locked into his vision for them when they were created that the circles fell apart when Chávez advocated new programs or organizations other than the circles (Hawkins and Hansen 2006).

Other scholars argue that even though Chávez created the conditions in which popular classes participate in civil society in higher numbers than ever before, that does not necessarily make him the patron and civil society the client. Hawkins and Hansen also found, for example, that people who participated in Chavista-associated organizations also participated in non-Chavista groups (Hawkins and Hansen 2006). Opinion is equally divided on the degree to which the workers' cooperatives formed after 2006 are Chávez tools. While some appear to toe the Chávez line, others act quite independently (Ellner 2008; Lupa 2010). If anything, civil society has become more complex in the Chávez era as different groups use their voices in different ways.

The emphasis on participatory democracy has also meant that the popular classes participate in a variety of ways and in many groups, not limited to marches of any sort or Bolivarian Circles or workers' cooperatives. Popular classes use, for example, community media as means to participate in civil society in participatory democracy. Catia TV's motto is *"No vea television, hágala"* (Don't watch television. Make it.). Community residents plan the programming, serve as on-air personalities, and run all of the equipment. After 2002, Chávez's government has invested more resources in microloans to community media outlets, both radio and television. The stations are largely on their own to find funding for ongoing operating costs, which usually means reaching out to the community, not the government. The government has not streamlined licensing processes for community media, which has lead to a host of small battles between community media and bureaucracy. Community media activists go so far as to assert that stations do not need a government license in order to operate legally. Said Carlos Lugo of Radio Negro Primero, "The community can themselves authorize a station and when the community recognizes the station, it is legal. There is no such thing as an illegal station—everyone has the right to communication" (Fernandes 2005). So while the government often expects community media to be dependent, to act like a client, to rally their forces to support a government cause, community media may or may not comply.

CHÁVEZ AND BOLIVARIAN REVOLUTION: SUCCESSES AND FAILURES—TRYING TO OCCUPY THE BARREN MIDDLE GROUND

The administration of Hugo Chávez and his Bolivarian Revolution are among the most divisive issues in Latin America. As scholars who have devoted our professional lives to the study of Venezuela and as people who live and work with Venezuelans on both sides of the issue, we are keenly aware of the strong feelings on both sides, and what Steve Ellner and Daniel Hellinger describe as the "barrenness of a middle ground between *chavistas* and the hardened opposition" (Ellner and Hellinger 2003: 216). We are also, however, aware that the issues are more complex and nuanced than many major media outlets and partisan supporters on both sides make them out to be. There are those who strive to occupy the barren middle ground of *ni-nis* (neither/nor) and give fair hearing and critical review to all sides of the argument for and against the Chávez government. Therefore, it is our desire in this section to give a sense of the intricacies of current Venezuelan reality and describe and present the arguments both for and against the achievements and/or failures of the Chávez administration. To achieve this goal, we will look at two key areas of debate at this point: (1) democracy and the democratic process and (2) poverty and state spending on the poor.

DEMOCRACY AND THE DEMOCRATIC PROCESS

One of the main charges against Chávez is one of authoritarianism. In the earlier years of the presidency, many based their assertions of authoritarianism on the fact that Chávez's rise to fame and popularity began with a coup attempt against the government of Carlos Andrés Pérez in 1992. A significant number of international observers in several elections, however, attested to the validity of Chávez's electoral success; they argued that Chávez's revolution failed as a military coup and succeeded as a popular electoral movement. In a string of elections from his initial installation in 1998 to his reelection in December of 2006, Chávez has won each with a significant majority of the voters. These elections are generally recognized to be free and fair as well. International observers from the Organization of American States, the European Union, and the Carter Center have praised the integrity of the National Electoral Council and the electoral process. In the election of December 2006, Chávez won reelection with 62 percent of the vote in an election where turnout was around 75 percent. After that election, the OAS Electoral Observation Mission was quoted as observing that "The democratic process emerges fortified after December 3" (Conway 2007: 51).

The strong turnout in many of the elections during Chávez's tenure through 2009 may be partly attributed to the effective connections that Chávez has built between himself and his supporters, particularly those in the lower socioeconomic strata of society. People of the lower classes, used to feeling left out of government, feel included in the Chávez program. This is what Chávez promised, and many believe that he has delivered. As Steve Ellner and Daniel Hellinger note, Chávez is particularly unique in the history of Latin America for the way in which he reached out to include the poor in designing new programs. Ellner and Hellinger note that especially during his first years in office, "Chávez displayed greater respect for democracy than many other leaders who have cultivated a charismatic relationship with the disenfranchised" (Ellner and Hellinger 2003: 218). Whether or not the programs are truly effective (a topic which we will discuss later), many who study Venezuela observe a majority of the individuals who voted for Chávez doing so freely, in a true participatory manner.

Opponents of Chávez have two problems with that argument. They note that the administration's tendency to disallow opposition candidates from participating in elections after 2007 represents a turn towards authoritarianism that undercuts otherwise democratic popular participation in election processes. Moreover, critics charge that his presidency represents a populist style of government that effectively "buys" the votes of the poor and the marginalized classes. Detractors argue that Chávez manipulates the people by pandering to them, offering overly expensive social programming that is neither in their best interest nor in the state's best interest.

Drawing comparisons to Juan Perón or Salvador Allende, opponents point out that the history of populism in Latin America has generally led to centralized, dictatorial leadership, deficit spending, and bankruptcy for the state and that Chávez's popularity was protected until 2008 by record oil prices ("Return" 2006).

Others note that it is condescending to charge that the majority of Venezuelan people are unable to make critical decisions about their leader and are so easily able to be "bought" by social spending. Greg Grandin, for example, notes that in the 2006 presidential election, Venezuelan voters rejected the idea of *"mi negra,"* the card that would have given them roughly $450 a month in cash directly from the national treasury, costing up to $16 billion a year. If the Venezuelan people were interested solely in populist-style handouts from the state, surely, Grandin argues, this would have been a better deal: "That this scheme was rejected should . . . end the notion that the majority gives their support to Chávez because of the baubles he dangles before them rather than their ability to critically judge, as much as any of us can, the world in which they find themselves" (Grandin 2007: 1).

In addition to questions of why the public votes for Chávez, detractors voice concerns about the level of public participation in balloting. Opponents note that while votes like the recall referendum of 2004 brought out record numbers of voters, other elections during Chavez's tenure have had less than impressive participation. Presidential elections since 1998 have always seen voter turnout at above 55 percent, but other voting was less well attended. The referendum to approve the new Bolivarian constitution, for example, saw voter turnout of only 37.65 percent, and municipal elections held in December of 2000 only saw a turnout of 25.1 percent. The poor turnout in some of the elections may have been due to election fatigue: Venezuela saw eight elections within the space of two years. Opponents of the Chávez government, however, argue that intimidation sometimes keeps people home and that elections with low participation are not true measures of citizen's sentiment.

Support for Chávez is easier to understand before 2006 within the context of opposition blunders. It was the opposition's reputation, not Chávez's, that was damaged by the 2002 coup and general strikes. Those errors made Chávez's victory in the recall referendum easier. Especially for Chávez supporters, it is hard to take U.S. concerns about democratic institutions seriously when that same U.S. government was among the first to recognize the unelected President Carmona after the coup. It is equally hard for supporters to credit concerns about the democratic process from an opposition that has seemed willing to throw the democratic process aside. A 2007 slate of proposed constitutional reforms included indefinite election, presidential appointment of state governors, and granted to the president the right to declare unlimited states of emergency. The reform failed on a 51–49 percent margin, with a high abstention rate, demonstrating that the Venezuelan public was not so enamored of their president that they would grant his every whim. Chávez enjoyed electoral success with a more narrow constitutional reform package (indefinite election only) in 2009. While Chávez may have authoritarian tendencies, results in elections show that Venezuelans still prefer democracy.

Beyond the issue of electoral success, critics claim that while Chávez may have been elected democratically, he does not govern democratically. U.S. governmental

Venezuela's President Hugo Chávez holds a copy of the national current constitution in his right hand and a copy of the proposal during the press conference in Caracas, Monday, December 3, 2007, where he acknowledged his defeat in a referendum that would have let him run for re-election indefinitely and impose a socialist system. Behind him is a painting depicting Venezuelan national hero Simón Bolívar. (AP/Wide World Photos)

officials have even been known to characterize Chávez as a democratically elected dictator, similar to Adolf Hitler ("Rumsfeld Says" 2006). The argument against democratic rule is many times supported with examples of significant structural changes to government that were made rapidly and, some would say, precipitously, with a result that favored Chávez. One such change was the government's expansion of the TSJ from 20 to 32 members in 2004. The Chávez government supported the need for the change in several ways: first, the administration defended the necessity to reign in anti-Chávez judicial agents on the courts who had not only blocked key legislation but who had also supported a strike at the national oil company that had cost the nation billions of dollars and who also had supported an unconstitutional coup against Chávez in 2002. In addition, the government defended the TSJ expansion by characterizing it as part of an ongoing plan to clean up a corrupt and inefficient judicial system that it had inherited in 1998. Chávez had indeed fired hundreds of judges upon his election in a move widely seen as necessary (Sullivan 2004).

The opposition, however, saw the move to expand the court as an opportunity for Chávez to pack the court with his nominees, a ploy that was characterized as an end-run around the system. The plan, while ultimately successful, was condemned by international monitoring groups like Human Rights Watch (HRW) as a betrayal of Venezuelan democracy. HRW noted in a 2004 press release that the 1999 constitution drafted by Chávez's own government guaranteed the independence of the judicial branch and the autonomy of the TSJ. To summarily change the rules by adding 12 new members while holding a supermajority in the congress (and not releasing the names of the nominees until the day of the vote), they argued, effectively undercut that principle. Miguel Vivanco, Americas Director of Human Rights Watch noted that "by packing the country's highest court, they are betraying that principle [of judicial independence] and degrading Venezuelan democracy" (HRW 2004). Venezuela's judiciary was absolutely not independent in 2004, and court packing made the problem worse, not better.

Another serious concern that Chávez opponents voice is the issue of freedom of expression. We have discussed the long-running difficulties between the Chávez government and the major media outlets. Owned and run by the opposition, all of the major television stations, radio stations, and newspapers in Venezuela were, since the moment of his election, unabashedly anti-Chávez, and attacked him regularly and with relish. Indeed, in the media outlets from 1998 to 2007, Venezuelans had very few media choices that were not vehemently anti-Chávez. In their 2003 study of both Chávez supporters and opponents, Friedrich Welsch and Gabriel Reyes found that both pro- and anti-Chávez Venezuelans watched the same television channels, read the same newspapers, and listened to the same radio stations. They all also agreed that all the media (with the exception of the tabloid-style newspaper *Ultimas Noticias*) were critical of the government (Welsch and Reyes 2006).

Perhaps because of this media blackout, and certainly because of the key role that the major media had played in the 2002 coup (the television stations showed soap operas instead of the pro-Chávez protests, and after the coup, the major newspapers simply did not print an issue to reflect), Chávez has incrementally made changes both in law and in policy that concern critics both in Venezuela and abroad. The 2004 Social Responsibility Law (see more in Chapter 5), was among the first measures that showed the Chávez government's willingness to control the content of broadcast and print journalism. Giving opponents pause especially was the component of the social responsibility law that allowed the government to levy "administrative restrictions" on television and radio stations. Equally disturbing to the media and others were new laws that made it a criminal offense to show disrespect for the president and other government authorities, an offense punishable by up to 20 months in jail. The measures, though not enforced, were widely condemned by human rights groups, international groups of journalists, and the Organization of American States. While not used, the laws were feared to have a chilling and intimidating effect on independent journalism in Venezuela. Continued changes to law and policy regarding freedom of expression will be discussed in more depth in Chapter 7.

Perhaps more troubling to some than the implications of the Social Responsibility Law are the changes to the national educational curriculum passed in August 2009 after nearly two years of debate and controversy. Parts of the law marked a definite step forward in equality in education. The law declared gender equity in education and asserted the right of people with disabilities to receive an equal education. It endorsed the "popular and ancestral knowledge" of indigenous, Caribbean, Latin American, and Afrovenezuelan people that strengthened their identity, something that Afrovenezuelan and indigenous rights advocates had argued for decades (Suggett 2009). Thousands of Venezuelans took to the streets in the days before the National Assembly passed the law, demonstrating equally vehement support and opposition. Venezuelans on both sides acknowledged that there is nothing politically neutral about national curriculum. Supporters of the law designed to create the "New Man" in Venezuela argued that the reforms proposed not only a more humane education but a more open, equal, and humane approach to human interaction by shifting the focus away from the good of the individual to community welfare. Students loved the informality suddenly common in relationships between teachers and students (Forero 2008). Such informality in interpersonal interactions and style of dress raised hackles with parents, elite and otherwise.

The informal attitude with which some teachers addressed their professions also extended to fashion, much to the dismay of some parents and other critics. The flip-flops and mid-rift-exposing styles worn by teachers encouraged disrespect so contrary to Venezuelan tradition. Critics further complained that the teachers did not have the pedagogical foundation necessary to teach. Teachers who had been in the system for some years echoed those complaints about new teachers. Experience and skill, they said, were sacrificed for ideology. Indeed, it was the fear of indoctrination that concerned opponents to the law the most. An editorial in *El Universal* said the law proposed a totalitarian vision for education, making the schools the mouthpiece for Chávez's constantly shifting version of socialism (Suggett 2009). Concerns about the quality of public education began before passage of the law in 2009. It remained to be seen in 2010 whether or not the state could the implement all aspects of the law thoroughly, given the economic crisis, and, as a result, whether or not opponents' concerns were valid. Nevertheless, the debate about the curriculum added to polarization and fueled the charges of authoritarianism.

POVERTY AND STATE SPENDING ON THE POOR

As we have previously discussed, Chávez rode a wave of popular sentiment against the traditional political and economic elite that had governed Venezuela. In a time in which a decline in oil prices and rampant corruption had made life very difficult for the average citizen, Chávez promised relief. Supporters assert they endorse Chávez because of his increased social spending on the poor. Before Chavez's election, through the 1980s and 1990s Venezuela had seen significant deterioration of social services. According to the United Nations Economic Commission on Latin America, between 1990 and 1997, Venezuela's spending on social programs was below average for Latin American nations. In addition, during that time, while all other Latin American nations (except Honduras) had increased spending on social programs, Venezuela had reduced spending. Spending on education, for example, had fallen from almost 4 percent of the gross domestic product (GDP) to less than 2 percent, and expenditures on health services had dropped from almost 1 percent to 0.21 percent (Parker 2007). Private schools and hospitals were available for those who could pay, but the great majority could not.

The first efforts of the new government to respond to the situation came from the "Plan Bolívar 200," which got the military involved in social projects. During the time between 1998 and 2001, for example, spending on education increased back up to 4.3 percent, and the government prohibited enrollment fees for public schools and initiated a program for free meals (Parker 2007). As time went on, however, the Chávez administration began the development of perhaps their signature program: the *misiones.*

After the general strike and the failure of the April 2002 coup, the Chávez government decided to put reform of social programs at the forefront of its programmatic priorities. Financed from both government ministries and from state oil revenue, the administration set up a series of "missions" that were designed to attack problems related to education, health, and nutrition. The missions received some organizational support from the government but were mostly designed to tap into already existing neighborhood groups and organizations (such as those that had organized to support Chávez during the coup attempt) and relied heavily on volunteers in the communities they served.

There were 27 missions in 2007, many named for prominent Venezuelans. Among the most popular were Misión Barrio Adentro (Urban Mission), which provides primary medical care in poor areas such as urban barrios, mostly through the use of Cuban doctors; Misión Robinson, which gave low-income adults the chance to finish secondary school; Misión Ribas, which provided scholarships and organized opportunities for low-income students to attend college; and Misión Alimentación (Nourishment Mission), which distributes food discounted as much as 39 percent to stores in low-income neighborhoods throughout the country. As of 2007, funding for the missions in total accounted for 3.5 percent of Venezuela's GDP, which may be the largest social spending program in recent Latin American history (Corrales and Penfold 2007).

For Chávez supporters, perhaps the most popular mission, and the one that best exemplified the type of real change and benefit that his administration has made in the lives of the poor, was Misión Barrio Adentro, the health initiative. Those who praise the program did so not only for the significant value in health care that it brings to the residents of the poor neighborhoods but also in the way that it involved community members in the design and implementation of the health care system. Proponents hold the program up as an example of the type of "participatory democracy" that the Bolivarian Constitution describes and the local Comites de Salud (Health Committees) who oversaw the health missions as an example of *cogobierno*, or "cogovernment," that actively involved the people (Alayón Monserat 2005). Committees in the communities assisted the doctors by volunteering in the clinic, by taking family medical histories, and by assisting with health education in the community.

The other, most obvious, benefit, for the community, was the access to free medical care, medicines, eyeglasses, and emergency services in the neighborhoods where they live. The program first brought doctors (some 20,000 physicians from Cuba) to

Patients wait to be seen by a Cuban doctor at a Barrio Adentro clinic in February 2005 in west Caracas. (Andrew Alvarez/AFP/Getty Images)

the poor neighborhoods all over the nation and expanded to rehabilitation centers and hospitals. From 1998 to 2007, the number of primary care centers for the poor jumped from 1,628 to 8,621, and the number of emergency rooms available to low-income patients nearly doubled (Weisbrot and Sandoval 2007). Many in the poor barrios had never had access before and were able to seek a doctor, not only for free, but in a convenient location. According to the Venezuelan government, during the period between February and October of 2006, Barrio Adentro provided free medical care to 3.2 million people and may have saved as many as 17,000 lives. Indeed UNICEF called Barrio Adentro a "model of comprehensive primary health care with active community involvement" (UNICEF 2005).

Criticism of Misión Barrio Adentro, as well as the other missions that form the social agenda of the Chávez administration, point out the problems related to cost and efficiency in the programs. Many fear that while some programs may be successful, they are not ultimately sustainable. Few, if any, attack the goals and success of the hugely popular Misión Barrio Adentro. What detractors note, however, is that the whole program fails without the Cuban doctors that Chávez has been able to secure from Cuba in exchange for oil. If the regime in Cuba were to change, the supply of Cuban doctors might dry up. Where would the government find 20,000 health workers willing to live and work in Venezuela's poorest urban and rural areas?

It is not true that Venezuela has a shortage of doctors, however. Venezuela boasts 1 doctor per 500 people, much better than the 1 to 1,200 average recommended by

World Health Organization. The reality is, however, that people living in the barrios had often never seen a physician. Class prejudice was part of the explanation for avoiding poor neighborhoods, but Venezuelan doctors traditionally viewed the barrios as dangerous as well, with some reason. When, in 2002, the government called on Venezuelan doctors to staff the clinics for Barrio Adentro, only 29 answered the call (Maybarduk 2004).

Cost is another significant issue for critics of the *misiones*. The Venezuelan government puts spending on Barrio Adentro alone in the billions. This type of spending is possible while oil revenues remain high. Detractors wondered, however, how the Venezuelan state could maintain the programs when oil prices inevitably fell when the economic crisis hit in 2008.

Critics also wonder if the state is getting true value for their money, especially in other missions. In his analysis of the mission dedicated to eradicating illiteracy, Misión Robinson, Francisco Rodríguez found cause for skepticism about the value of the program. According to Rodríguez, the Venezuelan government claimed that somewhere between 1 and 2 percent of the national labor force was employed by the government as trainers in the literacy campaign and taught 1.5 million people how to read and write. Using data from the Venezuelan National Institute of Statistics, however, Rodriguez and his coresearchers found no evidence of the dramatic reduction in illiteracy claimed by the Venezuelan government. According to the data, for the time period in which the government claimed to have taught 1.5 million people to read, the illiteracy rate only dropped by 0.9 percent, about the same as it had during the administration of President Caldera, who did not embark on a massive literacy campaign (Rodriguez 2007). If this is true, as Rodriguez suggests, the program was not only a failure, but an expensive one. According to the Ministry of Finance, the Venezuelan government invested $50 million in Misión Robinson. Rodriguez casts further doubt on the whole program by pointing out that while the government claims to have taught 1.5 million people to read and write, the 2001 census, carried out two years before the start of the program, showed that only 1.08 million Venezuelans were illiterate.

The successes and failures in the Chávez era have created a climate in Venezuela of polarization and mistrust where few dare to sit in the barren middle ground. Split on issues of politics and economic policy, the Venezuelan people are more divided than at any other time in recent history. The global importance of Venezuela's foreign and oil policy also mean that more international attention is paid to Venezuela and its business than at any other time in the last several decades. Venezuela sails into uncharted territory as it enters the new century with the world watching. Many challenges face the nation after the first decade.

REFERENCES

Alayón Monserat, Rubén. 2005. "Barrio Adentro: Combatir la Exclusión, Profundizando la Democracia." *Revista Venezolana de Economía y Ciencias Sociales* 3: 219–244.

"An Opposition Gagged." 2007. *Economist.* June 27. http://www.economist.com/node/925 7733?story_id=9257733.

Briggs, Charles. 2001. "Modernity, Cultural Reasoning, and the Institutionalization of Social Inequality: Racializing Death in a Venezuelan Cholera Epidemic." *Comparative Studies in Society and History* 43: 665–700.

Buncombe, Andrew. 2005. "Assassinate Chavez, Pat Robertson Tells a Stunned America." *The Independent (London)*, August 24. http://www.independent.co.uk/news/world/americas/assassinate-chavez-pat-robertson-tells-a-stunned-america-504100.html.

Bustamante, Paula. 2003. "Venezuela Strike Declared Amid Petition Drive." *Agence France Presse.* February 3. http://www.accessmylibrary.com/coms2/summary_0286-22271727_ITM.

Carter Center. 2005. *Observing the Venezuela Presidential Recall Referendum: Comprehensive Report.* Atlanta, GA: The Carter Center.

Chávez Frías, Hugo. 1998. "Acta Compromiso." *CONIVE.* http://www.conive.org/chavez.html.

"Chávez's Battle to Keep the Oil Flowing." 2003. *The Economist.* August 2. http://www.highbeam.com/doc/1G1-106195748.html.

CIA. 2010a. "Chiefs of State and Cabinet Ministers of Foreign Governments." https://www.cia.gov/library/publications/world-leaders-1/world-leaders-v/venezuela.html.

CIA. 2010b. "World Fact Book: Venezuela." https://www.cia.gov/library/publications/the-world-factbook/geos/ve.html.

Clement, Christopher I. 2007. "Confronting Hugo Chávez: U.S. 'Democracy Promotion' in Latin America." In Steve Ellner and Miguel Tinker Salas, eds., *Venezuela: Hugo Chávez and the Decline of Exceptional Democracy.* New York: Rowman and Littlefield.

Conway, Janelle. 2007. "Observing Democracy." *Americas* 59: 50–52.

Coronil, Fernando. 1997. *The Magical State: Nature, Money, and Modernity in Venezuela.* Chicago: University of Chicago Press.

Coronil, Fernando, and Julie Skurski. 2006 "Dismembering and Remembering the Nation: The Semantics of Political Violence in Venezuela." In Fernando Coronil and Julie Skurski, eds., *States of Violence.* Ann Arbor: University of Michigan Press.

Corrales, Javier, and Michael Penfold. 2007. "Social Spending and Democracy: The Case of Hugo Chávez in Venezuela." *LASA Forum* 1: 20–22.

Ellner, Steve. 2008. *Rethinking Venezuelan Politics.* Boulder, CO: Lynne Rienner.

Ellner, Steve, and Dan Hellinger. 2003. "Conclusion: The Democratic and Authoritarian Directions of the *Chavista* Movement." In Steve Ellner and Dan Hellinger, eds., *Venezuelan Politics in the Chavez Era: Class, Polarization, and Conflict.* Boulder, CO: Lynne Rienner.

Fernandes, Sujatha. 2005. "Growing Movement of Community Radio in Venezuela." *Znet.* December 26. http://www.venezuelanalysis.com/print.php?artno=1637.

———. 2007a. "Political Parties and Social Change in Venezuela." www.venezuelanalysis.com/analysis/2295.

———. 2007b. "A View from the Barrios: Hugo Chávez as an Expression of Urban Popular Movements." *LASA Forum* 1: 17–19.

Forero, Juan. 2008. "In Venezuela, Creating a 'New Man.'" *The Washington Post*, May 19. http://www.washingtonpost.com/wp-dyn/content/article/2008/05/18/AR2008051802330.html. Accessed February 13, 2010.

———. 2009a. "Chávez Wins Removal of Term Limits." *The Washington Post*, February 15. http://www.washingtonpost.com/wp-dyn/content/article/2009/02/15/AR2009021500136.html.

————. 2009b. "Venezuela's Determined Voice of Dissent." *The Washington Post.* February 25. http://www.washingtonpost.com/wp-dyn/content/article/2009/02/24/AR2009022403721.html.

————. 2009c. "Venezuela's Drug Trafficking Role Is Growing Fast, U.S. Report Says; Government Corruption, Aid to Colombian Rebels Are Cited." *The Washington Post*, July 18. http://www.washingtonpost.com/wp-dyn/content/article/2009/07/18/AR2009071801785.html.

Fox, Michael. 2006. "Indigenous March in Support of Chávez in Venezuela." *Venezuelanalysis*, June 11. http://venezuelanalysis.com/news/1784.

García-Gaudilla, María Pilar. 2007. "Social Movements in a Polarized Setting." In Steve Ellner and Miguel Tinker Salas, eds., *Venezuela: Hugo Chávez and the Decline of an "Exceptional Democracy."* New York: Rowman and Littlefield Publishers, Inc.

González de Pacheco, Rosa Amelia. 2003. "Encuestas, cacerolazos, y marchas." In Patricia Márquez and Ramón Piñago, eds., *En esta Venezuela: Realidades y nuevos caminos.* Caracas: Ediciones IESA.

Grandin, Greg. 2007. "Countervailing Powers." *Latin American Studies Association Forum* 38: 1.

Haggerty, Richard, ed. 1990. *Venezuela: A Country Study.* Washington, DC: GPO for the Library of Congress.

Hawkins, Kirk, and David Hansen. 2006. "Dependent Civil Society: The Círculos Bolivarianos in Venezuela." *Latin American Research Review* 41: 102–132.

Hellinger, Daniel. 1991. *Venezuela: Tarnished Democracy.* Boulder, CO: Westview Press.

————. 2003. "Political Overview." In Steve Ellner and Daniel Hellinger, eds. *Venezuelan Politics in the Chavez Era: Class, Polarization, and Conflict* Boulder, CO: Lynne Rienner.

————. 2006. "Tercermundismo and Chavismo." *Stockholm Review of Latin American Studies* 1: 4–17.

————. 2007. "Electoral Politics in Bolivarian Venezuela." In Steve Ellner and Miguel Tinker Salas, eds., *Hugo Chávez and the Decline of an "Exceptional Democracy.* Lanham, MD: Rowan and Littlefield.

HRW. 2004. "Venezuela: Chavez Allies Pack Supreme Court." Human Rights Watch. www.hrw.org/english/docs/2004.

"Hugo Chávez Scores Hollow Victory." 2009. *Montreal Gazette.* February 18. http://www2.canada.com/montrealgazette/features/viewpoints/story.html?id=0e6756a4-20c2-404c-82c2-ddb5d4ad4c9e.

IFES. 2005. "Election Guide: Venezuela. International Foundation for Electoral Systems." http://www.electionguide.org/country.php?ID=231.

Ishibashi, Jun. 2004. "Hacia una aperture del debate sobre el racism en Venezuela: Exclusión e inclusión estereotipada de la persona 'negra' en los medios de comunicación." Centro de Investigaciones Postdoctorales, Facultad de Ciencias Económicas y Sociales, Universidad Central de Venezuela.

Kelly, Janet. 1995. "The Question of Inefficiency and Inequality: Social Policy in Venezuela." In Louis W. Goodman, Johanna Mendelson Forman, Moisés Naím, Joseph S. Tulchin, and Gary Bland, eds., *Lessons of the Venezuelan Experience.* Baltimore, MD: Johns Hopkins University Press.

Kozloff, Nicolas. 2005a. "A Racial Democracy?: Venezuela and the Politics of Race." *Venezuelanalysis*, October 15. http://www.venezuelanalysis.com/articles.php?artno=1577.

———. 2005b. "Venezuela's War of Religion." *Venezuelanalysis*, October 24. http://www.venezuelanalysis.com/analysis/1430.

Lombardi, John V. 2003. "Prologue: Venezuela's Permanent Dilemma." In Steve Ellner and Daniel Hellinger, eds., *Venezuelan Politics in the Chavez Era: Class, Polarization and Conflict.* Boulder, CO: Lynne Rienner.

Lopez Maya, Margarita. 2002. "Venezuela after the *Caracazo*: Forms of Protest in a Deinstitutionalized Context." *Bulletin of Latin American Research* 21: 199–218.

Lupa, Noam. 2010. "Who Votes for Chavisimo? Class Voting in Hugo Chavez's Venezuela." *Latin American Research Review* 45: 3–32.

Márquez, Humberto. 2005. "Venezuela's Indigenous Peoples Protest Coal Mining." *Inter Press Service*, April 5. http://www.venezuelanalysis.com/articles.php?artno=1414.

Márquez, Patricia. 2003. "The Hugo Chávez Phenomenon." In Steve Ellner and Daniel Hellinger, eds., *Venezuelan Politics in the Chávez Era: Class, Polarization and Conflict.* Boulder, CO: Lynne Rienner.

Maybarduk, Peter. 2004. "A People's Health System: Venezuela Works to Bring Healthcare to the Excluded." *Multinational Monitor* 9–13. http://www.multinationalmonitor.org/mm2004/102004/maybarduke.html.

Montañez, Ligia. 1993. *El racismo oculto de una sociedad no racist.* Caracas: Fondo Editorial Tropykos.

Moreno, Alejandro. 1998. Editorial. *Heterotopia* 4: 5–16.

Parker, Dick. 2007. "Chávez and the Search for an Alternative to Neoliberalism." In Steve Ellner and Miguel Tinker Salas, eds., *Hugo Chávez and the Decline of an "Exceptional Democracy."* Lanham, MD: Rowan and Littlefield.

Pearson, Tamara. 2009. "Venezuela Passes New Electoral Law." *Venezuelanalysis*, August 2. www.venezuelanalysis.com/news/4681.

Ramirez, Antonio. 2006. "An Introduction to Venezuelan Governmental Institutions and Primary Legal Sources." http://www.nyulawglobal.org/globalex/venezuela.htm#_3._Judicial_Power.

"Return of Populism." 2006. *The Economist*, April 15: 39–40.

Roberts, Kenneth. 2003. "Social Polarization and the Populist Resurgence." In Steve Ellner and Daniel Hellinger, eds., *Venezuelan Politics in the Chávez Era: Class, Polarization and Conflict*. Boulder, CO: Lynne Rienner.

Rodriguez, Francisco. 2007. "Sharing the Oil Wealth? Appraising the Effects of Venezuela's Social Programs." *LASA Forum* 1: 22–25.

"Rumsfeld Says Chávez Rise 'Worrisome.'" 2006. *Agence France Presse*, February 2. http://demopedia.democraticunderground.com/discuss/duboard.php?az=view_all&address=102x2082212.

Suggett, James. 2009. "Venezuelan Education Law: Socialist Indoctrination or Liberatory Education?" *Venezuelanalysis*, August 21. http://www.venezuelanalysis.com/analysis/4734.

Sullivan, Kevin. 2004. "Chavez Tightening Grip on Judges, Critics Charge." *The Washington Post*, June 20. http://www.washingtonpost.com/wp-dyn/articles/A54913-2004Jun19.html.

TSJ. n.d. "Sobre el Tribunal." http://www.tsj.gov.ve/eltribunal/sobretribunal/organizacion.shtml.

————. 2010. "Gestión Judicial." http://www.tsj.gov.ve/index.shtml.

UNICEF. 2005. "Venezuela's *Barrio Adentro:* A Model of Universal Primary Health Care." www.unicef.org/french/infobycountry/files/IPlusQuarterlyE-newsletterJanMarch2005.

U.S. Department of State. 2009. "Background Note: Venezuela." http://www.state.gov/r/pa/ei/bgn/35766.htm.

"Venezuela Passes Controversial Election Law." 2009. International Foundation for Electoral Systems. http://www.electionguide.org/country-news.php?ID=231#anchor_4767.

"Venezuela's Oil Blacklist." 2007. *American Public Media: Marketplace*, May. http://marketplace.publicradio.org/shows/2007/05/01/AM200705012.html.

Weisbrot, Mark, and Luis Sandoval. 2007. The Venezuelan Economy in the Chávez Years. Center for Economic and Policy Research. http://www.cepr.net/.

Welsch, Friedrich, and Gabriel Reyes. 2006. "¿Quiénes son los revolucionarios? Perfil socio-demográfico e ideopolítico del Chavecismo." *Venezuelan Politics and Society in Times of Chavismo* 1: 4–17.

Wilpert, Gregory. 2003. "Community Media in Venezuela." *Venezuelanalysis*, November 14. http://www.venezuelanalysis.com/analysis/221.

————. 2004. "Racism and Racial Divides in Venezuela." *Venezuelanalysis*, January 21. http://www.venezuelanalysis.com/articles.php?artno=1091.

Economy

OVERVIEW

Dependency and Development

Economists understand financial statistics like doctors understand blood pressure, heart rate, weight, and cholesterol levels (see Venezuela's economic information in Table H in the "Facts and Figures" section in the back of this book). Such statistics are measures of basic health or, in this case, measures of basic economic health. The news for Venezuela in 2009 was not exactly good. In this chapter we will first briefly review the evolution of Venezuela's dependent status in the global community then assess oil and its consequences in the 20th and 21st centuries. We will evaluate the role of labor before finally reviewing economic policies in the Chávez era, oil policies, monetary policies, land reform policies, energy policies, and more.

Though the GDP (the sum of the gross value of all of the producers in the economy) has risen substantially since 2000 to a total of $313.8 billion, GDP growth is slowing down, and inflation is skyrocketing to 31.3 percent, making it difficult for more and more Venezuelans to afford goods and services. Industry (primarily oil) makes up over half of Venezuela's GDP, services make up 38 percent, and agriculture makes up only 4 percent, and this in a country with tremendous agricultural potential. While we will assess the connections between political policies, land, and agricultural production later in the chapter, what is significant to note here is that food to support the slowly growing population represents a portion of the growing percentage of imported goods.

By far, however, the most important statistics many Venezuelans monitor are the number of barrels of oil produced daily, the price per barrel, and Venezuela's place in the rankings of the world's oil producers. Since the early decades of the 20th century, oil has been the nation's life blood. It pays for education, road construction, social services, the arts, health care, nonpetroleum industrial development, and future petroleum exploration. Since the early 20th century, Venezuelan politicians base, at least in part, their political success on their ability to sow the oil. However, one cannot understand Venezuela's dependency on oil production and its consequences without realizing that said dependency evolved within a specific social, political, and economic context. Since the colonial era, Venezuela has been a nation defined by its production of raw materials for export, first to a mother country and then to the developed, industrial world. President Hugo Chávez Frías (1998–) has had little success altering the nation's dependency on the production of the most important raw material, petroleum. Just as "sowing the wealth" created formulas that lead to political and social clientelism throughout the 20th century, planting the oily crop in the 20th century has yielded nothing more than new clients.

Spain established its colonies in the Americas using a mercantilist economic policy. Nations who used mercantilism maintained that there was only a fixed amount of wealth in the world. Countries competed with each other to obtain greater shares of the wealth, at the expense of other nations. Colonies enhanced mother countries' wealth so long as colonies did not compete with mother countries for a share of the global wealth pie. Colonies, therefore, produced raw materials to serve the mother countries' economic interests. That basic economic equation defined the relationship between all Spanish colonies and Spain and between Portugal and Brazil. Cacao was the commodity that Spain expected from Venezuela. Cacao defined not only economic relationships with the mother country but also shaped social and political relationships. The white elite held all political and economic power and owned most of the productive land. People of color—indigenous, African descent, or mixed race—labored.

When colonialism ended, dependency shifted from Spain and Portugal to other North Atlantic nations who continued to use Latin America's rich resource base for the production of raw materials to fuel the engine of industrialization. Like all new Latin American nations desperate for loans to build their economies after the devastating wars for independence, Venezuela embraced its role as a producer of raw materials, coffee in the 19th century, for export to the North Atlantic in exchange for economic support. The social and political relationships constructed in the colonial era continued in the 19th century to support the economic model.

In the 20th century, economists and political scientists began to refer to Latin American and similar raw material–producing nations as third world nations, developing nations, or emerging nations. The International Monetary Fund (IMF) and other world organizations use multiple criteria to assess levels of development, including the level of industrialization, GDP, per capita income, export diversification, and integration into the global financial system. As of 2009, only one Latin American nation—Chile—had nearly managed to shift categories, from developing to developed, resolving one longstanding economic legacy of colonialism (Forero 2009).

Oil defines the 20th-century Venezuelan economy. The development of the oil industry did not change any of the patterns of relationships between Venezuela and North Atlantic nations. If anything, oil production was made easier because Venezuela had long since embraced its role as a producer of raw materials for the North Atlantic. Venezuelan social and political relationships—understandings of who had power, who did not, who worked with their hands, and who did not—also facilitated Venezuela's evolution as one of the world's most important oil-producing nations.

A NOTE ON THE INFORMAL ECONOMY

Since the economic crisis of the 1980s and the 1990s, more and more Venezuelans have turned toward the growing informal economy for employment, commerce, or for currency exchange. The informal economy is the system of employment and commerce that exists outside employment and commerce systems regulated by the government. Income earned from sales or employment in the informal sector are not available to the government for taxation. Likewise, those who deal in the informal economy do not have access to protections against abuse in employment or unfair economic practices (usurious interest, for example) expected in the formal economy. The growth in the informal economy since the 1970s is a global phenomenon. A 2004 World Bank study found that 57 percent of all employed in Latin America and the Caribbean were employed in the informal economic sector; 78 percent of Africans worked in the informal economy (Becker 2004: 8). It is also the sector of the economy with the greatest job growth in recent decades. In 2000, 83 percent of new jobs created in Latin America and the Caribbean were created in the informal economy (Becker 2004: 18). In Venezuela, like many countries worldwide, food vending on the street and window washing and trinket selling at intersections are examples of informal employment. The old cattle areas in the east still produce dairy products like *queso de mano* that are not easily obtained outside of the area. People with connections to ranchers purchase the *queso* directly and resell it to a network of clients in cities like Puerto La Cruz and Barcelona. All over the country, women with artistic skill make and sell jewelry and other handmade products. Those with more resources to invest and connections to Caracas or points north purchase and resell goods like shoes or purses. All are examples of informal economic activities. Some people's primary employment is in the informal sector. Others use the informal economy to supplement income earned in the formal economy.

We should also note the role of the informal economy in the currency exchange system. The official currency is the bolivar, which is estimated at 4.3 per U.S. dollar, Lyons and Crowe 2010). Dollars come in handy for Venezuelans. In case of emergencies, dollars can be used to purchase goods not easily available in the formal sector. Dollars can be sold at a profit, at a rate higher than the official exchange rate. For many years, it has become normal for people, like scholars, who travel regularly to Venezuela to sell their dollars to trusted friends in order to obtain bolivars (VEB) necessary to function on a daily basis. Since 2000, President Chávez instituted a series of monetary controls to try to prevent the sort of capital flight that marked the

People walk through vendors that fill a main street in Caracas, Venezuela. In 2004, more than half of all adult Venezuelans without formal employment sought out a living as maids, cabbies, or street peddlers. (AP/Wide World Photos)

economic crisis of the 1980s and 1990s, when billions of dollars forever left the Venezuelan economy. Though the controls had some basis in reason, they have made it difficult for people who need dollars for legitimate purposes (necessary foreign travel associated with employment, for example) to obtain them. The devaluation of the VEB in early 2010 further spurred the informal currency exchange system. In sum, the informal economy has become a permanent feature of the Venezuelan economic scenario. It takes on greater importance when the formal economy contracts, as it did in the 1980s and 1990s, then again in the later years of the first decade of the 21st century.

INDUSTRY

Oil in the 20th Century and Beyond

President Juan Vicente Gómez (1908–1935) laid the foundations for modern Venezuela's economy, lubricated by oil. Before Gómez could invest in oil, he had to invest in infrastructure, roads, and fiscal reform. One British engineer suggested that Venezuela did not have roads, except near major cities. He had a point. So bad were the roads that existed that it cost $4.00 to $5.00 (approximately $85.00 2003 dollars) to transport a bag of coffee overland from Táchira to Maracaibo and only $0.40

(approximately $7.50 2003 dollars) to ship the same bag of coffee from Maracaibo to New York (McBeth 2008: 17, 426). By 1924, after spending 55 percent of the Ministry of Public Work's annual budget on road construction since 1910, roads connected most isolated communities. A highway finally connected Caracas to the Andes in 1934 (McBeth 2008: 18). Gómez saw himself as the champion of a modern, progressive Venezuela, and as such fiscal responsibility became a priority. Yet he governed a nation in which *caudillismo* defined relationships between the president and state governors, and regional challenges to his authority were not uncommon in the early years. In that context, it is not surprising that Gómez used alliances greased by concessions, monopolies, land, livestock, and cattle transactions to cement and centralize authority (Yarrington 2003: 12). Of course the president took his cut. Gómez became one of the wealthiest men in Latin America, controlling the soap, paper, butter, match, and cotton industries; he became the exclusive supplier of meat to Puerto Cabello and other urban markets and was the primary shareholder in the Companía Anónima Venezolana de Navegación (Coronil 1997: 82; McBeth 2008: 61). His close associates, often family members, similarly benefited. Nevertheless, by 1912 Venezuela paid its outstanding debt as outlined by the 1903 Washington Protocols that ended the Cipriano Castro–era blockade crisis. In 1918, congress passed the Ley Orgánica de Hacienda Nacional, which created internal revenue sources through taxation capable of equaling customs, in essence laying the foundation for Venezuela's modern financial system.

Such reforms were essential because Gómez and his advisors insisted that Venezuela's future lay with greater financial integration with North Atlantic networks. Arístides Tellería, president of the senate in 1911, said the congress should pass laws that would "flatter the foreigner so that he will come to our shores to instruct us in their scientific advances and participate in our wealth" (McBeth 2008: 40). Venezuelans defined wealth not in terms of manufactures but in terms of production of raw materials. As early as 1909, foreigners had an easier time obtaining mining and agricultural concessions than they had under the Castro presidency. In 1910, the United Fruit Company received a 25-year contract with no tax obligations that enabled Gómez "to think with pride that we [Venezuela] have opened the vast hinterland of the country where you [Gómez] will build together with all good Venezuelans the future of our beloved Venezuela" (McBeth 2008: 41–42). That same year, congress passed a mining law that required companies to pay minimal taxes on oil extracted— only 2VEB per ton. Royal Dutch Shell sunk the first commercial oil well in 1914, and by 1925 oil overtook coffee as the nation's leading export (Coronil 1997: 78).

On the surface, the move toward oil seems like a shift to yet another raw material—first wheat, then cacao, then coffee, and finally oil. Oil, however, meant a fundamental reordering of the economy and, in a sense, national identity. As stated by Venezuelan intellectual Domingo Alberto Rangel, "no event in Venezuela can be separated from oil . . . It is the fundamental force that shapes national life. All aspects of the Venezuelan economy are the legitimate or bastard children of that substance that irrevocably stained our history" (Tinker Salas 2009: 2). Before oil, Venezuela understood wealth in agricultural terms, which preferenced rural areas in the national imagination. Oil quickly became the symbol of Venezuela's wealth, present and future, and the state's primary job became to protect and then sow that wealth for future generations. That remains the role of oil in the national psyche and the national economy to this day. Oil wealth, however, was and is urban, not rural. Cities boomed where mere suburbs had existed before. Puerto La Cruz before the refinery and the offshore platforms was no more than a small fishing village. Maracaibo soon rivaled Caracas as the nation's most important urban and commercial center. Its population nearly doubled from 45,000 in 1920 to 80,000 in 1926 alone (Tinker Salas 2009: 61). Oil realigned the national economy and national imagination away from agriculture and toward urban-based commerce and real estate. The traditional, land-owning elite quickly made the transition from rural-based land wealth to urban commercial and real estate wealth. The elite who once demonstrated wealth through ownership of slaves (a colonial import) demonstrated wealth in the era of oil through its ability to consume imported luxury goods (cars, for example) and later parked their money in dollars in international bank accounts. The middle class grew parallel to both the growth of the oil industry throughout the country and with urbanization. Old Venezuelan political structures did not serve this middle class's needs—liberal democracy was in order. It was oil, more than any a modern military controlled by the president, a modern road network, or political favors, that definitively defeated Venezuelan regionalism and *caudillismo*, centralized political and economic authority in one Venezuelan state, recreated the Venezuelan elite, and provided the foundation for the discourse on democracy after Gómez died in 1935 (Coronil 1997).

Oil has been both a blessing and a curse that has dogged Venezuela since 1914, a permanent dilemma that has at least two parts (Lombardi 2003). The first part of the dilemma is how to properly manage the wealth. Gómez and his economic ministers knew that they were dependent on foreign oil companies to extract oil. The money for Venezuela came in the form of concessions sold, taxes, and royalties. If Venezuela exerted more direct control over the oil, it risked alienating the oil companies. If the state left the companies with too much latitude, the nation lost

---

BARROSO NO. 2, "THE ROAR THAT FROZE THE BLOOD"

Venezuela's first gusher was Mene Grande in 1914. Its output paled in comparison to the monster strike near La Rosa at Barroso No. 2 on December 14, 1922. On that morning, as drillers drilled deeper into a well once thought dry, the ground began to shake. Drillers heard a noise that "sounded like the passage of a thousand freight trains." As the well exploded 200 feet into the sky, workers dove for cover to avoid rocks and falling debris. Homes three kilometers away were spattered with oil. Oil coated the town of La Rosa; it "covered the trees, coated the vines and in ever-growing streams flowed through the underbrush like black serpents" (Tinker Salas 2009: 55). Venezuela was forever stuck in oil.

income and possibly legitimacy in the eyes of the population. Different national policies on oil and on the companies throughout the 20th century and into the 21st century should be seen within the context of that dilemma as the Venezuelan state alternately tried to control the companies and leave them with more latitude. By the late 1910s, Gómez realized that the dilemma was the predicament that would define the remainder of his presidency, or the rest of his life. Because his control over Venezuela was personalist cloaked in some modernity, he could not play populist political games or rally the companies against exploitators of Venezuela's national patrimony. Gómez did not have a popular base, so he needed the support of the companies and the small, yet growing, commercial elite associated with the oil industry. He also needed a greater share of the profits. The 1920 oil law championed by Development Minister Gusmerindo Torres appeared to straddle the fence. It separated oil from other subsoil resources and defined extraction as different from other industrial activities because oil, once sold, left Venezuela forever. Oil industry taxes, according to Torres, should be different, too. In a nod toward the argument that the state should assert greater control of oil as national wealth and patrimony, Torres claimed for "the nation, as landlord, the right to charge a rent for the use of its subsoil" (Coronil 1997: 80–81). The royalties charged using the law, in effect until 1943, were still low, however, an average of 9 percent, and the companies received tax exemptions on imports brought into the country. In the end, the companies paid less in royalties than the value of the tax exemptions granted. Torres said that " the companies exploited the petroleum, and the government paid them for carrying it away" (Coronil 1997: 82).

There was much oil to carry away. By 1930, Venezuela was the world's third largest oil producer. In 1917, the nation produced only 120,000 barrels of oil. By 1930, that number skyrocketed to 136,669,000 (Brown 1985: 365). Though crude prices dropped 30 percent at the beginning of the Great Depression and the companies tried to reduce production, by the time Gómez died in 1935, Venezuela was second only to the United States in global petroleum production (Tinker Salas 2009: 40). Royal Dutch Shell, the nation's largest producer, extracted 8.7 million tons of oil in 1935 (McBeth 2008: 1, 44). Agriculture in 1935 had fallen to 18 percent of GDP (from 27 percent in 1920), and oil represented 70 percent of all exports (Coronil 1997: 117–118). By 1940, Venezuela was a net importer of food (Tinker Salas 2005: 150). Soaring production numbers meant, for some, greater questions about Gómez's political model. There were three, possibly four, serious conspiracies against Gómez between 1921 and 1931 (McBeth 2008: 6). As soon as he died, political debates became intertwined with economic policy questions because many understood that Gómez had paid the nation's foreign debts but had stolen the subsoil. Democracy, advocates argued, would unify Venezuelans and enable them to reconquer the subsoil for the people, not a for select group of cronies. Intellectual Arturo Uslar Pietri stated that reckless national investment in oil production would produce a "suicidal dream":

> Venezuela would become an unproductive and idle nation, an immense petroleum parasite, swimming in a momentary and corrupting abundance and propelled toward and imminent and inevitable catastrophe. (quoted in Coronil 1997: 105)

A better, more democratic use of the resources would be to sow the oil, to reinvest in agricultural activities, insisted Uslar Pietri. Sowing the oil became the metaphor that defined economic and political policies throughout the 20th century and into the 21st. Uslar Pietri understood the phrase in agricultural terms, which made perfect sense in a nation that was still smarting over the recent shift in economic models and the social and demographic consequences the shift had produced. Later generations of politicians and economic theorists understood the phrase in terms of industrial development other than oil, investment in other natural resources, and investment in the arts, education, health care, or other forms of social spending. Oil's economic might remains the most important political tool in Venezuelan politicians' arsenals in 2010. That brings us to the second part of the permanent dilemma, how to spend the wealth. Every post-Gómez administration faced scrutiny about how it "sowed the oil" to make constituents happy (e.g., Chávez sowed the oil in social services, but the electrical grid suffered). Other administrations sowed the oil in universities, forsaking nonoil industrial development. High international petroleum prices throughout the 20th and the 21st century have meant social and political stability. Falling prices not only produced economic instability but social unrest and political change. So long as Venezuela's economy remains dependent on the "fundamental force" or "irrevocable stain," Venezuela will remain trapped in both parts of the permanent dilemma.

Sowing the Oil before OPEC and Punto Fijo, 1935–1958

In order to sow the wealth, the Venezuelan state had to control the wealth more effectively than it did under Gómez. Development Minister Manuel Egaña tried to levy an income tax on the oil companies (Royal Dutch Shell, Creole [part of Standard Oil], and Mene Grande [part of Gulf]) in order to increase revenues, but it was not until World War II that President Roosevelt issued orders to force U.S. companies to comply with Venezuelan law. The 1943 Petroleum Law reordered the relationship between Venezuela and the companies and was a crucial step in the conundrum of wealth management, in sowing the oil effectively. The law granted the companies new, large 40-year concessions, fixed a higher royalty to be paid by the companies: one out of every six barrels of oil extracted by the companies belonged to Venezuela. When it added royalties to the income and other fixed taxes that were part of the 1943 law, the Venezuelan state thought that it should receive 50 percent of the profits oil yielded to the companies. The law also required the companies to build refineries in Venezuela instead of refining oil overseas (Coronil 1997: 107–108). President Isaías Medina Angarita saw that clause as fulfilling his obligation to sow the wealth by using the companies to jump-start industrialization. Not until 1960 and Venezuela's participation in the establishment of OPEC (Organization of Petroleum Exporting Countries) would there be substantial change in Venezuelan petroleum policies.

The companies were not exactly pleased with the changes, but by then the companies much preferred to work with Venezuelan political leaders to compel them to moderate policies rather than openly oppose Venezuelan economic policies. There was substantial public pressure on President Rómulo Gallegos during the *trienio democrático* (1945–1948) to nationalize the oil industry. However, Development Minister Juan Pablo Pérez Alfonzo assured the companies that:

> The defense of our national economy and the necessity of using foreign capital for the development of our national resources can be harmonized without trouble . . . it is in [the country's] best interest to permit development of its oil petroleum resources under the present arrangement of foreign capital and technicians. There is no intention to nationalize the industries or expropriate properties. (Tinker Salas 2005: 151)

The companies styled themselves as the ideal corporate citizens to protect their privileged place in Venezuela. They invested in infrastructure—roads, sanitation, water, electricity, schools, sports facilities, churches, and hospitals—in essence assuming some of the functions of the state in order to avoid labor upheavals, community protest, and expressions of nationalism (Tinker Salas 2009: 2). So successful were the companies at becoming corporate citizens in Venezuela, despite political change, that the author of an article in *Fortune* magazine asserted that "If there had been no perfect illustration of what U.S. capital and technical resources could do for the world's underdeveloped areas, it would have been necessary to invent the Republic of Venezuela" (Tinker Salas 2005: 149). Within the context of the cold war, the United States perceived the companies' oil operations as instruments of U.S. foreign policy, and from the U.S. perspective, given the confluence of evidence, the companies' policies had worked in Venezuela.

Cozy relationships between the companies, Venezuela, and the United States continued during the dictatorship of Marcos Pérez Jiménez. Nelson Rockefeller and Creole's president, Arthur Proudfit, negotiated on behalf of Venezuela with the Truman Administration for favorable tariff arrangements. In return, Venezuela reduced duties on nearly all U.S. imported goods—cars, radios, televisions, planes, and trucks, for example. As Venezuelan governments had done a century before, Pérez Jiménez sacrificed Venezuelan markets in favor of favorable relationships with the North Atlantic. By 1957, Venezuela imported $695.4 million in consumer goods from the United States (Tinker Salas 2009: 219). Simultaneously, oil production soared. By 1955, the companies produced 2,157,216 barrels of oil a day. Creole was the leading company (with 3,000 wells and 14,000 employees and over 9 million barrels produced daily), followed by Shell and Gulf. Venezuela earned, from Creole alone, $232 million in taxes and royalties, a total of $7 billion from all companies between 1948 and 1957. The profits began to transform the urban landscape. Caracas's population doubled to 1.2 million by 1957. The construction industry boomed, with modernist styles favored above all others, as we will discuss in Chapter 6. The elite could shop at a Christian Dior boutique after 1955, the first in Latin America. Public investments (wealth sowing) totaled $685 million in 1957–1958, though much of that was siphoned off in corrupt enterprises (Tinker Salas 2009: 220).

Creole Petroleum Corp. well in the Jusepin field of eastern Venezuela, March 1944. (Library of Congress)

Other Industrial Development before the Pact of Punto Fijo

The profits from the 1943 law allowed Acción Democrática (AD) to create the Venezuelan Development Corporation (CVF), which in turn created the Steel and Iron Department to plan for a future iron and steel industry. In 1948, U.S. Steel discovered La Parida (She who Gives Birth) renamed Cerro Bolívar, an iron mountain containing 400 million tons of 65 percent pure iron ore (Coronil 1997: 191). Soon thereafter, the CVF realized the hydroelectric potential of the Caroní River. The military coup that led in 1950 to the dictatorship of Marcos Pérez Jiménez derailed all efforts to exploit those discoveries. Because Pérez Jiménez dissolved the CVF and effectively centralized all government-sponsored development activities under his personal authority, iron and steel exploitation activities shifted to the private Iron Syndicate with deep ties in the Caracas elite and with 170 stockholders in 1952. They curried the support of German investors and the U.S.-based Iron Mines and U.S. Steel.

After the syndicate proved that existing technology and the Caroní's hydroelectric power could mine the iron ore and refine it into steel, the state began its own iron and steel operations organized through the Office of Special Studies of the President of the Republic. The Commission for the Study of Electrification of the Caroní led to hydroelectric development. In 1954, Pérez Jiménez announced Venezuela would build a steel mill on the same day U.S. Steel began shipments from its Cerro Bolívar. In 1955, he ordered the dissolution of the Iron Syndicate. The construction of steel operations were marred by corruption and poor design; they were not productive until long after the end of the Pérez Jiménez dictatorship. Hydroelectric operations, however, proceeded efficiently under the leadership of Rafael Alfonzo Ravard. He later became president of a revitalized CVF and designed and directed the Guayana Regional Development Corporation (CVG), a holding corporation that controlled all the major industries in the Guayana region and a model for effective relationships between the state and local and foreign capital (Coronil 1997: 193–199).

OPEC and Nationalization

Despite Venezuela's close relationship to U.S.-based companies, it was not blind to changing international petroleum dynamics. The companies began to explore new petroleum deposits in Guatemala, Colombia, Ecuador, Peru, and Bolivia. In 1949, Venezuela sent a delegation to the Middle East to encourage the Arab states to increase royalties and taxation to the benefit of Venezuela in a more competitive global market (Tinker Salas 2009: 218–219). The trip also produced greater information sharing among the oil-producing countries that continued throughout the Suez Canal Crisis (1956–1958), with its rather significant effects on international oil production and prices. The closure of the Suez Canal worked toward Venezuela's advantage in 1956; but the reopening of the canal in 1958 produced a global glut (Tinker Salas 2009: 221). The economic woes only served to intensify political instability at the end of the Pérez Jiménez regime. When his regime ended, foreign creditors held $1 billion in recallable debt, compounding an instant increase in unemployment by 250,000 people when the new government ended Pérez Jiménez's construction projects. With nationalist sentiments running high, interim president Edgar Sanabria unilaterally and without negotiation raised the income tax rate charged to the companies from 26 to 45 percent, which increased the Venezuelan share of oil profits to 60 percent (Hellinger 1991: 98–99). When the United States refused to increase its share of global imports from Venezuela, President Rómulo Betancourt (1959–1964) sent a delegation to the First Arab Oil Congress in 1959. In the series of meetings that led to the establishment of OPEC (1960), Iran, Iraq, Kuwait, Saudi Arabia, and Venezuela redefined petroleum royalties and profits. The OPEC nations defined the royalty as "compensation for the intrinsic value of oil as a nonrenewable resource . . . Profits were to be shared after discounting the company's operating costs and distributing the royalty" (Coronil 1997: 50). The net effect for producing nations was an increase in profits. The deed, however, was done. According to Development Minister Pérez Alonzo, "the governments of the consuming countries never believed that Arabs, Iranians, and Venezuelans could agree on anything. All their computers were unable to calculate this equation" (Tinker Salas 2009: 228).

By the time Venezuela collaborated with the Middle Eastern countries to establish OPEC, its share of global oil market had already shrunk. In 1955, Venezuela produced 38.4 percent of the world's crude and 24.3 percent in 1965. The average price per barrel dropped from $2.65 in 1957 to $1.81 in 1969. Venezuela compensated by increasing production to a high of 3,708,000 a day in 1970. Oil represented 66.4 percent of state income in 1967 (Hellinger 1991: 100). Through the 1960s and 1970s, with the growth of the Venezuelan form of democracy born at Punto Fijo (see Chapter 2), the companies decreased their social spending, though approximately 25 percent of the total Venezuelan population lived in or near an oil camp in the 1960s (Tinker Salas 2009: 4, 13). If anything, despite the ability to leverage more profit out of the companies, the state's increased involvement in the economy and the increased social spending inherent in sowing the oil made the country more, not less, dependent on petroleum production.

Through the 1960s, Venezuela tried to maintain its special relationship with the United States and its oil conglomerates despite the growing relationship with OPEC. When the United States decided to make Canada, not Venezuela, its preferred oil supplier, Venezuela largely gave up the complicated dance with both the United States and OPEC and worked instead to strengthen OPEC. By the end of the decade, OPEC gained the right to set reference prices, or unilaterally establish the price with which to calculate royalties and profits regardless of the actual price of oil on the world market. The cartel countries could raise reference prices and increase their national incomes. The cartel also began to establish fixed production levels. The reference price system and production levels permanently altered the global petroleum playing field, making oil policy part of international gamesmanship between producing and consuming nations, minimizing the semi-autonomous political and economic power of the oil conglomerates (Hellinger 1991: 123). The cartel's new powers produced profits unimagined when the fourth Arab-Israeli War (1973) and the Arab oil embargo placed much of the global oil supply out of the reach of consuming nations. The price of Venezuelan crude skyrocketed to $10.31 per barrel, and government income increased 170 percent, setting the table for the 1970s Golden Age of Oil, Saudi Venezuela (Hellinger 1991: 122).

OPEC's move to set reference prices enabled the cartel nations to successively move toward nationalization of their oil reserves. President Carlos Andres Pérez initiated the process in Venezuela in 1974 when he appointed a commission incorporating multiple sectors of the economy (labor, FEDECAMARAS, etc.) to negotiate with the companies the process of nationalization in order to shift the management of Venezuela's subsoil wealth definitively in favor of Venezuela, not the companies. Political opinion was not at all unified, and debate was heated in congress in 1975. Nevertheless, nationalization officially became the law of the land on January 1, 1976 at a ceremony at Zumaque No. 1 in Mene Grande. Nationalization created PDVSA (Petroleos de Venezuela, Sociedad Anónima) primarily as a holding company composed of three corporations that were, in essence, the companies as they had been before. Creole became Lagoven, Shell became Maraven, and Mene Grande (Gulf) became Meneven. The companies' corporate cultures also remained intact. PDVSA and its subsidiaries continued to rely on foreign technical and advisory expertise, and the United States remained the primary buyer for Venezuelan crude. Commercialization agreements further protected the companies, making sure that they received 88 percent of PDVSA production proportional to their status prior to nationalization. The profit margin for the nation in those agreements was so small that the only way to develop markets or deposits separate from the companies' established markets was to increase production in existing sites to raise money to propel exploration and

President Carlos Andres Pérez, far right, raises the Venezuelan flag over a western oil field in a ceremony marking the formal takeover of his nation's nationalized oil industry in Caracas, Venezuela on January 2, 1976. On New Year's Day, Venezuela took over concessions and property of more than 20 private, mostly U.S.-owned companies under terms of a nationalization law. (AP/Wide World Photos)

extraction in new locales. Nationalization, instead of providing Venezuela with income to diversify its economic infrastructure, actually reinforced the economy's dependency on oil production while simultaneously increasing social expectations about politicians' ability to sow the oil (Hellinger 1991: 122–124; Tinker Salas 2009: 228–299). Instead of resolving the permanent dilemma, nationalization made it worse.

Sowing the Oil in the 1970s—Cars and College

Nevertheless, the 1970s were definitely golden years. Gambling on future profits and President Pérez's popularity, the Venezuelan congress passed a law that allowed Pérez to spend oil profits at his discretion (Mommer 2003: 133). Public spending increased by 96.9 percent between 1973 and 1978, and by 1978 only 10 percent of all Venezuelans lived in poverty (Buxton 2003: 115). Some of the spending came from new profits from oil, but Venezuela borrowed a great deal in the 1970s, gambling that international petroleum conditions that existed in the 1970s would last indefinitely. The challenge for COPEI (Comité de Organización Política Electoral Independiente) President Rafael Caldera (1969–1974) AD President Pérez (1974–1979) and COPEI President Luis Herrera Campins (1979–1984) was how to sow the wealth in the form of oil profits and loans in order to ensure political legitimacy as consistent with the permanent dilemma. Development experts in Venezuela in the 1970s understood that Venezuela's dependency on oil for revenue created significant long-term economic problems; the question was, for those experts and to a certain degree government officials, how to use oil wealth to alleviate that dependency, to diversify the nation's economic foundation. Public investment in the economy eclipsed private investment in the economy, reaching 61.2 percent in 1977 (Hellinger 1991: 144). Pérez wanted to create the "Great Venezuela" through a combination of social spending and state-sponsored industrialization in multiple arenas. By 1981, state enterprises other than petroleum represented 7.2 percent of gross national product (GNP) and 10 percent of wages and salaries paid in the national economy (Hellinger 1991: 145). The quality of the state-run enterprises varied substantially from the efficient PDVSA, which we will deal with in a bit more depth later, to joint state-private enterprises to state enterprises so inefficient and costly that "if a Martian visited the earth, she might ask whether they really [had] profit as their goal" (Hellinger 1991: 145). Of interest to us as programs exemplary of the period are education and automotive projects, the latter representative of state-private enterprises. Since 1935, intellectuals and politicians had urged Venezuela to invest more heavily in education, particularly higher education, to spur development. Since the formulation of the automotive policy in 1962, politicians and economists had perceived establishing a functional auto industry as a path toward development and economic diversity. Politicians sowed oil wealth into both plans, college and cars, in the 1970s, with mixed results.

CORDIPLAN (Oficina Central de Coordinación y Planificación de la Presidencia de la República, or Central Office for Coordination and Planning of the President of the Republic), created in 1958, was the central planning organization for the nation until 1999. According to its fourth national plan, "education . . . must contribute to the creation of a critical consciousness and to the spread of innovations, turning itself into a medium of personal and social development" (Albornoz 1977: 297). Practically speaking, Venezuela needed its own technocrats—engineers, technology specialists, business and economic experts—to truly own and manage its national resources. Furthermore, education spending was simply good politics. As the population perceived education, primarily higher education, as a means toward social mobility, state spending in education enhanced the legitimacy of the state by providing said means. Therefore, in 1976, Venezuela dedicated 16.1 percent of the national budget to education spending, quadruple the amount spent in 1964. Oil directly paid for education, taking into account that in 1975 approximately 84 percent of national income came from oil revenue (Albornoz 1977: 295, 300). In that context, education policy was economic policy.

As far as expensive policies go, Venezuela received positive short-term returns on its investment, rather quickly. Between 1970 and 1980, the literacy rate increased from 76.3 to 83.9 percent, and to 94 percent by 2005 according to the United Nations Educational, Scientific and Cultural Organization (UNESCO 2006). Primary public school enrollment increased from 1.5 million students in 1969 to 1.8 million in 1975 (Albornoz 1977: 301). In order to generate the highly skilled population that Venezuela needed, state investment in college was crucial, and the state spent its education budget to meet the demand. Thirty-four percent of the 1976 education budget went to higher education (Albornoz 1977: 301). By the early 1980s that percentage had increased slightly to 35.5 percent, though the total amount budgeted for education began to fall, representing an overall decrease in higher education spending (Lorey 1992: 65). Enrollment in public higher education institutions nearly doubled from 64,200 students in 1969 to 110,223 in 1975, and numbers continued to rise through the late 1970s and into the early 1980s (Albornoz 1977: 301; Lorey 1992). The number of university graduates increased by 41 percent in the 1970s, with the numbers of graduates in engineering, related technical fields, business, and economics-related degrees increasing most rapidly. Engineering represented 28.5 percent of all degrees granted by the early 1980s (Lorey 1992: 75). However, increasingly difficult economic conditions through the 1980s eroded higher education enrollments. By the mid-1980s only 4 percent of students sitting for university entrance exams came from households that endured critical poverty (Buxton 2003: 117). Education, in those circumstances, could not provide the promised social mobility, reaffirm the political legitimacy of the state, or adequately serve the technical needs of the state.

Success in diversifying the economic base through development of other industries was equally ephemeral, though Venezuela began industrial projects with as much gusto as it had invested in education. The most successful project, the CVG, had its roots in the period prior to Punto Fijo and owed its success in part to its MIT (Massachusetts Institute of Technology) trained management's ability to insulate it from political gamesmanship. The corporation and its subsidiaries developed Venezuela's iron, steel, and aluminum resources, planned and sponsored the development of Ciudad Guayana (population 750,000 in 2009) to house industrial workers and support continued economic development. The cities of Puerto Ordaz and San Felix also boomed.

The Venezuelan automotive industry met with less success. Automotive industry policy began in 1962. Its proponents argued that the ideal way to pursue Venezuelan development was to craft and enact policies that mirrored successful industrial development in the United States, hence the interest in cars. The auto industry could create both investment and employment opportunities. Ideally, sowing the wealth in the auto industry could foster technological independence and reduce costly imports (Coronil 1997: 240). Using import substitution industrialization, transnational corporations, primarily the Big Three (Ford, General Motors, and Chrysler), established assembly plants in Venezuela in the 1960s that produced Big Three cars with Big Three parts imported into Venezuela. Entry into the Andean Pact in 1973 pushed Venezuelan planners into action because participation in the pact required Venezuela to coordinate auto production, assembly and otherwise, with other pact nations (Colombia, Peru, Ecuador, and Bolivia). Throughout 1974 and 1975 officials from CORDIPLAN, the Development Ministry, and the Foreign Commerce Institute worked with a 1969 plan drafted by three AD economic specialists connected with corporate interests to create the plan that became Venezuela's auto law in May 1975.

The law incorporated elements of the economic idealism that inspired policies in 1962, with constraints that served to limit development in practice and that echoed

An American car parked alongside a church on the island of Isla Margarita. (Raymond Wijngaard/StockPhotoPro)

the political and corporate connections of the law's authors. The law preferenced those companies already engaged in some form of auto production in Venezuela and the car-buying tastes of Venezuelans; Venezuela would not work with the growing Japanese auto industry to produce smaller, more energy-efficient cars but with the U.S. auto industry to learn how to build 1970s Detroit Big Three gas-guzzling cruisers. The law established timetables to increase the percentage of auto parts locally produced with locally manufactured materials and eventually required the Venezuelan auto industry to export parts (Coronil 1997: 240–243). The Venezuelan industry would initially purchase major parts (engines, for example) from non-Venezuelan auto producers that fit certain model types, primarily Big Three model types. Venezuela would then learn how to make the major parts on their own and become automotively self-sufficient. Transnational corporations (primarily the Big Three) could participate directly in the Venezuelan parts and auto markets if they partnered with Venezuelan firms.

Major forms of capital were less than enthusiastic in their support of the Venezuelan plan. Venezuelan investors preferred to place their capital in proven Venezuelan ventures—real estate, banking, and commerce. Foreign investors' response was complicated by the consequences of the oil crisis on transnational auto companies. The Big Three in particular began efforts to seek new markets in which to make and sell cars to combat the auto economic catastrophe produced by the 1970s oil embargo. They wanted to make "world cars . . . standardized auto models assembled from components produced in different countries" (Coronil 1997: 245). According to *Business Latin America:*

> Corporate strategy should be mapped out for the area as a whole, so that bids in one country are prepared with regional priorities in mind . . . Concessions that would make the home office wince would look quite different to management if they gain firm access to a related project. (Coronil 1997: 245–246)

In other words, if the Big Three accommodated Venezuela in one area, they extracted payment in another. The 1975 law appeared to bend in favor of the Big Three, but to them, given their emerging policies and practices, this was not enough. One GM official bluntly stated in 1980 that they would not invest "a penny" in Venezuela (Coronil 1997: 251).

The auto law, in essence, established a quota system that limited transnational corporations' ability to develop their products (parts and completed vehicles) and markets as they saw fit. In both words and deeds, the transnational corporations that were already engaged in part or auto production resisted any implementation of the 1975 law and eventually forced the government to reduce the amount of local product in parts or in completed autos—nullifying the intent of the law. Because the Venezuelan demand for cars only grew during the 1970s, and the small local industry could not meet the demand without new imports, the government remained convinced of the need to create a local industry. The controversial bidding process for major new automobile projects began in 1976 and continued through 1978 and escalated into a so-called Motor War that eventually involved other Andean Pact nations. In the end in the early 1980s Ford suggested that the Andean Pact nations should continue using 1960s import substitution assembly strategies to produce Big Three vehicles and not pursue producing engines or complete automobiles until "local market volume justified production" (Coronil 1997: 278). Venezuela could continue to export parts, such as wheels made from Venezuelan aluminum. Venezuela did not object to these terms and in so doing acquiesced to North Atlantic economic terms and conceded that it would remain an oil producer and assembler of parts but not an equal partner in the industrial, global economy.

Oil wealth, Fernando Coronil argues, empowered the Venezuelan state to assume that it could undertake ambitious economic projects, often poorly organized and not well thought out in terms of resources and manpower. In so doing, Venezuela alienated foreign capital resources (the Big Three in the scenario just described) and also sacrificed the managerial, economic, and technical expertise associated with foreign capital. The state forgot its historical ties to private capital inside and outside of Venezuela and the historical expectations of unified, interconnected, transnational corporations. President Pérez admitted as much when he noted that transnational automobile corporations do not act based on their individual corporate interests, but instead for the interests of the transnationals as a whole (Coronil 1997: 284). Moreover, Venezuelan politicians made economic decisions based on electoral considerations, not best economic practices. If there has yet been a time when Venezuela had the opportunity to resolve the permanent dilemma, it was the 1970s. Instead of saving Venezuela, economist Bernard Mommer argues, oil drowned the nation (Mommer 2003: 133).

PDVSA the Conglomerate

By the early 1980s Venezuelan-owned industries obtained 60 percent of their capital from loans and only 19 percent from their own earnings (Hellinger 1991: 146). Debt numbers, rising sharply during the Pérez administration, ballooned during the Herrera Campins administration from $9 billion to $24 billion (Coronil 1997: 370). Additional credit became difficult to obtain, the 1983 devaluation of the bolivar did nothing to increase productivity, and more capital flew north than monarch butterflies from Mexico. In a search for capital, the state tapped PDVSA's $5.5 billion investment fund. That, combined with rising oil prices and falling international demand and plummeting prices, limited PDVSA's ability to invest in Venezuela. The combination of circumstances propelled PDVSA to engage in a policy of internationalization. Using this policy, PDVSA began to invest in refineries, acquire affiliates, and sign long-term contracts in other countries that had the effect of sending many of the company's profits abroad and insulating them from the economic turmoil inside Venezuela. Citgo in the United States is a PDVSA-owned and managed company, for example (Mommer 2003: 134–135).

At the same time, PDVSA created strategies that made it more an international oil conglomerate than a state-owned industry. It began to work to avoid limitations imposed on the industry by OPEC membership. When world oil prices began to fall in the early 1980s, OPEC instituted a quota system to limit member nations' production to prop up international prices. PDVSA, in this case in collusion with the state, employed a variety of tactics to maintain or increase Venezuelan production despite OPEC quotas, including redefining certain types of crude so that they would not count in OPEC quotas. In 1989, PDVSA initiated a program of *apertura petrolera* that allowed PDVSA to partner with foreign companies, enabling them to bid on not completely explored fields and new concessions in the Orinoco basin and also to manufacture synthetic crude not subject to OPEC quotas (Tinker Salas 2009: 230; Mommer 2003: 136).

More than policies made PDVSA a conglomerate domestically and internationally. It was the attitude. Since nationalization, the state, in most cases, refrained from interfering with how PDVSA extracted the oil and managed its operations so long as the company delivered profits to the state. PDVSA had retained the foreign companies' management structures and their corporate culture predicated on "bonds of obligation and loyalty among [PDVSA] employees . . . a strong sense of group solidarity that transcended traditional class boundaries" (Tinker Salas 2009: 11). As such, PDVSA executives perceived themselves as uniquely qualified petroleum experts empowered to establish company policies and practices without interference from the state. If anything, PDVSA thought politicians and the general population were a "disruptive force" in the pursuit of PDVSA's drive to create corporate autonomy, to increase production, and to protect profits (Tinker Salas 2009: 229). As the company became more of an international conglomerate than a state enterprise and instituted tactics that alienated company profits from state use, policies and attitude perfectly paralleled each other.

NEOLIBERALISM

We assess in greater depth elsewhere the profound social and political consequences of the institution of neoliberal economic policies in 1989. For now we need to assess neoliberalism in strictly economic terms. Neoliberal economists presume that economic growth provides the path toward human progress. Governments should not interfere in free, increasingly global markets. All steps that a government can take to remove impediments to the free flow of capital—for example, deregulation, tariff or subsidy removals, or deunionization—are considered positive steps. Neoliberals also perceive privatization of industries and services as a public good as it removes inefficiencies inherent in the public sector. The government should even reduce social spending in education and public health. The most important role of the government is to provide the infrastructure to support laws necessary to protect property rights and contracts (Robbins 1999: 100). Much neoliberal policy has its roots in economic liberalism that developed during the Enlightenment and was championed by Adam Smith in *Wealth of Nations.* The 20th-century neoliberal prophet was Milton Friedman of the Chicago School of Economics. Already by the 1970s, Chilean dictator Augusto Pinochet had incorporated some neoliberal economic policy into Chilean economic practices. By the 1980s, international lending agencies like the IMF (International Monetary Fund) and the World Bank adopted neoliberalism as the panacea to the debt crisis that enveloped the developing world, not just Latin American countries. The lending agencies conditioned loans on the implementation of neoliberal practices (deregulation, privatization, decreased public sector spending, etc.) in order to spur private sector investment and free market practices.

As we noted in Chapters 2 and 3, Carlos Andres Pérez campaigned for a second term as president in 1988 on a promise to reject any neoliberal IMF reform package as conditional to new loans. Upon election, accepting an IMF package is exactly what Pérez did. In addition to slashing subsidies and public spending (the measures that directly led to the *caracazo*), he freed the exchange rate, reduced tariffs, lifted requirements on local content in exports, embraced foreign capital in utilities, and began the process of privatizing 64 public enterprises (Hellinger 1991: 146). The *apertura petrolera* allowed foreign oil conglomerates to reenter the Venezuelan petroleum marketplace. So much did U.S. oil executives like *apertura* policies, particularly under the leadership of PDVSA President Luis Giusti during the Caldera administration (1994–1999), that they named Giusti the Petroleum Executive of the Year in 1998 (Parker 2005: 42). The neoliberal policies led to economic growth at an average annual rate of 7.4 percent between 1990 and 1993, but poverty rates continued to rise (Buxton 2003: 118). Inflation rates exploded to 103 percent in 1996 (Ellner 1998: 126). In 1996, President Rafael Caldera announced a second neoliberal

IMF austerity program that included a 600 percent increase in the price of gasoline (Coronil 1997: 384). That measure proved to be as politically explosive as the price increases that were part of the first *paquete* and had to be scrapped. The damage of both *paquetes* combined with a century of wealth mismanagement had been done, however. By the middle of the 1990s, the small elite class, the ones historically connected to the international marketplace, had made the most of the advantages neoliberalism provided them and substantially improved their investment portfolios and beefed up their U.S.-based bank accounts. The middle class had been nearly wiped out by spiraling inflation and the associated price increases. The number of poor exploded, and the suffering was worse as the reforms eroded the safety nets—subsidies, public health care—that protected them. The long-term picture was made more bleak when one considers the long-term economic consequences of successive cuts in education spending. The economic context with its damning social consequences produced dramatic political change and the election of Hugo Chávez Frías in 1998. As we shall see, as much as he has tried to manage the economy to build a new Venezuela, many of his economic tools and tactics are old. The permanent dilemma remains.

LABOR

Oil and Society, Labor and Otherwise

A U.S. observer of early Venezuelan oil works in the 1910s noted of Venezuelan laborers that "the companies won't teach the natives [Venezuelans] all of the tricks of the trade. They're afraid if the natives get to know it all of the countries down here will kick the Americans and the English out and run the fields themselves" (Tinker Salas 2009: 111). For Venezuelans, control of the oil meant not only control of the subsoil resource but, as we have already seen, the acquisition of the expertise to manage the resource effectively. Early on at least, some international observers recognized that the Venezuelans were not only entirely up to the task of learning all of the physical and intellectual skills associated with oil production but said observers also acknowledged the economic global consequences of said skills. In this section, we will analyze the evolution of Venezuelan labor in the 20th and 21st century, from a force alienated from the means of a production and stigmatized by race and class, to a powerful political force, and finally to a force fragmented both by politics and a large informal economy.

Understanding the evolution of labor in the oil industry, the industry that dominated the 20th century and continued to shape 21st-century Venezuela, requires some understanding of Venezuelan concepts of race and class. We deal with those issues in some depth in Chapter 5. It is worth noting here that the development of the oil industry took place within the context of charged debates about Venezuelan identity predicated in reevaluating and denigrating the role of people of color and the poor in Venezuelan history. Routinely, as we have noted, Venezuelan elites categorized the poor and people of color as backwards, as barbarians responsible for Venezuela's lack of progress in North Atlantic terms. If they were only less lazy, less indolent, and less drunk, Venezuela would be an orderly, progressive nation, or so the argument went. A 1921 conference of Venezuelan agricultural, cattle, merchant, and industrial interests concluded that Venezuelan labor was "debased, addicted to gambling, inefficient, and lacking in morals and 'fulfillment of their duty'" (Tinker Salas 2009: 96). When foreign oil officials described Venezuelan laborers as indolent and lazy, as petty criminals and gamblers unable to work in the tropical Venezuelan environment, they only echoed stereotypes Venezuelan elites had fostered since the colonial era (Tinker Salas 2009: 95, 110).

Labor and Race in the Development of the Oil Industry

The labor and wage hierarchy implemented by the companies reflected stereotypes about Venezuelan labor that explained, in part, the companies' preference for immigrant labor. A 1918 Venezuelan immigration law strictly prohibited the immigration of all except those of European descent. However, company demands required them to ignore the law to facilitate the immigration of thousands of West Indian, Mexican, Chinese, and Middle Eastern employees, who all found their places in the work hierarchy (Tinker Salas 2009: 108). U.S. employees served in professional and skilled labor capacities in Venezuelan oil fields (tool pushers, riggers, machinists, carpenters, and fabricators); West Indians performed work that ranged from physical labor to office help; the companies assigned Asians to service positions (mess hall, laundry, etc.); Venezuelans filled a few office positions, but most formed the majority of the unskilled labor force (Tinker Salas 2009: 96).

Companies clearly thought immigrant labor was more capable than Venezuelan labor. They thought West Indians in particular were "more trustworthy and hardworking than Venezuelan labourers" and lacked the negative "Latin characteristics, such as excitability, irresponsibility, etc." (Tinker Salas 2009: 100, 111). West Indians also spoke English and were familiar with the British administrative structure, which was akin to company hierarchy and bureaucracy. Because of their history with the West Indians within the context of colonialism, company officials, especially British company officials, thought West Indians were more likely to be more pliant, more accommodating employees less likely to join labor unions. Just because North Atlantic oil officials thought West Indians made better employees did not mean that they decided not to impose Jim Crow–style segregation in oil operations. West Indians lived in separate quarters, ate in separate dining rooms, belonged to separate social clubs, and even used different water fountains and bathrooms. Violation of those policies were one of many reasons for dismissal and placement on the infamous "blacklist." Those placed on the blacklist could never find work in any of the camps with any of the companies.

Wages and benefits varied by category, nationality, and skill. Most Venezuelans worked without the security of contracts, hired by intermediaries as day laborers called *peones*, a derogatory term in the Venezuelan context. Though in the early decades, living conditions in the camps were extremely poor for all workers regardless of nationality, by the late 1930s through the 1950s, living conditions also reflected wage and occupation hierarchies as well as North American ideas about segregation. The U.S. company employees lived in communities that mirrored suburbia in the United States, carefully planned, efficiently administered, and representative of a "modern economic and social order" complete with sports facilities and commissaries that functioned like North American supermarkets (Tinker Salas 2009: 4–5). Some Venezuelan professional junior staff associated with the companies were allowed to live inside the camps' gated communities, but they were segregated from U.S. senior staff. The remainder of the Venezuelan work force lived outside camp walls in conditions that reinforced their subordinate status in the company.

Women Workers

We should also note that while men composed the overwhelming majority of the formal labor workforce associated with the growing oil industry in the early 20th century, female employment in the informal sector increased dramatically. Women worked as food vendors, cooks, seamstresses, and laundresses, but many more women became part of the active sex trade associated with each oil camp in the country. The sex trade eventually became big business. Some companies actually distributed condoms to their employees every week. Politicians did not work to eradicate the trade but instead to make sure they got their cut. They also began efforts to control the spread of venereal diseases. Authorities required sex trade workers to submit to weekly health exams and to carry health cards as proof of good health. Even so, by 1947 the national health ministry estimated that 64 percent of people who had to be hospitalized had syphilis and 37 percent had other venereal diseases. Companies began to randomly test employees for venereal diseases and fire those who were sick. Unions demanded treatment instead (Tinker Salas 2009: 66–67).

Though *muchachas*, "girls" or domestic servants, may have spent their days laboring in conditions less sexually exploitative than sex workers, *muchachas'* jobs were no less difficult. The title *muchacha* is demeaning and disrespectful, roughly equivalent to calling all African American men "boy," regardless of age, as was common through much U.S. history. *Muchachas*, like Indian *ayahs* who worked for British imperial authorities in India, found themselves as cultural go-betweens. Daily and constantly, the U.S. or British wives of company employees demeaned *muchachas'* intellectual and cultural capabilities. At the same time, said wives relied on the *muchachas* as cooks and nannies, to run errands, and to interact as necessary on behalf of the English-speaking family with the Venezuelan world outside of the camp. Wives often preferred English-speaking West Indian *muchachas* to their Venezuelan counterparts, using the same stereotypes to justify their choices. Whether Venezuelan or West Indian, domestic servants lived in the shantytowns that mushroomed outside of walled oil camps in conditions that had little in common with the middle-class suburban comfort enjoyed by their employers (Tinker Salas 2009: 113–116).

Nationalism and the Beginning of Labor Activism

As the Mexican oil industry began to decline in the 1920s because of economic pressures (not as a consequence of the Mexican Revolution), more Mexicans experienced in the industry moved to Venezuela (Brown 1985: 385). By the middle 1920s President Gómez began to worry that Mexicans employed in the Venezuela oil industry transplanted Mexican revolutionary tendencies to Venezuela. Gomez's later interactions with Mexico and with intellectual and Mexican Minister of Education José Vasconcelos in particular, indicated that his preoccupation crossed the border into paranoia and possibly vendetta; he had Vasconcelos followed when he traveled abroad. However, Venezuela's growing labor troubles were entirely homegrown (Tinker Salas 2009: 125). In all of the fields, British or U.S. controlled, Venezuelan laborers complained about poor pay, lack of medical care (petroleum work is dangerous), inadequate housing, and discrimination.

Complaints occasionally escalated to strikes and other forms of labor unrest. In 1925, strikes engulfed the Shell-operated oil fields at Mene Grande and La Rosa. At the same time, railway workers went on strike against three foreign-owned railway companies in the Caracas area, with the support of the press and the general public. The police had to disperse a riot related to the strike with clubs and pistols (McBeth 2008: 204). Such violence against strikers and their supporters was not unusual. Neither the companies nor Gómez hesitated to use violence against strikers. The violence eventually caught the attention of the Pan American Federation of Labor and the International Labor Organization, though neither their complaints nor strike activity provoked many concessions from the companies (Ewell 1984: 69–72).

The West Indians and Chinese found themselves in a terribly uncomfortable place in the middle of growing tensions between workers and the companies, unable to

---

MENE

Not all Venezuelans were equally enthusiastic about Venezuela's early dependence on the oil industry. One of the earliest and most cogent critiques took literary form in Ramón Díaz Sánchez's *Mene* (1934). Written in four parts, the novel uses four stories to examine the social and cultural consequences of rapid Venezuelan dependence on oil exports and the role of the industry in Venezuela. In sum, Díaz Sánchez suggests that Venezuela sold its soul to the devil when it opened its wells and its doors to the companies. He poignantly argues that human, cultural, and social costs paid by Venezuelans and West Indian immigrants far outweighed any profit obtained from oil. Two characters (a West Indian immigrant and a Venezuelan married to an engineer from Kansas City) commit suicide after their relationships with the company and North Americans goes sour. Díaz Sánchez used those characters, among others, to represent Venezuela. No Venezuelan characters enjoyed a happy ending in *Mene*. Díaz Sánchez's point was clear.

speak Spanish to communicate with the Venezuelans, and rejected by the British and the Americans on racial and national grounds. The Venezuelans, in particular, combined their frustration over subordination to North Atlantic interests with their own prejudices against darker hued peoples. The result was frequently violent, with the West Indians as the victims. Though the overwhelming majority of company employees were Venezuelan, government officials worried that the comparatively small population of West Indians only exacerbated Venezuela's "race problem." Venezuela needed to "defend the race" from outside influences (West Indians) that could produce a "lamentable regression" to Venezuela's "ethnic nucleus," causing "grave prejudice" to Venezuelan society (Tinker Salas 2009: 135). West Indians did seek nationalization in Venezuela at a higher rate than other foreign nationals did. By 1936, in an attempt to diffuse tensions that were spreading through the camps on multiple issues, not just the nationality and race of laborers, the government ordered that 75 percent of all company employees, blue and white collar, had to be Venezuelan (Tinker Salas 2009: 117).

The legislation of 1928 did little to halt the companies' and government's abuses of workers' rights. A 1936 labor law was the first law to provide any real protection for workers. The new López Contreras administration passed the law in the wake of a massive strike in 1935 by oil workers celebrating of the death of Gómez. In Lagunillas and Cabimas, workers rioted and looted and took vengeance on police for years of suffering and abuse. In the end, 200 people died. The riots and looting caused millions of bolivars in property damage (McBeth 2008: 369). The 1936 law established the right to unionize, bargain collectively, and mandated the eight-hour workday. It also allowed for a form of workers' compensation in case of injury on the job. The government did not always follow the law, however. Unions called a general strike in December 1936 that lasted until January 1937. López Contreras ended the strike without considering workers' demands and retained the right to cancel labor syndicates—a union's legal right to exist. In 1937, López Contreras exiled 47 labor leaders and prolabor politicians accused of communist activities. Others he imprisoned. López Contreras's actions had a chilling effect on the formation of new unions and the growth of union membership. The number of unions decreased from 246 to 155 between 1939 and 1940, and membership fell from 69,139 (1939) to 36,326 (1940) (Ewell 1984: 82).

AD and the Venezuelan Labor Movement—1944 to 1958

Simultaneous to the slow growth of the union movement in Venezuela was the much more successful development of the AD political party. AD coined the phrase "to divide is to locate," which meant that there should be multiple unions in any given industry so that workers could join the union that best suited their political leanings (Ellner 1993: 2). AD proposed that the political fracturing of the total labor movement was acceptable because it allowed the strongest political party to gain the largest number of adherents in the movement. By 1944, AD felt politically strong enough to move to control Venezuela's labor organizations. At the March 1944 Second Workers' Congress, AD proposed the formation of a national labor organization with leadership divided between AD and the communist party. When negotiations between the parties broke down, AD pulled out of the conference. At that point, President Medina Angarita found the congress in violation of the constitution because it established a formal relationship between labor and a political party. He suspended national recognition of all unions that remained at the congress, undercutting the communists in all labor matters, weakened the party, and opened the political and labor field for AD. At the same time, AD began to organize peasant unions. By 1945, there were 77 syndicates with 6,279 members (Ewell 1984: 82–83).

When Rómulo Betancourt became president in 1945 after the fall of Medina Angarita, not only did the event mark the beginning of Venezuela's first experiment with democracy but the beginning of a long relationship between AD and Venezuelan labor, industrial and rural, and a more formal relationship between union labor and the companies. Unions signed their first formal contract with the companies in 1946 (Tinker Salas 2009: 3). During the *trienio*, AD acted as if it owned the labor, peasant, and student movements, though the companies had to remind Betancourt of small communist party successes in unions in rural oil camps (Ellner 1993: 2; Tinker Salas 2005: 155–156). Unions and parties had to overcome their differences in order to survive the 10 years of dictatorship between the fall of the *trienio* and the beginning of Venezuelan-style democracy in 1958.

Dictator Marcos Pérez Jiménez forced the AD underground during most of the period between 1948 and 1958 and restricted the activities of other political parties, complicating their ability to work with labor. Even so, the parties worked together with labor in a 1950 oil workers strike in Zulia and Anzoategui. The government besieged workers' camps to end the strikes through starvation. The strike ended in 10 days, but the working relationship between the parties with labor endured (Ellner 1993: 3). The assassination of an AD underground leader and the death of a second chilled AD/PCV (Partido Comunista de Venezuela) labor activities until 1956. In that year, Pérez Jiménez founded the Confederación Nacional de Trabajadores (CNT)—his own labor movement. He increased social security benefits and began the construction of low-income housing units (*superbloques*) in an effort to undercut worker support for other unions. In response, COPEI, AD, the PCV, and the URD (Unión Republicana Democrática) formed a workers' committee that demanded the dissolution of the CNT, the removal of the labor minister, and the enforcement of the 1936 labor law (Ellner 1993: 4).

The foundations laid in 1956 enabled the parties working with labor to play a significant role in the resistance in December 1957 and January 1958 that led to Pérez Jiménez's departure on January 23, 1958. The worker's committee then became the Comité Sindical Unificado (CSU, Unified Labor Committee) and worked to support the Wolfgang Larrazabal–led junta through 1958. Sometimes they assumed the civil functions of the police in the absence of real police in the first weeks; they called general strikes and blockaded Caracas to thwart coups against the junta. In return, Larrazabal recognized unions and returned confiscated union property. Together with FEDECAMARAS (Venezuela's most important business organization, roughly equivalent to a national chamber of commerce), the CSU constructed the Pacto de Avenimiento Obrero Patronal, which urged the creation of labor-management committees to "settle industrial disputes and for the signing of industrywide contracts to standardize working conditions and benefits" (Ellner 1993: 6). Businesses agreed to avoid layoffs whenever possible and recognized the right to unionize. The government followed up in November 1958 with Decree 440, which mandated industry-wide collective bargaining at the regional or national level when business, government, or the majority of workers through their leadership requested it. If workers and businesses failed to reach a contract through collective bargaining, an arbitration process would decide contracts (Ellner 1993: 6–7). Those two developments laid the groundwork for relationships between unions and business through the Punto Fijo period, or between 1959 to 1989.

Labor in the Era of Punto Fijo, 1959–1989

What strikes most outside observers about labor in Venezuela in the era of institutionalized democracy (1959–1989) is labor's relative passivity. As industries grew during the 1960s and 1970s labor did not, by and large, publicly demand greater percentages of industry profits. Labor did not decry the growing income inequality that separated blue from white collar workers in the 1970s. It was not until 1989 that national disturbances with their roots in inequality rocked the nation. Organized labor, however, had nothing to do with fomenting any sort of class consciousness that fed the *caracazo* riots. CTV (Confederación de Trabajadores de Venezuela) officials actually accused participants in the demonstrations of being "loafers, thieves, and vagabonds" (Ellner 1993: 82). An assessment of the close relationship between organized labor as represented by the CTV, the government, and business is the focus of this section of the chapter.

From the beginning of the 1960s, the CTV styled itself as the spokesperson of the popular classes. It used its support for increases in the minimum wage and for application of the labor law to workers in the informal economy as evidence of its grassroots agenda. However, the CTV never functioned in the labor market without measuring its actions or consulting with the government and/or FEDECAMARAS. Through much of its history, outside observers might argue that the CTV's relationship with the political system, particularly with AD, was incestuously close. AD's equally close relationship with FEDECAMARAS made for a kin relationship that undercut labor's independence. By the 1970s, in an institutional agreement with COPEI, AD controlled the CTV presidency and COPEI controlled the secretary-general position. That institutional pact within the CTV became foundational to the national political institutional pact between AD and CTV that lasted through the 1980s. Moreover, AD controlled the CTV's executive committee through the 1980s. Other parties (MEP and MAS, for example), tried to find their voices in the CTV's National Congresses, but with little to show for their efforts (Ellner 1993: 13, 46, 227).

Additional labor protections gained through legislation in the 1960s and the 1970s reinforced labor's tranquility. The 1966 Law of Worker's Representation gave labor a seat on the board of directors of state-run companies and institutes. It was hailed as labor earning a "seat at the table," but has since come to be seen as legislation that facilitated the CTV's co-optation (Ellner 1993: 38). The 1974 Ley contra Despidos Injustificados (Law against Unjustified Layoffs), passed during the Pérez administration, was even more important to labor. The law ordered companies to pay double severance to any employee laid off without cause. Layoffs with cause required a single severance payment. A tripartite commission (labor, employer, and government) determined whether layoffs were justified or not (Ellner 1993: 206). The 1974 law did not mandate *estabilidad absoluta* (absolute job security) that labor had sought since 1959. It did, however, create *estabilidad indirecta* (indirect job security) because the threat of double severance served as a deterrent to layoffs. Pérez's administration also implemented a minimum wage for the first time in Venezuelan history. The minimum wage had been part of the 1936 Labor Law, but it had never been enacted. In addition, Pérez mandated scaled wage increases, apprenticeship programs, and obligatory employment of people to run building elevators and clean restaurant bathrooms in efforts to reach full employment (Ellner 1993: 51).

Legislation and the relationship between political parties, labor, and business were not enough to prevent all strikes in the 1960s, 1970s, and 1980s. Telephone and public transportation worker strikes in 1960 and 1962 are notable because they marked the end of unity between the political parties in labor issues that had been the norm in the Pérez Jiménez years. There were relatively few strikes in the 1960s, Steve Ellner argues, because the force used to control guerrilla activities (see Chapter 2) served as disincentive to any disgruntled laborers. The government's reluctance to recognize the legal right to strike also served to dampen labor's willingness to walk out. The overwhelming majority of strikes that occurred between 1958 and 1990 were declared illegal. The state recognized only seven strikes as legal in 1972 and declared 172 illegal. There were no legal strikes in 1983 and 200 illegal ones, involving 59,749 workers losing 2.9 million work hours (Ellner 1993: 49–50). The 1980 strike in the textiles industry over pay and working conditions is one example of one of the many illegal strikes. What makes that strike notable is that it shut down the entire textile industry, the first strike in decades to consume an industry completely. The CTV condemned the strike instead of supporting the workers. (Hellinger 1996: 115). By the 1980s, most strike activity originated in unions that were not associated with the CTV. Causa R became a political force in the state of Guayana and was extremely influential in the unions representing nonpetroleum heavy industries. Health workers and teachers—primary, secondary, and college—also did not hesitate to strike in the 1980s in response to state spending cuts combined with the consequences of currency devaluations.

Despite the growing number of illegal strikes, increasing poverty rates, and the growing importance of the informal economy in the 1980s the CTV preferred social harmony to challenging the government or FEDECAMARAS. Its revision of the AD "labor thesis" established in the early days of the Betancourt presidency, which defined the working class as a revolutionary force that would bring democracy and development, is an example of the accommodations the CTV was willing to make. In 1981, the CTV instead proposed *cogestión*, or shared control between workers and management, as the preferred goal for labor in the context of classical capitalism. That position made sense for the organization that had by the 1980s $1 billion in assets (Hellinger 1996: 113). The CTV appeared to side with the Pérez administration against participants in the 1989 *caracazo*, which showed just how out of touch the national labor organization had become. To try to regain its status as the spokesperson of the popular classes, the CTV called a general strike on May 18, 1989 that shut down the national economy completely for one day, the only strike of that scale until that point in Venezuelan history. That general strike did not mark a new trend for the CTV, however. Throughout the second administration of President Pérez, neighborhood associations, student organizations, and non-CTV unions led disturbances that targeted the state more than they did business. The CTV's hegemony in labor was a bit frayed, its alliance with FEDECAMARAS and the government shaken, but it remained the most important official labor confederation in Venezuela.

The Special Place of Oil Workers in the Labor Hierarchy

Oil workers, blue and white collar, saw themselves (and perhaps still see themselves) as the aristocracy of Venezuelan labor. They embody the modernity to which Venezuela strives in their discipline, efficiency, work ethic, and meritocracy. Their pay and benefits, PDVSA contract employees insist, reflect their special place in the labor market as those most closely associated with the industry that is national wealth, oil (Tinker Salas 2009: 5, 11). The origins of PDVSA's high pay have more to do with social harmony during a political transition than with efficiency and work ethics. President Betancourt in 1960 argued that in order to ensure economic productivity and social harmony during the critical early years of Venezuelan democracy, oil workers should earn salaries comparable to their U.S. counterparts (Ellner 1993: 132). When the oil industry acted on Betancourt's salary recommendations, Venezuelan oil workers earned substantially more than any other skilled or unskilled labor in Venezuela. Practical reality reinforced oil industry myth and culture and further reinforced within oil corporate culture the concept that oil workers were and should always be exceptional within the labor movement and in society as a whole.

In the 1960s and the 1970s, oil workers, through their union, Fedepetrol, won rights no other group of labor gained. Oil workers earned the protections that follow:

- The contractual right to *estabilidad absoluta* (absolute job security, roughly equivalent to tenure in education in the United States).
- The right that companies would only hire from lists submitted by the union.
- The right that union dues had to be deducted from employees' salaries.
- The right to a 40-hour work week.
- A reduction in the work assigned to contractors rather than contracted employees.
- A tripartite commissions to mediate disputes.
- A limitation on the number of employees not covered by union-negotiated contracts to only the top executives.

Other unions in other parts of the labor market eventually obtained some of the guarantees granted to oil labor, but no other union obtained as many rights and guarantees enjoyed by oil labor.

Over time, PDVSA labor became more and more white collar instead of blue collar, reflecting the company's corporate conglomerate identity. In 1963, 43.7 percent of labor was white collar. That number had increased to 53.8 percent in 1975 and 66.6 percent in 1989 (Ellner 1993: 138). High salaries for blue and white collar workers did not protect all of them from the economic crises of the 1980s. PDVSA tried to cut costs by trying to work around union rules on labor contracted out of the corporation as it was cheaper than PDVSA, union-protected labor. There were some strikes within the industry against PDVSA by the late 1980s, when workers became displeased by not only the presence of subcontractors but also by the elimination of benefits like commissaries. Employees understood salary reductions within the context of currency devaluations and inflation. Even so, PDVSA labor's position at the top of the labor hierarchy remained unchallenged at the end of the 1980s (Ellner 1993: 142). Oil labor, more than any other labor in the workforce, had the skills and the income to survive the economic crisis that continued through the 1990s.

Things Fall Apart, or Do They?: Labor in the 1990s and the Chávez Era

The 1990s could have marked a time of dramatic change for labor. Certainly economic and social conditions favored new relationships between workers, union, and the state. In the 1980s Causa R had become a political force in the state of Bolívar in part because of its advocacy of *nuevo sindicalismo* (new unionism). In the early 1990s, it began to have some success in Caracas, too. *Nuevo sindicalismo* offered a strong critique of the moral decay that had become part of the AD-CTV-FEDECAMARAS partnership and offered a new project to develop new union leadership from within the working classes, not based on ideology but instead on worker democracy (Hellinger 1996: 118). Causa R was a grassroots organization that attempted the inverse of standard Venezuelan union and political policy: to represent workers rather than to direct them. Political scientist Luis Salamanca said of Causa R when it became a political force in Bolívar, "it was not a political party in search of votes but a workers' union asking for the support of the electorate" (Hellinger 1996: 119). *Nuevo sindicalismo* dominated SIDOR (the iron and steel industry, Siderúrgica de Orinoco), with its 12,000 employees, until the CTV orchestrated an intervention that removed the most important new union leaders. One, Andres Velasquez, became the governor of Bolívar in 1989, elected in a landslide representing Causa R and reelected in 1992 with 70 percent of the vote (Hellinger 1996: 123). Even with its electoral success in the 1990s, Causa R worked to protect its grassroots foundations against party institutionalization. It allowed anyone to run on its slate for political, union, student organization, or neighborhood association positions so long as the candidate promised to put the interests of the constituency ahead of any other interests (Hellinger 1996: 125). However, in Venezuela's institutionalized labor and political system, grassroots efforts could not have much success nationwide, no matter their success regionally.

At the same time that *nuevo sindicalismo* appeared to draw strength away from the CTV and the traditional labor movement, President Pérez's bumbling allowed the CTV to regain some credibility without having to change its role substantially in the political-labor-business relationship. The CTV supported the 1990 labor law that strengthened workers' rights and benefits over the opposition of President Pérez. Pérez, whose credibility in the eyes of the populace was already extremely dented because of the implementation of neoliberal economic reforms, supported an executive order that would have allowed the president to establish salaries insufficient to cover the cost of living that constantly increased because of inflation. That move was easy for the CTV to oppose. A corruption scandal forced Pérez out of office in 1993, allowing the CTV to remain loyal within the system once the president most associated with unpopular initiatives left office (Burgess 1999). When AD established an unofficial pact with President Rafael Caldera (COPEI, 1994–1999) in exchange for a pledge from Caldera to refrain from massive layoffs as part of a new wave of neoliberal reforms, it sealed the CTV's complicity in the collapse of Venezuela's "exceptional" democracy in 1998 (Ellner 2005: 54).

We have assessed elsewhere in this work how blind the political parties had become to real class and race divisions in Venezuela and how that facilitated, at least in part, Hugo Chávez's electoral successes in 1998, 1999, and 2000. During the electoral processes, Chávez called CTV leadership a "trade union mafia" that "slavishly defended the positions of AD and COPEI" (Ellner 2005: 54). Though, as we have seen, the situation was a bit more complex than that, the accusations rang true enough with a substantial percentage of the electorate. The door was open for a new labor movement in Venezuela—sort of. Some scholars argue that from the beginning of his presidency Chávez worked to control the CTV. When those efforts failed, he pushed for the creation of an alternative labor union (Shapiro 2007). Though Chávez has never been an objective bystander in labor politics during his presidency, we also cannot discount the role of internal divisions within the labor movement in the development of labor and political strategies throughout the early years of the 21st century. Chavistas were not unanimous on what to do with the CTV in the early years of the Chávez presidency. Some wanted to dissolve the CTV completely. Moderates, who prevailed at least initially, argued that the CTV should be allowed a place at the table, as it were, in order to include them in labor and policy discussions. Legislation secured benefits sought by advocates from the left, including generous severance packages, broadened social security benefits, and a limitation on night shift work to 35 hours a week (Ellner 2005: 55).

New Chavista labor leaders worked to limit the authority of traditional labor in other ways consistent with arguments made by Causa R and neoliberals in decades prior. Causa R had always been suspicious that automatic payment of union dues stipulated by union contract had been a vehicle that drove toward corruption in unions. Neoliberals had never liked contractual obligations to hire established percentages of union labor in oil and other industries. Neither new unionists nor neoliberals approved of permanent job security for union officials that allowed them to take leaves of absence that extended indefinitely in some cases, divorcing leaders from any real contact with labor. However, Chavistas criticized these tactics not because they shared neoliberal ideas about increasing labor efficiency and limiting unions' influences in a free economy, but as a way to undercut traditional labor leadership and its alliance with AD. When Chávez's choice to lead PDVSA proposed a new 2000 collective bargaining agreement with PDVSA, workers included stipulations that addressed those critiques, and opponents to the contract described the deal as neoliberal and unacceptable (Ellner 2005: 58).

In the early years of the Chávez presidency, a powerful group of labor independents had the ability, Steve Ellner argues, to definitively move labor away from its close relationship with the state, AD, or Chavistas. The union representing SIDOR workers was the most prominent of the independents. SIDOR by then was privatized, no longer a state-run enterprise. In May 2001, that union led a three-week strike against SIDOR that temporarily crippled the economy in Ciudad Guayana and other industrial cities along the Orinoco. Chavistas supported the union's moves; when the strike ended favorably for the union and workers, Chávez recognized the strike as a success (Ellner 2005: 59). In the months that followed and preceding October 2001 CTV elections, independents and labor leaders sympathetic (but not directly associated with) Chávez's MVR (Movimiento Quinto República) worked through elections in the CTV to avoid the creation of a labor confederation parallel to the CTV. At the same time support coalesced around a new labor organization, the FBT (Bolivarian Workers' Force) and its chosen candidate for CTV president, Aristóbulo Istúriz, university professor, former Causa R mayor of Caracas (1992–1996), and cofounder of the PPT (Homeland for All) party that ran Chávez as its candidate in 1998. At the same time, AD unionists created the FUT (Frente Unitario de Trabajadores) and ran their own candidates for key CTV positions. When the voting concluded amid widespread accusations of electoral fraud and voter intimidation, the FUT had won 64 percent of the vote and retained control of CTV positions. Independents and Chavistas who had been arguing for moderation in relations with the CTV insisted that they had no choice but to separate from the labor confederation. In the process, they began to grow closer to Chávez and the MVR (Ellner 2005: 62). The general strikes in 2001, 2002, and 2003 finalized the divorce.

Though the CTV had always maintained a close relationship to the state, particularly to AD, and a cordial relationship with FEDECAMARAS, it had always publicly maintained the appearance of independence. It insisted that it was the voice of the working class. FUT/AD's manipulation of the CTV elections in 2001 demonstrated that FUT/AD did not understand the CTV as an independent voice for labor in the society, regardless of which politician lived in Miraflores. FUT, AD, and the other political opposition to Chávez saw the labor confederation as tool in a greater political game to reconstruct the political system as it had been before 1998. From that perspective, the general strikes were not about improving working conditions for labor (the role of general strikes historically, globally) but about manipulating the system for political gain. Immediately after FUT won the CTV elections, the new FUT/AD president of CTV, Carlos Ortega, began to work with FEDECAMARAS to form an alliance that led to four general strikes: December 2001, April 2002 (which produced a failed coup attempt), October 2002, and December 2002 through February 2003. In all four cases, CTV workers and business owners joined forces to call for the ouster of President Chávez or immediate elections. The upper middle class and the elite were the most ardent supporters of the work stoppages. During the April 2002 strike, the FBT planned a counter general strike (also using the general strike as a political tactic) to oppose the coup and the brief presidency of FEDECAMA-RAS leader Pedro Carmona. The independent labor leaders opposed the general strikes because the alliance with FEDECAMARAS invalidated labor's voice in any negotiations with businesses. Moreover, Ortega called the general strikes (whose goal was to shut down all labor in the country, in all industries) without consulting other labor leaders.

We deal with more of the devastating consequences of the 10-week December 2002 to February 2003 general strike elsewhere. The consequences for labor were dramatic. CTV's support for the strike permanently undercut the labor confederation's credibility with much of the working class. Those labor moderates within the MVR and FBT who had continued to argue for moderation and continued relationships with the CTV despite the earlier general strikes either left the MVR or conceded the finality of the divorce. Finally, the labor independents were ready for the definitive break (Ellner 2005: 63–64). The independents, who were neither pro-Chávez or anti-Chávez like most political independents (approximately 40%–50% of the population at that time) argued that the new labor confederation that had to form after the break with the CTV had to retain its independence from the state in order to protect its credibility in the eyes of the working classes. Only with massive grassroots support would the confederation succeed, with careful planning. The Chavistas in the FBT argued that the political exigencies of the moment did not allow for the sort of time the independents requested and insisted that a close relationship to the state was necessary for the new confederation's survival. The latter arguments won the day in the formation of the UNT (Workers' National Union) (Ellner 2005: 64).

The UNT styled itself as a labor confederation who's loyalty to the workers would be unquestioned. The UNT tried to address policies and enact practices that would preclude the corruption that had become endemic in the CTV. Though the UNT's relationship with the MVR was close, their ideas about labor policies were not always identical. Chávez was, however, heartened when the UNT assumed a strong position in favor of worker control of businesses in bankruptcy or on the verge of bankruptcy. In the wake of the 2002–2003 general strike, there were many businesses nationwide owned but Venezuelans and foreigners with thousands of employees in exactly that situation. The UNT insisted that the companies should bear the economic burden created by the strike. Some leaders of CTV unions, however, allowed for the suspension of collective bargaining, worker layoffs, and the termination of fringe benefits associated with the duration of the strike (Ellner 2005: 66–67).

By far the most controversial decision enacted by Chavistas in the wake of the 2002–2003 general strike was the purge of PDVSA, the industry at the heart of the strike, of all employees who supported or who were suspected of supporting the strike that resulted in a "criminal" paralysis of Venezuela's most important industry. Eighteen thousand PDVSA employees, mostly white collar, many highly skilled engineers and technicians, immediately lost their jobs. Many discovered that they were blacklisted and could never legally work in Venezuela again in any industry. Thousands of other employees were graylisted, suspected of supporting the strike because of their employment in the industry and unable to find jobs in the industry for years after the strike. The UNT took the vendetta against general strike and coup supporters even farther and called for their purge from positions of public administration. Those public administration employees and PDVSA employees who signed a recall petition to recall Chávez as president also found their jobs threatened. When Chávez won an August 2004 recall election, the situation finally began to ease. Chávez said in April 2005 that "the list [of those who signed against him] should now be buried" (Ellner 2008: 160). All purges through the years allowed Chavistas to occupy positions in PDVSA and public administration, in a new chapter in the old book on political and labor clientelism in Venezuela (Ellner 2005: 67–68). By 2006, the UNT had replaced the CTV as Venezuela's primary labor confederation, representing 76.5 percent of collective agreements (Janicke and Fuentes 2008).

The political exigency that created the UNT and pushed leaders associated with the MVR to the forefront did not resolve the fundamental rifts between labor leaders on crucial issues of theory (the relationship between labor, the state, and society) that had been percolating since at least the 1970s. The UNT suffered severe organizational and factional difficulties at its 2006 congress and did not reconvene another congress until December 2009. At that conference, leaders insisted that they would pursue a grassroots approach to labor organizing efforts (the strategy preferred by labor

Striking oil workers wave Venezuelan flags as they pass oil tanker Pilin Leon, which sits anchored in Lake Maracaibo, in support of the general strike against President Hugo Chávez on December 6, 2002. (AP/Wide World Photos)

independents in earlier years). They vowed adherence to the principles of "Organisational and political autonomy, independence from the state and capital, internal democracy, worker solidarity, internationalism, unity, gender equality and the rejection of 'class conciliation,'" though many of the leaders in the December congress were closely associated with the Chávez administration (Janicke 2009a).

Though some critics may justifiably question the UNT's commitment to independence, events in recent years may well have forced the UNT to rethink the benefits of a close relationship between labor and the state. The 2008 strike against SIDOR by an independent labor union, in addition to decrying poor working conditions and wages in the iron and steel industry, also brought back to the nation's attention the question of labor's relationship with political parties and the state. Labor questioned the state's relationship with management when the Chavista governor authorized the use of tear gas and rubber bullets against strikers (Janicke and Fuentes 2008). A strike against Mitsubishi because of poor working conditions lasted from January through September 2009. Two workers died when police tried to remove workers who had occupied the plant in Barcelona. The Labor Ministry appeared to collude with Mitsubishi to block the return to the workplace of 150 employees who had supported the strike, leading labor to accuse the Labor Ministry of approving practices akin to those of the pre-Chávez era (Suggett 2009c).

It is clear that union confederations have not found the formula to promote unity within the Venezuelan labor movement. Beyond theory, however, are the problems with the economy's structure. In 2008 only 20 percent of employees in the marketplace were represented by any sort of union. At least 47 percent of workers worked in the informal economy—outside formal labor law or union protections (Janicke and Fuentes 2008). The growth of worker cooperatives during the Chávez presidency marks another factor that complicates labor cohesion. Some scholars see the cooperatives as Chávez's strategy to complete his control over civil society (Shapiro 2007). Explosive growth certainly allowed for plenty of opportunities for mismanagement and corruption. The UNT does not like the cooperatives because most of them eliminate the traditional worker-management relationship, which means cooperatives' structures do not lend themselves to unionization (Ellner 2008: 187). Participants in the cooperatives argue that they provide economic opportunity and autonomy (Ceaser 2005). The jury is still out as to whether or not workers' cooperatives provide vehicles for economic growth or prove to be a political ploy. What is sure is that cooperatives propose a labor model that is somewhere between the formal economy and the informal economy that traditional labor law and organizations cannot yet support.

In November 2009, President Chávez called for a Fifth Socialist International Congress that would be "an instrument for the unification and the articulation of the struggle of the peoples to save this planet" (Sabado 2009). Presumably, said congress would also have to address complicated labor issues. As the labor market becomes more complex, it appears that what Venezuela needs is a new labor paradigm to deal with challenges presented by the labor in the formal, informal, and other sectors of the economy. It remains to be seen whether the new actors, often working with old ideas, have the creativity necessary to help Venezuelan labor face the 21st century.

ECONOMICS AND POLITICS IN THE CHÁVEZ ERA

At the beginning of this chapter we described oil as the permanent dilemma that undergirded Venezuelan economic policy and made Venezuela perpetually dependent on oil production. Sowing the oil wealth became fundamental to political policy and further trapped Venezuela in the permanent dilemma. Though political scientists, economists, and historians will write dozens and dozens of volumes about the Chávez administration, the one thing that is clear thus far is that he has not been any more successful than any of his predecessors at resolving the permanent dilemma. Chávez has to sow the wealth to try to achieve political and social stability, just as his predecessors did. Instead of writing a new book on Venezuelan economic independence, Chávez is adding a new chapter to the same book that Venezuelan presidents have been writing since 1908.

TRADE AND FINANCE

Industry, Trade, and Finance in the Revised Relationship between the State and PDVSA

The *apertura petrolera* and PDVSA's internationalization were thorny political and economic issues for many at the beginning of the Chávez presidency. The company's direct contribution to the state had decreased in the 1980s and the 1990s. Moreover, any profits PDVSA earned from units that functioned in other countries, like Citgo, remained with those companies and were never repatriated to Venezuela and PDVSA. The company also restricted information available about production and labor efficiency available to the general public. That further tainted the company's image. PDVSA appeared to be a company responsible for the nation's most important patrimony, a nationalized raw material, that did not seem to consider itself accountable to that nation (Parker 2005: 42). As we have previously noted, that public image was not inconsistent with PDVSA's self-image.

Once president, Chávez had to revitalize the economy without alienating foreign lenders. He continued debt payments on schedule (unlike Argentina a few years later), maintained high currency reserves, and tried to control inflation. New income for new programs (and debt payment) had to come from increased revenues, which meant, above all, increasing oil revenues. He moved to strengthen the relationship with OPEC that had deteriorated as a result of PDVSA's international policies and quota skirting. The administration did not reneg on any contracts with foreign companies developed during the *apertura*. The 2001 Hydrocarbons Law, however, worked toward channeling more of the nation's resources back to the nation rather than the company through new tax and royalty policies and a mandate that the majority of stocks in mixed (PDVSA and foreign) corporations be held by the state (Parker 2005: 44). Through legislation, Chávez had the ability to influence oil policy that could begin to redirect resources back toward the nation. Chávez appointees to the Ministry of Energy and Mines could further influence the creation and implementation of policies. The person occupying the office of the presidency had had the ability to appoint the president of PDVSA and exercise some influence over appointees to the board of directors since the creation of the company with nationalization of oil in 1976. Chávez used that authority to choose a PDVSA president, Ali Rodríguez, sympathetic to Chávez's economic project and to begin to appoint to the board members similarly sympathetic.

The confluence of appointees and legislation led to the creation of a political and cultural divide between those in Venezuela who sought an alternative to neoliberal economic politics and increased control of the nation's oil wealth on one side. On the other side of the divide were company employees and their supporters who not only did not approve of policies that threatened PDVSA's autonomy but who also questioned the petroleum expertise of individuals appointed to lead the industry. Many Venezuelans throughout the country found themselves somewhere between the two extremes; they appreciated the need for the nation to more closely control its resources, which required a new approach to PDVSA, but they also questioned the qualifications of some individuals appointed to head the industry and noted the

Emir of Qatar Sheikh Hamad Ben Khalifa Ben Hamed Al-Thani, right, talks with Venezuelan President Hugo Chávez during a private meeting at the Hilton hotel in Caracas, Venezuela, Wednesday, September 27, 2000. (AP/Wide World Photos)

heavy-handedness with which some appointees were brought into, or removed from, the industry.

We noted previously the alliance between Carlos Ortega of the CTV and FE-DECAMARAS that resulted in a series of general strikes beginning in 2002. The third party in that alliance was PDVSA executive Juan Fernández. In early December 2002, along with the leadership of all of the fractious opposition parties, they called for an indefinite general strike that began with the PDVSA managerial class. PDVSA management shut down the industry, making worker support for the strike irrelevant. Other oil companies working contracts in Venezuela also soon shut down either in support of PDVSA or because the strike disrupted their subsidiaries or supply chains. Businesses in middle-class and elite neighborhoods across the country shut down in sympathy. Banks closed in early January 2003. The value of the currency plunged 30 percent over the course of the strike. As oil and gas became scarce, trucking shut down and people began to worry about food shortages. Many grocery stores closed. By mid-January, 2003 the strike cost Venezuela $50 million a day (Thompson 2003).

As economic conditions became more precarious and social tensions escalated, public opinion turned against PDVSA and other strike proponents, something that some members of the opposition acknowledged as possible as early as the third week of the strike (Axtman 2002). Some people began to think that instead of using oil to empower Venezuela, PDVSA was using the nation's oil in a siege campaign whose

Employees of Venezuela's state oil company PDVSA demonstrate in support of the company in the dispute it holds with U.S. energy giant ExxonMobil, in front of a Mobil petrol station in Maracaibo, Venezuela, on February 13, 2008. PDVSA said it suspended oil supplies to Exxon-Mobil in retaliation for the U.S. energy giant's securing court orders to freeze billions of dollars in global PDVSA assets. The court orders were issued as part of the arbitration sought by ExxonMobil to gain compensation for the Venezuelan government's nationalization of key oil fields in the Orinoco basin. (RAFAEL NAVARRO/AFP/Getty Images)

only victims were Venezuelans. Business owners who remained sympathetic to the strike began to open their businesses on shortened schedules in order to avoid bankruptcy. Chávez used his bully pulpit to demonize PDVSA, CTV, FEDECAMARAS, and other organizations who supported the strike, and then he used the military to begin to reopen closed-down oil fields. By early February, when the strike ended, Venezuela was again exporting approximately 2 million barrels a day, far below pre-strike numbers but substantially higher than the 150,000 barrels exported daily at the height of the strike (Ellner 2008). In total, the strike cost PDVSA $12.8 billion. The company lost 1 to 3 billon more in property damage to equipment associated with the oil industry (Camacho 2005). Some say the heavy equipment was purposefully sabotaged by strike supporters when they left in December 2002. Others say the sand buildup in the deposits ruined the equipment when production began again. Data was lost, too. When employees who remained with the company returned to work after the strike, they found many computers destroyed.

Chávez was the biggest winner in the strike. PDVSA, CTV, FEDECAMARAS, and the opposition parties supported the strike as an attempt to discredit Chávez and, if not end the presidency, force a recall vote. Instead, Chávez used the strike to clean house in PDVSA's management and definitively subjugate the company to the authority of the state, and to Chávez himself. The company became a vehicle for a

Venezuelan National Guards soldiers stand guard outside the offices of the government oil monopoly, Petróleos de Venezuela S.A., in Caracas, December 5, 2002. In a televised address the same day, President Hugo Chávez told Venezuelans and international clients that he would use the military to keep Venezuela's oil industry working. (AP/Wide World Photos)

clientelism in the 21st century, just as other state-run companies and other confederations like the CTV had been vehicles for clientelism in the 20th century. Many Chavistas occupied the positions left by the dismissed strike loyalists. The company became crucial in Chávez's Socialism for the Twenty-First Century program. In 2007 alone, PDVSA spent $14.4 billion in social projects (Alvarez and Hanson 2009). In clear cut ways, in education, health care, grants, and microloans to cooperatives, Chávez used PDVSA to sow the nation's patrimony for millions of Venezuelans who became, some would argue, blind political clients in service of a tyrant (Corrales 2006). Other scholars argued that by the close of the first decade of the 21st century, it was too soon to tell if those who benefited from oil's largesse would be as loyal as presumed (Ellner 2008).

After 2006, Chávez moved to alter Venezuela's relationship with foreign companies working inside Venezuela and with countries who purchase Venezuelan oil. Chávez began to close the *apertura* but without completely exiling foreign companies from production in Venezuela. Foreign companies had to accept 60 percent state ownership in mixed Venezuelan-foreign operations established during the *apertura*. All employees, however, became PDVSA employees (Ellner 2008). Also in 2006, the state nationalized CANTV, the phone company partly owned by Verizon. In 2009, Venezuela completed renationalization of SIDOR. Internationally, Chávez sought to diversify markets for Venezuelan oil to lessen its dependency on the U.S. market. Specifically, PDVSA signed contracts with China and Iran. In Latin America, Venezuela signed a variety of preferential agreements associated with oil production, exploration, and/or export with Argentina, Brazil, Colombia, Bolivia, Ecuador, and Cuba. However, the U.S. remains the primary market for Venezuelan oil (Alvarez and Hanson 2009).

The only constant in Venezuelan oil policy is that Venezuela remains dependent on oil production. In February 2010 Chávez appeared to reopen *apertura* when he signed new concessions for oil development in the Orinoco Belt with Chevron along with companies from India, Spain, Japan, and Malaysia. Geologists consider the deposits in that region to be substantial, but only time will tell how much oil the reserves will actually yield. In the meantime, Venezuela reaped signing bonuses of $500 million or $1 billion from each company. As much as Venezuela needs help developing its oil fields, the world needs Venezuelan oil and will pay the price (Romero 2010).

Indeed, the global economic crisis that began in 2008 demonstrated quite clearly the flaws in any economic system tied to the export of raw materials. When oil prices soared in 2007, the IMF estimated GDP growth at 8.4 percent (Alvarez and Hanson 2009). In that good year, Chávez severed Venezuela's relationship with the IMF and the World Bank, saying that Venezuela no longer wanted the aid of institutions tainted with U.S. imperialism (Tran 2007). In 2008 when prices began to fall, late in the year PDVSA lost a $5 billion line of credit. In early 2009, Chávez suggested he would be open to more foreign investment in oil reserves, though little was forthcoming (Alvarez and Hanson 2009). Soaring oil prices and thorough control of PDVSA allowed Chávez to think that he had moved Venezuela past the traps of the permanent dilemma. Instead, social policies, foreign spending, military spending (see Chapter 7), clientelism in the company, and a bleak global economic picture seemed to indicate that Chávez was just as stuck in Venezuelan tar as any president had ever been.

Banking and Monetary Policy

The Banco Central de Venezuela's (Central Bank of Venezuela, BCV) history dates back to 1939. It performs all of the functions of other central bank or federal reserve systems worldwide, like managing the money supply and credit and issuing bank notes. Changes in laws that govern the BCV have evolved with domestic and global economic changes. The most important change occurred in 1992, when it became a legal public entity rather than a corporate entity. BCV was governed by a president and six-member board appointed by the Venezuelan president and confirmed by a vote of two-thirds of the Venezuelan senate, a process similar to the process of appointment to the leadership of the Federal Reserve Board in the United States. By law, the BCV cannot provide direct credit to the government (Banco Central de Venezuela 2009). The BCV is not the same as the Banco de Venezuela (Bank of Venezuela). The Banco de Venezuela was one of the oldest privately owned banks in the country. In 2009, Venezuela purchased the bank from the Spanish Santander group. Ali Rodríguez, then finance minister, said that Venezuela would use the bank to "strengthen the public financial sector" (Suggett 2009b).

Monetary and banking policy have been crucial to Chávez's economic policy from the beginning of his administration. As we noted, in the early years Chávez worked toward moving the economy away from neoliberalism and toward something he began to call "Socialism in the Twenty-First Century" after 2006. Early problems were more practical, less grandiose. The currency devaluations and inflation in the 1980s and the 1990s resulted in the permanent loss of billions of dollars in capital flight. By early 2003 the value of the VEB had plummeted from 772VEB to the U.S. dollar to 1,853/US$1. International monetary reserves had fallen by US$2 billion (Fletcher 2004). In a bid to cauterize further hemorrhaging and build some confidence in the currency, and within the context of the 2002–3003 PDVSA general strike, in 2003 Venezuela instituted strict foreign currency controls (*control de cambios*). It pegged the exchange rate at 1,600VEB/US$1. Included in the currency control regulations were stipulations that required sale to the BCV of "all foreign currency coming into the country from transport services, travel, wire transfers, leases, dividends and from all other services as well as commercial, industrial, professional and personal activities" (Fletcher 2004: 46). The state placed similarly strict restrictions on the amount of foreign currency legally available to importers and to private citizens who needed foreign currency for travel for personal, academic, or business purposes. The result, as we noted previously, was brisk business in currency exchange in the informal economy. Restrictions also added to problems in the food supply as food importers had difficulty obtaining the currency necessary to do business. Those circumstances added to inflationary pressures and did not decrease pressure to further devalue the bolivar.

By 2006, monetary policy analysts worried that policies in addition to foreign currency controls hampered economic stability. Specifically, they worried that new laws in 2005 limited the BCV's ability to establish and control monetary policy and strengthened the state's direct role in the economy. The state also began to transfer funds away from the BCV into Fonden, a state-controlled treasury bank (*Venezuela Monetary Transparency: Country Report* 2006). In 2006 and 2007, rising GDP and oil prices masked soaring inflation rates, up to 22 percent in 2007. By 2007 the BCV had officially devalued the currency to 2,150VEB/US$1. Coins were worth nearly nothing. Prices became difficult to calculate and understand. In early 2008, the state instituted a new currency somewhat euphemistically called the *bolívar fuerte* (strong bolivar). The VEB (*bolívar fuerte*) simplified the currency system by eliminating zeros. The official exchange rate became 2.15VEB/US$1 instead of 2,150. Even then, however, the informal black market exchange rate was closer to 5.60VEB/US$1 (Zissis 2008). The new currency did nothing to restrain inflation, either. In July 2009, *The New York Times* declared Caracas the most expensive city in Latin America, in part due to continued soaring inflation (Kristof and Romero 2009). In January 2010, Venezuela devalued the VEB to 4.3/US$1 for most transactions, but subsidized the VEB at 2.6/US$1 for imports of food, medicine, and other items deemed essential. Finance Minister Ali Rodríguez admitted that the most recent devaluation would do nothing to stop inflation (then at 27 percent annually) but might instead make it at least temporarily worse (Crowe and Lyons 2010).

The banking industry found further cause for concern in 2009. In 2009, the government began to investigate fraud claims in various banks. Those investigations resulted in the closure or nationalization of eight banks that represented 8 to 10 percent of the banking sector. In addition to the nationalizations or closures, the investigations resulted in the arrest of 10 banking executives. Not all of the executives arrested were associated with opposition political parties. Some were part of the new Bolivarian bourgeoisie, or the new client network who are beneficiaries of contracts with state-run enterprises. However, when combined with the nationalization of Grupo Santander and the creation of the state-run Banco de Venezuela mentioned previously, state relationships with the banking industry indicate increased direct state participation (Janicke 2009b).

LAND REFORM

Kai Rosenberg, a German Jew who moved to Venezuela when he was 18, admits that a touch of insanity might be necessary to grow cacao in Venezuela. He has fought armed intruders, squatters, and a fungus in his crop, all for the sake of the old fashioned version of black gold in Venezuela. European connoisseurs of cacao drool at the thought of the small quantity of cacao still produced in Venezuela in terms parallel to those that enologists use to describe the finest grapes for wine. President Chávez, however, is less enthusiastic about old school black gold and the land use patterns associated with it. He said of one grower that "This gentleman is getting rich while workers are living in poverty" (Romero 2009).

Land issues in Venezuela are much more complicated than Kai Rosenberg's ability to grow cacao or presidential rhetoric about worker poverty. In part, questions of land date back to the first decades of the oil boom in the 20th century. Urban populations exploded in the 20th century. By 1960, only 35 percent of the population was rural; since then, the rural portion of the population has declined to 12 percent (Wilpert 2005). In addition, food production, a practice intricately tied to the issue of land, did not increase proportionately to match urban growth. Related to the issue of how land was used was the issue of land ownership. In 1937, an agricultural census found that 4.4 percent of rural property owners owned 78 percent of the land; 95.6 percent of owners owned the remaining 22 percent. Ninety percent of peasants worked land they did not own (Ewell 1984: 83). A land reform program initiated in 1960 distributed land to 200,000 families over 20 years. This program, however, did little to alleviate either the problem of concentration of land in the hands of few or the issue of food production but cost $333 million to the Venezuelan state before 1964 (Harris 1969; Wilpert 2005).

The Tragedia de Vargas (Vargas Tragedy) one year into the Chávez presidency in 1999 brought to the forefront the environmental consequences of urban land use. The mudslides that encompassed 300 kilometers of heavily populated territory on the Venezuelan coast near Caracas cost at least 30,000 lives and displaced at least 300,000 people. Not all Vargas residents rebuilt on the hillsides. Chávez encouraged the resettlement of untold numbers to cities and rural areas in the interior of the country, which brought back to the forefront the issue of land ownership, urban and rural. Simultaneously, inflation, currency devaluations, and monetary control policies simultaneously increased the price of food, most of it imported as noted earlier. In that context, land reform was not just a matter of ideology but economic policy and food sovereignty.

By far one of the most controversial laws in the early years of the Chávez presidency was the 2001 Land Law that Chávez said would address the land distribution problem, the land use problem, and eventually the food production problem. Critics from the beginning decried the law as socialist and a threat to private property rights. Between 2001 and 2005, the state focused redistributions on public lands, redistributing 4.9 million acres, and did not begin expropriating privately owned lands until 2005 (Gindin 2005). At that point, government attention focused on large private landholdings of 12,350 acres or more. Even before 2005, however, owners of large properties complained about squatters encroaching on private property, taking land out of commercial use and shifting production toward yucca, corn, sesame seeds, and other domestic crops grown by squatters. Land development experts who supported land reform in theory worried that the Venezuelan process had been hampered by a less than complete registry of land titles or data on arable land. Those farmers who had received public lands had received neither the credit nor technical support necessary to make the land productive. In sum, experts and Chávez critics worried that the reform would harm food production rather than help it (Forero 2005).

Parallel to the issue of food production is food distribution. Chávez began in 2003 to increase government control of food distribution. Real food shortages became common in 2007. Venezuelans could purchase luxury food items but found it difficult to purchase eggs, milk, sugar, or, much to everyone's dismay, coffee (for more on the cultural significance of coffee, see Chapter 6). When items became available, lines formed quickly and supplies disappeared. In some cases, the staples were only available through the state-supported Mercal markets established in 2008, part of PDVAL (Venezuelan Production and Distribution of Food, a subsidiary of PDVSA). Administration officials and those who oppose Chávez differ on the reasons for the shortages. The administration insisted that the shortages were not that bad; when they occurred they reflected the lower classes' increased purchasing power and merchant-class hoarding. The opposition argued that price controls on staple items decreased their profit potential, which provided a substantial disincentive for investment in crops and machinery. Fear of land expropriation, furthermore, led to stockpiling of food supplies. No matter who was right or wrong, what was apparent to the population was that multiple groups were playing politics with food ("Venezuela Food Shortages" 2007).

In 2008, the administration passed a Food Security Law that stated "It is indispensable to guarantee to all Venezuelan citizens access to quality food in sufficient quantity. For true and revolutionary rural development, it is necessary to overcome the traditional market conception of foods and agricultural products. This vision is a detriment to the fundamental right that all Venezuelans have to feed themselves" (Isaacs et al. 2009). The language reflected the socialist rhetoric common after 2006 and also the increased tension associated not only with land ownership and use but also with food. In 2009, the administration pushed ahead with another round of expropriations, targeting both land held by individual landowners and by companies. It planned to distribute credit to new landowners to develop their properties (Suggett 2009a). As of yet, however, it remains difficult to cut through the political subterfuge to determine the success or failure of land reform or to assess the land and food subsidy policies connections to food shortages. What we can say is that land and food issues contribute to continued economic instability that affect all Venezuelans, regardless of class.

Turn Out the Lights

Complicating the economic picture in 2009 and 2010 was a major drought. The problem was not so much that the drought limited food production (it did, but as most food is imported, food problems were more economic than climatic). The major issue was that the drought limited the hydroelectric capabilities of the Guri Dam on the Caroni River, which produces 73 percent of all electricity in Venezuela. Blackouts throughout the country began during the fall of 2009 and continued into 2010. President Chávez used his radio and television programs to urge water and electricity conservation before declaring an Electricity Emergency in February 2010 ("Chávez Declares an Electricity Emergency" 2010).

Blackouts deepened the economic crisis for several reasons. Measures to conserve energy included closing commercial businesses or limiting their hours of operations. The government also partially shut down state-run aluminum and steel industries. The energy crisis cost businesses and industries untold millions of dollars and constrained capital flow into consumer sectors of the economy. The great fear, however, was that the water levels in the reservoir above the Guri Dam could drop so low that power production could become impossible. Such a situation could idle the entire Venezuelan economy more drastically than even the 2002–2003 PDVSA strike did.

The rains began in May 2010 and lasted through July with unusual force. Though Venezuelans initially celebrated, by July as saturated grounds gave way to mudslides in Guanta just to the east of Puerto La Cruz and the overflowing headwaters of the Neverí to the west of Barcelona displaced thousands, people sang "Rain, rain go away." Rain, however, did not resolve the underlying problems associated with insufficient power resources. The recent memory of power outages combined with even higher inflation meant that economic issues dominated daily conversations. A kilo of fish cost the equivalent of 8$U.S. dollars in the summer of 2010, an obscene and impossible amount of money for many Venezuelans. The discovery in June 2010 of 1,197 tanker containers of spoiled PDVAL food in Puerto Cabello fed further economic discontent ("Town Councillor Reports Loss of 1,600 Tons of Rice in Carabobo" 2010). By late summer 2010 with the unofficial exchange rate fluctuating between 5 VEB and 9 VEB to 1$U.S. dollar daily, no one expected economic relief any time soon.

CONCLUSION

Once, it rained oil. At least that is what the oil workers at La Rosa thought when that well exploded into production in 1914. Venezuelans believed that glorious black rain would definitively end the nation's dependency on North Atlantic economies that had been the norm until that point in Venezuelan history, colonial or national. Alternately a blessing and a curse, Venezuela's heavy crude trapped the nation into an interminable permanent dilemma, impenetrable to any political party or leader's political or economic tactics in the 20th or 21st century. Venezuela is like a fly trapped in a spider's web. The more the nation struggles to free itself, the more hopelessly enmeshed it becomes. Even if President Chávez, political leaders of all political stripes, and all Venezuelans find a way out of the most recent crisis, changes in the global community may further conspire to make Venezuela petroleum's victim. If industrialized nations manage to change their economic and social structures to limit their dependency on oil and other fossil fuels that damage the environment, Venezuela will suffer economically, politically, and socially in ways yet unimagined. Maybe that crisis could finally liberate Venezuela from oil.

REFERENCES

Albornoz, Orlando. 1977. "Higher Education and the Politics of Development in Venezuela." *Journal of Interamerican Studies and World Affairs.* 19: 291–314.

Alvarez, Cesar J., and Stephanie Hanson. 2009. "Venezuela's Oil-Based Economy." *Council on Foreign Relations.* http://www.cfr.org/publication/12089/.

Axtman, Kris. 2002. "Anti-Chavez Groups Barely United." *Christian Science Monitor*, December 23. http://www.csmonitor.com/2002/1223/p06s01-woam.html/(page)/2.

Banco Central de Venezuela. 2009. "History of the BCV." http://www.bcv.org.ve/english version/c3/index.asp?secc=history.

Becker, Kristina Flodman. 2004. "The Informal Economy." *World Bank*. http://rru.world bank.org/Documents/PapersLinks/Sida.pdf.

Berglund, Susan. 1985. "Mercantile Credit and Financing in Venezuela, 1830–1879." *Journal of Latin American Studies* 17: 371–396.

Briceño de Bermúdez, Tarcila. 1993. *Comercio por los Ríos Orinoco y Apure: Segunda mitad del siglo XIX*. Caracas: Fondo Editorial Tropykos.

Brown, Jonathan. 1985. "Why Foreign Oil Companies Shifted Their Production from Mexico to Venezuela in the 1920s." *American Historical Review* 90: 362–385.

Burgess, Katrina. 1999. "Loyalty Dilemmas and Market Reforms: Party-Union Alliances under Stress in Mexico, Spain, and Venezuela." *World Politics* 52: 105–134.

Buxton, Julia. 2003. "Economic Policy and the Rise of Hugo Chavez." In Steve Ellner and Daniel Hellinger, eds., *Venezuelan Politics in the Chavez Era: Class, Polarization, and Conflict*. Boulder, CO: Lynne Rienner.

Camacho, Carlos. 2005. "Minister: 2002–2003 Strike Cost PDVSA U.S. $12.8 Billion." *Business News America*, July 27. http://www.bnamericas.com/news/oilandgas/Minister:_2002-2003_strike_cost_PDVSA_US*12,8bn.

Ceaser, Mike. 2005. "In Venezuela, a Bid to Empower Poor Barrios." *The Christian Science Monitor*. http://www.csmonitor.com/2005/0901/p11s01-woam.html.

"Chavez Declares an Electricity Emergency." 2010. *The New York Times*, February 8. http://www.nytimes.com/2010/02/09/world/americas/09venez.html?ref=americas.

CIA. 2008. "Country Comparison: Oil Production." *The World Factbook*. https://www.cia.gov/library/publications/the-world-factbook/rankorder/2173rank.html.

Coronil, Fernando. 1997. *The Magical State: Nature, Money, and Modernity in Venezuela*. Chicago: University of Chicago Press.

Corrales, Javier. 2006. "Hugo Boss." *Foreign Policy* 152: 32–40.

Crowe, Darcy, and John Lyons. 2010. "Chavez Devalues Venezuelan Currency." *Wall Street Journal*, January 9. http://online.wsj.com/article/SB126305109903923235.html.

Ellner, Steve. 1993. *Organized Labor in Venezuela, 1958–1991: Behavior and Concerns in a Democratic Setting*. Wilmington, DE: Scholarly Resources.

———. 1998. "Izquierda y politica en la agenda neoliberal venezolana." *Nueva Sociedad* 157: 125–136.

———. 2005. "The Emergence of New Trade Unionism in Venezuela with Vestiges of the Past." *Latin American Perspectives* 32: 51–71.

———. 2008. *Rethinking Venezuelan Politics: Class, Conflict, and the Chavez Phenomenon*. Boulder, CO: Lynne Rienner.

"Energy Prices." 2009. *Bloomberg*, December 28. http://www.bloomberg.com/markets/commodities/energyprices.html.

Ewell, Judith. 1984. *Venezuela: A Century of Change*. Stanford, CA: Stanford University Press.

Fletcher, Erin. 2004. *Bolivar Distorted: The Effects of Exchange Controls on the Venezuelan Economy or Perhaps Chavez Spent Too Much Time Reading Machiavelli and Not Enough Time Reading Adam Smith*. Durham, NC: Duke University.

Forero, Juan. 2005. "Venezuela Land Reform Looks to Seize Idle Farmland." *New York Times*, January 30: 3.

Forero, Juan. 2009. "Chile to Move on from Developing to Developed Status." *National Public Radio*, December 21. http://www.npr.org/templates/story/story.php?storyId= 121701830.

Gaceta de Guayana. 1857. Ciudad Bolívar. December 12: 1. Archives of the Archdiocese of Ciudad Bolívar.

Gindin, Jonah. 2005. "Venezuela's Land Institute Recovers Land for Redistribution." *Venezuelanalysis*, March 14. http://www.venezuelanalysis.com/news/998.

Grau, Pedro Cunill. 1987. *Geografia del popblamiento venezolano en el siglo XIX, tomo I.* Caracas: Ediciones de la Presidencia de la Republica.

Harris, Edward R., Jr. 1969. "Financing Land Reform: Funding Land Redistribution in Developing Countries, Maintaining Fiscal Solvency in the Face of Heavy Costs." *American Journal of Economics and Sociology* 28: 193–204.

Hellinger, Daniel. 1991. *Venezuela: Tarnished Democracy.* Boulder, CO: Westview Press.

———. 1996. "Causa R and the Nuevo Sindicalismo in Venezuela." *Latin American Perspectives* 23: 110–131.

Isaacs, Anna, Basil Weiner, Grace Bell, Courtney Franz, and Katie Bowen. 2009. "The Food Sovereignty Movement in Venezuela, Part Two." *Venezuelanalysis*, November 26. http://www.venezuelanalysis.com/analysis/4954. Accessed February 9, 2010.

Janicke, Kiraz. 2009a. "Venezuela's National Union of Workers Holds Extraordinary Congress." *Venezuelanaylsis.* December 7. http://www.venezuelanalysis.com/news/4989.

———. 2009b. "Venezuela Takes Over Another Bank, Arrests Ex-Head of National Securities Commission." *Venezuelanalysis*, December 13. http://www.venezuelanalysis.com/news/5001.

Janicke, Kiraz, and Fernando Fuentes. 2008. "Venezuela's Labor Movement at a Crossroads." *Venezuelanalysis* April 29. http://www.venezuelanalysis.com/analysis/3398.

Kristof, Gregory, and Simon Romero. 2009. "Why Is Caracas Latin America's Most Expensive City?" *New York Times*, July 16. http://economix.blogs.nytimes.com/2009/07/16/why-is-caracas-latin-americas-most-expensive-city/.

Lombardi, John. 1982. *Venezuela: The Search for Order, the Dream of Progress.* New York: Oxford University Press.

———. 2003. "Prologue: Venezuela's Permanent Dilemma." In Steve Ellner and Daniel Hellinger, eds., *Venezuelan Politics in the Chavez Era: Class, Polarization and Conflict.* Boulder, CO: Lynne Rienner.

Lorey, David E. 1992. "Public Policy and Economic Development in Latin America: The Cases of Mexico and Venezuela." *Higher Education.* 23: 65–78.

Lyons, John and Darcy Crowe. 2010. "Chavez Devalues Venezuela's Currency." *Wall Street Journal.* http://online.wsj.com/article/NA_WSJ_PUB:SB126305109903923235.html.

"Markets and Data: Currencies." 2009. *The Economist.* http://www.economist.com/markets/currency/md_conv.cfm.

McBeth, Brian. 2008. *Dictatorship and Politics: Intrigue, Betrayal, and Survival in Venezuela, 1908–1935.* Notre Dame, IN: University of Notre Dame Press.

Mommer, Bernard. 2003. "Subversive Oil." In Steve Ellner and Daniel Hellinger, eds., *Venezuelan Politics in the Chavez Era: Class, Polarization and Conflict*. Boulder, CO: Lynne Rienner.

Parker, Dick. 2005. "Chavez and the Search for an Alternative to Neoliberalism." *Latin American Perspectives* 32: 39–50.

Pérez Villa, Manuel. 1976. "El gobierno deliberativo: hacendados, comerciantes, y artesanos frente a la crisis, 1830–1848." In Miguel Izard, ed., *Política y economica en Venezuela, 1810–1976*. Caracas: Fundación John Boulton.

Pinero, Eugenio. 1988. "The Cacao Economy of the Eighteenth-Century Province of Caracas and the Spanish Cacao Market." *Hispanic American Historical Review* 68: 75–100.

Robbins, Richard. 1999. *Global Problems and the Culture of Capitalism*. New York: Allyn and Bacon.

Romero, Simon. 2009. "In Venezuela, Plantations of Cacao Stir Bitterness." *New York Times*, July 29. http://www.nytimes.com/2009/07/29/world/americas/29cacao.html.

———. 2010. "Sealing Shift: Chávez Gives Contracts to Western Oil Companies." *New York Times*, February 11. http://www.nytimes.com/2010/02/12/world/americas/12venez.html?hpw. Accessed February 11, 2010.

Sabado, Francois. 2009. "Chavez Calls for Fifth International: Decisive Lessons from Stalinism and Social Democracy." *Venezuelanalysis*. November 27. http://www.venezuelanalysis.com/analysis/4956.

Shapiro, Charles. 2007. "Venezuelan Labor Struggles to Find Its Autonomy (Is Labor Lost)." *Georgetown Journal of International Affairs* 8: 19–27.

"Strike Paralyzes Venezuelan Aluminum Industry." 2009. *Latin American Herald Tribune*. http://www.laht.com/article.asp?ArticleId=348311&CategoryId=10717.

Suggett, James. 2009a. "Venezuela Accelerates Land Reform." *Venezuelanalysis*, March 12. http://www.venezuelanalysis.com/news/4289.

———. 2009b. "Venezuela Buys Bank of Venezuela for US $10.5 Billion." *Venezuelanaysis*, May 25. http://www.venezuelanalysis.com/news/4467.

———. 2009c. "Venezuelan Auto Workers Decry Possible Firings of Union Leaders as Plant Reopens." *Venezuelanalysis*. September 24. http://www.venezuelanalysis.com/news/4814.

Thompson, Ginger. 2003. "Strike's Effects Tear at Social Fabric in Venezuela." *New York Times*, January 16.

Tinker Salas, Miguel. 2005. "Staying the Course: United States Oil Companies in Venezuela, 1945–1958." *Latin American Perspectives* 32: 147–170.

———. 2009. *The Enduring Legacy: Oil, Culture, and Society in Venezuela*. Durham, NC: Duke University Press.

"Town Councillor Reports Loss of 1,600 Tons of Rice in Carabobo. " 2010. *El Universal*. June 17. http://www.eluniversal.com/2010/06/17/en_eco_esp_town-councillor-repo_17A4040171.shtml.

Tran, Mark. 2007. "Venezuela Quits IMF and World Bank." *The Guardian*, May 1. http://www.guardian.co.uk/business/2007/may/01/venezuela.imf.

UNESCO. 2006. "EFA Global Monitoring Report 2006." http://unesdoc.unesco.org/images/0014/001497/149782e.pdf.

"Venezuela Food Shortages Despite Oil Revenue Boom." 2007. *The Irish Times*, November 14: 12.

Venezuela Monetary Transparency: Country Report. 2006. Oxford: Oxford Analytical. "Venezuelan Oil Production Down to 2.3 Million Barrels a Day." 2009. *El Universal*, December 16. http://english.eluniversal.com/2009/12/16/en_eco_art_venezuelan-oil-produ_16A320 2771.shtml.

Wilpert, Gregory. 2005. "Venezuela's Land Reform: Land for People, Not for Profit." Land Research Action Network. http://www.landaction.org/display.php?article=334.

World Bank. 2009. "Data Profile: Venezuela." http://ddp-ext.worldbank.org/ext/ddpreports/ ViewSharedReport?&CF=&REPORT_ID=9147&REQUEST_TYPE=VIEWADVANCED.

Yarrington, Douglas. 2003. "Cattle, Corruption, and Venezuelan State Formation during the Era of Juan Vicente Gomez, 1908–1935." *Latin American Research Review* 35: 9–33.

Zissis, Carin. 2008. "Venezuela's Inflation Woes." *Council of the Americas*, January 8. http:// www.as-coa.org/article.php?id=850.

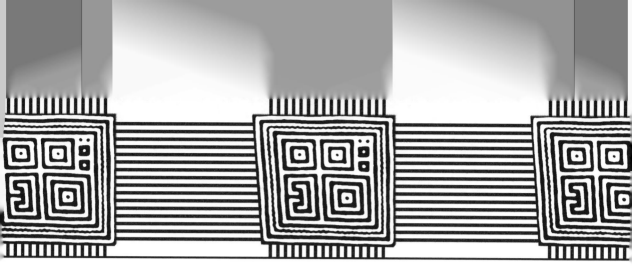

Society

INTRODUCTION

In the novel *Ana Isabel: A Decent Girl* that we discuss in Chapter 6, a young girl of good family navigates the difficult process of finding her place in Venezuelan society as a young woman. Ana Isabel is guided in this process both by her family and by the nuns who run her private school; both groups admonish her to follow society's rules and become a decent, honorable girl. In order to achieve this objective, Ana Isabel must cultivate her beauty, for decent girls are well-groomed and beautiful. In addition, she must stop playing with her friends, the poor children of the neighborhood, as they are *indecentes* (indecent). Ana Isabel chafes at these expectations, feeling sad she cannot play freely with her poor friends yet feeling out of place in her religious school, where all of the other girls are much wealthier than she. Ana Isabel first resists the pressure to be confined to her house and her school and wonders why poverty makes people indecent, but in the end she bends to society's rules.

Ana Isabel's story, and her struggle to conform to the expectations of society, show how religion, education, social class, and women's experiences are inextricably linked in a package of traditional societal norms. Teachers certainly would have urged Ana Isabel's brother to avoid contact with anyone *indecente*, but he did not have worry about his physical appearance and would have continued to run freely through the neighborhood. The rules were different for girls who wanted to achieve social mobility. Though Ana Isabel's story takes place at the beginnings of the 20th century, many of the same rules still apply in Venezuela in the 21st century. Expectations of beauty and decency still apply to women, and religion still plays a key role both in education and in family relationships. Being *decente* still matters. This chapter will outline both the historical background and contemporary societal expectations in religion, social class and ethnicity, women's roles, and education.

Religion and Thought

RELIGION AND RELIGIOSITY

Juan Fuentes died in 1996 in Puerto La Cruz. Juan lay in his casket in the Fuentes family living room for the next two days before the funeral services while the family gathered from all corners of Venezuela. The family constructed an altar at the head of the casket. On the altar, they placed a statue of the Virgin of the Valley, the patron saint of eastern Venezuela, flowers, a picture of Juan, and a glass of water so that Juan's spirit would have something to drink in its journey to the afterlife. The family built another altar at the head of his bed in his bedroom with the same decorations, including the glass of water, in case the spirit visited the place Juan died instead of his body.

By the third afternoon after Juan's death, everyone who was going to attend the funeral had arrived. Elvira, the local religious specialist, gathered Juan's sons together so that they could tell their father goodbye before closing the casket. Casket closed, the sons and their cousins lifted Juan on their shoulders and carried him from the house two blocks to the local Anglican Church, dozens of family and friends following behind. The Anglican priest, with his new wife in attendance, presided over the rites in the church. Juan was not a churchgoer. When asked why the Anglican priest celebrated the official, church funeral, the sons' suggested they chose the Anglican Church because that was where their mother attended. She liked the Anglican priest, and his wife. She did not like the local Catholic cleric. After the funeral, the family left the priest at the church and carried the casket down the block. There they loaded it into a hearse for the trip to the cemetery. The family boarded rented microbuses.

If there ever was any spatial organization to indicate status in the cemetery on a hill in Puerto La Cruz, it is impossible to determine now. One really needs to be part mountain goat to navigate around and over the graves of all sizes in order to reach any given spot. But that is exactly what the mourners did. The sons and cousins carried Juan ever so carefully to his final resting place. Each son said a few words and placed a flower on their father's casket. Finally, that part of the formal mourning process was over.

The novena began the next evening and continued for nine evenings. During the novena, friends and family gathered in Juan's home to say the rosary for Juan, led by a young Catholic lay minister. As custom forbids the widow or direct blood relatives from serving guests, Juan's daughters-in-law served hot chocolate, made from beans grown in Juan's sister-in-law's cacao trees, and cookies to the women who prayed. They also served chocolate, cookies, and cigarettes to the men gathered outside. People of all religious persuasions participated. Catholics, Anglicans, Protestant evangelicals, even the local *bruja* (witch) came to pray the rosary and pay their respects to the family. Through the nine nights, Juan's sons took turns staying up all night in the house, which remained well-lit, to make sure Juan's spirit did not come back. Elvira always knew which son stayed up all night. At the end of the rosary on the ninth night, she gathered the sons together and told them it was time for the last goodbye. She then incensed every square inch of the property, starting in Juan's bedroom. The family took down the altars and stacked the rented chairs. At midnight, the process was finally over. Juan's family had done everything they could to secure a safe transition for Juan's soul to the great beyond.

There are themes in this story that are useful to help us understand religion in Venezuela. Religiosity—that is, the way people feel and express a relationship with the supernatural—is and always has been important in Venezuela. Institutional religion has not always been important in Venezuela. Indeed, it is perhaps the historically weak position of the Catholic Church in many parts of Venezuelan society that has contributed to Venezuelans' often complicated expressions of faith. Venezuelan religiosity can incorporate Catholicism with a personal devotion to a variety of saints, some recognized by the Church, others not. Religiosity can incorporate elements of indigenous and African traditions as well. Venezuelans go to mainstream Protestant churches, like the Anglican Church (Episcopal in the United States), and more and more, Venezuelans find spiritual value in Protestant evangelical traditions. In many cases, people incorporate elements of many religious traditions in the creation of personal and communal religious identity in ways that seem odd to people in the United States but completely normal in Venezuela. This section explores the religion in Venezuela in all of its wonderful complexity.

THE CATHOLIC CHURCH IN THE COLONIAL ERA

We sketched the broad outlines of the official role of the Catholic Church in the colonial era in Chapter 2. In theory, the Catholic Church's official mission was the religious indoctrination (civilization) of the indigenous population and pastoral care of Spaniards and their descendents. The Church also retained the obligation to convert the slave population. In Caracas, the Catholic religious brotherhoods, *cofradías*, served as the Church's surrogates in that capacity in a way that also allowed Afrovenezuelans to create and maintain some cultural and economic autonomy as we will discuss later in this chapter.

Royal patronage, the right granted by the Pope to the Spanish crown to allow the crown to appoint priests and bishops in the Americas, in practice meant that the lines between Church and state became blurred. Absent a strong state, the elite's agenda became the Church's agenda. In Caracas and the surrounding area, the Church as an institution served primarily the needs of the *mantuano* elite. Priests in Caracas and in the surrounding areas made the values of the *mantuano* elite their own. As the elite did not want to risk their status by intermarrying with individuals of impure blood, bishops frequently allowed marriages between elite who were closely related, despite canonical prescriptions against such marriages. Clergy at the cathedral in Caracas performed three marriages uniting members of elite families every year after 1720. In most years, at least one of those three marriages united first cousins (Ferry 1989). In the areas where distance or expense prohibited obtaining the bishop's permission to marry kin, elites preferred common law relationships with cousins to Church-sanctioned marriages, with the full knowledge of local clergy. Only when the Church sent Spanish bishops, not associated with local elites and local clergy, on inspection tours did such practices and relationships fall under scrutiny. Once the bishop went away, so, too, did the worry (Waldron 1989).

Clergy and the Church as an institution in Caracas benefited substantially from their close relationship with the elite. When an elite family decided that a daughter should enter the convent, her dowry (cash, household goods, houses, and slaves) went to the Church. The Church charged fees for weddings, baptisms, and funerals. Elaborate funerals for the elite with processions, music, incense, choirs, and multiple clergy cost more than simple funerals for average *caraqueños*. The elite, in their wills, left funds to pay for numerous masses in honor of favored saints to ensure safe passage of the elite soul to the afterlife. The elite ordered the construction of chapels in honor of their dearly departed and endowed chaplaincies to staff the chapels. The elite left funds for the purchase of religious statuary art. The elite used their resources to finance the Church, and in return, the elite expected financial support and loyalty from the Church and its clergy as necessary. When the Caracas elite of the colonial era became the national elite in the 19th century, their close relationship with the Church continued.

Outside of Caracas, the Church's mission remained the evangelization of the indigenous population through the colonial era, and, south of the Orinoco, into the national period. Through most of the colonial period, most areas outside of Caracas had no ecclesiastic relationship with the bishopric of Caracas (Venezuela). The east became part of the bishopric of Puerto Rico, and Mérida and Maracaibo became part of the bishopric of Santa Fé de Bogotá. It was not until the late 18th and early 19th century that those areas gained their own bishoprics. By the national period, there were three Venezuelan bishops—in Caracas, Mérida, and Ciudad Bolívar.

In the east, evangelization could not begin in earnest until Spaniards gave up using indigenous populations as forced labor in pearl fisheries. Slave raiding into indigenous territories for indigenous slaves sold back to Spanish Caribbean properties also slowed Spanish missionary efforts. Those few attempts at missionization in the first several decades of colonization frequently proved fatal—for the missionaries (Alvaro Huerga 1996). The first Franciscan monasteries to survive in the east were established on the island of Margarita in 1593 and in Cumaná in 1638. By the mid 1700s, there were at least 26 mission communities in the east, plus three Spanish communities (Gómez Candeo 1967).

Ideally, the missions were supposed to civilize indigenous Venezuelans through conversion to Christianity, but numerous pressures complicated that agenda from the beginning. Missionaries complained that there were never enough missionaries to complete the task. In addition, runaway slaves and nonmission Carib Indians occasionally attacked missions. More intense was pressure from Spaniards who saw mission Indians as a cheap labor supply. Understaffed, underfunded missionaries found it difficult to counterbalance competing pressures (Gómez Candeo 1967).

We know, however, that indigenous Venezuelans converted to some form of Catholicism that became important to their cultural identity. When indigenous Venezuelans in Mérida moved to take advantage of shifting economic conditions, they took images of their favorite Catholic saints with them. Through the mid-19th century, when clergy did not serve the needs of indigenous populations in old mission communities in the east, indigenous Venezuelans petitioned the bishop to send them a priest who would serve their community interests, as Catholic Indians (ACB 1845). Exactly how indigenous Venezuelans understood Catholicism or how they incorporated elements of indigenous religious belief systems, we really do not know. What we do know is that even though the Church as an institution was not often as wealthy or influential as it could be in Caracas (given the relationship with the *caraqueño*-cum-national elite), religiosity was important.

CHURCH, STATE, AND SOCIETY IN THE 19TH AND 20TH CENTURY

It was only during the national period that the bishop of Caracas became the Archbishop of Caracas, with primacy over the other two, huge Venezuelan dioceses. The Diocese of Guayana incorporated all of eastern Venezuela, from the Caribbean coast (including the island of Margarita) to the Brazilian border. Mérida included Barinas in the llanos, the Andean highlands, and all of the west, including Maracaibo. The financial dependence of the Church on the state in much of Venezuela limited the Church's influence as an institution in much of Venezuela throughout the 19th century. The Venezuelan state retained patronage rights over the Church in the 19th century. That meant that the Venezuelan political authorities, governors, and the president had the right approve Church appointments to important positions, like bishops and the archbishop. In subsequent decades, the national government prohibited the entry of foreign clergy (despite the understaffed Church's continued dependence on such priests), ordered all clergy and bishops to swear loyalty to the constitution, ordered the expulsion of the Jesuits, and required the Church to submit ecclesiastical budgets to congress for approval. The government, through patronage rights and Church poverty, assumed payment of priests' salaries. The state also funded ecclesiastical education and new church construction (RPB 1844). In 1853, congress passed legislation designed to normalize annual financial support of the Church distributed through the three dioceses as shown in Table 5.1 (ACB 1853).

Furthermore, Venezuela generally, and the Diocese of Guayana in particular, remained dependent on foreign clergy to staff local parishes. Disease and poverty were unfortunately the norm for those priests. Friar Salvador de la Gertrud was one of 22 Spanish priests who arrived in Barcelona in 1842 to serve the Diocese of Guayana. He survived until 1848. When the local authorities inventoried Friar Salvador's earthly possessions, all they found was one candle, four rotting bushels of corn, a

TABLE 5.1 Dioceses of Venezuela, 1853

Diocese of Caracas	Diocese of Mérida	Diocese of Guayana
University—2,000 pesos	University—2,000 pesos	Bishop—5,000 pesos
Seminary—2,000 pesos	Seminary—1,500 pesos	59 priests—13,400 pesos
Bishop—6,000 pesos	Bishop—5,000 pesos	
129 priests—34,000 pesos	115 priests—26,800 pesos	

horse, two burros, 56 pesos, and an image of the Good Shepherd on tin (RPB 1848). Friar Salvador died poor, in a poor parish, in a poor diocese, in a poor Church.

Clerical penury placed priests in a complicated position. As they had to figure out how to survive from one day to the next, that often meant that they had to choose which portion of their flock was more deserving of their time and efforts. As clergy in colonial Caracas chose to accommodate the needs of their elite parishioners, so, too, did many financially dependent clergy in the national period adjust to serve the elite. Clergy raised funds to build churches and cemeteries that reinforced the elite's concepts of social order. When, occasionally, clergy chose to defy elite expectations and serve the needs of the broader populations, some priests found their jobs or their lives at risk (Morse 2003).

Clerical penury combined with Venezuela's close adherence to class and race hierarchies explain much about cemetery construction in the 19th century. In the book in which he registered the deaths and burials for the parish, Friar Bernardino de San Hipólito from Aragua de Barcelona noted the consecration of a new cemetery in 1868 this way: "This is the cemetery I built" (Family History Library 1857). This cemetery, Friar Bernardino's cemetery, was no average cemetery. It represented the culmination of his life's work as a faithful pastor serving the needs of his parishioners, most specifically his elite parishioners. As the cemetery served the interests of the elite first, the elite took up the task of organizing the space inside the cemetery walls and made rules for the cemetery's proper use. According to the rules Aragua's elite wrote, the elite were buried near the east entrance of the cemetery, at the right as one walked in. The elite believed themselves to be the most privileged in society, so, they thought, it was only just and appropriate that they bury themselves in the most privileged position in the cemetery—at the right hand side, as Jesus sat at the right hand of God. The east entrance was important, too. At the day of the second coming, those nearest Jerusalem, nearest to the east, would first behold the Messiah. So it was that the elite should see the Messiah first from their special position. The elite ruled that poor children should be buried on the left side near the east entrance. Poor children should also have a shot at redemption, before their poor parents, the elite determined. Of those poor parents, the elite rules dictated that poor men would be buried on the west side of the cemetery, on the right. The rules segregated poor women, even if married to poor men, to the west side, far left corner, the position of least privilege in the entire cemetery. Only the elite buried their dead in marked graves, with expensive, elaborate tombstones made of marble and cement. The poor buried their dead, according to the elite's rules, in shallow, narrow, unmarked graves (ACB 1868).

Aragua's Nuestra Señora del Carmen cemetery became a microcosm of the greater social order. As in life, the poor and the rich lived *juntos pero no revueltos*, together but not mixed (Staples 1994: 116). On either side of a sidewalk in the cemetery, they existed in close proximity to one another, but not together, purposely segregated. As the elite entered the cemetery to bury one of their own, they mourned and grieved and felt reassured. The funeral procession, priest at the head, with acolytes, musicians, candles, banners, flowers, casket on a horse-drawn caisson, and many mourners, made its way slowly from the church, six long blocks. As they approached the gate, the streets were clean, kept that way by the security guard the elite employed. Cemetery staff made sure the cemetery walls and the arched entry shone white, as white as the elite that rested immediately inside the cemetery, to the right of the entryway, the place of honor anywhere. The place reconfirmed the elite's pride in themselves as a group—pride in their power, pride in their wealth—all made manifest in the gleaming marble and cement statues that towered above them.

The poor had to carry their dead wrapped in a shroud, by themselves—no acolytes, no candles, no horse and caisson. Maybe a priest accompanied them, there to sprinkle a few drops of holy water and to mumble a few words in Latin. Dressed in their frayed Sunday finest, the mourners entered the cemetery with their heads bowed in grief and in respect to the elite dead they had to pass in order to arrive at the unmarked shallow hole that was to be the final resting place of their equally beloved dead. Every time they entered the cemetery to tend that grave, the poor walked past those gleaming statues, and they knew what their place was in the social, economic, and political order in Aragua de Barcelona, Venezuela. They knew *aun en la muerte separados* (even in death we are separate).

Aragua was not unique in its class-specific funerary traditions. After 1876, all *caraqueños* buried their dead in the suburban Cementerio del Sur by order of President Antonio Gúzman Blanco (Landaeta Rosales 1994). González, Giráldez, y Cía charged 24 pesos for a first-class private funeral with six funeral carriages in 1875. Coffins ranged in price from 8 to 65 pesos. First-class burial fees at the Cementerio del Sur cost 60 pesos in 1875. By 1900, choice, first-class real estate in the first quadrant of the cemetery cost 60 bolivars (Bs) *per square meter* (García Ponce 1995). Anyone wanting to purchase large family plots or build large tombs could expect considerable expense at first-class rates. The Caracas elite could purchase statuary for tombs from six agencies dedicated to funeral art after 1904. The cream of the Caracas elite, however, chose to import statuary from Italy or other European locations (Landaeta Rosales 1994: 28). The Caracas poor buried their dead in the Cementerio del Sur in its sixth quadrant, in plots that cost 10 Bs per square meter (Landaeta Rosales 1994: 28).

Walls do not divide rich and poor in cemeteries now, but cost remains an indicator of class. Rituals, remarkably enough, have remained constant. Then, as now, most people above a certain age were buried within a day of death. Also customary for all above a certain age was the novena, or the practice of saying the rosary for the soul of the departed for nine nights in a row after the burial. Families placed flowers and glasses of water at home altars and in the bedrooms of the departed to make sure the soul had enough to drink in its journey. Family members stood guard at the home through the night to make sure the wandering soul did not come back. At the end of the ninth day ritual specialists (often lay people, not clergy) helped cleanse the house one last time to guarantee the deceased's peaceful rest. Children's bodies were often salted to preserve them to allow for a couple of days of drinking, music, and dancing. When the time for burial came, however, there were no elaborate processions for children. Neither did the family observe the novena, because children's souls went straight to heaven (García Ponce 1995; Aretz 1957: 99–100). Rituals associated with death were important for the living in Venezuela. The church and clergy, however, were not necessarily part of that process.

The construction of the Cementerio del Sur marked more than cement monuments to concepts of class. Gúzman Blanco's construction of the Cementerio del Sur was actually the culmination of a process that marked the end of the 19th-century process of state usurpation of church power. In 1828, Bolívar ordered the construction of cemeteries in the suburbs and prohibited burials in churches or church yards for the sake of public health. Such declarations caused major upheaval in Brazil and Guatemala, but did not cause a fuss in Venezuela (Reis 2003; Sullivan-González 1998). The government's decision to declare freedom of religion in 1834 to encourage foreign (British) investment in the country and to accommodate the needs of foreign businessmen did not cause controversy as it did in other Latin American nations (Mecham 1966). Though the Church's hierarchy protested when the state required clergy to sign loyalty oaths or when the government expelled foreign priests, the government's actions did not cause an uproar among the general population. Only President Guzmán Blanco's moves to expropriate Church property, suppress Church-supported schools in favor of secular education, mandate civil registry of births, marriages, and deaths, and declare civil management of cemeteries in 1874 caused open controversy between the Church and the state. When Archbishop Guevara y Lira refused to sing a Te Deum mass in honor of Liberal party victories, Guzmán Blanco exiled the Archbishop to Trinidad. Guevara y Lira finally resigned his post when it became clear to him, Guzmán Blanco, and the Pope that the parties could not resolve the dispute any other way.

After the controversy, the already weak Venezuelan Catholic Church did not have the strength to challenge the state as it became increasingly authoritarian in the late-19th and early-20th centuries (Mecham 1966). That does not mean that the Church as an institution or individual Catholics did not make moves to adapt to 20th-century socioeconomic and political realities. To better serve the growing Venezuelan population in the 20th century, in the 1950s the Church began to add dioceses. There are now 37 dioceses. Individual Catholics at the lay and institutional level spoke against the worst state excesses of the 20th century, though the Church as an institution prospered during the dictatorships, particularly in terms of education. A self-identified Catholic student movement was part of the larger student movement that opposed Juan Vicente Gómez in the 1920s and 1930s. A pastoral letter issued in 1956 by the archbishop mildly critical of Marcos Pérez Jiménez began the process that led to his downfall (Levine 1976).

Pacted democracy beginning in 1958, and oil revenues brought benefits to the Church it had not had in its history in Venezuela. The government tripled the subsidies paid to the Church, granted the Church the legal status necessary to own property, reduced the state's role in the appointment of bishops, and regularized rules to bring in foreign clergy. Though there were still not enough clergy present to serve the needs of Venezuela, the situation was better in the 1970s than it had been in 1870, when only 734 priests served all of the Venezuelan Catholic faithful. The legal, ecclesial, and material concessions made by the state to the Church cemented official Church support for state policies, even in the 1980s and the 1990s when it became obvious to most that pacted democracy in Venezuela had lost legitimacy in the eyes of most of the population (Levine 1976). The Church in the 1970s did not favor encouraging lay participation in social action or community organizations but instead encouraged groups, like the Legion of Mary, dedicated to fomenting piety. In so doing, the official Venezuelan Catholic Church turned its back on liberation theology, the theology predominant in many Latin American countries in the 1970s, which suggested that the Church must change tack and tackle social causes, like poverty, with lay people, through Church-driven community organizations and social action.

There were, however, clergy that urged the Church to abandon its comfortable relationship with the state in order to tackle social issues. The most famous of those clergy was the Belgian priest Francis Wuytack. Father Wuytack worked in the Caracas barrio of La Vega. He was expelled from the country in 1970 after he participated with his parishioners in protests against poor living conditions and unemployment. The Church hierarchy affirmed the legality of Father Wuytack's expulsion and criticized him for becoming involved in politics. Though numerous clergy criticized the hierarchy and supported Father Wuytack's ideas and actions through open letters and sermons, the hierarchy did not change its position. The Jesuits in Venezuela also urged the Church to move away from a position of comfortable compliance with the state and toward social action. In one article, a Jesuit spokesman suggested that those individuals who worked to protect the social, economic, and political privileges of the few risked dangerous social consequences. Though the spokesman directly referred to lay people who benefited from privileges, his argument also implied criticism of Church hierarchy (Levine 1976). The controversies in the 1970s largely reflect patterns well established in Venezuelan Church history. The Church, as an institution, retained its close association with the national elite and the government. Individual clergy could voice support for alternative agendas that supported more closely the needs of their poor parishioners, but in so doing clergy risked losing their voice. At least that is what Father Wuytack discovered.

POPULAR RELIGION AND RELIGIOSITY

Nineteenth-century debates about the political influence of the Church or 20th-century debates about Church complicity with the state had little or nothing to do with how Venezuelans constructed their ideas about faith and the daily role of religion in their lives. Nineteenth-century chroniclers in Maracaibo in the state of Zulia in the far west noted that residents in that growing community constructed their calendars around religious festivals. Corpus Christi; Holy Week; the Virgins of Carmelo, Imaculada, and del Carmen; Santa Lucía, San Benito, the Sacred Heart of Jesus, San Francisco, Our Lady of Mercy; and, above all, the day of the Virgin of Chiquinquirá were all celebrated with enthusiasm by Zulians (Bermúdez Briñez 2001). Another way to look at religiosity is through understanding the careful preparation and precise execution of rituals associated with death and burial, regardless of social class. Venezuelans believed (and many continue to believe) that the only way to guarantee safe passage of the soul from the body to the afterlife was through proper, respectful burial. That was not easy in 19th-century Caracas, particularly for the poor. The poor had to carry their dearly departed on wooden slabs on their shoulders, often without coffins, through the Caracas hills to the cemetery, and in the rain during those months of the year when rain is the norm (García Ponce 1995). Slipping and dropping the dead was considered extremely shameful. Rituals in the 19th century were remarkably similar to those followed by Juan Fuentes's family in the late 20th and early 21st century and included the novena, home altars, and non-clerical ritual specialists (García Ponce 1995; Aretz 1957). Ensuring safe passage of the soul was the most important duty the living undertook, proving the importance of religiosity, not religious institutions, in the lives of everyday Venezuelans.

Religiosity in Venezuela, then, is part of popular religion broadly and popular Catholicism a bit more specifically. Popular religion refers to the complex processes through which people construct their relationships with the supernatural, sometimes with the direct guidance of religious institutions. In many more cases, the institutional presence is indirect, at most. National, regional, local, class, race, ethnic, and gender considerations can influence popular religion as much as any religious institution can. Catholicism lends itself to the development of rich popular religious traditions. Religious scholar William Christian notes that Roman Catholic canon law "leaves ample room for customary practice that accumulates at all levels" (Christian 2006: 260). Catholicism allows for the construction of smaller catholicisms, national, regional, local, or personal applications of faith in which the faithful can incorporate elements of non-Catholic regional identity or racial identity into their relationship with the divine. Sometimes, such processes change the way the faithful and the Church understand the divine. The Virgin Mary, for example, was a secondary figure in European Catholicism before the age of exploration. Marian devotion in the Americas quickly surpassed Marian devotion in Europe in part because of the importance of female deities in indigenous religious systems. In many indigenous religions, male and female deities existed in complementary pairs. Female gods were as important as male gods. Monotheistic Catholicism did not, obviously, have female gods, but indigenous Americans forced into Catholicism looked for something or someone in Catholicism who could represent for them what the female indigenous deities had in the past (Viera Powers 2005). Mary fulfilled that purpose. Some argue, for example, that Our Lady of Guadalupe, the most important saint in the Mexican tradition, is a Catholic incarnation of the Aztec deity, Tonantzín. The location of

Guadalupe's shrine is the same as the location of Tonantzín's shrine. Important images commonly included in Guadalupe images were also images associated with indigenous deities. None of that makes Our Lady of Guadalupe any less Catholic, but all may have served to help indigenous Mexicans construct conceptual bridges to help them move from polytheistic indigenous traditions to monotheistic Catholicism (Poole 1995).

In most cases, images of Mary quickly lost their association with indigenous religions and became thoroughly Catholic, but there were (and are) as many representations of Mary as there are national, regional, and ethnic identities in Latin America. Africans brought as slaves also found Catholicism to be malleable. One of the important distinctions between slavery in Latin America and slavery in the United States was that Spaniards came to the point that they did not question Africans' humanity as the English did. Africans were definitely lesser humans in the Spaniards' perspective, but they were still humans with souls. Because Africans had souls, the Church had the spiritual obligation to care for those souls. That religious duty placed the Church in a complicated position in Latin American slave-holding societies. If the Church pushed evangelism too hard among the slave populations, it ran the risk of alienating slave owners, the elite, the all important financial contributors to Church wealth. That is, in part, why official evangelism among slaves dropped on the Church's priority list and officially sanctioned but locally governed religious brotherhoods, *cofradías*, assumed greater significance. Catholic saints became the vehicles through which African-descended Latin Americans constructed religious identity, drawing from African polytheistic religious traditions. Afrobrazilians, for example, granted the Catholic God the status of a major saint in their religious pantheon, but the Catholic God was not supreme over all in the Afrobrazilian cosmology (Reis 2003). But even though Afrobrazilian Catholicism was different from catholicisms throughout Latin America, that does not mean that individuals who used different influences to construct different religious identities understood themselves to be any less Catholic. Catholicisms became fundamental parts of personal, local, regional, national, and ethnic identities.

Venezuela was no different from anywhere else in Latin America in terms of construction of popular (from the folk) religious identities. The Virgin of Coromoto has been the official national saint since 1942 (Pollack-Eltz 1994). Her story parallels the story of Our Lady of Guadalupe in Mexico. As in Mexico, an image of the Virgin appeared to Indians and served as a catalyst to encourage Catholic devotion. The story goes that in 1651 and 1652 the Virgin appeared to the Coromoto chief and his family in two different locations in the llanos. Just like Our Lady of Guadalupe, the Virgin of Coromoto left a small image of herself that a child carried to Church authorities (Our Lady of Coromoto 2003). Though she is officially the national patroness, Coromoto is best understood as a regional saint, most important to people in the llanos. Her official sanctuary is in Guanare in the state of Portuguesa. Other images of the Virgin are more important for other regions. Our Lady of the Divine Shepherdess (Divina Pastora) is the patron saint of the state of Lara and its capital, Barquisimeto. The Virgin of Chiquinquirá is favored among Zulians in the far west. The eastern coastal areas remain largely devoted the Virgin of the Valley, somehow brought by the sea. Though it is said that fishermen are her most ardent devotees, people throughout the east pay her special homage. Devotion to all images of the Virgin is intensely personal. The faithful talk with their favorite versions of Mary as a spiritual mother who has the ability to act in their lives just as a biological mother

VIRGIN OF COROMOTO

Devotion to the Virgin of Coromoto by Venezuelans both in Venezuela and abroad is a good example of the practical religiosity of the Venezuelan people. Venezuelans show their love for the patroness not only in pilgrimages to her official shrine in Guanare, but also by visiting her Facebook page (http://www.facebook.com/pages/Virgen-de-Coromoto-Patrona-de-Venezuela/29224636834).

The Virgin's Facebook page is a space for her devotees (in the language of the site, "likes") to offer her prayers, give her thanks for blessings, and publicly express their love for her. Since August of 2008, when her Facebook page was created, with photos of the Sanctuary and basilica in Guanare, the Virgin has gained 45,248 Facebook likes in Venezuela and in countries such as the United States and Italy.

A crowd estimated at 150,000 gathers around the Virgin of Coromoto cathedral near Gunare, Venezuela Saturday, February 10, 1996 to take part in a mass celebrated by Pope John Paul II. The church, about 250 miles southwest of Caracas, is dedicated to the Virgin Mary and built on the site where she is believed to have appeared before an Indian chief in 1652. (AP/Wide World Photos)

would. The faithful ask the Virgin for favors, to grant health or jobs, and then make pilgrimages to the Virgin's sanctuaries to express gratitude. Dedication to different Virgins also reinforces regional identity, as each region considers its Virgin the most beautiful, most miraculous of all Venezuelan Virgins.

San Juan and San Benito are the saints most closely associated with Afrovenezuelan identity and culture in the Barlovento coastal areas in central Venezuela and in the Maracaibo basin. San Juan became the patron saint of the Barlovento region in the 1700s. The celebration of the saint's day falls on June 25, roughly coinciding with the cacao harvest, the summer solstice, and the beginning of the rainy season, perfect times to allow a festival. The three days of the celebration, starting on June 23 and ending on June 25, came to be associated with symbolic expressions of freedom within the context of slavery that were so important for Afrovenezuelans that slave owners realized that suppression of the celebrations could provoke open rebellion (Guss 1993). Devotees used African-style drums made of complete tree trunks and dancing to honor a Catholic saint whose image was placed in a central, public location during the celebrations. Celebration of San Juan's day continued after the abolition of slavery as a cornerstone in the construction of combined local, racial, and religious identity. As residents in Barlovento began to move to Caracas in the mid-20th century in search of new economic opportunities, they continued to come home for the celebration to reconnect themselves with the roots of their identity, even as they began also to see themselves as urban *caraqueños*.

For Afrovenezuelans in the Maracaibo basin, celebration of San Benito serves a similar function to the celebrations devoted to San Juan in Barlovento. The faithful describe San Benito as a *negro* like all other Afrovenezuelans who can save his faithful from danger and cure all sorts of ills, but who requires people to fulfill promises made to him, punishing those who do not. The celebration of the saint's day roughly coincides with the winter solstice in December, culminating on December 27. Drumming, dancing, and singing accompany the procession of an image of the saint through the streets as he collects on the promises through monetary contributions made by the faithful or toasts offered to the members of the procession (Pollack-Eltz 1994). In communities like Gibraltar or Bobures in the mid-19th century, the style of drumming associated with the celebration of San Benito also came to be even more closely associated with Afrovenezuelan identity and resistance to regional and national authorities who wanted to replace local autonomy with regional and national authority (Linder 2007).

The only figure in Venezuelan popular Catholic religiosity that transcends racial and regional boundaries is not even officially a saint. The Vatican recognized José Gregorio Hernández as "venerable" in 1985 but has yet to make him a saint. That technicality does not matter to Venezuelans. José Gregorio was born in 1864 in the state of Trujillo. He studied medicine at the Universidad Central, and with state funding completed his studies in Europe. As a doctor in Caracas in the late 19th and early 20th century, he was widely known for his piety and his concern for the poor. He ran a free medical clinic for the poor and supplied medicines for them out of his own pockets. According to the legend, José Gregorio was delivering free medicine when he was struck by a car and died in 1919. Nearly immediately after his death, people began to visit his grave to ask for favors of all sorts in addition to healing.

A statue of José Gregorio Hernández stands at the entrance to his hometown of Isnotu, Venezuela. Many feel the humble, learned, and religious man who gained fame early this century for giving free treatment and medicine to the poor deserves to be made a saint by the Roman Catholic Church. When Pope John Paul II visited in February 1996, he received a petition signed by five million people—nearly one of every four Venezuelans—urging him to declare Hernández a saint. (AP/Wide World Photos)

Soon, word spread of miracles. Today, innumerable Venezuelans all over the country regard him as their most important personal protector. He is part of the court of María Lionza, a spiritualist religion unique to Venezuela that incorporates African, indigenous, and historical figures. As proof of his sainthood, José Gregorio's spirit does not possess mediums in trances. As he is a saint, he sends other doctors to aid the faithful (Pollack-Eltz 1994).

MARÍA LIONZA

Venezuela's most unusual contribution to Latin American popular religion is the cult of María Lionza. The religion began sometime during the early part of the 20th century in Caracas, though its most sacred space is Sorte Mountain south of Caracas. Despite its modern origins, the religion draws heavily on Venezuelan colonial and postindependence history for ideas and religious figures. María Lionza assumes two forms in the religion. The first, most common, is that of a strong, young, indigenous woman, said to have been the daughter of an indigenous leader. She is depicted naked, holding up a human pelvis while riding a tapir. The second version resembles the Virgin Mary, complete with a blue scarf on her head. In either form, she reigns over a court of spirits with the aid of the Indian Guaicaipuro and the Negro Miguel, indigenous and African leaders who died at the hands of the Spaniards in the early decades of the colonial period. The three together are called the *tres potencias*, or three powers. Particularly when María Lionza is symbolized as the Virgin Mary, the *potencias* represent the three components of Venezuelan identity—European, African, and indigenous. Additional spirits in the court include Simón Bolívar, Andres Bello, the Negro Primero, the Negra Matea (Bolívar's nanny), José Gregorio Hernández, and other Catholic saints.

As a whole, the religion reflects complex popular conceptions of sacred national identity, including ideas about race and gender, as well as popular ideas about pressing problems. The cult of María Lionza is not a religion guided by an established hierarchy that somehow shapes understanding of religious or social issues. The spirits field questions directly from believers about family disputes, romantic problems, financial issues, or medical ailments. People who need help assisting a family member in jail seek guidance from the spirit of Juan Vicente Gómez. Those with political questions ask Simón Bolívar. Believers' intense devotion to the spirits generally and the *tres potencias* specifically, their care of María Lionza spiritual centers in Caracas and other urban areas, and the importance of pilgrimage to Sorte within the belief system demonstrate the priorities of María Lionza faithful. For them, the cult of María Lionza is their vehicle for understanding a relationship with the supernatural, just as Virgin de Coromoto may be key in that relationship for someone in Mérida, or San Benito may be a focal point for an Afrovenezuelan in Maracaibo (Pollack-Eltz 1994; Placido 2001).

Statue of indigenous goddess María Lionza created by Alejandro Colina. (TimeLife Pictures/Getty Images)

PROTESTANTISM IN VENEZUELA

During the last decades of the 20th century, evangelical Protestantism became a player in the Venezuelan religious and political arenas. Protestantism in Venezuela, however, is nothing new. The establishment of freedom of religion in 1834 allowed British Anglicans in Caracas to establish a chapel to serve the needs of foreign Protestants. Other mainstream Protestant denominations followed. As part of the broader Western efforts in missionization in the developing world, mainstream denominations sent missionaries to Venezuela in the late 19th and early 20th century, though their efforts bore little fruit. Only the Anglican Church gained a tiny foothold. With the discovery of gold in El Callao in the llanos, mining companies imported West Indian labor, primarily from Trinidad. Trinidadian laborers brought their religion with them. When oil companies imported West Indian labor in the Maracaibo basin, that also led to the establishment of a small Anglican community.

All sorts of missionary efforts gained momentum beginning in the 1960s. The Church of Jesus Christ and Latter Day Saints (Mormons) also began actively evangelizing in Latin America. Groups like New Tribes Mission began missionary efforts with indigenous populations throughout Latin America, including Venezuela. In most of Latin America, Protestant populations began to grow rapidly concurrently with urbanization in the 1960s and the 1970s. In the late 20th century, however, it was not the mainstream churches but churches loosely called *evangélico* (evangelical) that grew in Latin America. Most Latin American *evangélicos* are Pentecostal Christians. By 1993, 10 percent of Latin Americans self-identified as *evangélico*, most in Brazil, Chile, and the Central American nations (Garrard Burnett 1993). Just over

---

MISSIONARY WORK

Protestant missionary efforts among indigenous populations in Venezuela have frequently aroused controversy in the 20th century because, critics argue, such efforts represent a form of cultural imperialism.

When in August of 2005 American televangelist and protestant evangelical Pat Robertson remarked on his television program that the United States should assassinate Venezuelan president Hugo Chávez, it was only one shot in an ongoing struggle between U.S. evangelicals and the Venezuelan government.

One missionary group in particular, the New Tribes Mission, which entered the country illegally in 1946 and moved into the southern territories of Amazonas State, had been of particular concern. Over the years, investigations by anthropologists and documentary filmmakers had found the mission guilty of systematic destruction of indigenous language, religion, family structure, and culture while only providing negligible improvements to standards of living. There had also been accusations against the mission of espionage and of building a state within a state with airstrips, hospitals, and a communications network not accessible to the Venezuelan government. In October of 2005, Chávez expelled the New Tribes Mission from Venezuela.

28 percent of all Latin Americans were Pentecostals in 2005 ("Overview: Pentecostalism" n.d.). The growth of evangelical Protestantism in Venezuela began in the 1980s simultaneously with the economic and political unraveling of the Venezuelan state. Evangelical groups, along with other grassroots social movements, found the space to organize when the clientele-based political party system fell apart. By the early 1990s, 5.34 percent of all Venezuelans were *evangélicos* (Smilde 2004).

At the same time the Evangelical community grew in Caracas, Hugo Chávez's MBR-200 movement began the campaigns that eventually led to Chávez's election in 1998. Journalists and critics comment frequently on Chávez's efforts to court *evangélicos* and his use of biblical language. His adaptation of Jeremiah 5:21, "Hear this, O foolish and senseless people, Who have eyes, but see not, Who have ears, but hear not" became Chávez's most popular campaign slogan (Smilde 2004). According to David Smilde, *evangélicos* do not give over their vote as a group easily. They argue that God granted humans "free will to choose to help God in his project or not" (Smilde 2004: 81). As a result, *evangélicos* feel free to vote their conscience based on their interpretation on how any given candidate acts according to God's will. Indeed, when one nationally prominent *evangélico* leader threw his support behind AD candidate Alfaro in 1998 and promised the *evangélico* vote, most of the rest of the *evangélico* community cried foul, not because they did not like Alfaro (most people did not like Alfaro) but because promising votes violated the free will of individual *evangélicos* (Smilde 2004). Some *evangélicos* chose not to vote for Chávez in 1998 because they thought that his violent past might predict either a violent or authoritarian future, either in contradiction with God's will, as they saw it. Other *evangélicos* became enthusiastic Chávez supporters. They acknowledged the violent past but argued that Chávez's dedication to the Bible indicated that God had called Chávez to the presidency. As a whole, however, *evangélicos* were not any more inclined to vote for Chávez than non-*evagélicos.* Their voting tendencies directly paralleled the tendencies of the nation as a whole (Smilde 2004).

Chávez's actions after the elections indicated a continued willingness to court Venezuelan *evangélicos* at the perceived expense of the Catholic Church. By 1999, the congress enacted legislation that allowed *evangélicos* to teach religion in public schools. Chávez cut in half the portion of the subsidy the Catholic Church received that came from the budget of the executive office (Smilde 2004). *Evangélicos* participated with other civil society groups in roundtable discussions about national reconciliation after the April 2002 coup attempt. Though *evangélicos* appreciated indirect government support and inclusion in public dialogues, they rejected formal inclusion in the government. The government tried to organize a Bolivarian Interreligious Parliament with representatives from all Venezuelan religious groups. The government's goal was to channel social projects and funds through the parliament, but the major *evangélico* organizations and the Catholic Church refused to participate. They distrusted the government officials associated with the projects. *Evangélicos* furthermore did not want to associate with organizations with whom they had major theological differences, specifically Rev. Sun Myung Moon's Unification Church (Smilde 2004). While Chávez thus far has failed in attempts to officially incorporate *evangélicos* into the state and to create with them a relationship similar to the relationship between the Catholic Church and the state in centuries prior, the fact that he tries indicates the social significance of the *evangélico* population in Venezuela.

PRACTICAL RELIGIOSITY

We started this section with a description of a burial and end it with another. One of Juan's sons, his wife, and their small daughter died in a car accident in 2005, something that happens all too frequently on Venezuelan highways. The family meticulously followed all of the rituals for Javier, Mariela, and Carla just as they had for Juan. This time, the official funeral was held at the Catholic Church. They had a new priest that Juan's widow liked better, though she still regularly attended the Anglican Church. The new Anglican priest and his wife attended every night of the novena, as did dozens of friends and relatives of all religious persuasions. There were more *evangélicos* in the family in 2005 than there had been in 1996, a situation that was a bit odd for most of the non-*evangélicos*, but that certainly did not matter in the time of tremendous grief. The rituals had to be properly observed. After the novena was over, the family decided to keep a small altar in Javier and Mariela's bedroom in the family house, with their pictures, flowers, and a glass of water. Juan's widow, Tata, still goes into the bedroom to talk to her son in front of the altar. She asks him to visit her in her dreams. Javier has become part of her personal religious pantheon, her way to construct a relationship with the divine, right up there with Jesus, José Gregorio Hernández, and the Virgin of the Valley.

Tata's sister speaks with anyone bearing a religious tract, *evangélico*, Jehovah's Witness, Mormon, Catholic—it does not matter. She places the tracts on her home altar with her statues of the Virgin of the Valley and José Gregorio Hernández. All represent the sacred to her, even though the groups who authored the tracts would not share her assessment. *Evangélicos* are supposed to give up the popular Catholic devotions when they convert, but it is certainly possible that they could save a small image of their favorite saint, a little José Gregorio Hernández, because you never know when you need more healing help. Anyone who needs a blessing these days may well seek one in a Mormon temple, from a Catholic priest, and at an *evangélico* church (Smilde 2007). They could also talk with a Maria Lionza spirit. Latin Americans' ability to adapt their religious beliefs according to the options available to them in some sense demonstrates remarkable religious creativity and in many cases a sense of religion that is more practical and less theoretical than in other areas of the world. As religions grow and change in new circumstances, the Venezuelan religious realm will only become even more dynamic.

REFERENCES

Acereda La Linde, Manuel. 1963. *Historia de Aragua de Barcelona del Estado Anzoategui y de la Nueva Andalucia, Tomo Segundo*. Caracas: Imprenta Nacional.

ACB. 1845. *Archives of the Archdiocese of Ciudad Bolívar.* Caja V, Libro 9, item 56, July 4.

ACB. 1853. *Archives of the Archdiocese of Ciudad Bolívar.* Caja I, Libro I, March 18.

ACB. 1868. *Archives of the Archbishop of Ciudad Bolívar.* Caja I, Libro I, item 21.

Aretz, Isabel. 1957. *Manual de Folklore Venezolano.* Caracas: Ministerio de Educación.

Alvaro Huerga. 1996. *La evangelización del oriente de Venezuela: Los anexos del obispado (Los anexos del obispado de Puerto Rico).* Ponce, Puerto Rico: Pontifica Universidad Católica de Puerto Rico.

Bermúdez Briñez, Nilda. 2001. *Vivir en Maracaibo en el siglo XIX.* Maracaibo: Biblioteca Temas de Historia de Zulia, 2001.

Caulín, Fray Antonio. 1987. *Historia de la Nueva Andalucia,* ed. Pablo Ojer, S.J. Caracas: Fuentes para la Historia Colonial de Venezuela.

Christian, William, Jr. 2006. "Catholicisms." In Martin Austin Nesvig, ed., *Local Religion in Colonial Mexico.* Albuquerque: University of New Mexico Press.

Family History Library. 1857. 1995784. Roll 12. " Libro de Confirmaciones hecho por el Ilustrísimo Sr. Dr. José Manuel Arroyo, Dignísimo Obispo de esta Diócesis de paso por esta ciudad de Aragua a 31 de Mayo de 1857 de tránsito para Ciudad Bolívar, Confirmaciones No. 2, 1857–1915."

Ferry, Robert. 1989. *The Colonial Elite of Early Caracas: Formation and Crisis, 1567–1767.* Berkeley: University of California Press.

García Gavidia, Nelly. 1987. *Posesión y ambivalencia en el culto a María Lionza: Notas para una tipología de los cultos de posesión existentes en la América del Sur.* Zulia, Venezuela: Editorial de la Universidad de Zulia, 59–62

García Ponce, Antonio. 1995. *Los pobres de Caracas, 1873–1907: Un estudio de la pobreza urbana.* Caracas: Instituto Municipal de Publicaciones.

Garrard Burnett, Virginia. 1993. "Introduction: Rethinking Protestantism in Latin America." In Virginia Garrard Burnett and David Stoll, eds., *Rethinking Protestantism in Latin America.* Philadelphia, PA: Temple University Press.

Gómez Candeo, Lino. 1967. *Las misiones de Píritu: Documentos para su historia.* Caracas: Biblioteca de la Academia Nacional de la Historia.

Guss, David M. 1993. "The Selling of San Juan: The Performance of History in an Afro-Venezuelan Community." *American Ethnologist* 20: 3, 453.

González Oropeza, Hermann, S.J. 1997. *Iglesia y Estado en Venezuela.* Caracas: Universidad de Andrés Bello.

Landaeta Rosales, Manuel. 1994. *Los cementerios de Caracas.* Caracas: Fundarte Alcaldía de Caracas.

Levine, Daniel. 1976. "Democracy and the Church in Venezuela." *Journal of Interamerican Studies and World Affairs* 18: 1, 3.

Linder, Peter. 2007. "Drumming Rebellion: Political and Social Violence in the Sur del Lago de Maracaibo on the Eve of the Federal War, 1839–1858." Paper presented at the XVII Congress of the Latin American Studies Association, Montreal, Canada, September 8.

Maradei Donato, Constantino. 1985. *Noticias historiales de nueva Barcelona /Fernando del Bastardo y Loayza.* Caracas: Academia Nacional de la Historia.

Mecham, J. Lloyd. 1966. *Church and State in Latin America: A History of Politico-Ecclesiastical Relations.* Chapel Hill: University of North Carolina Press.

Morse, Kimberly J. 2000. "Aun en la muerte separados: Class, Clergy, and Society in Aragua de Barcelona, Venezuela, 1820–1875." PhD diss., The University of Texas at Austin.

———. 2003. "When the Priest Does Not Sympathize with the Pueblo: Clergy and Society in El Oriente Venezolano, 1843–1873." *The Americas* 59, no. 4: 511–535.

Our Lady of Coromoto. 2003. "Nuestra Señora of Coromoto." *Hispanic Heritage Plaza 2003.* http://www.hispaniconline.com/hh03/mainpages/religion/mary_venezuela.html.

"Overview: Pentecostalism in Latin America." n.d. *The Pew Forum on Religion and Public Life.* http://pewforum.org/surveys/pentecostal/latinamerica/.

Placido, Barbara. 2001. "It's All to Do with Words: An Analysis of Spirit Possession in the Venezuelan Cult of Maria Lionza." *The Royal Journal of the Anthropological Institute* 7, no. 2: 207–224.

Pollack-Eltz. Angelina. 1985. *María Lionza: Mito y Culto Venezolano.* Caracas: Universidad Católica Andrés Bello.

———. 1994. *La religiosidad popular en Venezuela.* Caracas: San Pablo.

Poole, Stafford. 1995. *Our Lady of Guadalupe: The Origins and Sources of a Mexican National Symbol, 1531–1797.* Tucson: University of Arizona Press.

Prato-Perelli, Antoinette da. 1990. *Las encomiendas de Nueva Andalucia en el siglo XVII: Visita hecha por don Fernando Riva Agüero, Oidor de la Audiencia de Santo Domingo, 1688, Tomo I.* Caracas: Biblioteca de la Academia Nacional de la Historia.

Reis, João José. 2003. *Death Is a Festival: Funeral Rites and Rebellion in Nineteenth-Century Brazil.* Trans. H. Sabrina Gledhill. Chapel Hill: University of North Carolina.

Registro Principal de Barcelona. 1844. "Aragua 1837-1844," Libro 26, item 4, 4v.-5v., October 7.

Registro Principal de Barcelona. 1847. "Aragua 1845-1850," Libro 24, *No. 13, Protocolo Principal Para la Oficina Subalterna de Registro en el Mes de Febrero de 1847*, item 4, 6v-7v, July 10.

Registro Principal de Barcelona. 1848. Civiles, Sucesoriales, Inventorios, Particiones, 1845-1850, Libro 22, "Juzgado de Paz de Caigua, Civiles, Mortuaria intestada del Reverendo Fray Salvador de la Gertrud, 1848."

Smilde, David. 2004. Contradiction Without Paradox: Evangelical Political Culture in the 1998 Venezuelan Elections. *Latin American Politics and Society* 46, no. 1: 75–102.

———. 2007. *Reason to Believe: Cultural Agency in Latin American Evangelicalism.* Berkeley: University of California Press.

Staples, Anne. 1994. "Policía y Buen Gobierno: Municipal Efforts to Regulate Public Behavior, 1821–1857." In William H. Beezley, Cheryl English Martín, and William E. French, eds. *Rituals of Rule, Rituals of Resistance: Public Celebration and Popular Culture in Mexico.* Wilmington, DE: Scholarly Resources, Inc.

Sullivan-González, Douglass. 1998. *Piety, Power, and Politics: Religion and Nation Formation in Guatemala, 1821–1871.* Pittsburgh, PA: University of Pittsburgh Press.

Vieira Powers, Karen. 2005. *Women at the Crucible of Conquest: The Gendered Genesis of Spanish American Society, 1500–1600.* Albuquerque: University of New Mexico Press.

Waldron, Kathy. 1989. "The Sinners and the Bishop in Colonial Venezuela: The 'Visita' of Bishop Mariano Marti, 1771–1784." In Asuncion Lavrin, ed., *Sexuality and Marriage in Colonial Latin America.* Lincoln: University of Nebraska Press.

Social Classes and Ethnicity

WHO IS VENEZUELAN?: RACE AND CLASS IN VENEZUELA

In July 2009, the Venezuelan population numbered some 27 million people (CIA: The World Factbook: Venezuela 2009). Two percent of that population was indigenous (Minorities at Risk: Assessment for Indigenous Peoples in Venezuela 2009). Most indigenous Venezuelans lived in the far eastern, southern, and western regions of the country. The most important groups were the Wayao (Guajiro) in the far west, the Yanomami and Pemón in the south and southeast, and the Warao, who live in the Delta Amacuro in the far east (Minorities at Risk: Assessment for Indigenous Peoples in Venezuela 2009). The Wayao maintained their cultural autonomy until the 20th century because of their ability to serve as economic middlemen between colonial powers before independence and between Venezuelans in the country's far west and Colombians in that nation's far east. The Amazon-dwelling Yanomami are, by far, the most famous of all Venezuelan indigenous groups in part because of their resistance to wildcat gold miners and also because of anthropologists' fascination with this remote group. The Pemon Indians live in the Gran Sabana, the vast, geologically unique region where Angel Falls is located. For the Pemón, well-managed ecotourism in the region could be a blessing because it would bring a regulated number of people into a delicate landscape that the Pemón still use and would provide a market for Pemón baskets. Botched ecotourism could damage ecology and culture. Not until the 20th century did the Venezuelan state and missionaries take any interest in the Warao in Delta Amacuro. The results proved detrimental to the Warao.

In addition to the indigenous populations, there are small populations of Italians, Germans, Arabs, Portuguese, and Chinese in Venezuela. When someone from the United States travels to Venezuela, however, they do not notice the tiny, rural indigenous population or the diffuse population of foreigners. What one notices is that Venezuelans are not white in the U.S. sense. They range in shades from blond-haired, blued-eyed folks through all possible hues to mostly dark. Census data, however, do not capture Venezuelans' hues. Census data reflect indigenous and foreign populations. All others are defined as "Venezuelan."

TABLE 5.2   Population of the Four Largest Indigenous Groups in Venezuela

Group	Location	Population
Guajiro/Wayao/Wayuu	Zulia	200,000
Warao	Delta Amacuro	18,000
Pemon	Gran Sabana	14,480
Yanomami	Amazonas	12,000–14,000

It is also easy for visitors coming into Caracas to see the poverty. Quite literally millions of people lived stacked in *ranchitos* on the hillsides that surround the city. Approximately 40 percent of the Venezuelan population lives in poverty (CIA: The World Factbook: Venezuela 2009). For the most part, those who live in the *ranchitos* are not white. Those who live in the elite neighborhoods on the east side of town are primarily white. One can see clearly in Venezuela that class has color even if Venezuela does not "count" color in its census data. Those realities took centuries to construct and they have concrete political consequences.

AD candidate Luís Alfaro Lucero played the race card against Hugo Chávez Frías in the 1998 election. Playing to elite Venezuelans' most deep-seated prejudices, Lucero demonized Chávez. Lucero and those who supported him called Chávez a mixed breed and a monkey, making fun of Chávez's hair. Political cartoonists drew Chávez with extraordinarily thick lips. Lucero supporters openly characterized Chávez's supporters in equally racialized terms, as ignorant monkeys who blindly followed the chief ape. In so doing, Lucero and his elite supporters exposed deep-seated classism and racism in Venezuela. Race and class are intimately entwined and fundamentally important topics in Venezuela today. To understand how it could be that a presidential candidate could use openly racist language in 1998 we need to explore a bit more history.

The first theme we need to understand is that Venezuelans of European descent (whites) and indigenous Venezuelans, Afrovenezuelans, and the mixed-race descendents of all of the above do not share much common history. That is to say that often they did not embrace shared agendas and similar identities. Most often, the story of race in Venezuela is about how one group has tried repeatedly to use others for the purpose of creating a modern Venezuela, whatever the definition of the moment was. We are just beginning to understand the extremes to which elite Venezuelans went in order to expropriate the labor of Indians and Africans and their descendents through at least the first third of the 20th century. We are also just beginning to understand how Indians and Africans and their descendents understood their role in Venezuela, how they constructed their identities, and how they resisted the demands placed upon them. That history is hard to recover. We are obligated to try, however, if we are to understand the open racism and classism that mark Venezuela in the Chávez era.

We need to examine the terms *racism* and *classism* a bit more. Racism exists when one person or group stigmatizes another based on racial composition and visual characteristics. Racism exists overtly against those of identifiably different racial groups that retain a separate ethnic identity—Guajiro Indians or Afrovenezuelans from Barlovento, for example. Racism also exists against mixed race Venezuelans who happen to have darker skin, curly hair, or thicker lips. The overwhelming majority of Venezuelans share those characteristics to one degree or another. Few Venezuelans are white. In addition throughout Venezuelan history, many people, especially people of color, have also suffered poverty. Race became associated with class. White became the color of the elite, while *pardo* (brown) became the color of the poor.

There were no Jim Crow laws in the Venezuelan national period, no legal barriers separating the races as there were in the United States. However, the social barriers associated with race (and class) were just as strong. A tutor for high school students in Puerto La Cruz recently reported the following story: students frequently met each other to talk outside the tutor's apartment between lessons. One day, a dark-skinned student flipped open a cell phone to make a call just as a white student entered. A bit later, the white student pointedly asked the tutor who the other student was. "They," he said, "aren't supposed to have those things" (personal communication with the author). The incident demonstrates exactly how pernicious racism is in Venezuelan society. It also demonstrates the importance of class, or money, in the process. *Blanqueamiento*, or racial whitening, existed in theory from the colonial period. It means using money to buy the attributes associated with both higher classes and lighter colors. Money whitens, so the saying goes. Who knows whether or not the young student with the cell phone thought of the phone in terms of anything other than the modern convenience that it is. We can guess that the second student saw the phone as a symbol of inappropriate whitening.

INDIGENOUS VENEZUELANS IN THE COLONIAL ERA

But why? To figure that out we need to go back to history. There were dozens of indigenous groups occupying Venezuela when the Spaniards arrived in 1498. Some groups were seminomadic hunter-gatherer peoples. Other groups used agriculture to subsist. No group created an empire the equivalent of the Inca in Peru or the Aztec in Mexico. At best, groups in the center and center-west formed a loose confederation of communities that shared common culture but who did not share loyalty to one leader. Of the colonial indigenous Venezuelan experience there was no single pattern that held true for the territory that became Venezuela. Some indigenous Venezuelans on the coast suffered immediate exploitation and demographic devastation when Spaniards raided those populations for slaves to use in other Spanish colonies. Others, like the Wayao Indians of the Guajira Peninsula in far western Venezuela, retained their autonomy well into the 19th century in part because of their ability to serve the mercantile interests of first Spaniards and other Europeans colonizers in the western Caribbean and then later Venezuelans and Colombians (Linder 1999). The fact that the Wayao occupied an inhospitable spit of land certainly aided their cause. Of course, all Venezuelan indigenous populations suffered the consequences of disease from the early days of the colonial process. Because we do not have a solid grasp on how many indigenous Venezuelans there were before the arrival of Europeans, we cannot know precisely the scope of the losses. We do know this: indigenous populations with resources coveted by Spaniards (and later Venezuelans), land or labor, suffered more than others. As Spaniards' and Venezuelans' land and labor needs shifted as their populations grew, new indigenous populations felt more pressure.

The indigenous populations in the central valleys and in the Andes attracted Spaniards because the Indians occupied fertile lands and because those indigenous populations lived in settled communities and had agricultural skills Spaniards appreciated. Spaniards quickly incorporated those indigenous Venezuelans into *encomiendas*. Disease, malnutrition, and hard labor meant that by the end of the colonial period there were either no Indians in the central valleys or only a tiny indigenous minority who did not live according to a defined indigenous cultural identity. They had become part of the larger poor and mixed race population (Cunill Grau 1987).

The situation was different in eastern Venezuela. Spaniards did not begin the process of trying to settle in eastern Venezuela until the 1600s. Spaniards needed indigenous labor to grow sugar, coffee, and tobacco and to care for cattle and other livestock on their plantations and ranches. A report from a Spanish cleric in 1688 indicated that Spaniards held from 6 to 233 Indians in *encomienda* or *apuntamiento* on their plantations in the east (Prato-Perelli 1990). Few *encomiendas* included Indians from one ethnic group but instead combined Indians from the 15 or more different ethnic groups common in the east, a process that most certainly led to cultural change at the least. Spanish clerics also established dozens of missions throughout the east, 26 in what became the province of Nueva Barcelona (Anzoategui state) before 1797 (Caulín 1987). Indigenous Venezuelans associated with each mission had access to crown-protected land, or *resguardos*, not for sale or for use by any population other than the missions' indigenous populations. The crown ordered the size of each *resguardo* to measure one league, or approximately seven miles, from the center of the community center in all cardinal directions. Officials then connected the four points in a circle (RPB 1783a). So long as indigenous populations had access to *resguardo* land and as long as Spaniards remained uninterested in *resguardo* land, indigenous Venezuelans in the east had the ability to move back and forth between *encomienda* employment and mission communities as they needed, retaining indigenous languages and customs.

Encomenderos complained that indigenous Venezuelans who were supposed to be part of *encomiendas* preferred to live on their own lands, *resguardo* or otherwise, and in their own homes, not in homes built for them by *encomenderos* in *encomienda* communities. Indigenous Venezuelans were supposed to follow Catholic edicts, but *encomenderos* noted in a 1688 report that the Indians continued to practice indigenous religious rituals. Indians even preferred the indigenous corn-based diet with *arepas* over the Spanish diet. Much to *encomenderos'* great dismay, indigenous Venezuelans in the east simply did not stay put and adopt Spanish ideas about civilization, religion, and labor. Neither did Indians in other parts of the larger colony. The report indicated that Indians from the Caracas area, Píritu, and the island of Margarita all lived in Cumaná in the far east (Prato-Perelli 1990). The Spaniards' problem is strong evidence of indigenous assertion of agency and identity through strategies that involved some indigenous physical mobility, despite exploitative *encomienda* and *apuntamiento* conditions. As a result, in 1800 at the end of the colonial period, 60,000 of the 131,000 people who lived in the east were indigenous. The majority of the remaining population was mixed race. Geographer Pedro Cunill Grau also counted 6,000 individuals of African descent, and a tiny white minority largely associated with the elite in Cumaná and Barcelona (Cunill Grau 1987).

Indigenous Venezuelans in Mérida in the Andes also used physical mobility and community formation to cultivate cultural identity, though not without adapting some Spanish practices. Spaniards forced indigenous Venezuelans to live in 15 new towns with *resguardos* in different microecological regions, highlands to lowlands, that served the purposes of 100 different *encomiendas* in the early 1600s. As in the east, each new community included Indians from different ethnic groups, which led to some cultural change (Samudio A. and Edda 1990). Like Indians in the east, these Indians moved into *encomienda* communities but did not remain in one place. They moved to other communities for climate reasons or to search for better economic opportunities, often to the city of Mérida itself. Women moved just as much as men did. Women worked as domestic servants and as weavers. Men not engaged in agricultural labor worked as craftsmen or in animal-based transportation. Andean Indians adopted Catholicism more completely than indigenous Venezuelans did in the east, often bringing images of their adopted patron saints with them when they voluntarily moved to create new communities not sanctioned by the Spaniards. No matter what, Andean Indians played the hand dealt to them by Spaniards in ways that preserved some autonomy, though with cultural change (Samudio A. and Edda 1990). By 1815, the *Gazeta de Caracas* noted that the populations of Timotes and Mucuchíes were so substantial (10,000 of the 15,000 people in Mérida) that they could be referred to someday as the República de Mucuchíes y Timotes. In total, there were approximately 282,000 indigenous Venezuelans at the end of the colonial era, or 29 percent of the total population (Cunill Grau 1987). All had suffered some degree of demographic decline and recovery. A few groups disappeared completely. Many changed. No one pattern held true for all.

SLAVE AND FREE, AFRICAN AND MIXED RACE IN COLONIAL VENEZUELA

Just as there was no single pattern that defined the indigenous experience in colonial Venezuela, there was also no single pattern that defined the African or mixed race experience in the early centuries. In some areas, like the Andes, there were few slaves. That was certainly not the case in the central valleys and the west. As the indigenous population dropped in those areas in the 1600s and 1700s and elites switched from wheat to cacao, the slave population grew exponentially. At the beginning of the 19th century, before independence, Venezuelan slave owners owned 58,000 slaves, many engaged in cacao cultivation, living in the coastal areas that extended roughly from Barcelona in the east to Coro in the west (Cunill Grau 1987). The mixed-race population, free people of color roughly defined as *pardo*, was 435,000, or almost 47 percent of the total population in the late colonial era. Adding the population of people of color to the slave and indigenous populations indicates that 775,000 of the 975,000 people who lived in Venezuela on the eve of independence were not of solely European descent (Cunill Grau 1987).

German Welsers brought the first slaves to Venezuela from Puerto Rico in the mid-1500s to search for the gold that the Welsers never found. According to tradition, among the original number was the Negro Miguel, who in 1553 formed Venezuela's first *cumbe* (runaway slave community) and led Venezuela's first rebellion of slaves and Indians. He became one of the major figures in the unique Venezuelan religion led by the mythical María Lionza (Tronconis de Veracoechea 1992). By the early 1600s, Spaniards brought African slaves to Venezuela in ever greater numbers to support the production of brown gold, cacao. Venezuela's dependence on cacao produced two societies, urban and rural, both in their own ways defined by hierarchy. Both also allowed for the development of a culture of people of color, some free, some slave. In rural areas, that culture retained some African elements dismissed by later generations as barbaric at worst, folkloric at best, but that was nonetheless part of the Venezuelan fabric.

Urban Venezuelans of Spanish descent in Caracas, Cumaná, Valencia, Coro, Mérida, or Barcelona relied heavily on domestic slaves. Humboldt described the Venezuelan elite as a "true aristocracy" who disdained manual labor and interracial interaction (Humboldt 1941: 308). Indeed, the Venezuelan urban elite measured the status of a household in the number of slaves who worked in it. Thirty-five percent of Caracas households had an average of 5.8 slaves in 1759 (Ferry 1989: 72). One of the most famous colonial-era paintings is of a *mantuana*, *caraqueña* elite woman, leaving church on a Sunday morning with three slaves to attend her. Slaves did not only work in domestic service. Because the elite abhorred what they called vile labor, slaves and free people of color worked in trades reserved for European guild members in other colonies. Slaves and people of color were carpenters, blacksmiths, tailors, and cobblers (Rojas 2004). As skilled craftsmen, slaves had the financial means to more easily purchase their freedom and the freedom of other family members. Slaves and free people of color dominated urban marketplaces as vendors, craftspeople of all sorts, washerwomen, water carriers, and muleteers. The urban working class, almost all people of color, lived in cramped quarters with more than one family sharing a dwelling (Waldron 1989).

Poverty was normal, but so, too, were forms of cultural expression. People of color, free and slave, belonged to their own *cofradías*, religious brotherhoods and mutual aid societies, from as early 1611. Members of *cofradías* pooled resources to purchase the freedom of fellow members, pay medical bills, or to pay for burial rituals. And though the *cofradía* structure was Catholic, members used *cofradías* to protect some African cultural practices. People of color incorporated into Corpus Christi processions masks, costumes, and instrumentation that had more in common with African practices than anything European. Indeed, the church officials tried to forbid some such practices without any success (Vílchez Cróquer 2007). Free people of color also belonged to colonial militias in the mid 1700s which also allowed some people of color some social mobility and respectability through militia service, though we know much less about free people of color and colonial militias in Venezuela than we do about *cofradías*.

The possibility of some respect and autonomy within the larger population of people of color meant that people of color could reach the wall that separated them from white elite. *Pardos* could purchase material goods associated with higher status, better clothes, or perhaps even slaves. They could socioeconomically whiten themselves, but legal whiteness was more complicated to achieve. A 1795 royal decree included regulations to purchase legal white status, *cédulas de gracias al sacar*. Once granted a *cédula*, a person of color, legally whitened, had access to education, to become clergy, or to serve in public office. Without the *cédula*, people of color could not even serve as doormen at the *cabildo*. White *caraqueños* resisted the granting of *cédulas* altogether. They inundated colonial authorities with gloom and doom predictions of the chaos that would befall the colony if people of color were able to legally whiten themselves and enjoy the privileges that came with white legal status. People of color throughout the Spanish Americas submitted only 20 such petitions throughout the colonial period, 11 from Caracas (Twinam 1999). Legal barriers between races extended into marriage. A 1778 royal decree allowed elite parents to block marriages between white and nonwhite children (Seed 1988). By then, however, the Caracas elite had married endogenously for a century, often marrying first cousins to protect familial property and honor defined in terms of racial blood purity (Ferry 1989). Elite men did not marry women of color, but they did not hesitate to make women of color into concubines no matter how much church officials protested (Waldron 1989). The marriage decree and elite resistance to legal whitening made official social barriers that had long been unofficial. Though the colonial urban elite depended on the skilled and unskilled labor of slaves and people of color, as much as 71 percent of the population of Caracas, the elite absolutely refused to allow most people of color to cross the racial and class-based chasm that divided them (Cunill Grau 1987).

WHITE VENEZUELANS IN THE COLONIAL ERA

The white population was also not homogenous, not all truly elite. Those born on the Spanish mainland or those who traced their roots in Caracas to the earliest days and maintained their blood purity controlled the most colonial power, social, economic, and political. Thousands of immigrants from the Spanish Canary Islands, *isleños*, arrived in the 1700s, swelling the ranks of the white population. They were many of the small farmers who supported Juan Francisco de Leon's protest against the Guipuzcoana Company in 1749. The *isleños* and others like them at the lower end of the white socioeconomic spectrum found themselves in a complicated position in Venezuelan society during the colonial era and through the 19th century. Whiteness gave them access to privileges—education, for example—that people of color did not have. But because their familial history was not sterling, because there were doubts about their racial purity, or because they lived tainted with the stain of illegitimacy, they could never be truly elite. Poorer whites could see the power associated with truly elite status. With luck, lower-class whites could own two or three slaves. But the truly elite families who staffed their Caracas townhomes with 20 slaves and had another 150 on the cacao plantation did not consider themselves the social equals of the *isleño* with three slaves. Poorer whites could almost taste the power the truly elite had, but few ever truly achieved it.

LIVING TOGETHER IN THE COLONIAL ERA

The urban elite's ability to live as an aristocracy depended on the product of rural cacao plantations. Most cacao plantation owners preferred to live most of the year in Caracas to avoid the plantations, which were associated with barbarism generally and slavery and disease specifically. Whereas in urban areas white Venezuelans and people of color lived in close proximity, *juntos pero no revueltos*, slaves, free people of color, runaways living in *cumbes*, and Indians interacted regularly and with limited white supervision in the coastal plantation zones. Free people of color who were formerly slaves formed many of the towns along the coast later recognized by the crown.

Living conditions for those living in the cacao-growing zones were worse than experienced by people of color in the cities. Disease in the rural population, slave or free, was all too common. Plantation records indicate that owners had to budget for medical expenses incurred by slaves. Sometimes owners through their local overseers relied on indigenous medical practitioners, and sometimes on Western medicine (Ferry 1989). The harvest season for cacao fell in the off-season for subsistence crops (black beans and corn), so laborers worked hardest while underfed (Cunill Grau 1987). Malnutrition made laborers even more susceptible to disease.

Despite the hardships, slaves developed expectations, a concept of rights associated with slavery as it existed in cacao-growing Venezuela. Slaves and people of color associated with cacao plantations actively engaged in the illicit sale of cacao beans to smugglers. Cacao sellers avoided crown-licensed retail venues and used the beans to purchase clothing, food, or alcohol directly from the smuggler. One visitor to the coast noted that no more than one third of the harvest reached plantation storehouses. One can only assume that middlemen pilfered more beans between the storehouses and legal ports in La Guaira (Ferry 1989). Many slaves had access to their own *conucos*, kitchen gardens, in which they grew plantains, yuca, corn, rice, kidney beans, black beans, and bananas for subsistence and for market purposes (Brito Figueroa 1985). Slaves grew their own cacao trees in the shade of their own plantain trees. With limited white supervision, some economic autonomy, and little interference from church authorities, people of color developed Afrovenezuelan culture, or cultural practices with African origins but modified in new, multi-ethnic settings. African cultural influences affected language, food, dances, drumming, and religion throughout the coastal regions. San Francisco de Yare's "Devil Dances" and Barlovento's celebration of the saint's day of San Juan today attract cultural tourists from around the world because of the cultural fusion the celebrations incorporate (Romero 2007). From the colonial era to the present, the festivals are important celebrations of unique Afrovenezuelan identity.

Free people of color learned how to work the colonial system in order to create and preserve their own communities. Free people of color petitioned the crown for land grants to establish the town of Curiepe in the heart of the cacao zone in 1711. Juan del Rosario Blanco led the effort. Blanco was a captain in the militia unit composed of free people of color, or *morenos libres*. He spent his early years as a slave in Caracas and became a recognized leader in the population of people of color there before working with other members of his militia unit to obtain the land grant and establish Curiepe. Blanco used intimate knowledge of Venezuelan domestic politics and colonial fears in the process. He was probably the illegitimate son of a member of the Caracas elite who lobbied to obtain the land in years prior to 1711, so it may not be a coincidence that Blanco worked to gain legal rights to the same land his father failed to win. The literate Blanco included in his petition a detailed description of the land and coastline. He suggested that the land could become an ideal pirate base if not settled and defended properly. He argued that his group of militia of free

A man dressed as the devil dances to a drum in San Francisco de Yare. Devil dancing is the town's traditional way to commemorate Corpus Christi, with rhythmic dancing to drums and chants that symbolize the eternal struggle between good and evil. The tradition dates to 1740 when priests used it to include slaves of African origin, who were not permitted to worship in the same church as their white masters, into church celebrations. Devil dances became a unique expression of Afrovenezuelan culture, incorporating African cultural and religious concepts with Catholic ones. (Getty Images)

people of color could do both. Blanco's land claims did not go unchallenged. A group of immigrants from the Spanish Canary Islands argued that the free people of color would multiply if granted the land, which in and of itself was a problem. Worse, the *isleños* charged, the people of color on the coast would aid Spain's adversaries and not defend Venezuela. All complaints failed, and in 1721 the crown granted Blanco's militia company the permission they requested. Curiepe grew as more free people of color moved to the area (Ferry 1989).

Even though Venezuelan slavery may appear different to our understanding of plantation slavery in other places, it was slavery, nonetheless. Slaves' reliance on *conucos* for subsistence meant that owners did not feel the obligation to provide additional food for slaves, which left them vulnerable during the cacao harvest season and when *conuco* crops failed. The law empowered local authorities to use a wide range of punishments on slaves, including physical torture (Brito Figueroa 1985). Owners used local authorities and bounty hunters to hunt and catch runaways, and once caught, runaways wore iron bibs to prevent further unauthorized travel (Ferry 1989). And the labor was hard. Workdays often started at 4:00 a.m. Slaves cleared and prepared ground to plant new trees with crude tools, tended existing trees, picked cacao beans then roasted them, and dug and maintained irrigation ditches, all in a tropical environment that was swarming in mosquitoes and that was miserably hot and dry part of the year, hot and wet the other part. Authorities and bounty hunters caught some runaways, but not all of them. *Cimarrones* fled to Caracas or as far south as the llanos, but many runaways stayed in the region and became part of the larger rural population of people of color somehow dependent on cacao cultivation.

Rebellions happened, and when they did they often incorporated not only slaves but also free people of color, *cimarrones*, and sometimes indigenous Venezuelans. Because slaves and people of color developed some concepts of rights and some small degree of autonomy, when colonial conditions changed in the 1700s, slaves and people of color revolted because they argued that authorities violated their rights. They also revolted against slavery as an institution, but in many cases resisting slavery through revolt was just one of many causes that provoked slaves and people of color to act. There are other characteristics of the 18th-century conspiracies or rebellions that are important. Conspirators used their cultural skills to plan and execute rebellions. For example, continued use of African languages helped conspirators organize the thwarted 1749 rebellion that incorporated people of color from Caracas and the rural areas that surrounded it, discovered immediately after the León Revolt (García 1995). The rebellions also made clear the fluid connections between slaves, free people of color, and, in the case of the Coro rebellion in 1795, indigenous Venezuelans. The groups shared economic, cultural, and familial ties that helped them establish the common cause necessary to start and sustain a rebellion. Absentee landlordism aided conspirators' agendas. Not only could people of color plan rebellions, but they also could execute them in rough terrain that they knew well but that was unfamiliar to those who aimed to end rebellions. Consequently, some rebellions simmered for years before finally being put down.

The legacies left by rebellions are extremely important to us because they were much more than rebellions against slavery. They demonstrated concepts of autonomy, rights, a complex process of identity formation, and an understanding of the broader colonial structure. Conspirators used Dutch smugglers upset with the Companía Guipuzcoana to arm rebels in a 1732 uprising (Brito Figueroa 1985). No matter how much the white elite wanted to dismiss people of color as subhuman barbarians, the rebellions proved the intellectual capability of people of color. No matter how much the elite feared people of color, the economic survival of the colony depended on them. That meant that the wall between people of color and the elite had to be maintained. Rural or urban, Venezuelans lived *juntos* but absolutely not *revueltos*.

ESTABLISHING THE RULES ABOUT COEXISTENCE AND INTERACTION AFTER INDEPENDENCE

No wonder people of color fought for both sides during the independence era. Both sides promised favors and positive changes for people of color who fought. Certainly people of color wanted change. Once the wars ended, however, positive changes for people of color were not something new national authorities were willing to grant given the tremendous need for labor. That said, the independence era marked the beginning of the end of slavery as an institution. The general upheaval of the wars allowed untold numbers of slaves to run away, effectively emancipating themselves. No new nation state with little real power was ever going to make those people of color slaves again. The Congress of Angostura did not abolish slavery in 1819 as Bolívar wanted, but by 1822 Venezuelan national authorities faced realities and passed a "Law of the Free Womb." Children born to slave mothers after that date were born legally free (called *manumisos*), but served their mothers' masters until the age of 18. The congress later amended the law and made the age of majority 25 in order to eke a few more years out of the dying institution, moribund by the time José Gregorio Monagas finally declared emancipation in 1854. After freedom, former slaves and *manumisos* became day laborers, sharecroppers, or *conuqueros* (farmers of small plots of land near a town, or *conucos*). Many became debt peons to the same masters to whom they had been slaves or *manumisos*. They became part of the large mass of the Venezuelan poor people of color.

Just because the elite had to let go of slavery does not mean that they changed the way they thought about people of color. Aragua de Barcelona was one of the three *villas de españoles* in the Nueva Barcelona province, surrounded by communities established as indigenous missions. Its fortuitous position at the crossroads between the main road east from Caracas and the north-south highway between Barcelona and the port of Ciudad Bolívar meant that it was a merchant hub. Aragua's elite owned cattle ranches, sugar and tobacco plantations, and farms that raised foodstuffs marketed locally and nationally. Though they depended on free people of color to perform most labor associated with ranches and plantations, they relied heavily on slaves for domestic labor and as status symbols. Of the 1,885 people counted in a church census in 1834, 341 were slaves (Acereda La Linde 1965: 221–236). During the 1820s and the 1830s, Aragua's priest kept separate ledgers to record baptisms of people of color and white *aragueños*. In the period that he filled one ledger for white baptisms, he filled two for people of color (FHL 1832). Just because Aragua's population of color, free and slave, was large does not mean that Aragua's elite was willing to soften its position on issues of equality, even in 1852 on the eve of emancipation.

In that year, Manuel Barrios sued his master, Comandante Manuel Baca, for his freedom. Manuel argued that his mother's owner granted Manuel freedom at birth because the mother saved the owner's life during the independence wars. The owner ordered the babe baptized as free. Manuel also claimed that his father, a member of the elite and son-in-law of the owner, publicly recognized Manuel's paternity and treated him with favor. As the story went, Manuel stayed with the owner's family through another generation, but always with the assumption that he was free. When the second generation did not honor the relationship and tried to sell Manuel as a slave, Manuel sued. He lost (RPB 1852a).

It was not so much that Manuel's case was a weak one. He and his lawyer built a solid case with witness testimony to support some of his claims to freedoms. Other evidence and witnesses (the baptismal certificate and baptismal godfather) disappeared.

The real problem was that if Manuel won, not only did he gain his freedom but he also damaged the racially divided foundation upon which the Venezuelan elite had constructed society. Everyone knew that elite men had children with women of color, but fathers did not acknowledge those children. Manuel claimed his father had publicly recognized Manuel's paternity. That also meant that Manuel's original owner, a charter member of the elite, not only knew about his son-in-law's activities but also condoned those activities. Throughout Venezuelan history, the elite constructed a wall to divide themselves from the masses, the poor people of color. Legal codes in the colonial era reinforced those walls. Only proper social behavior and marriage patterns in the national period maintained the walls. If the blood of the elite flowed through the veins of people like Manuel, that was not something the elite recognized as advantageous to people of color. Under circumstances like these, miscegenation was potentially devastating to the elite. Manuel argued the opposite. He argued that because his original owner declared him free and because elite blood flowed through his veins, he had the right to claim not only his freedom but upward social mobility as well. Manuel argued for the destruction of the wall. Of course he lost.

INDIGENOUS VENEZUELANS IN THE 19TH CENTURY

For indigenous Venezuelans, the 19th century was perhaps worse than the colonial period, but as we said before, there was no single uniform pattern that applied to the entire nation. The national elite's drive to use more indigenous land and labor defined events throughout much of the period. It should be noted, however, that there is a tremendous amount of work to be done to understand the reality lived by indigenous Venezuelans throughout the 19th century. Too much is unknown. We know that some indigenous groups managed to retain some cultural autonomy supported by access to *resguardo* land. Some did not. Sometimes the land lost its connection to ethnicity. Doug Yarrington argues that *resguardo* lands were important to the development of the smallholder coffee economy in the state of Lara in the west, but those who used the land did not claim any distinct indigenous ethnic identity (Yarrington 2003). Farther east in the regions south of the Orinoco, the Venezuelan state tried to sponsor the construction of mission communities using Capuchin missionaries from Spain. Many missionaries refused to go into the territory. The mortality rate for those who did was extremely high. As a result, most indigenous groups south of the Orinoco remained outside the reaches of the state until the early 20th century, when missionaries tried yet again.

Indigenous Venezuelans in the east, north of the Orinoco, did what they could to retain autonomy throughout the 19th century. Píritus, Caribs, Cumanagotos, Chimas, Guaribes, and Chacopatas made their homes in 35 landed indigenous communities in Barcelona Province in 1829. Fourteen of the 35 communities were Carib (Maradei Donato 1985). A census taker in 1829 noted that the Caribs continued to live according to Carib customs. Many did not speak Spanish. Those that did, according to the census taker, preferred not to. They continued to survive simply off of subsistence agriculture (corn, yuca, and other tubers), fish, and meat from hunting (*Memoria* 1873). The census taker believed that the state had the obligation to

> improve Indian society in this province . . . it was necessary to improve their lot in life by awakening their intellectual faculties, blunted by their culture. In [his] humble opinion, the most effective use of resources to achieve this aim would be to send them priests and to use local officials to force the Indians to work every day to improve their lot. (*Memoria* 1873: 35)

So it was that the state assumed that indigenous Venezuelans would become more civilized if they worked under the direction of their social and racial betters. While they had *resguardo* land, Indians had no incentive to work the way the national elite wanted. In the Province of Barcelona alone there were 14 elite challenges to indigenous land rights between 1840 and 1855. In each case, indigenous parties demonstrated clear understandings of their rights and interests as separate and apart from the elite community in the Province of Barcelona; they demonstrated clear understandings of law and local power relationships, and they manipulated the law and power relationships to their advantage. Conflicts usually involved primarily land on the edges of the *resguardos* and land that all parties agreed was good agricultural or grazing land. As the cattle industry in the region grew in the 19th century, those indigenous communities that claimed prime grazing land faced the most problems with incursions (or *perturbaciones*) on the edges of *resguardo* land. Indians used laws passed by the Venezuelan congress in 1836 and 1838 that recognized the validity of colonial land holdings to resist elite land challenges.

In one extraordinary circumstance in 1852, the indigenous town council of San Lorenzo went en masse to Caracas to deliver a letter to President José Tadeo Monagas asking for his intervention in a particularly grievous case. Elites in San Lorenzo connected to provincial authorities used all sorts of dirty tricks to try to obtain a portion of San Lorenzo's *resguardo*. Worst was when local authorities in league with the elite invented charges to jail the Indians' lawyer, then set bail at price so high the only way Indians could pay was to sell the land (RPB 1852b). But the crooked local authorities underestimated San Lorenzo's indigenous council. Instead of wringing their hands in desperation or selling their land, they took their case to the top, to President José Tadeo Monagas. In the letter they presented to the president, the indigenous council wrote:

> We, the poor and ignorant aborigines of San Lorenzo, destitute of all social graces, without a trace of all that is that surrounds civilized men, believe that Pablo Figueredo, although not much brighter than ourselves, is a man of means and counts on invaluable assets and relationships that allow him to make a mockery of the sacrosanct rules of justice, to threaten us with untrustworthy agents of the public confidence . . . but we have reason and right on our side. (RPB 1852b: 110v)

The letter was a masterwork of prose that unequivocally demonstrated the indigenous community's understanding of elite perceptions of indigenous intellectual capacities and the council's ability to manipulate those understandings. It also quite astutely assessed the local political scene and local political and economic agendas. The local elite who invaded indigenous property, Pablo Figueredo, according to the council, was no more than the blind instrument of the more powerful Ruiz brothers. Figueredo was also the brother-in-law of provincial judge Joaquin Correa,

> whose fraudulent and damnable ingenuity has been the agent of destruction against the well being of hundreds of families . . . They all know theft well. They know that the unhappy Indians, to whose community we belong, cannot humanly pay the huge sum they have demanded, and it is also evident . . . that they plan to despoil us of everything, including our land that we have fertilized with the sweat of our brows. (RPB 1852b: 110r)

The council clearly understood the Figueredo was not the real problem. The problem lay in the connections between Figueredo and those more powerful than he. Those people had obvious agendas. Their true aim was to obtain all of the *resguardo's* land, not one small sliver of it. How were the Indians of San Lorenzo going to come up with the money to bail out their lawyer if not through the sale of land?

The letter also clearly demonstrates that its authors were masters of flattery who understood that the state (and elites) saw indigenous Venezuelans as lesser humans incapable of caring for themselves. They also understood that Venezuela wanted desperately to be perceived as a modern state that protected the weak, governed by law and not whim. They knew well the image the state wanted to present and crafted their appeal to meet that image. The council said to President Monagas:

> Without dispute, it is the most noble prerogative of the head of a wise, philan-thropic, liberal and republican government to aid through omnipotent care men like the aborigines of our forests and communities, who lack normal means to defend themselves, to be aided by sweet and benevolent institutions that hold sacred and sacrosanct the ideal of equality before the law. We do not doubt that you will labor in favor of the invalids, the indigenous people of San Lorenzo. (RPB 1852b: 111v)

It worked. The day after the audience with the council, through his secretary of state, President Monagas informed the supreme court of eastern Venezuela to make sure indigenous rights were protected. Monagas emphasized that all Venezuelans had the right to government protection, but that indigenous Venezuelans were par-ticularly entitled to the protection of the state. Higher courts should repair the dam-age done by lower courts (RPB 1852b). Even though the case was not over yet, San Lorenzo's council went home with a major victory and a presidential guarantee that protected the *resguardo*.

Other communities were not as lucky (or as plucky) as San Lorenzo. Despite best efforts to keep land, indigenous communities often lost land through schemes like the one employed by the elite in San Lorenzo. For other communities, even when they won their court cases and kept their land, they had to sell to pay legal fees. In the end, the state dissolved all *resguardos* in 1882. Only those Indians in the far south and the far west retained any right to any land, and only if they agreed to live according to the rules of the Venezuelan state, which only desired to "give them a civilized life" (Sánchez P. 2002). Indigenous Venezuelans lost the leverage they had to use in relationships with the elite who still considered indigenous Venezuelans as barbarians. Without land, it became even easier for the elite to exploit indigenous labor. The Guajiro Indians in the far western part of the nation finally lost their autonomy in the late 1800s with the rise of the sugar industry in Zulia and increased demand for labor. Colluding with local authorities, "merchants and *hacendados* (plantation owners) developed a system that resembled chattel slavery . . . Indians were bought and sold as property and subject to violence and coercion" (Linder 1999: 219). Guajiro slaves, alienated from family and culture, found resistance to their situation difficult. It was not until after President Juan Vicente Gómez died in 1935 that national authorities intervened to end the practices, but by then the damage to Guajiro identity and autonomy were permanent (Linder 1999).

BLURRING THE LINE BETWEEN RACE AND CLASS

In 1853 Manuel Carreño, father of the pianist and composer Teresa Carreño, published a book in Caracas that soon became all the rage among the elite throughout Latin America. His *Manual de urbanidad y buenas maneras* was a book about proper comportment in a host of situations in the most minute detail, from appropriate dress to table manners to how to greet people on the street. Social inferiors, Carreño insisted, must always cede the sidewalk to social superiors (Carreño 2005). Social inequality was not morally good or bad in Carreño's perspective. Inequality simply existed; therefore, there were rules to deal with it. The elite, that tiny percentage of the population that was white and controlled most property in the country, Carreño wrote, must maintain proper distance from the poor, the overwhelming majority of the population that was, for the most part, landless. Under no circumstances should the elite commiserate with the poor about their lot, as the fate of both classes was ordained by God. The classes were simply different. Both groups must accept that fact and behave accordingly. Poor people must also learn proper comportment, Carreño argued. The poor would receive heavenly rewards in return for their earthly sufferings, but while on this earthly plane the poor were obligated to honor and respect the rich. And when the poor felt particularly oppressed by their misfortune, they should never allow themselves to envy the rich but instead should accept that both poverty and wealth were part of the will of the divine (Carreño 2005: 414–416).

We know from our review of the history of race and class in Venezuela that there was nothing divinely inspired about the chasm that divided Venezuelan elite from everyone else, most of whom were people of color. Perhaps when Carreño suggested that the elite should hold their tongue when talking negatively about the poor, he responded to more common elite discussions about the poor that were openly slanderous. The elite characterized the poor as "improvident, lazy, and scornful people who shirked all responsibility when it came to work." So of course the appropriate solution, the elite thought, was to make the poor work through enforcing vagrancy laws. Making the poor work and teaching them the value of hard labor would create progress; the nation would become modern and the elite would prosper (Wright 1990: 49). Of course, the poor worked already. They had to in order to survive. They just did not work the way the elite wanted them to.

The elite saw their problem in terms of class (the problematic poor) and race. Positivist thought came to dominate first elite and then state discussions on national development by the 1860s, at the same time that positivism dominated similar debates throughout Latin America. Developed by French philosopher Auguste Comte, positivism was a philosophy with foundations in Darwin's theory of evolution. Comte and his Venezuelan devotees argued that race, climate, and other natural factors determined the fate of any given society. Positivist theorists interpreted the success of Anglo-Saxon (white) societies in North American and Europe as evidence to suggest that the white race was the most evolved, producing the most progressive and modern societies. Venezuelan society had failed thus far because it was not white enough. Not only were the poor lazy, but they were not white. That meant that the future of national development hinged on immigration, preferably immigration from northern Europe and not the swarthy Mediterranean Europeans. State-sponsored immigration project after project failed miserably throughout the 19th century. Instead, gold mining in El Callao south of the Orinoco and the oil industry in the late 1800s and early 1900s attracted thousands of immigrants from Trinidad and other Caribbean islands—people of color, not whites—even though the state passed immigration codes designed to discourage Caribbean immigration (Wright 1990).

Eventually, the Venezuelan elite had to accept the fact that Venezuela was not going to become a white nation. So how, then, were they to understand the Venezuelan past and rationalize the present and future when they knew they were doomed to be a nation full of poor people of color who the elite understood to be detrimental to the development of a modern and progressive Venezuela? Simple: Rewrite history. Venezuelan intellectual José Gil Fortoul accepted that the Venezuelan majority was not white, but he argued that the process of racial mixing that occurred over the centuries wiped out all traces of unique African and indigenous identity. White was better, of course, but the average Venezuelan was acceptable, too (Wright 1990). About the same time that Gil Fortoul constructed his arguments, state authorities in Zulia employed their best efforts to eradicate popular celebrations of carnival heavily influenced by Afrovenezuelan cultural practices (Linder 2007). Residents all along the coast still celebrated Corpus Christi with devil dances. African drums dominated the musical sounds all along the Barlovento, not far from Caracas. And Gil Fortoul probably wrote after eating an *arepa* stuffed with black beans and plantains for breakfast, ingesting indigenous and African contributions to Venezuelan cuisine.

Gómez apologist and intellectual Laureano Vallenilla Lanz stretched the intellectual gymnastics one step farther. He argued that it was pointless to think in terms of pure race. After all, Spain experienced centuries of racial mixing with Romans, Visigoths, and Moors before beginning the American experience. He argued that racial mixing in Venezuela created a Venezuelan type that incorporated the best elements of African, indigenous, and European races and discarded negative influences. Yes, he created, in theory, a positive Venezuelan national identity that allowed for *arepas*, *platanos*, and *caraotas negras* (arepas, plantains, and black beans), but Vallenilla Lanz also never questioned the principle of white superiority and the need for more European immigration. More white would only improve the Venezuelan mix. More dark would not (Wright 1990).

It is extremely difficult to underestimate just how important both men's ideas were to the development of modern Venezuelan ideas about race, history, and identity. Both men categorically denied the fundamental roles indigenous and Afrovenezuelans played in the creation of Venezuela in the colonial or national period. They talked about slavery as an institution but did not talk about the cultural and demographic contributions of Africans to the nation. They either could not see or denied indigenous or Afrovenezuelan expressions of culture in the world in which they lived, and if they did see them, they wrote them off as folklore at best, barbaric in need of revision at worst. Worse still, their writings, Gil Fortoul's *Historia constitucional de Venezuela* in particular, became the basis for national histories and social science curriculums taught to children throughout Venezuela through almost all of 20th century. Finally, if Venezuelans came to believe that if separate races did not exist, that all were Venezuelans, then racism could not exist.

There was one other reason that the state adopted the theory of raceless Venezuela. Vallenilla Lanz wrote during the first frenzy of oil extraction when Gómez rewrote subsoil laws to allow North American companies tremendous latitude in how they exploited Venezuelan resources. Venezuelan intellectuals legitimately feared that Gómez allowed the companies to rape the country's resources. Gallegos calls his one North American character in *Doña Barbara* Mister Danger, a man without morals who views Venezuelans with the utmost contempt. The North American engineer in Ramón Díaz Sánchez's *Méne* marries a local girl, raises her expectations by moving her into the fancy company enclave, which looked like U.S. suburbia, complete with a country club, then goes back to the United States never to return to his Venezuelan wife. Antonio Arráiz was even more pointed in his criticisms. He argued that North Americans took oil out of Venezuela with ease because they viewed Venezuela as a primitive nation of "unreasonable people," "monkeys," and "blacks" incapable of exploiting their own resources:

> One million three hundred sixty thousand bolívares go to them [North Americans] from Venezuela; from the poor, obscure, remote, and diffuse Venezuela. A little republic populated by monkeys and blacks, a hot place where coconut trees grow and where these people have, poor souls!, this rich thing that is petroleum, which they allow to be exploited. (Coronil 1997: 103–104)

Venezuelan media of the era clearly indicate that the Venezuelan elite shared similar ideas about the Venezuelan mixed-race population. The journal *Fantoches* included scathing cartoons that made fun of people of color who attempted to whiten themselves economically (Wright 1990). Nevertheless, in order for Venezuela to appear progressive and modern in the eyes of the all-important North Americans, the nation had to embrace the idea of the raceless Venezuelan—not so much whiten the nation, but instead strip the African and indigenous out so as to remove the racial stain.

The reality was that the Venezuelan elite never gave up their negative ideas about the poor and people of color. Venezuelans of different races did not exist, after all, according to the new theories. The Venezuelan state continued to blur the lines between class and race à la Gil Fortoul and Vallenilla Lanz when it classified indigenous Venezuelans as *campesinos*, peasants, in the 1960 Agrarian Law (Sánchez P. 2002). Officially, indigenous Venezuelans did not have a distinct racial or ethnic identity. They were part of the larger socioeconomic class. Of course a law could not make the ethnic identities of thousands of indigenous Venezuelans disappear. The law meant that the last of the indigenous Venezuelans who had land in remote areas of the country due to their race or ethnicity could no longer claim land that way. Indigenous Venezuelans became part of the larger racially undefined Venezuelan class, at least according to the law.

Because the same language about Venezuelan identity became part of Venezuelan curricula, generations of Venezuelans embraced it, though lived experience often proved otherwise in subtle and not so subtle ways. When in Venezuela, visitors might be shocked to hear the phrase *"trabajar como un negro para vivir como un blanco,"* or work like a black to live like a white. They might be even more shocked to have someone explain that the phrase had nothing to do with race. It was only about work. But the implications of the phrase are patently obvious. People of color work, whites do not. Moreover, if one wants to live like a white person, one has to work awfully hard. The phrase links class and race in a way that blurs the distinction between the two in a way that is completely apt in Venezuelan society. It also endorses and idea of racial whitening that in many cases still did not work in the late 20th century. The reality is that most Venezuelan extended families include individuals who are lighter skinned with green eyes and individuals who are quite dark. Even so, in the all-important realm of personal beauty, Venezuelans frequently think lighter skin is more beautiful than darker skin, lighter colored eyes more attractive than dark eyes, and straight hair more attractive than curly hair.

So of course racial issues did not go away in the 20th century with new language. Talking about racial issues just became much more complicated. That is why novels like *Méne* (1936) about oil workers and the oil industry and Juan Pablo Sojo's *Nochebuena negra* (1943) about the Barlovento coast were so subversive. The novels exposed Venezuelan (and North American) racism for what it was and did not shy away from discussing the consequences.

But the dialogue about race took place in the intellectual world outside of the mainstream. The discussion also primarily addressed the darkest members of society, those with a distinct ethnic identity, or Afro-Caribbean immigrants. Intellectuals did not challenge the validity of the raceless Venezuelan identity. And only occasionally did the discussion, such as it was, go public. In 1945, three elite Caracas hotels denied occupancy to North American (and African American) singer Robert Todd Duncan, his wife, and accompanist even though the hotels had confirmed vacancies by phone prior to the party's arrival. Suddenly, upon seeing the Duncan party, the three hotels were all booked up. Duncan had unwittingly trespassed into the Venezuelan white world. Though Duncan took the refusals in stride and found a fine hotel elsewhere in Caracas, the incident publicly embarrassed Venezuela. Within a week the Venezuelan legislature passed a law prohibiting racial discrimination in any form (Wright 1990). Venezuelan authorities then patted themselves on the back. Though they believed that the hotels' actions were atypical in racism-free Venezuela, the law addressed the appearance of racism. Problem solved. And if laws could not solve the problem, sowing the oil could. In 1978, the anthropologist who did much to chronicle Afrovenezuelan culture, Angelina Pollack-Eltz, stated that "economic conditions . . . had improved so markedly that blacks now had equal opportunities with racial groups for work and social advancement" (Wright 1990: 125). Money did whiten, Pollack-Eltz suggested.

Opportunities did not necessarily mean equality. A 1974 editorial by another Venezuelan anthropologist, Miguel Acosta Saignes, addressed the myth of Venezuela's racial democracy. Acosta described the experiences of a friend, a successful black surgeon, who had never fit into the *caraqueño* social world and had never been invited to join the elite social clubs. Money did not whiten Acosta's friend. He may have been able to purchase the material goods associated with elite status, but he never became elite. Racism against people of color at all socioeconomic levels in Venezuela was pernicious and persistent. Acosta suggested that the Venezuelan elite cloaked their racism in classism. White Venezuelans said they had nothing in common with people of color because poverty meant that people of color lived differently from

Wayu indigenous women look at a voter lists as they wait to vote in a referendum on the rule of Venezuelan President Hugo Chávez in Maracaibo, Venezuela, Sunday, August 15, 2004. (AP/Wide World Photos)

whites (Acosta Saignes 1974). Add divinely inspired language, and Acosta described an argument remarkably similar to the one Manuel Carreño made in 1853. And so it was, and is, that the Venezuelan elite lived in fancy gated homes on the east side of Caracas, or Lecherías in Puerto La Cruz. They drive in their late model cars to high paying jobs in high rise buildings, driving right past the roads to Tronconal in Puerto La Cruz, or as far west as 23 de Enero in Caracas, where their domestic servants live. *Juntos pero no revueltos.*

REFERENCES

Acereda La Linde, Manuel. 1965. *Historia de Aragua de Barcelona, del Estado Anzoátegui y de la Nueva Andalucia Tomo Segundo.* Caracas: Imprenta Nacional.

Acosta Saignes, Manuel. 1974. *Ultimas Noticias,* December 15.

Bermúdez Briñez, Nilda. 2001. *Vivir en Maracaibo en el siglo XIX.* Maracaibo, Venezuela: Biblioteca Temas de Historia de Zulia.

Brito Figueroa, Federico. 1985. *El Problema Tierra y Esclavos en la Historia de Venezuela* Caracas: Universidad Central de Venezuela, 115.

Carreño, Manuel. 2005. *Manual de urbanidad y buenas maneras.* Bogotá, Colombia: Panamericana Editorial.

Caulín, Fray Antonio. 1987. *Historia de la Nueva Andalucia*, Pablo Ojer, S.J., ed. Caracas: Fuentes para la Historia Colonial de Venezuela.

CIA: The World Factbook: Venezuela. 2009. https://www.cia.gov/library/publications/the-world-factbook/geos/ve.html.

Coronil, Fernando. 1997. *The Magical State: Nature, Money, and Modernity in Venezuela.* Chicago: University of Chicago Press.

Cunill Grau, Pedro. 1987. *Geografía del poblamiento venezolano en el siglo xix.* Caracas: Ediciones de la Presidencia de la República.

Ferry, Robert. 1989. *The Colonial Elite of Early Caracas: Formation and Crisis, 1567–1767.* Berkeley: University of California Press.

FHL (Family History Library, San Marcos, Texas). 1832. Roll 1995768, *Bautismos, No. 9 1827–1838, Libro de Bautismos de Blancos, Año de1827, Bautismos, No. 10, 1827–1832, Libro que se hacen en esta Iglesia Parroquial de San Juan Bautista de Aragua, provincia de Barcelona, y comienza desde hoy 7 del Julio de 1827, Bautismos, No. 11, 1832–1839, Libro que se hacen en esta Iglesia Parroquial de San Juan Bautista de Aragua, provincial de Barcelona, y comienza desde hoy día 1 de febrero de 1832.*

———. 1857. Roll 1995784, Roll 12, item 5, *Libro de Confirmaciones hecho por el Ilustrísimo Sr. Dr. José Manuel Arroyo, Dignísimo Obispo de esta Diócesis de paso por esta ciudad de Aragua a 31 de Mayo de 1857 de tránsito para Ciudad Bolívar, Confirmaciones No. 2, 1857–1915.*

García, Jesús. 1995. *La diaspora de los Kongos en las Americas y los Caribes.* Caracas: Fundación Afroamerica.

Humboldt, Alejandro de. 1941. *Viaje a las regiones equinocciales del nuevo continente hecho en 1799,1800, 1801, 1802, 1803, y 1804 por A. de Humboldt y A. Bonpland.* Tomo 2. Translated by Lisandro Alvarado. Caracas: Biblioteca Venezolana de Cultura.

"Indigenous Communities from Venezuela," 2010. *Native Planet.* http://www.nativeplanet. org/indigenous/ethnicdiversity/latinamerica/venezuela/indigenous_data_venezuela_ wayuu.shtml.

Linder, Peter. 1999. "'An Immortal Speculation': Indian Forced Labor on the Haciendas of Venezuela's Sur del Lago Zuliano." *The Americas* 56, no. 2: 191–220.

———. 2007. "Drumming Rebellion: Political and Social Violence in the Sur del Lago de Maracaibo on the Eve of the Federal War, 1839–1858." Paper presented at the XVII Congress of the Latin American Studies Association, Montreal, Canada, September 8.

Maradei Donato, Constantino. 1985. *Noticias historiales de nueva Barcelona /Fernando del Bastardo y Loayza.* Caracas: Academia Nacional de la Historia.

Memoria de la Dirección General de Estadística al Presidente de los Estados Unidos de Venezuela en 1873. 1873. Caracas: Imprenta Nacional.

Minorities at Risk: Assessment for Indigenous Peoples in Venezuela. 2009. http://www.cidcm. umd.edu/mar/about.asp.

Morse, Kimberly J. 2000. "Aun en la muerte separados: Class, Clergy, and Society in Aragua de Barcelona, Venezuela, 1820–1875." PhD diss., The University of Texas at Austin.

Prato-Perelli, Antoinette da. 1990. *Las encomiendas de Nueva Andalucia en el siglo XVII: Visita hecha por don Fernando Riva Agüero, Oidor de la Audiencia de Santo Domingo, 1688, Tomo I.* Caracas: Biblioteca de la Academia Nacional de la Historia.

Rojas, Reinaldo. 2004. *La rebellion del Negro Miguel y otros studios de Africania.* Barquisimeto, Venezuela: Zona Educativa del Estado Lara Fundación Buria.

Romero, Simon. 2007. "Venezuela Dances to Devilish Beat to Promote Tourism." *New York Times.* http://www.nytimes.com/2007/06/12/world/americas/12venez.html.

RPB (Registro Principal de Barcelona). 1783a. Resguardos Indígenas, Años 1783–1786, 1838–1839, 1840–1844, 1846–1850, 1856, 1851, Libro 1, "Oficina Principal de Registro del Estado Anzoategui, Copia certificado de las diligencias de la mensura de la resguardia del pueblo "San Buena Ventura de la Margarita," practicada el año 1783."

RPB. 1844. Aragua 1837–1844. Libro 26. October 7.

RPB, 1847. Aragua 1845–1850. Libro 24. "No. 13, Protocolo Principal Para la Oficina Subalterna de Registro en el Mes de Febrero de 1847." July 10.

RPB. 1848. Civiles, Sucesoriales, Inventorios, Particiones, 1845–1850, Libro 22, "Juzgado de Paz de Caigua, Civiles, Mortuaria intestada del Reverendo Fray Salvador de la Gertrud, 1848."

RPB. 1852a. Registro Principal de Barcelona, Expedientes Civiles, Año 1852, Libro 30. "Civiles, El Procurador Municipal Solícita la Libertad de Manuel Antonio Barrios al Servicio de Gervacio Sosa como esclavo, 1852."

RPB. 1852b. Resguardos Indígenas, Años 1783–1786, 1838–1839, 1840–1844, 1846–1850, 1856, 1851, Libro 10, "Juzgado Cantonal de Onoto, Civiles, Interdicto promovido por los naturales de San Lorenzo contra Pablo Figueredo por un terreno titulado "La Sabaneta," parte de los resguardos de San Lorenzo. (Sentencia definitiva a favor de los indígenas, 1852). Contiene: Copia certificado de las diligencias de la mensura primitiv10a de los resguardos del pueblo de San Lorenzo de Güere, expedida en 1838. Representación original de los indígenas al Presidente de la República inpetrando justicias y comunicación del Poder Ejecutivo Personal. Copia certificada del titulo primitivo de terreno "Los Botalones," diversos croquis de los terrenos en discusión."

Samudio A., and Edda O. 1990. "Seventeenth-Century Indian Migration in the Venezuelan Andes." In David J. Robinson, ed., *Migration in Colonial Spanish America.* Cambridge: Cambridge University Press, 1990.

Sánchez, P., Domingo. 2002. "From Article 4 of the Law of June 2, 1882 in 'Una nueva realidad para los indígenas de Venezuela' " Paper presented at the Tercero Congreso Virtual de Arqueología y Antropología—Red NAYA—Buenos Aires. http://www.centrelink.org/SanchezSpanish.html.

Seed, Patricia. 1988. *To Love, Honor, and Obey in Colonial Mexico: Conflicts over Marriage Choice, 1574–1821.* Stanford, CA: Stanford University Press.

Tronconis de Veracoechea, Ermilia. 1992. "Aspectos de la esclavitud negra en Venezuela y el Caribe (1750–1854)." In *Primer Congreso Internacional de Historia Económica y Social de la Cuenca del Caribe, 1763–1898.* San Juan, Puerto Rico: Centro de Estudios Avanzados de Puerto Rico y el Caribe, 1992.

Ann Twinam. 1999. *Public Lives, Private Secrets: Gender, Honor, Sexuality, and Illegitimacy in Colonial Spanish America.* Stanford, CA: Stanford University Press.

Vílchez Cróquer, Haydee. 2007. "Las cofradías de Negros durante la colonia: Un espacio de libertad." Paper presented at the XXVII International Congress of the Latin American Studies Association. Montreal, Canada.

Waldron, Kathy. 1989. "The Sinners and the Bishop in Colonial Venezuela: The 'Visita' of Bishop Mariano Marti, 1771–1784." In Asuncion Lavrin, ed., *Sexuality and Marriage in Colonial Latin America.* Lincoln: University of Nebraska Press.

Wright, Winthrop. *Cafe con Leche: Race, Class, and National Image in Venezuela.* Austin: University of Texas Press.

Yarrington, Douglas. 2003. "Cattle, Corruption, and Venezuelan State Formation during the Era of Juan Vicente Gomez, 1908–1935." *Latin American Research Review* 35: 9–33.

Women and Marriage

OPPRESSION AND ADORATION: WOMEN IN EDUCATION, POLITICS, AND BEAUTY PAGEANTS

In July of 2001, Linda Loaiza López was rescued by Caracas police from the apartment of Luis Antonio Carrera, where she had been held for four months. During those four months, Loaiza was continually raped and tortured. Graphic photos taken at the hospital, and widely published throughout Venezuela, showed the near destruction of Loaiza's eyes, ears, and genitals. Carrera was arrested later that month. His police records showed a previous arrest for torture of a woman in 1999.

Despite the mountain of evidence, however, the case did not resolve itself quickly. Carrera was a member of a wealthy and influential family, a fact which helped delay his arrest until September of that year. Even then, he was held under house arrest.

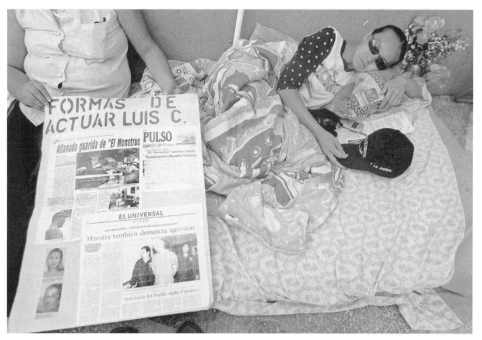

Linda Loaiza López in the midst of a 2004 hunger strike in front of the Supreme Court of Justice. Loaiza reported that she was kept in captivity by a man for four months in 2001 and was submitted to diverse tortures and abuses. The strike demanded justice against her attacker. (Luis Acosta/AFP/Getty Images)

Carrera's family moved to help him escape in November, an attempt that culminated in a manhunt and his recapture. The family next turned their attention to discrediting the victim and working behind the scenes to beat the charges. This effort was successful. After three years, in October 2004, Carrera was acquitted and set free.

Attorneys for Carrera had based their defense on Loaiza's supposed position as a "sex worker," which they said made her vulnerable to violence by her customers. An unreliable witness did not help her case, either (Gomez Q. 2004). The defense explained that Carrera, "because of the needs that all men have" contracted Loaiza as a prostitute (Gomez Q. 2004: 21). He liked her, the defense postulated, and let her stay in his apartment. Carrera claimed that she continued to work as a prostitute, and that her injuries came from her other customers.

The defense had no evidence to support this claim. The prosecution, and Loaiza herself, asserted that while poor, Loaiza was not working as a prostitute when she was taken captive by Carrera. They argued that Loaiza's injuries were so severe and so deformed her appearance (brain injury, severe burns and bites to the eyes and ears, facial lacerations with severe swelling) that she could not possibly have been freely coming and going from the apartment without others noticing, much less working as a prostitute. Rosa Cádiz, the judge in the case, finally sided with the defense, however, ruling that Carrera was to go free despite all of the evidence because in part Loaiza had "lied about the way in which she originally met Carrera" (Gomez 2004: 21). In

---

THE CEM: *CENTRO DE LOS ESTUDIOS DE LA MUJER* OF THE UCV

The *Centro de los Estudios de la Mujer*, or Women's Studies Center, at the UCV was founded in 1992 with a mission of achieving equality for women in society through research activities, instruction, collection of data, and outreach activities throughout Venezuela. The CEM not only offers both undergraduate and graduate degrees in women's studies, but also pursues an active political, legislative, and social justice agenda. The CEM pays particular attention to court cases that deal with women's rights and violence against women.

In October of 2004, the CEM published a document denouncing the sentence given to Carrera and a calling for the resignation of the Judge Rosa Cádiz. In an example of the CEM's outreach to community organizations, the document was signed by 42 women representing 18 different agencies from a wide strata of Venezuelan society, from the Socialist Bolivarian Women's Force (Fuerza Boliviariana de Mujeres), of the poorer neighborhoods and slums, to the economically elite Women's Federation of Venezuelan Attorneys (Federación Venezolana de Abogadas).

---

addition, Cádiz ordered an investigation of Loaiza, her father, and sister on charges of prostitution.

No one really believed the tale of unknown men attacking Loaiza. As to the truth of Loaiza's job on the day of her kidnapping, for most women in Venezuela, the issue was beside the point. Kidnapping and torture are criminal acts no matter the woman's profession. For women at the Centro de Estudios de la Mujer (CEM, Women's Studies Center) at the Central University in Caracas, the sentence seemed to send two clear messages: "First, if you are a prostitute, it doesn't matter what happens to you. Second, to every raped woman: don't go to the police. What's the point?" (CEM n.d.).

After the shocking and unreasonable verdict, women's organizations across the nation came together in protest. That the presiding judge in the case was a woman only made it worse for many observers and showed how deep the divide can seem between the classes in Venezuela. The case was seen as not only a blow to women's rights but as an example of "undue influence peddling and arrangements to please an influential family against a poor and destitute woman" (Gomez Q. 2004: 21). In the end, Loaiza and the protesters did win a hearing with the supreme court, who vacated the verdict and granted a new trial. The end would please few, however. Even with the new trial, Carrera was convicted only of assault and deprivation of liberty, not of the more serious charges of rape, torture, and attempted homicide. As a result, Carrera only received a sentence of six years.

This story shows the problems evident in the state of women's rights and the gender inequities still visible in Venezuela today. In many ways women have made great progress in education, civil rights, and political representation in the last 60 years. In other ways, however, women still fight battles against systems that view feminism and women's rights as an affront to national cultural norms and Christian family values. This is especially true for women of the lower economic classes. The judge in the Loaiza case, Rosa Cádiz, was an educated, middle-to-upper-class woman who had benefited from the significant progress of the 20th century in women's rights. On the other side of the judicial bench, however, the victim, Loaiza, did not receive those same benefits, either from the social system or the judicial system.

Such is the ambiguous state of women in Venezuela. Women attend university in record numbers and are venerated as beauty queens and goddesses yet lack many fundamental rights. Venezuela had a female presidential candidate in 1998 (Irene Sáez, a former Miss Universe) yet lags far behind other Latin American nations in female representation in congress and other wings of government. In the middle of it all, many women hold the nation together through hard work and grit. Some Venezuelan women may be vain and/or politically and economically disadvantaged, but they are extremely assertive. Outsiders may be appalled by the wage gaps, but Venezuelan women work through them and still manage to accomplish something. If some government office is giving away something, traditionally it will be a woman who finds out, then figures out how to work the bureaucracy to make something happen. Many women work three jobs to get their kids ahead. Women run neighborhood associations and always have. Women invade abandoned property to establish new homes. They are the ultimate survivors. In order to understand how this system works both for the women involved and for the nation, we will begin with a bit of historical context.

PUBLIC VERSUS PRIVATE: SOCIAL AND HISTORICAL CONTEXT

Since colonial times, women in Latin America have been associated with the home and with private life. A woman's life has traditionally been assumed to be interior: she is in charge of the house, the children, and the religious and spiritual life of the

Former Miss Universe Irene Sáez, later mayor of an affluent Caracas municipality, portrayed herself as the one person who could wrench Venezuela out of its poverty in the 1998 presidential elections. After leading presidential polls for months, Saez lost the election to former coup leader Hugo Chávez. (AP/Wide World Photos)

family. Men, on the other hand, take care of the public, or outside, world: jobs and careers, politics and financial issues. The patriarchal family has always constituted the core organizing unit in Latin American society, with the father serving as the head of the household, like a benevolent despot, and the mother taking charge of domestic tasks.

This model is often said to be based on, or at least reinforced by, the teachings of the Catholic Church, which is the historically dominant Latin American religion. Earlier, in the section on religion, we discussed how women not only found themselves left out of the circles of power in their lives but also in their deaths, consigned to the back corners of the cemeteries built by the elite and clergy of the church. Many scholars have discussed how the church offers the example of the Virgin Mary to devout women as an example of purity, motherly love, and self-sacrifice. Women are encouraged to follow the example of Mary and in return receive spiritual salvation in exchange for their subordinate lives on earth.

Being private and following the example of the holy mother also means staying within the bounds of traditional *pudor* or honor (decorum, modesty, humility and purity) and *recato* (prudence, caution, and shyness) (Castillo 1992). The expectations for the traditional Latin American woman are formed from the expectation of immobility and silence, not just in the home but personally as well. A woman is expected to be physically enclosed in the home and also to keep her opinions, her feelings, and her thoughts to herself.

Whatever the root of women's association with an ideal private life, the prevalence of this idea is even found in the language. The term *mujer pública* or "public woman" in Spanish is a term for prostitute. The implications are very clear. Decent women do not meddle in public matters, and "public women," as the case of Loaiza shows, neither deserve nor receive society's protection. There are also class implications associated with ideal feminine behavior. The ideal incorporates multiple assumptions about women's proper behavior that are at odds with Venezuelan reality, past or present. The ideal assumes, for example, that women marry. In reality, in both the colonial and national periods, women frequently did not marry even if they maintained households with men. Because the lower classes adopted the elite's association between marriage and property, the property-less lower classes did not see the purpose of marriage. As a result, many women spent at least some portion of their adult lives as the heads of households. They had to work to support children as domestic servants, food vendors, seamstresses, cigarette or cigar rollers, or, yes, prostitutes. The bottom line is that women's economic conditions often forced them into public lives. Combine that with the fact that women were often not married, no matter what the reason, and the elite found it easier to condemn lower class women as *mujeres públicas* without honor. Such ingrained ideals certainly influenced the way the judge and the elite public perceived Linda Loaiza López.

But even though the elite frequently defined lower-class women as without honor, even though the law left unmarried women without the property rights that elite married women had until 1873, poor women still asserted their own versions of honor and rights. When Hilario Alquinidiguez laid hands on Vicenta Puerta and slapped her around after a street party in 1869, Vicenta pressed charges. She said she would not allow the affront to her honor go unchallenged (RPB 1869). Vicenta embodied everything the elite thought was wrong about lower-class women. She was single. She partied. She was seen as immoral, disregarding male superiority. But she also certainly understood that she had individual rights, and she also knew she had the right to defend them. But most importantly, she asserted her honor. At the same time that Vicenta asserted her honor and filed charges against Hilario, unmarried women with long-time companions sued those companions for familial support. Unmarried women did not have traditional property rights, but they still expected the men with whom they shared their lives to contribute to household expenses (Díaz 2004). In both cases, lower-class women took definitions of honor and property rights and redefined them in ways to suit lower-class women's purposes. They created paths for themselves.

There is one other stereotype built into the public/private woman dichotomy that we have mentioned previously but merits repetition. The ideal assumes that women, in order to maintain their honor (which also becomes associated with their families' honor) must live private lives. Certainly the title character in Teresa de la Parra's novel *Ifigenia* struggled against the idea that women must remain submissive domestic creatures, restraining their intellect and public activity. Society condemned the protagonist of *Doña Bárbara*, Gallego's novel, because she was so publicly assertive.

Yes, polite society did expect certain restrained behavior from women. But restrained in Venezuela did not mean private in all circumstances. The reality is that elite women, even in the colonial period, lived rather active public lives. Because women were often significantly younger than their husbands at the age of marriage and because inheritance laws were generous to widows, elite women often found

LIGIA PARRA JAHN

"The Blonde with the Revolver," Ligia Parra Jahn, highlights continuing tensions between male control of family honor and progress in women's autonomy.

Parra Jahn lived in Caracas during the 1940s, a time of social change in Venezuela. As foreigners developed the Venezuelan oil industry and politics became more progressive, women found new opportunities to work outside the home. This meant that male heads of household had a smaller role as guardians of women's honor as they participated in public life.

In 1948, Parra Jahn, a secretary, fell in love with a charming Basque jai-alai player. Having been promised marriage, a sexual relationship began. When the athlete discarded her, Parra Jahn first hired a lawyer to enforce their marriage agreement and save her reputation. The Basque refused, though Parra Jahn was pregnant and, therefore, socially ruined. Desperate, Parra Jahn calmly walked into an office and shot him twice with a revolver. While this crime, if committed by a man, would have received no punishment, Parra Jahn received a jail sentence of seven years, becoming a symbol of women's struggle to control their own lives.

themselves in charge of significant property, cash reserves, and even businesses, upon the deaths of husbands. Mothers often made all-important marriage choices for their daughters and sons. Though legally women often had to manage property through male powers of attorneys, elite women bought and sold property, managed businesses, and made other major economic and familial decisions on their own, often quite publicly and without being condemned as public women without honor (Ferry 1989; Morse 2000). Rosa Cádiz, the judge in the Loaiza case, could not have become a judge as a woman in any time prior to the late 20th century. That is certain. But Judge Cádiz may well have benefited from older ideas about elite women who could bend the rules on public behavior. Lower-class women, in the elite's view, could not.

All of this means that Venezuelan women did not share a common consciousness as women, even though all women suffered from limited legal and political rights, limited access to education, and common assumptions about domesticity, despite elite rule bending. In fact, history indicates that while in some cases women's movements are born and grow because of increases in education and drops in fertility, in Latin America, the impetus for major changes in women's public participation more often comes from social or political upheaval. In both the Southern Cone of Chile and Argentina and in Central America, repressive military dictatorships in the 20th century forced women in those areas to mobilize and organize. In Nicaragua, women became soldiers for the leftist revolutions and continued their work fighting for women's rights after the war. In Argentina, mothers came together to ask for the return of their disappeared children and husbands, marching around the central plaza in the capital. These Madres de la Plaza de Mayo continue as a political force today. In Venezuela, however, no Marxist revolution took place, and the last dictatorship of Pérez Jiménez was less brutal than the regimes in the Southern Cone or Central America. Lack of a common political or social cause meant that women in Venezuela have not been as highly mobilized nor as organized as those in countries who suffered more significant upheaval.

Entering the latter half of the 20th century, then, Venezuelan women faced the additional challenges of coordinating their efforts more effectively as they confronted a government with a set of very gender-biased institutions. One of the key goals of women's groups in the second half of the 20th century was the reform of the *código civil* or civil code. Between 1825 and 1873, the body of laws that governed Venezuela in all matters incorporated laws passed by the Venezuelan legislature, laws from the Spanish colonial era approved in 1808, and three sets of older colonial codes. The colonial codes provided the basis for national period laws regarding women, family, and property. Though the laws favored the rights of male heads of household, the courts did protect women in property and familial matters (Díaz 2004). That situation changed with the 1873 civil code. The code defined the Venezuelan family as the core unit of social organization and set laws governing all the relationships in the family. Though the code improved the legal situation of single women without children (they received recognition as legal individuals) and widows (they received the right to serve as guardians of their minor children), the code limited the rights of married women (Díaz 2004). The code in particular emphasized the power of the father over all other members of the family group. In legal terms, the man had complete control of his wife and children. Under the laws, women had no rights against her husband and no rights concerning her own children. A woman who owned property before marriage lost control of her property upon marrying. The 1873 civil code decreed that the only legally recognized marriage was a civil marriage (not church marriage), but it did not make provisions for divorce or remarriage (Díaz 2004). Amendments to the code in 1904 added divorce rules. Upon divorce, a woman had no hope for custody of her children or recovery of her property. The civil code also detailed accepted discrimination against children born outside of legal marriages. These children had no rights on issues of inheritance or support and no right to use their father's name.

The first efforts to have the civil code change came as early as 1937 but met with little success. Women, who did not yet have the vote, had little voice in government. While some petitions circulated in 1946 after women achieved suffrage, it was not until the 1980s that the code was finally changed. By 1982 the FEVA, or Venezuelan Federation of Female Lawyers, decided that the time was right to attempt to change the civil code. The main plan of action was to ensure that the changes guaranteed equal rights for husbands and wives with regard to property and children, and equal rights for all children, whether they were born inside or outside of legal marriages. The lawyers had an uphill climb, but ultimately formed a large coalition to fight for the change, including socialist women's organizations, political party subcommittees, and university groups. Finally, using the power of the *telenovela* (see Chapter 6), movement leaders wrote four short *novelas* dramatizing the issues in the reform proposals: children's legal status, property in marriage, family unity and decision making, and parents' responsibility for children. The whole drive culminated with a march to congress led by uniformed policewomen. In 1982, the reform legislation passed, though still with stiff opposition.

CURRENT POLITICAL AND SOCIAL STATUS

Despite the progress that led to the revision of the civil code in 1982, women's position in Venezuela can still cause obstacles as well as opportunities. In the 21st century, women increasingly graduate from universities and professional programs and are more visible in government. Conversely, however, a large number of women experience the deprivations of poverty and poor health as they struggle to support their families.

EDUCATION AND INCOME

During the time between 1974 and 1984, women in the middle classes in Venezuela benefited from increased educational and professional opportunities provided by oil revenues. Women's participation in higher education, for example, increased from

44 percent of all graduates in 1974 to 54 percent of all graduates in 1984. The growth in women's participation in higher education during that period brought with it an increased number of women in professional positions, such as in law, business, and politics.

This was good news, but the reality for many working women of the lower classes remained the same. Many Venezuelans could still not afford higher education, and so during the 1980s only 8 percent of all women of the appropriate age were enrolled in university. The majority of Venezuelan women continued to be employed in sex-segregated, low-paying service and manufacturing jobs. In addition, the poorest and least educated women had the largest number of children (Friedman 2000).

During the closing years of the 20th century, educational numbers for women in urban areas continued to improve slightly. By 2000, a greater number of women, compared to men, were literate. In addition, enrollment at the primary school level was approximately equal for boys and girls, with slightly more girls than boys enrolled at the high school level (International Fund for Agricultural Development [IFAD] 2003).

While enrollment in education improved, the overall economic situation for many Venezuelan women worsened. Since the economic collapse of the 1990s, this is especially true of women in the lower economic classes. During the 1980s and 1990s, the number of households living in poverty in Venezuela jumped from 46 to 62 percent, and those described as living in a situation of "critical poverty" increased from 14 to 30 percent (Paredes 2005). Unemployment numbers leapt upward, and the number of women working in the informal sector, in casual, temporary, or unpaid jobs, rose significantly. This forced women to suffer even greater inequities in pay; by 2005, the difference in salary for men and women in the informal sector had reached 40 percent (Paredes 2005).

The situation was particularly acute for women in rural Venezuela. As the IFAD reported in 2003, the majority of women in rural areas worked in the informal sector in agriculture, as well as in the industrial and service sectors, leaving them behind professionally, unprotected by labor law and isolated. Women in rural areas were typically landless workers who were forced to sell their labor to mid-size and large farms and industrial enterprises, picking coffee or cocoa seasonally or working as tobacco graders and dryers during harvest (IFAD 2003).

While both national and international aid organizations have worked in Venezuela to introduce income-generating activities to groups of rural women, it is worth noting that planners have not always paid attention to the daily burden of household chores. This burden increases women's work and the tasks they must accomplish. Sometimes referred to in development circles with the often-used phrase "the infinite elasticity of women's time," aid organizations expect women to take on more and more with no extra help. These organizations often forget that women, especially those who are heads of household, must not only work outside the home but also raise children, take care of extended family, and do back-breaking housework. They have little extra time to be entrepreneurs. Thus, even when microcredit or other revenue-generating programs are introduced in rural areas, women generally do not obtain sufficient incomes to advance beyond the subsistence level (IFAD 2003).

MARRIAGE AND HEALTH

In the last half of the 20th century and in the early years of the 21st century in Venezuela, women have felt the worst of the economic crisis. They have worked longer hours at more jobs with less return than their male counterparts in order to emotionally and financially provide for their families. The specific dangers associated with sexual health and domestic economic stability that women encounter complicate lifetime opportunities, economic or familial.

As reported by the United Nations, in Venezuela, premarital sex among young people is common, and the teen pregnancy rate is quite high. The UN also reports that 134 of every 1,000 young people in Venezuela between the ages of 12 and 18 have a sexually transmitted disease (STD). The STD and teen pregnancy rate was by far higher among the poor than among the middle or upper class, the UN confirmed (United Nations 1999). That situation did not change during the first decade of the Chávez administration. The 1999 UN report lamented the lack of sex education in schools, as did a 2006 report (Cevallos 2006).

Improved sex education may help some, but it does not address more profound sociological problems associated with teen pregnancy—when the burden of poverty and hopelessness falls most heavily on young women. In some cases, a pregnancy can make a romantic relationship between the parents more permanent, with the father taking economic responsibility for his child. It is just as normal, however, for the young woman to become a single parent with the support of her family, placing the burden on her shoulders.

In a case where two young people find themselves in a situation of unplanned pregnancy, cohabitation and, eventually, common-law marriage continue to be much more common than civil or religious ceremonies. Indeed, unofficial unions, sometimes called "consensual unions" are very common. These common-law marriages that exist outside of legal or religious marriage continue to be more widespread in Venezuela than in many other nations. A 2004 study found that, on average, 25.3 percent of Venezuelan women aged 20–29 were a member of a "consensual union" in the years between 1950 and 2000. This is a contrast with a nation such as Chile, where the number of women in consensual unions was 4.5 percent (Fussell and Palloni 2004).

The high prevalence of consensual unions in Venezuela is most concentrated among members of the lower and lower-middle economic classes. Those same groups had lower marriage rates historically in Venezuela as marriage was most associated with elite status and used to transmit property from one generation to the next and to protect blood purity. In most cases, then and now, people in common-law marriages do not take these unions any less seriously than a marriage sanctified by the church and certified by a judge. Consensual unions are often lifelong unions, and parents in common-law marriages follow the Hispanic tradition of granting both the paternal and maternal surnames to children just as they would if the children were born to an officially married couple. It is this prevalence of common-law (and therefore extralegal) marriage, however, that made the 1982 changes to the civil code, which recognized equal rights for partners (and children) of all marriages (legal and common law), so important. As Fussell and Palloni (2004) find, consensual unions tend to be concentrated among rural women, among less educated women, and among those who had premarital conceptions of babies. These women tend to be disadvantaged in the labor market and have little negotiating power in relationships. Changes to the civil code to recognize women's rights in these consensual partnerships was important and overdue.

Among the educated middle and upper classes in Venezuela, consensual unions or common-law marriage is not unknown but is less common. Many times, especially with educated urban women, consensual unions are the precursor to formal, legal marriage, much like in the United States or Europe (Fussell and Palloni 2004). In the case of middle-class women, and certainly in the case of members of the economic elite, civil and church marriage is a necessity. In these cases, the marriage is often accompanied by lavish parties and long announcements in the society pages of the newspapers, just as in decades past.

POLITICS

Women in Venezuela have struggled to achieve the type of political representation that women in other Latin American countries have attained. In 2007, 27 of the 167 members of Venezuela's congress were women, or only 16 percent. While this number is up significantly from the 1990s and is comparable to the 81 of 535 (or 15%) of women in U.S. Congress, it does not compare favorably with other Latin American nations such as Argentina. Argentina, whose women's movement got a jump start in organization during the repressive dictatorship of the 1970s, has an electoral law dictating that at least 30 percent of all candidates for congress must be women. This law generated striking progress in women's representation. In 2007, 88 of the 254 (35 percent) representatives in the Argentine Congress were women. As Cathy Rakowski notes, gains by women in the 1990s were jeopardized by the election of Hugo Chávez, who was slow to include women in his government administration and initially showed no inclination to endorse legislation beyond that dedicated to protecting motherhood (Rakowski 2003).

Work still also remains to be done on the nation's laws. In 1990, a National Women's Council was formed to work on the major legislative issues still affecting women in the nation. As of 1997, however, adultery was still a criminal offense, criminal law still did not recognize domestic violence between married couples, and laws against rape still carried exceptions for rape of prostitutes. A UN report from the same year noted that women had taken "a step backwards since 1992" in efforts to advance women (United Nations Development Programme 1995). The report cited high rates of female illiteracy as well as significant female unemployment and underemployment. The UN report also noted that while Venezuela had formed a National Council of Women, there was no evidence that the council functioned at the level of a ministry, as it had no real power to pursue or implement its own programs (Women's Anti-Discrimination Committee 1997). This snapshot is reinforced by UNIFEM, the United Nations Development Fund for Women, who in their 2000 report noted that Venezuela was among several Latin American nations who had seen backsliding in the gap in men's and women's wages and the ratio of men to women in political representation (Gonzalez n.d.).

Despite the fact that he was slow to take an interest in women's issues, Chávez has proved more welcome to the idea of changing the status of women in Venezuela. Chávez supporters often refer to the new constitution, written in 1999, as the "nonsexist Magna Carta," referring to its gender-inclusive language. The constitution makes a great effort, for example, to alternate the feminine and masculine forms of the word "president:" "*presidente*" and "*presidenta*" throughout its text. In addition, the creation of INAMUJER and the Ministry of People's Power for Women and Gender Equality are steps forward. The constitution laid out some ambitious plans for Venezuela's future, including an article that defines a law similar to that of Argentina's requiring that 30 percent of all congressional candidates be women.

Despite the good intentions of the constitution, however, many Venezuelan feminists emphasize the distance yet to go. The unreasonably high focus on physical beauty (discussed in Chapter 6) that leads most job openings to request a photo with a woman's application is still very much in place. While this widespread cultural expectation is legal, other activity continues in defiance of law. The article requiring 30 percent female participation in congressional elections, for example, was suspended almost immediately in 2000 by the male majority of the congress.

Additional laws have also been ignored until very recently. Article 41 of the Bolivarian Constitution, for example, went unenforced until July of 2005, when the Social Services Act finally ratified a financial allowance for low-income homemakers at the rate of 60 to 80 percent a month of the current minimum urban wage. In April of

---

INAMUJER

INAMUJER, the Instituto Nacional de la Mujer (National Institute of Women), is a government organization established in 1999 by the administration of Hugo Chávez, an outgrowth of Andrés Pérez's CONAMU (National Council for Women). Ten years later, Chávez announced the creation of a Ministry of People's Power for Women and Gender Equality in Venezuela that would include INAMUJER. This improved the power of the organization by making it a government ministry and providing a dedicated budget for its activities.

INAMUJER's mission is to define, supervise, and evaluate political and social issues that affect women. The organization plans, organizes, and executes programs and workshops in the areas of education, health, social security, and job training. INAMUJER is also very involved in legal issues, especially those of violence against women. INAMUJER provides legal assistance, seminars for men and women designed to reduce family violence, and offices where women can report instances of domestic violence to the institute. It is key to INAMUJER's mission to gain not only the passage of new legislation but also enforcement of laws that affect women.

2006, President Chávez announced that homemakers in the lowest income brackets would receive the 80 percent of the minimum wage every month (approximately 170 dollars U.S.) starting in June of that year. While this is certainly one positive step toward making up the economic difference between men and women in Venezuela, much change is still needed.

THE DIVIDING LINE OF SOCIAL CLASS

We have already noted the complicated relationship between class and gender issues historically. Unfortunately, the situation has not changed much. Economic differences not only persist between men and women in Venezuela but also divide women into groups defined by economic class. As we explained at the beginning of this section, the very infrastructure of Venezuelan society, the buildings and universities, ensure that citizens live *juntos pero no revueltos*—together but not mixed. Rosa Cádiz and Linda Loaiza López are both women of Caracas, but their experiences could not be more different. Women are united by many issues but are still divided by the line between rich and poor.

In many ways the width of the breach between rich and poor defines one of the sharpest dividing lines between groups in Latin America as a whole. The region has a poverty rate of over 35 percent, with one of the worst income distributions in the world: the income share of the richest 20 percent of the population is more than 15 times the share of the poorest 20 percent in most countries (UNDP 1995). For women in Venezuela, the situation is particularly severe. Women with the same level of education as men earn 20 percent less, and the number of poor female-headed households is more elevated in Venezuela than in other surrounding countries (Paredes 2005). Venezuelan sociologist Rosa Paredes links this situation to three key factors: first, the underlying discrimination that blocks women's initial entry into the labor market; second, women's primary responsibility for "unpaid, invisible, reproductive roles, activities that convert them into those principally responsible for the economic support of low-income households"; and third, the ignorance of government agencies that refuse to recognize or support women's efforts to enter and remain in the labor force (Paredes 2005: 35).

As mentioned earlier, women were the hardest hit by the economic crisis in the 1980s and 1990s. During this time, the number of women working in the informal sector (as housekeepers, laundresses, or nannies) rose significantly. Women's participation in the informal work sector provides another view of the difference between the economic classes. In Venezuela, as in other Latin American countries, it is common for professional women to employ female domestic servants in their home to clean, cook, and take care of their children. The difference in income between rich and poor makes it possible to hire domestic help for very little, so many professional women depend on servants to run their households. Yet when the women's movement organized to reform the labor laws in the late 1980s, the new proposal did not extend equal benefits to those women who worked in the informal sector. Whether from practicality or willful blindness, the elite women who drafted the reform were unwilling to acknowledge the work of the women who made it possible for them to have full-time careers by carrying out their families' domestic chores. This is one of the great ironies of the women's movement in Latin America: in some ways it can be said that advancement for elite women has been achieved on the backs of the women of the lower economic classes.

Today, we can see the difference between women of different social classes emphasized in the contemporary politics of the nation. The current president, Hugo Chávez, has frequently been accused of stirring up "class war" in the nation between the rich and the poor. Women of the lower classes tend to support Chávez, who has spent millions on social programs for the poor, in medical care, food programs, and education. These women participate in the "Bolivarian Circles" that Chávez has organized in the poorest neighborhoods, and they find leadership positions in Chávez's "Bolivarian Revolution." One of the most colorful examples of a woman who has become well known throughout the economic lower classes for her support of Chávez is "Commander" Lina Ron. Ron, a vocal and famous supporter of Chávez, runs one of the largest Bolivarian Circles, which regularly hands out cash and medicine to the poor. She calls herself a "revolutionary," wearing camouflage and speaking of the necessity of violence, telling the *Miami Herald* "Any time the fascists lift a finger against the poor they will be punished by our popular militias" (Brand 2004: 14A).

Lina Ron, a supporter of Venezuelan President Hugo Chávez, is shown during an interview with the Associated Press in Caracas, Venezuela, Friday, March 22, 2002. Ron said she would willingly become a martyr for Chávez's revolution. Thousands of street toughs nationwide had followed her lead, quashing dissent and alarming Chávez's numerous critics. (AP/Wide World Photos)

Perhaps a more representative example, however, of the type of woman who participates in the Bolivarian Circles and other grassroots organizing can be seen in a less-well known figure: Nora Lee Verenzuela. Verenzuela is the type of woman who can be found in the middle of any community, helping it survive and move forward. When interviewed in 2003, Verenzuela was working in a hotel and volunteering as a coordinator for Trabajo y Tierra (Work and Land), a neighborhood garden cooperative in Caracas originally funded by the Chávez government (Valencia Ramírez 2007). The cooperative produced food for participants in an effort to create a self-sustainable food supply, as well as for local sale, and looked to reclaim unused or misused areas in the parish. In addition, the cooperative sought to generate employment and use their funds for projects such as opening a restaurant. The idea for the organization had come from other grassroots sources: a local neighborhood assembly that, with help from the local Bolivarian Circle, sought aid from the municipal assembly. Trabajo y Tierra had received technical assistance from the military and two months of monetary assistance from the municipal assembly. The program continues today with support of the FAO, the Food and Agriculture Organization, of the United Nations.

Verenzuela, like many other neighborhood leaders, had a long history in working to help her community. Before joining Trabajo y Tierra, she had worked in neighborhood assemblies and local Bolivarian Circles. By 2006, Verenzuela had become the full-time director of the showcase garden of the program Organopónico Bolívar I, an organic garden that sits between the Bellas Artes Metro Stop and the Caracas Hilton and provides more than just produce to the surrounding community. When interviewed in 2006, Verenzuela showed off the healthy plants, cheap vegetables for sale, and nascent "safe zone" that the garden provided. When a reporter asked her about a young girl playing in the garden, she replied: "Her father is a street vendor. There were some problems, so she started hanging out here. She has her toys here, and we take her to school, and she does her homework afterwards. She likes it here" (Howard 2006). There are many women like Verenzuela working daily in low-profile positions, in working-class communities around Venezuela.

On the other side of the class divide, women of the upper and middle class continue to gravitate to the opposition. Chávez and his government appeal to the very poor whose practical, day-to-day needs continue to be addressed. For some elite women, however, Chávez's actions regarding the economy and free speech remind them of Fidel Castro during his more autocratic moments. Two of the poets mentioned in Chapter 6, Yolanda Pantin and Veronica Jaffé, who created the editorial house Pequeña Venecia, have been among the most vocal opponents of Chávez and his regime. Pantin and Jaffé have used the platform of the editorial house and its Web site to publish anti-Chávez petitions and messages to academics around the world. In one such message, written in three languages and addressed from "Venezuelan Writers, Artists and Academics to our Colleagues Around the World," the authors write that "instead of trying to achieve a national consensus, Chávez has used a poisonous speech, promoting violence, hate between social classes and the exclusion of vast sectors of middle class people branding them as oligarchs" (Agudo et al. 2004). Writers, businesswomen, and other professionals are among the most vehement op-

---

NIRVA CAMACHO

Examples of women participating in community organizing and social causes exist in many sectors of Venezuelan society. One woman actively involved in the struggle for increased recognition for Venezuela's African-descended minority is Nirva Camacho. Camacho, a psychologist, is coordinator of institutional relations for Afro-Venezuelan Network and is the head of the Afro-Descendant Women's Network. The women's network, which is made up of groups from 33 different countries, works to advance the cause of black women across Latin America.

In Venezuela, Camacho has undertaken numerous psychological and anthropological studies of Afrovenezuelan experience and is in wide demand as a public speaker. She also directs the Cumbe de Mujeres Afrovenezolanas, an Afrovenezuelan women's organization. The Venezuelan group is particularly concerned by the way that European standards of beauty and femininity affect Afrovenezuelan women in all aspects of their lives, including in matters of employment. In addition, the Cumbe de Mujeres Afrovenezolanas fights for more studies on the situation of Afrovenezuelan women in the areas of poverty, education, and health.

---

ponents of Chávez for these reasons. Indeed, the current political situation seems to have exacerbated the breach between the social classes in general, and between women in particular, in Venezuela.

THE GODDESS AND THE QUEEN

Miss Venezuela is not the only queen to reign in Venezuela. As explained earlier in this chapter, Venezuela's only home-grown religion is the cult of the goddess María Lionza. In the most popular legend, she was a Spanish girl who tried to save the Indian people from destruction but was destroyed for her efforts. After her death, she ascended to the peak of an Andean mountain as an *onza* (boar), where she could continue to protect the native people. Interestingly, among all South American cults, the religion represents the only example of a religious belief system with a central divine *female* figure (García Gavidia 1987). This helps explain why the cult interests us here. The religion is a longstanding and somewhat informal creed interested in providing tangible solutions to the everyday spiritual problems of its adherents. María Lionza represents a protective figure for the underdogs of society: women, the native people, persons of African descent, the poor, and the disenfranchised. It should not come as a surprise, then, that the majority of practitioners are found in those groups.

While some variation exists between groups that worship María Lionza and consider themselves *marialionceros* (those who adhere to the María Lionza religion), there is a basic set of beliefs that unites all believers. All sects of the religion believe in the centrality of a trinity of holy figures: María Lionza herself, the Indian Chief Guaicaipuro, and the black slave the Negro Felipe. María Lionza is the center of this trinity, and the highest deity, called "The Queen" (La Reina) by her adherents (Andrade n.d.). Members of the cult also interact with the goddess directly through members of the priesthood.

Unlike the dominant Roman Catholic Church, the cult of María Lionza allows the participation of female "priests," in the form of *materias* (mediums) who receive the spirits directly into their own bodies or *bancos* (mediators) who mediate, translate, and comment on the messages of the spirits to the faithful. While the *materias* and *bancos* are not exclusively female, most studies suggest that the number of female clergy is larger than that of men. This is important for two reasons: it allows women to assume positions of power in the religious structure that they may not find in other walks of life, and it allows women to earn a living through the cult. *Materias* and *bancos*, sometimes working in mother-daughter pairs, can charge significant amounts for vigils and rites. Even women who do not have the "gift" of talking to María Lionza and the saints can take advantage of the opportunity by offering religious items for sale. As one researcher found, "In the last ten years a new industry has installed itself around the cult with the fabrication on a grand scale of appropriate candles and lamps, fragrant essences for all types of baths and irrigations . . . and seeing as how one should not bargain for magical objects, since they lose their value in the process, the profits are high" (Pollack-Eltz 1985: 47).

Like the possibility of becoming beauty queens, the cult the goddess represents a uniquely Venezuelan opportunity to women. Like the beauty queens, María Lionza is lovely. She is also powerful, however, with the ability to grant requests and answer prayers. María Lionza offers to her followers the opportunity to gain respect and power through her by "putting on" her spirit like a royal crown.

OPPRESSION AND ADORATION: THE PARADOX

Much of the contemporary situation of women in Venezuela can seem paradoxical. As Roberto Hernandez Montoya observes, "We Venezuelan men have an ambiguous relationship with our women: we oppress them and we adore them at the same time" (Hernandez Montoya n.d.). In the same city on the same day, a woman may work as a municipal judge, but another woman may see her torturer go free because he accuses her of being a prostitute. There is opportunity, however. Whether through the national spectacle of the beauty pageant, or through homegrown religion, veneration of women does provide some space for mobility and power. And Venezuelan women have a history of creating their own spaces for mobility even when such a space does not seem to exist. Latin American feminist scholars have long railed against the process of objectification of women in a society that turns women into decorative trinkets. The Puerto Rican author Rosario Ferré's famous story "La Muñeca Menor" literally has the protagonist turning into a doll. In the Venezuelan case, however, the paradox of adoration and oppression allows the dolls constructed in the workshop of Casa Miss Venezuela (the Venezuelan Beauty Queen School) to come to life and gain economic and political power.

THE REVOLUTIONARY GAY MOVEMENT: SEEKING A PLACE FOR LGBT RIGHTS IN 21st-CENTURY VENEZUELA

In 2001, law professor Pablo Aure wrote a letter to the editor of the main Venezuelan newspaper *El Nacional* with the title "Generals in Panties." The letter called the armed forces "castrated and servile" and ridiculed the military for not standing up to President Chávez. This letter was accompanied by packages of women's underwear that appeared at the offices of more than 100 senior and mid-level military officers. This insult was considered so great that Aure was arrested, held for three days, and charged with a crime that held the possibility of 3–5 years in jail for insulting the armed forces (Wilson 2001: A16). What this incident shows is how strong *machismo* still is in Venezuela. The suggestion that the generals might wear women's clothing was a felony offence. This strong *machista* instinct has been a historical challenge for members of Venezuela's lesbian, gay, bisexual, and transgendered (LGBT) community. While relatively low-key and under the radar for many decades, the movement to recognize the rights of LGBT individuals in Venezuela has seen an upswing in activity in the early years of the 21st century.

The first gay rights organization of record was the Movimiento Ambiente Venezuela (MAV), formed in 1980, which focused on social work. This organization did not involve itself in political maneuverings, choosing rather to reach out to the gay community through health and counseling services (Fuentes and Janicke 2005). It was not until the election of Hugo Chávez in the late 1990s and the constitutional congress of 1999 that LGBT activists saw the opportunity to elaborate legal protections against the lesbian and gay community in the new constitution. MAV members worked to get inclusive and antidiscriminatory language into the 1999 constitution but were blocked by the lobbyists of Catholic Church and other members of the Constituent Assembly. As one MAV member put it, "the constitu-

---

FAT, GAY, AND PROUD

One indication of both the changing public attitudes toward the LGBT population in Venezuela and the power of the Venezuelan beauty pageant was the inaugural "Miss Fat Gay Venezuela" pageant held in 2009.

The pageant, which took place in Caracas, respected many of the social conventions governing the beauty pageant industry in the nation: there were separate contests for evening gown, swimsuit, and poise in answering questions. The pageant, however, smashed many other expectations by having all overweight male contestants.

The show skewered two taboos at once: the drive for physical perfection and the *machista* image of men as manly heterosexuals. While contestants admitted that they disapproved of the concept of pageants as a "meat parade," they embraced the opportunity to publicly celebrate acceptance of different sexualities and body types.

tion rejected the interests of the church, but the church still has a direct impact on discussions over abortion, euthanasia and the rights of gays and lesbians" (Fuentes and Janicke 2005).

The Catholic Church is not alone in its reticence to accept sexual orientation beyond that of the heterosexual variety. In their report titled "Situation of Gays," The Immigration and Refugee Board of Canada (IRBC), the International Gay and Lesbian Human Rights Commission (IGLHRC), and Amnesty International detail many of the obstacles that the LGBT community faces. Through 2009, members of the LGBT population continued to be in a "precarious" position in Venezuela. Problems included frequent assaults by citizens and private security, harassment, arbitrary arrests and beatings by police officers, as well as high rates of discrimination in employment and health services (IGLHRC 2006, 2009). In addition, murders, such as that of transgender activist José Luís Nieves (known as Dayana), are not unknown (Amnesty International 2000). These problems are particularly acute in rural areas and small towns (IRBC 2004).

LGBT activists are quick to note, however, that progress is being made in the 21st century. In 2002, President Chávez announced on his weekly television program that he thought a mistake had been made when the 1999 constitution did not include specific protections for gays and lesbians (Fuentes and Janicke 2005). With this implicit backing from the president, a new movement formed, the Movimiento Gay Revolucionario (Revolutionary Gay Movement. MGR) designed to work with the Chávez government to further both the aims of the socialist revolution and the LGBT human rights agenda. One of the leaders of MGR notes that under the Chávez government, the LGBT community has celebrated gay rights day every year and that starting in 2005, government ministers and CONAC representatives have participated (Fuentes and Janicke 2005).

REFERENCES

Agudo, Alvaro, et al. 2004. "Mensaje de escritores, artistas y académicos venezolanos. Caracas, 25 de febrero." http://www.pequenhavenecia.com/mensaje.

Andrade, Gabriel Ernesto. n.d. A Girardian Reading of the Myth of María Lionza. AnthroBase. http://www.anthrobase.com/Txt/A/Andrade_G_E_01.htm.

Amnesty International. 2000. "Venezuela: Possible Extrajudicial Execution/Fear for Safety-Dayana (Real Name José Luís Nieves)." http://www.amnesty.org/en/library/asset/AMR53/009/2000/.

Brand, Richard. 2004. "Comandante Lina at Helm of President's Paramilitary Neighborhood Groups." *The Miami Herald*, May 2: 14A.

Castillo, Debra. 1992. *Talking Back: Toward a Latin American Feminist Literary Criticism.* New York: Cornell University Press.

CEM. n.d. "Comunicado de la asamblea de mujeres reunida en la Universidad Central de Venezuela el viernes 22 de octubre." http://cem.ve.tripod.com/.

Cevallos, Diego. 2006. "Let's (Not) Talk About Sex." *Inter-Press Service*, April 18. http://www.aegis.com/news/ips/2006/IP060412.html.

Díaz, Arlene J. 2004. *Female Citizens, Patriarchs, and the Law in Venezuela, 1786–1904.* Lincoln: University of Nebraska Press.

Ferry, Robert. 1989. *The Colonial Elite of Early Caracas: Formation and Crisis, 1567–1767.* Berkeley: University of California Press.

Friedman, Elisabeth. 2000. *Unfinished Transitions: Women and the Gendered Development of Democracy in Venezuela 1936–1996.* University Park, PA: Penn State University Press.

Fuentes, Federico, and Kiraz Janicke. 2005. "Struggling for Gay and Lesbian Rights In Venezuela." *Venezuelanalysis*, December 5. http://www.venezuelanalysis.com/analysis/1512.

Fussell, Elizabeth, and Albverto Palloni. 2004. "Persistent Marriage Regimes in Changing Times." *Journal of Marriage and Family* 66, no. 5: 1201–1213.

García Gavidia, Nelly. 1987. *Posesión y ambivalencia en el culto a María Lionza: Notas para una tipología de los cultos de posesión existentes en la América del Sur.* Maracaibo, Venezuela: Editorial de la Universidad de Zulia.

Gomez, Q., Vannessa. 2004. "Una Sentencia incomprensible." *El Nacional*, October 22: B21.

Gonzalez, Gustavo. n.d. "Latin America: Scant Progress in Status of Women, says UNIFEM." TWN Third World Network. http://www.twnside.org.sg/title/scant.htm.

Hernandez Montoya, Roberto. n.d. "The Cult of Venus in Venezuela." http://www.analitica.com/bitblio/roberto/venus.

Howard, April M. 2006. "Feeding Ourselves. Organic Urban Gardens in Caracas Venezuela." http://towardfreedom.com/home/content/view/869/.

Immigration and Refugee Board of Canada. 2004. "Venezuela: Situation of Gays. Immigration and Refugee Board of Canada." http://www.unhcr.org/refworld/topic,4565c22547,45 65c25f563,3df4bec44,0.html.

International Fund for Agricultural Development. 2003. "Sustainable Rural Development Project for the Semi-Arid Zones of Falcon and Lara States." December 18. http:// operations.ifad.org/web/ifad/operations/country/project/tags/venezuela/1252/project%20 overview.

International Gay and Lesbian Human Rights Commission. 2006. Venezuela: Trans Activist Had to Leave the Country Due to Police Harassment and Is Asking for Protection." http:// www.iglhrc.org/cgi-bin/iowa/article/takeaction/globalactionalerts/268.

———. 2009. "Venezuela: Condemn Arrests of LGBT in Caracas." http://www.iglhrc.org/ cgi-bin/iowa/article/takeaction/globalactionalerts/1003.

Morse, Kimberly J. 2000. "Aun en la muerte separados: Class, Clergy, and Society in Aragua de Barcelona, Venezuela, 1820–1875." PhD diss., The University of Texas at Austin.

Paredes, Rosa. 2005. "Las mujeres en Venezuela: Estrategias para salir de la pobreza." *Revista Venezolana de Estudios de la Mujer* 24, no. 35: 17–42.

Pollack-Eltz. Angelina. 1985. *María Lionza: Mito y Culto Venezolano.* Caracas: Universidad Católica Andrés Bello.

———. 1994. *La religiosidad popular en Venezuela.* Caracas: San Pablo.

Rakowski, Cathy A. 2003. "Women's Coalitions as a Strategy at the Intersection of Economic and Political Change in Venezuela." *International Journal of Politics, Culture, and Society.* 16: 387–405.

Registro Principal de Barcelona. 1869. "Criminales, 26, 1861 al 1869, Libro 56, Contra Hilario Alquimediquez, por injurias de hecho de verificados en la persona de Vicenta Puerta, 1869."

Seed, Patricia. 1988. *To Love, Honor, and Obey in Colonial Mexico: Conflicts over Marriage Choice, 1574–1821.* Stanford, CA: Stanford University Press.

Twinam, Ann. 1999. *Public Lives, Private Secrets: Gender, Honor, Sexuality, and Illegitimacy in Colonial Spanish America.* Stanford, CA: Stanford University Press.

United Nations. 1999. "Summary Record of the 561st Meeting of the Committee on the Rights of the Child." http://www.unhchr.ch/tbs/doc.nsf/(Symbol)/af41e2ce3f2501208025 680300567afe?Opendocument.

United Nations. 2002. "Convention on the Rights of the Child." http://www.unhchr.ch/tbs/doc.nsf/(Symbol)/af41e2ce3f2501208025680300567afe?Opendocument.

United Nations. 2010. "Convention on the Rights of the Child." http://www.unhchr.ch/tbs/doc.nsf/(Symbol)/af41e2ce3f2501208025680300567afe?Opendocument.

UNDP (United Nations Development Programme). 1995. "Human Development Report 1995 of the United Nations Development Programme." http://hdr.undp.org/en/reports/global/hdr1995/.

Valencia Ramírez, Cristóbal. 2007. Venezuela's Bolivarian Revolution: Who Are the Chavistas? In *Venezuela: Hugo Chávez and the Decline of an "Exceptional Democracy."* Steve Ellner and Miguel Tinker Salas, eds. Lanham, MD: Rowman and Littlefield.

Waldron, Kathy. 1989. "The Sinners and the Bishop in Colonial Venezuela: The 'Visita' of Bishop Mariano Marti, 1771–1784." In Asuncion Lavrin, ed., *Sexuality and Marriage in Colonial Latin America.* Lincoln: University of Nebraska Press.

Wilson, Scott. 2001. "As Military Men Get Panties in the Mail, a Law Professor Lands in Jail." *The Washington Post*, January 29: A16.

Women's Anti-Discrimination Committee. 1997. "Venezuela Appears to Have Taken Step Backwards on Women's Advancement, Women's Anti-Discrimination Committee Told." 1a—Press Release WOM/940. 323rd Meeting. January 22. http://www.un.org/News/Press/docs/1997/19970122.wom940.html.

Education

EDUCATION: A PATH TO MODERNIZATION AND EQUALITY

Throughout Venezuelan history, politicians perceived education as the path to modernity and as an antidote to social, racial, and gender differences. President Chávez is no different. In August of 2009, the administration of Hugo Chávez passed a new law that sought to reorganize the education system in Venezuela. As we will see later in this section, the new law covers everything from the official language of instruction in public schools to the rules governing which students will be admitted to state-run universities. One of the most controversial articles of the law is the provision that proclaims the secular nature of the school system. In the words of a member of the Education Commission of Venezuela's General Assembly, "religious education in schools is not going to be prohibited, rather it will not be obligatory in the curriculum" (Suggett 2009). Of particular concern to opponents is the provision in the new law that removed old rules allowing religious educational organizations to receive state money as long as they offered high-quality education free of charge to the public. This change in the role of religion in public education represented a major shift in the history of education in Venezuela. Whereas religious organizations, such as the Catholic Church, were formerly key in the foundation, development, and running of schools and universities, now their role would be limited.

HISTORICAL BACKGROUND

The Roman Catholic Church was one organization that vehemently protested the new law. The church is deeply interested in the education of Venezuelans, continuing a tradition that dates back to colonial times. As with many things in colonial Venezuela, the educational system was both originated and controlled by the Roman Catholic Church.. In the early days of the colony, the church provided tutors and organized schools, but only for the rich. Wealthy landowners sought out education for their sons, many times through the use of tutors. It was relatively common then, after the Venezuelan tutoring, for students to go abroad and study in Europe. This is the path that the Liberator, Simón Bolívar, took as a youth. Bolívar studied both with tutors and in a church-run elementary school in Caracas. Later, however, he traveled to Spain, France, and Italy to complete his studies.

The first opportunities for free and public education came in the 1800s after Venezuela's independence from Spain. After the war, Bolívar issued a series of decrees proclaiming the need for free public education. While most of Bolívar's proposed programs were never implemented, he still remains an important figure in Venezuelan education. The first real free education did not become readily available to the public until 1870 under the regime of Antonio Guzmán Blanco. His presidency marked the first real step forward for public education. Guzmán Blanco made free public education legally the responsibility of the nation, administered through national, state, and local governments. While not all of Guzmán Blanco's plans were carried out, the state organized and financed normal schools to train teachers and established a Ministry of Education. In 1891, the National University of Zulia was founded, followed by the National University of Carabobo. After this period of support, however, the Venezuelan educational system went through a tough period. Universities thrived, and university students were frequently part of the opposition to dictator Juan Vicente Gómez, but millions of poor and rural Venezuelans did not yet have access to a basic primary education. Finally, in the middle of the 20th century, dictator Marcos Pérez Jiménez slashed the national budget for education and often closed universities that he perceived as critical of his regime.

Real support blossomed again with the fall of Pérez Jiménez and the establishment of democracy in 1958. It is during this period that the ideals and goals of Guzmán Blanco were revived and put into action. Several universities were established, educational programs were broadcast on radio and television, and agricultural extension offices were formed to reach out to Venezuelan farmers. During the period from 1958 to 1980, massive state investment in primary education made six years of education a funded mandate. With the passage of the Ley Orgánica de la Educación (Organic Law of Education), in 1980, nine years of basic education became compulsory.

Private schools (both religious and secular) remained in Venezuela along with the public options, but though the public schools were relatively well funded and staffed, private schools continued to carry more prestige than public ones did. Wealthy families sent, and still send, their children to private schools rather than participate in public education, as they perceive a private education to be key for career success.

The Catholic Fé y Alegría schools that serve primarily the urban and rural poor were different, however. Founded by Chilean priest José María Vélez in 1955 in Caracas, the schools functioned under the notion that an ignorant people are a repressed, oppressed, and marginalized people. This vision affirmed that an educated people are a free and transformed people, the owners of their destiny (Fé y Alegría 2009). By 1964, the schools had educated over 10,000 students in Venezuela. There are now Fé y Alegría schools in Venezuela, Bolivia, Brazil, Chile, Chad, Argentina, Colombia, Ecuador, El Salvador, Spain, Guatemala, Honduras, Haiti, Panama, Nicaragua, Peru, Dominican Republic, Paraguay, and Uruguay.

CONTEMPORARY OVERVIEW

At the beginning of the 21st century, Venezuelan schools followed the 1980 Organic Law that established four levels of education: preschool, primary education, diversified and professional education, and higher education. A Venezuelan child may start in preschool at the age of three. Preschool in Venezuela is free but not required. At the age of five, a Venezuelan child must begin primary, or elementary, school. Students spend nine years in primary education.

COLEGIO HUMBOLDT

While religious private schools are still common in Venezuela, another long-standing choice in private education at the primary and secondary level are international schools. One well-established school that speaks to Venezuela's immigrant tradition is the Colegio Humboldt, established in 1894.

Located in the exclusive Altamira neighborhood of Caracas (two blocks north of the country club), the Colegio Humboldt is run jointly by an agreement between the German and Venezuelan governments. The school offers K–12 education. The coursework is multilingual (in Spanish, English, German, and French) and covers all of the main academic subjects in the sciences and humanities while taking an international approach. The school sells itself to the parents of prospective students on the basis of the "competitiveness" and "professional" ability that students will gain as well as the "opportunities" that students will have internationally as part of the school's network of international high schools and universities subsidized by the German government. These advertising points all feed the perception that private school education is the fast track to professional success.

After these nine years, students pass on to a third level of secondary, "diversified" education. The diversified level is where students choose to follow a technical track, and graduate after two or three years with a trade, or follow a more academic track and apply to university.

Due to lack of space in the public schools, the Venezuelan government only offers instruction for half a day at all levels. It is true that after the 1958 transition to democracy, the state funded the construction of many schools. However, the majority of these schools were built as temporary structures and were never meant to serve in the long term. Fifty years later, most of these schools are still in use. In the words of researcher Mariano Herrera, "we now have schools with zinc roofs in 60°C heat (140°F) that are falling into ruin" (Losego 2001). Even with the continued use of temporary structures, there are not enough schools for all children, and therefore schools are obliged to serve two different sets of students every day.

Part of the reason for the lack of adequate buildings for public schools may be traced back to the economic crisis of the 1980s. As UNESCO reports, government spending for education fell from 7.4 percent of GDP in 1983 to 3.8 percent in 1998 (Losego 2001). The lack of funding caused public schools to begin charging registration fees to students, fees that many living in poverty could not afford. These problems have meant that at the beginning of the 21st century, Venezuela's primary school graduation rate was significantly behind the Latin American average of 94 percent (Losego 2001). Lack of decent facilities and drops in spending are key reasons why private school education continues to be considered the path to success in life. These are also the reasons behind the Chávez administration's sweeping revisions.

After basic education, when it comes time for students to choose a university, there are several types of universities to choose from, including national (public) universities, private universities, polytechnic institutes, military university institutes, ecclesiastical university institutes, or pedagogical institutes. Venezuela is well supplied with choices of higher education; in 2000, there were 42 universities (21 public and 21 private) as well as 104 university institutes and colleges (some private and others public) (Márquez n.d.). Venezuelan universities (both public and private) are comprehensive and include within their structure many individual schools that grant professional degrees in areas such as engineering. Universities also offer graduate degrees in their schools. University colleges and polytechnic institutes generally offer three-year programs designed to train mid-level technicians and social service providers such as social workers. Pedagogical institutes train teachers, and military institutes and ecclesiastical universities train individuals for service in the military and the church. Men and women serve in the military.

There are no significant differences in course offerings or prestige across the board between public and private universities. Both offer a wide range of degrees, and there are both poorer and higher quality public and private universities, and the quality of education is equal between the best of both groups. The major difference between public and private universities is cost and financing. Private universities charge tuition and depend on tuition revenues and donations for their operating budgets. Public universities, by contrast, are funded by the Ministry of Education, which in 1991 covered 93 percent of the total expenditures of the public universities (Navarro 1991). No tuition is charged at public universities, which are functionally free, apart

LEY ORGÁNICA DE LA EDUCACIÓN 1980

The 1980 Organic Law of Education laid out some fundamental principles of public education in Venezuela. In addition to setting standards in practical matters, such as years of primary education, the law set forth a number of philosophical ideas. First, it declared education to be a fundamental right of all persons and the education of all persons to be the responsibility of the state, as well-educated citizens are necessary to the formation, security, and growth of the nation. The law recognized citizens' right to choose technical or pre-university education without discrimination based on race, gender, religion, or economic status. On this last point, the law recognizes the necessity of a free public education, and it makes preschool and basic education mandatory. Interestingly, the 1980 law prohibits any type of political propaganda in Venezuelan schools. As we shall see, in this, the 1980 law stands in contrast to the revisions begun in 2007 with the implementation of a "Bolivarian" curriculum that reflects the goals of the Chávez administration. The revisions culminated in the 2009 Ley Orgánica.

from some nominal fees. Low cost did not mean that working class populations attended public universities in large numbers. By the early 1990s, only 36 percent of public university students came from working-class households. Thirteen percent of students came from households headed by university professionals, or .25 percent of the total population.

Venezuelan university students, like university students throughout Latin America, honor a long and continuous tradition of student political activism. In Venezuela, the tradition dates back to the Gómez era, when student democracy advocates forced Gómez to close the universities for 10 years, beginning in 1914. When the schools reopened, students again challenged Gómez in 1928. Many of the leaders of that movement became important democratic political leaders in AD, COPEI, and other political parties throughout the 20th century. Though students in the 1970s, 1980s, and 1990s remained vocal advocates of social justice issues and insisted on academic freedom, university autonomy, and low cost public education, many of their activities became intertwined with the spoils system employed by AD and COPEI. Becoming part of campus AD and COPEI organizations meant much, much more than it did to be a Young Republican or Young Democrat on a U.S. college campus. Student political leaders could become important voices in off-campus political conversations. When the economic crisis of the 1980s and the 1990s led to deep cuts in public higher education funding, strikes, led by students, faculty, or both, commonly shut down universities across the country for weeks at a time, punctuated by demonstrations, tear gas, and tire burnings. In that context, student activism in opposition to President Chávez, which began in earnest in 2006 and involves major universities throughout the country, carries on a nearly century-old national tradition.

In order for Venezuelan students to get a seat at a university or institute, students must take a mandatory admission exam that tests both reading comprehension and mathematical reasoning. Then students are assigned scores, based both on their performance on the exam and on their grade point average from seventh grade until graduation from the diversified level. This score is then called the Academic Index. Students use this index to seek admission to universities and institutes. The length of time that a student spends in higher education varies. Technical majors take three years to complete, while professional degrees such as engineering or psychology may take up to six years. As in other nations, Venezuelan universities also offer graduate degrees: master's degrees, doctorates, and certificates of specialization.

EXEMPLARY PUBLIC HIGHER EDUCATION: THE UNIVERSIDAD CENTRAL DE VENEZUELA

Of the many universities available, the Universidad Central de Venezuela (UCV) is the largest and oldest and is considered by many the most prestigious. The UCV is a masterpiece of urban planning and the alma mater of 19 of Venezuela's presidents and many major cultural figures, including Andrés Bello and Rómulo Gallegos.

Venezuelan students talk near a wall decorated with a mural by French artist Fernand Leger at the Central University of Venezuela, March 4, 2000. Architect Carlos Raul Villanueva conceived of the sprawling campus as a "synthesis of the arts." Its buildings and walkways are decorated with the abstract sculptures of Francisco Narvaez, Henri Laurens, and Jean Arp. (AP/Wide World Photos)

The university traces its history back to 1696 under the name of Colegio de Santa Rosa (College of Santa Rosa), a catholic seminary that held classes in a chapel. In 1721, King Felipe V of Spain awarded the college official accreditation to give seminary degrees. It is this date that the university usually uses as the official date of its founding. Either of these dates, however, place the UCV as one of the oldest universities in the western hemisphere (UCV n.d.).

In 1826, the UCV took its current name and became a secular, public institution. In 2009, the university had an enrollment of 54,000 students, who attend the 11 different *facultades* (schools) in Caracas, 2 *facultades* in Maracay, and the 5 study centers and experimental stations around the nation. The main campus in Caracas offers degrees in a wide variety of areas, including agronomy, architecture, law, pharmacy, and medicine.

The UCV in Caracas forms a *ciudad universiaria* (university city), a small town within the capital. The current, impressive Caracas campus was designed by Venezuelan architect Carlos Raúl Villanueva and serves as a worldwide model of architecture and urban planning. Villanueva's vision was to synthesize functionality, art, and architecture and to use the opportunity to create a university city that functioned as an "outdoor museum" (Sennot 2004: 89). To this end, the UCV provides functional innovations, such as architecturally pleasing covered walkways for the Venezuelan rainy season, and integrates many major artworks from Venezuelan and international artists, including building-size murals by Alejandro Otero and Oswaldo Vigas, and sculptures from Alexander Calder, Henri Laurens, Jean Arp, and many others. For its integration of form, function, and artistic sensibilities, the campus of the UCV was named a World Heritage Site by UNESCO in 2000.

CHANGES TO THE EDUCATIONAL SYSTEM

At the beginning of the 21st century, the administration of President Hugo Chávez undertook a series of steps aimed at reforming the Venezuelan school system. One piece of this project was a new Ley Orgánica de la Educación passed in 2009. The law, both hailed and criticized by many, was designed to create more opportunity in education for the poor and to instill national values in students.

While the 2009 law is an important event in education reform in Venezuela, the Chávez administration began its efforts soon after the president's election in 1998. In his first years in office, Chávez did away with the practice of registration fees in public schools, used the armed forces to repair decaying schools and build new ones, and launched campaigns aimed both at young students and also adult learners. To achieve these objectives, the Chávez government raised the amount spent on education from the previously mentioned 3.8 percent, to 6 percent of GDP. These initiatives allowed an additional 350,000 children to enroll in public schools by 2001 (Losego 2001).

Another early program designed by the administration were the *misiones* (social missions) dedicated to educating adults. Three of the first *misiones* created in 2003 were the Misión Robinson, dedicated to eradicating adult illiteracy, the Misión Sucre, designed to provide scholarships and increase accessibility of university education, and the Misión Ribas, which supplies remedial high school education to Venezuelans who never completed secondary coursework ("Fact Sheet: Social Missions" n.d.). The Venezuelan government claimed huge gains in these areas after their implementation and development. In 2006, Misión Ribas reported having founded 297 cooperatives nationwide that served both urban and rural citizens. In that same year, Misión Ribas reported more than 25,000 graduates of the program who had moved on to *Misión Sucre* (Misión Ribas n.d.). Perhaps most impressive, however, are the achievements of Misión Robinson, which in 2005 announced that it had graduated 2 million citizens who were now able to read and write ("Literacy Campaign" 2003). Indeed, the Venezuelan Embassy in 2009 reported that "Venezuela is now considered a country free of illiteracy" ("Fact Sheet: Social Missions" n.d.).

After focusing on basic issues of adult illiteracy and public school fees, the Chávez administration launched a campaign to revise the curriculum for national standards in education. This new "Bolivarian" curriculum, implemented in 2007, applies to all schools in the nation, both public and private. The curriculum, as Chris Carlson reports, is "based on four fundamental pillars of learning and four programmatic themes. The four pillars are: 1. Learn to create 2. Learn to coexist and participate 3. Learn to value and 4. Learn to reflect" (Carlson 2007). "The four programmatic themes of the new curriculum are 1. Environment and Health (collective, individual, and mental health, and harmony with nature) 2. Inter-culturality (self identity and the recognition of national consciousness) 3. Information and Communication Technology (for the production of native content, free software, and the generation of knowledge); and 4. Liberation Work" (Carlson 2007). These changes to curriculum were effected not only by changes in teaching in the schools, but also through the creation of new textbooks by the Ministry of Education that became required in all schools, both public and private. Chávez has warned that private schools who do not use the new curriculum will be closed or taken over by the state (Carlson 2007).

The pillars and programmatic themes are somewhat open to interpretation on the part of individual schools. Overall, however, the goal of the new curriculum is to deepen students' appreciation of the uniqueness of Venezuelan cultural and intellectual heritage, to increase ecological awareness and to highlight the economic situation of Venezuela. Juana Sierra, principal of Fermín Toro school in Caracas, understands that the goal of the new curriculum is to train a different kind of citizen. In 2008, Ms. Sierra described this new citizen to *The Washington Post* as "A Venezuelan who's highly humanistic, with solidarity, who knows his history, who knows the Venezuelan Indian, who knows all the resources the fatherland has, who knows the history of oil, about why we're so dependent, about why we're underdeveloped" (Forero 2008).

Fermín Toro is one of the new "Bolivarian" schools in the nation. In September of 2007, concurrent with the launch of the new curriculum, the federal government opened 15 new schools across the nation with the designation of "Bolivarian" schools. These schools, in addition to using the new curriculum, offer full-day education and three free meals a day to students. According to the Chávez administration, the creation of new, specifically "Bolivarian" primary and secondary schools was

FERMÍN TORO

Fermín Toro, for whom Venezuelans have named various elementary and secondary schools as well as a university, was a colonial-era author, educator, and diplomat in the tradition of Andrés Bello and the writer-statesman.

Toro was born in 1806 in the Caracas neighborhood of El Valle to Spanish parents. He was raised and educated in Caracas by both church tutors and his uncle, the Marquis del Toro. As an educator, Toro directed the Liceo Venezolano secondary school in Caracas.

Toro, however, is most famous for his political and literary activity. Toro served in various government posts, including several terms as senator, as diplomatic envoy to England, France, and Spain, and as director of the treasury. It was Fermín Toro who served as plenipotentiary envoy to ratify the peace terms between Spain and Venezuela after the wars of independence. As an author, Toro is known for his journalism as well as his philosophical and legal studies, but he is most famous for authoring the first Venezuelan novel, *Los Mártires* (The Martyrs).

accompanied in the 2007–2008 school year by the conversion of 5,766 old schools to the Bolivarian model. The goal of the administration in 2007 was the conversion of all public schools in Venezuela to the Bolivarian model by the 2010 academic year as well as the construction of new schools (Carlson 2007).

Educational reforms, however, are not limited to the primary and secondary levels. The Ministry of Education at the beginning of the 21st century also sought to gain more control of higher education through changes to law and the creation of new institutions. In 2003, the government opened the Universidad Bolivariana (Bolivarian University). This university was created specifically to offer opportunities in higher education to the poorest of Venezuela's citizens, those who wish complete a degree in higher education but did not receive a high enough Academic Index to be admitted to one of the nation's main public universities. Bolivarian University's mission is to promote inclusion, and as such it has open admissions. Everyone is accepted, regardless of scores, work, or criminal history.

As the *Washington Post* reported on the occasion of the university's first graduation ceremony, the mission of the institution is not only to educate thousands of new doctors, lawyers, and teachers but also to promote "the sort of social activism that Chavez says can help Venezuela's poor majority to overcome decades of oppression by the rich" (Reel 2006). The Bolivarian University occupies space in Caracas that once housed the headquarters of PDVSA, the state petroleum company, and as such provides a symbol of the administration's ideology. The walls are bare of any advertising that would promote consumerism (these having been replaced by posters of Marxist revolutionary Che Guevara). The classrooms and offices that once held executives trained in free-market economics were converted to the promotion of socialism.

The Universidad Bolivariana had grown in 2006 to the largest university in Venezuela, with more than 180,000 students enrolled at the main campus in Caracas and at 190 satellite classrooms throughout the nation. Students graduate from a variety

Education mural in Mèrida, Venezuela. (Bildagentur/StockPhotoPro)

of programs in two or three years compared to four or more for the average graduate from the traditional universities. While the enrollment numbers are impressive, the Chávez administration reported that they hoped to enroll up to 1 million students by the year 2010 (Reel 2006). The government's hope is that so many Venezuelan students, trained with the methods and within the ideological framework preferred by the government, will go on to serve in the government's social missions. Many fear, however, that graduates from the Universidad Bolivariana may not be as qualified for many professional positions due to the abbreviated nature of their education. Will there be, skeptics wonder, long-term consequences for short-term expediency?

CONTROVERSY AND OPPOSITION TO EDUCATIONAL CHANGES

As with many of the new social programs and plans advanced by the Chávez administration, there has been considerable controversy about both the new curriculum and the creation of new schools. On the government side, the Chávez administration contends that the new educational plan will counter the influence of the United States and capitalist and consumerist values. According to the administration, the new curriculum will instill in Venezuelan children respect and appreciation for their national culture and identity, while responding to the forces of cultural globalization effected by imported movies, music, and television programs. Opponents, however, see the changes to the educational system as dangerous and nothing more than a government-supported campaign to brainwash impressionable children into supporting Chávez and his socialist policies.

Parents of children in middle- and upper-class neighborhoods especially are vehemently opposed to the changes to the curriculum. While the majority of children in the middle and upper class attend private schools, parents are fearful of Chávez's demand that private schools adopt the textbooks and program designed by the government. Parents are not only worried that the new textbooks contain "hidden Marxism" (Forero 2008) but also that they are inadequate in presenting a full view of Venezuelan history. Many complaints center on how the new curriculum glosses over events that show Chávez in a bad light (such as the 1992 coup attempt). Others are upset at the way that the new curriculum privileges indigenous and African culture in Venezuela over the contributions of European immigrants and their customs.

Opposition to the changes to the educational system came to a head in August of 2009 as the Venezuelan congress voted to pass the new Organic Law of Education. On the eve of the vote, opposition members walked out of congress in protest, and thousands of Venezuelans, including parents, members of teachers' unions, university students, and officials of the Catholic Church, marched in the capital in a series of demonstrations.

As mentioned before, Catholic Bishops were concerned that private Catholic schools could lose government subsidies, and university administrators protested that the new law would breach the autonomy of the university system and wrest control of university admissions from the institutions themselves. Journalists joined in protests as the Organic Law contained provisions that would allow the government to close down any media organization that was viewed as producing material likely to cause "terror" among children or damage the "mental health" of the public (Gunson 2009). Teachers' groups such as the Assembly of Educators objected to parts of the law that would allow the supervision of schools by "communal councils" based in the community. While the government defended the provision by touting it as a way for community members to be more involved in their local schools, teachers and school administrators feared that it would allow further government intrusion and meddling by those with no experience in education.

Indeed, the Venezuelan congress, in their passage of the law, noted that while the law does seek to promote specific values in students (social responsibility and participatory democracy), so, too, did the curriculum it replaces. Carlos Escarrá, a legislator in the congress that passed the law, argued that the new curricula would reverse the indoctrination that was present in earlier curricula, curricula that "educated students to be non-critical, non-committed to society, and divided into segments" (Suggett 2009). As with many issues in 21st-century Venezuela, both sides of the debate are vehement. Only time will tell whether the concerns of the opposition or the hopes of reform proponents are more prescient.

CONCLUSIONS

We can now see the answer to the questions Ana Isabel posed about her poor friends on the eve of the 20th century. Manuel Carreño would opine that the poor children of Ana Isabel's neighborhood (who would have been mostly people of color) were not decent because they were lazy, ignorant, and untruthful. The Catholic Church, as it had for centuries, would endorse this vision both through its teaching in schools and through the organization of cemeteries and other institutions.

Some things have changed since Antonia Palacios, the author of *Ana Isabel*, wrote her autobiographical novel. Some have not. The Catholic Church has made an effort to reach out to members of the lower economic classes, and education is much more widely available to all. Women have made progress in entering public society in business and in politics. Members of indigenous groups and of the lower economic classes have a stronger political voice in national decisions. However, women, regardless of class, still subject themselves to the cult of beauty. Venezuelans still perceive lighter skin as more attractive than darker skin. There is still a wide gap in understanding and communication between members of the upper and lower economic classes, and a great number of Venezuelans (many of color) are still poor and disenfranchised. The past century has shown progress, but much work remains to be done.

REFERENCES

Carlson, Chris. 2007. "Venezuela Launches New 'Bolivarian' Education Curriculum." *Venezuelanalysis*, September 19. http://www.venezuelanalysis.com/news/2616.

Fé y Alegría. 2009. http://www.feyalegria.org/.

Forero, Juan. 2008. "In Venezuelan Schools, Creating a 'New Man.'" *The Washington Post*, May 19. http://www.washingtonpost.com/wp-dyn/content/article/2008/05/18/AR2008051 802330.html.

Gunson, Phil. 2009. "Critics of Venezuelan Education Law Vow to Defy It." *Miami Herald*, August 17. http://www.miamiherald.com/news/americas/venezuela/story/1187084-p2. html.

"Literacy Campaign Misión Robinson Will Graduate 2 Million Citizens by 2005." 2003. *Venezuelanalysis*, September 16. http://www.venezuelanalysis.com/news/103.

Losego, Fabrice. 2001. "With Bolivar We Go." *UNESCO Courier*. http://www.unesco.org/courier/2001_6/uk/education.htm.

Márquez, Patricia. n.d. "Venezuela." Global Foundation for Management Education. http://www.gfme.org/global_guide/pdf/277–284%20Venezuela.pdf.

Misión Ribas. n.d. "Misión Ribas." http://www.misionribas.gov.ve/index.php?option=com_content&task=view&id=16&Itemid=29.

Navarro, Juan Carlos. 1991. "Venezuelan Higher Education in Perspective." *Higher Education* 21, no. 2: 177–188.

Paredes, Rosa. 2005. "Las mujeres en Venezuela: Estrategias para salir de la pobreza." *Revista Venezolana de Estudios de la Mujer* 24, no. 35: 17–42.

Reel, Monte. 2006. "Chavez Educates Masses at a University in His Image." *The Washington Post*, May 25. http://www.washingtonpost.com/wpdyn/content/article/2006/05/24/AR2006052402444.htm.

Sennot, Stephen, ed. 2004. *Encyclopedia of Twentieth-Century Architecture.* New York: Taylor and Francis.

"Fact Sheet: Social Missions in Venezuela." n.d. http://www.embavenez-us.org/factsheet/socialmissionsinvenezuela-12.11.09eng.pdf.

Suggett, James. 2009. "Venezuelan Education Law: Socialist Indoctrination or Liberatory Education?" Venezuelanalysis, August 21. http://www.venezuelanalysis.com/analysis/4734.

United Nations Development Programme. 1995. "Human Development Report 1995 of the United Nations Development Programme." http://hdr.undp.org/en/reports/global/hdr1995/.

Universidad Central de Venezuela. n.d. "Reseña Histórica." http://www.ucv.ve/sobre-la-ucv/resena-historica.html.

Valencia Ramírez, Cristóbal. 2007. "Venezuela's Bolivarian Revolution: Who Are the Chavistas?" In Steve Ellner and Miguel Tinker Salas, eds., *Venezuela: Hugo Chávez and the Decline of an "Exceptional Democracy."* Lanham, MD: Rowan and Littlefield.

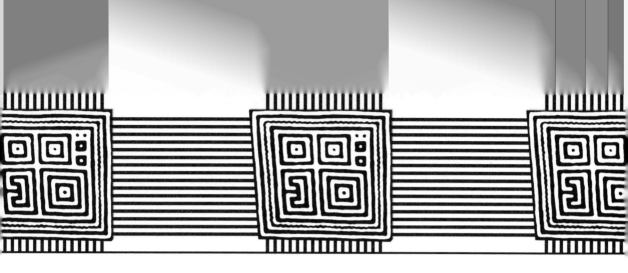

Culture

INTRODUCTION

On the third of May every year, many people in eastern Venezuela celebrate El Día de la Cruz (Holy Cross Day). In elaborate celebrations that stretch through the whole month of May, on Margarita Island and in places such as the city of Barlovento or San Juan de los Morros, Venezuelans eat traditional foods, dance, and sing *galerones* to the cross as it is decorated with flowers. The observance of Cruz de mayo (May Cross) combines pre-Colombian celebrations of fertility and spring with the Catholic remembrance of the cross of crucifixion. In the month of singing, dancing, poetry recitals, and dinners we can see examples of many elements of Venezuelan culture. The culture of a society envelops the knowledge, beliefs, morals, laws, arts, and customs of the people in the society (Tylor 1958: 1). As we will see in this chapter, the arts and customs of Venezuelan society cannot be separated from its beliefs, laws, or morals.

This chapter discusses different expressions of Venezuelan fine arts and popular culture and the connections between them. When we discuss Teresa Carreño, we should not only remember that she was the foremost of all Venezuelan classical music composers. It is also important to recognize that oil wealth funded the construction of the theater named in her honor, a theater recognized for attracting world-class musical and theater talents and for showcasing globally recognized Venezuelan talents like Huascar Barradas and the Simón Bolívar National Youth Orchestra. The people who came to Venezuela to work in the oil fields brought their musical styles with them, combined them with local Venezuelan styles, and in the end created a rich and varied popular musical culture heard in all corners of the country.

Additionally, kids today attend schools named in honor of Rómulo Gallegos, author of *Doña Barbara* and Venezuelan president. Though few people outside of Venezuela know much about Venezuela's literary heritage, more have seen the most recent *telenovela* version of the novel from 2007, produced by U.S.-based Telemundo. *Doña Barbara*'s appeal is not just Venezuelan, but international. Many of the *telenovelas*, or soap operas, enjoyed by Spanish-speaking audiences in the United States and throughout Latin America are actually produced in Venezuela. *Telenovelas* definitely are popular culture, but they can be based on classic literature or tackle complex social and political issues. Popular music can make you dance and think at the same time. This chapter incorporates many elements of Venezuelan culture, from language to food, art to baseball, and from the great Venezuelan writer Andrés Bello to the internationally popular *telenovelas*.

Language

Castilian, or as it is commonly referred to, Spanish, is the official language of Venezuela. The vast majority of Venezuelans speak Spanish, while about 1 percent of citizens speak various additional indigenous languages (*Venezuela* 1993). The Spanish spoken in Venezuela, however, is certainly not the same as that spoken in Spain, as it is a product of several hundred years of linguistic mixing. Indigenous languages have had their influence, as have other European languages. The Spanish spoken in Venezuela is also not exactly the same in all parts of the country. While huge differences are not common, changes in vocabulary, accent, speed, and some unique grammatical features do appear from one region to the next. A traveler who begins in Caracas will notice changes as he or she moves west to Maracaibo, and even more if he or she moves east or south into areas where more indigenous languages are still spoken.

PRELIMINARY EXPANSION AND DOMINATION OF CASTILIAN

When Ojeada and Vespucci arrived in South America in 1499, they found a land full of indigenous peoples speaking a variety of languages that fell, generally, into three linguistic families: Caribans, Arawak, and Chibcha. The colonizers who followed Ojeada and Vespucci, however, brought a new language that, like their economics and their agriculture, soon took over the linguistic landscape. When exploration of the interior began in the 16th century, Castilian went in with the explorers.

Language has long been recognized as a force of colonization, a force as powerful as weapons or disease. When a group that is stronger militarily, economically, religiously, or politically comes into contact with a group that is weaker in those areas, the weaker group generally has to adjust and assimilate into the dominant culture.

This assimilation includes adopting the language of the dominant culture. This was certainly true of the colonizing Spanish. They came with superior organization and firepower as we noted in Chapter 2, spreading a great deal of violence and forcing the indigenous groups to change.

The significant missionary efforts of the Franciscan friars aided the spread of Spanish by the 17th century. This is the power of religious assimilation. As the Franciscans worked to "civilize" the indigenous peoples by educating them and converting them to Christianity, they also worked to teach them Castilian Spanish. By the time Don José de Oviedo y Baños published his first history of Venezuela, he did so in Castilian Spanish, in a colony that was controlled by a Spanish-speaking government and economic structure. That is not to say, however, that the Spanish spoken in the colony was the same as that brought directly from Spain. Indigenous languages and words from African tongues crept into the language as the colonization process continued.

ANDRÉS BELLO CLEANS UP THE LANGUAGE

By the middle of the 1800s, the great Venezuelan intellectual Andrés Bello thought it was high time to clean up the language in Venezuela. Concerned by the lack of discipline in rules and grammatical structures and troubled by the creep in vocabulary words and the addition of foreign words, in 1847 Bello wrote the first modern *Gramática de la lengua castellana* (Grammar of the Castilian Language). This, he hoped, would help Castilian Spanish avoid the "barbarous" fate that had befallen the woefully "corrupted" Latin (Bello 1902: 43).

Andrés Bello was born in 1781 in Caracas to a well-to-do family. He had a quick mind and great connections and was expected to rise quickly in the Spanish royal service. This plan changed, however, with the wars of independence. Bello began work with the architects of the revolution, even tutoring Simón Bolívar for a time and developing a love for the idea of the Americas as a region with an identity separate from Spain. In 1810, Bello traveled to Europe with Bolívar and eventually found work with the Chilean government in Great Britain. While in Europe, he began to write. He was prolific and wrote on a great number of subjects, including language. While we will discuss his contributions to the literary world a bit later, of interest at this point is his *Gramática de la lengua castellana* (Grammar of the Castilian Language). This was the first scientific study of Castillian Spanish ever undertaken and has been, many times, credited with the standardization of spoken Spanish. It is, in fact, the first book of rules and grammar for Spanish in Latin America and has been recognized as a significant force in beginning to mark the difference between Latin America and the Iberian Peninsula when Latin American nations worked to construct national identities independent from their Spanish-speaking mother country. Bello understood the power of language. As Amado Alonso describes in his studies of Bello, the scholar was in agreement with the French Enlightenment scholar Jean-Jacques Rosseau, who said, according to Bello, that language's "cultivation and perfection form the base of all other intellectual advances" (Alonso n.d.). Bello wrote his text while in residence at the University of Chile and intended it as a gift not only for his own nation but for the whole continent. (The text bears the subtitle "Destined for the Use of all Americans.") As the scholar Amado Alonso explains, scholars of this era felt the obligation to teach what they learned for the betterment of all, and so Bello sought to take his knowledge of language and provide a text to improve the thinking of a continent (Alonso n.d.).

The *Gramática* begins with six *nociones* (notions) in which he outlined the most important elements of the study. In brief, these are: (1) grammar is an art that all well-educated people should know; (2) it is preferable that there be a standard, learned grammar among the provinces to ensure mutual understanding; (3) the language is properly called *castellano* (Castilian) and not *español* (Spanish); (4) one cannot underestimate the importance of pure language for expressing feelings, laws, contracts, and so forth; (5) language is a collection of individual signs, known as words; and (6) correct language use is the use of words together (Bello 1902). Through these principles, Bello hoped to bring the continent together and give it a language identity equal to that of Spain.

It is not lost on Venezuelans that the man credited with standardizing the colonizer's tongue as a foundation of Latin American identity was one of their own. Venezuelans quickly recognized Bello's contributions as a scholar. The most prestigious private university in the country bears his name: the Universidad Católica Andrés Bello. Two cities are named for him, as are countless grammar and high schools. What is most significant is that Bello proved that Latin Americans were the intellectual equals of Europeans in a crucial moment in Latin American history.

MODERN SPANISH IN VENEZUELA: WOULD BELLO BE PROUD?

While Bello was concerned about the corruption of Castilian on the continent, language is a living thing that is not so easily controlled. Despite his efforts to standardize the language, in the 150 years since the publication of his *Grammar*, changes have come to the Spanish spoken in Venezuela.

The philologist Angel Rosenblat notes a whole range of vocabulary differences in modern Venezuelan Spanish from the Castilian of the Spanish Royal Academy. He notes that many frequently used words in Venezuela, including yuca (cassava), *guanábana* (custard-apple), *arepa* (cornmeal cake), and *caiman* (alligator) are of indigenous origin, and probably originally come from the Caribbean islands of the Antilles through migration. Additionally, Venezuelan indigenous tribes have added words such as *butaca* (canvas chair) to the language. Rosenblat also notes differences in vocabulary within the country, where brown sugar can be *papelón* in Caracas but *panela* in the Andes. Venezuelan slang also tends to be littered with *groserías*, or foul language. Though there are generational barriers that separate those who use colorful language and those who do not, Venezuelans generally integrate more foul language in daily conversation than what is commonly accepted in the United States.

UCAB

The Universidad Católica Andrés Bello (UCAB), named for the great 19th-century intellectual, is one of Venzuela's premier universities. The UCAB is a private university run under the direction of the Jesuit Order of the Roman Catholic Church. As such, the UCAB stands as a enduring symbol of the church's interest in education in Venezuela. The choice of Andrés Bello for the name of the university is in keeping with the UCAB's stated mission to "work for the integration of Latin America and both save and enrich its common socio-cultural patrimony." (UCAB "Historia" n.d.) Just as Bello did, the university seeks to unite diverse elements of Latin American society while promoting an interdisciplinary ideal that creates dialogue between the arts and sciences.

The UCAB was founded in 1953 during the rule of Marcos Pérez Jiménez, who repealed a law prohibiting Catholic control of universities. While the main campus is found in Caracas, the university has extensions throughout the country, one of which, in Táchira, has been converted into a full-fledged institute, the Universidad Católica de Táchira.

Andrés Bello. (Library of Congress)

Differences in modern Venezuelan Spanish are not just limited to vocabulary, however. There are some differences in pronunciation of the language, especially in Caracas and on the coast, where many Venezuelans tend to "aspirate" or drop the final "s" in words or the "d" in between vowels. Venezuelans in the Oriente speak rapidly, and they abbreviate and combine words. For example, *para alla* (over there) becomes *pa'lla*, *para adelante* (go forward) becomes *pa'lante*. This can be in stark contrast to citizens of the Andes who speak slowly (comparatively) and fully pronounce letters and words.

In addition to changes in pronunciation, travelers who move west will find that in the Andes and in the area around Maracaibo, there are those who practice the *voseo* in Spanish, an extra subject pronoun similar to the informal *tú* or "you" in informal speech. The *vos* is not unique to Venezuela, as it is common in other South and Central American nations. Generally, the *vos* is used with the second person singular of a Spanish verb, the same verb conjugation as the *tú* form, with the stress moved to the last syllable. Therefore, in the Andes, one would hear *vos hablás.* In Venezuela, however, the *maracucho* version of the *vos* is unique in that it uses the *vosotros* forms of the verbs used in Spain. In this case, in Maracaibo, one would hear *vos habláis.* In either case, the *vos* is generally used as a slightly more polite way to address friends. *Orientales* (people from the east) never use the *vosotros*, so language becomes one of the other points that define the regional identities and differences that we discussed in Chapters 1 and 2.

INDIGENOUS LANGUAGES IN VENEZUELA: LANGUAGE DOMINATION AND SURVIVAL

Earlier we mentioned that one of the most important interactions in the spread of Spanish into indigenous communities in Venezuela happened (and still happens) between missionaries and the people that they are sent to convert to Christianity. These interactions, in many cases, determine how much of their native language an indigenous community will be able to retain. One case we can look to as an example of how these contacts occur is between missionaries and the Warao Indians of the Orinoco Delta area in Eastern Venezuela.

The Warao represent a different and unusual case in Venezuela, as they survived early domination by colonizers and missionaries in the 17th and 18th centuries by retreating into the swamps of the Orinoco Delta. This strategic retreat allowed the Warao to both remain more isolated than many other indigenous groups in Venezuela and to retain many of their linguistic and cultural practices into the early 20th century. The Warao remained mostly isolated until 1912, when Catholic and Protestant missionaries began arriving in Warao territory with neither the permission nor the knowledge of the Venezuelan government. After a few years, however, the Venezuelan government decided to use the religious organizations to their advantage, seeing them as the cheapest way to "civilize" the untamed forest and people.

Missionaries established the first official missionary stations in the Orinoco Delta in the 1920s. The stations included boarding schools and hospitals. The missionaries used the schools to entice parents to send their children to the missionaries as early as possible to start the process of civilization and create Venezuelan (not indigenous) citizens, which of course entailed learning Spanish. Indeed, teaching children Spanish was a priority, as the missionaries conceived of the Warao language as a particularly "backward" language that could not express "modern" ideas (Rodriguez 2008). The missionaries were particularly unimpressed by the lack of higher order numbers in Warao and the lack of words for things like airplanes and cars. In this interaction, it seemed more important for the Warao to gain words for modern concepts than to retain words for their traditional lives. This was seen as an evolutionary process (Rodriguez 2008). The assumption that Spanish was more civilized and on a "higher" evolutionary plane makes clear which language is the dominant and preferable one. Just as the missionaries represented a superior economic force, so, too, did they wield an intellectual argument designed to convince the Warao that their language was "unevolved" and "inadequate."

When missionaries collected and compiled the stories and myths of the Warao, they reinforced the ideas about Venezuelan superiority and Warao inferiority. Those who wrote down the myths only chose to record the tales of the Warao before the time of their encounter with "civilized men." Those stories that told of the Warao's encounter' with colonists and Warao attempts to make sense of current political relations were excluded. In this way, the missionaries gave the impression that the Warao language was only good for expressing old-fashioned ideas and expressions from a time when the Warao lived apart from complex ideas and interactions and therefore did not have the language to express them (Rodriguez 2008). This meant, of course, that if the Warao wanted to be able to live in the new, more complicated, more advanced nation, they had to be able to speak the new, better language.

While this process of language domination and colonization, repeated throughout the nation, was effective, there was resistance on the part of the Warao. The Warao, despite their marginalized position, have managed to retain some hold on their language, mostly through the continued production of poems and stories that tell their history, and traditional songs, or *hoa*. In 2008, there were still more than 25,000 native speakers of Warao in the Orinoco Delta, a testament to the resilience of the Warao language.

WARAO COUNTING SYSTEM

The Warao use a quinary/vigesimal counting system that uses the number five as its base, used in cycles of 20. This system stands in contrast to the decimal system used in most European cultures, which uses the number 10 as its base, but is a shared cultural trait between the Warao and other Amerindian cultures such as Nahuatl (Aztec) and Maya. Many believe that the quinary/vigesimal systems originated in the 5 fingers of one human hand and the 20 digits found on both hands and feet. It is perhaps this belief that has led many, such as the missionaries to the Warao, to consider the system primitive.

In a quinary/vigesimal system, numbers between 1 and 5 are used to indicate similar numeric concepts as in the decimal system. However, numbers above 5 are represented as 5 + 1 (6), 5 + 2 (7), 5 + 3 (8), and so on, up until 20. After 20, numbers are represented as multiples of 20—for example, 2 × 20 (40), 5 × 20 (100), or 5 × 20 + 3 (123).

OTHER INDIGENOUS LANGUAGES

Warao is one good example of an indigenous language still spoken in Venezuela. It is far from the only one, however. Article 9 of the 1999 Venezuela Constitution recognizes 31 indigenous languages. These languages have "official status for native peoples, and must be respected throughout the territory of the Republic, as constituting part of the cultural heritage of the Nation and humanity."

The native languages referred to in the constitution, mainly fall into two language families: Arawak and Cariban. The Arawakan languages in Venezuela include Wayuú, a language spoken by nearly 300,000 people in Venezuela and Colombia. To see what Wayuú looks like, we can offer the example of the first four numbers (1, 2, 3, and 4): *wane, piana, apünüin*, and *pienchi.* Additionally, the first line of the Catholic prayer to the Virgin Mary, the Hail Mary, reads, in Wayuú: *Najachijira Maréigua pia, María* (Landsnes n.d.).

The language in the Cariban family with the largest number of speakers is Carib, which has approximately 10,000 speakers in Venezuela, Brazil, Suriname, and Guyana. In Carib, the numbers 1–4 are *o'win, oko, oruwa*, and *okupaime*, and the first line of the Hail Mary in Carib reads *Mabuiga María buíntibu labu gracia* (Language Museum, n.d.). The Chibcha language family referred to earlier seems extinct in modern Venezuela, while other languages, such as Warao, do not belong to the larger families of languages but rather are isolated linguistic examples.

THE IMPORTANCE OF ENGLISH

Another language of both linguistic and political importance in Venezuela is English. In addition to the original indigenous languages of the nation, together with the colonial contribution of Spanish, increasingly English is becoming a language of national use. Examples of the inclusion of English in Venezuelan society can be seen both through the addition of *anglicismos*, or borrowed words, from English and the overt teaching of English as a second language. In his essay, Angel Rosenblatt notes the large number of words of English origin, especially in the areas of sport, business, and industry. Some of these words such as *chequear* (to check), Rosenblatt notes, have been in use for quite some time (Rosenblatt n.d.). Others, more related to daily living, are of more recent origin: household words such as *el living, el pantry, el closet*, or the more commonly heard *okey*. Venezuelans also use *chance*, though pronounced in Spanish (chan-se), the same way English speakers use the word.

This trend of increasing use of English has been noted, and recently decried by the Chávez administration, which sees the encroachment of English as a new form of colonial domination. As MSNBC reported in February 2008, the administration launched a campaign specifically designed to reduce the use of English by government employees. In a statement, the Communications and Information Ministry spoke to the need for Venezuelans to recover Spanish words that are "threatened by sectors that have started a cultural battle for the cultural domination of our nations" ("Venezuela's Chávez Fights" 2008). As part of this effort, CANTV, the nationalized state telephone company, printed up stickers and banners that read "Say it in Spanish. Say it with pride," hoping to wean workers away from *anglicismos* such as *el staff*, *el marketing*, and *el password*.

The reality remains, however, that many Venezuelans view learning English as key to success in business and their professional careers. English is widely taught to schoolchildren in public and private schools. Private schools generally begin instruction in English for children in the first year, at the age of five. In public schools, English instruction becomes mandatory beginning in the seventh year, continuing through the end of a secondary education. With so many Venezuelans learning English, we can expect the efforts of the Venezuelan government to meet with resistance when fighting the creep of English into the Spanish used in Venezuela. As Rosenblatt notes, however, "one of the most important aspects of the new Venezuela. The language is in constant renovation and movement with the changes in the world" (Rosenblatt n.d.).

CASE STUDY: LITTLE VENICE

Language does not only refer the sounds we use to construct words but also to the words we use to convey ideas. Ideas become foundational to the construction of identity, so the words people choose imply political, social, and economic power. As we saw previously in the case of the Warao, language can be used to hold on to indigenous culture, or to erase indigenous culture. This tension over the meanings behind language decisions reaches to the 21st century in Venezuela, as we can see in the case of the country's name.

The story of Venezuela starts in 1499 when a Spanish expedition led by Alfonso de Ojeda and the mapmaker Amerigo Vespucci reached the northern shores of the South American continent. Coming aground on the hump of South America, they proceeded westward, eventually reaching the extensive inland sea now known as Lake Maracaibo. There the expedition found a community of indigenous people who had built a city of huts on stilts above the lake. Looking around, Vespucci was reminded of a certain city in his native land of Italy. Stepping forward, he declared that the newly discovered land would be known as "Veneziela," or "Little Venice." The name that Vespucci chose for the new Spanish territory tells us much about international relations, contemporary politics, and cultural conditions in Venezuela today. The word "Veneziela," a name that is at the same time both diminutive and derivative, is a name that to many Venezuelans today denies the historical and cultural uniqueness of the region. The name implies that there was nothing special enough about Venezuela to those explorers for it to merit its own name. In other places in Latin America, the local word for the land discovered was taken and adopted by the arriving Europeans as the name of the place. For example, Spaniards called the part of New Spain that corresponds with modern day Mexico "Mexico" fairly early in the colonial process. The name comes from "Mexica," the name of one of the native peoples who populated large portions of colony. In contrast, Spaniards forced Venezuelans to become a small version of somewhere else, without a name native to the people or the area. What is more, the name of the nation continued to change over time. The original "Veneziela," with the suffix *-iela*, which suggested smallness, changed to *-uela*, a suffix that insulted or put down the noun that it was attached to. When this happened, the name of the nation went from bad to worse, "Little Venice" to "Faulty Venice" or "Inadequate Venice" (Herrera Luque 1970).

Modern Venezuelans still struggle with the baggage associated in all the connotations of the label given to them by Vespucci. Writers fight to create new images, and politicians speak loudly about independence from foreign influence. In 2001, the poet Yolanda Pantin wrote of her nation that it is a "country named with the desire to subjugate it, pejorative / because one is the name that one bears" (Pantin 2004: 279). Venezuela spent much of its history, colonial or national, dominated by western (European and U.S.) economic, social, and political influences that often overlooked Venezuela's unique and rich heritage. There is, of course, much original thought and production in the Venezuelan cultural tradition to celebrate. Recovery of Venezuelan uniqueness and power in the face of U.S. and European influence in the last 25 years, therefore, can be seen as a driving force for much current cultural production and political activity in Venezuela.

We can see examples of this effort in the 1999 constitution, which brought to fruition President Hugo Chávez's drive to officially change the name of the country from the República de Venezuela (Republic of Venezuela) to the República Bolivariana de Venezuela (The Bolivarian Republic of Venezuela). This project goes to the heart of the problem of how Venezuela sees itself, and how the rest of the world sees it, in different ways. The change takes the old, derivative language, embraces it, and makes it Venezuela's own, not someone else's. The new label for the country puts the family name of Venezuela's most famous son, the Liberator Simón Bolívar, first. His name appears in adjective form, creating a new and alternate description of the nation, not as a small version of a European city, but as a follower of the man who fought for independence against those same Europeans. This new designation for the country presents the image of a leader who sought to unify South America against the influence and intervention of the industrializing Western nations. As such, it is an appropriate lens for viewing the current foreign policy of the populist and frequently confrontational president, the former General Hugo Chávez, who has declared his administration to be carrying out a "Boliviarian revolution." Indeed, Chávez, like Bello 150 years prior, understands that there is nothing neutral about language. Chávez understands, just as Bello did, that the language a nation uses says much about its identity, both political and cultural. Language conveys meanings to citizens in the nation and broadcasts multiple messages to the international community. Language is power.

REFERENCES

Alonso, Amado. n.d. "Introducción a los estudios gramaticales de Andrés Bello." http://homepages.wmich.edu/~ppastran/etexts/ABello/Gramatica_Bello.pdf.

Bello, Andres. 1902. *Gramática de la Lengua Castellana.* Paris: Roger y Chernovitz Editores.

Herrea Luque, Francisco. 1970. *Los viajeros de Indias: Ensayo de interpretación de la sociología venezolana.* Caracas: Monte Avila.

Language Musuem. n.d. "Carib." http://www.language-museum.com/encyclopedia/c/carib.php.

Landsnes, David G. n.d. "AVE MARIA in 404 lingue." http://www.christusrex.com/www1/pater/JPN-guajiro.html.

Pantin, Yolanda. 2004. *Poesía reunida 1981–2002.* Caracas: Editorial CEC.

Rodriguez, Juan Luís. 2008. "The Translation of Poverty and the Poverty of Translation in the Orinoco Delta." *Eurohistory* 55, no. 3: 417–438.

Rosenblatt, Angel. n.d. "El Castellano en Venezuela." http://www.analitica.com/BITBLIO/rosenblat/castellano.asp.

Tylor, Edward. 1958. *Primitive Culture.* New York: Harper.

Venezuela: A Country Study. 1993. Washington, DC: Library of Congress.

"Venezuela's Chávez Fights Use of English Words." 2008. MSNBC. http://www.msnbc.msn.com/id/23350305/.

Etiquette

Just six years after Bello published his *Gramática*, Manuel Carreño published his *Manual de urbanidad y buenas maneras* (Manual of Urbanity and Good Manners). Though language may change, Carreño insisted that good manners are a constant. The fact that his *Manual* remained in print in 2009 after its first publication in 1853 suggests he may have had a point. Though some of Carreño's advice seems out of date (the overwhelming majority of Venezuelans have no use for advice about how to treat domestic servants), other counsel, on relationships with in-laws, for example, is always wise (Carreño 2005). The essence of much of Carreño's instruction still influences Venezuelan etiquette. Carreño argued that adhering to the details of formality, paying close attention to social obligations, choosing language carefully in public, and maintaining appropriate relationships inside the home produced the respect necessary for society to function. Respect remains a bedrock Venezuelan virtue, even though class-bound rules Carreño describes often do not.

RESPECT AND THE FAMILY

Venezuelans understand the family in much broader terms than the nuclear unit common in the United States. Venezuelan families incorporate parents, children, uncles, aunts, cousins, grandparents, godparents, and even coaches and neighbors in some cases. The Venezuelan concept of family, as for many Latino cultures, is malleable and not bound by blood relationships but open to manipulation according to circumstances. For example, a child could be raised by his mother as well as the neighbor.

Both women are mothers to him, and the children of the neighbor are his siblings in all but blood. One of the authors of this text married into a Venezuelan family. That author, as far as she is concerned, has two mothers-in-law, one father-in-law (the blood one is deceased), five brothers-in-law, and one sister-in-law combining all siblings. Three months after she and her husband married, a respected elder neighbor asked when she was going to give him grandchildren. The blood relationship does not matter. The broad understanding of family matters. All elders take seriously their responsibilities toward children, blood or not. Elders provide love and material support, serve as mentors, and teach respect. That also means that children can expect discipline, if appropriate, from all elders, not just parents.

Respect and loving formality mark relationships between parents and children, younger people and their elders. When children of any age greet their parents and elders they ask that person to convey God's blessing:

"*Bendición, Mamá.*" (Blessing, Mama.)
"*Diós te bendiga, hijo.*" (May God bless you, child.)
"*Bendición, Tío.*" (Blessing, Uncle.)
"*Diós te bendiga, hija.*" (May God bless you, child.)

When Venezuelans who live away from home call, the first phrase out of their mouths is "*Bendición.*" Not asking for the blessing conveys disrespect not just to God but to the elders. When Venezuelan parents discipline their children (and corporal punishment is not unusual) the most common reasons are ones associated with respect—flagrant disobedience and talking back are all understood as forms of disrespect not tolerated by parents. The phrase that commonly accompanies the discipline is "¡*Respeta, pues!*" (Have respect!).

Venezuelan elders believe that by instilling respect in children, elders establish foundations for respectful relationships to exist beyond the family. Venezuelans use formal titles to remember respect. Parents certainly expect children to treat teachers with respect. The common form of address for grade school teachers is *maestro* or *maestra* (teacher). Students address high school and college professors with *profesor* or *profesora* (professor). Depending on the context and the relationship, the diminutive *profe* could either demonstrate respectful affection or disrespect.

Greetings combine Venezuelan insistence on respect with affection. A firm handshake is always appropriate between men and between men and professional women. If a woman and a man know each other, even in a professional setting, it is not unusual to add a brief kiss or cheek touch to the right cheek to the handshake. Men and women who consider themselves friends can add a brief hug. Women can always add the hug and cheek kiss to greetings with other women. Men who are friends add the backslap hug. Concepts of personal space in conversations in public are similar to concepts in the United States; appropriate distances between conversation participants are similar. Venezuelans can be comfortable, however, with reduced personal space when they become more animated in conversations, despite the fact that Venezuelans use hand gestures to emphasize speech more frequently than North Americans do.

ETIQUETTE AND GROWING UP

We began Chapter 5 with a description of the rituals associated with burial. Many of the traditions associated with etiquette revolve around the broad definition of the Venezuelan family, the life cycle, and food, a topic we will discuss in depth later in this chapter.

When a baby is born, traditionally women visit the new mother in the hospital or at home shortly after the birth. They always bring a small gift. In Caracas and in other large cities, it is becoming just as common for women to simply call the new mother and offer congratulations. New fathers have their own tradition, and this one has not changed. In the hospital, instead of offering cigars to everyone as fathers traditionally did in the United States, Venezuelan fathers offer alcohol and toast to *los miaos*, or the baby's first pee, a sign of health. Fathers and their guests do not hide the fact that they are drinking alcohol in the hospital. It is not unusual for hospital staff to participate in *los miaos*. To turn down the drink would be both a sign of disrespect and bad luck for the baby.

Wishing the baby good health is very important. While in other nations it may be more common for visitors to comment on a new baby's beauty, in Venezuela compliments to the new child more often revolve around his or her vigor and well-being. A comment such as "*¡es tan gordita!*" (she's such a chubby little thing!) is meant to be taken both affectionately and as a commentary on the baby's obvious good health. A baby who is eating well is a happy, healthy baby to be praised. Words like *gordita*, then, can be used as nicknames for children for many years.

According to Catholic tradition, parents ask particularly honored family members or friends to serve as the child's godparents. Godparenthood is not only symbolic but a responsibility godparents and godchildren take seriously, as godparents assume extra moral responsibility for the well-being of the child. Symbolic of that relationship is the gift of an *azabache*. An *azabache* is a small black rock that mothers

---

AZABACHE

The use of *azabache*, or jet, as an amulet is not unique to Venezuela. Indeed, the use of jet dates to prehistoric times. The first known amulets shaped out of the material date from 13,000 BC. Jet is used for luck and good health around the world.

Jet is a semiprecious gem that is made of fossilized wood. Jet is deep black in color, hence the English expression "jet black." Jet has been considered to have positive magical properties for thousands of years. This may be because of jet's unique qualities: jet is warm to the touch, conducts electricity, and is flammable. For those who believe in the power of jet, the gem confers long life and a cure for depression. In Latin America, *azabache* is particularly valued as a protection against the evil eye, violence, and bad luck. In Spain, Brazil, and other parts of the Latin world, the gem is carved into a *higa*, an amulet shaped in the form of a hand with the fingers making the sign of the cross.

tie around the left ankle of their babies to prevent the negative effects of *"mal de ojo,"* or the evil eye. Many people throughout Latin America think that the excessive envy of others can cause physical illness in small children. In Venezuela and other Caribbean basin countries with an African heritage, people believe that an *azabache* can protect babies from *mal de ojo*. When the *azabache* is a gift from the godmother, it symbolizes her moral obligation to project the child from harm. Godparenthood also ties the godparents and the parents together. Once united in the ritual relationship, individuals no longer refer to each other with their proper names but as *compadre* and *comadre*, and they pay extra attention to their mutual well-being.

A child's circle of fictive kin can grow with each major milestone in the Catholic life cycle—first communion, confirmation, marriage. With each ceremony, gift giving is common. Families host celebrations in which etiquette dictates that the family of the child provide food, drink, and sometimes small *recuerdos* (gifts) to all of the guests. Some major life cycle celebrations combine sacred and secular traditions. Venezuelans are rapidly adopting the Mexican *quinceañera* tradition, or huge parties to celebrate a young woman's coming of age at the age of 15. A *quince* begins with a Catholic mass and culminates in a dinner and dance in which the young woman of the hour and her attendants dance a carefully choreographed first dance. The gifts the girl's godparents give her symbolize their ongoing relationship with her. The *arras*, or gold coins, which are given to the girl, represent the godparents' blessing and symbolize good fortune. Other gifts are consistent with Venezuelans' beauty-driven culture; breast implants are becoming an increasingly common *quince* gifts from parents to daughter.

ETIQUETTE, FAMILY, AND THE DAILY RHYTHMS OF LIFE

Venezuelan families are remarkably close. While it is becoming unusual for parents to have more than two children, the extended family, blood or not, remains foundational in Venezuelan life. The emphasis on respect does not create emotional distance. On the contrary, Venezuelan families tend to demonstrate affection more effusively, and more physically, than what might be traditional in many North American families. Grown children curl up next to their mothers so mothers can groom children they did when the children were small. Grown sons kiss fathers. Visiting close friends and family are opportunities to demonstrate affection. Grown children, cousins, nieces, and nephews living in the same town as elders visit elders unannounced to make sure that the elders are alright and to chat. Not calling in anticipation of a visit is not considered rude. Hosts, kin or not, of course, offer food and coffee. To not offer food and coffee is a way to deliver an insult and demonstrate disrespect. Kin living far away from a most honored family member try to find time at least once a year to visit for a few days. If that honored family member lives near a beach, he or she can expect visits around carnival, Holy Week, during the Christmas and New Year holidays, and in August when people commonly take vacations. Venezuelans do not see such open demonstrations of affection or visits as inappropriate or a burden. For Venezuelans, such common demonstrations of affection reinforce the ties that bind family together.

It is not unusual for grown children to live with their parents much longer than is common in the United States. Economic realities mean that if children can go to college they attend college in their hometown and live at home. Even after graduation, children stay at home until they have established a more stable economic foundation, even after marriage. After children move out of the house, and even if they live long distances from parents, families make every effort to come together at least once a year either for Christmas or the New Year. New Year's Eve is a major family holiday in Venezuela. During the weeks around Christmas and through New Year's, families prepare traditional holiday foods in anticipation of the visits and as gifts for friends. Holiday favorites are *pan de jamón* and *hallacas*. *Pan de jamón* is a sweet bread with ham, olives, and raisins braided inside. *Hallacas*, as we discuss in the food section, are roughly equivalent to Mexican tamales. Inside plantain leaves (instead of corn husks) is a corn meal *masa*, pulled pork, olives, and other ingredients. Every family's *pan de jamón* and *hallaca* recipe is a bit unique. When someone brings a family *hallacas*, the host offers at least coffee in return and another food gift if possible. The only respectable *hallaca* is a homemade *hallaca*. Venezuelans never offer as a gift a *hallaca* they have not made.

On New Year's Eve, many hands are in the kitchen preparing the huge feast for all of the gathered family members. The kitchen, as it is so often, becomes the gathering place and the heart of all family activity marked by laughter and tremendous affection. Dinner begins at approximately 10 p.m. On the table, in addition to everything else, are enough grapes for each person to have 12 grapes representing the 12 months of the year. As midnight approaches, the grapes are distributed and the toasting begins. Each person, in addition to offering a toast, slowly eats their grapes and offers a wish with each grape. The feast culminates at midnight with a great toast, hugs, and kisses. Then everyone leaves the house to wish all of the neighbors a happy New Year. The festivities in the street can last well into the wee hours of the morning. Neighborhoods host additional events, like softball games and street carnivals for children, during the day on New Year's Eve or New Year's Day to reinforce the deep ties between friends and neighbors. As with everything, family is not just about blood but about all the ties that bind. The etiquette and celebrations associated with Christmas and New Year's reinforce those ties. Because Christmas season continues through Epiphany, or 12 days after Christmas, Venezuelans have much nationally respected time to embrace family.

ETIQUETTE, FAMILY, AND DATING

Just as family play an important role in other areas of life, so too does the Venezuelan family play a large role in dating and courtship. To a larger extent than in other nations such as the United States, young Venezuelans expect members of their families to be involved in their social lives and in their love lives, especially as they decide who they will settle down with and marry.

Young peoples' social networks are very commonly composed of family members. Brothers, sisters, and cousins often go out together in groups to parks, to cafés, and to clubs. These groups of extended family provide a ready-made group of friends for young people to hang out with as well as providing a sense of security for parents when younger children are ready to venture out. Since teenagers will often meet members of the opposite sex in the company of their extended family, it is logical then that their choice of boyfriend or girlfriend will gain the approval of those cousins or other family members. Venezuelan young people use social media (Facebook, for example) as frequently as young people in the United States do. Just like in the United States, Venezuelan youth use Facebook not only to communicate with "friends" but to keep in touch with boyfriends and girlfriends. "Friends" lists frequently include siblings and cousins, so even virtually the family is part of the courtship process.

It is also very common for older family members to meet potential mates very early in the friendship. Especially where the couple feels that the relationship could get serious and lead to marriage, men and women expect to meet parents and family members, and family members expect to be included in the courtship process. Parents and families generally expect that sons and daughters will find a mate from a family with similar social standing and from the same ethnic group. Once a child's choice of mate has been approved by the family, that person becomes family too.

CLOTHING

As we have noted, Venezuelans (like most Latin Americans) tend to be formal people publicly, and that certainly extends to how Venezuelans dress when they go out in public, preceded, of course, by close attention to personal hygiene. In public, men do not wear flip flops and low-slung shorts, but they can wear jeans or more informal clothes when they run errands. For women, there is no public "dress down" occasion where one can wear less makeup or wear running shoes. Women make a point to arrange their hair and put on makeup even to do simple errands like going to the market. High heels are appropriate for nearly all occasions. All clothes must be carefully pressed, including the uniforms children wear to public and private schools. Because of Venezuelan clothing etiquette, it is usually fairly easy to spot people who are not Venezuelan—they are the ones wearing comfortable shoes.

PARTIES AND OTHER GATHERINGS, FORMAL OR OTHERWISE

No matter what, in all contexts, if one is offered a cup of coffee one has to accept. Coffee for Venezuelans is symbolic of hospitality. One can never reject hospitality. Likewise, any food proffered in any context must also be accepted. At the table, if someone asks to pass the salt or other table condiments do not pass the condiment from one hand to the other, but place the salt in a place that can be reached. It is commonly thought that those who pass condiments from hand to hand will end up fighting. How food is served varies. Some homes serve food "family style," when people at the table serve themselves from bowls. In other houses, the hosts or mothers place the food on the plate of each individual. In either case, it is most appropriate to eat some of everything. If enough food is left after all have eaten, it is appropriate to ask for seconds. If one is invited to a party and takes a covered dish and any of the dish remains, do not expect to take home the leftovers. Asking for them is perceived as extremely rude. The only faux pas worse than asking for the leftover food is asking for an unfinished bottle of wine or alcohol. However, if the host offers a plate of multiple leftovers, you must accept because rejecting food is always perceived as disrespectful.

TIME AND TRAFFIC

Venezuelans are not punctual people. The word *ahorita*, roughly translated as "now," more or less, best encompasses the Venezuelan concept of time. If someone says they will arrive *ahorita* that could mean 15 minutes, an hour, or three hours. Certainly a party scheduled to begin at an appointed hour will not begin until at least a half an hour after the appointed time. Arriving on time is actually considered improper. Venezuelans' flexible concept of time is actually practical when one considers traffic in most Venezuelan cities. Traffic can easily make simple errands last hours. One can make a commitment to arrive at a particular point at a particular hour, but traffic can easily make the *ahorita* concept of time a practical reality.

The traffic generated by all of the nation's cars presents another series of problems, that of etiquette on the road. Non-Venezuelan drivers are most frustrated by Venezuelans lack of respect for traffic signals. No one stops for a yellow light, and Venezuelans run red lights regularly. Many busy intersections, even in the largest cities also lack traffic signals, and an understood rule of "no guts no glory" governs these intersections. In busy traffic, a driver with more guts will creep out to break the flow of cars moving in the other direction, and that will last until the driver at the cross street decides a suitable interval has passed and noses his car or truck out.

Buses are part of all the traffic, and many Venezuelans ride public transportation. On the bus it is still considered appropriate to give up one's seat for an older rider, a pregnant woman, or someone traveling with small children. How to ask the bus to stop depends on custom in any given city. Most routes have commonly accepted bus stops, even though those stops may not be marked. The driver may shout the name of the stop and someone wishing to get off at that stop loudly repeats the stop's name. If the driver does not shout the name of a stop, it is acceptable for a rider to shout "*parada, por favor*" (stop, please) and the driver will stop as he is able. In Ciudad Bolívar, riders clap loudly twice to ask for a stop. For buses as well as cars, the flexible concept of time makes practical sense as traffic and multiple stops can make short trips last an hour or more.

Carreño defined urbanity as the accumulation of rules that one has to observe to communicate dignity, decorum, and elegance in actions and in words and to demonstrate benevolence, care, and respect that are owed to others (Carreño 2005: 46). As hurried and chaotic as life has become for Venezuelans, they still hew reasonably close to Carreño's principles. Those are pretty fair principles to use as guideposts in life, in Venezuela or otherwise.

ETIQUETTE AND LANGUAGE
FOR PROFESSIONALS

As noted earlier, respect for others is highly valued in Venezuelan society. This emphasis on courtesy and formality is especially noticeable in the use of language in professional contexts. Formal titles, for example, that demonstrate respect are expected in most business or government settings. Unlike in many informal North American settings, professionals should never be referred to by first name. At a minimum, professionals should be referred to as *Señor* + (last name) for men or *Señora* or *Señorita* + (last name) for women. There is no word in Spanish that is the equivalent of "Ms." The difference between *Señora* (Mrs.) and *Señorita* (Miss) has traditionally been married status. However, in modern times, since the suffix *-ita* is diminutive, it is common to refer to any woman over the age of 30 as *Señora* regardless of her marital status.

It is also preferred to refer to most professionals with a college degree as *Licenciado* or *Licenciada* (graduate). *Doctor* can apply to someone who is a medical doctor or to someone who is in charge of a government entity or business; if a contact is an engineer or an attorney, it is appropriate to use their title of *Ingeniero* or *Abogado*. It is always best to use a formal title in Venezuelan professional contexts to avoid unintended disrespect. Additionally, visitors from North America (who may be more used to informal communications) should be prepared to present themselves with any relevant professional titles to which they are entitled. Business cards, letters, and other messages should contain this information so that all involved will have all relevant information necessary to communicate politely.

For professionals who will be working in Venezuela, it is advisable to learn as much Spanish as possible before beginning work in the country. This is not only advisable from a practical standpoint—as many of the business, government, and educational institutions publish materials and information only in Spanish—but also as a sign of respect for the nation's culture. Efforts by non-Venezuelans, especially North Americans, to speak Spanish are greatly appreciated, even if the speaker's accent is terrible and the Spanish is very bad. While many upper-class Venezuelans are themselves bilingual in English or another language, they will greatly appreciate the effort of the speaker to acknowledge their country's native tongue. Professionals who carry business cards should be sure to have one side of their card translated into Spanish, and when presenting their card in Venezuela, they should be sure to do so with the Spanish side up.

Efforts, such as learning Spanish, will help foreign professionals in Venezuela cultivate contacts in country, an activity that is of utmost importance. As in many Latin American nations, Venezuelans, especially from older generations, prefer to do business with people they know well and are comfortable with. Being able to speak the language will help develop the relationships necessary to be successful in many contexts.

Developing a network of contacts in Venezuela is a long-term enterprise. Those intending to work in business, government, or research should be prepared to spend a significant amount of time getting to know members of their professional community in order to build credibility and reputation. This will increase a professional's chances of success in their field. Venezuelans value face-to-face contact and would, in general, prefer to get to know new colleagues through meetings and conferences rather than through electronic communication. While younger generations are becoming more comfortable with electronic media, attention should be paid both to in-person encounters as well as to follow-up touches such as thank-you notes in order to build long-term relationships. It is then important to remember that in many cases, respect and trust will have been placed with the individual, not necessarily with the company or the organization. For this reason, it is best for businesses to maintain the same professional contact who originally made the connections in Venezuela (Katz 2008).

REFERENCES

Carreño, Manuel. 2005. *Manual de urbanidad y buenas maneras.* Bogotá: Panamericana Editorial.

Katz, Lothar. 2008. "Venezuela." *Negotiating International Business.* Booksurge. http://www.booksurge.com/.

Literature

Rómulo Gallegos is certainly the most well-known of all Venezuelan authors. His most famous work, *Doña Bárbara*, is a must read for all Venezuelan school children and common fare in university-level Spanish language literature courses in the United States, too. Latin American film buffs know the 1943 version of the book made by Mexican movie master Fernando de Fuentes with the beautiful María Félix in the title role. Venezuela, however, has a long and rich tradition of literature that goes well beyond that classic novel.

ANDRÉS BELLO: WRITER, PHILOSOPHER, JURIST, EDUCATOR, ALL-AROUND INTELLECTUAL HERO

Intellectual and creative activity marked the era of Venezuelan independence. One of the most important literary figures in Venezuela and Latin America was Andrés Bello. We have already mentioned Bello in the context of his contributions to the standardization of Spanish as a language. This, however, is not the limit of his contributions. Bello was always a well-rounded renaissance man, typical of the writer-statesman that is such a familiar figure in Latin America. Bello was a great poet, writing first neoclassical poetry that describes the beauty of the plants and animals of his native land. The most famous of these poems is the *Silvas Americanas* (*American Woods*) that he wrote in the years between 1826 and 1827. This collection of poems sings the praises of country life with real depth of feeling and love for Venezuela.

Bello's contributions, however, go far beyond poetry and language. In 1823 Bello published an entire *Biblioteca Americana* filled with essays on every subject ranging from poetry to science, history to art, showing the breadth of his knowledge. In addition, Bello wrote the first detailed standard textbook on international law, titled *Principios de derecho internacional* (*Principals of International Law*), for which he has been called the founder of Latin American international law (Helguera 1994). For his contributions to the language, to literature, to the law, and to all intellectual pursuits in Venezuela, Bello is considered a true hero of independence.

THE 19TH CENTURY AND INTELLECTUAL AUTONOMY

Andrés Bello's death in 1865 left a void in the Venezuelan literary world. His legacy, however, was not limited to his contributions poetic and legal forms, but is better understood in terms of defining Venezuelan intellectual autonomy in a Latin American context. Nineteenth-century authors followed his intellectual legacy. We have already noted that Manuel Carreño's 1853 *Manual de urbanidad y buenas maneras* rapidly became a Latin American bestseller and remains a popular guide to etiquette. More important in the conversations about politics and state formation were the newspapers. Throughout the middle decades of the 19th century, a dedicated group of highly educated intellectuals publicly debated the important issues of the day in the press and through the publication of scholarly monographs. The Sociedad Económica de Amigos del País (Economic Society of the Friends of the Nation) was at the heart of said intellectual activity. Such societies, designed to promote the material progress in countries, were not new by the time President Paez created the Caracas chapter in 1829 (Pacheco Troconis 2003). Similar societies began in Spain in the late 18th century for similar purposes, though history (and Napoleon) did not allow said societies much success at that time. Society members' definition of a modern Venezuela became clear in the topics of the books they wrote; topics included the state of education, the lack of roads and the economic consequences of said problem, navigation, mathematics, mineralogy, banking and currency, property rights, agriculture, population and immigration policy, geography, and history for the purpose of creating a modern, educated, autonomous Venezuela (Pino Iturrita 1993: 19). Newspapers provided another vehicle for intellectual discourse on Venezuelan modernity in editorial, essay, and sometimes literary forms. The most important of those newspapers were *El Copiador*, *La Oliva*, *La Bandera Nacional*, *El Liberal*, and *El Venezolano* published by die-hard Venezuelan Liberal leaders Leocadio Guzmán and Tomás Lander.

The diversity of ideas about what Venezuela should and could be politically and economically fascinated scholars; one group's vision of modernity was not necessarily shared by all. The Economic Society of the Friends of the Countries and many of the newspaper editors argued that modern Venezuela's future lay clearly with a more complete economic relationship with the United States and western European nations. Fermín Toro (1806–1865) argued that all that was Western (U.S. and European) was not necessarily positive. In *Ideas y necesidades, Europa y América* and *Reflexiones sobre la ley del 10 de abril de 1834*, Toro suggested that if Venezuelan leaders tried to adopt too quickly Western political and economic constructs and forsake Venezuelan constructs, then conflict might ensue. Industrialization in Europe, he noted, had not brought universal economic and social benefits. Impending imperialism might do more harm than good to Venezuela and other Latin American nations (Pino Iturrita 1993: 19–20).

While political scientists and other critics might look back at Toro's writing and determine that he was absolutely prescient, the writing of most 19th-century intellectuals sided with the theories proposed by the society and the newspaper editors and their views about modern Venezuela's future. By the late 19th century, the challenge faced by prolific intellectuals was how to understand Venezuela as modern when so much about Venezuela was not modern when measured against Western standards. We discussed the late 19th-century philosophy of positivism more completely in Chapter 5. Positivists tried to minimize the contributions of people of color, indigenous or African, to Venezuela. They clearly argued that urban was to rural as civilization (modern) was to barbarism. Though Rómulo Gallegos wrote in the 20th century, his writing belies the profound influence of Venezuelan positivism, despite Gallegos's occasional nods toward Toro-style skepticism of the United States and western Europe. Gallegos—author, politician, ideologue—wrote *Doña Bárbara* in 1929, hoping to provide a story for the nation to follow: an optimistic story of how rational thinking and modernization could help Venezuelans escape their "barbarous" and "uncivilized" past and move forward into the 20th century.

Gallegos's hero and symbol of rational thinking and modernization was Santos Luzardo (a name derived from the words for "saint" and "light"), a recently graduated lawyer from the Central University of Venezuela in Caracas. Santos, the man of reason, Christianity, education, civilization, urbanization, and progress, returns to his family home on the southern plains to find the ranch taken over by an evil and troubled woman called Doña Bárbara (whose name derives from the word for "barbarism"). She represents irrationality by virtue of her control over men, through her implied communion with pagan spirits, her connection to the land and wilderness, and immoral sexual behavior because she bore a child out of wedlock. While these two are the main characters of the piece, there are other persons of interest in the novel. These include: Marisela, the daughter of Doña Bárbara, who represents the salvageable, innocent raw material in Venezuela who may yet be saved from corruption, and Juan Primito, a worker on the ranch who represents the superstition and ignorance of the majority of "native" Venezuelans. The final key character is Mister Danger, an American who speaks horrible Spanish and shows contempt for all the Venezuelan characters. In this, Mister Danger stands in for all the Westerners who show up and automatically assume that they are better than the "ignorant natives."

It goes without saying that in the end, Santos drives Doña Bárbara away, gets the ranch back, and wins the girl, thereby proving that civilization triumphs over barbarism. Venezuela (in the person of sweet, innocent Marisela) is saved and led down the proper path. But if we take a closer look, we can see that the story of the novel and the author have more to tell us than that. When Gallegos chose to have the barbarous wild personified by a woman, he incorporated one of Venezuela's oldest cultural and religious traditions. Any visitor to Caracas can tell you that one of the most interesting statues (or disturbing, depending on your outlook) on the way into the city is the statue of the indigenous goddess María Lionza.

María Lionza is the defender the wilderness and the jungle, the poor and the marginalized. Since the time of the Spanish Conquest, the goddess has served as a protective figure of the land and nation. In the famous statue, she is depicted naked, astride a tapir defiantly hoisting a pelvic bone over her head. Though many Native American religions incorporate goddesses, in all of South America María Lionza is the only central female goddess of any native religion.

The representation of women as agents of chaos, representative of irrationality and sexuality, tied to the land and the body (as opposed to the mind), is not confined to the pages of Gallegos's novel. Indeed this theme can be found throughout Venezuelan society. Maybe this is part of why there was such a strong urge to reject the barbarous wilderness in the early 20th century. Rationality, technology, and modernization were the way and were the province of men. It is ironic, therefore, that in Gallegos's novel, Mister Danger, the representative of the imperial powers (who introduced the new modernity and technology), is an ally of the barbaric woman, Doña Bárbara. Gallegos and many Venezuelan intellectual and political leaders held ambivalent attitudes about Venezuela's relationship with the modern, civilized, and industrialized West (the United States and western Europe). On one hand, leaders

---

HUGO CHÁVEZ AND "MISTER DANGER"

One indication of the importance of the novel *Doña Bárbara* as a cultural touchstone was Hugo Chávez's constant use of the title "Mister Danger" (a reference to the character in *Doña Bárbara*) as a nickname for U.S. President George W. Bush. Bush was a frequent target of Chávez on his television program *Aló Presidente*, where Chávez often attacked him for the invasion of Iraq and for promoting free trade policies in Latin America. Calling Bush "Mister Danger" was Chávez's shorthand to suggest that the U.S. president was crafty yet arrogant, ignorant, violent, and untrustworthy. Emphasizing his comparison, Chávez, in one famous episode of his program on April 10 of 2006, spoke directly to Bush: "You don't know much about history, you don't know much about anything. A great ignorance is what you've got. You're an ignorant Mr. Danger . . . you're a donkey, Mr. Danger." This last was repeated in English (presumably underlining the point that Bush would not understand the message in Spanish).

like Gallegos craved the benefits of civilization, everything that Santos Luzardo represented, and detested all things barbaric. That said, Gallegos and others like him did not want to give up Venezuelan uniqueness—local culture and knowledge—in the process of modernization. Perhaps the message of *Doña Bárbara* is that the ideal path to civilization is not to follow the American model but to create the Venezuelan hero who embraces the civilized, educated world, but with a unique Venezuelan perspective. Santos Luzardo went home to tame the Venezuelan wilderness to make it productive. He did not turn his back on it or build a highway over it.

WOMEN WRITING THE 20TH CENTURY AND BEYOND

Gallegos wrote female characters as archetypes—characters that reminded readers of ideas. Sometimes the ideas implicit in the archetypes were gendered (women as irrational sexuality), and sometimes the ideas (barbarism) were not. In short, Gallegos used women to write about ideas; he did not write about women. Three 20th-century women writers, Teresa de la Parra, Antonia Palacios, and Yolanda Pantin, strongly suggest that becoming modern means rethinking gender roles. Each in their own way write about the struggle implicit in the limitations placed upon women as women. They are close observers of the consequences of race and class in society. They understand that all three categories—race, class, and gender—shape how all Venezuelans experience life in different ways. These three authors cannot understand modern Venezuela without being realistic.

Teresa de la Parra

Teresa de la Parra wrote during the period central to the creation of the modern Venezuelan state. Parra was born in 1889 and raised in the context of the debates about modernity, during which positivism became the dominant intellectual construct. Parra spent her early years on a ranch outside of Caracas before leaving with the family for Spain as a young woman. After the children completed their educations, the family returned to Caracas. Once they were back in Venezuela, Parra noticed a change. She felt a huge distance between herself and her mother and her grandmother—a distance in generation and perspective. In an autobiographical note to a friend, Parra said that her mother and grandmother were from another time, one where all women were extremely religious, shy, and uneducated. Parra was never like that, and neither were her friends. The new young women had a "new mentality" that meant that they didn't have to live with the same customs and prejudices as their parents. Parra and women like her read books, had their own opinions, had new ideas about who they could marry, and were not as devout in their religious observances (Pantin and Torres 2003).

All of these ideas show up in Parra's novels, *Ifigenia: diario de una señorita que escribió porque se fastidiaba* (*Ifigenia: Diary of a Young Girl Who Wrote Because She*

Was Bored) (1924) and *Las memorias de Mamá Blanca* (*Mamá Blanca's Memories*) (1929). *Ifigenia* is the tale of a young woman who returns home from France when her father dies. She is of that new, modern generation, educated in Europe, full of ideas of marrying for love, thinking for herself, and the importance of reading and education. She is naïve and sheltered, and she is completely unprepared for the shock of her traditional grandmother and aunt upon her return to Caracas. They expect her to be a traditional girl, shy, religious, and retiring. She never gets to leave the house, except to go to church. This, of course, is why she is so bored, and why she starts to write. Ifigenia sulks for a while, until her family decides that she can amuse herself by looking for an acceptable husband. In the end, the novel is a small tragedy. Ifigenia is forced by her family to choose between a traditionally "acceptable" husband who is overbearing and mean, who does not think she should speak, much less read, and who she really does not love, and a man who has more modern notions about love and relationships. She has a chance to run away with the man she truly wants, but she fails in her convictions, choosing to stay in the safe but loveless relationship.

Teresa de la Parra received much criticism for *Ifigenia*, but the novel was wildly popular with the younger generation. Traditionalists of the day worried the novel would give young girls dangerous ideas about love and marriage. Especially devout Catholic figures of the Venezuelan state expressed deep concern for the moral values that the novel expressed. Today, authors, especially women authors in Venezuela, see the novel as an important contribution to the Venezuelan literary canon because of its full characterization of women, one that does not picture them as dolls but as complete emotional and intellectual people.

Parra's second novel was much better received and continued to explore the process of creating a modern nation from the perspective of a young girl. In *Memorias de Mama Blanca*, a woman remembers what it was like growing up on a ranch outside the city and how different it was from the city of the present day and the modern world of the early 20th century. What makes this novel especially interesting is how different it is from Gallegos's novel about a rural location. Gallegos shows all the characters in his book as archetypes of civilization or barbarism, not as real people. In *Mama Blanca*, Parra lets the reader in to see what the people see and feel. The novel, like *Ifigenia*, is narrated by the young girl who is the main character, Blancanieves. We see through her eyes how the children play and love and observe the world around them. We also see how much Blancanieves (Snow White) does not understand how her mother could have saddled her with such a name, hates having her hair done to conform to traditional ideals of beauty, and is confused by racism and class structure. Gallegos's novel is a big novel, with big ideas. Parra's novel is more intimate, about the small things that made rural life, as seen through the eyes of a child.

Teresa de la Parra was, for a long time, the "token woman" author that everyone referred to in Venezuelan literature, the female author so good she could not be ignored. She took advantage of that position, however. During her lifetime, she gave a lecture on "The Influence of Women in Forging the American Soul"—citing women all the way back to the Spanish Queen Isabel and Cortés's slave Marina (Parra 1991:

471). A pioneer for women as well as a great author, she stepped in at a time when Venezuelan society was changing and introduced a woman's voice into the ongoing discussions on what it meant to be a nation.

Antonia Palacios

Teresa de la Parra was a child of privilege and, in part, her ability to publish in the early 20th century was due in part to her privileged background—she had money and clout that lower-class women did not have and, therefore, Parra could push to have her voice heard. Other female authors were not so fortunate. For many, the development of a community of writers has had much to do with female writers' success. Antonia Palacios is representative of that process. Overcoming a difficult childhood and lack of formal education, Palacios grew to become not only one of the most important writers of her generation but a key mentor of young authors in the second half of the 20th century.

Born and raised in Caracas, Palacios's childhood was difficult because her father's epilepsy caused lost income and familial economic instability. Her desire to write came as a result of her need to exorcise what she described as the "ghosts" of that childhood marked by poverty and illness. In the 1920s, however, due to family connections, Palacios had occasion to meet the important Venzuelan authors Miguel Otero Silva, Arturo Uslar Pietri, Pablo Rojas Guardia, and María Teresa Castillo. These intellectuals encouraged the young woman's literary aspirations. Through this support, Palacios learned the value of having writers as mentors. This was a lesson that she applied later in her life.

In 1932, Palacios married the author and publicist Carlos Eduardo Frías, who was also supportive of his wife's desire to write. Palacios's marriage gave her the opportunity to travel. When Frías was named to the National Delegation to France in 1936, Palacios met the great Latin American poets Pablo Neruda and César Vallejo. This time would be very important in her literary career. After this point, she began a flurry of literary activity, publishing articles and papers in magazines and newspapers across Europe. She also began to write novels. Upon the couple's return to Venezuela, between 1939 and 1945 Palacios served actively in the women's cultural movement, serving as an officer on various national committees. In 1945 she traveled to Havana and met with the great Cuban author Alejo Carpentier.

Palacios wrote her most famous work, *Ana Isabel, una niña decente* (*Ana Isabel, A Decent Girl*), during this time period. Like her other early stories, this semiautobiographical novel provides the reader with a window into the formative decades of the 20th century. Ana Isabel, an eight-year-old girl, observes life in Caracas as it grew larger and more cosmopolitan in its customs and as family practices began to change. Palacios brings the reader into the normal spaces occupied by a young Venezuelan woman of the middle class: the home, the school, and the church. The reader sees how the connections between these spaces, like the rules that go with them, trap the young girl.

One key technique that makes the novel stand out is how Palacios uses the protagonist's innocence and awakening consciousness to explore the inequities and social problems of the period. Ana Isabel explores such questions as: what makes a girl "decent" and why is there such pressure to be a "decent girl"? The reader is invited into the text, to laugh and cry for the young girl as she struggles to understand the mystifying rules. It is this connection that the novel forges with its readers that has made it so popular for so long. The way that Ana Isabel explores, and in many ways rebels against, the boundaries created for her by society is reminiscent of Ifigenia, who similarly chafed at the arbitrary rules of gender and class.

Both authors, Palacios and Parra, also explore the emphasis on outward physical beauty in women and how those rules constrain the movements and choices for women. Much of *Ifigenia* focuses on the importance of social etiquette and the constriction of a woman's free movement (and Ifigenia's objection to these constrictions). Additionally, as in *Ana Isabel*, Parra's other famous work, *Memorias de Mama Blanca*, also uses a child's perspective to illustrate how female children are trained in the importance of beauty as they mature. Blancanieves, Parra's protagonist, is taught to agonize over her hair, while Ana Isabel, like Ifigenia, mourns the loss of her freedom.

In 1975, Palacios became the first woman to receive the Venezuelan National Literature Prize (the nation's highest honor for literature) for her collection of short stories *El largo día ya seguro* (*The Now Sure Long Day*). One year later, she was named to the jury of the prestigious International Novel Prize Rómulo Gallegos. By this time, Palacios was no longer a "token woman" but a major figure in Venezuelan literature and was ready to share her wisdom with others, as she had been mentored throughout her career. Beginning in 1978, Palacios began directing a literature workshop at the literature center CELARG (Centro de Estudios Rómulo Gallegos, or Rómulo Gallegos Center for Latin American Studies) in Caracas. This workshop quickly became the most prestigious and productive place for young writers in the capital to hone their craft. The list of participants in the CELARG workshop is long and significant; famous Venezuelan authors such as Armando Rojas Guardia, Miguel Márquez, and Yolanda Pantin passed through its embrace. The CELARG workshop then evolved into a literary group called Calicanto (Lime and Song) that met at Palacios's home. This group met until 1980, and is generally considered to be one of the great influences on the writers of the generation of the 1980s in Venezuela.

The Calicanto workshop produced its own journal, titled *Hojas de Calicanto* (*Pages from Calicanto*), edited by Palacios, who also included her own works. By this point in her career, Palacios had turned to poetry, writing a type of "story-poem" with a strong interior focus. These poems continue Palacios's description of life as a middle-class Venezuelan woman, but in a fluid way, with spaces and images that seem to flit just beyond the grasp of the reader. Themes of lost innocence and youth are common in these poems. Especially in her last collections of poems, the reader finds a poetic voice aware of impending death. The fluidity of imagery and language in these poems shows how not only language but life itself slips away from an individual. Despite this feeling of life slipping away, however, the poems in these collections show an image of death that continues identity beyond this life, with consciousness as an infinite light leading others forward.

Palacios has been hailed by authors including Yolanda Pantin, Elizabeth Schön, and Elisa Lerner for her generosity to young authors. Indeed, upon Palacios's death, Lerner noted that "She was a very close presence for the writers of my generation . . . I can't say enough about the generosity and continuous encouragement she gave me" (Ramos n.d.). Palacios is considered a true leader in the education of the next generation of writers in Venezuela.

Yolanda Pantin

One of the most well-known and successful writers to move through Antonia Palacios's Calicanto workshop was Yolanda Pantin. Pantin was, at that time, a university student just finding her voice as a poet. Since that time, however, she has become one of the key authors, editors, and scholars of literature working in Venezuela in the early years of the 21st century.

Pantin was born in 1954 in a suburb of Caracas to a middle-class family. She spent her childhood going between a city home and her family's farm in Aragua. After early studies in the visual arts, in 1972 she enrolled in the Universidad Católica Andrés Bello and there began to participate in what would become, for her, the first of a series of poetry groups. It was as part of this group of young poets, who called themselves Rastros (Leavings) that she began to seriously write poetry. These first works earned her admission into Calicanto. In 1980, Pantin published an essay chastising the old guard of Venezuelan poets, accusing them of having had no new ideas since 1958. Soon after, Pantin, along with several other poets, left Calicanto and formed the poetry group Tráfico (Traffic). During this time, Pantin wrote poetry particularly interested in the urban reality of women and their feelings of being trapped at home, themes common in the works of Parra and Palacios. The poems in her 1983 collection *Correo del corazón* (*Letters from the Heart*) describe the repetitive nature of daily living and the isolation of individual women in apartments of the city. Instead of celebrating marriage and family, the poetry focuses on the banality of the everyday life of a housewife. These scenes of quiet desperation are presented in a conversational and easily accessible style that was meant to be read by a wide audience and spoken aloud in poetry readings.

Pantin worked with the members of Tráfico until 1984, as the group looked to reimagine both the role of the poet and the role of poetry. They wanted to bring poetry back to the streets, back to the common people, and to rediscover "the language of the tribe" (Nichols 2000). To achieve this goal, the poets wrote verse that included everyday language and scenes from everyday life. The group read poetry on street corners, on television, and in public parks, sometimes drawing a live audience of 2,000 people and a television audience of thousands more. Pantin was the first member of the group to leave, however. She felt that the militant social message was beginning to overshadow the production of poetry and that the pressure to write poetry that fit the group's manifestoes stifled her creativity. She had, in fact, come to see value in some elements of the previous generation's poetic production.

Pantin's poetry after her association with Tráfico has two main themes: a return to the world of her childhood and an extended consideration of the figure of the vampire. The vampire, both as physical construct and as an idea, provided Pantin in recent years with a way to explore love, danger, life, and death both in her poetry as well as in drama and novels. Pantin's work shows a particular interest in the figure of the psychic vampire, who drains not the blood but the vital force and energies of its victim. The poetry suggests that unhealthy love relationships are like that of vampire and victim.

Conversely, however, the main character of Pantin's most popular children's book is a playful bat named "vampire." Pantin's most recent collection, *País*, from 2007, traces her family history in Venezuela and considers its place in the nation as the country struggles with its identity. Pantin's childhood memories in the collection mix with political commentary and observations of the divisions affecting Venezuela in the first years of the 21st century.

Pantin is not just a poet and author of children's literature, however, she is also a leading scholar and critic. In 1999 she received with Ana Teresa Torres a Bellagio Center Residential Grant from the Rockefeller Foundation to live in the Bellagio Study Center in Bellagio, Italy. There, she and Torres wrote and edited the definitive chronological, critical anthology of Venezuelan women writers in the 20th century. In addition, as we will cover later, she has increasingly entered the world of politics by writing essays of political commentary.

RATÓN Y VAMPIRO

Yolanda Pantin is a serious author whose participation in politics has grown considerably in the 21st century. She is also, however, the author of several award-winning children's books, among them two about a mouse and a vampire bat: *Ratón y Vampiro se conocen* (*Mouse and Vampire Meet*) and *Ratón y Vampiro en el castillo* (*Mouse and Vampire in the Castle*). The first introduces the bat to the mouse and leads them through the difficult process of getting to know someone who is different from themselves. The book begins with Vampire crash landing outside of Mouse's house, and ends with them as fast friends. In the book, the two find their similarities as they describe their experiences to each other; Vampire talks about the world of night creatures, and Mouse tells stories about life during the day. The friendship continues in the second story as Mouse and Vampire have an adventure in a castle and make a new friend (a ghost). Teaching tolerance and courage, the two books have proved very popular and in 2009 were in their third edition.

WORKING TOGETHER: LITERARY GROUPS

We have just seen examples of some of Venezuela's finest individual authors. We should note, however, that one of the most interesting characteristics of literature in Venezuela in the past century is the fact that writers tend to come in groups. In fact, for some time, the concept of the group has been the rule rather than the exception among authors. As with Palacios's Calicanto, we can see this in Caracas, but it is equally true all over the country. Many times having colorful and striking names, almost always publishing big, long manifestos that declare what they're all about, these literary groups are a uniquely Venezuelan way of creating art.

The first group on record was a trio of writers who called themselves Cosmópolis. These writers, Luis Urbaneja Archepohl, Pedro César Dominici, and Pedro Eimio Coll, got together in 1894 to promote a nationalist agenda and debate some of the modernist ideas of the Cuban leader José Martí. They did this by publishing a journal, writing articles and poetry, and debating among themselves. The original group was followed by a whole string of others. The next group, La Alborada (Music at the Break of Day) included the great Rómulo Gallegos and challenged the literary establishment by promoting a type of anti-European and nationalist literature in search of a truly American form of expression.

In fact, most of the literary groups who would follow Cosmópolis and La Alborada were confrontational, rebelling against those who came before. Most of the groups went so far as to write and publish manifestoes, stating their ideologies publicly. This seems to have been a way for the artists involved to brainstorm new ideas, organize their thoughts, and agree as a group to move forward with new artistic, and sometimes political, vigor. In the example of the literary group Válvula (Valve), which appeared in 1928, the members not only rebelled against the writers who came before them but were also the first literary group in Venezuelan history to openly rebel against the sitting government, in their case the dictatorship of Juan Vicente Gómez. This was a dangerous tactic for the group, and it did cause trouble for the group's members. In spite of this, Válvula launched the careers of three important Venezuelan authors: the novelist, short story writer, and later diplomat Arturo Uslar Pietri and the poets Antonio Arráiz and Miguel Otero Silva.

After the fall of the Gómez dictatorship, a series of literary groups interested in following European trends emerged, including Viernes (Friday), which included the great poet Vicente Gerbasi, in 1948. This turned out to be too boring for the next generation, however, who wanted to explore surrealist poetry and metaphysical ideas. A few groups started out in this direction, notably Sardio in 1955, which was a group of poets, writers, and visual artists, including Ramón Palomares and Guillermo Sucre. The exploration of surrealist themes, with their juxtaposition of unexpected images and synesthesia (combination of senses like smell and taste), was cut short by the intrusion of world events in 1959. Venezuelan artists and intellectuals could, at this point, hardly ignore the revolution taking place just off their coast in Cuba, led by Fidel Castro.

Tabla Redonda (Round Table) and El Techo de la Ballena (The Roof of the Whale), inspired by the events in Cuba, were out to completely reject the political and cultural establishment. Most of the members of Tabla Redonda were militant communists; the poet Rafael Cadenas and the artist Jacobo Borges led the group in a revolution that called for complete artistic freedom. Most artistic movements come with rules and parameters for the creation of art. Surrealist art, for example, seeks to re-create a dream state and dislikes any faithful or figurative representations of reality. Tabla Redonda sought to create an environment where artists could create whatever type of art they wanted, without any guidelines at all.

Shortly after the appearance of Tabla Redonda, another group of even more radical writers published a "premanifiesto" (Vera 1985: 55) in a Caracas journal. This new group, called El Techo de la Ballena, was out to reject practically every literary idea that had come before. In the premanifiesto, the group identified itself as "guilty of purification" (Vera 1985: 63) and avowed that their germs were the instrument that would inoculate the nation against bad art. El Techo de la Ballena mounted combined literary and artistic expositions with titles like "Homage to Necrophilia" and staged surprise meetings on the streets with confrontational poetry and odd images. The members of this group included Salvador Garmendia and Juan Calzadilla, who would, ironically, go on to become major establishment figures in Venezuelan literature.

After the previous two groups, the scene moderated somewhat, but the tradition of working in groups continued. Through the 1960s and 1970s Trópico Uno (Tropic

Writer Salvador Garmendia speaks in an interview in Caracas, Venezuela in 1993. Garmendia won the National Prize for Literature in 1972, and the Juan Rulfo Prize for his work in 1989. (AP/Wide World Photos)

One) tried a version of humorous and ironic art, and En Haa (In Awe) formed, it seemed, with the simple idea of getting their members' work published. En Haa never published a manifesto, leading some to wonder if there wasn't some fatigue in the literary community at this point from all the confrontational and aggressive tracts being written.

By 1981, though, the groups were ready to rebel again. In 1981, the poetry group Tráfico formed, with the publication of a blistering manifesto titled *Sí, manifiesto* (*Yes, Manifesto*). They were quickly followed by another group, named Guaire (the name of the highly polluted river that runs through Caracas), in 1982. These young people were concerned with the everyday life of the urban citizen of Caracas and the pollution and traffic of the city. These two groups contained some of the writers who continue to be major literary figures in Venezuela today: Yolanda Pantin, Armando Rojas Guardia, Miguel Márquez, and Rafael Castillo Zapata in Tráfico, Rafael Arráiz Lucca, Leonardo Padrón, and Nelson Rivera in Guaire.

These young people, the members of Tráfico and Guaire, all college students and recent graduates, were products of a boom in government sponsorship of the arts. The middle years of the 1970s were the heights of the oil wealth for Venezuela. So, during that time, like never before, the state sponsored artistic activity. This included building theaters and museums and starting poetry workshops. All the members of Tráfico met at one poetry workshop at the state-run CELARG. In a very real way, oil money created Tráfico. They are just one example of the effect that the oil money had on the arts in that period.

The tradition of groups does not stop there. Until the end of 2004, citizens in Caracas could tune into radio station 97.7 to hear the broadcast of a new group of

---

ARTISTS DENOUNCE CHÁVEZ

The "Message from Venezuelan Writers, Authors and Academics" was originally published online on the February 25, 2004. The strongly worded message, signed by 264 people, took the administration of Chávez to task for a number of perceived failings. Included among these were: the creation a totalitarian state through complete control of all public sectors, the militarization of public administration, the violation of the Venezuelan constitution, the destruction and militarization of the Venezuelan oil company PDVSA, the destruction of the Venezuelan economy and an increase in poverty, the operation of an unbalanced and irrational foreign policy, and brutal repression of dissent.

This message was only the first in a series of similar public group communications from writers and academics in Venezuela. It was followed by a declaration on the March 2, 2004, "Against Violence, for Democracy and Peace," also signed by hundreds, and then in March of 2008 with a full-page advertisement in the newspaper *El Nacional* that accused the administration of practicing "cultural apartheid" and limiting access to those who had signed previous messages.

writers and artists who call themselves Texto Sentido (Text Sense). The radio broad-casts ended in 2004, but the group continued until 2006. In fine 21st-century style, this group of writers and poets maintained a Web site at www.textosentido.org, where one could find their manifesto, works by the writers themselves, and interviews with writers from previous generations like Yolanda Pantin and Leonardo Padrón.

In other nations, both in the Americas (North and South) and Europe, you can find the occasional group of artists in history who get together to produce art. In Venezuela, however, this is a long-standing tradition that goes all the way back to independence and reaches to the present day. These groups—multidisciplinary com-binations of authors of novels and short stories, painters, and movie makers, many of whom have gone on to become important figures in social and political circles—show how important art is in public culture in Venezuela. Art and literature in Venezuela has not been, traditionally, a private and solitary exercise. It is the kind of activity you do with friends, the kind of production you get together to discuss. It should not be a surprise, then, that, unlike in the United States or in other Western societies, the writer is not an ivory tower figure but a public one, many times a writer-statesman.

PUBLIC POETRY AND THE WRITER-STATESMAN

Rómulo Gallegos is not the only Venezuelan to embody the image of the writer-statesman. Arturo Uslar Pietri is another fine example of how intellectual ability as an author often goes hand in hand with a public life in politics in Latin America. Pietri studied political science and writing at the Central University of Venezuela. After graduating, he moved to Paris with the Venezuelan diplomatic delegation, where he simultaneously exercised the professions of diplomat and writer, publishing a historical novel set in revolutionary Venezuela. Pietri's whole career was devoted dually to writing and serving the Venezuelan state. He wrote seven novels and many essays and short stories while serving as minister of education, minister of the inte-rior, founding a political party, and running for president, among other activities. This is the tradition of the writer-statesman, and Venezuela is not the only Latin American country that has this tradition. The novelists Mario Vargas Llosa in Peru and Carlos Fuentes in México are two modern examples in other Latin American nations of writer-statesmen. Both are men who first built careers as novelists and later entered the political arena, never giving up literature. Since the early colonial days of renaissance intellectuals like Andrés Bello, through 20th-century figures like Rómulo Gallegos, the novelist/president of the republic, the writer in Venezuela has had the power to show some political clout as well. This has continued to be true even through the present day.

In 1989, a group of writers, including the poet, critic, and children's author Yo-landa Pantin, the poets Veronica Jaffé, and Antonio López Ortega, as well as the poet and journalist Blanca Strepponi began a small publishing house called Pequeña Venecia (Little Venice). The publishing house had a hard-copy publishing end (paper books) and also ran a Web site at www.pequenhavenecia.com. The original idea of this press was to publish poetry that might otherwise not get published by the big state-run publishers in the country and to bring new voices into the Venezuelan literary marketplace. As time passed, however, and the political situation in the country became more complicated, the authors found a new use for their forum.

After the election of Hugo Chávez, the authors found that they did not agree with many of the policies and ideas of the new president, and they used their positions in the country to speak out. On the Web site and in print they posted a series of texts. First, in 2004 they published a "Message From Writers, Artists, and Venezuelan Academics to Our Colleagues All over the World" in three different languages. This message denounced Chávez and his policies. It was signed by 220 Venezuelan intellectuals. The Web site and the press also published a series of essays by prominent Venezuelan writers, such as Pantin and Jaffé, attacking the Chávez administration on various issues.

Interestingly, one of the essays in particular criticizes Chávez's own use of poetry in his speeches and on his radio program. Chávez and members of his administration quote poetry often in their speeches, one indication of the importance of literature to communication in the country. Interestingly, however, the criticism of Chavez was not that he should not use poetry; the essay criticized him for using it incorrectly (the authors of the essay believed that the president was taking the quotations out of context). In Venezuela, poetry is normal political language, and writers and cultural intellectuals feel qualified and duty-bound to speak on political and social issues. In the tradition of the writer-statesman, literature has a place at the table in the political dialogue in Venezuela.

REFERENCES

Helguera, J. León. 1994. "Bello and Bolivar: Poetry and Politics in the Spanish American Revolution." *American Historical Review* 99: 1008–1009.

Nichols, Elizabeth Gackstetter. 2000. *Rediscovering the Language of the Tribe in Contemporary Venezuelan Poetry.* Lewiston, NY: Mellen Press.

Pacheco Troconis, Germán. 2003. La sociedad económica de Amigos del País de Caracas, el conocimiento agronómico y el progreso agrícola (1830–1844). *Tierra Firme*, July, 21, no. 83: 335–350.

Pantin, Yolanda, and Ana Teresa Torres. 2003. *El Hilo de la Voz: Antología Crítica de Escritoras Venezolanas del Siglo XX.* Caracas: Fundación Polar.

Parra, Teresa de la. 1991. "Tres Conferencias: Influencia de las mujeres en la formación del alma americana." In Velia Bosch, ed., *Obra (Narrativa, ensayos, cartas).*Caracas: Biblioteca Ayacucho.

Pino Iturrita, Elias. 1993. *Las ideas de los primeros venezolanos.* Caracas: Monte Avila Editores.

Ramos, María Elena. n.d. "Antonia Palacios, la vida desalojada." *Verbigracia.* http//:noticias.eluniversal.com/verbigracia/memoria/Ni151/tributo.

Vera, Elena. 1985. *Flor y canto: 25 años de poesía venezolana (1958–1983).* Caracas: Biblioteca de la Academia Nacional de la Historia.

Art

Due in part to the wealth generated from the petroleum industry, Venezuela has a well-developed and internationally recognized contemporary art community. University training in the arts nationally and scholarships for studies abroad have been accessible to aspiring artists since the middle of the 20th century, and state funding for museums and exhibitions of the visual arts has also been available and relatively constant. Venezuela's artistic heritage, however, dates to a time long before the discovery of black gold. Three to five thousand years ago, people living in South America began to create art by drawing on rocks.

MYSTERIOUS ROCK ART

The continental areas of northern South America contain one of the largest concentrations of prehistoric rock paintings in the Americas. These drawings appear throughout the Venezuelan territory, in the Andes areas of Barinas, Táchira, and Mérida, on the northern coast from Falcón to Miranda, in the Cordillera Central in Carabobo, Aragua, Vargas, and Miranda, and in Bolívar and Amazonas state in far southern Venezuela along the Orinoco River. In all, more than 650 rock art sites have been discovered in Venezuela (Scaramelli and Tarble 2006).

Scholars group the rock art of Venezuela into five types: (1) petroglyphs, which are carvings or line drawings in rock, (2) geoglyphs, which are works of art made by moving or arranging stones or earth or other objects within a landscape, (3) grinding basins and cupules, which are hemispherical, cup-shaped, nonutilitarian cultural markings, (4) rock paintings, and (5) megalithic monuments, which are constructions involving one or several roughly hewn stone slabs of great size (Scaramelli and Tarble 2006).

One of the largest petroglyph sites in Venezuela is the Complejo Arquelógico Piedra Pintada at Vigirima in Carabobo State. This site has more than 165 clusters of petroglyphs and two megalith constructions. The petroglyphs represent pyramidal, square and snakelike shapes, waving over and around the rocks at the site. In a stylistic analysis of all the forms represented in 1999, faculty of the University of Carabobo found hunting scenes, female forms, representations of animals (deer, anteaters, frogs, monkeys, etc.), gods, stars, and unknown symbols (Delgado de Smith et al. 1999).

The Geoglyph of Chirgua is the only known geoglyph in Venezeula. It is also located in Carabobo, north of the community of Chirgua. It is a large figure of almost 60 meters, made up of several circles, one inside the other, with rectangular "arms" attached. Most have interpreted this geoglyph as a human figure. The geoglyph was created by excavating furrows on a hill.

Both the Geoglyph of Chirgua and the petroglyphs and megaliths at the site of Vigirima have been nominated as UNESCO World Heritage Sites and in 2010 were on the tentative list of that organization (Scaramelli and Tarble 2006).

The specific dates for and significance of this art remains a mystery. This is because the rock art sites lack reliable and specific archeological contexts. Without the presence of major archeological finds to help explain and help place in history the culture that produced the art, we may never know who, when, or why the art was produced.

ARMANDO REVERÓN REMAKES THE VENEZUELAN LANDSCAPE

Art served public purposes in colonial and early 19th-century Venezuela. The church and the state used art to demonstrate big themes—piety, religiosity, elite prosperity, and patriotism, for example. One did not go to museums to view art (there were no museums) or buy art for personal collections. The first museum in Venezuela, the Museo de Bellas Artes (Fine Art Museum) was not built until 1938, and the current, gorgeous Galería de Arte Nacional (Gallery of National Art) is a product of the oil wealth of the 1960s and 1970s, with one location built in 1976 and moved to an even more impressive building completed in 2009.

The paintings in the colonial period are mostly religious in nature, the type found in churches and cathedrals. With the early days of the Venezuelan state, however, there was a shift from art for religion's sake to art for the sake of creating an image of the nation. During this time, artists painted patriotic portraits of national leaders, such as Simón Bolívar, to tell the national story. The foremost painters of this period was José Gil de Castro and Cristóbal Rojas. José Gil de Castro was a Spanish painter who in the 1820s produced many of the most famous portraits of Bolívar (which are now featured prominently behind Chávez in television addresses and photo opportunities). Cristóbal Rojas, a Venezuelan painter working in the later 1800s, studied both in Caracas and later in Paris, where he spent all of his time in the Louvre, learning from the classical masters. Rojas is famous for his 1883 painting *La muerte de Girardot en Bárbula*, a canvas that shows a hero of Venezuelan independence, Atanasio Girardot, trying to lift the national flag during the Battle of Bárbula. This iconic painting has become a national symbol in Venezuela, where Girardot is still highly regarded. Rojas has also gained wide recognition and acclaim outside of Venezuela in the 21st century. His painting *Los Lectores* sold at auction in 2009 for $1,172,500 after being appraised for $300,000, according to the auctioneer Sotheby's.

In addition to patriotic painting as a common form of 19th-century Venezuelan art, President Antonio Guzmán Blanco used statuary and public space to construct the idea of the modern and progressive Venezuelan nation. Guzmán Blanco had a decided affinity for French architecture that demonstrates a late 19th-century proclivity for perceiving all things French as modern. He also sponsored the construction of statues of Simón Bolívar in public squares throughout the country to combine a European architectural style with unique Venezuelan patriotic identity.

Venezuela did not see a real group of professional artists, who produced art for a market other than church or state, until the later years of the 19th century. The first of these artists was Armando Reverón. Reverón was born in 1889 and began his education in painting in Venezuela. He followed the traditional, realist style of the late 1800s for a time, and in 1910 was given a scholarship to go to Spain to study painting with the Spanish realist masters. While Reverón was in Spain, in 1912 a more rebellious group of young artists formed an artistic group called the Círculo de Bellas Artes (Circle of Fine Arts) to explore the ideas of impressionism, futurism, and cubism that were coming out of France. When Reverón returned from Spain, he joined the Círculo, though he was suspicious of the new ideas. The paintings that Reverón painted after this time show the formal background and the ideas of the new group.

Reverón's most famous paintings are impressionist images of the coast where he lived with his partner, Juanita Ríos, in the town of Macuto. Through the 1920s, 1930s, and early 1940s, he painted impressionistic landscapes in which the scene is only a fuzzy image and every figure seems to wash out. These landscapes are usually grouped into three categories: first a "blue" period, a "white" period, and then a "sepia" or brown period. In all the series of paintings, critics are fascinated with Reverón's ability to paint light and make it shine right out of the painting; one 1990s exhibition of his work in Colombia was called "Light and Warm Shadows" (Caballero 1997).

Armando Reverón's art is full of warmth and light, but his life was less tranquil. Many times described as "eccentric" and a clinically diagnosed schizophrenic, he was institutionalized twice during his life. Recently, art researchers have become interested by Reverón's less traditional methods of creation. One example is the models that the artist used in his later works. After his long series of landscapes, Reverón turned to a series of more figurative paintings with human images in them. The bodies in his paintings were mostly women; however, they were not posed by human models. Instead, he made life-sized dolls from cardboard and other found materials and used them to pose for his paintings. The house where he and Juanita Ríos lived was filled with these dolls; every room had a few posed artistically around. There are many photographs of Reverón with these dolls as well as other objects that he made from recycled materials. Recent exhibitions of his art have combined his paintings with these sculptures.

Reverón has always been considered an important artist to Venezuelans, but like the rest of Venezuelan cultural artistic production, he was neglected by the international community for years. Recently, however, he has received the attention he deserves. The Museum of Modern Art in New York staged a one-artist exhibition of his work in 2003, the first show of a single Latin American artist of the museum since Diego Rivera's show in 1940. This show was an indication of the new interest in Reverón's work and the work of other Venezuelan artists. Venezuelan citizens would say it is long overdue.

Nearly contemporaneously with Armando Reverón, another painter, Pedro Centeno Vallenilla, was creating a vision of a different element of Venezuela's reality: the indigenous peoples of Venezuela's colonial past. Centeno Vallenilla was born in 1904 in Caracas and trained at the Academy of Fine Arts before entering the diplomatic service in Paris and Rome. Centeno Vallenilla's work shows the influence of his time in Italy, using the mannerist style. While Centeno Vallenilla gained modest fame during his lifetime as an artist-statesman, he has been little studied in modern times (and has been widely dismissed as kitsch). Recently, however, a 21st-century controversy brought his work back into the spotlight.

After his return to Caracas in the 1940s, Centeno Vallenilla was commissioned to paint a series of murals designed to represent different aspects of Venezuelan nationality in the Palacio Federal (Venezuela's legislative capital building) and in the Círculo de las Fuerzas Armadas (The Venezuelan Military Academy). In these murals, Centeno Vallenilla created a famous series of fictionalized portraits of famous indigenous figures, including Guaicaipuro, chief of the Caracas and Teques tribes during the time of conquest and leader of the resistance against the Spanish.

One Centeno Vallenilla mural that recognizes the indigenous peoples' struggle is *Mapas y alegorías venezolanas* (*Venezuelan Maps and Allegories*). The painting displays a map of Venezuela in the center, with a portrait of an armed Simón Bolívar standing to the right and an indigenous leader, with a bow and arrows, on the left. This painting, and in particular the image of the figure on the left, was used in 2007 by the government of President Hugo Chávez in the reissue of the Venezuelan currency, the *bolívar fuerte* (Bs.F). The face of the figure now appears on the 10 VEB with a caption indicating that the indigenous leader is Guaicaipuro. The problem is that many disagree that the figure in *Mapas y alegorías venezolanas* represents Guaicaipuro.

The figure in the mural is not identified. Centeno Vallenilla did, however, undertake a series of commemorative medallions in 1955 for the exchange house Italcambio that depicted the great aboriginal chiefs of Venezuela. These medallions do bear the names of the chiefs they are meant to represent. When scholars compare the image of Guaicaipuro on the medallion with his name to the figure in the mural, they find little resemblance. By contrast, the same observers find that the medallion representing another leader of the resistance, the chief Paramacay, as much more similar to the image in the mural.

Is it important or a triviality? The reality is that no portraits of Guaicaipuro exist from the time of conquest, and so no one is sure what Guaicaipuro really looked like. All of Centeno Vallenilla's portraits of indigenous leaders are imagined and invented. While some find the discrepancy bothersome, others feel that the point is moot and the important thing is the recognition of indigenous resistance. Whatever the opinion, the controversy has generated a great deal of new attention for the art of Centeno Vallenilla both in Venezuela and in the international community.

ALEJANDRO OTERO AND THE GEOMETRIC REVOLUTION

Armando Reverón and those who followed him took landscapes and changed them. Landscapes went from being background imagery to an art form in and of themselves. By the late 1940s, however, the landscape movement had lost its momentum, and the art community searched for something new. The push for the new and the modern in art, especially in Caracas, mirrored what was going on socially and politically as well. Pérez Jiménez pushed the New National Ideal of modernization and futurism, and the art world took notice of his government funding. These same forces of modernization and social change that we see in Gallegos's and Parra's novels hit the art scene; Caracas transformed from a sleepy town to a large modern city.

Alejandro Otero, after having studied in Caracas, went to Paris to study art at the Sorbonne from 1945 to 1949. During his time there, he painted a key series of works called *Cafeteras* that looked at coffee pots from unexpected and unusual angles. The subject matter and the perspective of these paintings was completely different than the paintings that had come before, and shook up the artistic community back in Caracas. The geometric revolution took hold, and a new vogue took over Venezuelan art: geometric abstractionism. Alejandro Otero is considered the leader and foremost painter of the movement. In 1951, Otero founded the artistic group Los Disidentes (The Dissidents) and met the modernist architect Carlos Raúl Villanueva. Villanueva and Otero shared an artistic vision that included the importance of modernization and industry, and they went on to collaborate successfully on many projects.

Otero went on to produce a great series of abstract paintings. Otero's early paintings are colorful, containing bold stripes of geometric shapes, often on tall, skinny canvases. There are no recognizable figures, just pure color. The idea of these images seems to create rhythm for the eye. One series, which contains mostly black and white stripes over different brightly colored shapes is even called *Coloritmo* (*Color Rhythm*).

Beginning in the late 1960s Otero turned his attention to sculpture. His sculptures are similar to his paintings, preferring geometric shapes and forms, but show less interest in the bright colors of the paintings. One of Otero's sculptures, *Delta Solar*, stands in front of the Smithsonian's Air and Space museum in Washington DC. Alejandro Otero is considered the founder of modern art in Venezuela. He is respected for bringing the new vision to the nation, and for his contributions, one of the museums in the capital that shows new artists was named for him.

SOTO AND CRUZ-DIEZ: MAKING ART MOVE

Jesús Soto

Art critics suggest that kinetic art is to Venezuela as mural art is to Mexico (Traba 1994). Jesús Soto first hit the art scene as a participant in the geometric revolution, but before he completed his career, he made Venezuelan sculpture move. Soto was born in Ciudad Bolivar, in the interior of the country, to the southeast, and started by painting movie posters. He later moved to the capital, where he met and became familiar with the works of contemporaries Otero and Carlos Cruz-Diez. Like Otero and Cruz-Diez, he also later traveled to Paris, where he continued to expand his knowledge of abstract art.

Soto's major works begin in the 1950s. All of his work can be described as kinetic: his art took the geometric images of previous artists and then focused on energy and movement. The energy can come in two types: implied energy, or movement, where the work looks like it is moving, and actual energy, where the art actually moves. In his early pieces, he designed paintings and pieces that were static but created the idea of vibration and movement by placing squared and twisted wires in front of parallel lines.

In later work, Soto wanted to show actual energy with his interactive, public works. Starting in the 1960s Soto began a series of pieces that were designed with public participation in mind. In 1969, he created an installation called *Penetrable* (*Accessible*), which was made of hanging plastic and metal tubes. Soto designed the piece so that the spectator could enter and move the tubes around, changing their position, thereby changing the look of the work and creating movement. This type of public art, often called "op art" or "operational art," became an important part of Soto's career. In addition to murals and public sculpture, including mural for the UNESCO building in Paris in 1970, Soto created a large interactive sculpture for the 1988 Olympics in Seoul, South Korea.

Venezuelan artist Jesús Soto is seen in Maracaibo, Venezuela, on October 5, 2002. Soto, best known for creating optical movement in his paintings and hanging sculptures, died in Paris on Wednesday, January 19, 2005. He was 81. (AP/Wide World Photos)

Carlos Cruz-Diez

Just as Jesús Soto focused on energy in his artistic vision, Carlos Cruz-Diez also began to create kinetic op art. Cruz Diez started his career in advertising, studying in both universities in Venezuela and New York City in the late 1940s. He later worked in advertising in Caracas and as a designer and illustrator for the Venezuelan newspaper *El Nacional* before turning to art full time. Cruz-Diez's particular artistic style is distinctive. His work focuses on the movement of lines, producing a "moiré effect," which causes the lines to seem to move and change as the viewer moves around the piece of art. Cruz-Diez sometimes refers to this effect as causing "vibrations" in the viewer. Cruz-Diez's most popular pieces that show this effect are the *Physicromie* series, a collection of smaller (wall-sized) to larger (30-foot-long outdoor) pieces that use a series of colored lines. Many of these works appear in environments such as airports and on the sides of highways, so that people walking or driving by will experience the piece differently as they move. One such work, *Phisicromie Naranja*, appears in a traffic roundabout in Valencia, Venezuela. Cruz-Diez also has shown much interest in the properties and vibrations of light as it relates to color. Following this idea, the pieces in the *Transcromie* series are composed of colored pieces of colored plastic that allow the light to shine through them. These works are found in locations such as the Venezuelan stock exchange in Caracas.

GEGO AND THE RETICULATED IMAGE

Working at the same time as the artists of the kinetic movement, Gertrude Goldschmidt (1912–1994), known artistically as "Gego," was interested in the kinetic movement but sought her own vision and moved away from the lines and color favored by Soto and Cruz-Diez. Gego was born in Hamburg, Germany in 1912, the daughter of a Jewish banker. Her family fled Germany in 1939 as the situation became dangerous and settled, like many Jewish families, in Latin America, choosing to come to Venezuela. Gego lived and worked in Venezuela for the rest of her life. She began her career as an artist late—she began by studying engineering and architecture at the University of Hamburg, finishing an engineering degree before her family fled Germany. She only began a career in sculpture, in her 40s, after working for years as a furniture designer. However, as a reviewer of the *New York Times* noted, "as it turned out, the older she grew, the better she got" (Cotter 2007). In the late 1960s, Gego began to experiment with transferring two-dimensional images into three-dimensional images, or as she called it, "drawing without paper." This concept of moving drawings into sculptures produced her most famous and successful works and created delicate sculptures that played with light and shadows. In the 1960s and the early 1970s, Gego created a series of sculptures and installations that used suspended nylon and stainless steel strips that approximate a three-dimensional architectural drawing. Some of these pieces try to communicate the elements of nature as viewed in Caracas. For example, *Chorros* (*Streams*), presents a vertical rain of thinner and thicker aluminum wires with subtle and broad metal twists that change the wires' direction.

By the 1980s, her vision fully came together in her most famous series of works, the *Reticuláreas*, the most famous of which is a room-sized piece housed in the Venezuelan Museo de Arte Nacional. The room is filled with a web of aluminum and stainless steel lines of varying thickness that hang with no visible support. These lines weave through geometric shapes such as triangles and squares, reminding some of a grove of mangrove trees, others of an elaborate star chart. As Gego's life progressed and her arthritis grew worse, she also produced more whimsical pieces of woven wire and woven paper that also play with light and shadow.

Gego's work can be seen not only in Venezuela in the Museo de Arte Nacional but also in New York City at the Museum of Modern Art.

MARISOL: POP ART WITH A MESSAGE

Following the tradition of great Venezuelan sculptors, María Sol Escobar (known artistically as "Marisol" [1930–]) began work in the 1960s on a new path of three-dimensional portraits, using both traditional materials and found items to create a type of pop art that focused on people and their relationships.

Marisol, the daughter of art lovers, began her artistic education in Los Angeles, where she and her family had moved from Venezuela when she was 16 years old. Supported by her father, she studied art in Los Angeles, Paris, and New York. In New York, Marisol met the artists Hans Hoffman and William de Kooning and began to investigate the abstract expressionist style. Through the 1950s, Marisol learned to work with a "push and pull" dynamic, pairing raw and finished materials and images, using terra-cotta and wood in many of her pieces, like the sculpture *Queen*, which shows a terra-cotta crown of tiny figures on a wooden head.

In the 1960s, Marisol met the pop artist Andy Warhol and became interested in his work and that of other pop artists including Roy Lichtenstein. It is during this period that Marisol dropped her surname and began work on sculpture pieces like the famous *The Party*, a life-sized installation of figures all with her face. From that time onward, much of Marisol's work has included portraits of herself and other famous figures, as well as unknowns. These sculptures many times poke fun at the famous figures represented and offer both humor and social satire. As Eleanor Heartney observes, Marisol's "lifelong inclination has been to poke fun at the prosperous while conveying sympathy for the less fortunate" (Heartney n.d.). On the satirical side is a portrait of John Wayne commissioned by *Life* that portrays the famous macho cowboy as a stiff doll on a toy horse with a pole reaching down that suggests the figure is the top of a weathervane. Showing her sympathy for the disadvantaged is her work *The Family*, which was based on a vintage photograph of a rural Southern family in the 1920s showing both poverty and dignity. The fatherless family stands stiffly; some of them are painted flat, while others are made of carved wood that protrudes from the canvas, including the baby who sits quietly on his mother's lap. The whole piece is presented over a pair of doors that Marisol found on the street outside her studio.

In recent years, Marisol, who divides her time between New York City and Caracas, has continued to produce portraits that have a message. These portraits include a wide array of subjects, from respectful sculptures of other artists such as Georgia O'Keefe, to works that portray the poor in Cuba, or *Blackfoot Delegation to Washington*, a sculpture that shows Native Americans hoping to negotiate a land settlement in Washington, DC.

JAVIER TÉLLEZ: VIDEO PASSPORTS TO OTHER SPACES

Javier Téllez, one of Venezuela's younger new experimental artists, uses film to create interactive pieces of art. Téllez creates installations that may include videos, circus tents, live animals, and actors, all in an effort to produce what he, in the Whitney Museum's artist guide, called a "passport to allow those outside to be inside." Téllez's work blurs the distinctions between spectator and art, reality and fantasy, reason and insanity.

Téllez, born in Valencia, Venezuela in 1969 to psychologist parents, developed an interest in mental disorders at an early age. He regularly accompanied his parents to psychiatric hospitals as they visited their patients. This early experience shows in his work. Many of his first installations recreated hospital settings, and he often used psychiatric patients as performers in his videos and performances. In one of Téllez's famous early pieces, he had audience members sit in an enormous wooden birdhouse and watch a video recreation of patients being forcibly restrained in London's infamous Bedlam Hospital. In this piece, called *P.S. 1*, the idea was to imply that all involved (spectators, orderlies, and patients) were equally "cuckoo." This piece is an early example of Téllez's continuing theme of insiders and outsiders (in this case, the spectators and patients) and how the difference between the two is not as great as we are led to believe.

Téllez lived in Venezuela until 1993, when he moved to New York City. In New York, he continued to explore differences between people and separations that might or might not be real. In 2005, Téllez created a video documentary of a "self-organized circus" of patients from Mexicali's mental health center, who walked in a parade, wearing costumes, in protest of perceptions of mental illness. The procession ended at the Mexico/U.S. border, where human cannonball David Smith was shot over the border, emphasizing the concept of inside/outside and criticizing both nations' immigration policies. Combing these two different concerns, the film makes a bigger statement about exclusion and segregation as a whole.

In his recent works, Téllez has focused on physical rather than mental disability, such as in the piece *Letter on the Blind for the Use of Those Who See* from 2007. In this work, Téllez recreates on film the Indian parable of the six blind men who each touch different parts of an elephant and come away with different ideas of what an elephant is. In the film, Téllez has the men describe their experiences out loud, asking viewers to think about what each man is "seeing" with his hands. The idea of the work is to create a connection between the blind and "those who see" in the title so that the two may understand each other better.

MONUMENTS TO NATIONAL ART
AND NATIONAL PRIDE

On the 20th anniversary of the opening of the stunning Galería de Arte Nacional, the gallery published a full-color history of the museum with pictures of the collections. The volume, which celebrates Venezuelan art, says that while many important artists have come along in the 20th century, the three emblematic names in Venezuelan art are Reverón, Otero, and Soto (Balza 1996). We should add, however, that the Galería itself is emblematic of the importance of art in the Venezuelan national consciousness.

First, the gallery shows the results of the oil boom of the 1970s. During the 1970s and early 1980s, petroleum wealth allowed Venezuela to do more than simply construct new roads and hospitals. The middle classes of Venezuela expanded quickly, and they suddenly found themselves economically equal with people in western Europe, the United States, and Canada. This realization created a feeling that Venezuela should also be equal in terms of social and artistic programs. In his history of Venezuela, John Lombardi says that "as wealth generated by the petroleum expansion increased, the prosperous elite found that the good life promised by the imitation of North Atlantic models required more than the simple ability to duplicate consumer styles" (Lombardi 1982: 10). The other requirements of the "good life" included funding for the arts and education, and so government support for artists and museums increased. The Venezuelan government followed the lead of the French state, which has almost always supported national arts institutions and individual artists, and one way in which they did this was by building monuments to national art. The Galeria sits in a complex with a beautiful museum of modern art and an outstanding multistage theater complex, all built with oil money.

So the Venezuelans did not just spend their oil money on roads and consumer goods. They also did not spend the money on foreign art. It is tempting to translate the name of the gallery in English to "National Art Gallery." This does not give a truly accurate meaning, however. The museum is actually a "Gallery of National Art." The museum, a gorgeous stone and marble building with fountains, reflecting pools and gardens, wide halls, and excellent lighting, holds only work by Venezuelan artists. It is a patriotic celebration of national artists and a reminder of the place of art and culture in Venezuelan society.

This celebration continues into the 21st century. Under the administration of President Hugo Chávez and the administration's Ministerio del Poder Popular para la Cultura (Ministry of Popular Power for Culture), the Gallery of National Art has opened a new and larger location in Caracas, reflecting both the importance of art in the national culture and the growing nationalistic sentiments of the Chávez administration. Inaugurated in April 2009, the new 30,000-square-meter museum has a permanent collection of more than 7,000 works, of which 700 are on display at any time. The new museum is described in an article by Tamara Pearson as "the first museum institution in Latin America of this style and magnitude . . . this space is evidence of the importance that the government gives to Venezuelan art" (Pearson 2009).

POPULAR ART IN 21st-CENTURY CARACAS

Art researchers and other interested parties who travel to Venezuela in search of strong traditions in folkloric art are generally disappointed. The reason for this is that strong craft traditions are common in Latin American countries with large or influential indigenous populations. As we have described in other sections of this book, Venezuela's indigenous peoples are primarily rainforest or nomadic tribes who make small portable things.

Additionally, as Marguerite Mayhall persuasively argues, a general intellectual predilection for things European in the art community has meant that indigenous crafts have not been valued in the nation.

What Venezuela has seen in the 21st century in the area of popular art is an increase in the quality and amount of politically engaged street art and Web-produced artistic satire. On the walls of major cities and on the increasingly popular Web site *El Chigüire Bipolar*, artists use images to comment on national and international politics, as well as issues of race, class, and gender.

Especially in Caracas, graffiti and poster art appear as means of expression for many artists. Some graffiti murals glamorize the Chávez revolution, demonizing the United States and its allies. One such mural is that of street artist Carlos Zerpa, who created a stenciled image that shows the biblical figure of David holding the head of Hillary Clinton (in place of Goliath). When interviewed about his work, Zerpa explained that "it's a metaphor for an empire that is being defeated" (Romero 2010a). Zerpa belongs to a group of street artists known as the Ejercito Comunicacional de Liberación (Communications Liberation Army). This federation of street artists produces a wide array of images both in poster form and painted murals commenting on politics and society.

Street artists do not always produce work that supports the Chávez administration, however. Saúl Guerrero, one of Caracas' most prolific street artists, chose to paint a series of portraits of young Afrovenezuelans or poor Venezuelans on telephone booths in the prosperous neighborhood of Chacao. While Guerrero himself is quoted as only wishing to bring attention to social polarization, the artist's work was considered critical of Chávez, and pro-Chávez supporters attacked the artist for his work (Romero 2010a).

The Web site *El Chigüire Bipolar* (The Bipolar Capybara) is more specifically critical of the Chávez administration. The site is satirical in nature and has gained popularity for its comedy. The site's biggest success as of April 2010 was a five-part animated cartoon modeled after the U.S. television program *Lost* called "Isla Presidencial" (Presidential Island). The cartoon skewers all the presidents of South America, portraying Chávez and Bolivian President Evo Morales as star-crossed lovers, Colombian President Alvaro Uribe as an insufferable prude, and Argentinian President Cristina Fernandez de Kirchner as a temptress (who seduces Brazil's President Lula da Silva). Seventy-two-year-old King Juan Carlos of Spain also makes an appearance in which his dentures fall in the ocean. As of March of 2010, the program had been viewed 450,000 times, and the Web site was receiving more daily page views than the main Venezuelan daily newspaper, *El Nacional* (Romero 2010b).

REFERENCES

Balza, José. 1996. "GAN: el esplendor del silencio." In *Galería de Arte Nacional: Veinte años por el arte venezolano 1976–1996.* Caracas: Fundación Cultural Chacao.

Caballero, German. 1997. "Armando Reverón." *Art Nexus* 23: 123–124.

Centeno Vallenilla, Pedro. n.d. *Mapas y alegorías venezolanas.* Colección de Arte BCV. http://www.bcv.org.ve/BLANKSITE/c3/colecarte/centeno_index.htm.

Cotter, Holland. 2007. "Off the Page and in the Air: Drawing Transformed." http://www.nytimes.com/2007/04/27/arts/design/27gego.html.

Delgado de Smith, Ymile, et al. 1999. "Análisis Estilístico de Petrolgíficos del Parque Arqueológico Virigima." http://74.125.95.132/search?q=cache:umg6jgZgy6IJ:www.facyt.uc.edu.ve/petroglifos/Publicaciones%2520Petroglifos/Boletin%2520Soc.%2520Ven.%2520Ciencias%2520Naturales%2520(1999).doc+complejo+arqueologico+piedra+pintada&cd=24&hl=en&ct=clnk&gl=us.

Esteva-Grillet, Roldán. 2001. "Colloquio Multidisciplinario: La obra escultórica de Alejandro Colina." CELARG. http://nosabemosdisparar.blogspot.com/.

Heartney, Eleanor. 2001. *Marisol: A Sculptor of Modern Life.* http://www.tfaoi.com/aa/2aa/2aa661.htm.

Jiménez Maggiolo, Roberto. "El cacique Guaicaipuro y su nuevo billete." http://encontrarte.aporrea.org/columnata/escalio/81/a9107.html.

Lombardi, John V. 1982. *Venezuela: The Search for Order, the Dream of Progress.* New York: Oxford.

Mayhall, Marguerite. 2005. Modernist but Not Exceptional: The Debate over Modern Art and National Identity in 1950's Venezuela." *Latin American Perspectives* 32, no. 2.

Pearson, Tamara. 2009. "Venezuela Opens National Art Gallery." http://www.venezuelanalysis.com/news/4402.

"Pedro Centeno Vallenilla." n.d. http://www.bcv.org.ve/BLANKSITE/c3/colecarte/centeno_index.htm.

Romero, Simon. 2010a. "Artists Embellish Walls with Political Visions." *The New York Times*, April 11.

———. 2010b. "A Political Site Skewers Chávez and Politics." *The New York Times*, March 2.

Scaramelli, Franz, and Kay L. Tarble. 2006. "Zone 2 Venezuela." In *Rock Art of Latin America and the Caribbean.* ICOMOS. World Heritage Convention.

Traba, Marta. 1994. *Art of Latin America 1900–1980.* Baltimore, MD: Johns Hopkins University Press.

Music

TERESA CARREÑO: CLASSICAL HEROINE

As previously mentioned, the Galería de Arte Nacional is just one of the monuments in a collection of buildings in central Caracas dedicated to the national arts—visual, literary, and musical. The venerable Ateneo, or literary club, is located there and is the main bookstore of the now state publishing house, Monte Avila. The biggest set of buildings in the area, however, is the complex of theaters, offices, and classrooms dedicated to one of Venezuela's great classical performers and composers: Teresa Carreño.

Teresa Carreño was born in 1853 to a musical family. Her father, the etiquette expert, Manuel Carreño, dedicated much of his life to her musical education. In 1862, she began traveling and performing with the family. In 1863, at the age of 10, she even famously performed on the piano for Abraham Lincoln in the White House. Traveling with the family to Europe, Carreño continued her studies in piano in Germany with the famous artists Gottshalk and Rubenstein. A multitalented artist, she debuted as an opera singer in 1876 but later decided to devote herself to the piano and to composing. She was considered one of the foremost international pianists of her time and toured the world constantly, giving concerts and premiering her compositions.

In between her international appearances both as a pianist and opera singer, Carreño returned to Venezuela in 1885 and gave a series of concerts, composed a patriotic anthem in celebration of the anniversary of Simón Bolívar's birth, managed an opera company, and helped found a conservatory of music. This level of activity was typical of Carreño, who was an extraordinarily productive and energetic woman. Her nickname, originally given during her time in Berlin, was the "Valkyrie of the Piano." When she died in 1917, Carreño had composed more than 40 pieces for voice, piano, and orchestra. She had been married four times, had borne five children, and had written a book. Together with Aldemaro Romero and Moises Molero, she is considered the most famous classical musician and composer from Venezuela.

CLASSICAL MUSIC IN CONTEMPORARY VENEZUELA: CREATING OPPORTUNITY

Young people still visit the Teresa Carreño cultural complex to learn and perform, as classical music retains an importance and relevance in Venezuelan society that is considered by some Europeans as a model for other nations. Indeed, in a November 2005 report, the BBC quoted the director of the Berlin philharmonic as swearing that Venezuela's youth orchestras were doing the "most important work in classical music anywhere in the world" (Gould 2005).

Venezuela maintains a state-funded system for the training of young classical musicians that dates to the 1970s, when Venezuela began public support for the other fine arts. José Antonio Abreu founded the state music system in 1975. He thought that if Venezuelan kids from Catia could play counterpoint rhythms on the *cuatro* (traditional Venezuelan four stringed ukulele-like guitar) they could also play them on the violin. Now celebrating more than 30 years of success, the system is a source of national pride that has inspired similar programs in 23 other nations. Unlike other nations, where support for classical music is in decline, the youth orchestra system in Venezuela has survived regime changes and political upheaval and has seen its budget grow in recent years to 23 million dollars annually. In its more than 30 years of life, still lead by Abreu in 2009, El Sistema (The System) has trained more than half a million musicians.

Part of the success of the program arises from its popular roots. The program trains children as young as two years old, inviting them to come to concerts and providing them with special seating areas where they can move to the music in a child-friendly environment. Visiting specialists from North America and Europe continually express admiration and awe at the technical skills exhibited by the students in the program—some as young as eight years old. According to the *Boston Globe*, one recent visit by the dean of the New England Conservatory left the gentleman so impressed that he signed an agreement to bring students of the American conservatory to study in the Venezuelan program. This visit then led the New England Conservatory to fully adopt the El Sistema program in Boston. In October of 2009, 10 students started in what the conservatory is calling El Sistema USA (Edgers 2009).

The Venezuelan system prides itself on training students from all social classes. The program uses its funds to provide free instruments, scholarships, and free transportation to students from the poorest of Caracas' neighborhoods. In June of 2005, the *Boston Globe* reported the example of one student who came to the program at the age of 15 after nine arrests for armed robbery and drug offenses. Eight years later, the student had become one of the clarinetists in the Caracas Youth Orchestra, a tutor for younger clarinetists, and a mentor for two other abused and reformed delinquent students who were turning their lives around (Lakshrananan 2005). Clearly, the system of youth and children's orchestras has trained musicians and changed lives in Venezuela, and it has kept classical music alive and well in the nation. When the program began in 1975, there were two symphony orchestras in Venezuela. Since that time, the number has grown to more than 200, with at least one professional orchestra in every state in the nation.

ABREU AND EL SISTEMA

José Antonio Abreu is yet another example of the Latin American renaissance man—in this case, the musician-statesman. Abreu received a PhD in petroleum economics from the UCAB in 1961 and went on to study music at the national conservatory, graduating with a degree in composition and organ performance in 1964.

Abreu's vision, grounded in this unique interdisciplinary training in economics and music, was of a program that would give new opportunities to economically disadvantaged children and those young people with special needs. From the beginning, Abreu saw music as a weapon against poverty and despair. Music, as Abreu notes, does not recognize poverty, disability, or class difference. "A child," he has been quoted as saying, "can reach the first line of an orchestra by merit alone . . . an orchestra is a meritocracy and team. It teaches our kids how to live in society. Music makes our children better human beings." (Lakshranan 2005) El Maestro, as the children call him, began the program in 1975 with 11 students in a garage. In 2008, 300,000 participated in El Sistema.

By far the most famous graduate of El Sistema is Gustavo Dudamel, who debuted as the music director and conductor of the Los Angeles Philharmonic Orchestra in 2009 at the age of 28. Dudamel, from Barquisimeto, is the son of musicians and became part of the system in Venezuela as a violinist at a young age. By the age of 13, he began conducting youth orchestras in the system, and by the age of 16, upon the invitation of Abreu, began conducting the system's premier orchestra in Caracas, the Simón Bolívar Youth Orchestra. In 2004, Dudamel won a conducting competition in Bamburg, Germany, conducted the Gothenburg Symphony in 2005 at The Proms in London, the premier European orchestra event, and by 2007 was named the next music director of the Los Angeles Philharmonic (Wakin 2009; Ashley 2005). Dudamel's youth, passion, talent, Latino roots, and hair seemed to make him a good fit for Los Angeles. Dudamel's success also brought new global attention to El Sistema. Some music critics argue that the future of classical music does not lie in the United States or Europe but in Venezuela (Padgett 2009).

POPULAR MUSIC: THE NATIONAL SOUND

Salsa and merengue, imported from the Caribbean islands, are popular in Venezuela, though they have fewer home-grown composers or groups that have made unique

Venezuelan conductor Gustavo Dudamel conducts the Sinfonica de la Juventud Venezolana Simon Bolivar during the Lucerne Festival on Wednesday, March 28, 2007 at the Culture and Congress Centre KKL in Lucerne, Switzerland. (AP/Wide World Photos)

contributions to the style. The one imported variety of popular music that Venezuelans have really put their stamp on is the calypso. Brought from the island of Trinidad in the 1880s by Trinidadians who came to the area of El Callao to work in the gold mines, calypso grew in Venezuela with a unique style, rhythm, and lyric tradition. The calypso you hear in Venezuela, however, is recognizable by the distinctive steel drum sound associated with the islands combined with traditional Venezuelan instruments. Calypso in Venezuela is particularly associated with the holiday of Carnival, held immediately before lent. Carnival, both in the El Callao area and along the coast, is a local favorite and a tourist attraction.

Salsa, merengue, and calypso have their origins in other nations. While Venezuelans have made calypso their own, one truly native style of Venezuelan popular music is the *llanero*, a type of music that comes from the plains, or llanos, of the south of the country. This music started out as a rural musical tradition, began by the Venezuelan cowboys, the *llaneros* themselves. *Llanero* music is traditionally accompanied by a four-stringed guitar called a *cuatro* and sometimes a small harp. This music dates from the colonial era and has continued to the present day, though many times combining with newer instruments and interpretations.

Andrew Gonzalez, 18, a computer science major, learns to build a traditional Venezuelan cuatro *guitar in an extracurricular class at the Bolivarian University in Caracas, Venezuela, Tuesday, May 31, 2005. Venezuela's government offers free schooling at The Bolivarian University, named after independence hero Simón Bolívar, to thousands of students in a programs that aims to revolutionize higher education in the country. (AP/Wide World Photos)*

Also originally from the llanos but now a national rhythm is the *joropo*. *Joropo* is played with *cuatro*, harp, mandolin, and maracas. The style of dance that accompanies the music is a style learned by school children throughout the country. By far the most famous of all Venezuelan *joropos* is the "Alma Llanera" which may well be the unofficial Venezuelan national anthem. Certainly the lyrics, which speak to being the child of the sea, the herons, the roses, and the sun, are lyrics that speak to many Venezuelan hearts.

Another traditional form of music that continues to be widely performed are *galerones*. *Galerones* are slow songs that are sung in groups of singers, to the accompaniment of a *cuatro*, guitar, and bandolin. The singers involved in the performance of the *galerón* take turns, creating a conversation or counterpoint within the song. *Galerones* cover patriotic, religious, philosophical, or sentimental themes. *Galerones* are often performed as part of public celebrations and festivals, including the Cruz de Mayo celebrations common in the eastern portions of Venezuela. As part of the celebrations, a Christian cross is ornamented with flowers and other decorations and

---

"ALMA LLANERA"

"Alma Llanera" (Soul of the Plains) is sometimes known as Venzuela's second national anthem. Composed by Pedro Elías Gutierrez, the song speaks to Venezuelans with its references to the land and the water:

> I was born on the banks of the vibrating Arauca.
> I am a brother of the waves
> of the herons, of the roses,
> I am a brother of the waves,
> of the herons, of the roses
> and of the sun, of the sun.
> The lively song of the breezes in the palms has put me to sleep,
> and that is why I have a soul,
> like the most beautiful soul,
> and that is why I have a soul,
> like the most beautiful soul,
> of crystal, of crystal.
> I love, I cry, I sing, I dream
> of passionate carnations,
> of passionate carnations,
> I love, I cry, I sing, I dream
> to decorate with rubies the mane
> of the pony of my lover.

"Alma Llanera." Composed by Pedro Elías Gutiérrez. Lyrics written by Rafael Bolívar Coronado, 1914. Translated by the author.

placed in a public place. People then gather to recite poems, pray, and sing religious *galerones* to the cross.

The 1960s and 1970s marked a resurgence of folk music in Venezuela as elsewhere in Latin America and the United States. Part of the resurgence was renewed interest in *llanero* music, and there was an explosion of groups, composers, and interpreters of the traditional music. Of these, the most famous is the artist/composer Simón Díaz. Simón Díaz dedicated himself to the *llanero* tradition in Venezuela and popularized the music both in Venezuela and throughout Latin America, seeing its export to Argentina, Brazil, and Spain. A hugely popular artist throughout the 1960s and 1970s, Díaz was a multitalented artist, playing the *cuatro*, showing comedic talent, starring in plays and films, and hosting a series of television shows dedicated to popular music. One of his television programs, designed to teach popular music and culture to children, earned him the nickname "Uncle Simón" for many years. Díaz's music has been used in classical compositions and film soundracks. He has received many of the most prestigious artistic awards the nation has to offer and is a Venezuelan icon. Many Díaz compositions are popular throughout Latin America, but the most famous is "Caballo Viejo." "Caballo Viejo" is a bittersweet story of an aging horse (man) who finds love, despite perceptions of age-appropriate behavior. There are arrangements of "Caballo Viejo" in multiple Latin music styles, including merengue, *cumbia*, and *norteño*.

Díaz was followed by several other groups interested in recapturing the sounds of folkloric music, including the Gurrufío Ensemble. The Gurrufío Ensemble formed in the early 1980s, dedicated to combining Venezuelan traditional styles with modern improvisation techniques. The Gurrufío musicians are virtuosos on their instruments—harp, maracas, *cuatro*, mandolin, and flute—and together they continue to receive international acclaim with their *joropos*, *danzas*, and merengues.

Other important figures in contemporary Venezuelan folk resurgence were Ali Primera and Soledad Bravo. Bravo and Primera were part the wider Latin American Nueva Canción (New Song) tradition, a style of music that combined folk song traditions with contemporary music, often including a social or political messages. Of this 1970s movement, the Argentine Mercedes Sosa is, internationally, perhaps one of the most famous members, but the New Song movement also enjoyed (and still enjoys) great popularity in Venezuela. The Venezuelan singer Soledad Bravo began recording in the late 1960s and went on to collaborate with New Song founder Violeta Parra of Chile. While one of Bravo's most famous recordings is the hymn "Hasta Siempre," dedicated to the revolutionary Che Guevara, in general she has chosen songs and themes less overtly political. To this day, Bravo's voice is recognized as one of the best of her generation, and her recordings of Venezuelan rural folk songs about the small trials, tribulations, and joys of everyday life are as important ethnographically as they are musically.

Ali Primera, known as the "Cantor del Pueblo" (Singer of the People) specialized in a more specific and overtly political style of the New Song. Primera sang in the Venezuelan musical form of the *gaitero* music of Zulia. A somewhat controversial figure during his lifetime, Primera studied music at the Universidad Central de Venezuela and then received a scholarship from the Venezuelan Communist Party to study in Romania in 1968. There he recorded his first album, which was censored by the Venezuelan government of the time. He went on to record several more highly popular albums on his own label, and he returned to Venezuela in 1973. Most of his songs may be considered socially committed or protest songs, though he preferred them to be called *canciones necesarias* (necessary songs). He continued to record until a fatal auto accident took his life in 1985. Many of his fans still believe that his death was no accident, but an assassination, as the singer was always politically active and confrontational.

In recent years, Primera's songs have become even more relevant and politically amenable to the administration of Hugo Chávez. Primera's brother, José Montecano, is a fervent Chávez supporter and frequently uses Primera's music at pro-Chávez rallies and Chávez appearances. Perhaps because of this, the Chávez administration declared Primera's music officially part of the *patrimonio nacional* (national heritage) in 2005.

The Chávez administration's affinity for the leftist message of Primera's music is not the only way in which it has supported a resurgence of traditional popular music. In 2003, the pro-Chávez government enacted a new Social Responsibility Law that detailed a new ratings system for broadcast content, set time limits and other restrictions for advertisements, and mandated certain time slots for government-sponsored programming. In addition, part of the new law also included provisions for the content of radio and television programming. In recent decades, home-grown popular music had lost airtime on radio stations. Most stations had turned to a combination of American and European rock, pop, and rap, with little domestic content. Radio stations rarely, for example, played rap produced by Venezuelan groups like Luango Rap, with their politically and socially charged lyrics. The Social Responsibility

---

THE DEATH OF ALI PRIMERA

Ali Primera, self-proclaimed Marxist/Leninist revolutionary, was not only a singer/songwriter but also a leader in social justice movements to free political prisoners, stop government appropriation of land, and support leftist revolutions in Nicaragua, Guatemala, and El Salvador. As such, Primera was a thorn in the side of Venezuela's ruling elite, including the AD political party. To this day, the AD reject Primera's music as much as the leftist president embraces it.

The AD's longstanding dislike of Primera is perhaps why many Primera fans blame the AD for the singer's death. Primera was killed in an automobile accident on one of Caracas' major highways in 1985. For these fans, Primera's death is part of a chain of assassinations against leftist leaders in the 1980s, beginning with the massacre of Yumare—another disputed event in which nine revolutionary leaders were killed either in an armed confrontation (according to government sources) or through detention, torture, and execution (according to members of the left). This chain then continued with Primera's death and with the murder of the socialist labor leader Hemmy Croes.

Law, following the nationalist bent of the Chávez government, requires that at least 50 percent of all music played on the radio be Venezuelan, and half of that 50 percent must be traditional, or folkloric.

This new law, while a headache for some radio stations, has been a boon for the more traditional performers like Simón Díaz, who turned 81 in 2009 and is still going strong. The wording of the law is just vague enough to be a boon to some of the younger local talent as well, like the jazz artist and composer Huascar Barrada. Barrada, a flautist who leads his own jazz ensemble, mixes jazz, traditional, and pop music into a modern fusion. For Barrada, the new law has meant that his songs now appear in heavy rotation on many radio stations, and he is in great demand across the country, booked solid in concert halls into 2010.

Barrada and Díaz are not the only beneficiaries. Other young talent in Venezuela that mixes traditional and modern music are also benefiting from the exposure and opportunity generated by the new law. One example is the hot new artist Rafael Brito, a *cuatro* player who also mixes a hip hop sensibility with jazz, pop, and the traditional harps and of *llanero* music. Brito has seen his sales soar and his records top the charts. Franklin Cacique, member of the Saladillo de Aguirre group, which plays the *gaitas* of Zulia and the northwest, has noted that the new law has meant that younger musicians are returning to traditional music, "leading to the creation of more imaginative music, as musicians try to interpret Venezuelan music in different ways" (Forero 2005). Even Los Amigos Invisibles, a Venezuelan pop group that had worked together nearly 20 years by 2009, incorporates traditional instruments into techno pop compositions with fascinating and fun results.

This is the intent of the new law. The government hopes to generate production of national music to combat the perceived colonial imperialism of Western rock that has taken over the radio airwaves. Not everyone agrees with this project, however. There are many who find the new law overly intrusive, who do not like the idea of the government telling them what they get to hear. For these citizens, the law is another example of Venezuelan's eroding freedoms and the Chávez government's attacks on freedom of expression. Whereas music critics and consumers have, by and large, embraced the changes in music as a result of the law, its consequences in television, as we discuss later, have been less positive.

THE VOICE OF THE PEOPLE: COMMUNITY RADIO AND CONTEMPORARY RAP MUSIC

Proponents of the Social Responsibility Law contend that its aim is to promote the production of unique Venezuelan art and music while combating the cultural influence of imported artistic styles and artifacts. Some of the beneficiaries of the law have been established artists who continue to practice traditional forms of Venezuelan art, such as the musical *gaita* style, played on mainstream radio and television programs. New participants, however, have begun to use the media of community radio stations and the style of rap music to create new modes of expression for a wide range of the Venezuelan community.

Community Radio and Television

Much has been made of the way in which the economic elite control the major media outlets in Venezuela. By the late 1970s, a series of actions had led to a significant decrease in government regulation and oversight of Venezuelan media and a significant increase in the commercialization of radio and television stations. By the 1990s, control of Venezuelan media was centralized in a small number of conglomerates (Fernandes 2005). As in many other nations, television and radio stations controlled by big businesses reflected the interests of big businesses. As a result, barrio residents had become passive receptors of media, only seeing themselves portrayed in mainstream radio and television as perpetrators or victims of violence. Community radio, as developed in the 21st century, has provided an alternative that allows those Venezuelans left out of the official system to meet local needs.

The impetus for community radio stations comes from the Organic Telecommunications Law, passed in June of 2000, which set up the framework for community broadcasting. The law set aside bandwidth and government funding for community groups to broadcast radio or television signals. The law states that stations may receive government permission and start-up funds for their station if 70 percent of the programming is produced within the community, if the programming is dedicated to community issues, and if the station provides training to community members in running the station so that all members of the community can participate (Migliorelli and McNulty 2009).

Community radio is not necessarily a new phenomenon. For years, information and music had been transmitted throughout the barrio via a network commonly referred to as Radio Bemba, an age-old tradition of unofficial word-of-mouth communication in Caribbean countries. By the late 20th century, the Radio Bemba network in Venezuela had gone beyond word-of-mouth to become true radio, blossoming to 13 licensed community radio stations and another 170 unsanctioned stations (Fernandes 2005). The signing of the Organic Telecommunications Law permitted the legalization of the Radio Bemba phenomenon. By 2007, there were more than 300 licensed community radio stations (Rentner 2007).

In the 21st century, community radio stations have grown in popularity and relevance in the economically disadvantaged neighborhoods of the barrios, where the citizens have little connection to the glitzy world of the *telenovelas* and game shows shown on mainstream television. The community radio station Emisora Libre al Son del 23 de Enero, which broadcasts out of the infamously poor and downtrodden 23 de Enero barrio, is a good example of this phenomenon. The radio station is located in a former jail and is proud of its position as an alternative to the mainstream media, especially as a voice for its community.

When interviewed about the mainstream media and the role of community radio, Emisora Libre participant Juan Contreras was quoted as saying:

> negative things are always covered: if tomorrow five people are killed they say "Oh! Look at the violence in El 23 de Enero! They are killing people!" But for those same news sources, we are not important: the fact that a building where people were tortured and killed has been turned into a radio station isn't impor-

tant for them. If tomorrow there is a public concert with five bands and dancers from a local dance class, that's not news. (Howard and Dangl 2006)

The ability to make the decision to report positive items and events such as concerts, meetings, and workshops certainly is news to citizens of the 23 de Enero barrio, and represents a significant change.

Different community stations make different decisions about their programming, allowing a wide range of possibilities for musical, artistic, and political expression. Researcher Sujatha Fernandes gives the example of four young women who work on the community radio station Radio Perola, a station that lets young people express the station's hip-hop inspired message of "Maximum Power!" (Fernandes 2005). On Radio Perola, the four young women, aged 17 to 22, write and produce a program called "Public Power," which discusses life in the barrio, especially for women.

This is just one example, and just one station. Many barrios have community radio, and each station and each program is different. There are "talk shows, educational programs, cultural shows, sports segments, local history programs, children's shows, cooking shows, and a variety of music programs, including salsa, bolero, hip-hop, rock, and llanero or country music" (Fernandes 2005). Rap, especially of the socially committed variety, is very commonly heard on community radio, as is the music of Ali Primera, who had always found it difficult to find a place on corporate radio stations.

There are also social and political programs, which attempt to make visible issues that don't get much coverage in the mainstream media. The community radio station Radio Negro Primero (Black First Radio), for example, advertises itself as for "black men and women only," in an attempt to bring racial issues out of the closet, and six different indigenous groups have begun broadcasting in their indigenous languages across the nation ("Indigenous Community Radio" 2008).

The ethnomusicologist T. M. Scruggs, who has worked in Venezuela for many years, gives a great deal of credit to the "explosion" of new community radio stations for helping to revive active interest in producing new material. Scruggs calls this the "most important change," one that "has never been duplicated in the history of the Americas." Scruggs also notes that some new community television stations have been started up, giving the general community production power in visual media as well (Rentner 2007).

One possibly related issue to the topic of community radio is that of music sales. Perhaps because of the general public's increased perception that music is less the province of large corporations, and more public domain, music copyright is falling apart in Venezuela. While this phenomenon is not unique to Venezuela, in many nations the sale of official CDs is losing ground to MP3 downloads and illegal file sharing. In Venezuela, however, the most common way that music is bought and sold is through the production and sale of illegal copies of CDs sold in the informal market. Official music stores continue to close as the majority of Venezuelans, especially young people, buy their CDs off of blankets in subways or on the sidewalk. "It would be interesting" says T. M. Scruggs "to find out how many people, say, under the age of 30 in Venezuela own a CD that has liner notes or have ever even seen liner notes to a CD" (Rentner 2007).

Venezuelan Rap Music: New Social Commentary on Economics, Race, Class, and Politics

As we have mentioned before, music in Venezuela has been for many years a popular form for protest. The *gaita* form native to Zulia state has been used by many as a vehicle for both criticizing the government and bringing social inequities to the attention of a wide audience. Ali Primera is perhaps the most famous Venezuelan artist to use the *gaita* in this way in the 20th century.

As the 21st century began, however, the situation seemed different for many young Venezuelans living in the capital. As we noted already, the systems of production and consumption of music had begun to break down—the monopolies that controlled radio stations and the sale of music had begun to collapse. The sale of rap music from other countries, especially the United States, had increased dramatically. T. M. Scruggs notes that this fact should be understood in conjunction with an increased sense of Afrovenezuelan identity at about the same time. While Venezuelans had lived for many decades with the myth of racial democracy and "*café con leche*" (coffee with milk) equality, after 1998 the nation had its first nonwhite president and a constitution that recognized indigenous groups (if not African-descended Venezuelans). This has allowed for more of an Afrovenezuelan class identity to emerge, especially in the barrios of west Caracas (Rentner 2007).

Many of the groups working in the fusion of North American hip hop and Venezuelan Latin rhythm went collectively by the name of "Venezuela subterránea" (Venezuelan underground). Perhaps the most well known of these groups is the rap duo Vagos y Maleantes, composed of the artists Pedro "Budú" Pérez and Carlos "Nigga" Madera. Pérez and Madera grew up poor and *pardo* in the center of Caracas in the barrio of Cotiza. In 1995, as teenagers, they formed a musical group known as Barrio MC. This group, however, was forced to disband when two of the group members were killed in the continuing violence of the neighborhood and the third was sent to prison. It was at this time that Pérez and Madera struck out on their own using the stage names Budú and Nigga under the group name Vagos y Maleantes (Lazies and Thugs) (*Secuestro Express* 2005).

Perhaps Vagos y Maleantes' most famous song is the hit "Papidandeando," produced by U.S. hip-hop artist Carlos Julio Molina. "Papidandeando," is indicative of the duo's style in its integration of Latin rhythms with more traditional North American rap style. After the success of "Papidandeando," Vagos y Maleantes were ready to release their first album. In 2003 "Papidandeando" became the most sold album of the year in Venezuela, and their first video off the album, "Guajira," which pays homage to the socially conscious music of Ali Primera, remained in MTV Latin America's top 10 videos for a month (*Secuestro Express* 2005). In 2008, the Vagos y Maleantes duo would go on to collaborate successfully with hip-hop DJ Trece, calling themselves Tres Dueños, on a new series of songs such as "La Mala Vida" ("The Bad Life").

The three collaborators first met in 2005 on the set of the Venezuelan film *Secuestro Express* (*Kidnap Express*). The title of the film refers to the unfortunately common practice of express kidnapping—the term for a short-term kidnapping in which people are held for a short amount of time (perhaps just a few hours) in exchange for quick cash from the victim's family. Kidnappers usually set a ransom amount that can be raised in a short amount of time and that can be paid with less trouble than would be entailed for the family if official authorities were to become involved. In the film, two wealthy white college students are kidnapped as they leave a party at a Caracas country club. The kidnappers demand 20,000 dollars U.S. for the pair.

The director of the film, Jonathan Jakobuwitcz, cast Budú, Nigga, and DJ Trece in the roles of the three kidnappers, believing that "no actor could inhabit the parts better than real ghetto kids who have lived all their lives struggling with the misery, violence, injustice and hunger of Caracas" (*Secuestro Express* 2005). The film indeed does go out of its way to make specific points about the differences of class and race separating the abductors and their victims. None of the characters are drawn as completely positive or negative. Budú only participates in the kidnapping to be able to get the money his child needs for medical care, and while one of the upper-class victims is a terrible elitist snob, the other is a gentle soul who volunteers in her father's free health clinic.

The film *Secustro Express* is violent and messy, but like the music of the Vagos y Maleantes or the programming of a community radio station, it is vibrant and colorful. Positive messages and hopeful insights can be drawn from all of these contexts. While the process of engaging and discussing difficult social issues such as race and class may be painful, it is ultimately more productive than ignoring them completely.

REFERENCES

Edgers, Jeff. 2009. "New Movement for Conservatory." http://www.boston.com/ae/music/articles/2009/10/23/.

Fernandes, Sujatha. 2005. "Growing Movement of Community Radio in Venezuela." *Venezuelanalysis*, December 26. http://wwww.venezuelanalysis.com/analysis/1543.

Forero, Juan. 2005. "Venezuelan Strongman's New Gig: Nacional Disc Jockey." *New York Times*, October 3. http://www.nytimes.com/2005/10/03/international/americas/03venezuela.html.

Gould, Jens Erik. 2005. "Venezuela Youths Transformed by Music." *BBC News Americas*, November 28. http://news.bbc.co.uk/2/hi/americas/4457278.stm.

Howard, April, and Benjamin Dangl. 2006. "Freedom on Air: Venezuelan Jail Transformed into Community Radio Station." http://upsidedownworld.org/main/content/view/449/35/.

"Indigenous Community Radio Gets a Boost." 2008. VenWorld. http://venworld.wordpress.com/2008/01/19/indigenous-radio-gets-a-boost/.

Lakshranan, Indira A.R. 2005. "For Venezuela's Poor, Music Opens Doors." *Boston Globe*, June 22. http://www.boston.com/news/world/articles/2005/06/22/for_venezuelas_poor_music_opens_doors/.

Migliorelli, Liz, and Caitlin McNulty. 2009. "Community Media: The Thriving Voice of the Venezuelan People." *Venezuelanalysis*, July 31. http://wwww.venezuelanalysis.com/analysis/4678.

Padgett, Tim. 2009. "Venezuela's Famed Youth Orchestra Visits U.S." *Time.* April 6. http://www.time.com/time/arts/article/0,8599,1889570,00.html.

Rentner, Simon. 2007. "Interview: TM Scruggs. Venezuela and the Rise of Afro Venezuelan Music to the Present Day Chavez Era." http://www.afropop.org/multi/interview/ID/118/TM%20Scruggs%20on%20The%20Rise%20of%20Afro-Venezuelan%20music.

Secuestro Express. 2005. Production Notes. Los Angeles: Miramax. thecia.com.au/.../kidnap-express-secuestro-express-production-notes.rtf.

Simon, Bob. 2008. "El Sistema: Changing Lives through Music." *60 Minutes.* July 20. http://www.cbsnews.com/stories/2008/04/11/60minutes/main4009335.shtml?tag=contentMain;contentBody.

Food

Food in Venezuela is tied as much to tradition as to the land on which it is grown. Even taking into account Venezuela's growing dependency on food imports (discussed later in this chapter), traditional Venezuelan foods continue to be based on the crops grown in the nation. Given Venezuela's great geographic diversity, this means that the typical foods eaten on the coasts of Venezuela are different than those enjoyed in the Andes or in the Orinoco River valley. This section will give an overview of some of the most commonly enjoyed foods in Venezuela, while noting the differences in cuisine throughout the nation.

CORN AND RICE

As the Foreign Agricultural Service of the U.S. Department of Agriculture (USDA) notes on their Web site, rice and corn are the two most important grains in Venezuelan cooking. Corn is the more widely grown grain, accounting for 62 percent of all grain production in Venezuela (USDA 2009). Corn is produced mainly in the central plains states of Portuguesta, Guarico, and Barinas. As a result, several of the nation's most popular dishes, including those of Caracas, are corn based. Corn production in central Venezuela dates all the way back to the precolonial era, as corn formed a large part of indigenous diets before the arrival of the Spanish. As such, it is a window in to the culinary history of Venezuela.

Arepas

One of the most common and popular dishes in Venezuela is the *arepa*. As the Venezuelan Web site Venezuelatuya puts it "to speak of the *arepa* is to speak of Venezuela . . . it is part of our culture and our table every day, it is our most indigenous culinary expression and it is our daily bread" ("La arepa venezolana y sus variaciones" n.d.). While any visitor to Venezuela will notice the popularity of the *arepa*, they will also notice variations in the way in which *arepas* are prepared and served.

In eastern and central Venezuela, *arepas* are made of ground precooked corn meal mixed with water and salt, which is then formed into a round, disc shape. The dough is then either fried or grilled until fluffy on the inside and crispy on the outside. *Arepas* may be small, intended to be served as side dishes or appetizers to a meal, or large enough to be stuffed with other items. Small *arepas*, or *arepitas*, are generally the size of a half-dollar, and larger *arepas* are the size of a hamburger bun, hockey puck, or salad plate.

Arepas may either be eaten plain, like bread, or stuffed with a wide variety of fillings. *Arepitas* are often served with sour cream for dipping. In Caracas, *areperas*, or *arepa* restaurants, may list as many as 20 choices for stuffing a larger *arepa*, everything from avocado to octopus, sausage to *perico* (scrambled eggs with tomato and onion). Common choices, however, include beef, ham, black beans, and cheese.

Arepas are eaten at every meal. They can either accompany breakfast or be a breakfast in and of themselves, be a quick meal for lunch (being very portable for a busy worker or a tourist with a lot to see), and are equally at home in a basket in an upscale restaurant as an accompanying bread with supper. One of your authors was even offered a basket of corn *arepas* as an appetizer before a meal in a Chinese restaurant in Caracas.

While the chubby corn *arepa* is ubiquitous in the eastern and central parts of the country, the Andean *arepa* is slightly different. Especially in the Venezuelan city of Mérida, *arepas de trigo*, or wheat, are at least as common as their corn-based cousins. An Andean *arepa* is also round but is generally flatter than the corn-based *arepa*. The wheat arepa is prepared with a mixture of wheat flour, egg, milk, and melted butter. These *arepas* are not meant to be stuffed but are generally eaten as a snack or as a bread accompaniment to a meal.

INDIGENOUS CULTIVATION OF CORN

Corn is not only central to the modern Venezuelan diet but has been cultivated by indigenous groups in Venezuela for thousands of years. As such, corn (with sweet potato and manioc) formed the basis of the diet in Venezuela long before the arrival of the Spanish. Arawak, Carib, Guajiro, and Timote all cultivated corn.

Tribes such as the Piraoa of modern day Bolívar and Amazonas States in southern Venezuela still cultivate corn in a traditional fashion. Choosing areas of secondary forest growth (an area that has already been used once and has regrown), each family in the tribe clears one-half hectare of land. The family then plants corn, sweet potato, or manioc. After four years, the plot of land is then abandoned and left fallow for 15 years.

Corn grown in this way is consumed by the family, though any extra may be sold or traded to neighboring families who grew other agricultural products.

Arepa de queso—a fried cornmeal cake filled with cheese. (Rui Dias Aidos/Dreamstime.com)

Cachapas

In addition to the arepa, another popular corn-based dish is the *cachapa. Cachapas*, like *arepas*, are eaten widely in Venezuela but are most common in the central part of the nation. *Cachapas* are made of corn and wheat flour, mixed into a sweetened batter. To this batter are added fresh corn kernels. *Cachapas* are then fried or grilled on an iron skillet known as a *budare*, which may also be used to cook *arepas. Cachapas* are often topped with butter and *queso de mano*, a soft, creamy cheese that is easily spreadable over the hot *cachapa. Cachapas* are popular for breakfast or snacks in Venezuela. They are common "road food." *Cachapas* are common fare all year round at roadside restaurants. The best are the ones made fresh during harvest season.

Hallacas

Together with *arepas* and *cachapas*, a third important culinary item made with corn is the *hallaca*, a traditional Christmas staple. The preparation and consumption of *hallacas*, in many parts of Venezuela, is similar to that of *tamaladas*, or tamale parties in other parts of the Hispanic world. Indeed, an *hallaca*, with its cornmeal dough, filling, and banana leaf wrapping, is similar to Central American tamales in many respects.

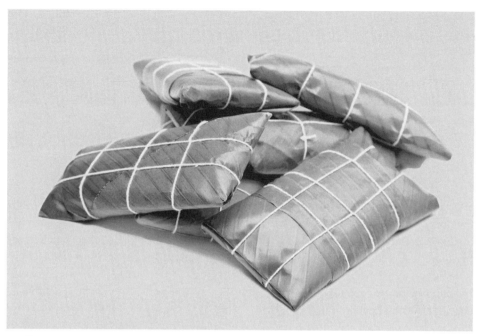

Hallacas—Venezuelan Christmas traditional food. (iStockPhoto)

As the process for making an *hallaca* is both labor-intensive and extensive, it invites the full participation of whole families over an extended period of time. Since the process is so labor intensive, many *hallacas* are made at once, in order to last the whole holiday season. For many Venezuelan families, making *hallacas* is a party that marks the start of the holiday season. It is a tradition that transcends race and class and indeed is many times offered as an example of Venezuela's syncretic, or mixed, heritage.

The main ingredients of the *hallaca* can be traced back to the three main constituent ethnic groups present in the nation. The corn was a staple of the indigenous tribes long before the arrival of the Spanish colonizers; the olives, capers, and raisins are the contribution of the Spanish; and the banana leaves represent the culinary heritage of the African slave population.

The preparation of *hallacas* can be divided into three parts: the preparation of the *guiso*, or filling; the preparation of the dough and the banana leaves; and the assembly and cooking of the *hallacas*. First, the filling is prepared by combining a variety of meats—chicken, pork, beef, and bacon—in large stew pots. These meats are then cooked slowly over a low heat for a full day with various seasonings such as onion, garlic, capers, tomatoes, raisins, olives, and sweet peppers. The fillings of an *hallaca* vary from family to family. The next day, the dough—made of corn flour, oil, salt, and broth—is mixed and kneaded. The banana leaves are also washed and dried. When both filling and dough are ready, an assembly line is put in place.

The assembly line, which can integrate all the members of the family, from the youngest to the oldest, takes a banana leaf, spreads a thin layer of dough on the leaf, places a mound of filling in the center, then folds the dough around the filling. The final step is to wrap the leaf around the dough and tie a string around the banana leaf, creating a neat package. This package will then be boiled or steamed and allowed to sit so all the flavors can meld.

There is some traditional rivalry between Venezuelan families about who makes the best *hallaca*, but the traditional Venezuelan saying that puts all debate to rest is: "*la major hallaca es la que hace mi mama*" (the best *hallaca* is the one my mom makes).

Pabellón Criollo

Rice is Venezuela's second most important grain crop and is the basis of another common dish, *pabellón criollo*. *Pabellón criollo* is known as Venezuela's national dish and is generally thought to date back to colonial times in Venezuela's culinary heritage. The *pabellón*, unlike the previously discussed foods, is not a single food item but an entire plate of food. While some regional differences may appear around the country in the preparation and presentation of the *pabellón*, it is recognizable as specifically Venezuelan in any iteration.

A *pabellón criollo* generally consists of white rice, black beans, and slow cooked beef known as *carne mechada*. White rice and black beans, staples of Venezuelan cooking since colonial times, are served side by side on the plate. Different regions may add different seasonings to the beans, such as garlic, onion, smoked pork, or even sugar, but the beans with any seasoning are integral to the dish. Next to the beans is the *carne mechada*. *Carne mechada* is a commonly enjoyed type of slow-cooked beef, simmered for hours with onions, garlic, sweet peppers, and tomato until one can pull it apart with forks. *Carne mechada* is also a common *arepa* filling.

Variations of this dish then include the common addition of fried plantains, or *tajadas*. These plantains are then placed on the sides of the dish, bracketing the plate. Therefore, this type of *pabellón* is often referred to as *pabellón con barandas*, or *pabellón* with guardrails, as the bananas look like they are keeping the other items from sliding off. Another variation is the addition of a fried egg on top of the dish, which is known as *pabellón a caballo*, or *pabellón* horseback riding, as the egg "rides" on top. It goes without saying that *arepas* often accompany a meal of *pabellón criollo*.

FRUITS AND VEGETABLES

In the eastern parts of Venezuela and along the coast, where there are lower elevations and higher average temperatures, one finds a very wide variety of indigenous fruits and vegetables, including mango, papaya, avocado, banana, coconut, melon, pineapple, and guava. In these warmer, lowland regions, the variety and size of these fruits is impressive, and they are widely consumed; a Venezuelan "fruit salad" as listed on a menu may consist of an entire platter of sliced, fresh fruit in comparison to the small cup of chopped, canned fruit that many North Americans might expect.

PARCHITA AND TAMARINDO

Two types of fruit that might not be familiar to those living outside of tropical climates are the *parchita*, or passion fruit, and the *tamarindo*, or tamarind.

Parchita is common throughout South America. The fruit has a hard outer shell and soft, pulpy, seedy interior. As the seeds are edible, it is common to slice the fruit in half and serve the fruit in halves with cream and sugar, as well as straining the pulp for a tangy, sweet juice. *Parchita* grow on trees, which also produce a unique and beautiful white and purple flower.

Tamarindo, while native to Africa, is also very popular in Venezuela. Tamarind fruits are pods, grown on very large trees (up to 100 feet tall). Each pod has many seeds within a juicy pulp. Tamarind beverages are made by opening the pods and removing the seeds. The surrounding pulp is then used by boiling the pulp with water and sugar and then chilling. The resulting drink has an earthy, tangy flavor.

One might expect to order the *ensalada de frutas* (fruit salad) and receive a small side dish, but in reality, one receives enough delicious fruit for an entire meal.

In the west, and especially in the higher elevations of the Andes, potatoes and yuca, or cassava root, are more widely grown than other vegetables. The yuca in particular is a very versatile and commonly consume root somewhat similar to the potato. Yuca, as seen in the market or in many of the fruit and vegetable stalls that line Venezuelan streets, is a large, dense, root vegetable covered in a tough, brown skin that must be removed before cooking. Yuca may be fried or boiled and is also made into a flat bread called *casabe* or (after mashing) into sweet doughnuts called *buñuelos*. Yuca is also a key ingredient in another common Venezuelan dish, the *sancocho*.

Sancocho is a hearty Venezuelan stew that combines yuca with other fruits and vegetables—often cabbage, carrots, potato, sweet potato, and plantain. The stew may also include a variety of types of meat or fish, many times depending on the region where it is being prepared. Chicken is common, but a *sancocho* being prepared in the Venezuelan llanos, or plains, will be heavy on the red meat, while a *sancocho* prepared on the beach may have fish or shellfish. *Sancocho* is a comfort food and is known to many as "*levanta muertos*" (raise the dead) for its perceived healing powers.

MEAT AND SEAFOOD

In the eastern parts of the country and along the coast, seafood predominates. Common seafood offerings include shrimp, fresh sardines, and *pargo*, or red snapper. These all can be prepared in a wide variety of ways and may appear at any meal. One of your authors has been served many delicious breakfasts of fried sardines, rice, and

---

THE WORLD'S LARGEST RODENT . . . AS FISH?

Venezuela was founded as a Catholic nation, and many follow the religious tradition of not eating meat during the period of Lent, 40 days before Easter. During this period, a very popular protein is the flesh of the capybara. While capybaras (known in Venezuela as *chiguire*) are actually the world's largest rodent, and have the furry aspect of a mammal, in Venezuela, for religious purposes, they are considered fish.

Capybaras are, like beavers, semi-aquatic, and they spend most of their time in the water. Colonists in Venezuela recognized this and used the fact as a loophole in the Lenten dietary restrictions. In the 1600s Venezuelans sent a request to officials at the Vatican, asking that the capybara be classified as a fish. The Vatican agreed (likely never having seen a capybara). Today, though, meat is only restricted on Friday during Lent, many Venezuelans still eat capybara during this time.

---

tajadas by her mother-in-law. Sardines or snapper can also be baked with tomatoes, garlic, or onions; grilled over an open flame; or, perhaps most deliciously, fried. A very popular meal is freshly caught fried red snapper in a beach side café.

Cazón, which refers to a small type of common shark, is also very common, and in addition to being found in some eastern and coastal *sancocho*, it forms the filling for Margarita Island's most popular empanada (a type of Latin American turnover). An empanada with *cazón* is made by preparing a filling of fresh *cazón* with onion and garlic, adding olives or raisins as desired. This filling is then covered in a round piece of cornmeal pastry folded into a half-moon and then baked.

In the grasslands of the llanos, beef and game such as deer are commonly eaten. As we discussed in Chapter 1, the llanos are an area where a great deal of ranching occurs. Men and women are accustomed to ready access to beef and are surrounded by wide open spaces, so it is likely not surprising that red meat, both from the ranch and as a product of hunting, is a staple of the *llanero* diet.

Two famous contributions to Venezuelan cuisine from this region center around meat. These are the *parrilla llanera* and the *desayuno llanero*. The *parrilla llanera*, or plains grill, is generally a widely mixed array of meat grilled on an open fire. This type of meal may consist of beef, pork, chicken, and sausage, and it often includes organ meats as well as cuts of meat more familiar to North American diners such as chops or steaks. When dining in a restaurant, the meal is often rolled up to the table on an actual functional grill so that all the meat remains hot while the diners eat. A diner can have a few bites of a steak, then move to a piping hot pork chop and then a *morcilla* (blood sausage). When eaten alfresco in the llanos, however, the *parrilla* may even include such exotic meats as a *babo*, a whole roasted freshwater caiman. Side dishes, such as yuca or *casabe*, do accompany a *parrilla llanera*, but they are secondary in importance to the meat. The *desayuno llanero*, or plains breakfast, is similar in its emphasis on meat as a staple of the *llanero* diet. In this hearty breakfast, the meats are accompanied by the traditional *arepas*, but in contrast to the *parrilla*, more dairy is eaten in the form of cheeses, milk, and butter to accompany the meal.

In the west and in the mountainous Andean region, the types of meat eaten vary from that of the coast and the southern plains. Coastal seafood is less common, as is beef, given restricted grazing lands. Some meats and fish more commonly found are goat and rabbit. *Tacarí del chivo* is a popular preparation for goat, where the goat meat is marinated and then stewed with red wine, tomatoes, garlic, and onion over time. *Tacarí* is often accompanied by rice and fried round coins of plantain banana known as *tostones*.

Trout, while not native to Venezuela (the U.S. government made the Venezuelan government a gift of breeding trout in 1937), has become an increasingly popular dish and tourist attraction for Venezuelans in Andean Mérida, where the clear, cold streams are perfect for the freshwater fish. As trout is a specialty item in Mérida, it is found in many restaurants, with many preparations—fried, baked, and wrapped in bacon.

BEVERAGES

While coffee may certainly be considered the most popular and culturally important beverage in Venezuela, other options, both alcoholic and nonalcoholic, are available. Fruit juices made from the indigenous fruits are very popular, and while locally produced rum is always a good bet, whiskey is probably more popular.

Juices and Nonalcoholic Drinks

Due to the wide availability of a variety of high-quality fruit, fruit juices are a common beverage choice either alone or to accompany a meal. Juices are available in restaurants but also at an array of sidewalk stands and shops that specialize in the drinks. A simple juice is known as a *jugo*, whereas a *batido* is a mixture of juice, water, and ice. The *batido* is generally thicker than a simple juice. If milk is added to a *batido*, it is known as a *merengada*. *Jugos* and *batidos* of *tamarindo* (tamarind), *parchita* (passion fruit), and *lechosa* (papaya) are as common as in many other Latin American nations. One unique juice beverage found in Venezuela, however, is *papelón con limón*, which is a *jugo* of raw cane sugar mixed with water and lemon or lime. This tart, refreshing drink is associated with very hot weather and is best drunk in the heat of an afternoon.

Chicha is a beverage similar to a juice, and like *batidos* and *jugos* it is commonly drunk both at home and purchased from street vendors and shops. *Chicha*, particularly popular in the Andean cities of Mérida and Trujillo, is a drink made of boiled rice, sugar, milk, and chopped ice. To prepare *chicha*, one soaks the rice in water overnight with cinnamon, then cooks the rice in the water until soft. Then the rice, water, milk, and sugar are blended until the beverage is thick and creamy, with an eggnog-like consistency. Some recipes call for adding evaporated milk for extra creaminess.

While carbonated beverages are consumed in Venezuela, and one can surely find North American brands such as Coke and Pepsi, the Venezuelan beverage market is atypical in its consumption of colas. Market research shows that most Venezuelans prefer flavored sodas to colas, and when they do drink a cola, they tend to choose the national brand, Frescolita. The most popular flavored soda choices include orange and guaraná (a berry native to Venezuela and Brazil) (Producto Online 2002). Another popular nonalcoholic drink in Venezuela is Maltín Polar, a nonalcoholic beer beverage produced by Venezuela's largest beer brewer, the Polar Brewery. Maltín is an ale-style beer with hops, but its is alcohol free. It does have caramel flavoring, and its final flavor is somewhat like that of root beer.

Rum and Whiskey

Rum has been produced in Venezuela since 1896 at the Hacienda Santa Teresa in the valley of Aragua, only 50 miles from Caracas (Yannitsas 2004). Rum is a distillate of sugar cane, and the fertile low-lying valleys of the central states of Venezuela provide the perfect climate for sugar cane production. The production facilities and sugar cane fields of Santa Teresa are located, for example, in the Aragua Valley in the state of Miranda. Santa Teresa, along with Pampero and Cacique, continue to be the top-selling brands of rum in Venezuela and internationally. According to Consejo Nacional para la Promocion de Inversiones (CONAPRI) on their Web site, Venezuela exports 2.75 million cases of the 35 million cases of rum bought in international markets per year, and based on the growth in sales, CONAPRI estimates that the number will grow to 20 million cases per year by the year 2015. Venezuelan rum brands also hold 70 percent of the national market in Venezuela. All three Venezuelan brands produce and specialize in aged rum (meant to be sipped, not mixed as part of a rum and coke) that has been increasingly popular both in Venezuela and European nations.

While rum is produced locally in Venezuela, according to the BBC in a 2009 online report, imported whiskies outsell Venezuelan rum and other national liquors by a ratio of almost two-to-one. Rum may be Venezuelan, but Venezuelans prefer whiskey. The BBC reports that the Scotch whiskey industry reports annual sales of $151 million a year, making Venezuela the world's sixth largest world market for whiskey, consuming less than only the United States, Spain, France, Singapore, and South Korea (Grant 2009).

It is ironic that a nation that produces some of the world's finest rum chooses to drink whiskey instead. Some view the choice as tied to the perceived "high class" nature of whiskey. Venezuela began its love affair with scotch whiskey in the 1970s at the height of the oil boom, when drinking aged (12-year-old or older) whiskey became a status symbol for the newly rich. Though those days are over, in a nation increasingly conscious of class divisions, whiskey is a higher class drink than rum, and many flock to whiskey bars. This connection between wealth, luxury, and whiskey has also been reinforced by Hugo Chávez, who, in October of 2007, denounced the consumption of whiskey on his radio and television program *Aló Presidente*. President Chávez denounced the importation of whiskey as antirevolutionary and compared whiskey to other luxury items such as Hummers.

AGRICULTURAL PRODUCTION AND PRICE CONTROLS

One of the modern-day challenges facing Venezuela in the area of food and drink is the decline in agricultural production. As we have discussed in other chapters, at the beginning of the 20th century, before the advent of the oil industry, agriculture was the engine of the Venezuelan economy, and the majority of the food that Venezuelans consumed was produced in Venezuela. As the *Nations Encyclopedia* notes, at the beginning of the 21st century, however, agriculture is one of the country's weakest sectors, employing only 13 percent of the labor force and accounting for only 5 percent of GDP ("Venezuela-Agriculture" 2009).

In the 21st century, the drop in agricultural production has led to food shortages in the nation. As reported by All Headline News, by 2007 Venezuela was importing 60 percent of the food it consumed, and a Datanalisis poll of that year showed nine basic food items in short supply in Venezuela: sugar, beef, powdered milk, eggs, rice, corn flour, sardines, and beans. This led Venezuela in January of 2008 to import more than 74,000 tons of food to meet the needs of the citizens (Hernandez 2008).

Many inside and outside Venezuela say that the food shortages caused by the drop in agricultural production are linked to price controls put in place by the Chávez administration. In an effort to keep prices low for the economically challenged social classes, the administration set controls on prices that stores may charge for basic food items, keeping those prices low for consumers. For producers, however, costs of production continue to rise. For producers whose costs exceed the price they are allowed to charge for their product, there is no sense in planting new crops. A good example of this dynamic is corn, featured earlier as a staple in several of the national dishes. As the Foreign Agricultural Service of the USDA reports, corn consumption rose between 2005 and 2009, but production, which dropped sharply in 2001, has remained flat ("Venezuela-Agriculture" 2009). The lack of increase in production is blamed on government price controls. While Chávez has blamed hoarders for the food shortages, advocates for the agricultural sector say that the food shortage problem will not be solved until the government removes the price controls that stifle production.

REFERENCES

Hernandez, Vittorio. 2008. "Venezuela Imports 84,000 Tons of Food to Avert Crisis." January 22. http://www.allheadlinenews.com/articles/7009793809.

Howard, April M. 2006. "Feeding Ourselves. Organic Urban Gardens in Caracas Venezuela." http://www.towardfreedom.com/environment/869-feeding-ourselves-organic-urban-gardens-in-caracas-venezuela.

"La arepa venezolana y sus variacines." n.d. http://www.venezuelatuya.com/cocina/arepa.htm.

Morton, Julia F. 1987a. "Passionfruit." *Fruits of Warm Climates.* Miami, FL: Purdue University Press.

———. 1987b. Tamarind. *Fruits of Warm Climates.* Miami, FL: Purdue University Press: Miami, FL.

Producto Online. 2002. "Guerra Sin Refrescos." http://www.producto.com.ve/225/notas/mercadeo.html.

U.S. Department of Agriculture. 2009. "GAIN Report." http://www.fas.usda.gov/gainfiles/200904/146347724.pdf.

"Venezuela-Agriculture." 2009. http://www.nationsencyclopedia.com/economies/Americas/Venezuela-AGRICULTURE.html.

Yannitsas, Athena. 2004. "From Venezuela, Rum with a Pedigree." *Hispanic* 17: 10–13.

Sports and Leisure

BASEBALL: THE NATIONAL SPORT

One of the great Venezuelan national spectacles is baseball. While the specific origins of the game in Venezuela are a bit murky, it is clear that baseball was being played in Venezuela by the end of the 19th century (Bjarkman 2005). Most believe that baseball was brought to Venezuela by upper-class students who had learned the new game while studying in American universities. By 1895, a group of brothers, Amenodoro, Emilio, Gustavo, and Augusto Franklin, organized the first baseball club in Venezuela, Caracas BBC, structured around a group of friends who had been practicing and playing together every Sunday for three months. As Leonte Landino observes in Peter Bjarkman's *Encyclopedia of Baseball*, the brothers wanted to promote the new game, and organized a public exhibition on May 22, 1895 (Bjarkman 2005). By November of the same year, the owner of the Caracas Beer Company built the first official stadium, with standard measurements according to U.S. rules.

During the late 1800s and early 1900s, upper-class boys (being the only ones who could afford the equipment) played games every Sunday. The events were popular outings for families, and the sport began to spread to other cities. In 1917, the baseball club in Magallanes was founded, a team that still exists in Venezuela's top professional league today. In 1912, a U.S. immigrant, William Phelps, brought baseball equipment to his department store in Maracaibo. Working with a local sports director, Raul Cuenca, Phelps helped introduce the game to the area, and it spread rapidly. By 1920, Maracaibo had more than 10 stadiums and 30 different teams. Maracaibo was also the first area to start charging a small fee to attend games. Soon other teams had begun charging admission and paying players. Players began to come from other countries, such as Cuba, to play for the Venezuelan clubs.

The first professional tournament was played in Caracas in 1927, and in 1930 the Venezuelan Association of Baseball was founded. By 1935, the game had become so popular that the dictator Juan Vicente Gómez ordered the organization of the baseball club Maracay BBC in the state of Aragua. Gómez personally played for the

Maracay club, which ensured a high number of wins for the team, as opposing teams were loath to beat the leader's squad. Over the years, Magallanes, and the series of teams representing Caracas, built up a fierce rivalry still present today. Many analysts compare the intensity of the competition between the two teams to the Boston Red Sox–New York Yankees rivalry in the United States.

By the middle of the 20th century, baseball had a solid place in Venezuelan culture, making Venezuela a rarity in South America—in Venezuela, baseball is more popular than soccer. The enthusiasm for the sport began producing a type of talent that drew U.S. baseball scouts. Perhaps the most famous Venezuelan baseball player is one of the first to play for a U.S. major league team: hall-of-famer Luis Aparicio, who played for the Chicago White Sox. Aparicio, a native of Maracaibo, began a long line of superior shortstops who went on to play in the United States. Players like Chico Carrasquel in the 1950s, David Concepción in the 1970s, Ozzie Guillen in the 1980s (named manager of the White Sox in 2003 and the first Latin American manager to ever win a World Series), and Omar Vizquel and Alex González in the 1990s and early 21st century helped establish Venezuela as a fountain of shortstops. In all, the number of Venezuelan players on major league baseball rosters jumped from 14 in 2000 to 51 at the beginning of the 2006 baseball season.

In 2006, there were approximately 800 Venezuelans playing in the major league organizations (major and minor league teams). Acknowledging just how important Venezuela is to the major leagues, in 2007, 9 major league teams had full-time academies in Venezuela to cultivate Venezuelan talent, while 13 major league teams sponsored Venezuelan summer league teams (Biertempfel 2007; Otis 2005).

International interest in Venezuelan players does not detract from fanaticism for baseball in Venezuela. The major professional league in Venezuela consists of eight teams: Caracas Lions, Navigators of Magallanes, Lara Cardinals, La Guaira Sharks, Oriente Caribes, Zulia Eagles, Aragua Tigers, and Aguirre Pastora. The league perennial powerhouses are the Lions and Navigators. Caribes fans have much in common with Kansas City Royals fans: great love, but little to cheer about. The professional league's season begins just after the U.S. baseball season's conclusion in October and finishes in January. It is not unusual for U.S. major leaguers, Venezuelans and non-Venezuelans, to head south to play in the Venezuelan professional leagues during the major league off season. At the end of the regular season, a championship series with the top five teams is played. The series, played round-robin style, eventually produces two teams who play a seven-game series to determine the league champion. The league champion then goes on to represent Venezuela in the Serie del Caribe (Caribbean Series) against teams from Mexico, the Dominican Republic, and Puerto Rico. The World Baseball Classic, created in 2006 by Major League Baseball, has become another international venue for Venezuela to showcase its talent. Venezuela was one of 16 nations participating in the first World Baseball Classic. The Venezuelan team made it to the semi-finals in the 2009 World Baseball Classic. The Japanese have won both tournaments.

Venezuelans follow their teams, and the players who have gone on to play in the United States, with keen interest, passionately and unabashed. Americans

CHICO CARRASQUEL

Alfonso "Chico" Carrasquel Colón, the first in a continuing line of great Venezuelan shortstops, was the first Hispanic player selected to play in Major League Baseball's All-Star Game.

Carrasquel was born in Caracas in 1928 and played for his hometown Cerveceria Caracas. When he was 17 years old, he hit the very first homerun in Venezuelan Professional Baseball League history while playing for the Caracas club. In 1949 he was drafted by the Brooklyn Dodgers, with whom he had some communication problems (due to limited English), and was later traded to the White Sox (who had a bilingual pitcher). Carrasquel played for the Sox from 1951 to 1955. In 1950, Carrasquel finished third in the balloting for Rookie of the Year, and was also considered for MVP honors. In 1951, he played in the MLB All-Star Game.

After his time in the United States, Carrasquel returned to Venezuela, managing several teams and leading the Venezuelan national team to the 1982 Caribbean Series championship. In 1991 the Venezuelan Professional Baseball League renamed a stadium in his honor in Puerto La Cruz.

Luis Aparicio, left, Chicago White Sox shortstop, poses with Chico Carrasquel, Cleveland Indians shortstop, before the season opener in Chicago, Ill., April 17, 1956. Carrasquel was traded to Cleveland and was replaced by Aparicio. Both men were born and raised in Venezuela. (AP/Wide World Photos)

accustomed to the pastoral and relaxed atmosphere of a U.S. baseball game are often surprised at the energy and raucous mood of a Venezuelan contest. Scantily clad female dancers perform between innings to extremely loud music. Spectators are extremely vocal in their pleasure (or displeasure) with players and officials and use shouting, whistles, and horns to get their point across. It is also not unheard of to either celebrate or protest by throwing beer and ice on the field or in the stands.

Baseball is such an integral part of Venezuelan culture that it should not be a surprise that the modern events that have affected the nation have touched the sport as well. The economic crisis of the late 1980s and 1990s, for example, actually made baseball more popular as a pastime and potential attractive career option for young Venezuelan men. As a scout for a U.S. team recently revealed to an interviewer: "When I got started [in Venezuela] I would ask dads, 'why won't you lety your son play baseball?' They'd say 'Are you crazy. That's not going to lead anywhere. He's going to go to college.' Now the dads seek me out and as me, 'Can you check out my son?'" (Ortiz 2005). The increased interest in the sport has created a boom in Venezuelan baseball (as evidenced by Venezuela's 2000 victory in the Little League World Series) and excites scouts for U.S. major league teams, who can sign a young Venezuelan prospect for a fraction of the cost of contracting a player of similar talent from the United States.

Once in the United States, Venezuelan players continue to have increasing success. This success, and the income that comes with it, however, can be a mixed blessing. Because of the scheduling of the U.S. and Venezuelan baseball seasons, for decades it had been the norm for Venezuelan stars to play for a U.S. team, and then return home to play "winter ball" in Venezuela. This system allowed Venezuelans to enjoy their national players not only on television with their U.S. teams, but also in person

---

JOHAN SANTANA

One of the finest major league pitchers of the 21st century is Johan Santana. Santana was born in Tovar Mérida, Venezuela, where he was discovered and sent to the Houston Astros' baseball academy in 1995. Santana stayed at the academy until 1999, when he was named athlete of the year. In 1999, Santana was the number-two overall pick in the Major League Baseball draft, taken by the Minnesota Twins.

By 2006, Santana was considered one of the top five pitchers in Major League Baseball. Santana won pitching's most prestigious award, the Cy Young in 2004 and 2006. In 2006, he became the first pitcher since 1985 to win the pitching triple crown (lowest ERA, most strikeouts, and most wins). In 2008, Santana signed a six-year $137.5 million contract with the New York Mets.

Santana is not only highly successful on the field but is also active in charitable work. His Johan Santana Foundation supports children's causes in both the United States and in Venezuela. In Venezuela, Santana has helped to build schools, hospitals, and sports facilities.

with a local club. A sharp increase in the crime rate, however, has meant a change in this system. Violent crime in Venezuela, and especially in Caracas, has been a steadily increasing problem for the last 20 years. Precise estimates on the numbers of kidnappings and murders are hard to come by, but Mark Ungar reports that, for example, the percentage of violent crimes as figured per 100,000 citizens rose from 13 percent in 1990 to 21 percent in 2001 (Ungar 2003). In addition, most analysts agree that since 2001, kidnappings nationwide have increased at least fourfold, while homicides have doubled (Duidley 2006).

These numbers have particular relevance for Venezuela's returning baseball heroes and their families. As celebrities, their incomes are well known and they have increasingly become targets. In 2005, pitcher Ugueth Urbina's mother was kidnapped from her Caracas home by men wearing police uniforms. The kidnappers demanded 6 million dollars in ransom money from the ballplayer. While Urbina's mother was finally recovered by a massive police operation in February of 2006, the incident highlighted the precarious position of players and their families. The Urbina kidnapping was not the only incidence of violence connected to baseball, and some players have recently begun to make difficult decisions regarding their residency. Fewer athletes now travel home for the Venezuelan baseball season, and more make their home with extended family year-round in the United States. For those players who still want to return home, or whose families refuse to move, significant increases in protection have become necessary. Bodyguards, alarm systems, and restrictions on movement have become the norm. In 2005, Philadelphia Phillies outfielder Bobby Abreu returned to play for the Caracas Lions but went so far as to have security guards on the field protecting him.

SOCCER

Because of most Venezuelans' obsession with baseball, it has been hard for soccer, or *fútbol*, to find a following. Venezuela does support national teams that play in international tournaments, but historically those teams have never performed well. When, in one of the qualifying games for the 2006 World Cup, the Venezuelans almost beat Chile, the Chileans took the close score as a wake-up call, motivation to improve, not as a sign that Venezuelan soccer was improving. It was, and is, however slowly. Venezuela hosted the 2007 Copa América international soccer tournament. For Chávez, the Copa provided an opportunity to invest in soccer facilities in many cities and play host to the global community. For Venezuelan soccer fans, the Copa provided them the opportunity to show the world that their Vino Tinto (the team wears colors similar to the color of red wine) was no longer a minor league team as compared to the Brazilians, Argentines, or Mexicans. Reaching the quarterfinals in the tournament eventually won by the Brazilians was a good showing for Venezuelan soccer.

OTHER SPORTS

While baseball and *fútbol* attract national audiences, other sports emphasize Venezuelan regional or class differences. *Coleo* is a *llanero*, or cowboy, sport somewhat similar to rodeo in the United States. It traces its roots at least back to the middle parts of the 19th century and was known to be popular with the Monagas presidents (brothers José Tadeo and José Gregorio, 1848–1858), cattle ranchers from the eastern *llanos.* Judges let loose a bull in a *manga de coleo*, which is a long, narrow strip approximately 100 yards long with walls on each side. Four riders then chase the bull and compete with each other see how many times each rider can take the bull down only by grabbing its tail in the allotted five minutes. It is a dangerous sport, like rodeo. It is not unusual for riders to suffer trampling by the bull and other riders. Spectators, frequently inebriated, often fall off the walls of the *manga.* The bull, too, suffers and frequently goes directly from the *manga* to the slaughterhouse. *Coleo* is most popular in the eastern and southern llanos, especially in the state of Barinas. The national *coleo* federation hosts competitions that are becoming national in scope, with competitors from the states of Monagas, Yaracuy, Trujillo, Portuguesa, Apure, Cojedes, Miranda, Guarico, and Carabobo.

Coleo is a sport that celebrates Venezuela's *llanero* heritage. Sponsorships subsidize the modern version of the sport. Without those sponsorships, many *coleo* riders would not be able to compete. *Coleo* is not a sport associated with the Venezuelan elite.

Bullfighting

Another traditional pastime related to bulls is the *corrida de toros*, or bullfighting. The *corrida* is not properly considered a sport; it is rather an art form imported with the Spanish colonists that dates its popularity in Venezuela to colonial times. The first bullrings were constructed in the 18th century. These rings were commonly made of wood and seated a few hundred people. The first large bullring, the Circo Metropolitano, was built in Caracas in 1896. This was later replaced in 1968 with the Nuevo Circo de Caracas (Portal Taurino n.d.).

Bullfights occur in various locations around the nation, including in Trujillo, Maracay, Valencia, Maracaibo, and San Sebastian. There are 55 permanent bullrings in the nation, 25 bull breeding farms, and two bullfighter training schools (CAS n.d.), Bullfighting festivals normally form part of a city's festival in honor of the patron saint or Virgin, as in the case of the festival of La Chinita (Virgen de la Chiquinquirá) in Zulia. Bullfighting festivals feature a week of spectacle with *corridas* every night during the evenings. Each evening's entertainment includes four or five *matadores* facing an equal number of Venezuelan bulls. In the art of bullfighting, the quality of the bull, his strength and power, is as important as the skill of the bullfighter.

Perhaps the most famous of all the bullfighting festivals is the Feria del Sol (Festival of the Sun) in the Andean city of Mérida. The Feria del Sol, also known as the Carnaval Taurino de América (The Bullfighting Carnival of America) is a special celebration of Carnival that features a week of bullfighting along with other traditional activities such as concerts and parades. The Andean festival draws national and international fans and features bullfighters from Venezuela as well as from Spain, Mexico, and Colombia. Visitors to Mérida during this time should be alert to the presence of a wide array of steak specials in the city that will be cheap, but very chewy.

Carolina Moreno drops a bull during the Venezuelan women's national Coleo tournament in San Juan De Los Morros, Venezuela. (AP/Wide World Photos)

While the *corrida* continues to be popular with many in Venezuela, as in other nations, there are those in Venezuela who feel that bullfighting is a cruel spectacle that should be outlawed. An ancient tradition that pre-dates recorded history on the Spanish peninsula, bullfighting is a bloody art that always ends in the death of the bull. In 2007, an animal protection bill was presented in the Venezuelan congress that would have made it illegal to harm bulls. This bill has been fought very vehemently, however, not only by fans of bullfighting, but also by fans of the *coleo*, and was mired in committee as of 2010 (CAS n.d.).

Golf

Golf has become a political topic in recent years, as President Chávez has pushed to expropriate some or all of the land owned by the clubs and use it to build housing. The 2001 land reform laws limited the amount of property owned by any one individual and asserted the government's right to tax unused property. Chávez argues that those laws grant the right to expropriate golf courses (Campbell 2006). There is no doubt that housing shortages in Caracas, Maracay, and other major cities with golf courses under expropriation orders are real. However, many perceive the move to expropriate golf courses as another chapter in ongoing conflicts between Chávez and the political opposition, many of whom come from the traditional elite. In a 2009 article in *The New York Times*, President Chávez said that he respected all sports but that golf was not a people's sport (Romero 2009). Those who perceive a political agenda intertwined with a housing agenda may have a point.

LEISURE ACTIVITIES

Plazas and Parks

The overwhelming majority of Venezuelans find other ways to occupy their leisure time. An emphasis on family and a relative lack of disposable income means that most Venezuelans choose to spend their leisure time in family-oriented activities rather than in recreational sports or in playing expensive video games. As emphasized later in this chapter, public spaces, such as central plazas, historically have fulfilled an important place in Venezuelan society. Plazas and parks provide low-cost areas for families to gather and enjoy their leisure time.

Most major cities still retain some green spaces that attract families and tourists in the evenings and on the weekends. Parks and central plazas are central gathering places for families at these times. Vendors regularly sell locally produced arts and crafts, and food vendors sell empanadas, *tostones*, and ice cream from carts. In parks, local entrepreneurs rent small go-carts for short rides to children and sell balloons. Teenagers zip around on skates or ride around on bikes. Young athletic men and women jog, and young families walk around with children in strollers. In plazas, adults simply sit and enjoy the evening or afternoon while the children run around.

The Paseo Colón, a boardwalk on the beach in downtown Puerto La Cruz, is an excellent example of a coastal public space frequented by Venezuelan families and tourists alike. The Paseo offers a pleasant walking space with a view of the sea and is lined with food and craft vendors. In Caracas, the Plaza Altamira hosts both ice cream carts and evening concerts, while the Parque del Este remains a popular weekend destination for families who walk the paths and view animals in the small zoo. *Caraqueños* also visit Avila National Park, the mountain preserve that borders Caracas on the north. There, visitors use the mountain paths to hike, visit the streams and waterfalls, and appreciate the flowers, plants, and butterflies.

While the Paseo Colón, Parque del Este, and the Plaza Altamira remained popular leisure spots through 2009, increases in crime and concerns about both robbery and kidnapping meant that many Venezuelans had abandoned other previously popular public spaces by that year. The Plaza Bolívar in central Caracas was no longer considered safe, and many other parks were considered unsafe for joggers very early in the morning or late at night. These changes, due to concerns about crime, mark a truly significant change in Venezuelan public life.

Vacationing is not a popular pastime in Venezuela as it is in the United States. However, when Venezuelans do travel for recreation, Mérida in the Andes is a favored spot. The highest mountain in Venezuela, Pico Bolívar, is easily accessible from Mérida. Gondolas of the *teleférico* take tourists to the top of the world in Venezuela on a regular basis daily. The *teleférico* is especially popular on colder days when the mountain is cloudy at its peak. It is then that citizens form long lines for the gondola rides, hoping to see some of the only snow in Venezuela at the top of the mountain.

It is harder to get to Angel Falls, the tallest waterfall in the world, in Gran Sabana in the southeast, though it is a dream trip for many Venezuelans. More accessible is the duty-free zone in Maracay that has made Maracay a popular attraction for more and more Venezuelans in recent years. In addition, people in the central regions regularly visit the Colonia Tovar, the immigrant community established by Germans in the mid-19th century. Despite its touristy nature, the Colonia Tovar feels much more authentically German than it does Venezuelan and is a popular spot for honeymooners from the capital. Finally, however, the place that most Venezuelans go, and usually more than once, is Margarita, the small island state a three-hour ferry ride from Puerto La Cruz. Venezuelans from the eastern part of the country sometimes visit Margarita as part of a religious pilgrimage because the shrine to the Virgen del Valle (Virgin of the Valley), the most popular saint in the east, is on Margarita. The duty-free shopping on the island is pretty good, and the beaches are even better.

Venezuelans are devoted beachgoers, and many Venezuelan beaches are world class. Foreign tourists come to Venezuela to snorkel off the beaches in the west, especially off the islands of Los Roques. The beaches to the north and east of Caracas and between Puerto La Cruz and Cumaná fill with thousands of Venezuelans

Stained glass window in the Church of the Virgin of the Valley, Patron of the Island and Fishermen. (Pedro Gutierrez/Dreamstime.com)

during the Christmas and New Year's holidays, during Carnival, holy week, and in July and August when school is not in session. The Chávez administration invested resources in cleaning up the beaches in the east, installing running water for toilet facilities, constructing cabanas for shade, and providing small loans for locals who want to make a living through serving beachgoers. The investment has paid off, as the beaches in the east are cleaner and more family friendly than ever before. Vendors sell fresh fried *pargo* with plantains and rice. Small entrepreneurs load up inflatable rafts with beachgoers then tow them at fairly high speeds up and down the beach. Other entrepreneurs take beachgoers on tours through coastal inlets. Locals often pay fishermen to take them to the small islands off of the eastern coast, where they can enjoy the beach, make a *sancocho* over a *fogón* (campfire) with *chipi chipi* (small clams) and other seafood they catch and can swim with dolphins. Beach time really is time for family and friends—the way Venezuelans define leisure. The best beach times combine the visits with family from out of town, on a day that is not a national holiday so the crowds are less intense, with lots of food, beer, rum, whisky, and other libations, both alcoholic and nonalcoholic. By the time that everyone is exhausted and kids have built all of the sand castles they can build, buried each other (and their uncles and aunts) in sand *tortugas* (turtles) is when the sun sets most gloriously. Even for fair-skinned North Americans, there is nothing better than a day at a Venezuelan beach.

FESTIVALS: TRADITION AND MODERNITY COMBINE

Carnival

Carnival in Venezuela is not as famous as Carnival in Rio de Janeiro or Mardi Gras in New Orleans. Nevertheless, the days before Ash Wednesday and the beginning of Lent are just as important in Venezuelan popular culture. As we noted in Chapter 2, Venezuelans have celebrated Carnival for centuries. How Venezuelans celebrated Carnival became controversial in the later decades of the 19th century when modernizing elites tried to control lower-class behavior. Peter Linder suggests members of all classes in Maracaibo used Carnival as an opportunity relax or forget the tight rules that governed behavior of people of different classes. Everyone—men and women, young and old, rich and poor—dressed in costumes (often cross dressed) and engaged in water fights. The poor targeted members of the elite, who made the poor's lives more complicated the rest of the year, with water cannons (sometimes filled not only with water) and *cascaras* (egg shells) loaded with unpleasant substances. Some elite experienced home invasions annually. By the 1870s, government officials began to prohibit behavior not deemed class or gender appropriate (Linder 2006). Today, Carnival celebrations all over Venezuela echo earlier traditions. Water fights are normal. Cross dressing is part of the Carnival experience now as it was then. Cities still sponsor Carnival parades, but it is more common for Venezuelans to go to the beach than to go to a Carnival parade.

The most unique Venezuelan Carnival celebration occurs in El Callao. El Callao's history is unique. It is a gold mining community south of Ciudad Bolívar founded in the 1850s. Most of the original inhabitants were from the Caribbean, brought to work in the mines. With the immigrants came Caribbean-style Carnival celebrations, calypso, and crews of ornately and elegantly dressed women, men in devil attire. The celebration also includes *mediopintos:* men covered in black paint who randomly douse parade-goers with water, Venezuelan Carnival style. In the 1940s, bumbac drummer Carlos Small and Isidora Agnes (popularly referred to as "La Negra Isidora") teamed to revive and recreate a Carnival mixing Venezuelan elements into the celebration and into the music. Calypso became truly Venezuelan with the addition of the *cuatro*, maracas, and cow bells making Venezuelan calypso distinct from Caribbean calypso. Venezuelan calypso, however, is still sung in English, not Spanish, but it is mixed with a patois unique to El Callao, a combination of English, Spanish, and local indigenous languages. In 1954 Isidora Agnes established the Association of the Friends of Calipso, which promoted calypso and became an important sponsor of Carnival crews. Isidora Agnes's contemporaries and experts in Venezuelan folklore credit her with the particular elegance of *madamas*, the members of the women's crew in El Callao's Carnival. Many suggest that because of Isidora Agnes, a robust and unique Carnival tradition thrives in El Callao.

While the experience of Carnival in El Callao is among the most famous and well-established, different regions of the nation celebrate differently. In Mérida, the city organizes the Feria del Sol, which centers on the bullfighting ring in the city and showcases cattle and cowboy skills along with music, parades, and the election of Carnival queens. In many places in Caracas, Carnival is a child-friendly celebration and an opportunity for children to dress up in costumes (from princesses to Power Rangers) and engage in confetti fights. Carnival, whatever its expression, is an event of costumes, parades, and celebration before Lent.

Carnival (or for the Venezuelans, Carnaval) is an excellent example of the intersection of a wide range of cultural practices. The timing of Carnival is tied to religious beliefs of the nation and the Catholic tradition of Lent. The calypso music and dances reflect the practice of the arts in Venezuela, with their various national and ethnic influences. Traditional family activities during the period of Carnival, feasts, and beach vacations point to the importance of family ties and traditional foods. The election, at many a Carnival, of a *reina*, or Carnival Queen, gives a good example of the importance placed on beauty and the widespread appeal of pageants. The evolution, over time, of the practices of Carnival from a free-for-all festival of gender bending and law breaking to a more organized, codified, legal, and decidedly popular celebration, show how morals and laws have changed through the years. Finally, the regional differences in Carnival celebrations from El Callao to Caracas to Mérida to Maracaibo showcase the range of expression that exists within Venezuela. As Edward Tylor observed in his widely quoted definition of culture (mentioned in the introduction of this chapter), the culture of a society is all of its knowledge, beliefs, and expressions, which cannot be separated from each other and are better understood in their relationships and interconnections.

Dancing Devils of Corpus Christi

The festival of the Diablos Danzantes (Dancing Devils) is celebrated during the Catholic religious holiday of Corpus Christi, a feast that remembers Jesus Christ's institution of the Eucharist at the Last Supper. This celebration is traditionally recognized by Catholic communities with a mass, after which there may be a procession of the sacrament through town, finishing with the blessing of the sacrament. For those readers more familiar with the Protestant tradition, this celebration may be understood as a festival celebrating the institution of communion.

In Venezuela, in a variety of towns across the nation, a common celebration on the Thursday of Corpus Christi is a devil dance. Members of religious brotherhoods dress as devils (first protecting themselves with rosaries, crosses, and other religious items). It is common for these participants to wear brightly colored suits on their bodies and elaborate masks depicting demons on their heads. Women may be allowed to join the brotherhood but are generally not allowed to wear the devil masks. The men then dance toward the church of their town, representing the actions of the devil as he tries to lead humans down an evil path. At the church, all the dancers kneel, showing how the devil is ultimately defeated by God and the powers of good. The dancers are then blessed by the priest of the church ("Diablos de Yare" 2008).

The Venezuelan town of San Francisco de Yare has one of the oldest and most unique Corpus Christi dance traditions. The Diablos de Yare is one of Venezuela's most famous celebrations and dates back to the 18th century. In San Francisco de Yare, a religious brotherhood known as the Devils of Yare dances to the sound of the *caja*, a drum typical to the region. The brotherhood is known for their red suits, the elaborate palm crosses they wear, as well as for their devil masks, the number of horns indicating their rank in the brotherhood.

The Dancing Devil celebrations are the legacy of Venezuela's slave past. The Corpus Christi processions were begun by the *cofradías* of former slaves, who integrated the African drums and dances of their ancestors and families. As Haydee Vilchéz Cróquer has found, even for Venezuelan slaves, dancing was an acceptable activity in the eyes of slave owners (Vilchéz Cróquer 2007). Some heritage, therefore, could be preserved in music and dance. Corpus Christi processions represented to the early Afrovenezuelans a way to practice and preserve their cultural heritage.

Fiesta de San Juan—Tambores de Barlovento

The seaside city of Barlovento is known for its large population of citizens of African descent and its raucous celebration of the area's patron saint, Saint John the Baptist, in late June. The feast of Saint John the Baptist in Barlovento is celebrated annually with a festival commonly known as the Tambores de Barlovento (Drums of Barlovento), a three-day party of drumming, dancing, eating, and baptisms.

The term "Barlovento" refers not to one city, but a string of towns along the coast from Birongo to Curiepe that have come to be synonymous with black culture and folklore. Settlements of Afrovenezuelans in the area of Barlovento date back to the cacao plantations of the colonial period that made intensive use of imported slave labor. Long after the abolition of slavery in 1854, the descendants of slaves still live and practice the cultural traditions of their Bantu, Yoruba, and Mandingo ancestors in the area (Hamilton 2010). During the slave years, these three days of the feast of St. John the Baptist were the only three days that slaves were allowed a break from their labors. For almost three centuries, then, this time of year has been a special celebration and time to give thanks. Today, the Festival of San Juan centers in Curiepe, a community settled in the 1700s by a group of freed and liberated slaves (Fox 2006).

The main attraction of the festival is the continuous, day-and-night drumming of the *culo e' puya*. The *culo e' puya* is a long, narrow, hollowed-out wooden drum that is played by numerous people at once in syncopated rhythms handed down through the centuries. These drums are spread all through the town of Curiepe and along the coast, on street corners, in front of churches, along the roads, in front of houses. The drumming never stops. Older citizens hand off the drums to children, and the children hand off the drumming to their siblings or neighbors.

All of the drumming is accompanied by dance. While the drumming is a male-only activity, the dancing is for men and women—the women always dressed head to toe in white (the color of holiness in Santeria religion), the men in red shirts or with red handkerchiefs (Fox 2006). Food is plentiful as well; hot dogs, *empanadas*, and *tostones* are all eaten from street vendors as people listen to the drumming, dance, and wait for the procession of the statue of Saint John.

The culmination of the festival is the procession of the small statue of Saint John the Baptist through town. The saint is carried by bearers, and the citizens pray and wave red kerchiefs in his honor. He is carried to the sea, where many will be baptized. This is a solemn reminder that the Festival of San Juan is at its core a religious celebration, in honor of the saint who baptized so many.

It is because of this reason that so many residents of Barlovento decry the increasing commercialization of the festival. The increasing popularity of music and dancing has led major alcohol sponsors such as the beer company Regional to make major economic investments in advertising. Coca-Cola also recently tried to muscle its way into the festival by buying thousands of red shirts for people to wear. The company angered many by trying to get the bearers of the saint themselves to wear red Coca-Cola t-shirts. While this was roundly denied by the bearers themselves, it shows how the celebration has become a victim of its own success (Fox 2006).

REFERENCES

Biertempfel, Rob. 2007. "Pirates Feature Several Venezuelan Natives." March 27. http://www.pittsburghlive.com/x/pittsburghtrib/s_499694.html.

Bjarkman, Peter. 2005. *Diamonds around the Globe: The Encyclopedia of International Baseball.* Westport, CT: Greenwood.

Campbell, Duncan. 2006. "Caracas Golf Clubs in Hole as City Bids to Build Homes on Greens." *The Guardian*, August 31. http://www.guardian.co.uk/world/2006/aug/31/topstories3.venezuela.

Caracas Country Club. 2009. "Organization." http://www.caracascountryclub.org/index. php?option=com_content&view=section&id=6&Itemid=154.

CAS. n.d. "Bullfighting in Venezuela." http://www.cas-international.org/en/home/suffering-of-bulls-and-horses/bullfighting/venezuela/.

"Diablos de Yare, Máscaras y Jerarquías." 2008. http://el-nacional.com/www/site/p_contenido.php?q=med/29292/Regiones/Los-Diablos-de-Yare,-M%C3%A1scaras-y-Jerarqu%C3%ADas.

Duidley, Steven. 2006. "Crime Wave, Police Silence Worry Caracas." *The Miami Herald*, June 1. http://business.highbeam.com/6033/article-1G1-146512704/crime-wave-police-silence-worry-caracas-growth-crime.

Fox, Michael. 2006. "Venezuela's San Juan Festival: The Drums of Curiepe Ring On." *Venezuelanalysis*, June 26. http://www.venezuelanalysis.com/analysis/1809.

Hamilton, Dominic. 2010. "Fiesta de San Juan Bautista: Baptism by Beat." http://www.2camels.com.

Linder, Peter. 2006. "Drumming Rebellion: Political and Social Violence in the Sur del Lago de Maracaibo on the Eve of the Federal War, 1839–1858." Paper presented at the XVII Congress of the Latin American Studies Association, Montreal, Canada, September 8.

Ortiz, Jorge L. 2005. "As a Country's Baseball Dreams Soar, So Do the Nightmares." *San Francisco Chronicle*, July 12. http://articles.sfgate.com/2005-07-12/sports/17380203_1_kidnapping-attempt-violent-crime-venezuelan-cy-young-award.

Otis, John. 2005. "Everyone Has Big League Dreams." October 25. http://www.chron.com/disp/story.mpl/sports/bb/3413800.html.

Portal Taurino. n.d. "Plaza de Toros de San Cristóbal." http://www.portaltaurino.com/plazas/america/venezuela/caracas.htm.

Romero, Simon. 2007. "Venezuela Dances to Devilish Beat to Promote Tourism." *The New York Times*, June 12. http://www.nytimes.com/2007/06/12/world/americas/12venez.html.

———. 2009. "In Venezuela, Plantations of Cacao Stir Bitterness." *The New York Times*. http://www.nytimes.com/2009/07/29/world/americas/29cacao.html.

Ungar, Mark. 2003. "Contested Battlefields: Policing in Caracas and La Paz." *NACLA Report on the Americas* 37: 30–36.

Vílchez Cróquer, Haydee. 2007. "Las cofradías de Negros durante la colonia: Un espacio de libertad." Paper presented at the XXVII International Congress of the Latin American Studies Association. Montreal, Canada, September 8.

Popular Culture

THE MOST POPULAR OF CULTURE: THE *TELENOVELA*

While Venezuelans are very proud of their classic cultural traditions in music, literature, and the visual arts, another area in which they also have well-founded pride is in the production of high-quality, prime-time soap operas, or *telenovelas*. These programs

—S
—E
—L

are hugely popular in Venezuela, where 52 percent of the population reported watching them regularly in the late 1990s (Zona Latina 1999). The importance of the *telenovela* goes beyond simple national popularity, though. The programs are not just a favorite pastime in Venezuela; they also represent a significant export commodity. The love for Latin American *telenovelas* is felt as far away as China and Indonesia.

In fact, as Zona Latina notes, "the export market for Venezuelan *telenovelas* is estimated to be more than the national exports of automobiles, textiles or paper products" (Zona Latina 1999). Not every Latin American nation has the media capacity to produce full-scale programs, but Venezuela does. Venezuela has the third largest television industry in Latin America (after Brazil and Mexico), with a rate of international expansion greater than that of even Brazil (Fox 1997). The Venezuelan media industry exports their product to other Spanish-speaking countries as well as to the U.S. market for the Spanish language stations such as Univisión, Galavisión, and Telemundo. In addition, Venezuela sells its *telenovelas* to other nations around the world. The Venezuelan production *Topacio*, for example, was marketed to networks in 45 countries worldwide, including such unlikely places as Poland, Russia, China, the Philippines, and Turkey, according to Araceli Urbina and Asbel López. In this way, the *telenovela* is a source of national pride, national income, and national unity (Urbina and Lopez n.d.). One scriptwriter, Fernando Gaitán, says that the *telenovela* has become the South American continent's main channel of communication both within the borders of the continent and also with the outside world (Acosta Alzuru 2008).

For those unfamiliar with this type of program, an explanation is in order. The *telenovela* in Venezuela, and in Latin America in general, is very different than the soap opera in the United States, both in the way they are designed and their audience and popularity they enjoy. In Venezuela, the movie industry is small compared to the United States or Great Britain, and few big-budget films are made. What replaces the Hollywood-style movie industry in countries like Venezuela and Mexico is the production of the *telenovela*, which is really a 100-hour big-budget movie. Unlike an American-style soap opera that runs for 50 years, a *telenovela* has a set number of

---

PLOT OF *TOPACIO*

Named by *People en Español* as one of the 20 best *telenovelas* ever, *Topacio* is the story of two babies switched a birth. Rich plantation owners have a baby girl, and the midwife, believing the baby to be dead, switches the girl for a poor baby boy. The girl (whose name is Topacio), however, is not dead, but only blind. The boy, Jorge Luis, then grows up to be a rich doctor, and the blind girl grows up a poor orphan. Later, the two meet and fall in love. The forces of convention and social class conspire to keep them apart, but the two secretly marry and Topacio becomes pregnant. Topacio and Jorge Luis are separated, and Jorge Luis loses his eyesight. In the meantime, Topacio's mother has realized that Topacio is her long lost daughter and finds a doctor who can cure her blindness. Topacio and Jorge Luis are reunited, Jorge Luis regains his eyesight, and their baby son is born. Everyone, as they should in a good *telenovela*, lives happily ever after.

chapters, usually between 75 and 150. It is shown five or six days a week, some during the daytime hours, but also during the prime-time evening hours, over three to six months. This allows a *telenovela* to build a set of specific story lines to a climax, which will sometimes paralyze a nation as everyone sits down to watch what happens.

The Venezuelan *telenovela* usually follows a similar type of plot as an American soap opera. There are elaborate sets and locations where beautiful people dressed in fabulous clothing show love and jealously, hate and revenge. Everything is shot in glorious super-saturated color reminiscent of the glory days of 1950s Hollywood Technicolor in order that the glamorous beauty can be fully appreciated. Kind young men and women find happiness in the end, and bad guys get their just deserts. The typical soap opera revolves around a love story but has plenty of subplots with extra characters to keep viewers interested. The characters generally overcome great obstacles—social class, family conflicts, illnesses—to finally win love and fortune. There is always a happy ending, but there is also always a great deal of suspense along the way. People around the world seem to like the *telenovelas* because they deal with familiar problems, universal situations that work across lines of social class and cultural difference.

It would be incorrect, though, to dismiss the whole industry as only mindless entertainment. It is easy for the outside observer to forget that unlike U.S.-produced soap operas, Latin American *telenovelas* are the main source of income for the agencies that produce them. This means that the programs are very professional indeed. The *novela* market is able to attract the very best writers, directors, and actors that a nation has to offer—sometimes some of the nation's finest poets and novelists such as Salvador Garmendia. As a result of this, the dialogue and even the themes of the *telenovelas* many times rise above the average or superficial. In fact, more than one scholar has noticed how the *telenovela* has been used to communicate social and political messages. *Telenovelas* across Latin America in recent years have attacked issues of police corruption, urban violence, and the role of mafia money in government. The *telenovela* is, actually, a perfect forum for the discussion of social issues to a wide audience in Latin America. After all, when you have the attention of over half the population, you have a great opportunity to deliver a message.

Venevisión's 2003 *Cosita Rica* represents a *telenovela* with significant social commentary. This *telenovela*, written by the poet Leonardo Padrón (former member of the group Guaire), was another example of authors using their medium for political commentary. *Cosita Rica* was, on the surface, the story of the star-crossed lovers Paula and Diego. What really made this particular *telenovela* stand out, however, was the character of Olegario Pérez. The setting for the story was a cosmetics company called El Emporio Luján, which had recently been taken over by a new president, Olegario Pérez. Pérez was a former fisherman who, newly rich, still had rough manners, dressed badly (if expensively), and was generally presented as a buffoon. He was also a bad company president, running the company into the ground and playing at his desk instead of working. In the show, the cosmetics business is a metaphor for the Venezuelan government, and Pérez is very obviously Hugo Chávez (Acosta Alzuru 2010). Therefore show's opinion (and therefore that of the author, who is anti-Chávez) of the president was just as obvious.

During the run of the show, the wife of the former president of the company appears and tries to take control of the business from Pérez. This triggers a referendum from the executive board. This happened in the show, not coincidentally, at the same time that the country was preparing for a referendum on the presidency of Chávez. The similarity and connection was so obvious that government representatives met with executives of the television station and pressured them to have Perez's referendum vote *after* the vote on Chávez's presidency (Alcosta Alzuru 2010). They were worried that the vote on the *telenovela* could affect the real referendum vote on the presidency of the government.

Chávez won the referendum on his presidency in 2004, and in the show, so did Pérez. Padrón, the writer and poet, received criticism for this, for having seemed to have "sold out" to the government. Padrón even received one message accusing him of being "not worthy of being called a poet any more" because of the positive ending he had written for the referendum vote in a *telenovela* (Acosta Alzuru 2010: 62). It did not seem to matter to his critics that he made Pérez impotent for the rest of the program, further making him an object of pity and scorn.

The example of *Cosita Rica* shows just how important the *telenovela* is in the Venezuelan context. It was assumed to have the power to change the outcome of a presidential vote. The *telenovela* is entertainment, surely, but it is also an important type of national communication.

OTHER PROGRAMS AND ISSUES IN THE WORLD OF VENEZUELAN TELEVISION

While *telenovelas* are certainly the most famous and popular form of television programming in Venezuela, other programs are produced and watched in the nation. Sports programming, especially baseball, is very popular, as are variety shows, as in the example of *Super Sábado Sensacional*. The show, which has run every Saturday from 4:00 p.m. to 9:00 p.m. since 1970, is a mixture of entertainment but prides itself on being the first place musicians go to present new songs and albums. The music on the show is interspersed with comic and dramatic sketches as well as visits from beauty queens and remote reports from locations such as bullfights and street celebrations. Like the Venezuelan *telenovelas*, the variety show is exported, transmitted, as its web site brags, "in the majority of Spanish-speaking countries" (*Super Sábado* n.d.) around the world. Slapstick comedy shows like ¡*Que Locura*! are popular in Venezuela but are also exported and seen regularly in the United States on Univisión. Also notable in Venezuelan comedy is *Radio Rochela*, a show that had been on the air for 40 years by 2009. Historically, a *rochela* was a runaway slave community. The mere existence of *rochelas* challenged the authority of a social, economic, and political order that allowed slavery. Likewise, *Radio Rochela* over the course of its long history has similarly not hesitated to challenge political, social, and economic norms. Politicians as different as Carlos Andres Pérez and Hugo Chávez found cause to quibble with *Radio Rochela*'s thinly veiled political parodies.

In addition to the high-quality programming produced in Venezuela, other international programs do appear on Venezuelan airwaves. Thus, the previously mentioned Social Responsibility Law has had an effect on the content of television broadcasts as well, as the law is used to monitor content as well as the ratio of Venezuelan to foreign-produced programming. Reuters reports that the Venezuelan broadcasting regulator, Conatel, was widely ridiculed when in 2008 it began warning television networks not to broadcast the U.S. television program *The Simpsons* because the program was "infringing many things in the television and radio social responsibility law" (Reuters 2008). In 2009, the same thing happened with the animated series *Family Guy*, which Venezuelan Justice Minister Tareck El Aissami accused of promoting marijuana use.

FILM

Venezuela does not have as strong a tradition in film as some other Latin American nations. In 2009, the Venezuelan film industry was averaging only one film completed every four years. When we compare this number to the average of 42 films per year produced in Mexico, it becomes obvious the Venezuelan motion picture industry has not been as robust as in other nations (Johnson 2005). This situation is partially due to the great attention paid to the *telenovela* market, as described earlier. The vast majority of time, talent, and wealth in the visual entertainment industry in Venezuela, from writing to acting to directing, goes into the highly successful and highly lucrative production of soap operas.

This does not mean, however, that the Venezuelan film industry is nonexistent. Films, good films, are made in Venezuela, and in the early years of the 20th century, film, like many other things, has become a battleground in the political and cultural wars surrounding the presidency of Hugo Chávez.

Origins and History of Venezuelan Film

The first known Venezuelan film, *Children Bathing in the Maracaibo Lagoon*, dates back to 1897 (Alirio Peña and Peña 2009). That film was made by Manuel Trujillo Durán, considered by many the first Venezuelan filmmaker, documentary maker, and businessman who recognized the economic power that film would have. The economic power, however, would in future years mostly center on the television industry of the small screen, leaving the big screen for more politically motivated or artistically risky films.

After the very early years of Venezuelan film, filmmakers from 1924 to the end of the Pérez Jiménez dictatorship engaged in two main types of film: propaganda or the "film-spectacular" that took advantage of the new and exciting artistic media of sound. During this time period, the big screen format was also used for news reporting in the theater, for such events as World War II. After the fall of Pérez Jiménez, in the period from 1958 to 1980, filmmakers made more independent and artistic films. Long-form documentary films, especially those of Jesús Enrique Guédez, were popular, and the intellectual elite begin to appreciate experimental films that included social critique such as the film *Soy un delincuente* (*I Am a Delinquent*) (Alirio Peña and Peña 2009).

Filmmakers working in the period from 1990 to 2000 are known as the *"Cineastas de la crisis del cine nacional"* (Filmmakers of the national cinema crisis). The decade of the 1990s saw a law, the Ley de Cinematografía Nacional, designed to support national filmmakers, but the economic downturn of the *caracazo* and the subsequent economic crisis had a devastating effect on both ticket sales and monetary support for filmmakers in this period. The situation is considered to have turned around in the new century, with increased oil revenues and more government funding for nationally based filmmakers' efforts. Films of this period turn to a consideration of both political and social problems, with a particular trend toward both social realism and at times hyperrealism as in the case of the wildly popular *Secuestro Express* (Alirio Peña and Peña 2009).

Contemporary Film

Two of Venezuela's most well-known contemporary filmmakers are Solveig Hoogesteijn and Jonathan Jakubowitz. The two artists examine the social realities of modern-day Venezuela and both have enjoyed significant levels of success both in Venezuela and in the international motion picture community. Both filmmakers are particularly interested in the economic disparities between the social classes in the nation and the condition of groups that are marginalized by their poverty, gender, race, or religion.

Solveig Hoogesteijn

Hoogesteijn, the daughter of Dutch and German immigrants to Venezuela, grew up in Caracas, where she attended the prestigious Humboldt Secondary School. She then went on to study art, literature, and filmmaking first at the University of Munich and later at the UCV. Hoogesteijn's major film successes include *Santera*, the story of a Spanish social worker who travels to Venezuela to work in the prison system. In the film, the social worker finds herself drawn to a *bruja* in the prison who practices traditional religion. Hoogesteijn also directed the film *Maroa*, which was Venezuela's 2006 entry into the foreign language film category for the American Academy Awards.

Maroa tells the story of an 11-year-old girl named Maroa living in the barrios, who suffers under the violent whims of an abusive grandmother. After being arrested for petty theft and involvement in a shooting, Maroa is sent to a reform school where a kind teacher tries to involve her in El Sistema, Venezuela's famous youth orchestra program. A coming-of-age story and a feel-good story of how art can bridge the gaps between worlds, *Maroa* was a critical and commercial success. The young star of the film, Yorlis Domínguez, who was cast off the streets of a barrio, received special attention and positive reviews for her portrayal of the young musician.

Jonathan Jakubowicz

Jonathan Jakubowicz, the son of Polish Jews whose families fled to Venezuela as the Nazis took over, was born and raised in Caracas. He showed an early interest in film-making, taking a camera along on family trips around South America. Jakubowicz continued this interest as a young adult, attending a filmmaking workshop at the New York Film Academy in Manhattan. He then returned to Venezuela and received a degree in art from the UCV.

Jakubowicz's first major film was a documentary about the Jewish immigrant ships that reached Venezuela's shores during World War II. The feature, called *Los Barcos de la Esperanza* (*Ships of Hope*) was shown on HBO and the History Channel in both the United States and across Latin America. Jakubowicz followed up this initial success with a major feature film, *Secuestro Express* (*Kidnap Express*) that would prove both a massive box office triumph but also politically controversial.

The events in *Secuestro Express* occur one evening in which a young couple is kidnapped for quick ransom by a trio of desperate, poor young men. As the night progresses, the group sees robberies, drug deals, murders, corrupt police, prostitution, and abject poverty. They also see and debate the reasons for crime and economic inequality. The film paints a dismal picture of Caracas, its people, its crime, and its hopelessly divided class structure. The movie is also relentless, barely allowing the viewer to breathe in between violent images and actions.

Jakubowicz was moved to make the film after his own express kidnapping in which he and a friend were kidnapped and held at gunpoint overnight. The friends were driven from bank to bank so they could withdraw as much money as possible. "They took our car, all our clothes, our cellphones, everything," Jakubowicz has recalled in interviews. "My first reaction was rage and hatred. You obviously are filled with hate. But later, I understood that what had happened to me happened for a reason" (Forero 2005). Jakubowicz wanted to share that epiphany of hate and understanding with many.

Many, especially in Venezuela, apparently understood. *Secuestro Express* went on to become the highest-grossing film of all time in Venezuela, out grossing the likes of *Titanic* (O'Keefe 2006). The Chávez government was not as impressed. Possibly because of the highly negative impression that a worldwide market received of the nation, Vice President José Vicente Rangel denounced the movie as a "miserable film, a falsification of the truth with no artistic value" (O'Keefe 2006). Moreover, Jakubowicz was attacked in some media outlets with thinly veiled anti-Jewish slurs, and the government filed charges against him, citing the Social Responsibility Law. In addition to the government charges, a group of Chávez supporters additionally brought a civil suit against the film, seeking to have it pulled from theaters. Judges in the cases found in favor of Jakubowicz in the first round of hearings, but the director decided not to stick around for the appeals. As of 2010, Jakubowicz had relocated to Los Angeles to continue his filmmaking work.

Lights! Camera! Revolution!: La Villa del Cine

As part of the effort to protect and promote Venezuelan national art in the face of an onslaught of North American and European imports, the administration of Hugo Chávez has placed an emphasis on supporting the Venezuelan film industry. In the same vein as the Social Responsibility Law, mentioned earlier, which was designed to help promote more production in the area of Venezuelan music, in 2006 the government announced an 11-million-dollar investment in La Villa del Cine, a national film studio just outside of Caracas. The studio contains two film studios, postproduction areas with digital equipment, and studios for costume and setting design ("Villa de Cine" 2007).

With an official motto of "Lights! Camera! Revolution!" the studio hopes to create a new image for Venezuela in film. As the Venezuelan Information Office (which is funded by the Venezuelan government) reports, the idea behind La Villa del Cine was to create opportunities for local filmmakers and combat the many negative images of Latinos that Hollywood films portray. In addition, the government hopes that funding the studio will increase the number of Venezuelan films entering the international market (VIO n.d.). When the studio was built, the government was still stinging from the image of Caracas portrayed in *Secuestro Express*—a movie that leaves viewers with an image of Venezuela as violent, chaotic, corrupt, and hopelessly divided by social class. While that film was directed by a Venezuelan and featured Venezuelan actors, it certainly did not promote a shining vision of Venezuela.

By contrast, the first film produced out of La Villa del Cine was a short digital production about the Liberator, simply titled *Bolívar*, directed by Beto Benites. The Benites film is a glowing portrait of the independence hero. By 2009, the studio had completed 13 films, all of them in the same vein of positive storytelling. Observers note that there is one clear rule, to "divide the world into two categories: those who are for Chávez and those who are against him." The Venezuelan Minister of Culture does not disagree, noting that La Villa del Cine's mission is "defending Venezuela" (Margolis 2009). Critics contend that this means that La Villa del Cine is nothing more than "Hugowood"—built to promote the policies of Chávez.

One representative feature of La Villa del Cine is the film *Libertador Morales: El Justiciero* (*Liberator Morales: Dispenser of Justice*). The 2009 release follows the comedic and exciting adventures of an honest motorcycle taxi driver who battles Caracas traffic by day and Caracas crime by night. The film makes reference to the impossibility of the traffic (much of the humor derives from the fact that he actually obeys traffic signals) and uses Morales to teach lessons about good manners and standing up to criminal activity. The hero's name, as a nod to Bolívar, also makes a patriotic statement. The film also takes a much more positive and optimistic view of the systematic problems of security facing the capital. Crime and lack of effective police? Don't worry, the vigilante motorcycle taxi/crime fighter will save the day!

Additionally, *Libertador Morales* shows the significant background of the filmmakers in the *telenovela* industry. Beyond the criticism of La Villa del Cine as a propaganda factory for Chávez, the other major critique of the studio's output is that its features tend to look like "soaps on steroids." In contrast to the gritty *Secuestro*

Express, Libertador Morales does have the flamboyant, Technicolor look that Venezuelan *telenovelas* favor. In the battle to win Venezuelan and international hearts and minds, La Villa del Cine has some distance yet to travel. *Libertador Morales* was the studio's most commercially successful release of the year. It grossed $200,000 against the Hollywood release *Ice Age 3*, which grossed $11 million (Margolis 2009).

PAGEANTRY AND THE PRICE OF BEAUTY

Telenovelas are a popular spectacle that focus on social issues as experienced by beautiful people in beautiful locations. Venezuelans are beautiful, love beauty, love to watch it, and will go to many lengths to achieve it. In this, they are very successful— Venezuela leads the world in the production and export of beauty queens.

The Venezuelans are a people who are more concerned with appearance than are the people of any other Latin American nation. They lead Latin America in per capita spending on cosmetics, and a 2001 poll found that 65 percent of Venezuelan women think about their looks "all the time" (Omestad 2001). This obsession with beauty is not limited to any one social group or class. Georgetown University scholar Lee Parker conducted cross-class research in 2005 in Caracas to determine attitudes on beauty. The researcher found that universally women rated their physical appearance as a top priority or even a "duty." When one lower-class respondent was asked "Do you think beauty is something important? Physical appearance?" She responded "Yes. Not being pretty? Imagine that. Yes, yes, yes." Beauty is equally important to privileged women. In the same study, middle and upper-class women who were interviewed responded with the same level of enthusiasm and emphasis on appearance. One middle-class respondent to the survey mentioned that: "These days beauty is indispensable, of course. And if you're pretty and intelligent, all the better" (Parker 2009: 2). Even the internationally famous race car driver Milka Duno, who participated in the 2007 and 2009 running of the Indianapolis 500, feels the need to list "beauty" as top on her list of qualifications. Duno holds four master's degrees (in naval engineering, organizational development, naval architecture, and maritime business/marine biology), was the first female Latin American driver ever to be classified as "expert," and in two international seasons has earned three overall wins, six podium appearances, and 17 top-10 finishes. Still, on her Web site, the slogan is "talent, beauty and youth" next to a buxom cartoon of Ms. Duno with flowing hair.

Venezuelan women both worry and spend on their appearance. It is estimated that 20 percent of all average household incomes are spent on beauty products and enhancements, with even the poorest women saving for lipstick or surgery (Obiko Pearson 2006). Plastic surgery is increasingly common, even for the lower classes, and even for the remarkably young. Breast augmentation and rhinoplasty, or nose jobs, are becoming increasingly popular gifts for a young girl's *quinceañera*, or 15th birthday (the equivalent to a sweet 16 birthday in the United States). The Venezuelan Plastic Surgery Society is currently urging banks in the nation to begin providing financing to low-income patients for surgery to allow more Venezuelans to

RECORD-SETTING MISS UNIVERSES

While it is not surprising that a Venezuelan won the Miss Universe pageant, in 2009 it was a record-setting event. When Stefanía Fernández received the crown as the newly selected Miss Universe, it was the first time in the history of the pageant that a compatriot was the reigning queen presenting her with the crown.

In the 58 years between its founding in 1952 and 2009, the Miss Universe pageant had never seen a woman from one country pass the title on to a woman from the same country. However, in 2008, Dayana Mendoza, a native of Caracas, won the Miss Universe title. It was she who crowned Fernández in August of 2009.

Many in Venezuela hope that the reign of Fernández will be less controversial than that of Mendoza, who was plagued not only by the discovery of nude photographs from early in her modeling career but also by ill-considered comments about the high-quality of living conditions and the "relaxing" nature of life at U.S. detainee facilities at Guantánamo Bay, Cuba.

Miss Venezuela Stefania Fernández poses after being crowned Miss Universe 2009 at the end of the Miss Universe beauty pageant in Nassau, Bahamas, Sunday, August 23, 2009. (AP/Wide World Photos)

participate in the national drive for physical perfection. For modern Venezuelan women, the quest for beauty is a no-pain, no-gain proposition.

Beauty is also a competitive enterprise. Beauty pageants are held everywhere—in grade schools, in high schools, in corporations, and even in prisons. Young girls go

Driver Milka Duno of Venezuela walks along pit road prior to the start of the Rolex 24 auto race at Daytona International Speedway in Daytona Beach, Fla., in 2007. (AP/Wide World Photos)

to special schools to train for pageant life. This drive to win comes from very specific role models. In the past 25 years, Venezuela has produced six Miss Universes, five Miss Worlds, and five Miss Internationals. Miss Venezuela made the Miss Universe pageant's top 10 finalists for an uninterrupted 20-year span until 2003, and had back-to-back victories in 2008 and 2009 at the pageant. The reason for the dominance on the world stage is no mystery: Venezuela combines a population of great natural attractiveness with a willingness to mold that attractiveness ruthlessly.

Every year, thousands of young women compete to enter the Casa Miss Venezuela academy where the next Miss Venezuela will be trained and molded. Casa Miss Venezuela is a monument of a uniquely Venezuelan sort: a Vegas-style mansion given over to the construction of beauty. Osmel Sousa, Veenzuela's beauty pageant director, has run Casa Miss Venezuela for 25 years with industrial efficiency. For this efficiency, and for his success, Sousa is the undisputed captain of the beauty pageant industry in Latin America. Every year, Sousa and his scouts scour malls, universities, beaches, and bus lines for women who they think have the potential to be a "Miss." He is looking for diamonds in the rough—he does not expect perfection, only possibility. "I mold the person," he has been quoted as saying, "I derive my enjoyment by changing the women for the better. Otherwise it would be a bore" (Omestad 2001: 131). The scouts round up nearly 4,000 women. This number will be trimmed to 80. Once accepted to the program, and becoming resident in the mansion overlooking Caracas, the women under Sousa's command are set upon by a team of experts. The six-month training period determines which 26 women will represent Venezuela's 26 states.

Plastic surgery is an essential part of the process. Women have "small adjust-ments" made to noses, breasts, lips, chins, eyebrows, or, in one example, gums. One of the candidates in the 1994 pageant had 17 gum operations to produce a bigger-toothed smile (Knight 2005). Liposuction is also a common procedure, as is tooth whitening to combat the coffee stains leftover from Venezuela's other national vice. Plastic surgeons associated with the pageant estimate that one-third of all the con-testants undergo some form of plastic surgery (Knight 2005). Women in the pageant are then expected to follow restricted diets and exercise at least five hours a day. The contestants receive lessons in everything from how to walk to how to apply make-up. They are coached by a psychologist in public speaking and self-esteem. At the end of the process, the women compete against each other to wear the Miss Venezuela crown. This final competition is more popular than nearly anything else in Venezuela. Somewhere between 80 and 90 percent of the Venezuelan population watches the annual pageant, an extravaganza of beauty that is the model for other nations (Knight 2005).

While it would be convenient to view the Venezuelan pageant system as nothing more than exploitation of women, many women in Venezuela view the pageant as a means for furthering their careers. Successful participation as a "Miss" provides entry into a number of professional careers, both in Venezuela and abroad. The list of pageant participants who have gone on to careers in acting, modeling, journalism, and politics is extensive. Indeed, virtually all of Venezuela's top television personali-ties and models are alumni of the pageant. Especially for women of the lower and lower-middle class, whose professional career opportunities are limited, the pros-pects afforded by the system are enticing.

To offer just two examples of the type of "success story" generated by the Casa Miss Venezuela, we will mention only Patricia Velázquez and Irene Saez. Super-model and actress Patricia Velázquez proves that a woman doesn't need to win the Miss Venezuela pageant do get noticed. Born in Zulia state to hardworking but economically challenged parents, Velázquez was the fifth of six children. In 1989, she took the opportunity to enter Casa Miss Venezuela and placed seventh in the national pageant. The experience got her noticed by international modeling agencies, however, and she left soon after the pageant to begin a modeling career in Milan. Since that time, she has become one of the highest paid Hispanic models in history, representing L'Oreal in 2009. Velázquez also used her celebrity to pursue a successful acting career in hit movies such as *The Mummy* and on the U.S. television program *Arrested Development.*

A career in entertainment and fashion is not the only choice for alumni of the Miss Venezuela pageant, however. Irene Saez parlayed her success into a politi-cal career. Saez, then an engineering student at the University Central de Venezu-ela, entered the pageant in 1981 and won the Miss Universe title in the same year. After the obligatory world tour that included meeting then Prime Minister Margaret Thatcher, Saez returned home and switched her major to political science, earning a degree from the UCV in 1989. In 1992 she was elected mayor of Chacao, one of the five municipalities that make up metropolitan Caracas. As mayor, Saez was ap-plauded for drastic reductions in crime and improvements in public works. She was

Miss Venezuela, Irene Saez, reacts after she is named Miss Universe as Miss Canada, Dominique Dufour, right, congratulates her in New York City, July 21, 1981. (AP/Wide World Photos)

reelected in 1995 with 96 percent of the vote. In 1998, Saez became a presidential candidate in the important and controversial elections that year. Saez eventually lost to the current president, Hugo Chávez. Later, Saez was elected governor of the state of Nueva Esparta in 1999, only the second woman in Venezuela's history to hold that office, proving that the crucible of beauty pageant can lead to significant professional careers.

REFERENCES

Acosta Alzuru, Carolina. 2008. "Among Telenovela Writers." February 21. http://telenovelas-carolina.blogspot.com/2008/02/among-telenovela-writers-fernando.html.

———. 2010. La Telenovela de Venezuela: Polarización y Discurso político en "Cosita Rica." In *Bottom Up or Top Down? Participation and Clientelism in Venezuela's Bolivarian Democracy*. Dan Hellinger and David Smilde eds. Durham, NC: Duke University Press.

Alirio Peña, José, and Claritza Peña. 2009. "Nuestro Cine Venezolano." Cine 100% Venezolano. http://cine100por100venezolano.blogspot.com.

Forero, Juan. 2005. "Venezuelan Filmmaker Finds His Kidnapping Tale Resonates with the Masses." *The New York Times*, October 6. http://www.nytimes.com/2005/10/06/movies/06expr.html.

Fox, Elizabeth. 1997. *Latin American Broadcasting: From Tango to Telenovela*. Bedfordshire: University of Luton Press.

Johnson, Reed. 2005. Mexico Reaches Out. *Los Angeles Times*. September 5. http://articles.latimes.com/2005/sep/05/entertainment/et-mexfilm5.

Knight, Jane. 1995. "Venezuelan Tale of Beauty and the Beast." *Christian Science Monitor,* September 25. http://www.csmonitor.com/1995/0925/25015.html/(page)/2.

Margolis, Mac. 2009. "Lights! Camera! Revolution!" *Newsweek*, November 2. http://www.newsweek.com/2009/10/23/lights-camera-revoluci-n.html.

Obiko Pearson, Natalie. 2006. "Breast jobs and Beauty Queens." *Toronto Star*, January 5. http://www.staugustine.com/stories/010106/wor_3549122.shtml.

O'Keefe, Alice. 2006. "The Chavista War on Cinema." *New Statesman,* May 29. http://www.newstatesman.com/200605290014.

Omestad, Thomas. 2001. "In the Land of Mirror, Mirror on the Wall." *U.S. News and World Report*, 131.

Parker, Lee. 2009. "Social Class Embodiment: The Body as Site For Political Struggle the Case of Working Class Women in Revolutionary Venezuela." p. 2. http://www.clas.georgetown.edu/parker/doc.

Reuters. 2008. "Venezuela Axes the Simpsons as Bad for Kids." April 9. http://www.reuters.com/article/idUSN0840461120080409.

Secuestro Express. 2005. DVD. Production Notes. Los Angeles: Miramax. thecia.com.au/.../kidnap-express-secuestro-express-production-notes.rtf.

Super Sábado Sensacional. http://www.venevision.net/sabado/ Author's translation.

Urbina, Araceli Ortiz and Asbel López. n.d. "Soaps with a Latin Accent." www.unesco.org.

"Villa de Cine: Venezuelan Government as Film Producer." 2007. The Power of Culture. http://www.krachtvancultuur.nl/en/current/2007/december/villadelcine.

VIO. n.d. "La Cultura es el Pueblo: Venezuela's Investment in Culture and the Arts." http://www.rethinkvenezuela.com/downloads/cultura.htm.

Zona Latina. 1999. "Telenovelas in Latin America." http://telenovela.freehostia.com/historyoftelenovelas.html.

Architecture

VERNACULAR ARCHITECTURE

As much as 90 percent of buildings in the world likely fall into the category of "vernacular architecture," buildings that were not designed by a professional architect (Arboleda 2006). Barns, storehouses, schools, and homes around the world designed and built by the people who use them are examples of this type of architecture. Building without the intervention of a professional architect is by far the most traditional and widespread way to build, but for many years, scholars did not recognize this type of architecture as worthy of study. Indeed, in the 19th century, ethnographers visiting other cultures tried to use examples of vernacular architecture to prove the intellectual inferiority of the culture and the builders of the structures they described (Arboleda 2006).

By the late 20th century, however, many who studied art and architecture had begun to recognize the environmental, technological, and social importance of vernacular techniques. In the 21st century, there is a great deal of interest in the study of those techniques. Years of research have revealed that vernacular builders have a unique store of knowledge when it comes to day-to-day building practice, knowing how to adapt to changing environmental conditions. Venezuela has a long history of both vernacular and professionally designed architecture. This section will highlight vernacular architecture.

Indigenous Design

Indigenous architecture occupies a unique position in the built landscape of Venezuela. Indigenous builders have a different perspective than professional engineers or architects, and indigenous construction has evolved to produce both elegant and functional forms over time. The homes and other structures built by the Indian tribes of the nation are both a product and an instrument of their culture. They are the result of ancient traditions, improved with time as a response to the requirements of their social and physical environment. Consequently, they are well-fitted solutions to the demands of their social and natural environment. As such, the indigenous architecture of Venezuela has much to teach modern students of architecture (Gutierrez 2004).

Palafitos

Much indigenous architecture is particular to the natural environment in which it is built, "an architecture that belongs more to the lay of the territory and patterns of settlement than to the desires of the inhabitants" (Gaspirini 1986: 32). One example of this type of construction are the *palafitos* of the Warao. Venezuela takes its name from the similarity of the design of the indigenous inhabitants of the country and the architecture of Venice, as observed upon the arrival of the European explorers to the shores of South America. When Amerigo Vespucci arrived at Lake Maracaibo, he found indigenous tribes living in *palafitos*, houses constructed over the water that reminded him of Venice. Vespucci was impressed with these houses—with their strength and flexibility in the face of tropical winds and rain but also by the way they could house so many in an extended family (Gaspirini 1986).

While the few remaining *palafitos* on Lake Maracaibo are only for tourist display, many Venezuelan Warao continue to live in *palafitos* in the Orinoco River Delta. A traditional *palafito* generally consists of a large, open room constructed of mangrove logs sunk into the bed of the lake. The building is floored with planks of mangrove wood and then roofed in palm leaves. The sides of a traditional *palafito* remain open; however, the European influence has led to some *palafitos* with closed sides of woven palm leaves. The open construction is due to the extremely hot and humid climate. The open or woven sides allow air to circulate. Some more contemporary *palafitos* may have wooden sides or tin roofs; these, however, are not as effective in combating the heat. One extremely common feature of the Warao *palafito* is the open-air patio on one side of the house. This space serves as a dock for canoes, a meeting space, and play area for children.

Palafitos, like much indigenous housing in Venezuela, are communal space. Extended families share a single *palafito*, and the individual homes of family members may be connected by wooden walkways. Whether of the older or newer style of construction, the traditional style of transportation to and from a *palafito* for the Warao is a canoe on the water. Indeed, the name "Warao" means "canoe people" from "wa" (canoe) and "arao" (people) in the Warao language (Warao n.d.).

Shabono

While the Warao live in *palafitos* designed for air circulation and water transportation, the Yanomami of southern Venezuela have designed a different type of housing structure for the unique environment of the tropical forest of Amazonas State. The Yanomami live in *shabono* circular communal homes composed of individually constructed shed roofs, or *tapirís*, built of bamboo and roofed with bamboo leaves. The *tapirí* of the Yanomami is generally of a triangular type, made of two meter-long poles staked in the ground and brought together and tied to one pole in the front. This structure then holds up a lattice of bamboo poles over which a thatch of bamboo leaves is laid (Gaspirini 1986).

The *shabono* village house typically can shelter between 40 and 200 people (Hames 1992). The joined ring of lean-tos surrounds an open plaza in the middle. Multiple extended families share both spaces, both in the central plaza, and within the outer ring. Individual family spaces are noticeable not by dividing walls but by the individual hearth fires and by the hammocks that families string up to sleep and rest in. The structure is built with one main door to the outside and several smaller side doors. With the dense forest completely surrounding the *shabono*, the arrangement of the *tapirís* is reminiscent of a circle of covered wagons drawn in a ring for protection against the encroaching forest.

The design of the village housing is consistent with the requirements of life in the Amazonian forest. The lean-to is one of the easiest and fastest structures to build. Its use is especially appropriate for seminomadic peoples such as the Yanomami, who have no need for more permanent structures. The wise land use practices of the Yanomami, which call for them to rotate planting sites, also call for regular resettlement. The constant faint haze of smoke from the hearth fires provides effective protection from the aggressive forest insects, and the open communal space inside the structure aids in the common care of children and common work.

The open space in the center of the *shabono* is additionally important in Yanomami culture as ceremonial, celebratory, and official space. The central plaza is where religious ceremonies and funeral rites are performed, visitors are received, festivals and dances are celebrated, and children play.

La Churuata

The *churuata* is the collective housing structure of the Ye'kuana Indians of Bolívar State. The *churuata* is a large, round-walled structure topped with a conical roof of palm fronds. The structure may be as large as 30 meters in diameter, enough to house 60 to 100 people. The *churuata*, also known as an *ata*, is an important form of indigenous architecture not only for its elegance and for the technical mastery that it displays in the use of natural materials but also in the importance of the structure to the culture and social symbolism of the Ye'kuana.

The construction of the *ata* is begun with the construction of walls of *bahareque*. *Bahareque* is a building technique in which bamboo poles are placed vertically as the inner posts of a lattice form for the *ata* wall. To these vertical posts the Ye'kuana tie horizontal canes of bamboo in the interior and exterior of the space, forming a lattice, or skeleton. The lattice is then daubed with mud, which may be mixed with chopped pieces of grass or cane or bamboo. The structure is then allowed to dry. *Bahareque* is not used exclusively by the Ye'kuana. It is also common with other Venezuelan tribes, and in other South and Central American nations.

Modern urban engineers find the structural characteristics of *bahareque* very interesting. First, well-constructed *bahareque* has been found to be an extremely earthquake-resistant building material. In order for buildings to be highly earthquake resistant, they must have three qualities: they must be regular in height with exterior mortar walls, they must be very light, and they must allow for structural flexibility (Gutierrez 2004). Buildings of *bahareque* satisfy all of these requirements, especially those of the Ye'kuana. The exterior wall of a *ata* is of uniform height and is daubed uniformly on the exterior. The bamboo of the interior walls is very light, and the palm roof makes the building even more light than a roof of tile or tin, and the bamboo is flexible enough to bend with the earth's movement. In addition to the value of the antiseismic properties of *bahareque*, the construction material also provides good insulation from the tropical heat of southern Venezuela. The hollowness of the walls that ensure their lightness also provide pockets of trapped air, providing the insulation.

While the walls of the *ata* are of *bahareque*, the roof is a cone-shaped structure of woven palm fronds in a pattern that starts at the apex and flows down the sides to the edges. This roof is held aloft by a central post. It is a mark of a *churuata* that the weaving pattern of the fronds is smooth from top to bottom, allowing rain to run off the roof and providing an elegant profile to the house. This brilliantly designed and intricate weaving is not only visible on roofs but also in trade items such as baskets. Especially in the area of baskets, each individual weaver has a unique pattern and color scheme and will work images of animal and plant life into her weaving. Ye'kuana women have, in the 20th century, turned their traditional craft of the *wuwa*, an hourglass-shaped basket, into a successful commercial practice (Orinoco Online n.d.).

The roof and its central post have additional significance, however. When the Ye'kuana build an *ata*, they are reconstructing in miniature the great cosmic home provided to them by the creator, Wanadi. The central pillar is symbolic of the tree of life, uniting the earth below and the sky above. The beams of the roof are called the celestial beams, and they represent how the constellations wheel through the night sky; the main girder for the roof beams is always oriented in relation to the Milky Way.

The ring of space just around the central pole, which holds up the roof in the *ata*, is known as the inner circle. This is the circle that represents the *dama*, the sea at the center of the world. The next circle, or ring, in the *ata* symbolizes the *nono*, or the earth, where people live. It is in this second ring that the sleeping quarters are located and the outside pillars, or *sirichäneare* (support for the stars) placed (Moreira Lauriola 2003).

Each *churuata* additionally has a door oriented to face the rising sun. This architectural feature reflects the Te'kuana belief that each dawn reflects another victory of the sun and the forces of light over the forces of darkness. Anthropologists record ancient and elaborate sun-greeting rituals and dances that now are falling into disuse in the 21st century (Orinoco Online n.d.).

COLONIAL ARCHITECTURE

Colonial architecture in Venezuela is indicative of the economic situation that the colony found itself in during the period from the 16th to the 19th century. As we have discussed elsewhere, Venezuela was not the source of large deposits of precious metals, and the pearls ran out very early. Large-scale building projects and elaborate decorative flourishes imported from exotic locales were not appropriate for a colony that was struggling to find its place in the economic reality of the new world. Colonial architecture in Venezuela, therefore, is characterized by the use of local materials to create modest buildings with clean and simple lines. In this sense, colonial architecture in Venezuela is significantly different from the baroque extravagances of Mexico or Peru, which had Aztec gold and Inca silver to fund artistic excesses and flourishes.

The relative poverty of the Venezuelan colony also meant that the architecture of this period is largely anonymous, placing the architecture of this period once again in the category of vernacular architecture (Gaspirini 1965). Therefore, we will not talk about specific artists or architects but rather give a general overview of how the colonial city and space was organized.

The architectural scholar Graziano Gaspirini reminds us that in colonial Latin America, life revolved around two spaces: the patio and the plaza. One was a private family space and one was a public space. The plaza was (and in many places in

Venezuela still is) the center of urban life. During the colonial period especially, the plaza space would have been surrounded by public buildings representing the three main colonial powers: a church, the Spanish colonial government, and the armed forces. These were constructed to awe and impress the citizenry. In Venezuela, this was achieved not through great ornamentation or height but through "austere dignity" (Gaspirini 1965: 22).

The creation of an austere façade was achieved by reducing the size of windows in proportion to the size of the façade, making the wall seem even bigger. The windows were then additionally placed very far apart, increasing this effect. The space between windows was at times filled in with decorative pillars, creating arches that gave the illusion of further height.

It was, however, the entryway of either an official structure or a home in colonial times that received the most attention. While exterior walls were left blank or with minimal ornamentation to create the illusion of height and width, entryways and doors were fiercely detailed. Commonly, the doorway to a building was framed by a pair of ornamental pillars in wood or metalwork with scenes from nature worked into the material. These columns were at times *estípite*—columns wider at the top than the bottom—a style common in Latin America during the colonial era. Elaborately carved eaves and arches would frame the doorway above with additional artwork. Frontispieces contained all of the decorative elements missing from other parts of Venezuelan colonial buildings. In this way, colonial builders gained much expressive power with limited means.

The plaza in colonial Venezuela was not only important, however, as the site of official buildings. It was also the literal center of the city for planning purposes. Federico Vegas recounts the tale of how a Spanish general undertook the informal planning of the Andean Venezuelan city of Cegarra in this way:

> He went to the plaza and, standing on a corner, fired his musket through a maze of houses, aiming toward the outskirts of town; then he ordered his Aide-de-Camp: "see where the bullet's hits the ground? Go there and nail in a stake; then bring a cord from the stake into the plaza." He then repeated this operation from the remaining three corners of the square. (Vegas 1985)

The citizens then built their new houses along the straight lines of the strings. The downtown of Cegarra retains an elegant straight grid in the 21st century, a pattern repeated around plazas in most Venezuelan cities.

After the plaza, the other major feature of colonial architecture is the importance of the interior patio. If the plaza was the space for impressive displays of power, the patio in colonial Venezuela was a space for intimate family activity. Especially in urban settings, houses were constructed in U-shaped or enclosed rectangular configurations surrounding an interior patio. All the rooms of the home would have doors leading out to and windows looking onto this inner patio, and one continuous covered walkway would run around its circumference. This configuration allowed all members of the household open access to the patio as well as afforded air circulation. Traditional colonial patios then allowed for space for the cultivation of trees and flowers as well as space for family members to walk outside in a covered area in all weather.

Especially for women, this interior patio was an important space. As Ana Isabel finds out in Palacios's novel, "decent" girls do not play in the plaza with "indecent" children as they become women. Middle- and upper-class women of the colonial period and early 20th century were confined to the private space of the patio in order to guard their honor, or risk being considered a "public woman" if they ventured out.

THE ADVENT OF PROFESSIONAL ARCHITECTURE

Art Deco

The relative poverty of Venezuela as a colony meant that the vast majority of construction in that period was anonymous. With the discovery of petroleum, however, funds for urban development, education, and architectural experimentation grew exponentially. The first decades of the 20th century in Venezuela found an increase in the influence of European architectural styles, especially in the cities where the oil money pooled.

Modern professional architecture begins in Venezuela with the art deco movement of the 1920s and 1930s. Art deco, born in Paris, was widely popular throughout Europe and the Americas and had reached Venezuela by the 1930s. Art deco, as an architectural movement, is characterized by an emphasis on surface decoration, a combination of both curved and straight lines, and the use of a wide range of color. Many decorative elements in this style seek to represent the laws of aerodynamics, reflecting a worldwide interest in flight, airplanes, and other futuristic technology. This style is streamlined and modern (Jirousek 1995).

As Venezuela developed its petroleum industry, it was very open to a design aesthetic enamored of the future and technological wonders. This was especially true of urban elites who wanted to distance themselves from their "backward," rural, indigenous and Afrovenezuelan compatriots. The Venezuelan government was itself interested in modernizing the capital and willing to spend government funds on urban planning and architecture along the French model (Almandoz 1999). Several famous federal buildings still show the art deco design aesthetic, including the City Hall of Caracas, built in 1933 and designed by architect Gustavo Wallis. The façade of the hall shows the characteristic straight lines, in conjunction with curved lines in a sunburst pattern. Carlos Raúl Villanueva, who would go on to become the most important Venezuelan architect of the 20th century, also designed an art deco façade for the new Museum of Fine Arts in Caracas, with its decorative front wall and roof of distinctive art deco arches and bursts.

Villanueva and the Modernist Aesthetic

As the art deco movement faded, Venezuelan architects, including Carlos Raúl Villanueva, began to explore modernist architecture. Modernism, as an architectural movement, would then dominate Venezuelan architecture well into the 21st century. Marguerite Mayhall contends that this is Venezuela's particular architectural exceptionalism: "In contrast to many Latin American cities in which vernacular and local styles of architecture stand cheek and jowl with buildings in imported styles, Venezuela's capital city of Caracas conveys a strongly European modernist message" (Mayhall 2005: 140). This came about because the Venezuelan art and architectural community made a collective decision to embrace modernism not only as an aesthetic ideal but also as a way for Venezuela to reach toward a modern economic and intellectual future for its citizens (Mayhall 2005).

Modernist architecture does away with all of the embellishment of art deco, choosing to focus on shape, form, light, and transparency. Modernist architecture privileges functionality over decoration, seeking to produce buildings that provide useful space while allowing light and air to flow (Modern Architecture n.d.). The modernist architects of Venezuela sought to create a synthesis of the fine arts and industrial design that would change people's lives. In this way, modernism fit in with the plans of the dictatorship of Marcos Pérez Jiménez to move the nation into the future through education, industrialization, and modern ideas.

Villanueva is the most famous and successful practitioner of the modernist utopian aesthetic in Venezuela. As Mayhall notes, Villanueva studied in Europe at the Ecóle de Beaux Arts in Paris and with the noted French architect Le Corbusier. It was in Europe that Villanueva learned the concept of buildings as "machines for living in," the key to Le Corbusier's concept of modernist architecture (Howe n.d.). Villanueva brought these ideas home and would use them in a way that would communicate with the international architectural community. Integrating the modernist vision into his work, Villanueva worked closely with Alejandro Otero on many projects, including the campus of the Universidad Central de Venezuela (now a UNESCO world heritage site). The UCV campus is one example of the modernist idea of functional architecture, and the *superbloques* are another.

Working closely with Pérez Jiménez, Otero and Villanueva looked to redesign entire barrios, hoping to improve living conditions for Caracas' poorest citizens while at the same time effecting an improvement in the people themselves. Villanueva believed in socially transformative architecture, that the built environment could act as a "teaching vehicle" that could "modify and create" habits of conduct (Mayhall 2005: 144). One of the largest projects that Villanueva undertook in this area was in the *barrio 23 de enero*.

The project was to raze the poor *ranchitos* of a Caracas barrio and replace them with new, modern, attractive housing that would integrate schools and shops, changing people's lives for the better. With the funding of the Pérez Jiménez government, between 1953 and 1955 Villanueva designed 38 housing units, known as *superbloques*, or superblocks. These were high-rise, high-density housing for upwards of 60,000 people. The units were inaugurated in 1955 with the name *2 de diciembre* (December 2) in honor of the day that the dictator took power. Today their name instead reminds everyone of the day the dictator was forced to flee the country (23rd of January).

Villanueva modeled the design for the *superbloques* on the work of Le Corbusier, adjusting for the particularly Venezuelan environment and enlisting Venezuelan artists for the cause. The apartment blocks each contained 160 apartments on 16 floors. Each two superblocks bracketed a central plaza, where it was planned to locate schools, markets, and churches to provide a "village scale" (Moholy-Nagy 1964: 12).

Additionally, the superblocks were designed with apartments starting on the fourth floor above public space designed for restaurants, offices, libraries, and parking.

Of particular importance to Villanueva in this project was to break up the exterior view of the superblocks both by varying the height of the buildings, the silhouette of the buildings, and the visual exterior design. To this end, Villanueva employed the geometric muralists Alejandro Otero, Victor Valera, and Mateo Manaure to design colorful designs for each building.

Whatever the good intentions of Villanueva and his collaborators, the design ultimately failed. While the apartments continue to be used, and are indeed well lighted and ventilated, none of the community elements that Villanueva and Pérez Jiménez imagined have come to pass. Indeed, all of the plazas and park areas surrounding the *superbloques* in 2010 are now recovered by *ranchitos*, the multicolored *superbloques* rising from a sea of brick and tin.

MISIÓN HABITAT: 21st-CENTURY APPROACHES TO PUBLIC HOUSING

The *superbloques* were Pérez Jiménez and Villanueva's answer to the question of how to solve the housing problem in the cities of Venezuela. Modernist architecture was a grand utopian social project that was not only supposed to provide decent housing but change the way people thought and lived. The experiment, however, was ultimately a failure. Theories vary as to why, but the modernist superblock model did not achieve its hoped-for success in any of the countries where it was attempted.

In the 21st century, the administration of Hugo Chávez is attempting a different approach to solving the issue of decent housing for members of the lower economic classes. One of the many social missions of the administration is Misión Hábitat, a

---

BAHARQUE FOR LOW-INCOME HOUSING

Recognizing the potential of *bahareque* as an economical, renewable, earthquake-resistant material for low-income housing projects, the very seismically active nation of Costa Rica began a project to promote the construction of new homes using *bahareque* in 1988. In 1990, a group of 30 houses were built using *bahareque* in the city of Limón. Early test results indicated that the houses were seismically adequate.

The first test of the validity of the structures came in 1991 when an earthquake that registered 7.5 on the Richter scale struck Limón, with its epicenter directly in the area of the new *bahareque* houses. All of the houses resisted the strong shaking without the slightest damage, even in areas with significant liquification of the soil. Given the widespread destruction of the 2010 earthquake in Haiti, which measured 7.0, leaving many economically disadvantaged Haitians homeless, indigenous *bahareque* seems to offer one promising idea for future construction.

government mission dedicated to providing "adequate, safe, comfortable and sanitary" housing. The mission has as its goal housing for all Venezuelans by 2021, a quantity of some 800,000 homes (Misión Hábitat n.d.).

The mission additionally follows a "new urbanist" model, as opposed to the modernist model for the public housing. One theory as to why the modernist model was ultimately unsuccessful is that citizens do not like to be removed from traditional modes of living, around a plaza, for example, or being "warehoused" in high-density, high-rise buildings. Another theory holds that communities and individual citizens prefer to have more control over decision making and even construction of their homes.

The ideology of Mission Hábitat follows the new urbanist model in which communities are built using a traditional neighborhood model. This means that there is public space (like in the traditional plaza), that everything is within walking distance, and that houses and business are combined in a mixed-use format ("Principles of Urbanism n.d.). Additionally, the mission runs an Escuela de Constructor Popular (School for Vernacular/Citizen Construction), which gives instruction on building and architectural techniques, allowing individuals and community groups to both gain skills and have more input into the process of the construction of their housing, schools, and public buildings. Critics contend that despite the money spent, only a fraction of the planned housing has been built. Time will tell whether this approach to public housing is more successful than the modernist model.

REFERENCES

Almandoz, Arturo. 1999. "Longing for Paris: the Europeanized dream of Caracas urbanism, 1870–1940." *Planning Perspectives*, 14: 225–248.

Arboleda, Gabriel. 2006. "What Is Vernacular Architecture?" http://www.vernaculararchitecture.com/.

Ashley, Tim. 2005. "Gothenburg SO/Dudamel." August 8. http://www.guardian.co.uk/music/2005/aug/08/classicalmusicandopera.proms2005.

Bauchner, Joshua. n.d. "The City That Built Itself." http://www.canopycanopycanopy.com/6/the_city_that_built_itself.

Gaspirini, Graziano. 1965. *La Arquitectra Colonial en Venezuela.* Caracas: Ediciones Armitano.

Gasparini, Graziano and Luise Margolies. 1986. *Arquitectura Popular de Venezuela.* Caracas: Armitano.

Gould, Jens Erik. 2005. "Venezuela Youths Transformed by Music." *BBC News Americas.* November 28. http://news.bbc.co.uk/2/hi/americas/4457278.stm.

Grant, Will. 2009. "Will Venezuela Go Sour on Whisky?" January 1. http://news.bbc.co.uk/2/hi/americas/7804839.stm.

Gutierrez, Jorge. 1 August 2004. Notes on the Seismic Adequacy of Vernacular Buildings. 13th World Conference on Earthquake Engineering. Vancouver B.C. Canada.

Hames, Raymond. 1992. Variation in Paternal Care Among the Yanomamo. *Father and Child Relations: Cultural and Bisocial Contexts.* Piscataway, NJ: Transaction Publishers.

Howe, Jeffrey. n.d. "Le Corbusier: Villa Savoye." http://www.bc.edu/bc_org/avp/cas/fnart/Corbu.html.

Jirousek, Charlotte. 1995. "Art Deco." http://char.txa.cornell.edu/art/decart/artdeco/artdeco.htm.

Lakshranan, Indira A.R. 2005. "For Venezuela's Poor, Music Opens Doors." June 22. http://venezuelanalysis.com/analysis/1206.

Language Museum. n.d. "Carib." http://www.language-museum.com/encyclopedia/c/carib.php.

Mayhall, Marguerite. 2005. "Modernist but Not Exceptional: The Debate over Modern Art and National Identity in 1950's Venezuela." *Latin American Perspectives* 32, no. 2: 134–145.

Misión Hábitat. n.d. "Gobierno Boliviariano de Venezuela." http://www.gobiernoenlinea.gob.ve/miscelaneas/mision_habitat.html.

Modern Architecture. n.d. http://www.learn.columbia.edu/ha/html/modern.html.

Moholy-Nagy, Sibyl. 1964. *Carlos Villanueva and the Architecture of Venezuela.* New York: Praeger.

Moreira Lauriola, Elaine. 2003. "Ye'kuana." http://pib.socioambiental.org/en/povo/yekuana/print.

Orinoco Online. n.d. "Ye'kuana." http://www.orinoco.org/apg/lopeopleindiv.asp?lang=en&people=yekuana.

"Principles of Urbanism." n.d. http://www.newurbanism.org/newurbanism/principles.html.

Tylor, Edward. 1958. *Primitive Culture.* New York: Harper.

UCAB. n.d. "Historia." http://www.ucab.edu.ve/historia.1854.html.

Vegas, Federico. 1985. *Venezuelan Vernacular.* Princeton, NJ: Princeton Architectural Press.

Wakin, Daniel J. 2009. "A New Musical Marriage in Los Angeles." November 22. http://topics.nytimes.com/top/reference/timestopics/people/d/gustavo_dudamel/index.html.

Warao. n.d. Venezuela Virtual. http://www.mipunto.com/venezuelavirtual/000/002/020/005.html.

Contemporary Issues

In January of 2010, the nation's biggest baseball rivalry played out in Caracas: the Caracas Lions versus the Magallanes Navigators. Thousands tuned in to watch Venezuela's two largest baseball teams playing the country's favorite sport. In the 2010 championship series, however, politics added an extra element of excitement to the game when a group of student protesters unveiled a large sign that read: "LUZ-AGUA-INSEGURIDAD PRESIDENTE TAS PONCHAO" ("electricity-water-insecurity president you've struck out") ("Pancarta en juego" 2010).

This sign encapsulated not only the contemporary frustrations of many Venezuelans at the beginning of the second decade of the 21st century but also many of the themes that we have covered throughout this book. The students who held up the sign were continuing a tradition of political activism that dates back to 1914 and the dictatorship of Juan Vicente Gómez. The students chose the baseball game for their protest because they knew that so many would be watching—baseball is of great cultural, economic, and international importance in Venezuela. Finally, the expression that the students used to call President Chávez out—"*tas ponchao*"—is baseball terminology for "you've struck out." It is also slang, with the shortened verb "*estás*" and the word "*ponchao*" borrowed from English, mirroring the phrase "punched out," referring to the motion an umpire makes when a batter strikes out. The language reflects both English influence and the employment of nonstandard usage in a way that would make Andrés Bello shudder.

The phrase at the end of the banner reflects material already covered in this text. The words at the beginning are three of the contemporary issues that we will look at now. As the students suggest, a failing electrical grid and lack of supply of electricity, a drought and failing water supply, and an increase in crime are three of the most pressing contemporary problems facing Venezuela as it moves through the 21st century. When we add to these worries about corruption, political instability, and increased tension in foreign relations, we can see that Venezuela may have a rough road ahead.

INTERNAL ISSUES: INSTABILITY, INSECURITY, AND HUMAN RIGHTS

Crime and Punishment

In February of 2010, Evelyn González's son-in-law was shot and killed for the motorcycle he was riding. Her son-in-law, César Enriquz Suárez Pérez, was a detective in the municipal police force of Baruta (a neighborhood in southeastern Caracas). Baruta and Chacao are two of the wealthiest districts in the capital. This did not hinder two suspects from taking the detective's black Yamaha XT. When she appeared at the morgue to pick up her son-in-law's body, Ms. Gonzalez told reporters that crime in Venezuela is as common as eating an *arepa.* "It's our daily bread, it's a routine and I can't see a solution; they don't resolve anything" ("La inseguridad" 2010)

The tragedy of Ms. González's son-in-law is the kind of story that makes front page news in Venezuela on a daily basis. It is perhaps for this reason that so many Venezuelans view crime as a crisis. A 2008 Datanálisis poll showed that 56 percent of Venezuelans viewed crime as the nation's top problem, and a poll by UCV professor Roberto Briceño-León showed that 64 percent of Venezuelans feared being attacked in the streets (Forero 2008). Crime is certainly a large problem in parts of Venezuela, but the extent to which the level of anxiety is appropriate to the level of daily danger is a matter of some debate. Additionally, opinions vary as to the extent of the Chávez administration's culpability in the growth of the crime wave and in the continued failure of police forces to protect the public.

Certainly, there is no doubt that crime is a significant problem. In 2009, the U.S. Department of State listed an alarming set of statistics in its country description of Venezuela. Among these were the 2008 rating of Caracas as the murder capital of the world, the 78 percent increase in kidnappings since 2006, and the fact that well-armed gangs were known to "operate widely" (U.S. Department of State 2009). In 2007, INOSEC (Instituto de Investigaciones de Seguridad y Convivencia Ciudadana), a group that works closely with FEDECAMARAS released a report that included a similarly alarming set of statistics:

- Between 1998 and 2005 murder by gun increased by 175 percent
- The average murder rate (measured per 100,000 people, and including death for resisting arrest) had climbed from 28/100,000 under President Pérez (1989–1992) to 57/100,000 under President Chávez (1998–).
- Not including murders for resisting arrest, the average murder rate had climbed from 22/100,000 in 1994 and 19/100,000 in 1998 to 45/100,000 in 2006. (Pearson 2009)

Given this, it is perhaps no wonder that so many Venezuelans are so seriously worried about their safety and security.

There remains, however, a growing gap between the perception of crime and the reality. A 2008 Latinobarómetro report showed that the number of Venezuelans who reported having been a victim of violent crime had held relatively stable in the period between 1998–2008. In contrast, the number of Venezuelans who had reported crime as their number-one concern had multiplied by six times over the same period (Pearson 2009). What this meant was that visitors, especially in Caracas, were cautioned against walking even a few blocks and that Venezuelans were increasingly fearful of sharing public space. This situation did nothing to alleviate the already profound problem of political and social polarization.

Whether anxiety about crime is exaggerated or not, certainly the battle against both the violence and attendant corruption in the police forces were key issues facing Venezuela's future moving forward in the 21st century. Critics of the Chávez administration say too little has been done to fix the broken judicial and criminal systems in the nation. Corruption is pervasive in the police forces, and resources are both poorly managed and unequally distributed. The drug trade is also an increasing source of concern. In 2009, the United States alleged that possible connections between the Fuerzas Armadas Revolucionarias de Colombia (FARC) rebels in Colombia and corrupt officials in the Chávez government were allowing Venezuela to become a significant player in the drug trade (Forero 2009).

Modern restructuring projects, both systematic and technological, have been attempted, however. In 2000, one of the chief architects of New York City's successful war on crime was recruited to come to Caracas and help with a makeover of the derelict system. Police Chief William Bratton came to institute a "Plan Bratton" for the metropolitan police segment of the Caracas policing structure. This plan included decentralized "mobile law enforcement modules" (mini-police stations) and a statistical program for coordinating operations and tracking crime. While some progress did seem to be made, the program was eventually shut down because of lack of funding for the statistical program and because the modules were ultimately ineffective. In one particularly embarrassing incident for the program, in the poor neighborhood of Catia, several people were actually killed right in front of one of the modules.

In addition to trying the "Plan Bratton," in April of 2007, the government purchased three blimps to patrol the Caracas sky. These blimps, armed with cameras linked to a central command center, are able to look out for a wide range of wrongdoing in many of the parts of the city that are hardest to patrol. A certainly modern innovation, it may be too early to gauge the ultimate effectiveness of this law-enforcement tool. Currently, however, the major problem with the blimps has been that they are of little use in bad weather or at night when the cameras cannot see very much at all. Nighttime is by far the most dangerous time in the city and is the time when the majority of violent crimes occur. The less than successful nature of these projects, perhaps, points to the depth and pervasiveness of the problem, which by any estimation did not begin with the Chávez government.

Opposition parties have made much of the continuing problems with crime and the Chávez government's less than effective attempts to fix them. Additionally, the Chávez administration has not helped its case by being either slow, or completely unwilling, to release statistics relating to crime. That said, most believe that the epicenter of the problems is in the barrios, the poor neighborhoods where disenfranchisement is high and enforcement is difficult. Some note that economic elites have rarely in the past shown any great concern for insecurity in the barrios and wonder if the attention that media and opposition parties now pay to the problem is now just a ploy to demonize the poor or use them, and crime, as a political tool against Chávez. One way or the other, the Chávez administration, or any government that succeeds in taking power from the *chavistas*, will certainly face a significant uphill battle against the entrenched monolith that has become the problem of crime and corruption in the nation.

POLITICAL INSTABILITY

As we have discussed throughout this text, Venezuela's political landscape was dominated throughout the second half of the 20th century by a stable agreement between two political parties. In the first decades of the 21st century, however, many Venezuelans sense that the situation is much less sure. Members of the diverse opposition to the Chávez government have, as of 2007, yet to form an organized and effective coalition to present a real alternative agenda to the Venezuelan people, and the results of recent elections show this lack of cohesion. As we discussed in Chapter 3, the domination of the National Assembly by pro-government congresspeople has allowed for a large number of sweeping laws to be written and passed, causing a significant disquiet in many.

Perhaps chief among the changes that concern some in Venezuela were those approved in the February 2009 referendum that amended the Bolivarian Constitution. The constitutional referendum, which passed with 54 percent of the vote, lifted term limits on the office of the presidency, a move that many see as potentially dangerous for Venezuela's democracy (BBC 2009). The constitutional changes that passed in 2009 were not as sweeping as those reflected by the electorate in 2007. The fragmented nature of the opposition, combined with the Chávez administration's ability to mobilize a united National Assembly and state-controlled PDVSA, however, proved successful enough to score an election-day victory. Chávez has the right to stand for election again. The specter of *caudillismo* and the military dictatorships of the past are clear in many Venzuelans' minds.

The legislative elections scheduled for September of 2010 will allow an opportunity for political parties that oppose the government of Hugo Chávez to once again attempt to come together and offer an organized alternative. In January of 2010, the National Assembly was overwhelmingly dominated by members of the PSUV, a progovernment party. Future elections will tell whether the opposition will be able to come together and regain lost seats in the legislature.

Time will also tell whether the Venezuelan diaspora will continue. Perhaps because they feel that they lack a real voice in the future of their country, Venezuela may continue to see future problems with the flight of middle- and upper-class citizens to other nations. In the first years of the 21st century, a growing number of Venezuelans sought to leave the country. From March of 2006 to March of 2007, U.S. Embassy officials reported that inquiries for visas rose by one-third over the previous year, and requests to obtain U.S. passports (by Venezuelans claiming to be sons or daughters of U.S. citizens) had doubled over the previous two years. Canadian officials reported that visa applications for entry into Canada were up 69 percent in that same time period (Dudley 2007). Long visa application lines had also been reported around the Spanish, Portuguese, Australian, and Italian embassies.

Expatriate Venezuelans interviewed in the United States do not recount stories of direct prosecution or economic hardship. Rather it seemed to be a general sense of being stuck with no options. Ruth Capriles, now resident in Miramar, Florida moved after the December 2006 elections. "After that, I realized we're not going to be able to get rid of him . . . I finally reached a point where there was nothing else left to do but leave," she told the *Miami Herald* (Dudley 2007: 1A).

This problem reminds many of the current situation of Cuban expatriates in the United States and other nations abroad. If Venezuela is to find a way for the polarized sides in the political and social debate to come to the table, the opposition in Venezuela will have to find a way to create a viable coalition that puts up electable candidates that represent the point of view of those who oppose Chávez and his policies. Only in this way will those citizens who currently feel disenfranchised be brought back in to the discussion and reinvest their lives in Venezuela.

CORRUPTION

Corruption in the Security Forces

Part of the complex of problems linked to the security situation in Venezuela is corruption. Corruption is a large enough issue in the nation's police force to be a concern for Chávez supporters and opponents alike. Critics note that while huge amounts have been spent on social programs in lower-income areas of the nation, little if any funds have been spent to update, train, and better equip the police forces. Confidence in security forces is low, and accusations of dishonesty in the national and local police forces are widespread.

One highly publicized case that has brought the extent of the problem to public attention was the kidnapping, and subsequent murder, of three boys in the spring of 2006. The boys, children of a businessman who owned a chain of shoe stores in Venezuela, were kidnapped on their way to school. Witnesses saw the boys and their bodyguard seized by men wearing police uniforms at a roadblock on February 23. A video that later surfaced showed the boys being carried past a tollbooth in a car escorted by police-issued motorcycles. Although the police found the car involved in the kidnapping later the same day, they never searched the car for fingerprints and simply moved the car to a police lot, according to the family's lawyer. Other clues surfaced during the boy's disappearance, including a proof-of-life video, communications asking for telephone calling cards, and other information. None of this seemed to lead anywhere, however, until after the boys were found dead. "We get the impression that the police knew who was involved," the family lawyer was quoted as saying (Dudley 2006: 1A).

The discovery of the bodies of the young men created a firestorm of protest in Caracas. After massive street demonstrations, the Chávez government immediately rounded up 21 suspects, including six police officers. The immediacy of the arrests after a long delay further reinforced the public perception that the police had known all along who was responsible. The public believed that the police knew because members of the police force had been involved in the crime. The whole incident further gave the impression that the delay was designed to give the government an opportunity to cover up that involvement.

In a shocking admission, in 2009, Venezuelan Interior Minister Tarek Al-Assimi admitted that up to 20 percent of all crime in Venezuela was committed by the police forces. This, combined with the fact that between January 2008 and March 2009 police forces were implicated in 755 extrajudicial killings, means that the public has lost most of their faith in the police. Interior Minister Al-Assimi has his work cut out for him (Carroll 2009b).

Critics charge that many national and Caracas officers loyal to the opposition were purged after Chávez came to power and were replaced with officers loyal to Chávez. This, opponents argue, makes the administration that much less willing to bring those loyalist officers to task for corruption and problems in their departments. These measures, opponents would argue, are not the kind of actions that will gain

Venezuelan investigative police officers look at the bodies of three Canadian brothers and their driver found near San Francisco de Yare just outside of Caracas, Venezuela, Tuesday, April 4, 2006. The bodies of John Faddoul, 17; Kevin Faddoul, 13; Jason Faddoul, 12, and driver, Miguel Ribas, 30, were found near an electrical tower about 30 miles west of Caracas. (AP/Wide World Photos)

the confidence of the people who find their confidence in their police forces at such a low ebb.

While the problem in the national police forces is surely significant, supporters of the Chávez administration point out that blame surely must not be only heaped on the current government and that patience must be given in the effort to clean up the system. The problem of corruption and general inefficiency in the system, including the police forces in Venezuela, is not new to the current Chávez government. Indeed, the problematic issues of underfunding, and the related problems of poor organization and corruption, especially in poor neighborhoods, go far back into the days of *puntofijismo.* Indeed, in the case of the police forces, experts in criminology point specifically to the 1989 law of decentralization that took a set of police forces (20 in 1990) that previously had all the same command structure and set of rules and regulations and broke it up into more than 300 different municipal forces by 2003 (Ungar 2003). This means that in the case of Caracas, for instance, the federal district falls under the jurisdiction of the metropolitan police. Five other municipalities within Caracas, however, have their own forces. (Such is the case of Baruta, where the detective mentioned at the beginning of this chapter worked.) Given the tensions that have arisen from the social polarization then, it is not uncommon for police forces in the same city to patrol the same areas yet work under different command structures with different political agendas. This is, in short, a mess.

The 1999 Penal Code intended to clean up some of the problems associated with Venezuela's notoriously poor prison system may well have made a bad situation worse. Lawmakers designed the law to make Venezuelan penal law more consistent with other international standards for bail and provisional liberty. The judicial system was simply not prepared to implement the new law and process all of the prisoners in the system as the law required. As a result, thousands of prisoners awaiting trial were released as the law required but were not adequately screened, as some of them had been accused of violent crimes (Human Rights Watch 2001). Realistically, even if someone had not been a criminal before being detained in the prison system, it was entirely likely that the prison system turned him into a criminal. Additionally, Venezuelans worry that procedural details written into the law make it easy for those accused of crimes to obtain provisional liberty if the arresting officer does not file paperwork properly. Given the deep-seated problems with corruption in the police force and inadequate judiciary system, police may well have little incentive to follow the laws in all details.

As the first decade of the 20th century closed, some actions were being taken on this issue. Interior Minister Al-Assimi, mentioned earlier, has been given credit for making initial headway on some of these issues by early 2010. The minister made positive news headlines by implementing human rights training for officers and for providing more funding for community policing programs (Carroll 2009b). In addition, in an attempt to combat the structural confusion and corruption inherent in the old system set up by the law of decentralization, President Chávez announced in late 2009 the creation of a new, centralized national police force. This force will report back directly to the ministry of the interior, will be trained in human rights, and will give the nation an opportunity for a fresh start in policing. Again, time will tell if these efforts will be successful.

Corruption in the Financial Sector

Corruption in the system is not limited to the security forces. Much debate continues to center on Chávez's economic policies and the country's economic performance since his election in 1998. The country suffered a recession during the first years of the Chávez administration, rebounded economically through 2007, then suffered again along with the rest of the world with the global economic crisis. What has not changed in all of the ups and downs of the Venezuelan economy are the concerns about corruption both in the economic sector and in the security forces. As Chávez originally ran for office on an anticorruption platform, this issue is of particular resonance to many.

One significant ongoing criticism concerns the administration of the state's oil wealth, the lack of oversight, and the potential for corruption. Corruption has long been a problem in Venezuela on nearly every level of society, in politics, in the military, and in daily life. For this reason, many of the Chávez government's actions with regards to the state's oil wealth are of great concern. Much of the government's funding for social spending comes from the state oil company, PDVSA. In 2006, for example, $19 billion of the taxes that PDVSA paid to the Venezuelan government were designated for social projects. PDVSA itself then set aside an additional $4.5 billion for antipoverty projects. On top of that, PDVSA deposited approximately $100 million a week in a discretionary presidential spending fund that is outside the official federal budget. This is an enormous amount of money. Unfortunately, however, according to a state-appointed central bank director, "the government didn't establish rules for the use or necessary supervision, control or auditing of this fund." In a nation with such pervasive history of corruption, this is a real concern (Lakshrananan 2006).

There is no doubt that some of the money associated with PDVSA social funding goes to appropriate projects, like a bakery co-operative in Tierra Adentro, a working-class neighborhood in Puerto La Cruz. Participants used the grant to renovate unused space behind an Anglican church and then to purchase equipment and supplies. The bakery, in return, is supposed to produce baked goods for the neighborhood and run an apprenticeship program for barrio residents. However, the amount of money available to PDVSA for social spending with limited oversight produces legitimate worries.

Accounts similar to the PDVSA fund have also been created and administered without sufficient oversight. When interviewed about Chávez's Fund for National Development for the Country (FONDEN, Fondo de Desarrollo Nacional), which had received $4 billion in oil money, the bank and government officials in charge were unable to say how much of the money had been spent or on what projects (Lakshrananan 2006). The situation did not improve in subsequent years. In 2008 Gustavo Coronel noted that through that year, PDVSA was no longer reporting financial results to the U.S. Securities and Exchange Commission or to the Venezuelan people. This meant that while total income to the national treasury from PDVSA was estimated at $300 billion during the years from 1998 to 2008, there was no way to be sure of the exact amount and no way to know where the money had been spent (Coronel 2008).

Indeed, Coronel notes that three parallel state budgets existed through at least 2007: a formal budget totaling more than $55 billion that was approved by the National Assembly, a second budget of $10 billion derived from monetary reserves taken from the Venezuelan Central Bank, and a third of $15 billion built from funds taken directly from PDVSA for FONDEN. Of the three, only the first had been approved by the National Assembly and was therefore discussed publicly or subject to accountability (Coronel 2008). The lack of transparency is startling and troubling, and the potential for corruption with the amounts in play is appalling.

Coronel also reports on the ongoing accusations that some Venezuelan bankers profited from the lack of transparency inherent in the system, citing Venezuelan journalist Carlos Ball, who estimated that bankers loyal to the government could have profited up to $600 million through differences in currency rates and through preferential deals with the government (Coronel 2008). In one particular instance, the banker Ricardo Fernández Barrueco is believed to have amassed a billion-dollar fortune by making back-door deals to supply corn and transport services to Misión Alimentación, the social mission that provides food to low-income Venezuelans (Carroll 2009a).

Fernández Barrueco is one member of the so-called *Boli-burgesia* (Bolivar+ bourgoesie), bankers and businessmen loyal to the Chávez administration that have allegedly benefited from the lack of transparency to make their fortunes. This may have been the case. In late 2009, the Chávez administration launched a sweeping investigation and crackdown against seven banks. The investigation against the banks resulted in the closure of seven banks, the arrest of eight bankers, and the removal of Jesse Chacón, minister of science and technology, from office. Chacón's brother Arne Chácon, was one of the eight bankers arrested in the corruption investigation. Questions remain as to how Arne Chácon went from being a small businessman to a bank president. Most, however, suspect that his brother's long loyalty to President Chávez explains all.

While the investigations and arrest seem like progress in the fight against corruption, observers both in and outside Venezuela remain concerned about the breadth and depth of the corruption in the banking system and have doubts about how the investigations and prosecutions will proceed. While the 2009 inquiry began with a promise of transparency, as the scandal has grown, the government has become less willing to share information. Economist Jose Guerra observed in 2009 that this procedure will do little to increase public confidence in the government or in the government's willingness to battle corruption: "first you say you're going to take over four banks and that the process is going to be transparent . . . then a few days later you say you're going to take over a few more but that now it will take place behind closed doors. What do you expect will happen?" (Grant 2009). The next years will see whether anticorruption efforts in the banking or government sectors are successful. However, what is clear is that financial corruption is a serious and pervasive issue, one that is a concern to citizens whether they support Chávez and his programs or not.

FREEDOM OF THE PRESS AND FREEDOM OF ASSEMBLY

The area of communications continues to be a battleground as Venezuela moves through the new century. Pro-Chávez groups remain concerned by the vehemence and vitriol of the anti-Chávez rhetoric that is broadcast and printed by the privately owned media. By contrast, a variety of international and national organizations express increasing concern about state censorship and repression of the press through 2010.

One of the major stories in this battle is that of Radio Caracas Televisión (RCTV). At the time of Hugo Chávez's election in 1998, RCTV was Venezuela's most-watched television station, popular with viewers because of its *telenovelas*, sports programming, and variety shows. RCTV had broadcast out of its Caracas studios and across the nation since 1953.

RCTV was also, however, a strident critic of the Chávez administration. RCTV was instrumental in the 2002 coup, airing relentlessly critical editorial coverage of the government and refusing to cover pro-Chávez protests. Indeed, for the two days preceding the coup, RCTV cancelled regular programming and ran constant coverage of the general strike that had been organized to oust Chávez. Interspersed with this coverage were commercial advertisements exhorting citizens to attend the April 11 anti-Chávez protest march. When the march ended in violence, coverage shifted to non-stop criticism of the violence and the pro-Chávez marchers. When the coup against Chávez succeeded a few days later, the coup plotters specifically thanked both RCTV and Venevisión for their support (Edwards 2007).

This is the background to the Chávez government's decision in 2007 not to renew RCTV's broadcast license. The official explanation for the nonrenewal was that RCTV had violated the 2003 Social Responsibility Law by airing pornographic and violent programming during daytime hours. The closure was in fact technically legal, given that many found the station's programming racially and sexually offensive. Not many have chosen to believe this explanation, however, seeing the move instead as one that the government took to silence a vocal critic of the administration. Organizations such as the European Union and the journalist's group Reporters Without Borders loudly criticized the decision to remove RCTV from the public airwaves. The closure prompted large student protests both in Caracas and across the country.

Chávez supporters noted there were still many nongovernment-run options for television in Venezuela and that both major newspapers were still very critical of the government. In addition, supporters pointed out that RCTV continued to broadcast on their cable channel. However, many noted that the poorest of Venezuela's citizens did not have access to cable television and that the continued broadcast of RCTV for them in that medium was a moot point. While other television outlets remained independent, the closure of RCTV as a public station sent a clear message that was heard by others. Venevisión, Venezuela's second most popular station, began to take a significantly less critical stance on the government, removing its most outspoken critics of the government, or moving them to off-hours slots.

This was not the end of the story, however. In December of 2009, the National Communications Commision (CONATEL, Comision Nacional de Telecomunicaciones) ruled that all television stations that broadcast more than 30 percent of Venezuelan-produced content in Venezuela would be obliged, under the Social Responsibility Law, to carry President Chávez's frequent public broadcasts, known as *cadenas.* In January 2010, the Chávez government removed RCTV and five other cable television stations from the cable airwaves after the stations refused to carry the *cadenas.* In February of the same year, the five non-Venezuelan networks (three Mexican, one Peruvian, and one Chilean) were allowed to resume rebroadcasting; RCTV was kept off the air. This latest action against RCTV heightened concerns in Venezuela about press freedoms and sparked a series of sometimes violent student protests across Venezuela (RSF 2010a).

The international watchdog group Reporters Without Borders described the 2010 action as skewing public speech and as a means of coercion on media content (RSF 2010b). The Inter-American Commission on Human Rights (IACHR) additionally voiced concern about the "progressive deterioration of freedom of expression in Venezuela . . . and the rising intolerance of critical expression" (IACHR 2009). The IACHR was additionally concerned about the forced closure of 34 radio stations with anti-Chávez editorial stances and several acts of intimidation against the remaining anti-administration television station in Venezuela, Globovisión (IACHR 2009).

As with all things in contemporary Venezuela, the debate about media freedom is ongoing, complex, and fluid. Critics argue that no matter what RCTV or other radio and television stations did, closing the stations violates basic principles of freedom of speech. Yet Chávez made the moves as part of the broader tit-for-tat conflict with the opposition on numerous issues, including media freedom.

We should also remember the Chávez administration's efforts to promote community media. The opposition regularly accuses community media of being tools of the state, or "radio-electronic media of the state . . . employed for propaganda and political proselytism," even though evidence suggests that community media are not necessarily *chavista* lap dogs. (Schiller in press). Furthermore, the opposition has also tried to silence community media stations and journalists. Caracas mayor Alfredo Peña, a former journalist associated with the opposition, closed down the Catia TVe (a station run by lower-class Chávez supporters) in July 2003, claiming that it caused health hazards in the old hospital in which it functioned, a move also denounced by Reporters Without Borders (Márquez 2003). The station reopened in larger facilities later that same year. In July 2005, a RCTV reporter, Arturo Pérez, assaulted a Catia TVe reporter, stating "Stop filming me you spy, and tell your papa Chávez to buy you a new camera" (Schiller in press). Though Pérez damaged the Catia TVe reporter's camera, it continued to run. Catia TVe ran the footage of the scuffle repeatedly. Pérez later called Catia TVe the "the trash boot-licking network of the regime" in a letter posted on the Internet (Schiller in press).

What is clear is that free debate of issues cannot take place without open and free expression in the country. Many will continue to watch the situation unfold, looking to see whether state control over media expression continues to tighten. To critics, this will be further proof that the Chávez administration is becoming increasingly totalitarian. Attention will also be paid to the explosion of community media. Will those stations continue to exercise editorial independence? Will local broadcasts provide an outlet for free expression for citizens? Time will tell.

A February 2010 report on human rights in Venezuela issued by the Organization of American States (OAS) certainly did not provoke outbursts of optimism from democracy advocates. The 300-page OAS report, much more overtly critical than many OAS pronouncements, asserted that "the [Venezuelan] state has punished and silenced critics, among them anti-government television stations, demonstrators and opposition politicians who advocate a form of government different from Chavez's" (Forero 2010). Further, the report raises concerns about Chávez's ability to influence the judiciary and impede opposition candidates from running for elected office and disrupt the ability to govern of officials associated with the opposition. OAS officials encouraged Chávez to receive the report as constructive criticism with which to begin reforms. Given his tendency to find fault with those issue any sort of criticism, many in February 2010 did not think that the OAS report would result in any substantive changes in the Chávez administration.

ELECTRICITY AND WATER PROBLEMS

We mentioned at the beginning of this chapter and in Chapter 4 the energy crisis that wracked the nation in late 2009 and into 2010. Beyond the potential for economic disaster, the energy crisis has brought into painful relief real deficiencies in Venezuela's energy infrastructure that long pre-date the Chávez administration. Phased construction of the Guri dam at Coroní began in 1963 and ended in 1986. By 2010, the dam produced 73 percent of all Venezuela's electricity (Molinski 2010). Ten other much smaller dams produced the remaining 27 percent of power. Chávez initiated construction of a hydroelectric power plant in 2006, the first new investment in energy in decades (Business Wire 2006).

The energy problem, however, is more complicated than overreliance on one power plant and the consequences of drought. Venezuela has never been a nation known for energy conservation or for effective energy distribution. Access to electricity and running water has long been a problem for people living in urban barrios. It has long been common for people to tap into electric lines and run lines to their homes without consulting any sort of electric company. Many people, regardless of class, long before the 2009–2010 crisis made it a habit to collect water in rain barrels, just in case. The issue with electricity more so than water (which is more tied to environment than politics) is culture. Venezuelans presume that all forms of energy are part of the national patrimony and are and always shall be, therefore, cheap and abundant. Subsidized gas and electricity have fueled cultural expectations. As a result, Venezuelans, before the 2009–2010 crisis, did not habitually turn out the lights

Guri Dam, a hydroelectric power station in Bolivar States, Venezuela. (iStockPhoto)

when they left the room as mothers scold children to do in the United States. To the contrary, leaving the lights on was an easy solution for home safety problems.

In that context, then, the energy crisis is not so much a problem with the environment or natural resources as it is about management of national patrimony. Of course what caused the crisis was decades of poor planning, wasteful consumption, and a drought. Much of Chávez's success in the middle years of his presidency rested on his ability to link his leadership to the control of national patrimony. He could not control the rain. However, the cultural understanding of energy as patrimony that Chávez manipulated successfully undermined his popularity during the crisis. Like the sign said, Chávez "tas ponchao" ("Pancarta en juego" 2010). He took the hit in poll numbers. By February 2010, popularity ratings fell to an all-time low (for him) below 50 percent ("Venezuela-Colombia Relations" 2010).

There is no doubt that both sides played politics with the crisis. Conservation suddenly became a new call to patriotism for Chávez. Patriotic Venezuelans turned off the lights and took three-minute showers. Normal human behavior became treasonous, at least rhetorically speaking. The elite's language was equally hyped. Some focused on orders to limit the hours of shopping mall operations. The malls, the elite said, only represented 1 percent of all energy consumption, so closing the malls was an attack on the elite. The mayor of Chacao, one of the elite neighborhoods of Caracas, said, "By limiting the hours we can go to malls, [Chávez] is trying to slowly take away liberties, to create absolute control over things such as shopping" (Molinski 2010).

Most Venezuelans, however, were not concerned about limitations on their right to shop. In addition to reducing mall hours, Chávez has also ordered all government offices and some industries to cut use by 20 percent; metal production decreased 40 percent (Molinski 2010). Reducing government office hours (part of the 20 percent reduction) meant that all Venezuelans were limited in their ability to tend to simple yet vital business, like registering the birth of a child in the public registry office. Public security became an issue for all Venezuelans, regardless of class. In sum, the rains may fill up the dams, but they cannot solve the infrastructure problems that led to the shortage or wash away the political or social wounds the energy crisis aggravated.

FOREIGN RELATIONS: CHASING BOLÍVAR'S DREAM

Tercermundismo

Much has been made in these early years of the 21st century of what has seemed a turn to the left in Latin American politics. This was a disturbing trend from the point of view of many in the U.S. government. In October of 2002, House International Relations Committee Chairman Henry Hyde sent President George W. Bush a fiery letter warning of the danger of an emerging "New Axis of Evil" in Latin America Hugo Chávez and rounded out by Brazilian President Luís Inacio "Lula" da Silva and cold-warrior Fidel Castro (Baker 2003).

Incendiary rhetoric aside, what may emerge in coming years in Latin America is a new coalition of like-minded nations whose leaders agree on general ideology as well as key issues of economic cooperation and regional defense. While any long-term view of the future is muddy at best, what can be ascertained is a desire on the part of the Chávez administration to lead a new attempt to resurrect Simón Bolívar's great dream, that of a South America united and strong, able to compete head to head with Europe and the United States.

Generally, when speaking of those nations and their leaders who share a leftist ideology with Chávez and his government, analysts (as of 2010) tend to list the previously mentioned Fidel Castro and Lula da Silva, former Sandinista rebel and current President Daniel Ortega in Nicaragua, leftist President Tabar Vásquez of Uruguay, and socialist Presidents Evo Morales of Bolivia and Fernando Lugo of Paraguay. This group, however, hardly represents a united and monolithic front of ideology or policy. Rather, the leaders just listed range from radicals to pragmatic social democrats. The group, therefore, is important for our purposes for the way that it presents a group of receptive listeners to Chávez and allows him the opportunity to share his vision of what Dan Hellinger calls "*tercermundismo*" (Hellinger 2006). *Tercermundismo* is an ideology that suggests that throughout South America (and perhaps the world) nations should band together to form an economic and defensive unit to compete with the developed world.

In the first years of the 21st century, Cuba and Bolivia, with their leaders, Fidel Castro and Evo Morales, have been Chávez's closest allies in this ideological crusade. Looking toward the future, as Fidel Castro fades physically and his brother Raúl takes more control, it will likely be the Bolivian president who will be the most important collaborator Venezuela has in the project of uniting the continent. Evo Morales, Bolivia's first indigenous president, was elected on a socialist platform very similar to Chávez's: a new constitution, nationalization of the nation's natural gas industry, social justice and redistribution of wealth to the poor, and strong emphasis on indigenous rights. After his election, Morales became a logical and strong ideological ally of Castro and Chávez.

In the 21st century, new projects have brought the two nations closer together and suggest further cooperation. Chávez visits Bolivia frequently and has offered the nation up to $1 billion dollars in aid as Bolivia works through its economic changes. More specifically, in 2006, Chávez and Morales reached a military agreement whereby Venezuela would provide up to $22 million dollars to help Bolivia build 20 military bases. In a related agreement, Bolivian elite military troops were scheduled to come to Venezuela with advanced technology and equipment (Bridges 2006).

This type of military agreement between two Latin American nations would not normally generate much attention. In this case, however, many see the move by Chávez as indicative of a larger future plan for building a South American defense network. Bolivia, bordering five countries in the middle of the continent, is especially important strategically. Chávez has spoken of this goal before in public addresses. "We must form a defensive military pact between the armies of the region with a common doctrine and organization," he is quoted as saying during a military parade in

Bolivia's President Evo Morales, left, and Venezuela's President Hugo Chávez sing Bolivia's national anthem at an agreement signing ceremony in Barinas, Venezuela, Friday, April 30, 2010. (AP/Wide World Photos)

Caracas in 2006, a parade attended by Evo Morales and Argentine President Nestor Kirchner (Arostegui 2006).

Chávez's relationship with Argentina is also gaining a great deal of attention and may ultimately become more important than the relationship with Bolivia. Nestor Kirchner, the center-left president of Argentina from 2003 to 2007, became increasingly closer to Chávez during his tenure as president. In one example, when U.S. president George W. Bush toured Latin America in an attempt to rebuild support and ties in the region, Chávez embarked on an "anti-tour" through the continent. In the highlight of the "anti-tour," when Bush was in Brazil, just over the border in Argentina, Kirchner helped organize a 32,000-person anti-Bush rally in a soccer stadium in a working-class neighborhood where Chávez was the only speaker (Sreeharsha 2007). President Bush did not even visit Argentina on his Latin American tour.

While Kirchner declined in 2007 to run for a second term, the connections between the two nations remained strong. Mr. Kirchner's wife, the senator Cristina Fernández de Kirchner, won election to the presidency in 2007 and continued the majority of her husband's policies, enjoying the support of Chávez. Through 2009, the two nations maintain a good working relationship, signing more than 130 social, cultural, political, and economic bilateral agreements in the years from 2005 to 2009. This shows, in the words of Venezuelan Minister of Agriculture Elías Jaua, "We see a qualitative jump forward in this important relationship achieved between the governments of Venezuela and Argentina, from the arrival of President Néstor Kirchner continuing with the same enthusiasm by President Cristina Fernández de Kirchner" (Diarocrítico de Venezuela 2009).

Again, the idea of forming an alliance of South American nations to counter U.S. influence is part of Chávez's ideology of *tercermundismo*. Chávez likens his proposed alliance to NATO, "with our own doctrine, not one that's handed down by the gringos," as he said in a television address broadcast in Bolivia. Some see the construction of military bases in Bolivia as the first step in this plan. Chávez, however, envisions eventually "the armed forces of Mercosur" (Arostegui 2006). Mercosur is the South American trading group that includes Argentina, Brazil, Uruguay, Paraguay, Bolivia, Chile, Colombia, Ecuador, and Peru.

Increased economic cooperation may happen through Mercosur. The trade and customs agreement, which began in 1991 between Brazil, Argentina, Uruguay and Paraguay, admitted Venezuela as a member in 2006. Chávez would like it, however, to move more as a geopolitical force than as a regional group meant to ease the movement of goods, services, and money. When Venezuela formally requested to join Mercosur in 2006, Chávez made some uneasy with his large plans for the union, including a trans-South American pipeline and a new development bank for the region that would compete with the World Bank (an enterprise that Chávez considers dominated by U.S. interest).

In January of 2010, plans were announced for Venezuela to become a full member of Mercosur in March of 2011. Resistance to Venezuela's inclusion into the bloc continued to be felt from Paraguay, which continued to be suspicious of Chávez's plans for the continent. In January of 2010, Paraguayan Vice President Federico Franco expressed misgivings about Chávez's "imperial attitude towards Paraguay" (Franco

Presidents, from left to right: Cuba's Fidel Castro, Uruguay's Tabare Vazquez, Brazil's Luiz Inacio Lula da Silva, Argentina's Nestor Kirchner, Paraguay's Nicanor Duarte, Venezuela's Hugo Chávez, Chile's Michelle Bachelet, and Mexico's Foreign Minister Luis Enersto Derbez pose for a photo during a Mercosur summit in Cordoba, some 700 kilometers (434 miles) from Buenos Aires, Argentina, Friday, July 21, 2006. (AP/Wide World Photos)

2010). While Paraguayan President Fernando Lugo is a leftist and a Chávez ally, the Paraguayan National Assembly is dominated by the opposition. Relations between Chávez and Paraguay, therefore, are somewhat strained.

In addition to urging Mercosur to position itself as a "world power," Chávez has also reached out to other nations outside the South American area through another initiative, the Bolivarian Alternative of the Americas, or ALBA (Alianza Boliviariana para los Pueblos de Nuestra America) (McMahon 2006). ALBA can be seen as Chávez's new modern vision for not only the united South America that Bolívar dreamed of, but also as an additional way for the current Venezuelan government to organize the united front that will counter U.S. influence in the region. In its early stages of organization, Chávez sees ALBA as an alternative to the Free Trade Area of the Americas (FTAA) that the United States has been negotiating with nations in North, Central, and South America for some time. Over the years, the United States has signed individual free trade agreements with México, the Dominican Republic, five Central American nations, and three South American nations.

Chávez envisions ALBA as an alliance between the countries of the south that would allow them to have more leverage when negotiating with the United States. The agreement, he explains, would also foster cooperation in energy, banking, and agricultural matters. Chávez and other analysts compare the idea to the European Union. Like in the EU, the larger and more prosperous countries would help strengthen the economies of the less developed nations in the early years. This means that the proposal is attractive for some nations. In the first ALBA meeting in Barquisimeto, Venezuela in April of 2007, Daniel Ortega of Nicaragua, Evo Morales of Bolivia, Fidel Castro, and Haitian President René Preval were all in attendance. Ecuador and Honduras joined a short time later.

It remains to be seen whether ALBA will survive and prosper. The possibilities for the association to promote inter-Latin American trade and cooperation do seem promising. The benefits, in addition, for the less-developed countries, are significant. Bolivia, Cuba, and Nicaragua have all received aid from Venezuela as part of their association in ALBA. In the 2009 meeting of ALBA nations, a new currency, the Sucre (named for independence hero José Antonio de Sucre) was proposed, a move that member nations hoped would strengthen economies across borders as the Euro had in Europe.

VENEZUELA-COLOMBIA RELATIONS

While through 2010 the Chávez administration continued to build political and economic bonds with many South and Central American nations, Venezuelan-Colombian relations continued to deteriorate. A series of border skirmishes and intrusions that involved not only Venezuela and Colombia but also Venezuelan ally Ecuador have increased tensions in the 21st century.

The current set of events may be said to have begun with a Colombian operation to track down high-ranking members of the FARC a Marxist/revolutionary/terrorist organization that operates in southern Colombia. In March 2008, Colombian forces followed a FARC cell over the Colombian-Ecuadorian border into Ecuadorian territory, killing FARC leader Raul Reyes and 23 others, and arresting five (BBC News Americas 2008). The Ecuadorian government was furious over the armed, unauthorized intrusion into their territory.

Ecuadorian allies Nicaragua and Venezuela immediately broke diplomatic ties with Colombia, and Venezuela moved 9,000 troops to the Venezuela-Colombia border (BBC News Americas 2008). The situation continued to escalate, as Venezuelan troops began destroying footbridges across the Venezuelan-Colombian border. The Colombian government decried the destruction of these bridges, used by many pedestrians to cross from one country to another daily for work or shopping. In 2008 and 2009, Colombia accused Venezuela of hiding and aiding at least one leader of the FARC on its territory and of various human rights abuses. Venezuela accused Colombia of aggression and spying.

By November of 2009, the situation had deteriorated to a point where the Colombian minister of defense admitted that he considered Venezuela "an external threat" and that for the first time in decades his government was designing plans to prepare for an armed confrontation with Venezuela. For their part, members of the Chávez government accused the Colombian government of Alvaro Uribe of making secret deals with the U.S. military, planning destabilization raids into Venezuelan territory (El Universal 2009).

Military spending by both nations means that the war of words could easily become effectively lethal. Under Plan Colombia (1999–2005), the United States gave Colombia $2.8 billion targeted toward military spending to be used to enhance Colombia's ability to fight drug wars (Veillette 2005). Venezuela spent $4.3 billion on its military between 2004 and 2006, purchasing arms primarily from Russia and former Eastern Bloc countries. In 2008, Venezuela entered into a contract with Belarus to build an air defense system (Alvarez and Hanson 2009). To a casual observer, the situation appears to echo the cold war in terms of military spending patterns and alliances. If only history was just that in this case—history.

Some hope was placed either in Spain, as a third party mediator, or in the Union of South American Nations (UNASUR, Unión de Naciones Suramericanas), to negotiate a cooling off of tensions between the two nations. Even so, destabilization of relations between Venezuela and Colombia remains a concern for many in the region.

VENEZUELA AND THE UNITED STATES

Even more important to Venezuela than its relationship with Colombia is its relationship with the United States. The centuries-long relationship, deeply grounded in economic interdependence, has been threatened in the last 20 years by the political maneuverings of both governments. While, in 2010, distrust was high on both sides of the Caribbean, most analysts were hopeful for a future of increasingly good relations between the two nations.

Trade is of great mutual interest to both nations. The United States remains Venezuela's most important trading partner. In 2009, 46 percent of all Venezuelan exports went to the United States, and 25 percent of all imports into Venezuela came from the United States (U.S. Department of State 2010). In addition, through 2010, the United States remained the largest buyer of Venezuelan crude, with 12 percent of U.S. oil imports coming from Venezuela (U.S. Department of State 2010). Given what is at stake economically for both countries, it is the opinion of many observers that it is in their best interests to improve a relationship that has been fraught with disagreement since 1999.

Despite longstanding economic interdependency, Venezuela is one of several Latin American nations that has, in the first decade of the 21st century, begun to construct foreign and domestic policies that have not always been consistent with U.S. interests. President Chávez had a particularly tense relationship with President George W. Bush, highlighted by Chávez's speech at the United Nations in 2006, the day after President Bush's speech, in which Chávez noted that the room still smelled of sulfur (a reference to Bush being the devil). This was just one verbal shot at President Bush, who Chávez attacked regularly on his television and radio program *Aló Presidente.* Chávez, a fervent opponent of free-market capitalism and the neoliberal economic policies of free trade promoted by Bush, saw the U.S. president as a opponent in the fight against poverty in the developing world. Chávez also, as of 2010, continued to accuse the government of President Bush of assisting in the 48-hour coup d'état against Chávez in 2002. The Bush administration, for its part, accused Chávez of assisting the FARC insurgents in Colombia and of not doing enough to combat the drug trade within Venezuelan borders (Council on Foreign Relations 2008). Concern continued in 2010.

Moving beyond accusations, however, in 2006 and 2007 Venezuela moved toward more tightly nationalizing Venezuelan oil and the Venezuelan oil fields, a step that concerned many in the United States and Europe. Industry observers in the United States noted that the move would increase investor fear as it would make it more difficult for U.S. oil companies to access one of the largest long-term sources of oil left on the planet, the Orinoco heavy tar belt (Gould 2006a). To the extent that foreign dependence on oil also constitutes a national security issue, this move also heightened political as well as economic tensions between the United States and Venezuela.

The economic crisis that began in 2008 forced Chávez to reconsider the oil policies, and the election of Barack Obama precipitated a slight political thaw. By early 2010, Venezuela opened new oil concessions to foreign investment. Ambassadors who had been recalled in September 2008 (before the presidential election in the United States) went back to their respective posts in Caracas and Washington, DC in the summer of 2009. At the OAS Summit of the Americas in April 2009, Chávez and Obama pledged to construct a relationship based on mutual interest and to avoid overt confrontation. Though the relationship remained strained, in early 2010 there had been no events that threatened the tepid truce in the war of words that had marked the years prior. Because of the mutual economic ties that bind the nations together, it is unlikely that any political crisis will sever the ties.

CONCLUSIONS

Don José Oviedo y Baños gushed over the colony's economic potential in 1723. Venezuela was the most fertile colony, he said, with "delightful valleys," waters "clear and salubrious" (Oviedo y Baños 1987: 7). A century and a half earlier, explorers made their way into the challenging Venezuelan geography looking for the fabled El Dorado. Most found nothing but indigenous resistance, mosquitoes, and death. Census takers in 1829 described Caribs in eastern Venezuela as primitive savages in need of civilization. Politicians used the same words to describe Venezuelans rioting during the *caracazo* in 1989 and Warao Indians dying of cholera in 1992. The indigenous *cacique* Guaicaipuro is hailed as a hero who led the resistance to the Spaniards who tried to settle the valleys of Caracas. El Negro Miguel is lauded in national history, national myth, and in religious ideology as the hero of the first major slave rebellion. Ezequiel Zamora led either a race war or thwarted revolution in the mid-19th century, depending on interpretation. *Doña Bárbara* was positivist garbage or an anti-imperialist critique ahead of its time. Ali Primera was either a vile communist or the martyred voice of the people. The well at La Rosa either spewed oil to lubricate Venezuela's liberation from dependency or mired the nation forever in a curse. PDVSA belonged to the state or PDVSA was the state.

Historia (history) in Spanish means simultaneously history and story. Which of the preceding *historias* is Venezuela's *historia*? All of them. All of those histories, all of those stories, shape Venezuelans today because Venezuelans choose the history and the story they need in order to understand complex economic, social, and political reality. The problem is that people do not live simple black and white, either/or lives. They live "all of the above" lives in shades of gray. *Doña Bárbara* was positivist garbage *and* an anti-imperialist critique ahead of its time. PDVSA belonged to the state *and* PDVSA constructed a culture that defined the company as the state. The "ands" make reality all the more complicated. Either/or is easy. "*Ni . . . ni*" is hard.

Sure, scholars argue that some versions of reality have more foundation in evidence, but that does not mean much to people trying to understand immediate complexity. Evidence, or as the Venezuelan expression goes: *¿con que se come eso?* (what does one eat with that?) helps scholars and citizens alike make sense of the world. Evidence, however, also means little when national curriculums reinforce the story deemed "most appropriate" for the population at any given moment. Venezuelans shifted the stories they believed as their daily lives changed, and daily lives changed rapidly in the past 40 years. In that context, it is not hard to see why people have alternately demonized and idolized Hugo Chávez. Polarization, however—be it of race, class, or gender—has always existed in Venezuela, right there underneath the surface. It is just that politicians sowed the wealth in ways in the 20th century that made it easier to forget complicated, polarized, painful Venezuelan realities. As hard as the 21st century is for Venezuela, at least now it has the chance to "see" itself in ways impossible before. Real and positive change can happen with such vision. Venezuelans are asking questions about their history and their realities that they never asked before. This is good. Venezuelans are survivors. They embrace hard work. Creativity and innovation define them more than corruption and fear. *Gloria al bravo pueblo.*

REFERENCES

Alvarez, Cesar, and Stephanie Hanson. 2009. "Venezuela's Oil Based Economy." Council on Foreign Relations. Backgrounder. http://www.cfr.org/publication/12089/venezuelas_oil based_economy.html.

Arostegui, Martin. 2006. "Chávez Seeks anti-U.S. Military Alliance." *The Washington Times.* http://www.washingtontimes.com/news/2006/aug/1/20060801-104047-5464r/.

Baker, Steven. 2003. "The Gathering Storm." FrontPageMag.com http://97.74.65.51/read Article.aspx?ARTID=18473.

BBC News Americas. 2008. "FARC Rebels Arrested in Ecuador." http://news.bbc.co.uk/2/hi/7282723.stm.

———. 2009. "Chávez Wins Chance of Fresh Term." http://news.bbc.co.uk/2/hi/7891856.stm.

Bridges, Tyler. 2006. Bolivia-Venezuela Military Deal Raises Red Flags. *The Washington Times*, October 29, 4B.

Business Wire. 2006. "New Hydroelectric Plant in Venezuela, an Industrial Info News Alert." April 13. http://www.encyclopedia.com/doc/1G1-144423781.html.

Carroll, Roy. 2009a. "Aides in the Firing Line as Hugo Chávez Targets Bank Corruption in Venezuela." http://www.guardian.co.uk/world/2009/dec/07/hugo-chavez-bank-scandal-venezuela.

———. 2009b. "Deadly Force: Venezuela's Police Have Become a Law unto Themselves." http://www.guardian.co.uk/world/2009/sep/06/venezuela-police-law-themselves.

Council on Foreign Relations. 2008. "Linking Venezuela and FARC." Council on Foreign Relations Analysis Brief. http://www.cfr.org/publication/16306/linking_venezuela_and_the_farc.html.

Coronel, Gustavo. 2008. "The Corruption of Democracy in Venezuela." *USA Today Magazine*. http://www.cato.org/pub_display.php?pub_id=9254.

Diarocrítico de Venezuela. 2009. "Chávez-Fernández Profundarizarán Relaciones Comerciales." http://www.diariocritico.com/venezuela/2009/Agosto/noticias/167318/reunion-trimestral-chavez-fernandez-profundizar-relaciones-comerciales.html.

Dudley, Steven. 2006. "Crime Wave, Police Silence Worry Caracas." *The Miami Herald*, June 1, 1A.

———. 2007. "Exasperated by Chávez, More Venezuelans Leave: Middle and Upper Class Venezuelans are Leaving the Country in Droves." *The Miami Herald*, May 1, 3C.

Edwards, David. 2007. "Chávez and RCTV: Media Enemies at Home and Abroad." http://www.mediaaccuracy.org/node/8.

El Universal. 2009. Venezuela-Colombia Relations Keep Worsening. November 27. http://english.eluniversal.com/2009/11/27/en_ing_esp_venezuela-colombia-r_27A3125811.shtml.

Forero, Juan. 2008. "In Rampant Violent Crime: Political Danger for Chávez." *The Washington Post*, November 18. http://www.washingtonpost.com/wp-dyn/content/article/2008/11/17/AR2008111703098.html.

———. 2009. "Venezuela's Drug Trafficking Role Is Growing Fast, U.S. Government Says." *The Washington Post*, July 19. http://www.washingtonpost.com/wp-dyn/content/article/2009/07/18/AR2009071801785.html.

———. 2010. "Venezuela, President Chávez Criticized in OAS Report." *The Washington Post*, February 24. http://www.washingtonpost.com/wp-dyn/content/article/2010/02/24/AR2010022401884.html.

Fox, Michael. 2006. "Venezuela Unveils Monument for Victims on Coup Anniversary." *Venezuelaanalysis*, April 14. http://www.venezuelaanalysis.com/news/1697.

Franco, Federico. 2010. "Paraguay's Vice-president contrary to Venezuela joining Mercosur" January 7. http://en.mercopress.com/2010/01/07/paraguays-vice-president-contrary-to-venezuela-joining-mercosur.

Gould, Jens. 2006a. "Venezuelan Slums Rife with Crime." *Washington Times*, August 22. http://www.washingtontimes.com/news/2006/aug/21/20060821-101841-9580r//?page=1.

Gould, Jens. 2006b. "Venezuela Tightens Oil Grip." *The Christian Science Monitor*, April 14. http://www.csmonitor.com/2006/0414/p06s01-woam.html.

Grant, Will. 2009. "Venezuelan Banking Scandal Widens." BBC News. http://news.bbc.co.uk/2/hi/business/8401020.stm.

Hellinger, Daniel. 2006. "Tercermundismo and Chavismo." *Stockholm Review of Latin American Studies* 1: 4–17.

Human Rights Watch. 2001. "Venezuela's Implementation of the International Covenant on Civil and Political Rights." Human Rights Watch. http://www.hrw.org/backgrounder/americas/venezuela_un.htm.

Inter-American Commission on Human Rights. 2009. "Press Release 55/09. IACHR Expresses Concern Abour the Deterioraton of the Situation of Freedom of Expression in Venezuela." http://www.cidh.org/comunicados/english/2009/55–09eng.htm.

"La inseguridad es tan común como comerse una arepa." 2010. *El Nacional*, February 10.

Lakshrananan, Indira A.R. 2006. "Critics Slam Oil Windfall Spending." *Boston Globe*, August 13. http://www.boston.com/news/world/latinamerica/articles/2006/08/13/critics_slam_venezuelan_oil_windfall_spending/.

Lombardi, John V. 2003. "Prologue: Venezuela's Permanent Dilemma." In Steve Ellner and Dan Hellinger, eds., *Venezuelan Politics in the Chavez Era: Class, Polarization, and Conflict*. Boulder, CO: Lynne Rienner.

Márquez, Humberto. 2003. "Venezuela: Opposition Mayor Shuts Down Community Television Station." *IPS—Inter-Press Service*, July 16. http://ipsnews.net/interna.asp?idnews=19274.

McMahon, Colin. 2006. "Venezuela Urges Bloc to Rival U.S." *Chicago Tribune*, July 22. http://articles.chicagotribune.com/2006-07-22/news/0607220073_1_uruguay-and-paraguay-mercosur-venezuelan-president-hugo-chavez.

Molinski, Dan. 2010. "Energy-Rich Venezuela Faces Power Crisis." *Wall Street Journal*. http://online.wsj.com/article/NA_WSJ_PUB:SB126291736012720909.html.

Oliver, Christian. 2007. "Venezuela Launches Zeppelin to Tackle Rampant Crime." Reuters. http://www.reuters.com/article/idUSN1935089920070419.

Oviedo y Baños, José. 1987. *The Conquest and Settlement of Venezuela*. Berkley: University of California Press.

"Pancarta en juego de Caracas-Magallanes contra Chávez." 2010. http://www.noticias24.com/actualidad/noticia/139831/la-polemica-pancarta-contra-chavez-que-origino-un-enfrentamiento-en-el-caracas-magallanes/.

Pearson, Tamara. 2009. "Crime in Venezuela: Opposition Weapon or Serious Problem?" *Venezuelanalysis*, March 30. http://www.venezuelanalysis.com/analysis/4338.

RSF.2010a. "Five Cable Television Stations Allowed to Resume Broadcasting but RCTVI Still Suspended." Reporters Without Borders. http://www.rsf.org/spip.php?page=article&id_article=36202.

————. 2010b. "Six Channels Suspended over Chávez *Cadenas.*" Reporters Without Borders. http://www.rsf.org/spip.php?page=article&id_article=36202.

Schiller, Naomi. In press. "Catia Sees You: Community Television, Clientelism and Participatory Statemaking in the Chávez Era." In David Smilde and Daniel Hellinger, eds., *Bottom Up or Top Down? Participation and Clientelism in Venezuela's Bolivarian Democracy*. Durham, NC: Duke University Press.

Sreeharsha, Vinod. 2007. "Hugo Chávez Denounces Bush in a Rally in Argentina." *Knight Ridder Tribune Washington Bureau (DC)*, March 9, 1.

Ungar, Mark. 2003. "Contested Battlefields: Policing in Caracas and La Paz." *NACLA Report on the Americas* 37: 30–36.

U.S. Department of State. 2009. "Country Specific Information." http://www.travel.state.gov/travel.

U.S. Department of State. 2010. "Background Note: Venezuela." http://www.state.gov/r/pa/ei/bgn/35766.htm.

Veillette, Connie. 2005. "Plan Colombia: A Progress Report." CRS Report for Congress http://fpc.state.gov/documents/organization/50264.pdf.

"Venezuela-Colombia Relations Keep Worsening." 2009. *El Universal*, November 27. http:// english.eluniversal.com/2009/11/27/en_ing_esp_venezuela-colombia-r_27A3125811. shtml.

Weisbrot, Mark, and Luis Sandoval. 2007. "The Venezuelan Economy in the Chávez Years. Center for Economic and Policy Research." Center for Economic Policy and Research. http://www.cepr.net/content/view/1248/8/.

Glossary

This section provides brief definitions or descriptions of common terms, places, things, or phrases associated with Venezuela. Words and phrases have been selected to assist readers who seek further clarification of terms used in the book. Special attention has been paid to Spanish words and phrases and commonly used acronyms.

AD   Acción Democrática, one of the two major political parties in Venezuela after the Punto Fijo accords and before the election of Hugo Chávez.

Adeco   Supporter or member of the AD party.

Agüardiente   "Firewater," a general term for fruit-based alcohol.

Ahorita   A term that literally means "a little time" but in practical terms in Venezuela may mean any amount of time at all, from five minutes to three hours, the Venezuelan concept of punctuality being very flexible.

Aló Presidente   Weekly television program of President Hugo Chávez in which he conducts interviews, gives speeches, and at times sings.

Andean Pact   A free trade agreement whose members include Bolivia, Peru, and Colombia.

Andino   Meaning "of the Andes." A description of regional identity.

Angel Falls   The world's tallest waterfall, located in the Guiana highlands.

Anglican Church   The Church of England, known in the United States as the Episcopal Church.

Anglicismo   A word in Spanish borrowed directly from English.

Apertura Petrolera "Petroleum opening," a program that allowed PDVSA to partner with foreign companies, enabling them to bid on incompletely explored fields and new concessions in the Orinoco basin, and also to manufacture synthetic crude not subject to OPEC quotas. President Hugo Chávez began the process of closing the *apertura* in 2006.

Arawak One of the three indigenous linguistic families of Venezuela.

Arepa Corn meal biscuit that is fried or grilled, then many times filled with meat, cheese, or vegetables, eaten throughout Venezuela.

Ata Round collective housing, made of *bahareque* and palm of the Ye'kuana people of Bolivar state. Also known as a *churuata*.

Audiencias Royal offices that functioned as subregional headquarters of viceroyalties.

Azabache A small amulet of the fossilized wood jet that mothers tie around the left ankle of their babies to prevent the negative effects of "*mal de ojo*," or the evil eye.

Bahareque Building technique that uses vertical wooden posts and horizontal bamboo canes to create a lattice. This lattice is then daubed with mud, sometimes mixed with grass or bamboo cane bits. Commonly used to build an *ata*.

Barrio Literally, "neighborhood." Often used to specifically refer to the collections of low-income slums in major cities in Venezuela.

Batido A juice drink made of juice, pieces of fruit, water, and ice.

BCV The Banco Central de Venezuela (Central Bank of Venezuela) an institution founded in 1939. The BCV performs all of the functions of other central bank or federal reserve systems worldwide, like managing the money supply and credit and issuing bank notes. Changes in laws that govern the BCV have evolved with domestic and global economic changes. The most important change occurred in 1992 when it became a legal public entity rather than a corporate entity.

Bolivar When used with a lowercase "b," refers to the currency of Venezuela. Changed to *bolivar fuerte* in 2008.

Bolivarian Circle A loosely knit political and social organization of workers' councils in Venezuela originally begun by President Hugo Chávez in 2001.

Blanqueamiento The concept of "racial whitening," in which "white" as a concept is accepted as modern, advanced, and civilized, and "black" as a concept is understood as unsophisticated, inferior, and uncivilized. In order for society to progress, therefore, the "black" must be made more "white."

Bruja Literally "witch," in Venezuela and other Latin American nations, commonly used to refer to women who practice herbal medicine and are believed to communicate with earth spirits and other potencies.

Budare A cast-iron skillet used in Venezuela and Colombia to cook *arepas* and *cachapas*.

Buñuelos Small sweet doughnuts made of boiled and processed yuca root, fried and covered in sugar.

Cabildo   Autonomous municipal council, the lowest administrative unit in the Spanish colonial government. Indigenous communities continued to use cabildos to govern themselves in the 19th century.

Cacao   Is the dried and fully fermented fatty seed of *Theobroma cacao*, from which cocoa solids and cocoa butter are extracted. They are the basis of chocolate.

Cachapas   A sweetened corn pancake often topped with butter and soft cheese eaten throughout Venezuela.

Café con Leche   Literally "coffee with milk." When referring to race, short-hand for the widely held national conception of racial equality that holds that all Venezuelans are of mixed blood and that there are no racial problems in Venezuela.

Calypso   A Venezuelan style of calypso, a type of music found in Venezuela during Carnival that incorporates *cuatro*, maracas, and cow bells.

CAP   Carlos Andrés Pérez, president from 1974 to 1979 and from 1989 to 1993.

Caracazo   The series of nationwide riots in 1989 caused by the economic changes in the neoliberal reform package introduced by President Carlos Andrés Pérez.

Caraqueño   Resident of Caracas.

Caribans   One of the three indigenous linguistic families of Venezuela.

Carne Mechada   Beef slow-cooked with onions, garlic, sweet bell peppers, and tomatoes until so soft it can be shredded with a fork.

Casaba/Casave   Flat bread made of the yuca root.

Casa Miss Venezuela   The training academy for Miss Venezuela candidates housed in a Caracas mansion.

Castilian   The standard literary and official form of Spanish, which is based on the dialect of the Spanish province of Castile.

Caudillo   Strongman. Political/military leader who holds authoritarian power.

Caudillismo   System run by a caudillo.

Causa R   A grassroots organization formed in the 1970s to promote land reform. In the 1980s, Causa R became more active in a wider political sense, integrating dissident union members, neighborhood organizations, and students. Causa R candidates went on to stand for election. Candidates could be part of the Causa R ticket if they promised to put the common electorate's interests above that of big business and the Punto Fijo political machine.

Cazón   A small shark variety commonly eaten in *sancocho* and empanadas.

Cédulas de Gracias al Sacar or Cédula   A permission for a slave to purchase legal white status, giving him or her access to education and the right to become clergy or hold political office.

CELARG   The Centro de Estudios Latinoamericanos Rómulo Gallegos, or the Rómulo Gallegos Center for Latin American Studies.

CEM   The Centro de Estudios de la Mujer (Women's Studies Center), an institute located at the UCV in Caracas.

Cerro Bolívar An iron mountain containing 400 million tons of 65 percent pure iron ore.

Chibcha One of the three indigenous linguistic families of Venezuela.

Chichi A nonalcoholic beverage of milk, sugar, and rice.

Churuata Round, collective housing of the Ye'kuana people of Bolivar state. Also known as an ata.

Cimarrones Black runaway slaves.

CNAC Centro Nacional Autónoma Cinematografía (National Autonomous Center for Cinematography).

CNE Centro Nacional Electoral (The National Electoral Council). The CNE is responsible for organizing, administering, and supervising elections and referendums at all levels: local, state, and federal.

Cofradía Religious brotherhood and mutual aid society.

Coleo A rodeo-style cowboy sport showcasing ranching skills popular in the plains of Venezuela.

Communal Council Neighborhood-based elected councils that initiate and oversee local policies and projects toward community development in groups of 400 families or less. Communal councils coordinate existing community organizations as well as promote the creation of new work committees, cooperatives, and projects.

Community Radio Radio stations that are run by members of marginalized and disadvantaged communities, usually poor neighborhoods or ethnic minorities. Seventy percent of programming must be produced by members of the community, programming must be dedicated to community issues, and the station must provide training to community members in running the station.

CONAC Consejo Nacional de Cultura (National Council of Culture). A government ministry responsible for supporting visual arts, film, dance, literature, theater, and other means of cultural production.

CONAPRI The Consejo Nacional para la Promoción de Inversiones, or the National Council for the Promotion of Investment.

Conucos Kitchen gardens, especially used by slaves for subsistence and market purposes.

Conuqueros Farmers of small plots of land near towns or *conucos*.

COPEI Comité de Participación Electoral Independiente. The Christian Social Democratic Political Party of Venezuela founded by Rafael Caldera in 1946.

Copeyano Member or supporter of the COPEI political party.

Cordillera Central Mountain ranges that stretch from western to eastern Venezuela along the coast, encompassing the cities of Maracaibo, Mérida, and Caracas.

Creoles In this case, individuals born in the Americas of Spanish descent. Not to be confused with the term as used in other contexts to mean a language born of the mixture of European languages and African languages (as in Haiti) or the style of cooking (as in Louisiana).

Criollo   Spanish term for creole.

CTV   Confederación de Trabajadores de Venezuela (Venezuelan Worker's Confederation). Venezuela's largest group of labor unions, founded in 1936. Closely associated with the AD political party.

Cuatro   A small, four-stringed guitar used in traditional Venezuelan music.

Cumbes   Free communities created in the Spanish colonial era by slaves who escaped from plantations.

Cupules   Cup-shaped, nonutilitarian, man-made cultural markings in stone.

CVF   Corporación Venezolana de Fomento—Venezuelan Development Corporation.

Decente   Literally "decent." Used in Antonia Palacios's novel and in other contexts to mean well-mannered, high-class, and Caucasian.

Distrito Federal   The specific term for federal district where the offices of the federal government are housed in Caracas.

El Paquete   The package of free market economic reforms proposed by Venezuelan President Carlos Andrés Pérez in 1989 in response to recommendations of the International Monetary Fund.

El Sistema   The famously effective state-run music system in Venezuela that has trained economically disadvantaged children to become classical musicians since 1970.

Empanadas   Turnovers of cornmeal dough filled with meat, fish, or cheese.

Encomendero   The owner of an *encomienda*.

Encomienda   Economic and political system through which the Spanish crown gave creole land owners the right to use the labor of a certain number of indigenous people. The landowner gained the work of the indigenous people and in theory was responsible for their welfare and their conversion to Christianity.

Estabilidad Absoluta   Absolute job security. Similar to the concept of tenure in the United States.

Evangélico   Literally "evangelical." In Venezuela, many who belong to the Pentecostal church use this term to refer to themselves and their beliefs.

Exceptionalism   Venezuelan exceptionalism was a theory popular through the early 1990s that argued that Venezuela's economic, political, and social stability created a healthy democracy unusual in cold war–era Latin America.

FBT   Fuerza Bolivariana del Trabajo—Bolivarian Worker's Force. A labor organization formed in the early years of the 20th century.

FEDECAMARAS   Federación de Cámaras y Asociaciones de Comercio y Producción de Venezuela (The Venezuelan Federation of Chambers of Commerce). A cartel that controls commerce, wages, and working conditions in 12 different sectors of the Venezuelan economy.

Fedepetrol   Venezuelan petroleum workers' union.

Gaita   A musical form native to Venezuela that features the *cuatro*, a four-stringed guitar. *Gaitas* are commonly used in religious settings and are also popular forms for protest hymns. They are most often associated with the Christmas season.

Galerones   Slow songs sung by groups of singers usually as part of public celebrations and festivals.

General Strike   A strike action by a critical mass of the labor force in a city, region, or country. In the case of those that have happened in Venezuelan history, general strikes have meant the shutdown of the Venezuelan economy.

Geoglyph   Work of art made by moving and arranging rocks or earth within a landscape.

Guaraná   A berry native to Venezuela and Brazil. Popular as a flavoring for Venezuelan soda.

Guiana Highlands   An area in southern Venezuela of flat-topped mountains known as *tepuis. Tepuis* are only found in the Guiana Highlands.

Hacendado   Land owner, owner of a hacienda.

Hallaca   Meat and vegetable–filled corn cake wrapped in banana leaf. Traditionally served at Christmas time and prepared by the whole family.

Iberian Peninsula   The peninsula at the southwestern point of Europe that is home to Spain and Portugal.

IMF   International Monetary Fund.

Import Substitution Industrialization   A trade and economic policy based on the premise that a country should attempt to reduce its foreign dependency through the local production of industrialized products.

Indecente   Literally "indecent." Used in Antonia Palacios's novel to mean not well-mannered, lower-class, and nonwhite.

Isleños   Immigrants from the Spanish Canary Islands to Venezuela.

Joropo   Song style from the llanos of Venezuela that uses the *cuatro*, harp, and maracas. The unofficial national anthem "Alma Llanera" is a song in *joropo* form.

Jugo   Simple juice of fruit juice, water, and ice.

Junta   A group of military officers who rule a country after seizing power.

Juntos pero no Revueltos   "Together but not mixed together," a term used to refer to the living conditions of whites and people of color (free people of color, slaves, and indigenous people) in urban areas.

Kinetic Art   Art that contains moving parts or depends on motion for its effect.

La Guaira   One of Venezuela's major ports, hampered by a lack of natural harbor but close to Caracas.

La Negra   "The black woman" a common term of endearment that harks back to slave days in which the woman of color was a slave lover who the elite white man kept on the side but could never marry. Therefore carries the double connotation of true affection and exploitation for many. Used (perhaps intentionally, perhaps unintentionally) by Manuel Rosales in 2006 when he called his debit-card scheme "*mi negra*" (my little black one).

La Villa del Cine   The state-owned movie studio opened in 2009 by the government of Hugo Chávez.

Licenciado/a   Many times abbreviated to "Lic." A title used by college graduates in professional situations.

Llanero   Cowboy resident of the llanos or a musical style of the llanos that uses the *cuatro* and a small metal-stringed harp.

Llanos   The Venezuelan plains, located in the southwestern part of the country.

Machismo   From the Spanish word "macho" for male animal, machismo is a term used to describe prominently exhibited or excessive masculinity. As an attitude, machismo ranges from a personal sense of virility to a more extreme male chauvinism.

Maiquetía   City on the northern coast of Venezuela where the Caracas airport is located.

Maisanta List   A blacklist of petroleum workers who signed petitions against President Hugo Chávez.

Mal del Ojo   The "evil eye," a curse of bad luck that many believe may be placed on a person.

Mantuano   Name given to the white elite of Caracas, descendant of the original Spanish colonizers.

Manumisos   Children who served their mothers' masters until the age of 18 or 25 who were born to slave mothers after the 1822 Law of the Free Womb.

Maracucho   Person from the Venezuelan city of Maracaibo.

MAS   Movimiento al Socialismo. A social-democratic political party in Venezuela founded in 1971 that emphasizes a socialist message.

MBR   Movimiento Boliviariano Venezolano (Bolivarian Venezuelan Movement), the party of the coup plotters of 1992 Hugo Chávez and Francisco Arías Cardenas.

Megalithic Monuments   Large stone constructions built by arranging one or more rocks.

MEP   Movimiento Electoral del Pueblo, a left-wing political party in Venezuela founded in 1967. MEP later merged with PSUV in 2007.

MERCOSUR   Mercado Común del Sur (Common Market of the South), a regional trade agreement among Argentina, Brazil, Uruguay, Paraguay, and Venezuela.

Miaos   A baby's first urination, a sign of good health for a newborn baby and a cause for celebration.

Miraflores   The location of the presidential offices and home. The Venezuelan "White House."

Misiones   In the Venezuelan context, refers to the collection of social missions designed and implemented by the administration of Hugo Chávez to deliver social services such as literacy tutoring, medical care, subsidized food, and housing assistance to the poorer economic classes of Venezuela.

Morenos Libres   Free people of color during the era of slavery.

Mototaxi   A taxi service on motorcycle. Popular especially in Caracas, where traffic is so heavy that a motorcycle is often a faster way to travel than car. The passenger sits behind the driver of the motorcycle. Mototaxis are not only faster, but often cheaper than automobile taxis.

Mujer Pública   Literally "public woman." A common, if somewhat dated, euphemism for prostitute. Points to the general expectation in Latin America that decent women are not active in public contexts such as politics or business.

MVR   Movimiento Quinta República (Fifth Republic Movement). Political party founded by Hugo Chávez.

Novena   Catholic tradition of saying the rosary in honor of the dead for nine nights after the funeral.

Nuevo Sindicalismo   "New unionism," a movement begun in the 1980s that offered a strong critique of the moral decay that had become part of the AD-CTV-FEDECAMARAS partnership and offered a new project to develop new union leadership from within the working classes not based on ideology but instead on worker democracy.

OAS   Organization of American States.

Op Art   Short for "operational art," a type of kinetic art that depends on viewer participation for its movement. In op art, viewers move parts of the art piece around to create different experiences of the artistic piece.

Orientales   "Easterners," description of people from the eastern area of the Venezuelan territory.

Orinoco Delta   A fan-shaped delta of the Orinoco River in eastern Venezuela, formed as it splits into numerous distributaries, called *caños*, which meander through the delta on their way to the sea. The delta includes large areas of permanent wetlands as well as seasonally flooded freshwater swamp forests.

Pabellón Criollo   Considered by many the national dish of Venezuela, consists of white rice, black beans, carne mechada, and may come with fried plantains or a fried egg on top.

Palafito   Traditional style of indigenous housing built over the water in Zulia state and the Orinoco River Delta of eastern Venezuela.

Pan de Jamón   A sweet bread, braided with ham inside, many times also with raisins or olives. It is most commonly eaten during the Christmas season.

Papelón   Raw cane sugar. It is heated into a liquid format and poured into a mold. Once cool, papelones are easy to preserve for long periods of time.

Papelón con limón   A drink of the juice of raw cane sugar mixed with lemon or lime.

Pardo   A rough definition for mixed-race, free people of color during colonial times. During modern times, used to describe mixed-race people.

Parrilla Llanera   A meal of mixed grilled meats popular in the southern plains.

Partidocracia   A combination of "party" and "democracy." Political governance controlled by political parties. Used generally to describe the period 1959–1998.

Patria Boba   The ineffective and short-lived "Foolish Republic" of 1812, led by Francisco de Miranda.

PCV   Partido Comunista Venezolano (Venezuelan Communist Party).

PDVAL   Producción y Distribución Venezolana de Alimentos: Venezuelan Production and Distribution of Food, a subsidiary of PDVSA. The Mercal markets are part of the PDVAL system. In the summer of 2010 a number of PDVAL tankers loaded with rotten food were found in various ports in Venezuela.

PDVSA   Petróleos de Venezuela, S.A. is the national oil company. It ran primarily as an independent corporation until a failed general strike in late 2001 led to greater direct government control of the company and its profits.

Pemón   An indigenous tribe native to Venezuela's Gran Sábana region, known for their cultural linkage to the unique landscape of the area.

Permanent Dilemma   Phrase coined by John V. Lombardi that describes the continuing economic problem of Venezuelan leaders using oil profits to make their supporters happy (clientelism) while neglecting important but less popular projects in infrastructure or development of new industry.

Petroglyph   A carving or line drawing in rock, usually dating to prehistoric times.

Plaza   A public square in a city or town, surrounded by government buildings, offices, and shops. Especially important in Venezuelan culture as a central place for public gatherings.

PODEMOS   Por La Democracia Social, a social-democratic political party in Venezuela

PPT   Patria Para Todos, a leftist political party in Venezuela.

PSUV   Partido Socialista Unida de Venezuela (United Socialist Party of Venezuela). In 2010 the ruling political party and largest left-wing party in Latin America.

Public Woman   See "*mujer pública.*"

Puntofijismo   Adjective describing the system of power-sharing that existed under the Punto Fijo agreement.

Punto Fijo   Term used to describe the power-sharing agreement made in 1959 between Venezuela's three major political parties of the time, AD, COPEI, and URD. In the agreement, the parties agreed to share governance no matter which party won the democratic elections. The agreement also protected interests of the Catholic Church and the military. It is this agreement that is widely believed to have provided long-term stability in Venezuelan politics.

Punto Fijo Pact   A formal arrangement arrived at between representatives of Venezuela's three main political parties for the acceptance of the 1958 presidential elections and the preservation of the rising democratic regime.

Quinceañera   The celebration of a girl's 15th birthday, traditionally associated with the transition to womanhood.

Radio Bemba   A term for the centuries-old tradition of word-of-mouth communication used by ethnic minorities and the poor for the transmission of information.

Ranchito/Rancho   Housing usually made of cement blocks, from one to three stories high, found in the low-income barrios surrounding major cities.

RCTV   Radio Caracas de Televisión. Formerly Venezuela's most popular television station. A source of great controversy given its support of the 1992 coup and the subsequent nonrenewals of its license by the Chávez government.

Reference Pricing   The system in which OPEC reserves the right to establish the base rate for oil regardless of market conditions.

Resguardo   Indigenous land protected through order of the Spanish crown. Some indigenous communities protected their resguardo rights until the national government dissolved most of the resguardos in the 1880s.

Sancocho   Stew made of a variety of different meats, yuca, and mixed vegetables.

Santería   A religious belief system that fuses polytheistic West African religious beliefs brought to the Americas with Catholicism. Thought to have originated in Cuba, Santería has grown more popular in Venezuela in the second half of the 20th century and the first years of the 21st century.

Santero/a   A follower or practitioner of Santería.

Sembrar el Petróleo   "Sow the oil," the famous call by writer-statesman Arturo Uslar Pietri for the Venezuelan state to reinvest oil profits in infrastructure, education, and the arts.

Shabono   Communal housing utilized by the Yanomami people consisting of a ring of lean-to homes around a central plaza.

SIDOR   Siderúrgica del Orinoco—The biggest Venezuelan steel corporation located in Ciudad Guyana in Bolívar State.

Sow the Oil   See "*sembrar el petróleo.*"

Superbloques   "Superblocks," a type of modernist architectural and urban planning construction that was often used in the construction of public housing. Superblocks were oversized city-block-sized structures that sought to integrate multiuse spaces such as shops and housing.

Tajadas   Fried plantains, a common part of a *pabellón criollo*.

Tacarí del Chivo   A stew of goat meat marinated and cooked with red wine, onion, tomato, and garlic.

Tachirense   A person from the western state of Táchira.

Tapirí   The individual family lean-to, a ring of which makes up a *shabono*.

Technicolor   While the word Technicolor is a trademark for a special process of using color motion pictures by means of superimposing the three primary colors to produce a final colored print, in common speech the term is generally used to refer to vibrant, lurid, and flamboyantly colored images. This is because the trademarked process produces such vibrant colors.

Telenovela   Latin American–style soap opera with a limited amount of episodes.

Tepui   A Pemón Indian word for "plateau," a unique type of table-top mountain found only in the Guiana highlands area of southern Venezuela.

Tercermundismo   "Third worldism," a term that describes the plan of Hugo Chávez to unite underdeveloped nations in an economic and defensive bloc to oppose the powers of Western capitalist powers in Europe and North America.

Tostones   Fried round coins of plantain banana.

Trienio Democratico/Trienio   Three year democratic period between dictatorships (1945–1948) under the presidency of writer-statesman Rómulo Gallegos.

TSJ   Tribunal Supremo de Justicia (Supreme Justice Tribunal), the highest level of judiciary in Venezuela.

UCAB   Universidad Católica Andrés Bello, one of the nation's important religious, privately run universities, located in Caracas.

UCV   Universidad Central de Venezuela (Central University of Venezuela), the nation's oldest and most prestigious university.

USB   Universidad Simón Bolívar, a selective, public, experimental university in Caracas.

VEB   *Bolivares fuertes*, official currency of Venezuela.

Vernacular Architecture   Architecture that describes structures made by local builders without the help of a professional architect. Includes primitive architecture, indigenous architecture, and folk, popular, rural, and traditional architecture.

Viceroyalty   An administrative unit used by the Spanish crown for managing the colonies. Venezuela was part of the Viceroyalty of New Spain.

Warao   An indigenous tribe of Venezuela with a unique language and culture, living in the Orinoco Delta region.

Wayuú   One of the languages of the Arawak language group. Also the name of the tribe that speaks the language.

Writer-Statesman   The centuries-old Latin American tradition that confers political clout and influence on literary and cultural figures. Authors are not only allowed, but expected, to participate in social commentary and politics, many times holding elected or appointed public offices or writing extensively in newspapers on public policy.

Yanomami (or Yanomamo)   An indigenous tribe of Venezuela with a unique language and culture, living in far southern Venezuela in Amazonas State, in the tropical forest.

Ye'kuana   An indigenous tribe of Venezuela with a unique language and culture, living in the southern part of Venezuela in Bolivar State, on the Orinoco River.

Yuca   Cassava root, used in a variety of Venezuelan dishes, including *sancocho*, also commonly fried or boiled to be eaten by itself.

Facts and Figures

TABLE A.1. Basic Facts and Figures

Country Info	
Location	Northern South America, bounded to the north by the Caribbean Sea, to the west by Colombia, to the south by Brazil, and to the east by Guyana.
Local name	República Bolivariana de Venezuela
Government	Federal republic
Capital	Caracas
Head of state	Hugo Chávez
Head of government	Hugo Chávez
National holiday	Independence Day, July 5 (1811)
Major political parties	United Socialist Party of Venezuela (PSUV), A New Era (UNT)

Source: CIA Factbook, The International Institute for Strategic Studies, Transnacionale.org

TABLE A.2. Basic Facts and Figures

Demographics	
Population	26,814,843 (2009 est.)
Population by age	
0–14	30.5%
15–64	64.3%
65+	5.2%
Median age	25.5
Population growth rate	1.5 (2009 est.)
Population density	76 people per sq. mile
Infant mortality rate	21.54 deaths per 1,000 live births (2009 est.)
Ethnic groups	Spanish, Italian, Portuguese, Arab, German, African, indigenous people
Religions	Nominally Roman Catholic 96%, Protestant 2%, other 2%
Language	Spanish (official), numerous indigenous languages
Voting age	18 years
Voter participation	n/a
Literacy	93%
Life expectancy (average)	73.61
Fertility rate	2.48 children per woman (2009 est.)

Source: CIA Factbook, The International Institute for Strategic Studies, Transnacionale.org

TABLE A.3. Basic Facts and Figures

Geography	
Land area	352,144 sq. miles
Arable land	3%
Irrigated land	2,220 sq. miles (2003)
Natural hazards	Subject to floods, rockslides, mudslides, periodic droughts
Environmental problems	Sewage pollution of Lago de Valencia; oil and urban pollution of Lago de Maracaibo; deforestation; soil degradation; urban and industrial pollution, especially along the Caribbean coast; threat to the rainforest ecosystem from irresponsible mining operations
Major agricultural products	Corn, sorghum, sugarcane, rice, bananas, vegetables, coffee, beef, pork, milk, eggs, fish
Natural resources	Petroleum, natural gas, iron ore, gold, bauxite, other minerals, hydropower, diamonds

Source: CIA Factbook, The International Institute for Strategic Studies, Transnacionale.org

TABLE A.4. Basic Facts and Figures

Economy	
GDP	$353.5 billion (2009 est.)
GDP per capita	$13,200 (2009 est.)
GDP by sector	Agriculture, 4%; industry, 34.6%; services, 61.4% (2009 est.)
Labor force	Agriculture, 80%; industry/service, 20% (2004 est.)
Unemployment	10.9% (2009 est.)
People below poverty line	37.9% (end 2005 est.)
Major industries	Petroleum, construction materials, food processing, textiles, iron ore mining, steel, aluminum, motor vehicle assembly
Leading companies	Petroleos de Venezuela S.A. (PDVSA), Mavesa S.A., Sudamtex de Venezuela, Acetco, Banco Industrial de Venezuela, CA Nacional Telefonos de Venezuela (CANTV), Cativen, Cisneros Group of Companies, Cisneros, Gustavo, Electricidad de Caracas (EDC), ELECAR, Empresas Polar, Fospuca, Inelectra, Mendoza, Lorenzo, Otepi, PIGAP, Public Institution, SENECA
Exports	$51.99 billion (2009 est.)
Imports	$41.04 billion (2009 est.)
Export goods	Petroleum, bauxite and aluminum, steel, chemicals, agricultural products, basic manufactures
Import goods	Raw materials, machinery and equipment, transport equipment, construction materials

Source: CIA Factbook, The International Institute for Strategic Studies, Transnacionale.org

TABLE A.5. Basic Facts and Figures

Communications and Transportation	
Electricity production	113.3 billion kWh (2007 est.)
Electricity consumption	83.02 billion kWh (2007 est.)
Telephone lines	6.304 million (2008)
Mobile phones	27.084 million (2008)
Internet users	7.167 million (2008)
Roads	59,748 miles (2002)
Railroads	500 miles (2008)
Airports	406 (2009)

Source: CIA Factbook, The International Institute for Strategic Studies, Transnacionale.org

TABLE A.6. Basic Facts and Figures

Military	
Defense spending (% of GDP)	1.2% (2005 est.)
Armed forces	82,000 active; 8,000 reserve (2007)
Manpower fit for military service	5,391,582 males, 5,873,563 females (2009 est.)

Source: CIA Factbook, The International Institute for Strategic Studies, Transnacionale.org

TABLE B. Population of Major Cities

City	State	Population
Acarigua	Portuguesa	174,000
Barinas	Barinas	307,400
Barquismeto	Lara	1,018,900
Chacao	Miranda	71,400
Cuidad Guyana	Bolívar	789,500
Cumaná	Sucre	322,000
El Tigre	Anzoátegui	188,300
Guarenas	Miranda	245,400
Federal District (Caracas)	Miranda	2,097,900*
Los Teques	Miranda	236,500
Maracaibo	Zulia	1,891,800
Maracay	Aragua	443,300
Puerto Ayacucho	Amazonas	83,500
Puerto La Cruz	Anzoátegui	254,700
Punto Fijo	Falcón	169,000
San Carlos	Cojedes	89,000
San Cristóbal	Táchira	279,100
San Fernando de Apure	Apure	126,000
Turmero	Aragua	336,900
Valencia	Carobobo	1,408,400
Valera	Trujillo	137,400

Note: these numbers are 2009 projections based on the Venezuelan government's official 2001 census and may not reflect citizens resident in barrios and other informally constructed housing developments.
*As discussed elsewhere, the Federal District is comprised of 22 municipalities. The 2001 census records a total population for these 22 municipalities but not for others in the surrounding Caracas metropolitan area such as Baruta or Chacao.
Source: Census Office of the Venezuelan Government: 2001, Office of National Statistics http://www.ine.gov.ve/demografica/censopoblacionvivienda.asp

TABLE C. Total Population by Gender, Area, and Age Group as of 2001 Census

Age Group	Total			Urban Areas			Rural Areas		
	Total	Men	Women	Total	Men	Women	Total	Men	Women
Total	23,054,210	11,402,869	11,651,341	20,381,757	9,953,574	10,428,183	2,672,453	1,449,295	1,223,158
0–4	2,470,081	1,266,429	1,203,652	2,114,708	1,084,080	1,030,628	355,373	182,349	173,024
5–9	2,651,257	1,352,926	1,298,331	2,283,934	1,163,848	1,120,086	367,323	189,078	178,245
10–14	2,513,224	1,269,705	1,243,519	2,193,114	1,102,048	1,091,066	320,110	167,657	152,453
15–19	2,300,721	1,154,745	1,145,976	2,036,324	1,007,927	1,028,397	264,397	146,818	117,579
20–24	2,170,254	1,072,826	1,097,428	1,941,509	946,028	995,481	228,745	126,798	101,947
25–29	1,876,568	918,063	958,505	1,678,175	809,490	868,685	198,393	108,573	89,820
30–34	1,752,525	857,675	894,850	1,576,344	760,521	815,823	176,181	97,154	79,027
35–39	1,584,465	768,107	816,358	1,429,300	681,979	747,321	155,165	86,128	69,037
40–44	1,421,374	691,549	729,825	1,286,827	615,157	671,670	134,547	76,392	58,155
45–49	1,154,097	561,907	592,190	1,045,071	499,771	545,300	109,026	62,136	46,890
50–54	920,953	449,661	471,292	828,743	396,968	431,775	92,210	52,693	39,517
60–64	500,525	238,627	261,898	439,251	203,550	235,701	61,274	35,077	26,197
65–69	381,497	177,284	204,213	332,905	149,483	183,422	48,592	27,801	20,791
70–74	302,777	139,265	163,512	264,650	117,582	147,068	38,127	21,683	16,444
75–79	205,844	92,800	113,044	180,151	78,154	101,997	25,693	14,646	11,047
80–84	123,791	52,273	71,518	108,357	43,852	64,505	15,434	8,421	7,013
90–94	30,170	11,962	18,208	26,564	10,149	16,415	3,606	1,813	1,793
95 and older	11,258	4,344	6,914	9,676	3,592	6,084	1,582	752	830

Note: Does not include indigenous populations.
Source: National Institute of Statistics, Bolivarian Republic of Venezuela. http://www.ine.gov.ve/demografica/censopoblacionvivienda.asp

TABLE D. Total Population of Indigenous Peoples by Age and State of Residence as of 2001 Census

Age Group	Total	Amazonas	Anzoátegui	Apure	Bolívar	Amacuro	Monagas	Sucre	Zulia
Total	178,343	38,258	8,861	8,223	42,631	26,080	4,025	1,678	48,587
0–4	31,813	7,079	1,330	1,708	7,731	4,969	701	304	7,991
5–9	29,051	6,167	1,252	1,409	7,084	4,310	672	276	7,881
10–14	22,542	4,625	1,107	971	5,565	2,966	467	209	6,632
15–19	19,132	3,891	1,001	766	4,725	2,778	440	170	5,361
20–24	15,367	3,437	824	659	3,501	2,321	362	125	4,138
25–29	12,270	2,850	672	545	2,966	1,772	266	96	3,103
30–34	10,096	2,293	550	430	2,403	1,478	230	78	2,634
35–39	9,277	2,150	475	386	2,166	1,446	186	76	2,392
40–44	7,132	1,486	397	280	1,720	1,115	173	75	1,886
45–49	5,646	1,211	307	245	1,337	820	148	63	1,515
50–54	4,496	937	228	201	1,032	641	102	56	1,299
55–59	3,076	645	196	158	737	372	73	30	865
60–64	3,043	669	167	138	610	401	69	37	952
65–69	1,809	314	144	91	380	236	39	24	581
70–74	1,526	258	84	91	293	200	39	18	543
75–79	893	108	39	52	187	146	19	17	325
80–84	651	77	53	43	100	56	23	9	290
85–89	274	35	14	27	58	30	10	5	95
90–94	173	17	16	15	29	16	3	9	68
95 y Más	76	9	5	8	7	7	3	1	36

Source: National Institute of Statistics Bolivarian Republic of Venezuela. http://www.ine.gov.ve/demografica/censopoblacionvivienda.asp

TABLE E.   Human Development Index Indicators 2007

Life expectancy at birth (years)	73.6
Adult literacy rate (% age 15 and above)	95.2
Combined gross education enrollment ratio (%)	85.9
GDP per capita (PPP US $)	12,156
People not using an improved water source (%)	10
Children underweight for age (% under age 5)	5

Source: United Nations Development Programme. UNDP Human Development Report 2009. http://hdrstats.undp.org/en/countries/country_fact_sheets/cty_fs_VEN.html

TABLE F.   List of Presidents of Venezuela

President	Took Office	Left Office
Cristóbal Mendoza	1811	1813
Simón Bolívar	1813	1814
Simón Bolívar	1819	1830
José Antonio Paéz	1830	1835
José María Vargas	1835	1836
Carlos Soublette	1837	1843
	1839	1847
José Tadeo Monagas	1847	1851
José Gregorio Monagas	1851	1855
José Tadeo Monagas	1855	1858
Julián Castro	1858	1858
Manuel Felipe Tovar	1860	1861
Juan Crístomo Falcón	1863	1868
Antonio Guzmán Blanco	1870	1877
Francisco Linares Alcantara	1877	1878
Antonio Guzmán Blanco	1878	1884
Joaquín Crespo	1884	1886
Antonio Guzmán Blanco	1886	1888
Juan Pablo Rojas Paul	1888	1890
Raimundo Andueza Palacios	1890	1892
Joaquín Crespo	1892	1898
Ignacio Andrade	1898	1899
Cipriano Castro	1899	1908
Juan Vicente Gómez	1908	1935
Eleazar López Contreras	1935	1941

(*continued*)

TABLE F. List of Presidents of Venezuela (*continued*)

President	Took Office	Left Office
Isías Medina Angarita	1941	1945
Revolutionary junta	1945	1948
Rómulo Gallegos	1948	1948
Military junta	1948	1950
Government junta	1950	1952
Marcos Pérez Jiménez	1952	1958
Government junta	1958	1959
Rómulo Bentancourt	1959	1964
Raúl Leoni	1964	1969
Rafael Caldera	1969	1974
Carlos Andrés Pérez	1974	1979
Luís Herrera Campins	1979	1984
Jaime Lusinchi	1984	1989
Carlos Andrés Pérez	1989	1993
Octavio Lepage	1993	1993
Ramón J. Velázquez	1993	1994
Rafael Caldera	1994	1999
Hugo Chávez Frías	1999	—

Source: Bolivarian Republic of Venezuela. http://www.consulvenbucaramanga.com/presidentes.htm

TABLE G. Recent Elections and Referenda (Post 1989)

Election/Referendum	Date
Legislative	November 8, 1998
Presidential	December 6, 1998
Referendum	April 25,1999
Referendum	December 15, 1999
Legislative	July 30, 2000
Presidential	July 30, 2000
Referendum	August 15, 2004
Legislative	December 4, 2005
Presidential	December 3, 2006
Referendum	December 2, 2007
Referendum	February 15, 2009
Legislative	September 25, 2010

Source: IFES International Foundation for Electoral Systems. http://www.electionguide.org/country.php?ID=231

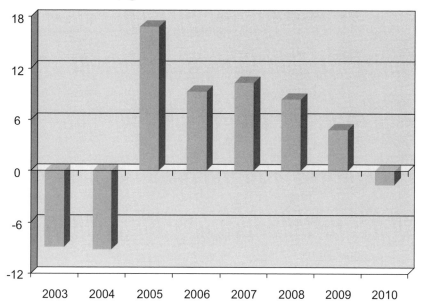

Percentage Real GDP Growth Rate 2003-2010

GDP growth on an annual basis adjusted for inflation and expressed as a percent.

CHART H.1.

Source: Index Mundi, http://www.indexmundi.com/venezuela/gdp_real_growth_rate.html.

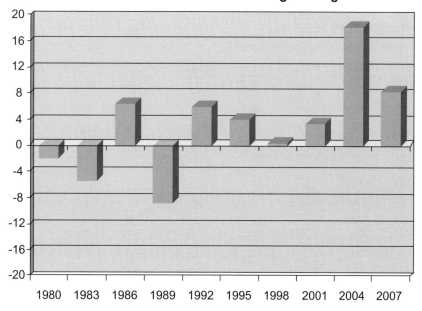

GDP Constant Prices – Percentage Change

Note: Annual percentages of constant price GDP are yearly based changes; the base year is country-specific.

CHART H.2.

Source: Index Mundi, http://www.indexmundi.com/venezuela/gdp_real_growth_rate.html.

TABLE I. Structure of the Venezuela Economy 2009

	1988	1998	2007	2008
(% of GDP)				
Agriculture	6.8	5.4	. .	. .
Industry	51.3	44.4	. .	. .
Manufacturing	18.1	20.8	. .	. .
Services	42.0	50.2	. .	. .
Household final consumption expenditure	68.3	57.6	53.8	53.9
General government final consumption expenditure	10.5	13.5	11.9	11.5
Imports of goods and services	27.2	22.7	24.7	20.2
	1988–1998	**1998–2008**	**2007**	**2008**
(average annual growth)				
Agriculture	0.5	3.6	3.9	1.1
Industry	3.2	1.9	3.9	8.4
Manufacturing	4.1	2.0	2.0	13.8
Services	0.9	4.9	11.0	2.2
Household final consumption expenditure	1.1	7.0	18.7	7.1
General government final consumption expenditure	3.4	5.8	5.1	5.7
Gross capital formation	8.1	7.7	26.6	2.9
Imports of goods and services	7.2	11.2	33.6	3.8

Note: 2008 data are preliminary estimates.
Source: World Bank: Venezuela RB at a Glance. http://devdata.worldbank.org/AAG/ven_aag.pdf

TABLE J. Data on Oil Reserves and Production with World Rank Comparison

Category	Amount	World Rank
Production	2,643,000 bbl/day (2008 estimate)	10
Consumption	7,760,000 bbl/day	24
Exports	2,182,000 bbl/day	10
Imports	0 bbl/day (2007 estimate)	210
Proved reserves	99,380,000 bbl (2009 estimate)	6
Distillation capacity	1.28 million bbl/day (2008 estimate)	No data

Sources: CIA World Factbook (https://www.cia.gov/library/publications/the-world-factbook/ geos/ve.html) and U.S. Energy Information Administration (http://www.eia.doe.gov/cabs/ Venezuela/Profile.html)

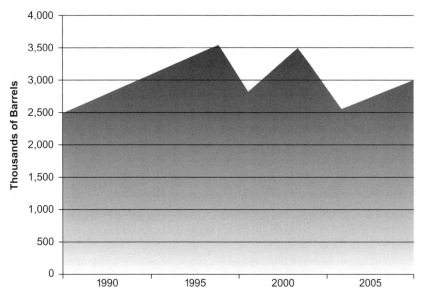

Venezuelan Oil Production

Original chart. Data taken from: http://www..eia.doe.gov/cabs/Venezuela/Oil.html

CHART J.

TABLE K. Important Macroeconomic Indicators of Agricultural Resources and Production, 1990–2000

Economic Indicator	1990	2000
Volume of agricultural production, index	100.2	115.2
Volume of crop production, index	97.4	114.4
Volume of livestock production, index	100.2	114.3
Arable land, 1000 ha	2,980	2,640
Permanent crops, 1000 ha	915	850
Irrigated land, 1000 ha	480	575
Fertilizer use, Mt	427,000	226,800

Source: Food and Agriculture Organization of the United Nations- FAO Country Profile. http://www.fao.org/countryprofiles/index.asp?lang=en&iso3=VEN&subj=4

Venezuelan Labor Force

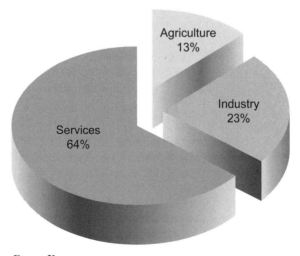

CHART K.
Source: Index Mundi, http://www.indexmundi.com/venezuela/labor_force.html.

TABLE L. Top Agricultural Exports (2007)

Rank	Commodity	Quantity (tons)	Value ($1000)	Unit Value ($1000/ton)
1	Cocoa beans	8,779	25,298	2,882
2	Beverage, dist. alcohol	10,362*	15,659	1,511
3	Wafers	3,787	11,777	3,110
4	Tobacco Products	6,453	11,454	1,775
5	Homogen. cooked fruit prep	5,031	10,914	2,169
6	Pastry	5,114	8,941	1,748
7	Beverage nonalcoholic	16,255	8,890	547
8	Rice milled	15,373	7,548	491
9	Coffee extracts	528	6,344	1,2015
10	Beer of barley	12,089	6,198	513
11	Sesame seed	15,688	5,515	352
12	Coffee, roasted	2,044	4,455	2,180
13	Food prep	2,239	4,157	1,857
14	Infant food	1,467	4,112	2,803
15	Breakfast cereals	2,067	3,800	1,838
16	Molasses	33,507	2,254	67
17	Flour of maize	2,810*	2,173	773
18	Plantains	10,410	1,579	152
19	Chocolate Prsnes	358	1,441	4,025
20	Food Prep, Flour, Malt Extract	600	1,273	2,122

*Unofficial figure.

Source: Food and Agriculture Association of the United Nations. FAO Stats. http://www.fao.org/ag/AGP/AGPC/doc/Counprof/Venezuela/venezuela.htm

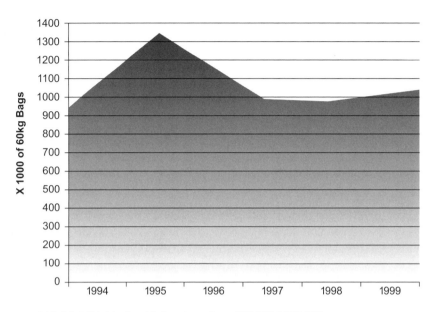

Coffee Production - Venezula

Original chart. Data taken from: http://www.fao.org/docrep/003/x6939e/x6939e07.htm

Chart L.

TABLE **M.** Top Agricultural Imports (2007)

Rank	Commodity	Quantity (tons)	Value ($1000)	Unit Value ($1000/ton)
1	Wheat	1,466,195*	423,425	289
2	Food prep Nes	107,771	292,693	2,716
3	Cake of soybeans	875,626	278,033	318
4	Cattle meat	68,381	269,469	3,941
5	Soybean oil	350,702	266,164	759
6	Cattle	268,045*	237,967	888
7	Beverage, dist. Alcohol	31,735	191,234	6,026
8	Milk, whole dried	62,772	169,806	2,705
9	Meat: cattle, boneless (beef and veal)	46,725	168,849	3,614
10	Malt	324,039	124,295	384
11	Maize	545,749	122,776	225
12	Sugar, confectionery	51,729*	107,645	2,081
13	Sugar, raw centrifugal	347,815	93,451	269
14	Beans, dry	91,479	76,591	837
15	Cheese of whole cow milk	13,755	66,698	4,849
16	Oil, Boiled etc.	97,061*	64,132	661
17	Chocolate Prsnes	15,865	58,285	3,674
18	Infant Food	11,733*	55,144	4,700
19	Wine	27,045	49,877	1,844
20	Palm oil	53,385	42,338	793

*Unofficial figure.

Source: Food and Agriculture Association of the United Nations. FAO Stats. http://www.fao.org/ag/AGP/AGPC/doc/Counprof/Venezuela/venezuela.htm

TABLE N. Poverty in Venezuela

Households Living In Poverty, by Year and Semester, 1997 and 1st Semester 2009

Semester and Year	Total	Undeclared	Not Considered Poor		"Poor"		"Poor: Not in the Extreme"		"Extremely Poor"	
			Total	%	Total	%	Total	%	Total	%
1997										
1st Semester	4,581,418	4,415,368	1,962,410	44.4	2,452,958	55.6	1,328,548	30.1	1,124,410	25.5
2nd Semester	4,790,520	4,626,926	2,403,507	51.9	2,223,419	48.1	1,329,287	28.7	894,132	19.3
1998										
1st Semester	4,871,926	4,689,391	2,392,445	51.0	2,296,946	49.0	1,311,676	28.0	985,270	21.0
2nd Semester	4,900,784	4,710,765	2,642,029	56.1	2,068,736	43.9	1,265,260	26.9	803,476	17.1
1999										
1st Semester	4,981,692	4,846,197	2,771,936	57.2	2,074,261	42.8	1,269,780	26.2	804,481	16.6
2nd Semester	4,953,821	4,836,058	2,806,986	58.0	2,029,072	42.0	1,212,227	25.1	816,845	16.9
2000										
1st Semester	5,000,526	4,899,702	2,861,841	58.4	2,037,861	41.6	1,221,994	24.9	815,867	16.7
2nd Semester	5,116,560	4,999,633	2,981,522	59.6	2,018,111	40.4	1,273,789	25.5	744,322	14.9
2001										
1st Semester	5,221,970	5,081,645	3,094,913	60.9	1,986,732	39.1	1,266,718	24.9	720,014	14.2
2nd Semester	5,412,497	5,286,079	3,222,415	61.0	2,063,664	39.0	1,321,459	25.0	742,205	14.0
2002										
1st Semester	5,769,181	5,596,809	3,276,246	58.5	2,320,563	41.5	1,392,417	24.9	928,146	16.6
2nd Semester	5,808,057	5,588,741	2,873,362	51.4	2,715,379	48.6	1,539,750	27.6	1,175,629	21.0

2003								
1st Semester	5,858,918	5,528,902	46.0	2,985,332	54.0	1,598,375	28.9	1,386,957	25.1
2nd Semester	5,901,012	5,575,633	44.9	3,074,301	55.1	1,678,924	30.1	1,395,377	25.0
2004								
1st Semester	6,004,141	5,624,147	46.9	2,984,988	53.1	1,665,380	29.6	1,319,608	23.5
2nd Semester	6,075,452	5,725,236	53.0	2,690,006	47.0	1,623,676	28.4	1,066,330	18.6
2005								
1st Semester	6,135,361	5,561,732	57.6	2,360,407	42.4	1,416,093	25.5	944,314	17.0
2nd Semester	6,221,917	5,941,102	62.1	2,251,303	37.9	1,341,236	22.6	910,067	15.3
2006								
1st Semester	6,319,445	6,058,468	66.9	2,006,345	33.1	1,387,664	22.9	618,681	10.2
2nd Semester	6,373,848	6,152,781	69.4	1,884,656	30.6	1,326,399	21.6	558,257	9.1
2007								
1st Semester	6,411,077	6,226,013	72.5	1,709,757	27.5	1,234,438	19.8	475,319	7.6
2nd Semester	6,488,505	6,327,141	71.5	1,804,628	28.5	1,307,201	20.7	497,427	7.9
2008								
1st Semester	6,565,279	6,390,194	72.3	1,769,805	27.7	1,292,594	20.2	477,211	7.5
2nd Semester	6,631,697	6,447,386	72.5	1,775,069	27.5	1,287,584	20.0	487,485	7.6
2009 (P)								
1st Semester	6,682,957	6,522,977	73.6	1,719,377	26.4	1,265,919	19.4	453,458	7.0

(P): Provisional figures.
Source: Instituto Nacional de Estadística, INE.
National Institute of Statistics- Bolivarian Republic of Venezuela.

TABLE O. Basic Health and Nutrition Indicators

Maternal mortality rate per 100,000 (2007)	56.8
Infant mortality rate per 1,000 (2007)	13.7
Neonatal mortality rate per 1,000 (2007)	10
Child mortality rate under 5 yrs per 1,000 (2007)	16.7
Chronic child malnutrition under 5 yrs (2007)	11.2%
Acute child malnutrition under 5 yrs (2007)	3.9%
General child malnutrition under 5 yrs (2007)	4.2%
Percent of newborns with low birth weight (2007)	8.9%
Antipolio vaccination coverage under 1 yr (2006)	73.6%
DPT vaccination coverage under 1 yr (2006)	64.6%
MMR vaccination coverage under 1 yr (2006)	93.4%
TB vaccination coverage under 1 yr (2006)	83.2%
Percentage of births assisted by medical personnel	95.0%

Source: UNICEF-Venezuela http://www.unicef.org/venezuela/spanish/overview_13275.htm

ELECTRICITY

TABLE P.1.

Electricity installed capacity	22.1 gigawatts (2005 estimate)
Electricity production	99.2 billion kilowatt hours (2005 estimate)
Electricity consumption	73.4 billion kilowatt hours (2005 estimate)

TABLE P.2. Production of Electricity by Source

Type	Percentage of Total
Fossil fuel	40%
Hydroelectric	25%
Natural gas	34%
Coal	<1%
Other	0%

Source: U.S. Energy Information Administration http://www.eia.doe.gov/cabs/Venezuela/Profile.html

TABLE Q. Social Missions (List as of February 2010)

Mission Name	Purpose/Mission	Year Launched
13 de Abril	Creation of socialist communes	2008
Alimentación	Subsidized basic food itemsLocal stores for subsidized foodNutrition educationSubsidization of national food producers	2004
Arbol	Reforestation projectsEnvironmental education	2006
Barrio Adentro I	Basic health care services for low income groups	2003
Barrio Adentro II	High-tech health care services for low income groups	2005
Barrio Adentro III	Hospital modernization and renovation in older neighborhoods	n/d
Che Guevara	Job training with socialist and revolutionary morals and ideals	2007
Ciencia	Development of a new model of science research under a collective, integrative, diverse model	2006
Cristo	Achieve zero poverty by the year 2021	n/d
Cultura	Decentralization, democratization, and "massification" of culture Bringing culture to the masses.	2004
Guaicaipuro	Restore the rights of indigenous peoples in Venezuela	2003
Hábitat	Create solutions with families and communities in the area of housing through construction projects, new urbanist projects, and education.	2004
Identidad	Provide identity cards for all citizens	n/d
José Gregorio Hernández	Provide basic services for citizens with mental and physical handicaps	2008
Madres del Barrio	Support single mothers living in poverty	2009
Milagro	Provide special eye surgery services to low-income patients	2004
Miranda	Train and organize military reserves	2003
Música	Consolidate El Sistema, provide more support for music education	2007
Negra Hipólita	Revive, rescue, and guarantee the rights of the homeless and those living in extreme poverty	2006
Niños y Niñas del Barrio	Attend to the needs of and defend homeless children	2008

HOUSEHOLD BUDGETS

TABLE R.1. National Results of 2005 Household Budget Poll: Typical Family Budget Structure by Expenditure

Food and nonalcoholic drinks	31.8%
Transportation	11.1%
Clothing and shoes	9.6%
Restaurant and hotel	6.9%
Miscellaneous goods and services	6.8%
Household goods	6.7%
Communication expenses*	5.9%
Entertainment	4.9%
Health	4.8%
Utilities**	4.1%
Educational expenses	3.0%
Rent/mortgage	2.3%
Alcoholic drinks/tobacco	2.1%

* Includes telephone and internet services
**Does not include telephone or internet
Source: Central Bank of Venezuela Office of Statistics–III National Poll of Family Budgets

TABLE R.2. Household Budget Expenditures by Locale Numbers as Percentage of Total Household Expenditures

Expenditure Category	Large Cities	Medium Cities	Small Cities	Rural Areas
Food and nonalcoholic beverage	27.8	29.1	34.1	60.6
Alcoholic beverage and tobacco	2.1	2.1	1.7	3.1
Clothing and shoes	9.1	10.7	12.9	7.8
Rent and mortgage	2.3	2.1	1.6	0.1
Household equipment and maintenance	6.8	8.1	6.4	5.0
Health costs	4.9	3.3	5.1	2.2
Transportation	12.5	12.3	9.5	6.5
Communications	6.5	5.6	5.4	2.5
Entertainment	5.3	5.4	4.7	2.5
Educational services	3.9	2.2	1.6	0.0
Restaurant and hotel	7.4	7.2	7.0	3.7
Miscellaneous goods and services	7.3	7.0	6.8	3.7

Source: Central Bank of Venezuela Office of Statistics–III National Poll of Family Budgets
http://www.ine.gov.ve/ine/enpf/enpf.asp

TABLE S. Telecommunications Indicators (in Comparison with Other Latin American Nations), 2009

	Ven. 2000	Ven. 2007 (total)	Ven. Upper Middle Income	Latin Am-Caribbean
Access				
Telephone lines (per 100 people)	10.4	18.5	22.6	18.1
Mobile cellular subscriptions (per 100 people)	22.4	86.7	84.1	67.0
Internet subscribers (per 100 people)	1.1	3.7	9.4	4.5
Personal computers (per 100 people)	4.5	9.3	12.4	11.3
Households with a television set (%)	82	90	92	84
Usage				
International voice traffic (minutes/person/month)[1]	1.9	—	—	—
Mobile telephone usage (minutes/user/month)	—	—	137	116
Internet users (per 100 people)	3.4	20.8	26.6	26.9
Quality				
Population covered by mobile cellular network (%)	—	90	95	91
Fixed broadband subscribe (% of total subscribe)	1.6	85.3	47.8	81.7
International Internet bandwidth (bits/second/person)	6	628	1,185	1,126
Affordability				
Price basket for residential fixed line (US$/month)	—	6.7	10.6	9.5
Price basket for mobile service (US$/month)	—	1.2	10.9	10.4
Price basket for Internet service (US$/month)	—	23.0	16.4	25.7
Price of call to United States (US$ for 3 minutes)	0.78	0.84	1.55	1.21

(continued)

TABLE S.   Telecommunications Indicators (in Comparison with Other Latin American Nations), 2009 (*continued*)

	Ven. 2000	Ven. 2007 (total)	Ven. Upper Middle Income	Latin Am-Caribbean
Trade				
ICT goods exports (% of total goods exports)	0.1	0.0	13.5	11.4
ICT goods imports (% of total goods imports)	9.4	12.1	16.2	15.9
ICT service exports (% of total service exports)	9.6	11.1	4.6	4.7
Applications				
ICT expenditure (% of GDP)	—	3.9	5.2	4.9
E-government Web measure index	—	0.47	0.37	0.44
Secure Internet servers (per 1 million people, Dec. 2008)	3.7	6.8	26.2	18.2

Notes: Use of italics in the column entries indicates years other than those specified.
— = Not available; GDP = gross domestic product; GNI = gross national income; ICT = information and communication technology; and MDG = Millennium Development Goal.
[1]Outgoing and incoming.
Source: World Bank: ICT Data at a Glance. http://devdata.worldbank.org/ict/ven_ict.pdf

TABLE T.   Weather Statistics for Caracas, Venezuela Weather Statistics: Caracas/Mqta. Aero., Venezuela

Temperature °C	**Latitude: 10.36N Longitude: 066.59W Altitude: 63m**											
	J	**F**	**M**	**A**	**M**	**J**	**J**	**A**	**S**	**O**	**N**	**D**
Maximum	29	28	29	29	30	30	30	31	31	31	31	29
Minimum	22	22	22	23	24	24	24	24	25	25	24	23
Mean	24	25	25	26	27	27	26	27	27	27	27	25
Precipitation	**J**	**F**	**M**	**A**	**M**	**J**	**J**	**A**	**S**	**O**	**N**	**D**
Total (mm)	28	17	22	29	36	53	57	50	54	56	54	54

(*continued*)

TABLE T. Weather Statistics for Caracas, Venezuela Weather Statistics: Caracas/Mqta. Aero., Venezuela (*continued*)

Other Weather Information	J	F	M	A	M	J	J	A	S	O	N	D
Sunshine (h)	233	218	242	183	202	207	242	245	228	208	195	211
Rel. humidity (%)	82	81	81	83	84	83	83	82	81	82	82	83
Wind speed (km/h)	8	8	8	8	7	8	7	6	6	6	6	6
Wind direction	E	E	E	E	E	E	E	E	E	E	NE	E

Number of days where	J	F	M	A	M	J	J	A	S	O	N	D
Precip. = 1 mm	4	3	2	3	4	7	8	7	7	7	6	5

The weather statistics displayed here represent the mean value of each meteorological parameter for each month of the year. The sampling period for this data covers 30 years from 1961 to 1990.
Source: The Weather Network http://www.theweathernetwork.com/index.php?product=statistics&pagecontent=C03094

TABLE U. Beach Conditions by Year and Holiday Season (Environmental Safety)

Year	Season	Total Number of Swimming Beaches	Safe for Swimming	Percentage of Total
2004	Carnival	412	274	66.5
	Holy Week	412	252	61.2
	School vacation	412	234	56.8
2005	Carnival	412	224	54.4
	Holy Week	412	115	27.9
	School vacation	412	132	39.3
2006	Carnival	412	157	38.1
	Holy Week	412	184	44.7
	School vacation	412	195	47.3
2007	Carnival	412	223	54.1
	Holy Week	412	198	48.1
	School vacation	412	190	46.1
2008	Carnival	437	236	54.0
	Holy Week	437	258	59.0
	School vacation	437	275	62.9

Source: Ministry of Popular Power for the Environment, General Directorate of Environment-Water, Bolivarian Republic of Venezuela http://www.ine.gov.ve/aspectosambientales/aspectosambientales/Estdambientales.asp

Major Venezuelan Holidays and Festivals

JANUARY 1

New Year's Day

The first day of the new year is an official national holiday, and all government offices are closed. Famous New Year's celebrations take place in Maracaibo with *gaita* music and dancing.

JANUARY 6

Epiphany (Paradura del Niño)

This religious festival is celebrated in the Andes region and marks the official end of the Christmas and New Year's holidays nationally. Based on the biblical tale of the child lost and found in the temple, the festival features processions with an image of the baby Jesus, music, and dancing.

FEBRUARY/MARCH
(40 DAYS BEFORE GOOD FRIDAY)

Carnival (Carnaval)

This week-long celebration before Lent features parades, music, and dancing throughout Venezuela but is particularly famous in El Callao. Carnival is an official national holiday, and all government offices are closed.

APRIL 19

Declaration of Independence from Spain

This day celebrates the signing of the Venezuelan Declaration of Independence. The day is an official national holiday, and all government offices are closed.

MARCH/APRIL

Holy Week (Semana Santa)

This holiday takes place 40 days after Carnival, one week before Easter. During this week-long vacation, all government offices are closed. This week is popular time for beach vacations and is a common time for pilgrimages to Sorte for devotees of María Lionza.

MAY I

Labor Day

This official national holiday, during which all government offices close, has, under the socialist government of Hugo Chávez, been a time of marches in support of workers' rights and wage increases.

MAY 3

Festival of the May Cross (Cruz de Mayo)

This religious celebration is a festival during which Roman Catholic adherents decorate the holy Christian cross with flowers and celebrate with dance and song.

MAY/JUNE

Dancing Devils of San Francisco de Yare (Diablos de Yare)

This is a religious festival of Corpus Christi held in San Francisco de Yare, Miranda State. The festival is famous for processions of elaborately costumed dancers.

JUNE 24

Battle of Carabobo

This is an official national holiday, which is a remembrance of the Battle of Carabobo, in which troops led by Simón Bolívar were victorious over the Spanish royalist forces. All government offices are closed.

JUNE 23–25

Festival of Saint John the Baptist—Drums of Barlovento (Fiesta de San Juan)

This celebration in honor of the patron saint of the city of Barlovento is known for its intricate drum music and dancing and is of particular importance in Afrovenezuelan culture.

JULY 5

Independence Day

This day celebrates Venezuela's independence from Spain. Parades and fireworks are common. This day is an official national holiday, and all government offices are closed.

JULY 24

Birth of Simón Bolívar

This holiday is a remembrance of the birth of the national hero and Liberator. The day is an official national holiday, and all government offices are closed.

AUGUST 3

Flag Day

This day recognizes the moment that national hero Francisco de Miranda arrived at La Vela de Coro and hoisted the "tricolor" (as the tricolored Venezuelan flag is known). On this day, processions of Venezuelan schoolchildren holding flags are common. This holiday was previously held on March 12, until it was changed in 2006 by order of President Hugo Chávez.

SEPTEMBER

The Miss Venezuela Pageant

This phenomenon is held traditionally in the second or third week of September and is a national event watched by nearly every Venezuelan citizen (and many international observers). The Miss Venezuela pageant is an unofficial holiday and a national celebration of beauty.

SEPTEMBER 8

Feast of the Virgin of the Valley (Virgen del Valle)

This celebration, in honor of the patroness of the eastern portion of Venezuela and of sailors, is characterized by religious celebrants traveling to honor the Virgin of the Valley at her shrine on Margarita Island, in the Valle de Margarita (Margarita Valley) near the city of Porlamar.

SEPTEMBER 8

Feast of the Virgin of Coromoto (Virgen de Coromoto)

This celebration, in honor of the official patroness of Venezuela, honors the first apparition of the Virgin in 1652. As patroness of Venezuela, this day is celebrated throughout Venezuela but is most important in the plains state of Portuguesa and the city of Guanare, where her cathedral is located.

OCTOBER

María Lionza Pilgrimage

This month is the common pilgrimage season to the mountain of Sorte in honor of the goddess María Lionza. Indigenous Resistance Day (also known as Columbus Day) is an important date during this pilgrimage for followers of María Lionza, who commonly arrive in groups at Sorte four or five days early or stay for four or five days after the 12th of October. During this time, followers of María Lionza pray and conduct ceremonies on the mountain.

OCTOBER 12

Indigenous Resistance Day

Commonly known as "Columbus Day" in other parts of the world, this day is recognized in contemporary Venezuela as both the of day of Columbus's arrival and a time to reflect on the damage done to indigenous groups by the colonial Spanish. It is an official national holiday, and all government offices are closed.

NOVEMBER

Feast of the Virgen de la Chiquinquirá

During this month, there are celebrations in the Zulia state in honor of the Virgen de la Chiquinquirá, also known as La Chinita, patroness of Zulia and Maracaibo. These festivals are known for the *gaita* music of the region specially composed in honor of the occasion. The celebrations culminate on November 19 with a *amanecer gaitera* (*gaita* morning) when musicians and citizens of Maracaibo gather on the banks of Lake Maracaibo at dawn to sing to the Virgin.

DECEMBER 25

Christmas Day

Christmas in Venezuela is a religious holiday and an official national holiday. Government offices are closed throughout the nation. Special meals of *hallacas* are eaten; music, including *gaitas*, is performed; and special Catholic masses are celebrated.

DECEMBER 26–27

Festival of Saint Benedict the Moor (San Benito el Moro)

This is a day in celebration in honor of the saint who cures illness and may save the faithful from danger in return for faithfulness. Religious processions featuring images of the black saint are common in the Lake Maracaibo area.

DECEMBER 28

Death of the Innocents (Día de Los Inocentes)

This religious holiday recognizes the death of the holy innocents at the order of King Herod. In some cities, people dress as bandits or clowns and run about town playing tricks and asking for money.

DECEMBER 31

New Year's Eve

This secular holiday is marked with large family gatherings, food, and community celebrations at midnight. Fireworks are common at community celebrations, as well as the traditional eating of 12 grapes in order to guarantee the fulfillment of 12 wishes.

Country-Related Organizations

These brief organizational profiles are designed to provide avenues for general readers seeking more information related to the country. As such, an effort has been made to provide sources that specialize in Venezuela and that communicate in English. However, given the relative scarcity of such organizations, some groups have been included that cover the region in general and focus in some specific way on Venezuela. Additionally, particularly useful sources whose communications are mainly in Spanish have also been included.

When possible, entries include the organization's full address, phone and fax numbers, general e-mail contact, and Web site. Contact information is followed by a very brief (two to three sentence) description of the organization.

BUSINESS AND ECONOMIC RESOURCES

Alianza Boliviariana Para Los Pueblos de Nuestra América (ALBA)

Web site: http://www.alternativabolivariana.org/

ALBA, the Bolivarian Alternative for Latin America and the Caribbean, is a trade pact whose members include Venezuela, Ecuador, Nicaragua, Haiti, the Dominican Republic, and Cuba. The organization is a joint Venezuelan-Cuban initiative based on fair trade as an alternative to the U.S.-sponsored Free Trade Area of the Americas. As might be expected from the anticolonialist stance of the organization, the information on the Web site is exclusively in Spanish, but it includes a depth of information on economy and history.

Banco Central de Venezuela (Central Bank of Venezuela)

Physical Address: Av. Urdaneta esq. Las Carmelitas
Caracas 1010—Venezuela
Postal Address: Apartado 2017, Carmelitas
Caracas 1010—Venezuela
Telephone: (+58-212) 8015111
Fax: (+58-212) 8611649
E-mail: info@bcv.ve.org Web site: http://www.bcv.org.ve/EnglishVersion/Index.asp

A public institution, the Banco Central de Venezuela performs all of the functions of other central bank or federal reserve systems worldwide, like managing the money supply and credit and issuing bank notes. The BCV Web site provides statistics, news reports, and a variety of information on the monetary and currency system in Venezuela.

Bolsa de Valores Caracas (Venezuelan Stock Exchange)

Edificio Atrium, Piso 1
Calle Sorocaima
Entre Avenida Tamanaco y Venezuela, Urbanización El Rosal
Caracas
(+58-212) 9055511
E-mail: webmaster@bolsadecaracas.com Web site: http://www.bolsadecaracas.com/eng/index.jsp

The Bolsa de Valores Caracas is the home of security and financial instrument trading in Venezuela. The Web site provides a wealth of information in English to those interested in the market in Venezuela. Among the items of information provided is a history of the stock exchange in Venezuela, a list of Venezuelan brokerage houses with their contact information, and detailed, up-to-date information on stocks listed on the market.

Caribbean Development Bank

Venezuelan Branch-(BANDES)
Avenida Universidad
Esquinas de Traposos a Colon
Torre BANDES
Piso 7 Apdo 2041 Caracas

(+58-212) 580108681

E-mail: vpromocion@bandes.gov.ve Web site: www.caribank.org

The Caribbean Development Bank works in its member nations (including Venezuela) to be a leading catalyst for development resources. The development bank's goal is the systematic reduction of poverty in member nations through social and economic development.

CONAPRI *(Venezuelan Council for Investment Promotion)*

POBA Intl A-263
PO Box 02-5255
Miami, FL 33102-5255
(+58-212) 9513692
(+58-212) 9514732
Fax: (+58-212) 9533915
Web site: http://www.conapri.org/English/index.asp

CONAPRI works to disseminate information concerning business opportunities in Venezuela. Its mission is to unite government and private initiatives to foster sustainable economic development in the country. CONAPRI provides various types of consulting and investor services.

ddex.com *(Directory of Venezuelan Exporters)*

Editores Milenium C.A.
Av. Francisco de Miranda, Edf. Samson, Piso 1
Ofc. 5, Los Ruices, Caracas 1071
República Bolivariana de Venezuela
Telf./Phone: (+58-212) 2399867 (master)
Fax: (+58-212) 2347441
E-mail: infoatddex.com / ddexmercadeoatgmail.com Web site: http://www.ddex.com

Ddex.com is a B2B (business to business) Web site designed to provide information on export products and import products of Venezuelan and foreign companies and industries in international markets. The organization seeks to form business relationships between exporters and importers worldwide and provides tools for the growth of our members and advertisers.

Global Exchange

2017 Mission Street, 2nd Floor
San Francisco, CA 94110

Telephone: (415) 255-7296
Fax: (415) 255-7498
E-mail: communications@globalexchange.org Web site: http://www.global
exchange.org/

Global Exchange is a U.S.-based organization that encourages the development
of alternative, local approaches to global economic problems. It endorses hands-on
education in global issues through "reality tours." The Global Exchange sponsors
reality tours surrounding a variety of topics, including Afrovenezuelan culture.

Organization of Petroleum Exporting Countries (OPEC)

Helferstorferstrasse 17
A-1010
Vienna, Austria
Web site: http://www.opec.org/home/

OPEC's 12 member nations (Algeria, Angola, Ecuador, Iran, Iraq, Kuwait, Libya,
Nigeria, Qatar, Saudi Arabia, UAE, and Venezuela) coordinate petroleum prices
and production policies and ensure profits to oil producers.

PDVSA

Web site: http://www.pdvsa.com/

PDVSA is the nationally owned oil company in Venezuela. Limited portions of
the Web site are available in English. In addition to listing the current price of a
barrel of oil prominently on the main page of the site, the site includes information about PDVSA-sponsored social development programs, news, and concessions
information.

GOVERNMENT RESOURCES

Embassy of the Bolivarian Republic of Venezuela to the United States

1099 30th St. N.W.
Washington, DC 20007
(202) 342-2214
E-mail: cultura@embavenez-us.org. Web site: http://www.embavenez-us.org/
index.php

The Embassy of Venezuela in the United States. The embassy provides general
information, information for travelers, history, and cultural information to Americans and Venezuelans.

Union of South American Nations (UNASUR)

Jr Libertad N° 804 Oficina 201
Telefax: (0051) (66) 311193
Ayacucho—Peru
E-mail: info@unasur.org Web site: http://www.unasur.org/

Founded in 2008, UNASUR is modeled after the European Union and seeks
to promote an integrated regional identity for South America. UNASUR's goals
include the creation of a unified energy policy, a lending bank of South America, a
unified South American defense policy, a South American parliament, and a common South American currency.

U.S. Census Bureau

4600 Silver Hill Road
Washington, DC 20233
Telephone: (301) 763-2255
E-mail: william.g.bostic.jr@census.gov Web site: http://www.census.gov/
foreign-trade/balance/c3070.html

While perhaps not the first place researchers might think to look, the Foreign
Trade Division of the U.S Census Bureau has, on its Web site and in its records,
extensive statistics pertaining to trade between Venezuela and the United States.
The Web site contains statistics from 1985 to the present, and more information is
available upon request from the organization.

U.S. Embassy in Venezuela

Colinas de Valle Arriba
Caracas, Venezuela
Telephone: (+58-212) 975-6411
Web site: http://caracas.usembassy.gov/

In addition to providing standard visa and passport information for Venezuelans
wishing to travel to the United States, the U.S. Embassy in Venezuela is a resource for
U.S. citizens in Venezuela from emergency services to absentee voting support. For
those U.S. citizens abroad during major U.S. cultural events, the embassy hosts activities to connect citizens to home. The embassy even hosts an annual Superbowl party.

U.S. Energy Information Administration

Telephone: (202)586-8800
E-mail: cabs@eia.doe.gov Web site: http://www.eia.doe.gov/cabs/Venezuela/
Background.html

The U.S. EIA provides both a brief background study of Venezuela on its Web site as well as significantly more detailed information about energy production and exportation. The energy information and report is updated frequently with information on petroleum, coal, and natural gas. A wide range of statistics in an easily understandable format is available, and extensive contacts in each area are listed.

SOCIAL AND CULTURAL RESOURCES

Ateneo de Caracas

Telephone: (+58-212) 5711314
E-mail: direccion-general@ateneodecaracas.org Web site: http://www.ateneode caracas.org/

The venerable Ateneo is one of the nation's premier cultural organizations. The Ateneo organizes exhibitions of visual arts, theater performances, musical presentations, literary readings, and educational programs. While the Web site is in Spanish, it has some features of note even for non-English speakers, including, under "*enlaces*," a link to the collection of the Ateneo's GBG Arts gallery that shows images of Venezuelan artists' work.

The British-Venezuela Solidarity Campaign

C/O W-ton TUC
P.O. Box 2917,
Wolverhampton WV2 2YA
Britain
E-mail:info@venezuelasolidarity.org.uk Web site: www.venezuelasolidarity. org.uk/

The VSC is a leftist organization based in Britain that has several goals: to promote and strengthen links with Venezuelan trade unionists, to coordinate solidarity activities within Britain, to promote news and documentaries raising awareness of Venezuela, and to organize solidarity tours to Venezuela. Their Web site contains information related to all of these activities in English.

The Carter Center

One Copenhill
453 Freedom Parkway
Atlanta, GA 30307
Telephone: (404) 420-5100 or (800) 550-3560
E-mail: carterweb@emory.edu Web site: http://www.cartercenter.org/ homepage.html

The Carter Center, founded by former President Jimmy Carter, is dedicated to improving human rights globally. Election monitoring and mediation are included in its many activities. It has monitored numerous elections in Venezuela since 1998 and mediated a variety of conflicts surrounding election disputes.

Centro de Estudios Latinoamericanos Rómulo Gallegos (CELARG)

Casa de Rómulo Gallegos
Av. Luis Roche con 3ra Transversal, Altamira
Telephone: (+58-212) 2852721
Web site: http://www.celarg.org.ve/Ingles/index.htm

The CELARG is the main cultural organization of the Venezuelan government. The CELARG organizes a variety of programs and workshops, theater productions, and readings. The CELARG does maintain a web site with categories and titles in English, though the content in English can be minimal.

The Centre for Research on Globalisation

PO Box 55019
11 Notre-Dame Ouest,
MONTREAL, Qc, H2Y 4A7
CANADA
E-mail: crgeditor@yahoo.com Web site: http://www.globalresearch.ca

The Centre for Research on Globalisation (CRG) is a left-leaning, independent research organization and media group of writers, scholars, journalists, and activists based in Montreal. The organization maintains a Web page that publishes news articles, commentary, background research, and analysis on a broad range of issues, focusing on social, economic, strategic, and environmental processes. In addition to the Web site, CRG is involved in book publishing, support to humanitarian projects, as well as educational outreach activities including the organization of public conferences and lectures. CRG also acts as a think tank on crucial economic and geopolitical issues.

Fundación Polar

Physical Address:
Segunda avenida, Los Cortijos de Lourdes
Edificio Fundación Empresas Polar, 1° piso.
Postal Address:
Apartado postal 70934.
Los Ruices. Zona postal: 1071-A. Caracas.
Telephone: (+58-212) 2027530

Fax: (+58-212) 2027522
Web site: http://www.fundacionempresaspolar.org/

The Fundación Polar is a major cultural and historic foundation that supports literary, educational, health, and other social development projects throughout Venezuela. The foundation publishes a wide range of literary and social texts and maintains an extensive library. While the foundation's Web site is in Spanish, projects are profiled with photos, and contacts at the foundation are likely to speak some English.

Human Rights Watch

Address: 350 Fifth Avenue, 34th floor
New York, NY 10118-3299
Tel: (212) 290-4700
Fax: (212) 736-1300
E-mail: hrwnyc@hrw.org Web site: http://www.hrw.org/en/americas/venezuela

Human Rights Watch is a 30-year-old, independent organization dedicated to defending and protecting human rights. HRW works by focusing international attention where human rights are violated. HRW conducts investigations and writes extensive reports with the goal of building pressure for action. HRW works worldwide, including in Venezuela. The Web site is continuously updated with news and reports and also contains extensive background information.

Instituto Internacional Para La Educación Superior En América Latina y El Caribe (IESALC)

Edificio Asovincar, 1062-A. Av. Los Chorros c/c Calle Acueducto,
Altos de Sebucan
Caracas
Apartado Postal 68.394
Venezuela
E-mail: iesalc@unesco.org.ve Web site: http://www.iesalc.unesco.org.ve/

IESALC is an organization of UNESCO devoted to the promotion of higher education, helping to implement in the Latin American and Caribbean region. The IESALC offices for the region are based in Caracas. The IESALC Web site provides information for Latin America and the Caribbean and therefore does so primarily in Spanish. Some articles and reports, however, are available in English.

Miss Venezuela Organization

Web site: http://www.missvenezuela.com/index.asp

The Miss Venezuela Organization runs the hugely successful and (in Venezuela) important Miss Venezuela pageant. The organization's Web site is mostly in Spanish but contains a wide variety of photos and links to the organization's Facebook page, where one can "like" and follow the contestants. The site also has a historical list of the Miss Venezuela competition and those winners who have gone on to international championships.

Organization of American States

17 Constitution Ave. N.W.
Washington, DC 20007
(202) 458-3000
E-mail: svillagran@oas.org. Web site: http://www.oas.org/en/default.asp

The Organization American States, of which Venezuela is a member, is the world's oldest regional organization and promotes democracy, human rights, security, and development throughout the western hemisphere. The organization seeks to achieve this through political dialogue, inclusiveness, and cooperation among its members. All member states, including Venezuela, have local offices of the OAS.

Pan American Health Organization

Regional Office of the World Health Organization
525 Twenty-third Street, N.W., Washington, DC 20037
Telephone: (202) 974-3000 Fax: (202) 974-3663
Web site: http://www.paho.org/English/sha/prflven.htm

The Pan American Health Organization serves at the Regional Office for the Americas of the World Health Organization (part of the United Nations system). The organization is an international public health agency with more than 100 years of experience in working to improve health and living standards of the countries of the Americas. It serves as the specialized organization for health of the Inter-American System. The organization's Web site includes information specifically about health issues in Venezuela and more widely about Latin America.

The Prout Research Institute

Avenida Sanz Calle Terepaima con Mosen Sol
Quinta Prout #11-20
Urbanización El Marques, Caracas Venezuela
Telephone: (+58-212) 8862323
E-mail: ivip@prout.org Web site: http://priven.org/index.php

The Prout Institute in Venezuela is a branch of Proutist Universal. The institute teaches a social and economic theory developed in 1959 by Indian scholar-author and activist Prabhat Ranjan Sarkar. Mr. Sarkar sought a practical alternative to the theories of both Marxist communism and capitalism. Prout is based on universal values recognizing and protecting the rights of all to the fulfillment of their basic needs; the protection of the environment, plants, and animals; and a dynamic, incentive-based, multitiered economy. Information on programs at the institute in Venezuela is offered in English.

The Section on Venezuelan Studies

Web site: http://svs.osu.edu/

The Section on Venezuelan Studies (SVS) is an official section of the Latin American Studies Association (LASA). The Section on Venezuelan Studies has two objectives: (1) to foster interdisciplinary communication and collaboration among scholars, students, and nonacademics whose work considers Venezuelan culture, politics, economy, ecology, social issues, and other aspects of Venezuela, and (2) to facilitate dissemination of information on Venezuelan studies among members and nonmembers through public events, conferences, and the media.

Simón Bolívar Youth Orchestra of Venezuela

Parque Central,
Torre Oeste, piso 18
Fesnojiv
Caracas, Distrito Capital
Venezuela 1010
Telephone: (212) 576-5511 / 573-7091 / 573-5091
E-mail: contacto@fesnojiv.gob.ve Web site: http://www.fesnojiv.gob.ve/en/home.html

The Simón Bolívar Youth Orchestra is the premier youth orchestra in the world. El Sistema, as it is known, was founded in 1975 by José Antonio Abreu. El Sistema supports music education throughout the country. Its musicians play in orchestras throughout Venezuela. The principal El Sistema orchestra has won world renown through concerts throughout Europe and the United States. Gustavo Dudamel, music director of the Los Angeles Philharmonic, is a graduate of El Sistema.

Teatro Teresa Carreño

Av. Paseo Colón
Complejo Cultural Teresa Carreño.
Los Caobos. ZP 1010.
Caracas, Venezuela.
E-mail: prensa@teatroteresacarreno.com Web site: http://www.teatroteresacarreno.gob.ve/

The Teresa Carreño Foundation's primary goal is to support the diffusion of high-quality art—all forms—throughout Venezuela. The theater in Caracas is the home to the foundation and many of the foundation's supported artistic activities. The Web site includes a complete list of concerts and other theatrical events scheduled in the various theater spaces in the complex including opera, musical theater, and ballet.

United Nations Children's Fund (UNICEF)

UNICEF Venezuela
Apartado Postal 69314
Altamira 1062
Caracas, Venzulela
Telephone: (+58-212) 2845648 Fax: (+58-212) 2868514
E-mail: caracas@unicef.org Web site: http://www.unicef.org/infobycountry/venezuela_25205.html

UNICEF works worldwide for the protection and betterment of children's and women's health and welfare. The UNICEF Web site in English gives a selection of articles about health and gender issues in Venezuela. The Web site also offers useful links to other Web sites, including the Venezuelan mirror site, which offers substantial statistics in Spanish.

United Nations Educational Scientific and Cultural Organization (UNESCO)

7 place de Fontenoy
75352 Paris 07 SP France
Telephone: 33 (0)1 45 68 10 00 Fax: 33 (0)1 45 67 16 90
Web site: http://www.unesco.org/new/en/unesco/worldwide/unesco-regions/latin-america-and-the-carribean/bolivarian-republic-of-venezuela/

UNESCO runs a wide range of programs in education, science and culture throughout the world and in Venezuela. The Web site contains detailed information about UNESCO's activities in Venezuela and a link to the UNESCO field office in Venezuela.

Venezuelan Film Commission

Email: venefilmcomis@cantv.net Web site: http://www.diatriba.net/venezuelafilmcommission/

The Venezuelan Film Commission provides information on production, services, and permits to those persons interested in making films in Venezuela. The commission works with the National Film Board (CNC, Consejo Nacional de Cine) to provide information and act as guide and host to international audiovisual producers.

Venezuelan Professional Baseball League

Web site: http://www.lvbp.com/scripts/home/index.asp

This site is only in Spanish, but it is a treasure trove for the Venezuelan baseball fanatic. It includes news, information about the league, statistics, and schedules during the Venezuelan regular season (Major League Baseball's off season) as well as information about the Serie del Caribe, a tournament involving all the national teams from the Caribbean basin nations.

TOURISM RESOURCES

Venezuelan Convention and Visitors Bureau

E-mail: http://www.venezuelavisitorsbureau.com/r4p.cfm Web site: http://www. venezuelavisitorsbureau.com/index.cfm

The bureau Web site has information about places of interest, locations for conventions and meetings, exchange rates, and other practical information for business travelers. The Web site also provides a contact page for those wishing to plan meetings or conventions.

Venezuela Information Office

2000 P Street NW
Suite 240
Washington, DC 20036
Phone: (202) 347-8081 Fax: (202) 223-8029
E-mail: vio@veninfo.com Web site: http://www.rethinkvenezuela.com/index.html

The Venezuela Information Office was, in 2010, run by the administration of Hugo Chávez and was dedicated to "educate the public about contemporary Venezuela." The Web site has information about the social programs, new legislation, economic issues, and issues of foreign relations of importance to the government. The site offers a very favorable view of the Chávez administration and its programs. It is a useful site to visit for opposing opinion for the negative press that the administration receives in mainstream Western media.

Venezuela Tuya S.A.

Centro Comercial Ciudad Tamanaco,
Torre D, Piso 2, Ofc D227, Chuao, Caracas 1064, Venezuela
Web site: http://www.venezuelatuya.com/siteinfo/comentarioseng.htm

Venezuela Tuya is a travel agency that provides a wide variety of services and information for international clients. Their Web site, additionally, is a good beginning resource in English with photos and basic general information. Included is a somewhat eclectic mix of information on the major geographical regions of Venezuela, major sites of interest, and natural wonders as well as recipes and information on Miss Venezuela.

CULTURAL EXCHANGE AND EDUCATIONAL RESOURCES

American Field Service—Venezuela

Avenida Francisco de Miranda Edo. TECOTECA
Piso 6, Of 6-A y 6-B
Urb. Los Palos Grandes
Caracas, Venezuela
(+58-212) 2840277
E-mail: info-venezuela@afs.org Web site: http://www.afs.org

The American Field Service is an organization that sends students internationally to participate in service projects. AFS volunteers work for peace and understanding in a diverse world by promoting justice, equality, and tolerance. The AFS office in Venezuela works with young people in Venezuela.

Amnesty International

Amnistía Internacional CCS18257 Av. Venezuela con Calle Sorocaima
Res Esedra P.B. Local #1, Casillero 936
El Rosal, Caracas 1060 Venezuela
E-mail: info@aiven.org Web site: http://www.amnesty.org/en/contact/
Venezuela/645

Amnesty International is a worldwide movement of people who campaign for internationally recognized human rights for all. Amnesty International works worldwide, including in Venezuela, to improve human rights through demonstrations, vigils, and direct lobbying. The Web site also publishes reports on Venezuela.

Fulbright Scholar Program

Council for International Exchange of Scholars
3007 Tilden Street, NW, Suite 5L, Washington, DC 20008-3009
Telephone: (202) 686-4000
E-mail: scholars@iie.org Web site: http://www.iie.org/cies/country/venezuela.htm

The Fulbright program is the flagship international educational exchange program sponsored by the U.S. government and is designed to increase mutual understanding between the people of the United States and the people of other countries. With this goal in mind, the Fulbright program provides participants—chosen for their academic merit and leadership potential—with the opportunity to study, teach, conduct research, exchange ideas, and contribute to finding solutions to shared international concerns. The Web site offers information about the program and general information about Venezuela.

Annotated Bibliography

GENERAL WORKS

Latin America Network Information Center (LANIC), http://lanic.utexas.edu/la/venezuela/.

LANIC is an online resource based at the University of Texas-Austin. The LANIC database lists hundreds of links to resources about Venezuela in English and in Spanish. These resources cover all areas of Venezuelan history, economy, culture, business, sports, and so forth.

CHAPTER 1: GEOGRAPHY

Animal Info, http://www.animalinfo.org/country/venezuel.htm.

A good online resource for environmental and animal issues, Animal Info highlights rare, threatened, and endangered mammals in Venezuela and other nations. The Web site includes information about biodiversity, ecosystems, land use, population, and protected lands of the country, as well as a listing of references used for further research.

CIA. 2010. "World Factbook-Venezuela." https://www.cia.gov/library/publications/the-world-factbook/geos/ve.html.

This online resource is a good source for facts and figures on geographical information as well as on population and other issues.

Perry-Castañeda Map Collection, http://www.lib.utexas.edu/maps/venezuela.html.

The Perry-Castañeda Map Collection of the University of Texas at Austin Library offers a number of public domain maps of Venezuela online. Maps include country maps, city maps, and thematic maps of Venezuela. Also includes links to other sites where Venezuelan maps may be found.

Veiga, Marcello M., Dario Bermudez, Heloisa Pacheco-Ferriera, Luiz Pedroso, Aaron Gunson, Gilberto Berrios, Ligia Vos, Pablo Huidobro, and Monika Roeser. 2005. "Mercury Pollution from Artisanal Gold Mining in Block B, El Callao, Bolívar State, Venezuela." In Pirronne, Nicola, ed. *Dynamics of Mercury Pollution on Global and Regional Scales: Atmospheric Processes, Human Exposure around the World.* Norwell, MA: Springer.

This chapter goes into specific detail on the processes that produce mercury pollution in the illegal wildcat goldmines of southern Venezuela. Provides technical data on pollution as well as efforts to alleviate the problem.

"Venezuela: A Country Study," http://www.country-data.com/cgi-bin/query/r-14501.html

This online resource (also available in print) is another good basic resource for facts and figures related to basic issues of geography, population, economy, and military issues.

CHAPTER 2: HISTORY

Bierck, Harold A., ed. 1951. *Selected Writings of Simón Bolívar.* 2 volumes. New York: The Colonial Press.

This two-volume translated collection of Simón Bolívar's letters and other writings is still the standard for historians interested in primary sources on the Liberator.

Díaz, Arlene J. 2004. *Female Citizens, Patriarchs, and the Law in Venezuela, 1876–1904.* Lincoln: University of Nebraska Press.

There are few monograph-length studies associated with any topic in the Venezuelan 19th century. Díaz explores how women in the 19th century appropriated concepts, like liberty, that came out of independence and reinterpreted them, carving out unexpected legal and political space in civil society.

Ewell, Judith. 1984. *Venezuela: A Century of Change.* Palo Alto, CA: Stanford University Press.

This is one of two standard texts on 20th-century Venezuelan history. Though some arguments represent earlier historiography, the book remains solid.

Hellinger, Daniel. 1993. *Venezuela: Tarnished Democracy.* Boulder, CO: Westview Press.

This is the second standard text for the 20th century. Its data on economic change in the 1980s is useful. Hellinger's arguments and evidence make events after 1989 easier to understand, even those that fall outside the direct scope of the work.

Lombardi, John V. 1982. *Venezuela: The Search for Order, the Dream of Progress.* New York: Oxford University Press.

This study is a good general overview of Venezuelan history. While the work is somewhat dated, the study is the one history that scholars and students have been depending on as a background history for years.

Lynch, John. 2006. *Simón Bolívar: A Life.* New Haven, CT: Yale University Press.

There are surprisingly few biographies of Bolívar. This one, simultaneously accessible and comprehensive, is the best to date. Lynch analyzes Bolívar as political, military, and social leader whose legacy is as complex as he was.

McBeth, Brian. 2008. *Dictatorship and Politics: Intrigue, Betrayal, and Survival in Venezuela, 1908–1935.* Notre Dame, IN: University of Notre Dame Press.

This is the best history to date of the presidency of Juan Vicente Gómez. Though McBeth primarily focuses on the multiple conspiracies that beset Gómez during his long presidency, the work also analyzes processes of state formation and economic development.

Morse, Kimberly J. 2000. "Aun en la muerte separados: Class, Clergy, and Society in Aragua de Barcelona, Venezuela, 1820–1875." PhD diss., The University of Texas at Austin.

Morse analyzes in this dissertation how the elite in an eastern Venezuelan community used clergy as well as concepts of race, class, and gender to construct a system of hegemony that lasted until the mid-20th century. The study also includes an assessment of economic and political conditions in Venezuela through the mid-19th century.

Racine, Karen. 2003. *Francisco de Miranda: A Transatlantic Life in the Age of Revolution.* Wilmington, DE: Scholarly Resources.

This is one of the few studies of Francisco de Miranda, one of the other early independence leaders in Venezuela. Racine's study is most useful in its transatlantic approach, assessing Miranda as an intellectual who was fluent in ideas derived from multiple contexts and whose loyalties were, for him, ultimately tragically Venezuelan.

Yarrington, Douglas. 1997. *A Coffee Frontier: Land, Society, and Politics in Duaca, Venezuela, 1830–1936.* Pittsburgh, PA: University of Pittsburgh Press.

This is one of the other studies associated with 19th-century Venezuelan history, this time focused on the development of coffee cultivation. Yarrington argues that one pattern does not fit for coffee cultivation throughout Venezuela. In central-western Venezuela, owners of small parcels of land used coffee cultivation to protect their economic autonomy while participating in the growing national and international coffee trade.

———. 2003. "The Vesty Cattle Enterprise and the Regime of Juan Vicente Gomez." *Journal of Latin American Studies* 35: 89–115.

This article is representative of new scholarship on Juan Vicente Gómez that looks beyond standard arguments on the relationship with the United States and corruption. Yarrington's assessment of Gómez's relationship with the British Vesty company suggests that the president used variable economic policies for different purposes.

Zahler, Reuben. 2009. "Complaining Like a Liberal: Redefining Law, Justice, and Official Misconduct in Venezuela, 1790–1850." *The Americas* 65: 351–374.

Historians are beginning use law and the courts as measures to understand state formation in the 19th century. Zahler argues that in Caracas courts served to reinforce the state legitimacy in a crucial period in the middle 19th century.

CHAPTER 3: GOVERNMENT AND POLITICS

Note: In the area of government and politics, those seeking to do research should keep in mind the comprehensive and substantial changes that have occurred in Venezuela in the years from 1989 to 2010, and indeed continue to occur. Because of this, researchers interested in contemporary politics must take extra care in ensuring that the information and data they find is up-to-date. In this instance, online resources are generally more up-to-date than printed texts.

CIA. 2010. "World Factbook-Venezuela." https://www.cia.gov/library/publications/the-world-factbook/geos/ve.html.

The CIA's "World Factbook" is a particularly good reference for politics and government in that it updates very frequently. Only available online, the "World Factbook" provides information on everything from geography to economics to the current governmental and political situation and structures.

"The Constitution of the Bolivarian Republic of Venezuela-1999," http://www.embavenez-us.org/constitution/constitution_titleI.htm.

The Embassy of Venezuela in the United States provides an English-language translation of the 1999 Bolivarian Constitution on its Web site. A useful resource for those interested in the specifics of the constitution.

Coronil, Fernando, and Julie Skurski. 2006. "Dismembering and Remembering the Nation: The Semantics of Political Violence in Venezuela." In Fernando Coronil and Julie Skurski, eds., *States of Violence.* Ann Arbor: University of Michigan Press.

Coronil and Skurksi's chapter on the Amparo massacre and the *caracazo* in this edited volume is, as of 2010, the most cogent analysis of those two critical events in Venezuelan recent history.

Corrales, Javier. 2002. *Presidents without Parties: The Politics of Economic Reform in Argentina and Venezuela in the 1990s.* University Park: Pennsylvania State University.

Corrales analyzes the relationship between presidents and political parties within the context of economic reform. He argues that a strong party system was still valid in Latin America in the 1990s.

Ellner, Steve. 2008. *Rethinking Venezuelan Politics: Class, Conflict, and the Chávez Phenomenon.* Boulder, CO: Lynne Rienner.

Rethinking Venezuelan Politics assesses the Chávez administration through 2007. Though it ends before the economic crisis that hit Venezuela in the last years of that decade, its analysis of the complex Venezuelan political landscape within the context of increasing polarization is worthwhile.

Ellner, Steve, and Miguel Tinker Salas, eds. 2007. *Venezuela: Hugo Chávez and the Decline of "Exceptional Democracy."* Lanham, MD: Rowman and Littlefield.

This is a good edited volume with chapters that assess what went wrong in Venezuela in the last two decades of the 20th century and early analysis of the first years of the Chávez presidency. The authors are political scientists, economists, and historians from the United States and Venezuela.

McCoy, Jennifer, and David Myers, eds. 2004. *The Unraveling of Representative Democracy in Venezuela.* Baltimore, MD: Johns Hopkins University Press.

A political science analysis of the pre-Chávez and early Chávez years, edited by the Carter Center's main representatives in Venezuela in the period leading up to the 2004 recall referendum.

Ramirez, Antonio. 2006. "An Introduction to Venezuelan Governmental Institutions and Primary Legal Sources." http://www.nyulawglobal.org/globalex/venezuela. htm#_3._Judicial_Power.

Though more outdated, this resource, written by a member of the St. John's law school faculty who received his law degrees at the UCAB and later worked for the Venezuelan prosecutor general's office, offers a more complete and detailed overview of the major branches of Venezuelan government. This source also offers a comprehensive bibliography of sources on Venezuelan law in English.

U.S. Department of State. 2010. "Background Note: Venezuela." http://www.state.gov/r/pa/ ei/bgn/35766.htm.

The U.S. State Department maintains a useful and frequently updated Web site with information about the Venezuelan government, the political situation, and foreign relations. As with the CIA Web site, descriptions and explanations may be brief but provide researchers with up-to-date data and a place to begin with more in-depth investigations.

CHAPTER 4: ECONOMICS

Coronil, Fernando. 1997. *The Magical State: Nature, Money, and Modernity in Venezuela.* Chicago: University of Chicago Press.

An anthropological and theoretical account of how Venezuelan politics and economics crashed in the pre-Chávez years. This is one of the main texts on pre-Chávez, 20th-century Venezuela.

The Economist. "Country Briefings: Venezuela." http://www.economist.com/countries/ Venezuela/.

This constantly updated Web resource offers free articles on economics and politics in English. For an additional fee, the service will provide even more in-depth country information and briefings in these areas. As a counterpoint to venezuelanalysis.com, this service offers a more conservative slant and perspective on events.

Ellner, Steve. 1993. *Organized Labor in Venezuela, 1958–1991.* Wilmington, DE: Scholarly Resources.

This is the standard text on labor history in 20th-century Venezuela. It is a sophisticated analysis of the complicated relationship between labor and political parties through the period of pacted democracy.

Karl, Terry Lynn. 1997. *The Paradox of Plenty: Oil Booms and Petro-States.* Berkeley: University of California Press.

Karl's is a clear analysis of the impact of oil dependency on the state. Long before the consequences of said dependency became apparent in the Chávez era, Karl argued that oil impeded rather than enhanced Venezuelan economic development.

McBeth, Brian. 1983. *Juan Vicente Gomez and the Oil Companies in Venezuela, 1908–1935.* Cambridge, MA: Cambridge University Press.

McBeth's first book is the standard text on the relationship between Juan Vicente Gómez and the oil companies in the initial decades of oil exploration in Venezuela. McBeth suggests that Gómez used the companies to consolidate political goals to modernize the Venezuelan state.

Tinker Salas, Miguel. 2009. *Enduring Legacy: Oil Culture and Society in Venezuela.* Durham, NC: Duke University Press.

In this text, Tinker Salas traces the history of the oil industry's rise in Venezuela from the beginning of the 20th century, paying particular attention to the experiences and perceptions of industry employees, both foreign and Venezuelan. It is as much a social and cultural history of oil as it is a political and economic one.

CHAPTER 5: SOCIETY

Briggs, Charles, and Clara Mantini-Briggs. 2003. *Stories in the Time of Cholera: Racial Profiling during a Medical Nightmare.* Berkeley: University of California Press.

Briggs and Mantini-Briggs's work is an outstanding, yet painful, study of the 1992 cholera epidemic that struck the Warao Indians in Delta Amacuro state. Briggs and Mantini-Briggs argue that layers of narratives (local, regional, national, and international) that deemed the Warao as barbarians impeded effective medical care and contributed to the tragedy.

Ellner, Steve, and Daniel Hellinger, eds. 2003. *Venezuelan Politics in the Chávez Era: Class, Polarization, and Conflict.* London: Lynne Rienner.

A good, in-depth analyses of the Chávez era, up until 2002. Very good for understanding many developments in a wide variety of areas, such as the Bolivarian movement, the economy, labor, oil, state reform, and civil society. Contains John V. Lombardi's important essay on the "permanent dilemma."

Fernandes, Sujatha. 2010. *Who Can Stop the Drums?: Urban Social Movements in Chavez's Venezuela.* Durham, NC: Duke University Press.

In this vivid ethnography of social movements in the barrios, or poor shantytowns, of Caracas, Sujatha Fernandes reveals a significant dimension of political life in Venezuela since President Hugo Chávez was elected. Fernandes traces the histories of the barrios, from the guerrilla insurgency, movements against displacement, and cultural resistance of the 1960s and 1970s, through the debt crisis of the early 1980s and the neoliberal reforms that followed, to the Chávez period. She weaves barrio residents' life stories into her account of movements for social and economic justice. *Who Can Stop the Drums?* demonstrates that the transformations under way in Venezuela are shaped by negotiations between the Chávez government and social movements with their own forms of historical memory, local organization, and consciousness.

Friedman, Elisabeth. 2000. *Unfinished Transitions: Women and the Gendered Development of Democracy in Venezuela 1936–1996.* University Park: Pennsylvania State University Press.

This work studies how the participation of women has developed throughout the 20th century by examining the organization of governmental and nongovernmental women's groups.

Levine, Daniel. 1981. *Religion and Politics in Latin America: The Catholic Church in Venezuela and Colombia.* Princeton, NJ: Princeton University Press.

Though a bit dated, this work still provides a useful analysis of the role of the Catholic Church as an institution in Venezuela in terms of the church's relationship with political structures, church hierarchy, and style.

Linder, Peter. 1999. "An Immoral Speculation: Indian Forced Labor on the Haciendas of Zulia's Sur del Lago Zuliano, 1880–1936." *The Americas* 56: 191–220.

Linder is one of a small cadre of historians who explores the history of race in Zulia during the late 19th and early 20th century. In this essay, Linder evaluates how sugar plantation owners illegally used the Guajira as slaves on sugar plantations beginning before and continuing through the Gómez era.

Morse, Kimberly J. 2003. "When the Priest Does Not Sympathize with el Pueblo: Clergy and Society in El Oriente venezolano, 1843–1873." *The Americas* 59: 511–535.

Morse's article is one of the only studies that analyzes the role of local clergy in conflicts in rural communities in 19th-century Latin America. Though in theory clergy were supposed to serve all people in a community, in fact poverty and ideology forced clergy to choose which part of the pueblo was more important. In some cases, clergy who choose to support the poor or indigenous populations suffered uncomfortable consequences.

Placido, Barbara. 2001. "It's All to Do with Words: An Analysis of Spirit Possession in the Venezuelan Cult of Maria Lionza." *The Royal Journal of the Anthropological Institute* 7, no. 2: 207–224.

This article is useful both in the detail it offers of the practices of the followers of María Lionza and also in the insights that it offers about the power of language and the place of women in the religion.

Pollack-Eltz, Angelina. 1991. "Pilgrimages to Sorte in the Cult of María Lionza in Venezuela." In N. Ross Crumrine and Alan Morinis, eds., *Pilgrimage in Latin America.* Vol. 4. Santa Barbara, CA: Greenwood.

Pollack-Eltz is a widely respected scholar of religion in general, and the devotees of María Lionza in particular. This article gives a useful overview not only of the practices of the pilgrimages themselves but also of the workings of the cult and the basics of the belief system.

Smilde, David. 2007. *Reason to Believe: Cultural Agency in Latin American Evangelicalism.* Berkeley: University of California Press.

Using Caracas as his case study, Smilde constructs an urban ethnography that seeks to understand why people convert to evangelical Christianity in cultural and personal contexts.

Wright, Winthrop. 1990. *Cafe con Leche: Race, Class, and National Image in Venezuela.* Austin: University of Texas Press.

This study provides an easily accessible overview of the subject of racial tensions in Venezuela as well as the Venezuelan tendency to downplay those tensions. Wright's work also covers the complex relation of race and social class.

Orinoco Online, n.d. http://www.orinoco.org/apg/loindex.asp?lang=en&first=true.

The Orinoco Online project is dedicated to preserving the legacy of indigenous societies in the Venezuelan Amazon. The Web site provides a description of the Amazon as well as information and images of 12 different indigenous societies.

CHAPTER 6: CULTURE

Acosta-Alzuru, C. 2010. "Beauty Queens, Machistas and Street Children: The Production and Reception of Socio-Cultural Issues in Telenovelas." *International Journal of Cultural Studies* 13: 2, 185–203.

In this, and other studies, Acosta-Alzuru outlines both the importance of the *telenovela* in Venezuelan culture and the way in which *telenovelas* often integrate important social issues in their stories.

The Ethnologue Report for Venezuela, http://www.ethnologue.com/show_country.asp?name=Venezuela.

This highly informative Web site provides a language map, showing where all of the indigenous languages of Venezuela are spoken. The Web site then provides a brief linguistic description of each language with the number of speakers of the language, alternate names of the language, classification, and other information. Of great use for those interested in indigenous groups or language studies.

Gallegos, Rómulo. 1948. *Doña Bárbara.* Translated by Robert Malloy. New York: Peter Smith.

An older, but still valid, translation of Gallegos's classic 1929 novel. Useful for those non-Spanish-speaking researchers wanting to discover more about the llanos and the literature of Venezuela. Generally available through libraries.

Gaspirini, Graziano. 1986. *Arquitectura popular de Venezuela.* Caracas: Armitano.

This text profiles a wide array of vernacular architecture in Venezuela, from indigenous construction to Andean cottages. The text is completely in Spanish, but even for nonreaders of Spanish it is well worth looking at for the amazing photos of indigenous construction in the deep jungle and for the very helpful schematic drawings.

Jiménez, Ariel. 2006. *Conversations with Jesús Soto.* New Haven, CT: Yale University Press.

This text reproduces a series of interviews with the artist about his art, particularly his kinetic sculptures. The book also contains a series of color photographs, tracing The artist's work through his career from the 1950s to the present.

Lewis, Marvin A. 1992. *Ethnicity and Identity in Contemporary Afro-Venezuelan Literature.* Columbia: University of Missouri Press.

This study uses a culturalist approach to study ethnicity and racial identity from a literary perspective. The study seeks to identify and analyze such features as the African past, myths, linguistic and thematic survivals, folk beliefs, societal inequities, and the development of an Afrovenezuelan worldview. The work analyzes two black and two nonblack writers: Juan Pablo Sojo, Ramón Díaz Sánchez, Manuel Rodríguez, and Antonio Acosta Márquez.

Lopez-Morillas, Frances. 1998. *Selected Writings of Andrés Bello.* London: Oxford University Press.

A good general introduction to the varied and prolific writing of Andrés Bello. This collection of translated texts includes poetry and essays. Selections include essays on grammar and philology, constitutional reform, the aims of education, international relations, historiography, Latin and Roman law, government and society, and many others.

Lowry, Glenn. 2007. "Foreword." In Luís Pérez Oramas, *Armando Reverón.* New York: Museum of Modern Art.

An introduction to the work of Reverón, introduced in English by a variety of essayists on the occasion of a major retrospective of his work at the Museum of Modern Art in New York City. The collection contains images of paintings and photos as well as the famous life-size dolls from Reverón's coastal home.

Mayhall, Marguerite. 2005. "Modernist but Not Exceptional: The Debate over Modern Art and National Identity in 1950's Venezuela." *Latin American Perspectives* 32, no. 2. 124–135.

In this study, Mayhall brings together politics, art, and architecture to show how the government and Venezuela's art and architecture community looked toward Europe for inspiration while seeking a particular Venezuelan identity.

Nichols, Elizabeth Gackstetter. 2000. *Rediscovering the Language of the Tribe in Modern Venezuelan Poetry.* Lewiston, NJ: The Edwin Mellen Press.

This study provides an overview of Venezuelan literature from the middle of the 19th century through the end of the 20th century. Using a cultural studies approach, the work focuses specifically on groups of poets working in Venezuela in the 1970s and 1980s in the urban environment of Caracas. The work of 12 different individual poets is analyzed, and translations of poems and manifestoes are provided.

Palacios, Antonia. 2004. *Ana Isabel, Una niña decente.* Caracas: Monte Avila Editores.

The most recent edition of Palacios's classic 1949 novel of a young woman learning what it means to be "decent" in early 20th-century Venezuela. As of 2010, this novel was not yet available in English.

Parra, Teresa de la. 1993. *Iphigenia: Diary of a Young Lady Who Wrote Because She Was Bored.* Austin: University of Texas Press.

An excellent translation of Teresa de la Parra's 1924 novel about a young woman returning to colonial Venezuela, her struggles for independence, and her ultimate surrender to convention. Also contains informative forward by Latin American feminist scholar Naomi Lindstrom.

Ramírez, María Carmen. 2006. *Gego: Between Transparency and the Invisible.* New Haven, CT: Yale University Press.

This study focuses on Gego's "drawings without paper" and "*tejeduras*" (woven paper pieces), tracing Gego's exploration of line and space. The work is a bilingual study and has essays on Gego's methodology, her remarkable life and career, and numerous color plates that attempt to capture Gego's work. There is also a comprehensive trajectory of Gego's life and work, a chronology of illustrations, and a selected bibliography.

Rodriguez, Juan Luís. 2008. "The Translation of Poverty and the Poverty of Translation in the Orinoco Delta." *Eurohistory* 55, no. 3: 417–438.

This excellent article both describes the Warao language and goes into depth about the missionary attempts to repress the indigenous language as part of expansion into Warao territory. Valuable both as insight into language colonialism and as information about the Warao language.

Suarez, Osbel. 2009. *Carlos Cruz-Diéz: Color Happens.* Madrid: Fundación Juan March.

This bilingual presentation of the work of Cruz-Diéz is a good overview of the artist's styles and work. Contains both scholarly discussion and analysis of Cruz-Diéz's art and photos of the work.

Torres, Ana Teresa. 2000. Gregory Rabassa, trans. *Doña Inés vs. Oblivion.* New York: Atlantic.

This is a fine translation of Torres's most famous novel. The novel is told in the voice of a bitter colonial lady seeking to wrench the family estate from the illegitimate mulatto son to whom her husband left the fortune. The novel traces decades of Venezuela's social and political history, and as one of the few major Venezuelan novels available in translation, it is an entertaining and worthwhile read.

The United Nations Educational, Scientific and Cultural Organization (UNESCO), http://www.unesco.org.

The UNESCO Web site is a useful resource for news and information on cultural events in Venezuela. This is especially true of early 21st-century concerns over freedom of the press. The UNESCO Web site archives on Venezuela (http://www.unesco-ci.org/cgi-bin/portals/archives/search.cgi?query=Venezuela) also contain useful links to a variety of other resources of cultural and educational interest. These are updated regularly.

Vegas, Federico. 1985. *Venezuelan Vernacular.* Princeton, NJ: Princeton Architectural Press.

This text is particularly useful for the full-color photos of Venezuelan vernacular architecture, both indigenous and nonindigenous. Also a useful reference for those who do not have the Spanish language skill to read the more detailed Gaspirini text.

Villanueva, Paulina. 2000. *Carlos Raúl Villanueva.* Princeton, NJ: Princeton Architectural Press.

This volume is part of Princeton's "Masters of Latin American Architecture" series. It is a profile of the complete work of the architect and includes many photos of the architecture described in this text as well as additional architectural projects.

CHAPTER 7: CONTEMPORARY ISSUES

Amnesty International, http://www.amnesty.org.

The "library" service of Amnesty International's Web site allows users to search for reports on human rights issues such as activism, death in custody, extrajudicial executions, indigenous peoples, law enforcement, and many other topics in Venezuela. Users can select not only a nation of interest but also the language that they desire the article to be written in.

Ellner, Steve. 2010. "Hugo Chávez's First Decade in Office: Breakthroughs and Shortcomings." *Latin American Perspectives* 37: 77–96.

Ellner's article is a retrospective and analysis of the first decade of the presidency of Hugo Chávez. Ellner suggests that while participation in the democratic process increased substantially, the economic foundations of the state are less secure. Elements of democracy other than participation also produced cause for concern.

GlobalResearch.ca, http://www.globalresearch.ca/.

The Web site GlobalResearch, based in Montreal, compiles a large array of constantly updated articles and news from and about Venezuela in its Latin America and Caribbean section. Articles on the Web site run toward a leftist, pro-Chávez slant. Of particular interest is access to the Chávez government's English-language newspaper the *Orinoco International*.

Hellinger, Daniel, and David Smilde, eds. 2010. *Bottom Up or Top Down? Participation and Clientelism in Venezuela's Bolivarian Democracy.* Durham, NC: Duke University Press.

This collection provides interdisciplinary perspectives on the significant changes to Venezuela's democracy at the end of the 20th century and the beginning of the 21st century. The chapters contained in the collection cover the political participation of religious, literary, artistic, and media actors. The work is useful as an overview of the way different groups within Venezuelan society have become politicized in contemporary times.

North American Congress on Latin America (NACLA), https://nacla.org/naclareport https://nacla.org/.

NACLA is an organization committed to "activist journalism"—journalism that seeks to provide information on stories that the organization considers to be "overlooked, underreported or covered up." NACLA provides two key resources: the NACLA report, with archives going back to 1967, and an Internet resource center. These resources cover all of Latin America including Venezuela.

U.S. Department of State, "Venezuela," http://travel.state.gov/travel/cis_pa_tw/cis/cis_1059. html.

Prepared by the U.S. Department of State and updated regularly, this Consular Information sheet provides current, if brief, updates on issues such as safety and security, crime, medical facilities, traffic safety, and road conditions. Also included is information on special circumstances such as foreign exchange controls and parallel market currency exchanges.

Vcrisis, http://www.vcrisis.com.

This Web site provides opinion and analysis from the position of the anti-Chávez opposition. The Web site provides links to other Web sites with articles about Venezuela, such as the OAS and Amnesty International as well as links to blogs such as the right-leaning Devil's Excrement blog.

Venezuelanalysis, http://www.venezuelanalysis.com.

This Web site provides constantly updated news and analysis from and about Venezuela. Articles on the Web site cover a wide range of topics including education, politics, and the environment. Until 2010, much content on Venezuelanalysis avoided substantial political bias, right or left. In 2010, however, the tone of the site changed and began to reflect a much stronger left-leaning and pro-Chávez political bent. The site can still be useful, if used with caution, as a counterpoint to the often anti-Chávez slant of Western mainstream media.

Thematic Index

Index

443